THE NOTEBOOKS OF GERTRUDE STEIN FOR *THE MAKING OF AMERICANS* 1903–1912

Leon Katz, editor

ISBN: 978-1798073827

The foreword, “A Year with AliceB. Toklas” by Leon Katz was originally published in *The Yale Review*, July 2012, Volume 100, Issue 3, pp. 1-22 and is reprinted here with the permission of John Wiley and Sons, Limited through PLSclear.

Contents

Foreword: A Year with Alice Toklas

Appendices

FOREWORD: A YEAR WITH ALICE TOKLAS[1]

Back in 1936, Thornton Wilder had warned Gertrude Stein to get her unpublished manuscripts into the safekeeping of the Yale Library because of the danger of another world war's breaking out on French soil. Charmed by the notion that all her work was to be safely harbored for later publication and study, Gertrude packed several cases of manuscripts, letters and miscellany and sent them off. The packing was done with characteristic Steinian abandon: neatly piled manuscripts were dumped into crates, and correspondence, carefully alphabetized and filed at the end of each year by Gertrude's amanuensis, Alice Toklas, was pulled out in drawerfuls and overturned into the crates. Finally, all the scraps of paper that Gertrude never threw away, budget lists, garage attendants' instructions about the Fords she owned during the 10's and 20's ("regardez le carburetor"), forgotten old dentist's bills, were tossed in, too. Alice remonstrated about their inclusion, but Gertrude used every hoarder's excuse: "You can never tell whether some laundry list might not be the most important thing."

Two packages in brown wrapping paper at the bottom of the armoire, lying among chunks of manuscript of her novel, *The Making of Americans*, fell into the crates along with all the other papers. Gertrude had forgotten what they contained, and Alice had never seen them, and merely assumed they were part of the manuscript. But she remembered that "Gertrude had a purse on a belt, with a pencil, loose coins, a small pocketbook that held gold coins, and one of the little notebooks. If anything came to her, she would write a word, sometimes a phrase, never a sentence. She didn't keep them. She had the habit of the purse on the belt from 1907 to 1914, when belts were out of fashion and she dressed differently."

Unidentified and a mess, they lay in the Library's custody uncatalogued and unexplored.But when the Notebooks were opened at Yale sometime later, they revealed a large number of miscellaneous sheets covered with notations for the novel, a mound of copybooks small enough to push into one's pocket, and a few larger school-children's notebooks.Sheets that had been torn out of the little books were found in the original manuscripts of *The Making of Americans* and the other works concurrent with it. When the small pads, the larger copybooks and the scattered scraps were assembled, they made up a continuity of discourse that may be regarded as Gertrude's only remaining unpublished work, her Notebooks.

The inked and penciled scrawls were the writing notes and comments she had made for herself, never intended to be seen by anyone else, and so recorded without any self-conscious concern whatever for the bluntness of their style or the injudicious

---

[1] From *The Yale Review*, June 2012. © 2012 by Yale University.

nature of some of their content. But the labor of assembling and organizing the Notebooks opened sluice- gates to the existence of a largely unknown Gertrude Stein. They were the notes from which she worked directly for most of her writing from 1902 to 1912, most particularly during the composition of "the long book," her mammoth novel, *The Making of Americans*.

Much of the Gertrude carefully concealed in her autobiographies is revealed plainly and sometimes unpleasantly in the Notebooks. And there's the story of her struggles with friendships, with loves, with private self-judgment out of which she gradually built her understanding of human nature, of herself, and of writing.Fathoming and clarifying that story became my devotion for a long, long time. There were first, of course, many interviews with surviving American relatives and friends in Baltimore, San Francisco and New York, (some still warmly remembering, some barely overcoming old antipathies,) archival research, and then, gratefully, a Ford Foundation grant to go to Paris for talks with Alice Toklas, then in her seventies, who could still, sometimes piously, sometimes less than piously, remember.

We spent a year together – during four particularly intensive months of that year meeting four days a week, never less than eight hours each day, Alice talking her profoundly beloved Gertrude, and I reading aloud, note by note, the gathered text, while she, unflagging, adumbrated. For her, who had never typed or even seen these notes – Gertrude's private memoranda – there were revelations; for myself, of course, incredible days of listening and watching and recording the little gnome of a woman left of what Gertrude had thought, in those early years, a beautiful one. Our sessions commenced in November, 1952, in dingy Paris six years after the end of the war. De Gaulle hadn't yet managed to get all the city's buildings - still covered in blankets of soot – cleaned up. Even the hallways of the city's buildings, even those of the reasonably well-to-do, were still untouched, some odoriferous. But once shutting the hall door of apartments like Alice Toklas's, you came into a world that needed none of De Gaulle's urgings to obliterate, finally, the war's effects. Alice was not living at 27 rue de Fleurus, which Gertude had shared with her brother Leo, the legendary address at which the Saturday Evening salons were held, and where the collection of School of Paris paintings was first assembled. This, the later apartment on rue Christine, Gertrude and Alice had lived in for only a few months before the war, and which they abandoned for Bilignin in the south of France for the duration. It was only a few months after returning to Paris that Gertrude died, in February of 1946, and Alice had been living alone in the flat for six years.

When I came to the door, instead of a greeting, there was a hurriedly muttered "Excuse me, please," and Alice was out through the great window of the salon to the adjoining roof from which she pulled out of the rain the third poodle owned by Gertrude and herself, Basket III, now very old, almost blind, and arthritic. Alice immediately got down on all fours, and with a drab green GI towel wiped each of his toes – not merely his paws, but each toe – and said, "Ah, we've come a long way," and almost apologetically, "Basket has lost his manners," by which she meant he could no longer contain himself. Her affection and care for the dog were entire.

Within weeks of that first meeting, Basket died. Oafishly, not yet knowing Alice, I was extending commiseration when she stopped me at once: "No. no, no, that's over, we wont talk about it any more." We never did. The loss of Basket was not to be shared with outsiders; it was to remain entirely her own.

When we settled to talk, she made her dislike of being interviewed about Gertrude immediately and abundantly clear. "I tried it twice," she said, once with an early biographer of Gertrude. "When we were finished with the interviews, she sent me a copy of her book, and I was appalled. It was primitive; she didn't understand Gertrude at all, not in the slightest degree." The recollection of it plainly pained her. The next was worse – another biographer, whose first question was "What was Apollinaire's influence on Gertrude Stein?" Apollinaire, poet, critic, whom Gertrude indeed knew in the early days in Paris, "but her connection with his poetry," Alice angrily insisted, " was nil, absolutely nil," and she wondered how anyone could have been so besotted as to dream that he or any other French poet could have had any connection with Gertrude's writing. "The next question," she remembered, "was really appalling." The story's been told many times of the rivalry between Alice and Gertrude's brother Leo, a contest fought silently, politely and unrelentingly for years, which Alice eventually won, displacing Leo in Gertrude's life. "Anyone should have known that," she insisted, "but his question was, What was the influence of Leo on Gertrude Stein? After that, I wanted no more interviews." But there was a third question, one which, for Alice, was thoroughly *verboten:* "What was Hemingway's relation to Gertrude Stein?" Clearly and publicly, Alice loathed Hemingway, and couldn't imagine, after Gertrude's reference in the *Autobiography* to Alice's writing Hemingway off as "yellow" – plainly intimating not his possible cowardice in the bullring but his cowering in the closet – how anyone could be so *maladif* as to confront her with that question. It was, for her, to be the end of interviews.

Her antipathy toward Hemingway was deep and lasting. Some weeks later when we met for our session, she got to him again. She hadn't yet recovered from the arrival in that morning's mail of a complimentary copy from the publisher of the brand new Carlos Baker biography of Hemingway, and was simmering about maladroit reminders to her of this despised one. Defending literature above *scandale*, I pointed gently to Hemingway's undoubted talent as a writer. "Writer of *what?*" ´ I thought possibly the latest Hemingway, just out: "Well, the Old Man and the Sea." Alice reared up, almost leaping out of her chair: "*The Old Man and the Sea has the EMPTIEST sea in all of LITERATURE!*" I let it go, dropped defense of Hemingway, and made a mental note to skirt in future all such molten dangers.

But overcoming her aversion to interviews, she had answered my note, intrigued by my claim to have Gertrude's notebooks. "I don't remember notebooks of Gertrude's." She had no reason to. But reminded of the brown paper bags at the bottom of the armoire, she remembered the bags entirely, was entirely curious about their contents, and entirely anxious for us to go through them together. And a few days later, our interviews began in earnest.

She sat in the little horsehair-covered chair measured for her in London (and one for Gertrude), both of us shivering slightly in the unheated apartment which Alice could not afford to heat. (Gertrude had replaced, before she died, steam heat with what she thought of as up-to-date twentieth century heat, electricity, prohibitively expensive after the war.) Damp Paris winters chilled to the bone, but Alice was rescued from the worst of them by calculated gifts from Pierre Balmain, whom Gertrude and Alice had befriended in his nonage before he became the celebrated Paris couturier. Each year, there was one gift for the summer and one for the winter, and for this winter, a six foot long, thickly woven woolen shawl in which she sat enwrapped, and - given her length – covered almost all of her. A single naked bulb hung from the middle of the ceiling over our parrying of question and answer, Alice having set the rule: if I knew to ask, she would tell everything, if I didn't, *tant pis*, her hooded look and her silent tongue would reveal nothing. Of the more than eleven hundred of Gertrude's separate notes, Alice responded to more than half, sometimes pushed unwillingly until she relented: "Katz, you're a detective."

Why "Katz?" It was a studied decision. The rules for proceding on the Notebooks were settled on that second day - what she would permit to be spoken of at all, what could be written down and used later, what, most especially, could be published - all this in the interest, as Alice stipulated, of avoiding embarrassment either to herself or to the good souls who might still be living when all this was to be public and out. "Yes," she was prepared to legislate, "you can use this; no, this you cannot." And on that second day, before we were to settle into the routine of Stein Notebook quote, then Katz question, then Toklas comment, Alice had one more question: "What is your feeling about first names?" I couldn't yet read her inflections or looks as well as I could later, and thought, with understandable inner suspicion, This could be a trap. Was I one of those gross types who coopted familiarity with celebrities long before it was either earned or welcome? No, I thought high- mindedly, and said so, and Alice took that as her cue: "I'll call you Katz," she concluded. And she remained for me "Miss Toklas."

But the formality no less than the censoring stipulations lasted only a few moments. The first note read aloud had, by chance, to do with Marie Laurencin. Gertrude mentions her incidentally in an early note, and Alice recalled: "Ah, Marie Laurencin – well!" and embarked at once on a lurid recap of Marie Laurencin, her mother, their scandals, their dark entanglements, and I, lowering my head, glared into my notepad, writing, assuming this exhumed irrelevance wouldn't survive her set restrictions. But looking up, there was Alice tossing her chair pillow up to the ceiling, catching and hugging it with all the might left in her, and laughing with glee: Oh, I WISH I could be ALIVE to see Marie Laurencin's FACE when she reads THAT!" That was the end of rules of engagement. It was also the beginning of loosened formality. We both smoked with abandon, and Alice, coming back from the kitchen promptly at eight each night with a bowl of hot soup (*beyond* mere soup - she, a notable cook, was currently writing her soon-to-be-legendary cookbook,) would stop at the salon door, take a long deep breath, and pay tribute to the cloud that threatened to obliterate the room: "Ah," she exhaled, "good grey smoke!" and would urge when I'd finished the soup: "Put away those awful white ones and have some of these *good red* ones." My brand was Chesterfields, hers Pall Mall. She could buy the red ones and many of her needs – impossible post-war on her straitened income - through the kindness of a devoted American living a sort of prewar life in Paris as a composer, but also as a postwar employe of the CIA, who had a functioning credit card for the Paris PX.

Her straitened income. Alice was left Gertrude Stein's estate "in usufruct" while she lived and so owned none of it, and was dependant for her – as she accurately saw it - mite of income on Gertrude's Baltimore executors. When Gertrude's nephew Allen Stein, who had been left the estate, died, inheritance passed to his son Daniel. For Alice, it was a mortifying turn. Allen's surviving wife Roubina – to Alice, "the Rumanian" - held her, according to the bitterly resentful Alice, captive to the letter of the will. Nothing in the flat was hers, not to keep, not to sell. And Alice suffered from the suspicion - if not the fact - that "the Rumanian" was unrelentingly vigilant, watching her every move lest an object, a painting, an anything of Gertrude's be converted by Alice into cash. Whether true of not, it was oppressively her feeling, and she inveighed against Roubina with the righteous abandon of victimhood. Still, there was, in her travail, a moment of victory.

Alice sold six of Picasso's drawings which – it was her certainty - he had given her. Roubina took umbrage, there was a brief legal tussle, but Alice won her contention. It was a seldom-known victory. More often the case was the Baltimore executors neglecting to send her her pittance on time. Sometimes months went by with nothing in the mail, and I remember Alice plainly fuming about having repeatedly to write to remind them. The indignity rankled, and in private conversation at least, she let fly.

That one was pretty regularly in evidence - the volatile, the chagrined Alice. Fathoming the rest of her was as tantalizing as fathoming Gertrude *by way of* Alice, and in the course of the year, gradual revelation produced a portrait of her at least as complex as the portrait of Gertrude herself. Gradually, day after day evoked a sprightly

Alice, a loyal friend, an astute avenger, a powerful ally, an emancipated heretic utterly indifferent to morality, an ascetic patrician absolutely insistent on manners, delicately attuned to the tiny, the lovely, the sensuous, the exquisite, coldly contemptuous of the mystically enraptured, the religiously ardent, the emotionally frenzied, the intellectually "deep." Her still-vigorous antipathies from the past were emotionally equal to her fervent empathies. And her sudden indifference to both – there *were* such moments – made me question her investment in either. Until, that is, her great moments of apparent *re*investment.

There were two such questionable moments, moments that tended to unhinge a bit one's faith in her total at-one-ness with Gertrude. At the end of one Notebook session that lasted late - I was leaving at midnight, no more metro - and Alice understandably fatigued, was lending me her Royal portable – the one that replaced the primitive mammoth Blickensdorfer – to type up my notes as well as (I volunteered) the new pages of the cookbook. It was the machine on which she had typed several decades of Gertrude's manuscripts. Taking it, and holding it respectfully, for a moment I may have looked to Alice as though I might possibly be on the verge of paying the thing homage. She caught the look, misread it, and commented, "Sometimes I look at that machine and hate every key on it." This sacrilege, startlingly out of key with Stein-Toklas legend, provoked from me only a lame: "Why is that, Miss Toklas?" She sighed, shrugged, "It's a long story," and that was all.

The puzzle reared again, again on leaving for the night when, both of us standing at the wall that held Picasso's paintings of pre-Cubist heads, and opposite, the wall with Picasso's earlier Young Girl with Flowers, and surveying through the open door to the vestibule more though lesser gems, thinking pretentiously something like 'riches ready to drop upon me,' I made comment of some inadequate kind, and she, with that same tired, jaundiced look, said matter-of-factly, in exactly the same vein: "Sometimes I hate all of these pictures each separately and all together." This, even more astounding, provoked the same "It's a long story," and no more.

To be sure, Alice's acid tongue was more quotable than the warm and kindly one, and because of the dozens of Notebook people on whom she was making comment, and her still-lingering feelings about many of them, the acid seemed more in evidence than the manna. But her feelings flowed as freely, and sometimes as deadly, when intermittently we were off the Notebooks altogether, not "interviewing" but just talking.

On one break, when talk moved to conversation about dance, there was this: "Whenever I see a poster on the kiosks of Martha Graham coming to Paris for one of her en*gage*ments, I could spit." (I worshipped Martha Graham.) "That's not *dance!* Dance is the ballerina coming on stage on toe, executing a few steps to a waltz, and going off" (like Karsavina, she meant, in Fokine's *Spectre de la Rose.*) "That's dance!" It was so for her, and profoundly so. Months later, when we were at Alicia Markova's performance at the Palais de Chaillot, there was the other Alice, the votary. Alicia Markova was one of Alice's particular treasures, and Alice seeing her perform - sadly assuming it was for her the last time - when the audience rose as one for a thunderous hand-clapping ovation, Alice, deeply deeply moved, stood too, and quietly, gently, not applauding, raised her arm high and waved farewell.

I too was caught – briefly, thank God – in Graham's plight: terminal contempt. We had talked about Michael, Gertrude's oldest brother, who back in the early 1900's would climb over the hills of Florence in search of genuine Renaissance furniture, and not particularly minding when the phenomenal forgeries of the craftsmen in those hills came up with superbly undetectable copies which Michael *could* detect and bought anyway. And among his finds was the great Tuscan table which Gertrude used all her Paris life as her writing table; and there it now sat in the salon in the rue Christine apartment where we were interviewing. A guest was with us that afternoon, a young Stein enthusiast like myself, and Alice was at her most genial, hosting. Sinfully, forgetting Michael's expeditions, I referred to the *Spanish* table at my elbow – *Spanish!* - and Alice whipped her head in my direction, and cried, *Spanish!!* And glaring, she corrected: *Tuscan!* And in that moment, I could see why Hemingway in *A Movable Feast* still remembered her after thirty years as *frightening*. For the rest of the afternoon she didn't speak to me or look in my direction, addressing only the guest, and for hours after, I remained an outcast, hopeless to talk to, who knew little and could remember nothing.

There was though, luckily, the other Alice who could forgive . Well out of the dumps the next day, I wondered still if another such *Spanish/Tuscan* lapse could finish her confidence and end our conversations. But on the contrary, confidence grew, and we were soon on track again, Alice spearing her enemies, flattering generously remembered friends, and giving wide berth to the Notebooks' cues that hinted at Gertrude's profound distrust of Alice's nature, and only gradually, over several years, accommodating her negative judgment of Alice's "type" to her deep feeling for her person.

Only once in our sessions did Alice bother to explain Gertrude's hostility toward her when they first met. (One has to put aside the English-pantomime tableau embedded in the myth perpetrated in *The Autobiography of Alice B. Toklas* of that first meeting when presumably "a little bell rang" and the two, transformed, were then forever one, and confront instead the brutal reality of the first note Gertrude wrote about Alice several weeks after that first meeting.) The note begins, and goes on for several pages, in this vein:

"Only one person as low as Alice in my experience is Zobel. She is low clean through to the bottom crooked, a liar of the most sordid unillumined undramatic unimaginative prostitute type, coward, ungenerous, ~~cons~~ conscienceless, mean, vulgarly triumphant and remorseless, caddish, in short just plain ~~rotten~~ low like Zobel but not dangerous not effective, no evil. Low but not evil. No evil intention."

I took care to forewarn her that this note was coming – "on the tapis," as she would say – for the next day, and that it would be well for her to be prepared for its contents. Well. whatever it is, it is, she said with a shrug, smiling. But the following morning, she called to say she could hardly sleep that night, and would I come some twenty minutes early so that she could have a look at the note to see just how bad it was. I rang early, the door flew open, and Alice, without looking at me but at my hand (assuming correctly that I would be holding the pages at the ready), "*Have you got it?"* grabbed them, ran into the bedroom, read it in solitude, and came back into the salon showing indescribable relief.

"Oh, this is all right! I thought it was quite different, I thought it was something else. No, this can be explained easily, and after what I expected, or rather feared, it comes as a relief." "What did you expect, Miss Toklas?" "I was afraid that Gertrude had accused me of disloyalty. That's the only thing that would matter. This is perfectly understandable, where it comes from, and why Gertrude should have thought so then, at the time it was written. I think you did very well to warn me of worse than was in it."

I couldn't imagine anything worse than was in it, but Alice then embarked on a gleeful explanation of the note's origins, its multiple enemy sources, its calumnies, and – most remarkable of all – its accuracies. "A good deal of it holds true. The evil, that's all right. The lack of morality that offended Gertrude, that was and is perfectly true." There was considerable conviction and unmitigated pride in Alice's cashiering of all the virtues and indulging all the vices in her friends and in humanity generally. Morality, she pronounced, was everything with most. "But not with me. I believe with Henry James, not in *morals* but in *manners*." And this, I learned, was – apart from her abiding love of Gertrude – her deepest, if not her proudest conviction. From the time of her arrival in Paris, it was not Gertrude alone but her close family circle, with their intellectual proprieties and uplifting devotions (Leo's academic "deep thinking," and sister-in-law Sarah's Christian Science pieties) who suspected or plainly recognized Alice's unnerving preference for "manners" over "morals." It was three years before Alice with much quiet labor could maneuver Gertrude herself into abiding her exceedingly tolerant judgmental norms.

But after skirting the potential shoals of this first "Alice" note, and as we read on for weeks, there were times when both of us flagged a bit in our devotion to Gertrude's written words and Alice's illumination of them. She at such times suppressed, under a fixed, jaundiced stare, her irritation at being badgered however politely and smilingly about her genuine responses to the more damaging of the

"Alice" notes. Whatever those responses were, they remained unuttered and undetectable, proof against all probing.

Still, Gertrude's animadversions told their own story. For several years, and long after their intimacy had begun, Gertrude's entries about Alice continued in the same vein, sometimes genuinely puzzled over Alice's "kind," , sometimes bluntly accusing, always consistent in her judgment of Alice as among the lowest and most ineffectual of "types," until the moment – after three years - when her judgment relented. But with none of these notes when read aloud to Alice did she bother to cavil. She had done so once, to the first note, when Gertrude, misguided or not, might have had her reasons; but afterward, feeling no urge to defend or excuse anything Gertrude had written, Alice, silent and unruffled, kept her counsel.

And yet, however cavalierly she dismissed morality, there was one sliver of it to which Alice was sworn: loyalty. Toward friends, it was absolute; toward Gertrude, sacred. And from this commitment, so far as one could tell, she never wavered. Whether it was to protect their old friend Bernard Fay who during the war had collaborated with the Vichy regime and was allegedly implicated in a death camp deportation, or for the ungracefully aging painter Sir Francis Rose, a pre-war darling of Gertrude's who was still in Paris, still scrounging shamelessly and still lying inventively and brilliantly, Alice was unfazed. Charged by Gertrude before her death to help the first escape his imprisonment and the other to survive his own behavior, Alice had little problem overlooking their moral quotients and fully serving Gertrude's charge. For Fay, she ducked investigation, knew nothing, explained when examined that she had no power, how could she?, to effect any release, any escape. But friends labored officially and unofficially, and however Alice joined or didn't join in their labors, Fay eventually got free. He was an untroubled presence in Paris life when we met for interview, once again a free citizen, possibly unreconstructed.

Irresponsible Francis, on the other hand, needed silent watching and care lest he unwittingly do himself irreversible harm. When she learned I was set to interview him next day, Alice, ever watchful, alert lest Francis's tongue in a fit of irrepressible inventiveness soil Gertrude's posthumous reputation for good, called anxiously, once again early in the morning, to plead and explain, "Katz, you have to promise: report to me everything Francis tells you. Francis is *unreliable,* his stories are *unreliable,* he invents, he will tell you whatever comes into his head. Be sure to report every word to me." I promised; and at the interview had the delight of listening to episodes in Gertrude's later life which Francis, their nominal spectator, recited with Proustian fluency. Passed on to Alice, she footnoted them with perfect equanimity, not a vestige of irritation with Francis's tongue, taking his inventive zeal as simple fact: "Ah yes, Gertrude dancing on the baby grand, yes, that was so-and-so's dance and at such at such an event; the Spanish shawl in which she wrapped herself, oh yes, it was a lovely shawl that belonged to Countess so-and-so," Alice reducing a hilarious portrait of

Gertrude tipsy at a party to each of its creative Franciscan ingredients. Francis's excesses, appalling to many who might otherwise have befriended him, had no impact at all on Alice; they were facts not to be judged but to be dealt with, nothing more.

. But her comments on her *betes noires* could be excoriating, and one could hear it in her smoothly growled extemporaneities (her voice was close to baritone; relayed phone messages from friends who didn't know her sometimes quoted a "Monsieur Toklas.") Alice's comments on those in Gertrude's circle whom she couldn't abide ranged from affable to ungentle to acid. "Later on," she noted about Annette Rosenshine, "[she] went Gurchieff, and afterwards she went Freud. Once Mike started to say, 'I dreamed last night,' and the Stinker [Annette] interrupted quickly. 'Don't say any more. I'll know too much about you.' Her Freud." On Leo's fasts: "I never saw anyone fast both for his health and his philosophy at the same time. At the beginning he did it for the number of days he said he would. Oh, the horrible calculation of it! ....Breaking his fast,.... he was under the impression that great thoughts had come to him, not realizing they were everybody's thoughts when fasting." And on the early days when she first met Gertrude and Leo, her feelings about both were ungentle: "Gertrude was at that time still in the 'deep-thinking' life, the kind that worries about 'issues' and deliberates on the ethics and morality of each little act.... It was boring and ludicrous....I had the impression at the time that 'deep-thinking' was the root of all evil, that the fallible minds of human beings were bound to go wrong." But afterwards, to Alice's relief: "When Gertrude would be in her bath in the morning, and I would call her, she always said, 'Let me alone, I'm meditating.' Not 'deep-thinking.'" And Alice shuddering at the devotions of Gertrude's sister-in-law Sarah Stein to her Christian Science proselytizing and equally to her adored Matisse: "Yes, Sally and her life of rapture... Mildred Aldrich once reported that she came to see Sally and she was in bed reading the Christian Science bible. ' Sally looked up, gave me the papal blessing and I left.' It was Mildred who called it the 'Little Eva' expression.... This was the Sarah I knew, where she was vacant and saintly, complete vacancy and saintliness... It was perfect when Sally was with Matisse." And on the flabby indolence of Picasso's mistress, Fernande Olivier: "Fernande would have gotten the worst of it in a harem, she would have come out badly." Cringing at the recollection of Leo's explaining the paintings to the gathered at the rue de Fleurus on the Saturday evenings: "The half-hour, not-rapid, quiet monologues of Leo's that bored people unless they were really ignorant and young,"

Listening to her in this vein, it was best, I would think, to corroborate from other sources; it wasn't likely but possible that her devotion to exactitude might slip during these episodes of demeaning the disliked. But they rarely if ever did. Her recollections were generally pristine (rare exception: one or two dates.) Of the hundreds of names scrawled in the Notebooks, Alice, whether she had known them personally or only through Gertrude's shared recollections – could recall almost all and place them precisely in Gertrude's pantheon. It became overwhelmingly clear that she had programmatically learned – had studied and reassembled - all the years of Gertrude's life from its beginnings until they met. When I confessed my astonishment at her prowess, she demurred. There was a time, she said, when she could remember her life with Gertrude day by day. "I could have told you every day of our life together. But after Gertrude died, there were three years when I didn't want to live." It was a desperate time, until she realized that she was going to stay alive after all. "And I thought I may as well start living again." And so she did, but found that a good deal of what she had remembered was gone. Still, I insisted, her remembering was remarkable. "Well, not what it was."

But for all the stores of recollection she brought to the interviews, Alice had little idea beforehand of how long Gertrude clung to her first damning impressions, so violently recorded in that first entry. From the beginning, she took no stock in Gertrude's newly-burgeoning psychological "system," regarding it as little more than echoes of Leo's "deep-thinking." "I know what you are," Alice recalled Gertrude telling her early on, fitting her into one of the system's early (soon expunged) categories . "You're an old maid mermaid" condemning Alice to one of the lowest of kinds - a "flavor" type. "Oh, rats!" retorted Alice. When the "flavor" entries came up in our sessions, Alice, laughing, added quickly, "But I got out early!"

But she didn't. She discovered during our sessions that in fact "flavor," Gertrude's condescending pejorative, clung to her for years. What it signified was the incapacity to do more than "taste" the value of anything but never to know it - either person or creative object - authentically. She saw Alice as a double personality, an "interesting mixture" of one who had a "*crudely material relation*" to the object as well as a *"passionate emotion about"* the object *("it is to eat.")* But Gertrude's rigid criterion for genuine understanding, whether of paintings or of people, was met - for example, by Picasso and (though only sometimes) by Matisse - by those who had a "*direct relation* to the object." The perception of Alice's crude materialism and crudely passionate emotion remained for years, and Alice without knowing it had this cross to bear. In Gertrude's fastidious judgment, Alice even much later when she was genuinely loved, continued, in this and in a host of similar respects, "low."

While I read those notes aloud, Alice withstood Gertrude's diagnoses of her failings without demur, tightlipped, challenging none. But in the scramble of names resurrected from the past, there was one in particular that came up regularly, sometimes coupled with Alice's, the two sometimes seen by Gertrude as one. These were the notes that eventually moved Alice to confess what may have been the most profoundly divisive episode in their lives..

A few years before I got to Paris, I went over a list of names with Emma Lootz, who shared a house with Gertrude for two years while they were medical students at Baltimore's Johns Hopkins, names mostly of fellow-students during those years. Lootz, a blunt-spoken one, checked off the list expeditiously until she got to the name of May Bookstaver. Glee and amusement: "I *knew* you were going to get to her!" I didn't particularly, but didn't disabuse her, who happily recited the woeful tale of Gertrude's love affair with May during those student days, the affair that became – not difficult to fathom – the subject of Gertrude's earliest story, QED. So significant an episode in Gertrude's life begged for corroboration. Mabel Weeks, close back then to Gertrude, met her during that summer in Italy, the summer of Gertrude's greatest desperation over the affair, and recalled for me compassionately (a contrast to Lootz's narrator's grin) Gertrude's considerable pain together with her torrents of what prim Weeks called her "Wildean justifications."

When Alice wondered how I had gotten all this, I told her of those two interviews, by then deposited at Yale, and she, more relieved, it seemed, than annoyed, loosed her recollections of how she herself had discovered the affair, and most particularly of the cost to Gertrude of her discovery. The narrative in *QED*, she began, "was simply *rapportage*, the story there is just as it happened. Gertrude pulled out all of May's letters and used them as they were." But those letters, she warned, would not be found in the Yale archives. "I destroyed them with a passion."

The jealousy and anger that exercised Alice was further exasperated by the understanding she had had with Gertrude that their pasts would be entirely known to one another; of buried secrets, there'd be none. But in 1933, when the American novelist Louis Bromfield was to be shown a manuscript deposited in the armoire, Gertrude pulled out by mistake the all-but-forgotten manuscript of QED, and possibly abashed by the discovery, urged it on Bromfield to read it presumably for its curiosity. Alice never having seen this, the earliest of Gertrude's works, and observing Gertrude's quick decision to get it away, took note. Some six months later, when it came back in the mail, she pounced on it, read it, understood at once, and her feelings of betrayal were violent. "I went almost mad. I destroyed every sign, every letter, of the recollection of May. If I saw hints of the letters *m* or *mm* shadowed on Gertrude's writing table [the Tuscan,] I sandpapered them off. And I went through manuscripts Gertude was writing then, and changed every mention of the word "may" to "can."

The most scrupulous of Stein scholars, Ulla Dydo, carefully checking through Gertrude's manuscripts at Yale, discovered that the "may/can" changes were in Gertrude's hand, not as Alice intimated, in her own. By that correction, a somewhat frightening suggestion emerges of Alice standing over a trembling Gertrude at her writing table following Alice's peremptory orders to eviscerate the offending "*may*s."

Or - more gently - of Gertrude alone at her table obeying, with tongue-between-teeth, Alice's vindictive edict.

"For a year and a half, I tormented Gertrude, and didnt let up even when we were in America for the lecture tour. When any of her old friends or relatives in America called, I answered the phone to say, Miss Stein is sleeping and cannot be disturbed. I didnt want her to see any of them. Then when we were in Chicago staying at Thornton [Wilder]'s apartment while she was lecturing at the University of Chicago, she suddenly turned to me one day, and said. 'Alice, if you don't stop this, our life together will be over.' I stopped at once. I never mentioned it again."

The outlandishness of her behavior during those eighteen months was palpable, but her recitation of it bore no hint of shame or *mea culpa* or self-justification. What had happened was the fact, it had happened, so it was. Her telling of it left her presentation of herself untouched, her *amour propre* undiminished. Alice was authentically equal to her boast: she had no morality whatever, and possibly regretted, if anything, only her manners toward her victim during those trying months.

But there were two moments during the reading of the notes that at last corroborated Alice's deepest certainties about Gertrude's feeling during those early years: one, the day after I had read so many of Gertrude's notes of carping and condemning and qualifying and acknowledging no warm feeling toward Alice, there was a note which read in passing: "and I love her." And Alice, who had been hoping it would never be said aloud for the profane, and at the same time dreading that it would never be acknowledged at all in these private texts, her eyes opening wide, "She says it?" "Yes." "Just like that." "Yes," followed by a long pause: "Well, then… !" Gertrude had said it bluntly, and privately, to herself, not in accommodating flattery directly to Alice, but definitively, to herself.

The second note again put it bluntly: Alice – unlike St. Katherine – (Gertrude was reading a life of St. Katherine just then) was at one with St. Therese. Alice was clearly gratified to hear the entry read aloud, though she could hardly have been surprise by it. Gertrude was already addressing intimate notes to her as "St. Therese." It wasn't difficult to know why, but I was anxious to set down Alice's explanation in her own words of Gertrude's meaning. (Great mistake, Costly mistake.) "In what sense were you St. Therese to Gertrude?" No response, but urged, and urged again, Alice with enormous reluctance and some anger responded, pained and hesitant, "Because I felt toward Gertrude as St. Therese felt toward the Christ. For me, it was the same experience and the same relation." A long pause, and then, blunt anger: "It was stupid of you to ask, young man." It was. The only rule for our question/answer sessions that still pertained. unspoken but understood: I was to have the courtesy never to encroach on her deepest privacy. I had, and was instantly chastised.

The last note was read, and the last comment appended in February, and Alice, finished for the time with our sessions, was complaining to me about the concierge who had been in the flat that morning, and had had the temerity to tell her that her face had gone bright yellow. It angered her, and she wanted flat contradiction. But he was right, I had to confess, and she ran to the bathroom to check in the mirror which, like aging Good Queen Bess, she had carefully not consulted in years. Reassured and laughing and appalled, she recognized – we both did – that the work on the cookbook and the winter chill and the the poring over Gertrude's notes till late hours had brought on a serious bout of yellow jaundice. But we were done with the notes for now, and Alice was soon recuperating under care, so I escaped to Italy from the winter gloom of Paris to interview Bernard Berenson, the doyen of Settignano in the hills overlooking Florence, who with his wife Mary, now deceased, had in the early days of the century dominated the Anglo-American colony there - the Steins and Houghtons and Hapgoods and Thorolds – who once gathered in those hills for summers of Italian sweltering bliss and discreet libidinal abandon.

Fifty years later, and absent the turn-of-the-century Anglo-Americans, BB lived royally under the solicitous care of his faithful secretary and caregiver Nicky Mariano in the quiet splendor of I Tatti, the villa he had already willed to his alma mater Harvard. It was to be turned after his death into a European annex for art students' study of mainly Florentine Renaissance painting, which was BB's celebrated expertise, and of his extraordinary library holdings.

"Come for luncheon," he called on the phone, and praying transportation up the hill from Florence would by rare exception – no strike, no *feria* – be running that morning, I made the trip not to Settignano but to Fiesole, where the Steins spent their summers, so I could walk, as they did, from their villas to BB's. And in the soft weather of the Italian hills, reveling in the pleasure of maneuvering those paths, I was remembering Alice's recollections of Gertrude on those walks stopping to stare directly into the sun not as a feat but as a familiar pleasure, and Gertrude telling Alice when she complained about stepping into a patch of cowflop and suffering the smell, Gertrude remonstrating, "Why? You love smells, don't you? [Alice's "flavor" type.] All smells. Well, that's a smell." And Alice remembering not loving it. The expansiveness, the sheer beauty of the landscape with its seven hills, like Rome's, embracing Florence, the landscape gentle, not overpowering, evoked the mental image of those early-in-the-century expatriates running about these hills, prompting one to call up not so much their reverence as their desecration.

Waiting lunch, BB gave me leave to wander through the library stacks and the great room with the covered-over murals – one of BB's embarrassing mistakes – forbiddingly ugly paintings which he had commissioned in the 1900's and which he couldn't bear to look at when they were finished, but had scruples about obliterating works of art. At table, now a frail one and as tiny as Alice herself, he presided, sage and wit, with verve, after his mandatory nap legislated by his devoted, adoring secretary and caregiver, Nicky Mariano . Without prompting or questions, he recollected stories about Gertrude and Leo which he recited as though – too bad for interviewers - they were already packaged and fixed in his head. (It was Mary Berenson's letters from those early years that told the whole complicated story of the Berensons' relation to the Steins; BB's remembered bits, as it turned out, did not.)

On Gertrude, there was the one about her badgering him for a half hour with diagnosis-cum-prognosis of his "character," not a word of which he could follow or understand. (What he had heard was surely that he was a "flavor" type like Alice, and that he "ran himself by his mind" rather than by his "bottom nature," a double debility in Gertrude's "system" that, after so many years of BB's recollection, still left him bemused.) Another, apparently equally worn performance, was mimickng his fright once again at the thought of the small brooch that held closed Gertrude's kimono, her single garment back then, slipping its grip. As for Leo, who till the end of his life lived penuriously but close to I Itatti, he was BB's genuinely valued friend. (BB's clout with the Fascists during the war protected Leo from harassment or deportation.) Still, in BB's packaged story, Leo came off badly. In his later years, he had gone deaf, and talking as he always talked in long, muttered paragraphs, now hearing no responses from interlocators, he never stopped. BB seeing him from a distance approaching the house, would run away and hide.. "I loved him," BB insisted. He was a saint, to be sure, but he had become insufferable.

But in Gertrude's pegging Berenson as a "flavor" type, she might well have been vindicated. In Samuel's biography of Berenson, Nicky Mariano tells of one of the last days of BB's life when he asked her to carry him to the window of his room to look at the villa's garden and the landscape beyond. Carrying the little that was left of him in her arms to view for the last time the splendor of that familiar landscape, like Alice at the last performance of Alicia Markova, BB raised his thin arm above his head, and waved farewell.

"Who do you think I am, Queen Victoria?" Alice barked into the phone a few days after I got back and was protesting to her that I'd been waiting to be "summoned." She was on edge to hear about the visit - the state of BB, what he said about Gertrude, about Leo, and most particularly about the state of the I Tatti gardens. Were they still mangled by wrong plantings, or better now than they were then? Alice loathed the villa itself, had no hope for its improvement, but the gardens – they were another matter; she shared BB's reverence for them. As for his recollections of Gertrude and Leo, Alice, alert for report of BB's every word, listened voraciously, nodding yes, that was BB, yes, yes, that's what he would think, neither agreeing nor disagreeing, only recognizing BB's feeling and opinion to be what they had always been. Happily confirmed, subject was filed and closed.

With Gertrude's notebooks put aside, the routine of visits continued nevertheless, but with much expanded venues and casts of characters. There were now visits out - to Balmain's Spring showing, where Alice was specially honored with a seat at the foot of the ramp, and where the parading models could catch sight of her and - violating for a moment the grim protocol of the frozen-faced mannequin - cheerfully waved Alice a big hello, and Alice feeling an irrepressible urge to pick the still-clinging threads from the hem of a grinning model's couture. And to Natalie Barney's Friday evenings in her seraglio of rooms where crowds of ancients wandered about, and Alice took the trouble to warn me about talking too long to one of her particularly disliked elderly pederasts. And a hostile young American, when I assured him I was working on Gertrude out of devotion, said flatly: "Man, you need a library card!"

Lunches expanded, and guests who once gathered for Gertrude's sake, now did so very much for Alice's sake alone, who was showing herself a redoubtable hostess once she had decided "to live again." For lunches and for 5 o'clock gatherings, she had simple techniques in hand that were a pleasure to watch in execution. Once it was for a roomful of guests, left-over surrealists from the Thirties, who babbled and babbled and fell silent, and did so repeatedly, when Alice, attuned to the millisecond of a too-long silence, interjected, as though continuing conversational flow, a "No," and then a "Well," to which she added any stretch of words that came into her head, whether about nothing or something, and somehow conversation would answer as though something had indeed been said, and again babble flowed. Her ability to fall in with a private guest's momentary mood – I watched it with Georgia O'Keefe and Dora Mahr – was a far cry from the cunning Gertrude noticed in the early days, when Alice so-to-speak sat at your feet and looked up worshipfully, turning you into "one of her old gentlemen so that you were then hers." That Alice was long gone. With an assured sense now, she maneuvered her interviews avoiding entirely the appeal Gertrude once condemned as groveling.

For Alice, who ate only once a day, when there were guests for lunch her tiny dining room was her pleasure and her empire. For it, she would bring in the current "Helene" – tribute to the old days with Gertrude, when whatever servant was current was rechristened "Helene" - to labor with her in the kitchen and serve at table and slip out afterward unremarked. The prohibitively costly electricity in the salon's wall-sconces was acknowledged and lit, and Helene under severe observation rendered the large salon and the tiny dining room immaculate. I - by then not so much a guest as simply there – came early once, and looking into the dining room, heard "eighty-four, eighty-five, eighty-six, go away, eighty-eight," Alice, proud chef, later explaining that that sauce was to be stirred exactly one hundred times, there was no losing count to say hello.

Alice for some reason took it into her head that afternoon to bait Janet Flanner, *The New Yorker's* Genet, a politically liberal American, and a friend who had written compassionate articles about Alice's life in Paris since Gertrude's death. But Alice, a lifelong unreconstructed Republican like Gertrude, all through lunch needled Flanner about niggers in America and thieving Arabs in Paris; but Flanner, taking no umbrage, graciously pretended not to hear.

It was the last *narishkeit* I detected in Alice who, before I left Paris, offered me a remarkable gesture of confidence, and, although regretfully nothing could come of it then, my gratitude for her trust remains intact. "Katz, why don't you come back next summer, and together we can go to Mallorca, where there is wonderful food and summer living to be had, and possibly I can recount for you my life together with Gertrude almost day by day." In pursuit of this, Alice, during the summer's "American invasion," waited for the day when Robert Hutchins and Thornton Wilder were coming to visit. Hutchins, Chicago University's president and head then of the Ford Foundation, could renew my grant for another year. But I had no prayer of extending my stay away from job and family for another year, and nothing could come of their visit. But there was consolation. Thornton Wilder took me that evening for another of his visits to a play he'd fallen in love with: "It's Kafka and Joyce!" He'd already sent a dozen copies of it to friends in America, including the producer Michael Myerberg. He'd made enough money, Wilder urged, on his own The Skin of Our Teeth; now he could afford to lose money on Waiting for Godot. The beginning of knowing the as yet not known Waiting for Godot, in a tiny theatre in Paris with no more than fourteen other viewers in attendance, and one of them, when Didi urges Gogo for the umpteenth time, "Let's go", calling out, "D'accord!" and with Thornton Wilder beside himself with pleasure, but with only one demurrer – Ah, it has to be played by clowns! (he got his wish the next year in Myerberg's Broadway production with Bert Lahr) was memorable compensation.

At our last meeting on the day I was leaving Paris, we exchanged my typed text of her cookbook and the borrowed typewriter, and she the Notebooks, which we had agreed she would not see all together until we were well finished with all talk. I was almost at the door ready to leave, when Alice, instead of saying goodbye, had one more thing to say. She had read the Notebooks right through the night before, and hearing Gertrude's voice describing mutual friends with such deadly precision, so exactly as Alice remembered them, especially the portrait of one, the redoubtable Claribel Cone so perfectly realized, she was intensely moved, and then, without guile, from her very center, it seemed, she was saying, "You know, Katz, we've been talking about Gertrude for a year, and in all that time I don't think I've ever been able to give you any idea of what it was like to live with her."

And then a truly rare thing happened. During all the interviews, one could tell from her eyes when she was concealing, when she was open, when plainly lying, but it never happened that one saw her entirely vulnerable, never. Now suddenly her face changed and became almost a child's face. And she said, "You see, when Gertrude came into this room, the room would light up, the day would light up, the year would light up – and my life would light up." There was indeed no more to be said but "Goodbye, Miss Toklas," and I left. It was extraordinary, on the very last day to see the absolute internality of this carefully guarded woman. Underneath all the guile, all the evasiveness, beneath all that, there was a truly guileless woman who simply loved, wholly, devotedly, loved. It could hardly have been more apparent: hers had been inwardly the most treasured of all blessings, an entirely fulfilled life. That was the greatest insight of all.

Leon Katz

1. INTRODUCTION

The full story of the writing of *The Making of Americans* is filled with people and events some quota of which has a peculiar and important place in the web of human associations that Gertrude used to build her psychological "system," the system which ultimately became the central matter of her novel. But it is also a titillating one, with the names of the great and near-great of Post-Impressionist, Fauve and Cubist artists dotting its pages, as well as less familiar but enigmatic personalities whose mysteries Gertrude yearned to unravel. All the people and incidents reviewed in the Notebooks were of significance in the construction of the schematic design, gradually completed during the writing of the novel's final version. The finished novel contains within its schemes and diagrams of characterization the residue of the hundred and more people evoked in the Notebooks, all of them wedged in one way or another into the book's elaborate and peculiar mosaic.

Its peculiar mosaic: The novel is compounded of three continuities. It was originally conceived as a conventional novel which would follow the progress of two immigrant German Jewish families—her own and the New York Steins, her cousins—being assimilated over years into the life of an "Anglo-Saxon," bourgeois America. Two attempts—two drafts—of the novel were begun, one in 1903 and the second in 1906, of which the first five chapters are still extant. [See *Fernhurst*, 137–172.] Early Notebook labors are expended on the planning of this narrative together with its characters, their sources drawn from Gertrude's family members, her early acquaintances and her later Radcliffe and Johns Hopkins colleagues. That planning is done in some detail in Gertrude's early notes, some even anticipating the last pages of the novel's narrative.

But it is suddenly interrupted and displaced by another continuity, one which becomes overwhelmingly the book's central concern. It is governed by Gertrude's ambition to build a universal characterological construct which would ultimately encompass, as she put it, "every one who ever was or is or will be living." That construct is carefully built over hundreds of pages, its principles and their instances carefully exemplified by the story's characters, and beyond them by multiple examples from any and all who existed among Gertrude's current acquaintance or distant memories.

But the motive that urged Gertrude to build such a system runs deep and goes far beyond its putative characterological formulations. It looks back to her childhood and adolescence, and to the disorientations she suffered confronted by painful questions about her relevance to "eternity," "identity," "existence" and being "important in living."

That becomes the novel's enterprise tracing the gradual building of the psychological "system," together with its eventual and inevitable undoing. But in the course of its pursuit, the novel's narrative is increasingly dimmed in its pages, dimmed but not abandoned. It remains the reader's most accessible path through the book's complexities.

A third continuity is Gertrude's self-interruptions for conversation with the reader. These consist of a running confessional of her concurrent thinking while writing and recounting frankly and unabashedly her own evaluation of her notional inventions for the book's composition. Rarely is an author at the same time both within and without his or her texts in the very moment of their telling, and rarely is a reader in fathoming that text, invited to sit so closely to the author's writing hand. The reader is never at a loss to know what the writer is up to, and what she thinks of what she's at the moment up to.

These Notebooks, then, are concerned with the writing years from 1902 to 1912 and trace the steps that led from the first draft of the novel to the unique craft of the finished work. When the final draft of the novel was completed, it was in effect a new work that subsumed the interests and preoccupations of the original versions—a new, unique and extraordinarily imposing composition.

***

As reader's aids for studying the Notebooks, there are appended sections tracing in detail (1) the novel's narrative of the two families, the Herslands and the Dehnings, and their moderately interwoven destinies, (2) Gertrude's intensely private but intensely urgent need for changing the book's direction, her gradual development of a characterology in response to that need, and Gertrude's gradual loss of confidence in her characterological venture, ending in "Impasse." The Impasse is in turn followed by a fundamental shift in her writer's intent that concludes with the extraordinary final chapter of the novel. The "David Hersland" chapter rejects the novel's earlier approach to characterology and begins the revolutionary use and justification for a language's privacy. Further appended to the Notebooks is a page-by-page Summary of the novel. Running through it are underlined headings marked GS to Reader, Gertrude's running colloquy with the reader, and the frank revelation of her own emotional and intellectual responses to her book's gathering complexities.

***

The detailed study of these years was made possible chiefly by the preliminary examination and tentative editing of the Notebooks at Yale University's Beinecke Library, and by the kindness of Miss Alice Toklas, who from November of 1952 through February of 1953 adumbrated and orally annotated the Notebooks out of her store of memories for about eight hours a day, four days a week. During that time, she was writing her cookbook too, and as a result of this double drain on her energies, she succumbed in the second week of March 1953 to a particularly bilious form of yellow jaundice. My obligation to her for her costly devotion to the job of clarifying

Gertrude's Notebooks is evident everywhere in these pages. What is further evident is her refusal to comment on any of the concerns of Gertrude's psychological ventures, and her determination to confine comment to her recollection of Gertrude's subjects, her comments and judgments ranging from her gentle nods of recollection to her unapologetic verbal jabs with skilled stiletto.

Professor Donald C. Gallup of the Yale University Library and Carl Van Vechten kindly permitted me to edit the Notebooks, and Professor Gallup's help, both with the materials in the Stein Collection at Yale and with supplementary information, was invaluable. This edition of the Notebooks was undertaken with the aid of a fellowship granted by the Ford Foundation, and by a subsequent grant from the National Endowment for the Humanities. For help with introductions to interviewees in France, Italy and the U.S., I am especially indebted to Marc Bourdelin, Lynn and Gail Belaief, Irvin Ehrenpreis and Kenneth Rexroth. To all the Stein associates and relations who were kind enough to grant interviews—all of whom are listed in the bibliography—my grateful acknowledgement. For the great encouragement and most generous practical assistance of the administration and staff of Manhattanville College, most particularly, of Mother Adele Fiske—my gratitude is abiding and profound. I owe a great deal. too, to the generosity of good friends Ulla Dydo and Edward Burns, extraordinarily knowledgeable Stein scholars, who provided invaluable information and assistance whenever called upon. To Edward Burns, who retains rights to Alice Toklas material, I am especially grateful for his granting permission for their use. My gratitude for the long and devoted labors of my assistants, Georgi Iliev and Benjamin Ian Smith, is great indeed.

***

A brief apology to sticklers for propriety. Given the level of discourse that seemed right for this publication, and to avoid the stiffness of referring everywhere to Gertrude Stein as either Miss Stein or by her full name, I've adopted the low expedient of referring to her as "Gertrude." I repeat: my apology to sticklers.

***

2. An Overview: "Saying Being"

In the prefatory paragraphs of the first draft, Gertrude announces that she is going to write a book reflecting the history of her own generation "so that we can know ourselves." [**First Draft; p. 1**; echoed in MA 3.] The sense in which she wished to know herself is slightly more particularized at the beginning of her description of her father, whom "we must soon be realizing so that we can understand our own being." [MA 42.] In the first design of the novel she conceived the answer to the problem of "knowing oneself" as consisting largely of tracing one's "traits" back to one's forbears for three or so generations. But it remained hardly an adequate answer to the problem that gave rise to her need to "realize" or "know" herself.

What became her intense need grew out of a series of anxieties in her childhood and adolescence that so frightened and shocked her that she never got over them. Worries familiar enough, she nevertheless returned again and again to the questions these "discoveries" aroused in her. "When I was about eight," she recalls in *Everybody's Autobiography*,

> I was surprised to know that in the Old Testament there was nothing about a future life or eternity. I read it to see and there was nothing there. There was a God of course and He spoke but there was nothing about eternity. [EA96.]
>
> It was frightening when the first comet I saw made it real that the stars were worlds and the earth only one of them, it is like the Old Testament, there is God but there is no eternity. [EA97.]

These anxieties, together with her later realization that whole civilizations had already lived and died, [EA96.] were worrisome in much the same way they have been for everyone who suffers the recognition of their cosmic unimportance.

> I was worrying then [during adolescence] about identity and memory and eternity.... if the stars are suns and the earth is the earth and there are men only upon this earth and anything can put an end to anything and any dog does anything just like anybody does it what is the difference between eternity and anything. As I was saying there was a God but there was no mention of everlasting. [EA98.]

Apart from these adolescent jolts, Gertrude experienced one less frequent, or at least less frequently recorded than those. "There are some," she writes at the beginning of *A Long Gay Book*,

> when they feel it inside them ... that there was once so very little of them, that they were a baby, helpless and no conscious feeling in them,

> that they know nothing then… [they] have from such a knowing an uncertain curious kind of a feeling in them that their having been so little once and knowing nothing makes it all a broken world that they have inside them, kills for them the everlasting feeling, and they spend their life in many ways, and always they are trying to make for themselves a new everlasting feeling.[1]

Her "broken world" and loss of the sense of everlasting are worth regarding closely. They are not the same as the Romantics' sense of disconnection, a literary posture which Gertrude did not imitate. Her disorientation was more depressing and found no relief in Nineteenth Century Romanticism's Byronic glooms. What she was overwhelmed by in the accumulation of all these experiences was not the picture of the ego dissociated and mourning in a hostile land, but a picture, made familiar later in Kafka and Beckett, of a landscape so enormous, so colorless and so uniform that it reduced human beings to things too small and unimportant to exhibit difference. On the one hand it causes it to appear to itself as impersonal and anonymous; on the other, it causes the discontinuity of human being from itself, so that even its intimate self-knowledge—as Gertrude would say, the knowledge of "himself to himself inside him"—does not put him into important and unbroken relation with "everlasting." As a consequence, Gertrude regards the chief activity of human beings to be the concealment from themselves of the desperate realization of their own nonentity and non-relation, of their rupture with eternity, and their isolated separation from the universal.[2]Their habitual way of accomplishing this concealment is through the various ways there are of inventing one's "importance," or—if altogether bereft of self-assurance—being capable of little more than asserting one's mere "existence."

The whole problem of fundamental human desperation as Post-Romantics saw it is centered on a complex of images different from those of the Romantics. It does not concern special egos but usual ones and everyone. The images they use take on their own characteristic tone, or posture—a sort of universally applicable shrug of

---

[1]*A Long Gay Book*, published in *Matisse, Picasso and Gertrude Stein with Two Shorter Stories*; (Paris: Plain Edition, 1933), p.13.

[2]In addition to treating this theme in the opening pages of *A Long Gay Book*, (pp. 13 to 17), Gertrude used it as the basis of her analyses of Harriet Levy and Dr. Clairibel Cone (two of the most important and extended analyses of personality she ever made) recorded in DB #57. The theme was taken up again in the Nineteen Thirties in *Everybody's Autobiography* [quoted above), and most elaborately in *Geographical History of America*, passim, in which her problem is resolved once again to her satisfaction. The resolutions sustained in the *Geographical History* are already implied—indeed, stated—in Weininger's *Sex and Character* [see below, p.278]. In the Nineteen Thirties, Gertrude in effect retraced the argument she had already accepted as conclusive during the writing of MA.

indifference. When the characters of Kafka or Beckett confront overwhelming desperation, they react with flat and emotionless diffidence. Kafka's heroes, since they refuse ever to give up their humanistic and rational morality in the face of the most extreme and universal monstrousness, are treated by their author as comic and quixotic posturers. Beckett's characters, brought to the last retch of inhuman misery, are contemptuous of themselves if they still bother to feel such a thing as rage. In a play called Listen to Me, Gertrude's characters have no names, only numbers, and they expend their days in trying to name who they are. Finally despairing of finding out what they mean by "I know I am," they give up their undertaking and go off with a kind of desperate joy to what appears to be an al fresco banquet.

The Nineteenth Century not only lyricized despair; it also adopted scientific naturalism as a diversion from its awareness of disorientation. "Darwin was... near... when I began knowing everything." [EA209.] By the Nineteen Thirties, Gertrude looked back on "Darwinism" as a forlorn excuse for an answer. She remembered also the hope held out by William James' *The Will to Believe.*

> There was of course science and evolution and there were of course the fact that stars were worlds and that space had no limitation... and civilizations came to be dead... since the earth had no more size than it had... and so was science and progress interesting was it existing but after all there was evolution and James' *The Will to Believe* and I had always been afraid always would be afraid but after all that was what it was to be not refusing to be dead although after all everyone was refusing to be dead.[EA210.]

Even William James' *The Will to Believe* for all its nudgings toward something like belief did not get rid of the old fear. The frightening certainty returned that everyone's life, one's own in particular, was not necessarily purposeful, but simply continued because "everyone was refusing to be dead." In the final pages of the Notebooks and in *A Long Gay Book*, Gertrude considers the question of everyone "filling days."[3]In it, people are shown covering the anxiety induced by the memory of their "broken world" by having babies or by religion or by self-preserving pride or knowledge or "creating." [LGB13–17.] But all these ploys are merely substitutes. Like the laws of science, "they do something to keep everyone from knowing that they are not going on living." [EA210.]

Gertrude gives the experience of the questionable terms of existence to the young David Hersland in *The Making of Americans* and makes it the most important

---

[3]Note #140; marginal notation in ms. of *A Long Gay Book* (for passage beginning on p. 35, par. 6): "filling being living." *Everybody's Autobiography*, p. 44: "The only reason why people work or run around... is that they will not know that time is something and that time can pass."

motivating factor in his failed life. [MA 743ff.] When he is very young, as she describes, he realizes that there is something exceptional, accidental and peculiar in the fact that he is living at all. He subsequently discovers that he was born only because of a family decision to replace a child who had died. It becomes necessary for him thereafter to scrutinize conscientiously and perpetually the meaning of the statement he persistently makes to himself: that he *needs* to be living. Subsequently he converts his quest for the meaning of his life into an equally determined quest for death.[4]He longs at the end only to be done with the torment of finding sufficient justification for life. In the dirge sung over the dead hero at the end of the book, Gertrude plays ruefully with the word "need." "Not anyone needed this thing, that he should come to be a dead one," but "*he* needed this thing." [MA 903.]

The greatest and most genuine solution to the whole problem was one that Gertrude attributed to "geniuses" and "saints," terms that she uses almost interchangeably for those who have won sufficient wisdom to transcend the pain of human contingency. For them the ordinary forms of human self-delusion are no longer necessary because they have achieved "self-relation" so complete that it does not need the supports of memory, or reflected images of one's identity, or spurious extensions of one's self in infinite relations with all time and all space.

> When one is completely wise that is when one is a genius the things that make you a genius make you live but have nothing to do with being living that is with the struggle for existence. Really genius[,] that is the existing without any internal recognition of time. [MA 903.]

But when Gertrude began her novel, she was not yet ready for the saintly wisdom of "existing without any internal recognition of time." She was still very much a product of the Nineteenth Century, and if the standard teleological comforts in their more familiar forms were already lost to her, when she asked the question "Who am I?" she still wanted a plain answer, and the answer she wanted was that she was linked with everything. "[I]t all had to do that inside you are separated away from connection and at the same time you do not think about that thing." [EA260] For the first two drafts of the novel (1903 and 1906–08) to "think about that thing" needed only "realizing" all of one's forbears for three past generations and all of one's own past, and then articulating in narrative one's self and one's own generation—so enfolding sufficiently the accident and irrelevance of the self into the stream of living.

> After all I was a natural believer in republics a natural believer in science a natural believer in progress and I began to write. After all I

---

[4]Theme of his quest for death begins on MA 835.

> was a natural believer just as the present generation are natural believers in Soviets and proletarian literature and social laws and everything although really it does not really make them be living any more than science and progress and democracies did me. [EA211.]

And so, the landscape in which she was to warrant her own being was to change entirely. The "family novel" was to be burdened with an alternate narrative that gradually superseded—without eliminating—the first. It was the narrative of the gradual building of a "system" which had become overwhelmingly compelling—to counter the accident, separation and irrelevance of the self with a coherent, universal, enclosing structure that resolved the dilemmas of concealed human anguish.

The urgency to develop so reassuring a system becomes the novel's second continuity—the author's own private progress gauged by her alone as she responded to the vicissitudes of her labors in her system's development. Only once, and only at her system's total unraveling, does she voice the pain of her loss when she cries, "I am important with this thing!" [MA 583] Establishing her "importance with this thing" had been her whole private objective.

***

"BEGIN THIS NEW THING," she instructs herself in her Notebooks in the summer of 1908. [NB-*C #4] What begins is the interspersing— within two years of text already written between 1906 and 1908 of a set of terms for character constructs assembled within a gradually developing system of groups, or as she called them, "kinds" of like human beings. Gertrude imagined the numbers of beings within each kind as "millions," and in turn, posited "kinds" themselves as numbered in millions. There was strategy in imagining the clustering of kinds and their instances in millions. It looked forward to an endlessly expanding cosmic diagram which—whether ultimately finished or never finished—would include each human's defined space within its scheme's universally classifying embrace. The comfort of such an embrace, whether of this scheme or another's, was in its strategy: human beings, knowingly or unknowingly, invested powerfully in such wide enclosure, whether for their genuine or illusory "refusing to be dead."

The beginnings of Gertrude's conscientious schematizings were tentative. In the early notes for the novel's second (1906) draft, she begins to group themes that in part define the subjectivities of her characters—their "feelings,"—as in feelings of anger, of pride, of vanity, and more significantly, feelings that lay at the heart of her initial and fundamental insights into human anxiety: their feeling for their "importance in living" or their self-negating feeling of having no importance at all, but of merely "existing"—as, for example, in Mr. Hersland's extremity of important feeling "as big as all the world around him," or his daughter Martha's feeling of hardly existing at all. Gertrude notes patterns in human behavior not only for her fictional characters but for the human aggregate, and these, collectively, become the thematic material which looks toward what was soon to become her fixed typological definitions of human being.

For Gertrude, themes like these became touchstones, introduced into the early pages of the novel as part of a soon-to-be- formal apparatus for psychological, or more specifically, characterological, analysis. But touchstones like "anger" or "vanity" were only the faintest beginnings of what was to become the substantial matter of the novel. The catalyst that led to the definitive change in the novel's purpose and method in 1908 was the book that fell into her hands during the previous winter.

It was probably Leo who first picked up a copy of Weininger's *Sex and Character* in a bookshop, although, as in the case of buying pictures, it's debatable whether Leo himself or he and Gertrude together first came across the book and bought it.[5] In any case, they were among the first of their acquaintances to read it, and for the rest of the winter until they set off for Florence in May of 1908, the book was the center of violent discussion. After their first enthusiasm, they sent copies to everyone, even to old friends in America.[6] Leo felt that Weininger was an example of pure genius, and since he was meeting regularly with Roche about once a week during that winter for hours-long discussions on set subjects, they used Weininger's book for a while as their focus, and as Leo adumbrated, Roche interlarded his copy of the book with Leo's notes and comments. Roche, when interviewed, still had his copy of the book with its record of months of deliberation. Leo responded for a time to Weininger's anti-feminism, and at the peak of his interest declared that if one could take women's minds off their wombs, they might be helped to some kind of development after all. [Roche, interview] But his interest in this project passed, and he returned soon to his more comfortable preoccupations with questions of consciousness, and composition in art.

Gertrude's response to Weininger left more considerable impress on her thinking. The book prodded her toward emulating his way of systematizing the description of relations among the people she was already using for character description in her notes. Like Weininger, she had already rejected the experimental psychology consisting of tabulating and enumerating bodily sensations to which she had been subjected at the Harvard Psychological Laboratory, and opted instead, like Weininger, for a psychology describing "the single and simple existence" in a single self, its "character" in this "unlimited" sense. It was also

> not something seated behind the thoughts and feelings in the individual, [Gertrude had already vowed, after reading Freud on the

---

[5]Toklas, Interviews, and Roche, Interview, disagree.

[6]Letters, E. L. Erving to GS, December 14, 1908 and May 3, 1909; Marion Walker to GS, (1909).

> Oedipus complex, to read no more] but something revealing itself in every thought and feeling.... This existence, manifested in every moment of the psychical life, is the object of characterology. [OW49.]

Weininger was now to make her goal explicit: to achieve a synoptic vision of the ego of each character so inclusive that his or her every act and sensation could be observed in its whole relevance to the complete field of the ego. The observer, passing beyond the need to separate one "aspect" of the self from another—a separation which can be accomplished only by the trick of abstraction—would seize on his *wholenes*s, and from that vantage be in a position ultimately to approach in each character "the last touch of [his] human being."

On the face of it, Weininger's book was widely taken as little more than a violent anti-feminist tract basing its argument on the characterological differences between "maleness" and "femaleness," and pushing argument into the outer reaches of the absurd by equating the highest possible reach of "being" with "total maleness" and the lowest with "total femaleness." [OW114.]

But far more significant than any of his terminological banalities that Gertrude took, enlarged or avoided altogether, the aspect of his work that struck her more forcibly was his immensely pertinent resolution of two of her problems: the conscious feeling of dissociation from the "everlasting," and that psych-lab description of men and women as bundles of factors, losing the sense of individual uniqueness (in her mantra, that "each one is *one*.")[7]

During the five months of labor on the "Diagram Book" and its attendant notations, [DB #1 through DB #64] the "system" took slapdash, rough, unsystematic, even bewildering, shape. But within that bewilderment, Gertrude was venturing to systematize.

***

BEGINNING

In the first pages of the "Martha Hersland" chapter [MA 290ff.], written in 1909 after her initial struggles with the building of her system were done, Gertrude recapitulated the unique process by which she had arrived at her understanding of individuals and their "kinds." The process began, as she reports, with the study of three women. The first of them was Annette Rosenshine, a forlorn creature, bent—just as the fashion was beginning that would overwhelm the new century—on finding herself. During the two years of Annette's stay in Paris, she and Gertrude settled into a routine painful to

[7]Refrain used in *Many Many Women*, published in *Matisse, Picasso and Gertrude Stein*, pp.119–198.

both but rewarding to Gertrude for its endlessly boring afternoon sessions in which she converted conversation into therapy, and equally rewarding for Annette who gratefully suffered the pain of Gertrude's unremitting therapeutic attacks.

The other two, Harriet Levy and Alice Toklas, also San Francisco renegades, arrived a year later, in 1907, and joining the Stein circle, gave Gertrude two further subjects for almost daily, excruciatingly intense study. While studying all three, Gertrude gradually discovered, and acknowledged willingly, the unreliability of her therapeutic ambition, and settled permanently for developing a system for psychological "description" and no more. Faced with continuing and futile labors with Annette and added to them the unshakable and incurable fears of Harriet Levy and the tantalizingly difficult to fathom Alice Toklas, Gertrude explains, through the intensity of her passionate, endlessly patient labor observing and listening for her subjects' defining characteristics, she discovered that the way to reach their self-revelation was through their inadvertent ways of repeating themselves.

***

REPETITION

"Always from the beginning there was to me all living as repeating." [MA 291.] The discovery of the ways "there can be seen to be kinds in men and women," and the "nature" and the "mixing of natures" in single human beings, begins with "loving [their] repetition." [MA 290.] What is repeated?

By "listening,"—not to what is said but to the rhythms and patterns of speech through which it is said; and by "looking"—not at the purpose of the body's intentional motion so much as at the characteristic rhythms and patterns into which its motions habitually fall—both one's general "kind" and uniqueness of self-reveal themselves inadvertently and unmistakably. "Listening can be dulling," writes Gertrude, but with patience, there is eventual reward through what she calls "the drama of emergence"—the eventual emergence of intelligible meaning through loving the repetition in her subjects—a repetition that is manifest in every action, every word, every sight and every moment of their being—one can, after long, patient scrutiny, realize the fundamental character of each one, and so, eventually, "the bottom nature of them, the mixtures in them, the strength and weakness of everything they have inside them, the flavor of them, the meaning in them, the being in them, and then you have a whole history of each one." [MA 137.]

But the patience needed for her method of "listening for repeating" had to be somewhat mitigated by the practical consideration that crowds of people—many currently known, many only remembered—were finding their place in the exemplification of her system. A few, to be sure, were intensely studied—Harriet Levy and Annette Rosenshine, Alice Toklas, Gertrude's brother Leo, her sister-in-law Sarah Stein, Matisse, Picasso, the Florentine art guru Bernard Berenson, and some few others. But there was also the more truncated, silent witnessing of the artists, friends, American visitors and strangers at the rue de Fleurus Saturday evenings, and the many remembered from her past. For these largely snapshot categorizings, some remained fixed while others were again renamed, again realigned. Endlessly, her Notebook entries debate with her preliminary determinations, and endlessly there is an enlargement, or an elision or a reversal of her conclusions about the nature of her many subjects, or the precision and inclusiveness of the typologically-determined naming of the groups themselves.

For the grounding—the first step—in coherent ordering of "kinds" and coherent descriptions of individual beings, Gertrude adopted Weininger's divisions of the psyche—the divisions he most persistently employed—of the three "levels" of "sex", "character" and "intellect." [OW33.] This tripartite division of the self remains the fixed template Gertrude uses for distinguishing the three separable agencies and their functions within the self.

***

"THREE LAYERS: 'SEX, MIND AND TEMPERAMENT"

The metaphor of the tripartite division of the "soul"—more recently dubbed the "psyche"—is, familiarly, Plato's. 'Plato locates the rational part of the soul in the head, the 'spirited' part in the breast, and the 'appetitive' part [according to a squeamish prelate-historian,] 'below the midriff'." Gertrude, in her opening note in the Diagram Book [DB #1], draws the vertical line of the three sometimes conflicting, sometimes harmonious components of being. Their viability for Gertrude's typology was confirmed by what she remembered as "that epoch-making—for me—conversation with Harriet [Levy] about Sally [Sarah Stein]," as she records in the Notebooks [NB10, #15.] It was one in which Harriet Levy described Sarah Stein accurately, according to Gertrude, as in the case of Annette, Gertrude found her accurate—"all but the bottom." In her rejoinder to Harriet, she apparently took the "bottom" into account, and doing so, found herself with an explanation of Sally's "success" as a human being that gave Gertrude the clue she needed: Sally, she explained, exhibited a sexual "type and temperament and ideal all flowing together to a perfect harmony." [NB11, #13.] What was also "epoch-making" was the realization that Sally's "harmony" was rare, almost unique. Gertrude preserves her sense of the radical uniqueness of each individual by regarding such internal harmony within "one" as the rarest of instances of character "success." Far more usual was—to put it in Weininger's forbidding example—this: The pure prostitute ought ideally to have no interest in "running herself by her mind" because she has none, damned, according to him, by her lack of all memory, all consciousness, and all sense of ethical distinctions. [Weininger 227–228.] But in fact, the most frequent failure, as Gertrude reiterated for a considerable number of both men and women of comparable types, lay in this very mistake of using their intellects as chief weapon in their struggle for power, for security and for self-esteem. All three "levels" of character structure—bottom nature, temperament and mind—became the particular objects of Gertrude's scrutiny for internal disharmonies; consequently, her endless exploration for the possibilities of permanent success or failure within "one," and intermittent and contradictory success or failure. To "make it come together" is, as Gertrude measures it, the ideal: the three entities equally "strong," equally functioning within their own purview and not presuming on the functions of the others, and the "self" legislating judiciously, without delusion or self-will, over such invasive presumption. (This is Gertrude icily speculating on the successes and failures of the many "selves" over whom she adjudicated.)

Although Gertrude remembers this "tripartite" insight as her own, post-Platonic tripartite disjunctions of human being had recovered analytic popularity among her turn-of-the-century psychologizing contemporaries—Weininger, Freud and Freud's followers—who also harnessed a three-level formula to exploit the psyche's internal battles and accommodations. Standard psychological lore for many centuries, it served intermittently at least since Plato's harried charioteer of the mind (his alternate metaphor: Reason struggling to keep on middle course between his two diverging steeds, Desire and Will.) As with Plato's own metaphor, each of Gertrude's three "levels" were understood to have volition of their own. But so envisioned, they opened the way for her subtleties and nuances of internalized battle formations in the psyche, playing games with the metaphor on which her contemporaneous "depth psychologists" thrived. Although she differs from those contemporaries in her terms—more or less homegrown—the dynamic of internal embattlement is the same: the individual "levels" attack, censor, mock, glower at, and shut the door on one another, possibly with less muscular aggressiveness in Gertrude's version than in the others.

But in her version, as in theirs, the bottom sexual nature (or its equivalent) powers and empowers. Gertrude gives its options wide, wide latitude. "Bottom nature" rules and doesn't rule; it masters, and it doesn't. Unlike the Freudian *id*, which is housed grimly and monomaniacally in the same substratum, Gertrude's "bottom nature" is as often as not defanged. "Some have… natures that never mix with the whole of them and in such ones the impulse in them comes from the bottom nature or from the other natures separate from each other." But if the other "natures" can in a pack control or ignore the bludgeonings of bottom nature, such psyches, as Gertrude notes with a measure of rue, remained for her "in pieces." And of these, Alice Toklas was Gertrude's prime instance. Bafflingly, there was no nature in Alice in definable control. She was permanently "in pieces," permanently indecipherable.

Gertrude's premise—that all the kinds divide in various ways into contrary pairs—grew first out of Weininger's thesis, in which the essential divide was between the Male and Female genders' characteristics. In her first enthusiasm for Weininger,

Gertrude succumbed to his example. In her earliest but scuttled plans for *A Long Gay Book*, women-in-relation were to be treated first, then men. And in the early pages of "this new thing," males and females were assigned their own distinctive natures. But she soon, as we've noted, qualifying Weininger's Male-Female gender cartoons, turned to her own experience, and invested the primary relation between lovers, for example, with her own fixed division between "dependent independency" and its binding opposite, "independent dependency". There are further and multiple divisions of "two main groups" which flourish in the pages of the Notebooks and in the novel, defining categorical opposites such as attackers versus resisters, masters (teachers) versus instruments (students), and so on. But the more such categorical divisions were added to her list, the more her system became rigid and delimiting, abandoning flexible insight for a language of systemic structural symmetries. It would be two years before the impasse of this procedure was borne in on her, when it provoked another radical change in the direction of the book.

***

Subversion

Still, beyond such symmetries, beyond "categories," Gertrude's native signature as "analyst" emerged of its own accord through her incredible consonance of feeling with the psychological portraits any of her subjects adopted as their reality. Concerning that "reality," suspicion lingered in Gertrude of prepared posturing attending self-portrayals. Gertrude's endless qualifications, measured nuances, subtle or bold contradictions and undoings of "types" through their "mixing" are fundamentally a ferreting-out of sophisticated or plain lying about the self. But what is hugely impressive about her procedures is the skill, rare indeed, of conforming in feeling so closely to her subject as though there is almost bodily proximity to her emerging subject's self-revelations. It is these passages in both the Notebooks and in the novel itself that, while making a mockery of acceptable psychological verbiage, catch the unmistakable intimacy and accuracy of Gertrude's infelicitously expressed recognitions rather than her formal system's verbiage reaching for the finish of definition.

So much is this consonance out of harmony with the objective naming of "states of feeling" or of "kinds," that it leaves the internal recognition of other selves to their own most intimate privacy—as Gertrude puts it: "the feeling of himself to himself inside him." Left so. the description of such recognitions is almost at the point at which the system's formal verbiage is eluded altogether. It imitates to the extent of possibility "inner motions," such as, for example, a sort of enlarging or contracting of the inner self in states or in moments of particularly inarticulable feeling. Some examples:

1. Mr. Hersland is as big as all the world, but then he "shrinks from his outside" [MA 117.]

2. "The way I feel resisting being in men and women. *It is like a substance and in some it is as I was saying solid and sensitive all through it to stimulation, in some almost wooden, in some muddy and engulfing, in some thin almost like gruel, in some solid, in some parts and in other parts all liquid, in some with holes like in air-holes in it, in some double layers of it with no connections of it between the layers of it. This and many many other ways there are of feeling it."* [MA 248.]
3. *"The spinster lives in the thing she isn't not alone the thing she isn't but the thing that has really no roots in her, it is not that she thinks herself something she isn't, but she is something she isn't. She does the things she is and she lives the things she isn't.... They live in their conception of themselves because what they are is with its accompanying train so small proportionally to their lives so to speak. Impossible to really tell spinsters the truth.... All this must be written up."* [NB-*J #3]

***

NAMING KINDS

Unlike more sober latinists and grecophiles like Freud and Jung and Fliess who were carefully honing classical nomenclature for service in their concurrently developing systems, Gertrude's namings of kinds were variously whimsical, commonplace, irreverent, sneering,—in a word, unguarded: Gertrude's personal delectations, her own associations. Some are Weininger's own, [Weininger, 29] but hers are gradually separated from his programmed meanings and given less of his ideological fixity. But Gertrude's are hardly free from fixities of her own. Her named "kinds" reflect the stratifications, given by those like herself familiar with the well-upholstered middle class's assignment of domestic roles and "characters," together with their casual biases. But there is another set of women's kinds related specifically to lesbians, ranging from the dominating Masculine Woman to the wholly passive Earthy Boy (for whom Gertrude records a single example—herself.) Named kinds of her own reflect her own casual biases, sometimes whimsical (male group of Persian tabby cats??) sometimes unintentionally prejudicial men who were unassailably upright ("Men of the World" or "Anglo-Saxons," or their opposites, "Bazarofs"—after the Russian nihilist in Turgenev's Fathers and Sons.)

Alice Toklas insisted that after reading Weininger, Gertrude went her own way. [AT response: in NB-A #15.] She is more than half right. The rigidly, ideologically determined characteristics of "maleness" and "femaleness" are darkly present at first, but gradually blur and become less relevant to her typology. Her determinants for who "fits" and who does not within her "kinds," are not, like his, categorically fixed. Certain touchstones of human behavior, its emotional tendencies, physical selves, act as subtle revelations which for Gertrude are the keys to "type," and it is these she takes note of, for their sometimes overt, sometimes hardly detectable, repetitiveness. They may signify—these are a few of her touchstones—degrees of "pride" or "courage" or "tenacity" or "cowardice" or "allying oneself to eternity," and so on. But it is through these signs, as they cluster around each of the kinds which either give them their precision at once, or over time their stumbles toward more precise group definitions.

***

Defining Kinds

The ideal construct of a group derives from its ideal representative—the person who for Gertrude is its precise example. But the inclusive definition of the entire group depends on multiple shadings—examples of those closest to that prime instance, those variously distant, and those "admixtures" who share characteristics with other groups. Once established, the near, far, and partial examples of its members are sorted by a set of secondary characteristics: weak or strong, "concentrated" or "unconcentrated," "aggressive" or merely "tenacious," and—a judgmental category of particular importance—"individuals" or merely "egotists." [NB-B #9; NB-E #2; MA 231.]

How do each of these judgmental oppositions relate to the particular nature of a particular group? One example: individuals vs. egotists. Whatever his type or kind, the "individual" has the capacity to transcend the possible limitations of his category "by being completely himself." The individual, we gather from Gertrude's notations, is one who has "become himself" with relish, with satisfaction, at best like Gertrude's beloved eldest brother Michael, as a paragon of casually maintained selfhood. The egotist, on the other hand, asserts who he is—rather than simply being himself, he must angrily, aggressively, assert it. But the egotist asserting aggressively what he imagines he is, might as easily be asserting what he is not.

Still, the distinction between the two is by no means simple or fixed. The egotist might by certain concomitant characteristics "achieve the greatest." Gertrude's examples are Matisse, Van Gogh, several others (among them, generously, Shakespeare.) Such "aggressive egotists," when they achieve, do so "because of brilliancy and direct attack" over and above what "unaggressive egotists" can muster.

[NB-*C #27, #28] Her personal dislike for Matisse's egotism is partially mitigated by his egotist's "brilliant attack" even though it led to such instances of plainly "brutal egotism" as his not lowering his upgraded prices for his early—and first—purchasers, the Steins. [NB-A #11]

But how essential the unique positioning of each individual is within kind, is demonstrated by one of Gertrude's most judgmental criteria, in which each candidate is weighed in the balance of her own—and one of her most fundamental—aesthetic criteria: one's "direct relation to the object." [NB-A #14] Not only is its purity in that relation judged, but the particular "admixtures" within individuals that determine connection or disconnection with it and with one another. That those distinctions suggest Gertrude's aesthetic judgments is obvious but irrelevant; they are relevant here only for Gertrude's calculations for their typological "placement." Here she enumerates the ways in which numbers of subjects fall short, and others qualify:

> ...all these people do not get their inspiration from their relation direct to the object but from their affection for the object. Alice is an interesting mixture, she has this affection and she has the emotion passionate that connects her with Sally [Sarah Stein], Mamie [Mabel] Weeks and Emily [Dawson.] [These] people get their sense again not from immediate contact with the object, but from a passionate emotion about the object. That is the reason all these have a dramatic, a practical and a crudely material imagination, and of these Matisse is the great creator. He truly said he painted his emotion, but in order to paint it, he had to have it attached to the crudely materialistic object; when he gets away from this, he is lost. He still makes lovely but not significant painting. Now Cezanne is the great master of the realization of the object itself. Pablo connects on to him. Renoir on the other hand is in direct relation so to speak with the beauty of the object, so is Leo. In Sally's case, the emotion about the object is never enough to make her creative [as a painter], she is therefore what I have always called her, a passionate partisan. Then in both groups, there are people like Alexandre [Heiroth] who are directly in relation to their own passion, that is also true of Alfy [Maurer], and so in that sense they are creative. Braque, Balzac, Chalfin, etc., are all more or less of Pablo's type, in all three of them they are to a more or less degree in actual creative relation to the object. The chances are also a man like Shakespeare was like Renoir, with the more vital reality of the man of the world. Vallotton stands between the affection and reality groups. This is what Pablo probably meant when he said that Matisse always gave the crude feeling of the object, but never really paints the object. [NB-A #14]

***

THE "TWO MAIN GROUPS:" ATTACKING VS. RESISTING

"More and more the two groups show themselves" [NB-*C #18]; that is, the two supergroups under which all others are subsumed. The one is the Earth or passively Resistant Group, which is "bohemian, murky, cowardly, and with dirty sexuality." Its "attack," when it ventures, is at best merely "practical," with little aggressive thrust. Its representative figure is Mr. Hersland in the novel. The other, the Attacking, or Power Group. is mundane ("bourgeois" and worldly, that is, as opposed to bohemian), has "clean" sexuality, and is unqualifiedly aggressive, "irrepressibly conflicting." [NB-*C #15] Simply, then, the basic contrast: those who "attack," those who "resist."

But what complicates the organization of the entire system is that one definition of the two main groups does not preclude others. Several times over, Gertrude recognizes new definitive contrasts that expand her basic oppositional alignment. In earlier entries in the "Diagram Book" [DB #8, #9, #16], the defining contrast is elementary and Weiningerian: Male characteristics as opposed to Female. But soon, the definitions of the overarching "two main groups" become more particularly her own. The distinction between the two groups' sexual orientation is enlarged: the Earth Group's "unconcentrated" or "diffuse" sexuality is opposed to the Attacking Group's "concentrated" sexuality; or the "type Anglo-Saxon and American" as opposed to—implied, not named, but an echo of Weininger's own anti-Semitism—the Jewish. [NB-*C #35.] Perhaps most significantly, the "clean" as opposed to what Gertrude calls the "sordid" or "*sale*" or just "dirty, bottom earth" type, of which she counts herself an example, is opposed to the sister she despised, Bertha, who is later described as an "unconcentrated mass," or a "mushy mass,"[MA 384; NB-B #12.] of being, the most mindless of beings, but at the same time, and paradoxically, the truly generic example of the clean, "courageous attackers."

At a considerable remove from Weininger's formula for mating "pairs" of friends or lovers is Gertrude's later notion of the dynamic of love, one far more complex than merely "attacking" and "resisting," and far more so than Weininger's proportionate "M" and "F" ratios for lovers, friends and enemies. For Gertrude, the two contrasting types are finally, and fundamentally, distinguished by the oppositions of their "need for loving," and their way of satisfying that need. Type I are those who love "only those who need them," and Type II are those who love only "the ones they need" To win, Type II of course must labor to "subdue" to the point of "owning" the loved one; Type I, not needing to subdue, wins by merely exhibiting "strength in domination." But as lovers, they are both dependent and independent, both, that is, bound, but in opposite ways. Type I is independent(ly) dependent; Type II is dependent(ly) independent. The embrace of the two conditions, as Gertrude defines them, bears some evidence of the recollection of her own experience with May Bookstaver, in effect the suffering she endured as Type II. [NB-C #12; MA 163.]

Gertrude envisions—and in fact, is soon to know again in her relations with Alice Toklas—a further refinement in her understanding of the two contestants who are engaged as much in battle as in concord: The "attacking" group "have to be cowed to be respectful, to know fear to love." But her own group, the "earthy," "have too intimate an acquaintance with fear to wish it; they love freedom, they wish to be conquered only by themselves for that is to conquer fear." [NB-*C #18] In an undated scribbled note to Alice Toklas [Note #73], Gertrude expands on this. Explaining to Alice Toklas, her own "St. Theresa" her own failure to overcome her ambivalence when she "wants to kiss [Alice] good-night," and the sadness caused in her by that very ambivalence, she confesses: "as it seems to me no creature holds me in bondage, I felt some little scruple, for fear I was not beginning to lose this liberty." She grieves that she is not yet capable of voluntarily surrendering her no-longer-wanted liberty [her "loneliness," she calls it too, in this note,] mourns her inability to wholly acquiesce. When, more than two years later, Gertrude confesses in the pages of her novel that she has at last abandoned her "scruple" about the loss of that liberty, she sings hosannas to her new-found freedom: "I am loving just now every kind of loving," for five pages swimming in her abandon, and concluding gleefully, "I am now a happy person." [MA 604–608.]

***

THE KINDS

Of the "millions" of presumably conceivable kinds, Gertrude, in the Notebooks, articulates and defines only twenty—twelve women's groups and eight men's. The range of the women's groupings echoes Weininger's—from the Lady to the Prostitute—but the understandings of them are remote from his. After enumerating the kinds in men and women—a flat, "listic" undertaking of small insight—but in her descriptions of these kinds, and in her analyses of individuals within "kinds," her insights into random human behavior and most of all into the fixities of fundamental human motive are far more perceptive than her otherwise rigidly denuded vocabulary might suggest. Buried inside those descriptions are subtle evocations of both individual and type that bear the knowing imprint of the novelist rather than the rigidities of the system-building classifier.

***

THE WOMEN'S KINDS

Pure Lady

Of the women's groups, the "Pure Lady" is a group apart. In its purity, it has features shared with few of the others: beauty, grace, sensitivity, the capacity to be tolerant. [DB #54] Of the "practical cold women," of whom Therese Thorold, the wife of the English minister Algar Thorold, is "the finest type of it," "They have the beauty of fine plaster cast," and combine their "flavor with strong lurid sexuality," and their sexual prowess is generally beyond that of almost all women in lesser groups. "They hold a man of a weak nature so completely because they satisfy him sexually entirely, and they can't be hurt by them because they care for something else. They are practical, tyrannical, beautiful, immobile, and more or less efficient." [NB-*C #31] Exhibiting less than their purity, they can succumb to even less admirable qualities: "ignorance of others, knowledge of themselves, and their power and technique of suffering." [DB #13] (The word "technique" is precisely chosen.) Their greatest quality is a kind of absolute certainty akin to the old man Heisman's, the old grandfather in the early pages of *The Making of Americans* who lives with the certainty of being "all there was of living and of religion." The "lady" in her undiluted state is rarely noted by Gertrude, who finds her more often in "admixtures" with other types: the "free soul," or the "pseudo-masculine," or the "Napoleonic," in all of whom "their reality is coexistent with the flavors they taste." [DB #30] This, the most accommodating and usual inauthenticity to which "pure lady" succumbs, characteristically subverts her authenticity. "Ladies and Flavor [groups] both have no knowledge of people. Ladies are not tactless because of their concentration and power. Flavors are tactless because of their reaching out and their ignorance of others" (a general key to the Flavor group.) Nevertheless, "all have the important feeling of themselves inside them, [and compared to all other women] are nearest to pure intelligence." [DB #35]

Mistress

The Mistress (that is, of a household, of family and servants, not of a lover), as a type is a step below "pure lady," and exhibits a "passion for intellectuality, culture, higher ideas, morality etc., [and is] strongly sexual, [and] mostly fairly stupid." She retains the feeling of conscious power as does the Lady group, [DB #54], but in her, it is associated with a characteristic "bridling," [i.e. a sort of harrumphing as though affronted], and she has, whether earned or not, a "consciousness of virtue." [Note #56] The true Mistress has no real intellect [NB-*J #9]; she has greed [NB-*C #40], and she has power, as Bertha's kind of independent dependent has, "only with those who love them" [Note #49]. And so, the Bertha "attacking" group "is always a mistress group in posse." [DB #60] But as a type, it can readily descend into the

Mistress Prostitute

The Mistress Prostitute group has little "head," much sentimentality, and much sordidness. Their iconic representative is BB's wife, Mary Berenson, "because there is the least head of all of their group [and] is the most utterly foolish." Hortense Federleicht, Leo's Baltimore piano-playing psychological protégée, qualifies too, as "the biggest nature of them all," because in her the group's inconsequential foolishness [DB #16.] "gave great temperamental musical expression," which in her "was the most closely wedded." [DB #6]

The group gives the appearance of being excessively frank, but in fact is usually reserved, and that reserve can take the form of hypocrisy, or even lying. They in fact encourage themselves not to know the truth. The reasons range from their empty-headedness, or their pathological lack of continuity, or their "emotional world living," or a mixture of all these, including plain sordidness. And at that extreme, they exhibit a puerile form of pedantry and a girlish lack of wisdom. What is characteristic of all of them is a wonderful capacity to keep going once they have started to so to speak improve upon their teachers. [DB #17] The absolute descent of the type is to the

Pure Prostitute

The Pure Prostitute is the mistress only to, and so of, the man who loves her. [DB #8] "They have power only when they are loved." [DB #36] "Their resistance to the lover is a subtle evanescence", and while "unconquered, have quite essential sweetness and emotional intelligence in its highest form." But once conquered, they become "commonplace," so that the prostitute without the "mistress" element can exhibit pure prostitute brutality. [DB #17, #54] "Egotists," as opposed to "individuals," they have nevertheless no "feeling of being important to themselves inside them." Those with a natural sense of their virtue, however conscious they may also be of their wickedness, are capable of accomplishing the "emotional leap," that is, the capacity to overcome or supersede rationality, out of, for example, a feeling of injury or resentment. [DB #41.] So emotionally justified, they can win through to a feeling and use of the weapons of power and sentimentality. For the pure prostitute, idealism functions as a sort of disease, because "they have not the sensibility [for it, and] when their idealism ceases, they become once again the pure prostitute," [NB-B #12] for "they have only the instrument quality of reliving, [that is, of emulating their mentor's beliefs.] And so, when that 'idealism' ceases, they revert…"

Gertrude, out of the same disconsolate feeling, remembers the other sorrow, the one more profound than Bird Stein: May Bookstaver, and she enlarges her into a "type:"

May's Group

May Bookstaver, through Gertrude's pained recollections, posits a group of her own. An "emotional sexual aristocrat," she has, paradoxically, "a lack of concentrated sexuality, although [her sexuality] has completely that appearance." It is "the intensest form of emotional sexuality, but it is not actual sexuality." Consequently, "when the element of emotional sexuality is removed, they sink into very commonplace people." The worst specimens of the group keep up the illusion longest. In fact, "it is [so persuasive] an illusion, [that] it [almost becomes] an actuality," but there is no basis for [that] apparent reality. The base, in fact, which has not much reality, is also "nothing much sexually." "So we have their high type of emotional intelligence and lack of real intellect." [DB #60.]

In retrospect, Gertrude concludes—winning a sort of victory over an old, still rankling defeat—that with little sexuality at "bottom" and less intellect at the "top," all that is substantial in the type is dramatic flair.

Mistress (Free Soul) Type

As distinct from the Mistress Prostitute—in fact, her opposite—is the "free soul" mistress group who have entirely the sense of their "importance inside them," The character of their resistance—so different from the other—comes out of their personal pride; "they own themselves;" they feel genuinely the "importance to themselves inside them." Independent and self-determined, the group genuinely earns its authority. But like all the Prostitute Groups, they maneuver an "emotional leap" from their sense of injury. [DB #17.]

Masculine Women

Four types of masculine women are defined: the True Masculine, the Lady Masculine, the Pseudo-Masculine Adolescent, and the Earthy Boy.

True Masculine

In an extended note on Mabel Haynes, her former rival with May Bookstaver, Gertrude defines her "masculine quality" as "not a concentrated one but an aggressive one, and so it makes for masculinity." "So far as I know," Gertrude adds, it is "the only really masculine type [of woman.]" It is masculine in its "strong instinct for allegiance," but since they're concentrated to attack, "they are rarely favorite with men." [NB-*C #14]

Lady Masculine

is one of the groups governed by exceptional self-delusion. Although they're the "Napoleonic type," they "do not conceive of themselves as evil" but actually think of themselves as moral. They have, so far as they are aware, no evil intention, "but they are tremendously willed, they have enormous power." Unlike the Lady group, which, though it also has power, is guided by a sense of right and dignity, the Napoleonic type has "the vulgarity of a misfit between their overpowering evil nature and their ideals. Can well believe Napoleon thought himself working for the glory of France." [DB #30] (Gertrude's idea of Napoleon was not far removed from Weininger's, who thought Napoleon "one of the three greatest criminals of all time.")

Pseudo-Masculine

In the pseudo-masculine group, "where boy and girl adolescent continues, and is not distinguishable," [DB #11], the sole example is Gertrude's friend Mildred Aldrich, about whom Gertrude's portrait in "A Family of Perhaps Three" describes Mildred, her sister and the woman she loved.

Practical Adolescent is another pseudo-masculine type among women. There's an extended explanation of this type in a note on "Emily [Dawson]'s dancing steps," concerning "the continuance of adolescence where boy and girl is not distinguishable."

[DB #29] The type is further developed at some length in the text of the novel [MA 174.] In brief: In some women, "the fear of coming adolescence" moves them to become "very lively so as to keep adolescence from giving sorrow to them." They dance "so that adolescence will be scared away." It is not from sentimental feeling, nor particularly "lightsome feeling," but rather an "aggressive liveliness," that makes for a "dance step every now and then in their walking," not realizing that they do it in order not to reach "the restlessness of adolescent living." All their lives they work at remaining in "just before beginning adolescent being," and so keep inside them, always, their anachronistic "school feeling."

Earthy Boy

Only one example of this type is offered: Gertrude herself. It is one of two entries in which she notes her sense of her own sexuality. As "Earthy Boy," the full note reads: "Me, not passionate adolescent, earthy boy." [DB #22] The other entry is more explicit but characterizes her as "pure servant female:" "Often men mistake in women like myself, because my temperament and point of view, intellect and consciousness, is masculine, and the erotic emotion is masculine, that the sexual nature is. My actual sexual nature is pure servant female. I like insolence. I find it difficult to work up energy enough to dominate," [NB-*C #30] (an accurate prevision of subsequent life with Alice Toklas.)

Servant Girl

But her sense of the "servant nature" as a type corresponds, a bit astonishingly, not to her own closely and realistically observed servant characters, the gentle Lena and the good Anna of *Three Lives*. Her descriptions of "servant nature" are in fact closer to the tremblings of the two old spinsters in Arnold Bennett's *Old Wives Tale* contemplating the low motives of their servants. The sum of Gertrude's own suspicions is more or less the same as theirs:

The typical servant girl nature is crooked in her attempts at overcoming the weakness of her "instrument" nature to attack (that is, a nature passive, imitative, willing to be used.) She has the practical anarchistic griminess that attaches to servant nature. There are two versions of her, the Bertha "attacker" and the earth type "resister." The attacking nature can be cowed, but not, like the resisting nature, humbled. Her base is indeed "earthy," and she herself is dirty, wallows in filth, and if she appeals, it is by her "dumb despair." [NB-B #5, #8; NB-G #11; NB-I #9; NB-*C #15; NB-*J #9 and Note #46.] The portrait is further enlarged in the pages of the novel. There she is "the little dirty shrinking lying little blonde hair nature" with "the scared little lying always in such a one. They need it to keep them going, to keep them cleaning and washing and working, to keep them from lying." And so, they need a directing mistress. Also, they have much trouble with their loving, so nobody stops them when they "go off loving." Most of them have the dependent's weakness, with no sense of responsibility, and just lie when anyone asks them anything. In later life, they tend to lose their "servant queerness," "just get married, and get old having many children coming out of them, and so the end of their living." [MA 172]

Gertrude makes considerable use of her contemptuous portrait of "the servant girl nature" in several of her more severe descriptions of women. The "servant girl" has the "bottom nature" of a woman like Neith Hapgood, the wife of the writer Hutchins Hapgood and an author in her own right, about whom Gertrude had ambivalent feelings. Whatever value her "top" and "middle" levels might have exhibited, her sexual bottom, "her servant girl nature" effectively sabotaged.

Sister Group/Spinster Kind

Both sister and spinster are essentially defined in relation to their core characteristic: their sentimentality or their lack of it. The more commonplace members of the Sister group "live to themselves and to others as ...what they ideally should be, and not by what they are.... They should have all the womanly virtues [Gertrude enumerates the 'womanly virtues' as mother, housekeeper, and 'sweet' disposition] partly because they have nothing else, partly because they suggest it to themselves and to others." And so, they are the very definition of sentimentality, which is: "changing the object without changing the emotion, and so one goes on and on for years thinking one has not done them justice." [DB #50, #52] The two sisters who were of deepest interest to Gertrude were the Cone sisters, Etta and Claribel. Of both she wrote a long piece, tentatively entitled in the Notebooks, "The Cone Sister's Tragedy." Of Claribel alone, she wrote one of her longest and most perceptive studies in the Notebooks, the entry that Alice Toklas, when she read it, recognized as the most deadly accurate of all. But displaced emotion finding a substitute object is hardly the whole of Gertrude's understanding of what she calls the "Sister" group, although little more is said of it in the Notebooks.

The Spinster group, of whom Etta Cone is "the perfect type," is dwelled on at length. Her essential spinsterishness lies in Etta's lack of generosity, which is largely invisible because of her "splendor and richness," and especially invisible "when she was in love with Ida Gutman," a time "when she became almost generous in her nature, for her love became heroic." Since then, notes Gertrude, she's become her own hero, "and her spinster state is complete." [DB #21, #22] "The illusion with them is the whole thing" Like Etta, they conceive themselves as heroes, but do nothing heroic. Of one kind, the sexually "unconcentrated" kind, "it is because of the negative quality of their sexuality, both maternal and mistress, that they are so completely an illusion, more complete because they are not more or less what they realise themselves as being, but they are practically not at all.... The illusion is therefore with them the whole thing." Fundamental to their being is the certainty that "they cannot find the right stimulus to produce [either] the attack or the engulf. They are not responsive. They are initial forces, essentially."

Alice Toklas is a prime example (and this is the particular *apercus* to which Alice responded with, "Oh, rats!" [AT response, in DB #56]) "Most of her is the elderly spinster mermaid with all her faults. I think Alice is the perfect example of the intellect with the sexual nature" [that is, the two levels—topmost and bottommost—in sad disharmony.] They [the type] "… completely feel themselves to be quite otherwise, and what they are is so small a proportion to what they are to themselves—they are completely self-centered and completely vain, they hold the world as a mirror up to themselves, and that mirror always completely flatters, which is the true mark of the spinster." As for the bottommost level, "the bottom dough of the female—or male as the case may be—has completely woodenized, solidified… made solidly into wood. Therefore, they have no fountain of expression, they have no profound sensibility, but they have a fairly deep superficial reaction [sic]. And this may have various forms." [NB-B #13; NB-*J #2]

Alice is only one of Gertrude's examples of spinsterish deluded vanity, but few of the other women's groups are scrutinized so particularly as hers. The note, however, was being written only a few months after their initial meeting. Gertrude's judgment obviously changed, gradually but completely, from the time of this entry in early 1908 to its entire reversal by the end of 1910. But in this early note, the scrutiny continues:

> [They have] no important feeling of themselves inside them. [Their] intellectual life is not connected with their nature. Slow in development, no instinct for culture…. This group has little power hold through the things they are not conscious of, consequently give the sense of a hole…. They also have a hardness. They are not affectionate, and have to be dominated to be won, and held, constantly dominated. They do not resist, they are not strongly maternal, they are cumulative in their effects. Recognition of them comes very slowly. They have no personal pride in them, no amour propre. They may be sensitive, they may not. [DB #47]

There's a particularly astonishing miscalculation in this early understanding of Alice. Almost the opposite of Gertrude's description here, Alice was never the one who had to be "dominated" to be won, and little defined her more than her *amour propre*, her personal pride. More accurate than Gertrude then imagined is the notation, "Recognition of [her] comes very slowly." [DB #47]

***

THE MEN'S KINDS

"We came to Paris to kill the nineteenth century," Gertrude famously wrote in *Everybody's Autobiography*. If it was so, in 1908, five years after her arrival, there was still a considerable way to go. Her designations for women's groups spell out the nuclear Victorian household of women: the lady of the house and her servants, the hangers-on: sisters and spinsters, and the unmentioned: masculine women and prostitutes. Her male groupings fare no better. Their categories are not only narrowly Victorian but narrowly German with the overlay of the European Jewish intellectual's own anti-Semitism, whose class distinctions snobbishly ignore distinctions of wealth, and focus instead on the difference between the sensitive ethical, enlightened intellectual on the one hand, (in Yiddish, the *edel*) and their opposite, the insensitive, unethical vulgarians (the *prost.*). Her male groupings reflect the gradations—moral, aesthetic and intellectual—between these extremes. But over and above this, there are, as with women, careful distinctions that weigh heavily in defining a man's fundamental "kind." Some of these, Gertrude relates almost entirely to men: the distinction, for example, between basic sexual natures: "*sale*", or "dirty" bottom natures, and "clean." This becomes, in the novel, the basic distinction between the father-figures of the two families: Mr. Hersland (*sale)* and Mr. Dehning (clean.) It becomes also, in the Notebooks, one of *the* malleable judgments visited on her male subjects. Picasso, for example, has proudly and appropriately his *sale* sexuality; the writer Hutchins Hapgood and the Swedish sculptor Edstrom are both utterly subverted by the same *sale* sexuality. As with women, there is also the primary distinction between the "power group," (or the "Bertha courageous attacker,") and Gertrude's own kind, the "earthy resisters." And in both men and women, there are the gradations of sensibility (belonging to the "middle" term—the "character" or "temperament") and its effects on the intellect. More and more. these dichotomies and oppositions grow in the system, both in the Notebooks and subsequently in the pages of the novel. Still, although the verbiage of these multiplying dichotomies becomes increasingly rigid, it allows, paradoxically, for more discerning descriptions of human beings in division within themselves—within a "kind," and—among themselves—between kinds.

The Man of The World

Uncle Jacob, the paragon of the Stein extended family, their wealthy Baltimore patriarch, is Gertrude's icon for "the man of the world." As a type, he is highly sensitive, not at all a passive "earth type" but vigorously "courageous," and although he assumes a conventional posture toward practical success, he is, as Gertrude is careful to qualify, a "high type" of such practical instincts.[DB #20] At his best, the man of the world "has an element of distinction: elegance, justice, action, *savoir faire*, mastery—the masculine version of Bertha at her best." [Note #45] Even in his "relation to the object," he has a vital reality as opposed to those who relate only to the beauty of the object. There is, on the other hand, a less sanguine version of the man of the world: the petit bourgeois, the clear, direct, insensitive, unethical "middleman," like the Bernheim who owns the picture gallery. But the true man of the world "adds distinction to this foundation." [Note #41] He adds sensibility. A step or two lower is:

The Anglo-Saxon

The Anglo-Saxon, like the man of the world, is part of the "attacking" group, "clean" sexually, practical and not sordid, strong in attack and hard, and like the Bertha courageous ones, has to be thoroughly beaten to be conquered. He is the quintessential courageous attacker, a "hard type." "The Anglo-Saxon and American [is the] absolute opposite of the earthy sordid, cowardly, tenacious prudent group" with which Gertrude—quite literally transcribing Weininger—identifies the "Yit" (the Jew) and herself. [NB-*C #35.] To practical Anglo-Saxon courage is added an inner sensibility, a genuine interior vision. "Always, they have real sensibility, real faith." His "prudishness is a conviction, a virtue and a defense." [NB-*B #7] But that interior vision is slow and blind. The mind progresses so slowly that it stops altogether, and the "practical worldly" takes its place, and that practical worldliness is unhappily expressed "by a passion for detail, a losing oneself in illustration."

The Idealist Kinds

There are four kinds of idealists, each characterized by a particular devotion: the ideal *of Beauty* (Oscar Wilde), *of Romance* (Byron), *of Power* (Edstrom), *of Intellect* (Hodder.) [DB #18] (Hodder was the brilliant Harvard philosophy student whose history Gertrude recounted in her earlier novella, *Fernhurst.*) As a type, the Idealist carefully but unknowingly divorces the reality of his past experience from his ideal, so that when recollecting that experience, by "conditioning," that is, by omitting major portions of what in the past was "unconditionally" experienced, he maintains the illusion of an unbroken fidelity to his ideal. "These then are lying, not by invention but by idealistic romantic dramatic sentimental omission." [MA 502.] But the unreality of their idealism is underscored in another way. The very young Walter Pach (who later became a celebrated American art critic and historian)

> "is very illuminating," writes Gertrude, "in his criticism of Leo's picture, I recognize the girl, I don't recognize the atelier, and then saying he and Henri [Matisse] believed in religion like the chinaman painting his soul at the end of his brush…. They none of them see the essential profound contradiction between their two expressions…. In their blindness their spiritual ineffectiveness comes from a deep and fundamental incompatibility. The more sensitive they are internally,

> the more definitive is this contradiction, the less sensitive, the more they succeed in practical results…. Also remember the slowness of their minds which helps their not seeing the two facts together and so realising their contradiction." [Note #45.]

There are, however, two genuine idealists in Gertrude's sense: the sculptor Elie Nadelman and Alexandre Heiroth, the Russian émigré who briefly and unhappily joined the Florentine circle. They, unlike most of the other Idealists, "do poignantly give [the] real sense of beauty directly, not derived." In contrast to them, there is the case of "George Eliot, Alice, et al" who have an "emotion toward beauty rather than a passionate realization of it." Written in 1909, a year and a half after Alice's arrival, Gertrude still designates her "a real flavor person" whom passionate emotion does not govern "excepting in relation to me." [NB-D #7] Two years later, in 1911, after Gertrude had undergone other mordant shifts in her understanding as well, she noted the "brutality" underlying fundamental human feeling, and in face of that deadly fact, considered that the genuine Idealist "can afford to be honest" about such realities, but those who are "not really Idealists would make a great mistake to be honest," since admitting this fundamental human fact "would be to have no real restraining power over themselves at all, for why should you not be a hog excepting for your nature, ideals or social conventions…. Of course, you can let yourself go if you know you won't go very far." [NB-I #12]

The Jewish Kinds

Gertrude calculates a careful distance from Weininger's animadversions against the Jewish mind and sensibility. She offers partial corrective, partial homage: "Real sensibility, [she writes,] real faith in the Jew is replaced by a lyrical, pretty quality and a passion for rather confused emotional and transcendental thinking and an intelligent facile practical intellect in their real business, whatever it is." [Note #45] Her more extended consideration of "the Jewish mind" is one of the most carefully exemplified in the Notebooks:

> Jews mostly run themselves by their minds. Now they have good minds but not great minds [and] your mind ought to be no more than a purveyor to you, because inevitably you are greater habitually than your mind. That is the secret of the inevitable mediocrity…. If it is not running yourself by your mind among the Jews, it is running yourself by your ethics, which is perhaps really nothing more than a crystalised mind…. The non-Jewish person runs themselves [sic] by their conventions and their training but they don't do it themselves to themselves, therefore they are freer than the more intelligent yid. [NB-A #3]

The Jew also suffers from incessant self-consciousness in directing himself. There are, as in all the groups, gradations downward. Alice, for example, has the "practical intelligence of the Helenising Jew, that is, self-knowledge but no consciousness of the significant, of the meaning of the things she knows." [DB #56] And among the lowest, there are the "coldly practical," the kinds of Jews who are "banal and vague and slow, who are the highly subtle forms of the kind of big thick vulgar Jewishness that runs theatres and trains ballet girls." [NB-G #16]

Oddly—more than oddly—the paragons of Jewishness with respect to the mind are Goethe and Frederick the Great. They are the only two in the Notebooks having both "great minds" as well as consciously running themselves "by the mind," the very perfection at which Jews inevitably fail. Leo and Berenson, for example, are Jews who suffer qualified failure in lapsing from the perfection. Leo has "neither resolution nor singleness of purpose enough," and has also "too much" of the kind of "enthusiasm and resolution", which merely "flavors and interrupts" the fully realized operation of his mind. And Berenson, though great in his "affections" for the good and the beautiful, "runs his mind… into being good," and so wears "a halo of goodness and superiority [which] is silly." [NB-C #20]

The Bazarofs/The Fanatics

With their nervous intensity, their *sale* sexuality, all the Bazarofs are "in essence ethical and fanatical, not by reason of affection for their object, but by reason of their realisation of its symbolism." Their "object" is not the thing itself— "it" itself—which they neither see nor know; what they see or know of it is what is "partly generalized." They know the reality and arrogance they have in themselves, and so are not susceptible to the reality in others. Since they have no touchstone for that other reality, they are not critical. They learn easily but are blind. Not slow, but facile. In their extreme blindness, as Leo put it, they reject the intellect altogether, and rush into sexuality and mysticism, an "abandonment" which altogether denies the intellect. [Note #41]

"The danger with the fanatics is the denial of their experience, this may make them moral enthusiasts [such] as Leon [Solomons], and Weininger. It may make them aesthetic visionaries as Raymond [Duncan, the dancer Isadora's brother, a Stein friend in San Francisco and Paris] & (I hope not) Pablo….But it is this quality in them that so often makes their genius sterile….Pablo may be saved by the intensity of his actual aesthetic experience, if he can hold to that, he will go on." [Note #45]. "Pablo is the highest type of [Bazarofian] because being low he has most reality. I believe he will work out of submission to unreality." [NB-*C #13.]

The process by which they pass over into (Bertha/Courage group) self-righteousness is this: their fear is "cut and hardened into a consciousness of virtue," and so, they assume fearlessness, and so, they reach self-righteousness. [NB-*C #19.]

Nevertheless, paradoxically, their self-righteousness, reaching fanaticism, can pass into genius. [NB-*C #35.]

Primitive Souls

They are "earthy," but unlike the more usual "earthy" kind, they are not merely ethical, but pagan or religious. They are not lovers of beauty like the "Idealist [of] Beauty" kind but are themselves beautiful. Characteristically, they have no feeling of importance inside them, they are at best modest, and have very little personal influence. But they have a "commonplace" side that makes for getting on. [DB #43]

Boy

The models for the "Boy" type of grown male are Walter Pach and Roche, the "earthy boy" rather than the passionate adolescent, with an "open boyish sweetness." They have no heroic element in them, only an unfinished, immature quality; with intelligence but no real intellect, and no instinct for success. They are in fact all stupid. As for Roche, "he is a translation, as Pablo says," by which he means, as Leo explained, his kind digest nothing "so [whatever he hears,] comes out as it went in." [DB #22, #25, #29, #53] Since they understand nothing but what is practical, nothing else but the practical comes out of them.

The "Persian Tabby Cats"

The Persian Tabby Cats, as a group are good, "'fin,' as the French say, tall and gentle." [NB-C #22] But though bearing a certain kind of elegance, they suffer from insensibility and "Persian lying." And they show "not a keen personal pride, but rather the pride of conceit, the lowest form of which passes over into the conceited pride of self-righteousness." And they have "an instinct for common-placeness," which they share with three other versions of the common-place: The actor, the doctor, and the clergyman. [DB #42]

The Masculine Prostitute

The Masculine Prostitute is a "passionate adolescent." [DB #21] Then: "me, not passionate adolescent [but] earthy boy." [DB #22]

The "Kantian" Man

One of Weininger's extravagant tributes in his book is to the philosopher Emanuel Kant's idealism: "The birth of the Kantian ethic, the noblest event in the history of the world, was the moment when for the first time the dazzling awful conception came to him: 'I am responsible only to myself; I must follow none other; I must not forget myself even in my work; I am alone; I am free; I am lord of myself.' "

Gertrude copied into her Notebooks the passage from Kant which Weininger quotes following his tribute. The Kant quote begins:

> Two things fill my mind with ever renewed wonder and awe the more often and deeper I dwell on them—the starry vault above me and the moral law within me....The second point of view enhances my importance, makes me an intelligence infinite and unconditioned through my personality, the moral law which separates me from the animals and from the world of sense, removes me from the limits of time and space, and links me to the infinite. [OW161.]

Kant defined for Gertrude the teleological end toward which her system necessarily moved for its ultimate justification, and perhaps more importantly, for its ultimate personal value. It provided an image of the ultimate human being, or as she called it, the "completed" human being, who escapes all contingency.

Since Weininger's interests are fundamentally ethical and metaphysical, his psychology of "character" moves unswervingly toward the definition of "ultimate" human being, which he defines in terms of consciousness. Ultimate self-consciousness embraces absolute memory, absolute self-comprehension and truth. Consequently, ultimate *cosmic* consciousness embraces absolute identification and unqualified relation of the self with the universal and the eternal. In effect, the "completed individual," then, is one whose consciousness—and therefore whose genuine existence—has moved outside of time and has thereby conquered it.

> Memory only fully vanquishes time when it appears in a universal form, as in universal men. The genius is thus the only timeless man—at least, this and nothing else is his ideal of himself; he is, as is proved by his passionate and urgent desire for immortality, just the man with the strongest demand for timelessness, with the greatest desire for value.... His universal comprehension and memory forbid the annihilation of his experiences with the passing of the moment in which each occurred. [OW 136–137]

The importance of this notion for Gertrude can hardly be overestimated. It appears at length in her work first in the portrait of the young David Hersland, but later—in her speculative writing of the Nineteen Thirties—this notion of the "completed individual" continued to be the basis of her repeated attempts to lay to rest her Nineteenth Century dilemmas concerning loss of uniqueness and "ever-lasting."

James' *The Will to Believe* was a disappointment to her hope that it, at least, might mitigate her large metaphysical desperations.[8] The logic in her speculative writing rests on her denial of pragmatism and her conscientious attempt to shore up against its ruins minimal certainties in precise accord with Kantian teleological idealism.[9] The whole encrustation of Gertrude's ideas and feelings in her writings from 1908 on emanate from the envisioning of this highest type of human being—the only true individuality—in terms of his achieving the ultimate escape from the contingency of time. Her later discussions of genius, of memory, of "human nature" as opposed to "human mind," and the hopelessness of "human nature" (for her, the fragmented, "diagrammed" aspects of human being) achieving "entity" out of itself, not merely its "identity," and her notion that the "human mind" alone and of itself can effect and know its own "entity"—all these discussions elaborate the basic definition in Kant, of the steps whereby the ultimately human redeems itself from the "mosaic" of factors currently accounting for human existence. And Gertrude follows this system of values to its end by insisting that this victory over time is achieved only by means of those qualities and capabilities of mind and spirit that belong to the genius or to the saint alone. In her writing of the Nineteen-Twenties and Thirties, the relevance of saints to her thought, the meaning, in *The Mother of Us All*, of Susan B. Anthony's "You may be married to the past one, no one can be married to the present one, the one, the one, the present one,"[10] the rationale of her insistence on her own genius (apart from its basis in personal idiosyncrasy) may be looked for in her emulation of the Kantian notion of unqualified and unlimited individuality, incapable of being known to others but only of being self-known, and the consequence to human being of such a creature coming to fruition.

Her enthusiasm for this concept was first expressed in her revision and enlargement of the portrait of the young David Hersland in the novel. In its first

---

[8]Refrain used in *Many Many Women*, published in *Matisse, Picasso and Gertrude Stein*, p.199.

[9]One of Weininger's extravagant tributes in his book to Kant's idealism: "The birth of the Kantian ethic, the noblest event in the history of the world, was the moment when for the first time the dazzling awful conception came to him: 'I am responsible only to myself; I must follow none other; I must not forget my self even in my work; I am alone; I am free; I am lord of myself.' "

Gertrude copies into her notes the passage from Kant which Weininger quotes following this tribute. It begins: "Two things fill my mind with ever renewed wonder and awe the more often and deeper I dwell on them—the starry vault above me and the moral law within me.... The second point of view enhances my importance, makes me an intelligence, infinite and unconditioned through my personality, the moral law which separates me from the animals and from the world of sense, removes me from the limits of time and space, and links me to the infinite." [Italics added.] [op.cit. pp.161–162.]

[10]*Saints and Singing, a Play*, published in *Operas and Plays* (Paris: Plain Edition, 1932); *The Mother of Us All*, in *Last Operas and Plays* (New York: Rinehart and Company, 1949), p.75.

version, he was to be merely "singular" as a Westerner—and in terms of that first version, it was eminence enough. In the 1908 notes for revision, his "singularity" is given Kantian dimensions. "Make David completed Individual," she instructs herself, and further, "must realise my hero by making him go through my development." [NB-MA #53] But as in the original plan of the book, he remains a defeated man, trapped by his ultimate longing for death.

But to give his failure further distinction, Gertrude added her own imagined characterization of Weininger himself. When she made the discovery of his suicide, everything fit anew: her own "sense of failure" at twenty-nine (that is, in 1903); Leon Solomon's "suicide" when he "chose" cancer and, more verifiably, chose to undergo a fatal operation at the age of twenty-nine; and finally Weininger's suicide after his "brilliant achievement," especially relevant, since that achievement rested so largely on the intellectual comprehension and expression of the victory the "singular" individual is capable of winning over death.

***

SENSIBILITY

Like "Flavor," "Sensibility" is less a group designation than a characteristic Gertrude uses to measure authenticity within types. Gertrude takes the measure, for example, of a group of artists and writers, and of some who are neither, whose lack of genuine sensibility produces work whose "vibrancy" is, in effect, like "wood" or "stone." The Notebooks are full of heavily judgmental passages on the artists populating her rue de Fleurus salon—whether in their paintings on its walls or milling about in attendance—whose value as artists is appraised and understood far more in psychological than in aesthetic terms—the psychology housed altogether in the language of her "system." An especially deadly but astute set of examples:

> [Max] Weber has the sensibility to color, he has not the constructive color sense, so as I said long ago about Manguin, he has the sensibility to works of art [but] he has no real sense of them. Derain and Sterne et al have a real intellectual sensibility but not a real intellectual process. That is what makes them what they are, they have this for the genius life. Leo F[riedman] & Pur[r]man[n] being less romantic *au fond* are more successful, their essential *commonplace* worldly efficiency is less interfered with, they have only the romantic or idealistic conception, they never except in their early youth attempt its realisation. None of these have a vital sensibility, they are wood or petrified wood or stone or metal, but they are always dead substance, they have no earth principle of vital growth, so they differ from the group [of] which Mike [Gertrude's oldest brother] forms an intermediate step to mine, which

> has. Nothing is within them, they are worldly because their reaction is always a readaptation, never a creation. [NB-A #10a]
>
> They are hard and mundane in ideal as well as in nature, they move directly to their end. In all of them, their minds are practical, detailed, unimaginative and commonplace. [NB-*C #32]

The rest of the male groups are given cursory definition, some none at all. They are defined largely by example, their definitions shrouded.

***

"CONNECTING"

"Always each one is of a kind in men and women. Always kinds are connected with other kinds.... I want to be going on and on and describe one and then another one and then connections between them." [MA 584.]

But over and above defining each one as one of the "kinds," there remains the problem of how individuals of different kinds can be definitively linked and at the same time remain uniquely themselves. What are the connections between the "kinds" themselves, what overlappings and parallels are there among them that serve to underscore the tightness of connections within the system's structure?

The answers are best ferreted out by returning to Gertrude's premise concerning the self's first need. Initially, the self's primary need is to obliterate recognition of one's initial state of being as meaningless or as equivalent to death itself. The first suggestion of this in the novel is attributed to members of families who appear in early pages of the second-draft, and who deal. though unconsciously, with strategies for accomplishing such concealment. [MA 56–58, 100–104ff.]

To review explanation once again: There are two self-generated, internalized self-definitions, either "the feeling of oneself as (merely)existing" (as in Martha Hersland) or "the feeling of oneself as important" (as in Mr. Hersland.) The feeling of mere "existence" is undeniably sustainable, but adding neither character nor value to the self, it remains a desperate and permanently self-defeating state of being. The feeling of "importance" overcomes the sense of nonentity and is personally uplifting but is inherently a lie. It uses the innumerable illusions available for enlarging self-importance, but whose substance, though delusory, builds a satisfactorily self-defined but essentially make-believe self. Still, self-invention is profoundly necessary the essential bulwark against confronting the reality of inanition.

Gertrude exhaustively counters her subjects' deluded inventions of themselves with her determinedly objective analyses. Once her subjects are recognized as of a "kind," or possibly an "admixture" with other kinds, they are then sorted by a set of secondary terms which may qualify, support, overwhelm, modify or negate initial perception.

A few of those secondary terms: lurid, dirty (*sale)* vs. clean, *efficient* vs. inefficient, passive vs. aggressive, weak vs. strong, concentrated vs. unconcentrated, aggressive vs. merely tenacious, sensibility vs. insensibility, successful vs. failure, important vs. unimportant—there are more.

These terms, though in common use, become in their usage here rigidified and restrictive, the meanings of some of them very particular to Gertrude. The loss of language offering quick intelligence to readers is indeed regrettable, but brave navigators eventually discover the depth of novelistic insight into human likelihoods stored in these pages, and eventually too the beauty of the language itself which, at a glance, seems as forbiddingly repetitious as its sense seems forbiddingly opaque. Further: connections, linkages, are recorded synoptically in the Notebooks, and the breadth of inclusiveness and density of a single entry sometimes requires a precise mental image—available at once to Gertrude, not to potential readers—of the diagrammatic interconnectedness of the entire system. Let's look at one relatively simple example as a paradigm for more complex and far more dense implicitly "diagrammatic" examples.

> Lurid male group. Hutch is a connecting link between Anglo-Saxon and lurid. Jaehne is a Bazarofian connecting to Hutch, Berenson to Vallotton, and through Vallotton to Jake Samuels. He also connects through Hutch to the idealists. [DB #28.]

Parsed:

"Lurid" is shorthand for the more extreme examples of *"sale"* or dirty sexual natures in males, the kind that "arouses fear" in Gertrude. [NB-*C #46] The "lurid male group" is almost the extreme of "resisting, cowardly, earthy" Alberichs who know their own cowardice, their own fear, their own lying, only too well. Their opposite, the Anglo-Saxon group, the "clean, courageously attacking" Siegfrieds, may be upright, but know themselves very little, rarely know, for example, that they're lying, but do it so well that they themselves and everyone else believes them. Hutch is at the midpoint between these two extremes, but actively shares in both. Who is he? Hutchins Hapgood, author, newspaper man, drama critic, novelist in the 1890's and early 1900's was deeply committed to radical movements in the U.S., a political idealist whom Mabel Dodge described as an intellectual anarchist pursuing at the same time God and social reform. Radical proselytizer, he wrote, among many books The Spirit of the Ghetto and The Spirit of Labor. And in old age, thinking himself the idealist who held still to the now-diluted moral values of his youth, called his autobiography A Victorian in the Modern World. But in Florence during Gertrude's summers there, she noted and wrote about the other Hapgood, the one who was a woebegone alcoholic, randy sexual Don Juan, and willing recruit to the blandishments of mysticism. In Mabel Dodge's jaundiced view, he was "an old bloodhound on a leash" held tight but only intermittently, by his wife, Neith Boyce.[11]

Gertrude in an astute, lengthy appraisal of Hutch, describes him as having on the one hand a "sexual base" that is "warm, passionate, idealistic, mystic, tolerant, sweet and lovable." But as distinct from his sexual base, his "character", or temperament, exhibits a "puritanical snob, hard, practical, intolerant… dogmatic… in short, about every quality a man can have that is incompatible with his ideal." Because of this "unself-recognized" incompatibility, "his sexual nature degenerat[es] into emotionality, liquor, mysticism." [DB #64] And so, she concludes in another note on Hutch, "there are innumerable ways to shipwreck." [Note #45]

But connective lines can run off in multiple directions. The simplest connection in this note pursues a basic line in a single direction, but takes it a jot further: Jaehne, a San Francisco German dealer in Oriental art and European antiques, close to Sally rather than to Gertrude, visited the Stein clan in Florence for a few days in the summer of 1907 while these "system" notes were in their earlier stages of composition. Gertrude had little more than a few days' glimpse of him, but her impression of his being a "Bazarofian" is confirmed by another source [R. Salinger interview with LK] who remembered that "there was something reptilian about Jaehne" A "reptilian" Bazarofian would be a step beyond even Hutch in the direction of the lurid, and so he is "connected," on the far—and even more lurid—side of Hutch's "Bazarofian" self.

The next batch—Berenson, Vallotton and Jake Samuels—are "connected" to these lurid males in a "line" away from Hutch's Bazarofian side, running in precisely the opposite direction, toward Hutch's affiliation with the "Anglo-Saxons" on his "bottom nature's" virtuously moral side. Closest to Hutch of the three, but still distant from Hutch's Bazarof, is the complicated Berenson. The celebrated connoisseur of Florentine art, the great lover of the "beauty" of the object rather than the object itself, is also (as Gertrude associates him with the same anomaly in Alice) one who for all his fine "flavor" and exquisite sensibility, has no "moral purpose," since like Alice he "chooses" beauty because he is "low," "for that is their [concept of] beauty," a basely "practical" and vulgarly "materialistic" sense of the beautiful. [DB #56] From that "lowness" BB clearly aspires to, and even exhibits, the values celebrated in the other direction, which eventually lead—beyond the Anglo-Saxon virtues—to the "Idealisms" in which the Nineteenth Century Romantics wallowed (and with which Gertrude had little patience, though she credited their lofty aspirations.) By intermediate steps, BB "connects" to that pristine height "through," first, Vallotton,

---

[11]Mabel Dodge re: "old bloodhound," re: HH

and then, closer yet to that height, Jake Samuels. Valloton, one of the Nabis group's painters whom Gertrude and Leo first bought and later remembered as one of their early mistakes, is nevertheless noted in the *The Autobiography of Alice B. Toklas* as "a gentle soul, a keen wit, [with] a great deal of ambition" but suffering from a feeling of impotence. [ABT 31.] Gertrude's definition of him is shrouded in one of the bewildering confusions of her system. Her respect for his "gentleness" and the genuineness of his artistic aspirations does not prevent her from seeing him as "temperamentally like Jaehne." But though his "temperament" is apparently as Bazarofian as Jaehne's, his gentleness and genuineness of aspiration place him in a line beyond BB in the direction of the Ideal.

An anomaly? Oddly, Gertrude's judgmental scheme here functions as neutrally descriptive, not as essentially evaluative. As with Matisse's "brutal egotism," whatever characteristic the self possesses at some extreme, even repellent, manifestation, it may well be the basis of "greatness." For Vallotton, Gertrude explains, "his greatness is his temperament, his sexual base and intellect [are] below it, and there is his great limitation as an artist." [Note #45] Because it is "great," Vallotton's disharmonious Bazarofianism doesn't prevent his being placed so far along this link of connections. This side of his temperament sets him—diagrammatically—on precisely the opposite track from Hutch's Bazarofianism.

Jake Samuels, Sally's brother, who lived at the time in San Francisco enduring an unhappy marriage and enjoying a happier political career, is one of Gertrude's paragons of the totally practical, a characteristic which at its purest can be the sign of the highest type of the Man of the World. In that purity, "the practical becomes complete before it passes over through… Jake Samuels into the men of the world who pass over to the pure idealists." [Note #41] And so, what would have registered to Weininger's horror, a practical Jewish politician emerges, in this particular linkage, as Gertrude's highest example of a male group's connection to an "Anglo-Saxon" ideal.

"Diagramming" these linkages rarely makes for simple linear design, as it does more or less in this relatively simple example. Far more frequently Gertrude imagines angular lines of linkage among her variations within types, in which a central character or group initiates lines of connection which, more than likely, run off in multiple directions. Consequently, her verbally described linkages, unless reduced to actual diagrammatic representation, remain bewildering, and—like as not—the diagrams themselves provide small deliverance. But the density and reach of those bewildering connections are everything; they are at the heart of the system, its ultimate justification. How?

They satisfy most significantly the triple obligation for determining the ego's ultimate definition: (1) as a wholly, yet qualified, identifiable member of a particular "kind," and (2) in this kind, as being attached to a definable network of similar or overlapping kinds, and (3) ultimately identifiable as "unique," by virtue of the number of nuanced and secondary characteristics merged with the defining terms of (1) and (2). And so, both the unique selves together with the representative selves merge—all together, defining "one." Consequently, Gertrude's most persistent mantra: "This one is one," signifies the total summary and privileged definition of a single self.

And so, the goal is a map, a geographical representation, a landscape of every kind of individual human being, each in its defined space, so hemmed in by similar but different types and kinds and with multiple qualifications and demurrers as to be recognizable both as wholly alike and as irreducibly unique—definition's conjunctive separations.

But the very process of constructing so comfortably symmetrical a system was at the same time undermining its own credibility. The more its logical likelihoods for fulfillment were pursued, the more her feelings were disturbed by gathering uncertainties. As early as MA 184, she is already querulous about the notion of "kinds." Still. she remains of two minds about her enterprise. "Is all this a fabrication?" But putting suspicion aside, she insists she's certain of all of it. [MA 362.] "When there will be a description of all repeating, then there will be contentment."

But that measure of certainty is effectively eroded during the writing of the "Alfred Hersland and Julia Hersland" chapter [MA 477–719.] Struggling with the problem of articulating the "whole" of Alfred Hersland, her attempt to stay within the orthodoxies of her system's terms and concepts fails her several times over. Its failure gradually makes clear to her her system's unsustainability. It suffers from two implicit difficulties: from the nature of language itself, and from her gradual re-recognition of her own uniqueness, her "separateness."

Language is as deceptive as it is revealing. In its designating meanings, Gertrude noted, there was an inevitable slippage of that meaning over time, separating statements from their former intent. The lesson was borne in on her when she included [MA 429–440.] the whole of the narrative copied from her story of *Fernhurst* written a few years earlier. Recognizing the anomaly of those earlier words (which she calls "categories,") "that once had meaning now have none," she concludes that "you have to lose words" to be faithful to present-tense, newly earned usage [MA 440.] And so, a new difficulty arises: only those words can be legitimately used that have in them currently "existent being."

As with language, so with systemic structure. The more Gertrude attempted to bolster her manufactured certainties, (as she did determinedly to define the "whole" of Alfred Hersland, from MA 508–719) the more those certainties continued to erode. Her test for their efficacy was, oddly, the universality of their acceptance: How many, how often, how thoroughly were her assertions believed? Was she at one with common understanding, or was she in her comprehension—and once again—separate and alone? And compounding these doubts was the growing suspicion that she herself had not yet grasped a definitive understanding of the "map" of human relations.

Confronting her failure, she is "unhappy," she reports, "that everyone is a little queer to me" [MA 482.] Compounding this is a more serious "disillusionment in living:" finding that "no one agrees with you completely in anything" [MA 482–483.] And there is the shock of discovering that even those fighting for you don't completely agree with you, so you "write for yourself and strangers." [MA 485]

Characteristic of her expressions of desperation: "Everything is in pieces, there is no use going on, everything is without end" and so there is "no reason to me why the world should go on" if in repeating "nothing gives me the sensation of a completed one.... It is pointless putting together kinds unless each one becomes a whole one to me" [MA 520.] The Alfred and Julia chapter is interrupted more than thirty times to lament the loss of the very certainties that had sustained her system. The difficulty of "realising" that no one had shared or currently shared her certainties, and that no one can share her isolation, gives her the feeling, she writes, of "a little boy realizing he is alone and howling" [MA 518–519.]

At this nadir, there's an intrusion into Gertrude's deliberations signifying a step toward manageable renovation. Alice Toklas as amanuensis had been sharing Gertrude's love and labor over the book but found voice only at this juncture to speak aloud long-gathering resentment: Gertrude. she complains,

> was still in the 'deep-thinking' life, the kind that worries about 'issues' and deliberates on the ethics and morality of each little act. This was the Stein thinking of Leo and Gertrude separately and together And it plainly offended me from the beginning. It was boring and ludicrous.... One of the jokes between Gertrude and myself was that I had stopped the 'deep-thinking' vein in her. I was discouraged to be in an atmosphere where intellectual processes were the basis of life, and in which Leo's endless notes and Gertrude's answers would be passing back and forth between them. I had the impression at the time that 'deep-thinking' was the root of all evil, that the fallible minds of human beings were bound to go wrong. [AT interview with LK.]

Gertrude reports the "upsetting" of her own way of thinking during this critical moment when she, with trepidation, was "being taught by some one that some have a way of feeling living that I have not ever been realising." But her new "way of feeling living" was not altogether new. It appeared to dissolve the structuring of "types" and "categories." It turned to unremitting focus on the observations of unprocessed manifestations of behavior, (once again: eating, drinking, sleeping, laughing, etc., as well as "thinking, talking, listening, knowing, feeling," etc.,) carefully unexamined literalness of the apparent—in a word, an ultimate "flattening" of intellectually-organized structures.

William James' Pragmatism, in inadvertent unison with Alice's misgivings, shares for Gertrude Alice's reflections on Leo's fundamental fault: his "thinking" untouched by the reality of his "experience." That charge against Gertrude's former mentor becomes her perpetual judgment of Leo's failed intellectual guidance. As James puts it,

> The world of concrete personal experiences to which the street belongs is multitudinous beyond imagination, tangled, muddy, painful and perplexed/ The world to which your philosophy-professor introduces you is simple, clean and noble. The contradictions of real life are absent from it.... In point of fact, it is far less an account of this actual world than a clear addition built upon it. It is no explanation of our concrete universe [W. James,1907, 8–9]

"Comment is not literature," Gertrude was to caution Hemingway in later years, although her Making of Americans is an unqualified example of comment *as* literature, since for its longest stretches, it is "comment" and almost nothing else. Turning her back on its "way of feeling living" to court its very opposite, was indeed confronted with trepidation. But Gertrude promises, at the conclusion of the following passage, to study carefully the likely consequences of being "taught:"

> I am now being taught by some one that some have a way of feeling living that I have not ever been realising. I like it although it is to me upsetting learning anything I am not naturally learning. I have been learning all my living very much that to me was upsetting as being not to me a natural thing to be learning.... I will be knowing sometime whether it is not a completely natural thing for me to be learning to be realising ways of feeling living with different kinds of living. [MA 621.]

The psychological resettings for the chapter's remaining analyses of "character" proceed in the old way, with neither hesitation nor confusion. But it is duty dryly done, genuflecting to abandoned commitments. The final chapter, "David Hersland," signals a most significant detour in her lifetime's writing divagations. The chapter begins with a lengthy divestment of old beliefs put aside for a new beginning, a profoundly new way of intimating her understanding of human behavior.

***

THE DAVID HERSLAND CHAPTER

The chapter begins:

> What am I believing about living. I am believing that I am not certain when I am saying something.... that I am meaning anything by what I am then saying, ... What is it I am knowing about living.... I am not certain that I am not knowing everything about being living. I am not

> certain that I am knowing everything about being living. [MA 723–724.]

It was clearly the moment for "beginning again." Two directions were explored simultaneously. One was already begun by extending the labors of the novel into the concurrently being written *A Long Gay Book* [MA 479ff.] In the other, Gertrude abandoned the calculated placement of "each one" within its grid of "kinds." The description of human being focused once more on the study of "each one as a whole one," each self altogether separate and distinct from all other "ones," its life's changes examined from their beginnings until death. This was indeed "beginning again." From the very beginning of her project, it had been implicit in its original intent—the ultimate way of knowing being through the knowing of the absolute totality of the life of "one."

The "one" was now to be David Hersland, and the scrutiny into the totality of his being became the sole object of the book's final chapter. It is literally an extended portrait of the "David" Gertrude knew, made up of a compendium of three actual selves: Leon Solomons, her colleague and collaborator at the Harvard Lab; her brother Leo; and herself. Foregoing the failed assumptions of her earlier scrutinies of selves, the David chapter redirects those assumptions—the first venture of many to come into ways of adequately "saying being."

The David portrait is focused on the interactions among the multiple components of his cognitive self over his lifetime. Its characteristics are reexamined in each of the periods of his aging. For David's portrait, there are five such periods (defined in erratically-sequenced and overlapping periods:)

> Childhood [MA 729–810, 836]
> Early School Days [MA 766–776, 842–849]
> College Years [MA 736–874]
> Julia and Alfred Relation [MA 86–99]
> David Alone and Death [MA 891–914.]

The cognitive life alone now defines the uniqueness of selfhood.

The meanings of David's invisible subjective impulses and inward intellectual gestures alone now constitute the whole of the essential "knowing" of his being. From that perspective, the studied self may, either over time or on the instant, feel multiple, contradictory responses to emotional confrontations, and so exhibit aberrations of response that render fixed character definition irrelevant. The "troubling,"—that is. the shock, for example—of David's discovery that he was born only to replace a son who had died—may at one and the same moment be recognized, denied, dismissed, suffered, or out of disinterest, almost forgotten. [MA 845–846] Gertrude circles her subject's initial responses replete with the particular emotional vagaries that precisely belong to him. Her understanding in turn reflects the new subtlety and precision of her recognitions of the self's stream of reactions, its fleeting specificities of response, to an original emotion:

> David Hersland.... being living is having meaning, he was one needing that being living is existing. He was one troubling, he was one not troubling, he was one needing that being living has not any meaning, he was one needing that being living is not existing. [MA 835.]

And in a lengthy passage on David's feelings about growing up, Gertrude, unravels the continuity—or possibly the simultaneity—of David's feelings of change as a boy, and then the certainty of his feeling, and then of his feeling something in the beginning and not feeling it, and his feeling sad, and then troubled, and deciding about the troubled ones he knows, and then, deciding about himself, but overall, concerning this whole matter, not completely interested. [MA 835]

But there remained a painfully unresolved question the answer to which plainly destroyed the possibility of reaching the goal to which she had devoted her entire project: grasping a "completed understanding" of all other selves. Of the many confessions to the reader written into the text of the novel, this confession is perhaps the longest and, for Gertrude, the most debilitating:

> There are so many being in living and there are so many that I am knowing by seeing and hearing being in living and each one of these is experiencing in being living and I cannot be feeling what way each one is experiencing, I who am suffering and suffering because of this thing. I am in desolation and my eyes are large with needing weeping and I have a flush from feverish feeling and I am not knowing what way each one is experiencing in and about some I am knowing in a general way and I could be knowing in a more complete way *if I could be living more with that one and I never will live more with every one*, I certainly cannot ever live with each one in their being one being living, in my being one being living. I tell you I cannot bear it this thing that I cannot be realising experiencing in each one being living, I say it again and again I cannot let myself be really resting in believing this thing, it is in me now as when I am realising being a dead one, a one being dying and I can do this thing and I do this thing and I am filled then with complete desolation and I am doing this thing again and again and I am now again and again certain that I will not ever be realising experiencing in each one of very many men and very many women, I can realise something of experiencing in some of them, in them as kinds of them but *I am needing to have it in me as a complete thing* of each one ever living and I know I will not, and I am one knowing being a dead one and not

> being a living one, I who am not believing that I will he realising each one's experiencing. *I do not want to realise each thing they are experiencing, I do not care anything about such a thing, all that I am needing to be one being living is to be realising completely how each one is experiencing, with what feeling, thinking, believing, creating* and I am very certain that I will not ever be completely with each one doing such a thing, I will be doing something in such a thing with kinds in men and women, with some of some kinds of them but not with each one not with every one, no certainly not with every one. No certainly not with every one, completely, certainly not, and more and more knowing some one experiencing and completely knowing that one makes it certain that if I could live with each one I could realise the experiencing in each one and I cannot ever live with each one, I certainly never will be living a good deal with each one ever having been living *[Italics added]* [MA 729.]

To "realise the experiencing in each one," as Gertrude mourns in this passage, was no longer attainable although its attainability remained for her a passionate yearning. But in the David chapter, she skirts the difficulty by effectively reordering the image of "the self." As she explains in her lamentation above, she has no interest in realising each particular external event in the life of her subjects. Now, their cognitive life alone encompasses the entire substance and uniqueness of the human self. And to accomplish the almost impossible feat of replicating her subjects' private cognitive life, *"I must find out,"* she writes, *"what is moving inside them that makes them them, and I must find out how I by the thing moving excitedly inside in me can make a portrait of them."* Having already determined that what she can know of another is limited by the compass and constraints of her own inevitably isolated "knowing," and that the certainty is gone that anyone can know of others whether they are experiencing "the full meaning of their living" [MA 737], she opts for a possible way, by way of *her own experience,* to venture on the comprehension and expression of another's subjectivity. To win that comprehension, it is her own subjectivity that becomes the significant center of her analysis. The understanding of her subjects is complete when, as she describes, she succeeds in "sinking into" the feeling of at-oneness with her subject's own "experiencing," her subject's own self-knowing and feeling.

Yet she can and cannot. "If I could live with each one, I could realise experiencing in each one, and I cannot." But overriding her quandary, she trusts her own "inner feeling" to substantiate the accuracy of her experience of other selves. Preparation for knowing the other, she had already explained, lay in the long, gradual procedure for "sinking-into" total accord. In *A Long Gay Book*, an image, a word, a phrase can recall for her that process and its ultimate and summary sufficiency. In the David Hersland chapter, not yet resorting to synoptic graspings at memory's telling phrases, Gertrude, at expansive leisure, turns her *apercus* this way and that, once again placing a precise "naming" of David's "boasting" within a pattern of possibilities:

> Mostly every one is needing some one to be one listening to that one being one being one boasting. David Hersland in a way was not one needing one to be one listening to him being one being one boasting. There certainly were some who were listening then to him. He was one in a way not really needing this thing and that was because he was one so clearly telling what he was so clearly feeling. He needed some to be listening while he was thinking, he did have very many to listen while he was thinking, he almost was not needing this thing. Some who are thinking are very much needing some one to be one boastingly listening, some who are thinking are needing some one to be listening to them and saying something and not really saying that thing. Some are needing to be having some one saying something and they are not seriously considering the serious thing they are needing that some one is saying while they are thinking. David Hersland could in a way be one of such of them. [MA 788.]

Since the renovated terms for describing human conduct now focus entirely on cognition, the key terms depicting that life, as Gertrude carefully enumerates in her text, are: *"[T]hinking…, listening, remembering, forgetting, feeling, meaning, and telling*" [MA 788.]

In the course of further explanations of David, Gertrude expands her relevant terms: *being certain, knowing, deciding, experiencing, liking, understanding*, as well as processes discernible to others such as *talking, looking, asking, advising eating (in relation to fasting and dying), loving, describing, being angered, being pleased.* These are the clusters of terms which signify, within the self and by the self, its internalized intentions and decisions as well as some few of its overt actions. They also reveal, sometimes gently, sometimes hardly discernibly, Gertrude's critical judgments of the successes and ineptitudes and delusions of David's cognitive life. His prowess and incapacities are tallied candidly in Gertrude's ironic and ultimately tragic portrayal of him.

Further: the radical "flattening" of language in this chapter reinforces a radical flattening of articulated reference to particulars of David's being. His "knowing" or "feeling" or "thinking" about "going on living" are not particularized in novelistic detail.; they're instead set within the context of other varyingly "flattened" contexts—"completely interested" or "not completely interested" or "going to be interested"—to arrive eventually at a positioning among them into which David momentarily fits. What is avoided is what was so carefully observed in *The Making of Americans*—descriptive detail and characterization of selves as definable among "kinds." What is left of fiction's persuasive guarantees of descriptive accuracy are Gertrude's private certainties born of her intense experience of "sinking-into" her subjects' own private "feelings." These intuitive discernments of her own, hidden or partially hidden in another self, become the substance of her portrait of David. Her new analytic terrain, then, is composed entirely of cognitive functions and their relation to one another, their mutual accord or contradiction of one another, their shadings of relevance to one another.

Stylistically, the chapter's prose foregoes any vestige of forward momentum, outdoing in all probability any instance in literature of so fixed a determination *not to proceed.* What governs this s*tasi*s is a deliberately altered relation between writer and reader. It ignores altogether the reader's habitual anxiety to grasp and proceed. Once a perception—a fact, a characteristic of David's—is evoked, Gertrude circles the conceivable contexts in which each momentary perception can be most fully "set." Only a step, one might suppose, beyond the prose of the novel's earlier pages. But the David chapter is more deliberately geared to what Gertrude calls "moment to moment" perceptions of her subject, each one separately and equally foregrounded, each related by proximity to its almost identical neighbor, and each unique to itself. Gertrude insists her portrait of David is not "repetitious." But though its forward motion is concealed, David's definitive portrait, from the beginning of his self-awareness until his death, is subtly, and deftly, fully accomplished.

The longest and most nuanced scrutiny of David is studied during the period of his college years. The wanderings within his mind become more complex, more outgoing and more rich during these years, and just as the "troubles" of his childhood and early school years produced tangled feelings of which he was not altogether aware [MA 845–846], so his more mature experiences as a college student became a time of hidden bewilderments concealed by increasing intellectual certainty and increasingly confident "clarity of thinking" and "boasting about it" [MA 786.] (The implicit ironies in this portrayal anticipate the mournful passages devoted to his dying, when the tragedy hovering over David's death is the failed potential of possibly crippled "genius.")

David's college years, then, encompass the gathering certainties not only of his "knowing" and delicate feeling, but of his "beautifully telling about it" to friends and acquaintances [MA 789–790] (Leo's "lecturing" to rue de Fleurus guests, which years later became Alice's exasperation.) Some of the new complexities studied: David's idealization of women, and in love, his submission to them [MA 736, 739–740] (echo of Gertrude's astute version of Leon Solomons in her earlier story, *Fernhurst.*) David's knowing "another one" and their both knowing and not knowing one another, and variations of these postures and their imagined certainties and uncertainties [MA 811–812;] David now living among many others (students and a hospitable family;) new friends and intensified uncertainty (once again, Gertrude's attribution of her own experience;) and David questioning which of them felt that he was genuinely one of them, and which, if any, did he feel "knew" him. [MA 741–742, 725–726] And again and again, the most troubling question of all resurfaces: the contention between the certainty that being alive has meaning, and the certainty that it does not. [MA 835.] Life's meaning and value, David imagines, can be "certain" if certain determinants can be known: knowing, for example, the intellectual perfection of "clear thinking," or knowing a woman possessing pure beauty, or sharing with him perfect love or perfect mutual understanding. [MA 824–826.] All fail but the one he himself can know: "clear thinking." But as Gertrude learned from William James, "clear thinking" as the equivalent of perfect knowing, is philosophy's delusion [W. James quote on page 41.] since it deliberately omits from its formulations the realities of common experience. Consequently, the major thread followed in the weave of David's cognitive prowess is precisely the rigidity of his commitment to "clear thinking," and its eventual despoiling of his flexibility of mind (studied in the long sequence MA 770–823,) and ending in acknowledgement of his need for "listening" and "telling" and "feeling," but mostly—persistently and perilously—his need for "clear thinking."

As for David's friends and acquaintances at college, his way of "listening" to them and "telling" them what he thinks and feels are both entree and barrier to mutual understanding and "liking" [MA 824.] He himself is puzzled, both certain and uncertain about the meaning of "liking." [MA 834.] And in his demand for perfection of understanding, he suffers the frustration of recognizing that, he cannot know what he yearns most to know of every friend: the whole reality of the friend's existence. [MA 811–812.] Or alternatively, David and a friend understanding one another and having feeling for one another, but neither speaking of it to the other [MA 825.] But the most deeply troubling quandary of all confronts David once again : the quandary that he needs in order to live: his ambivalence concerning his need to know that living itself has "certainty of meaning," and at the same time, his need to know that it does not—and further, that "living has not any meaning and that living is not [even] existing." [MA 835–836.]

This last recalls Gertrude's earliest speculations concerning "existing" [MA 99–115] in which she first notes two kinds of human being confronting the fundamental dread of recognizing human nonentity and settling for one of two alternative responses: either bolstering or inventing reasons for one's "importance," or succumbing to the feeling of merely "existing." But David tolerates the further desperation of living itself being equivalent to non-existence. This is Gertrude's unemphatic beginning of what is to become the increasingly overwhelming certainty of David's last days when he withdraws altogether from living, succumbing willingly to "non-existence."

But among college mates, he is still longing for and suffering the disappointment of not possessing a completely different consolation: since he is certain that no one "could completely listen to him unless they loved him," he suffers the awareness of one who *almost completely* loves him and so he realizes the incompleteness of her listening to "all of him." [MA 866–867.] And yet there is one he loves and shows it to her out of his perpetual need to love "a completely beautiful one" [MA 871–872.]

Gertrude (here seeing David in the guise of Leo as he rises to self-confident and rhetorical authority among classmates,) pays tribute to a brief intermission of good feeling—David escaping from habitual bouts with uncertainties. He emulates Gertrude's own victory over her confusions among "kinds," and recognizes that "each one is [indeed] one" [MA 872.] Outgoing, he is interested in disseminating advice among friends; he has "completely clear feeling" of whatever he is feeling and has mastered an "extraordinarily complete expression of it;" fighting self-contradictions, he works conscientiously at being certain that he is truly and entirely "one being living," and needs no further reassurance. [MA 878.] He is a study, in other words, of visible self-assurance and inner bewilderment.

Julia and Alfred's friendship begins the last phase of David's gradually "not needing" any of the props that had sustained him. The episode touches once again on narrative but is absent the substance of narrative. The constraints of this phase of portraiture are observed: inner propulsions alone are recounted, not their explanation nor their detail.

Gertrude begins the episode recalling relations between David and the Dehnings: Alfred (David's now married brother), Julia his wife, Julia's brother George, and Mr. and Mrs. Dehning. (Gertrude had originally planned for the friendship and falling out of David and Julia to be the climactic episode of the novel's narrative. It remains the most critical loss David suffers before his abandoning all relations.)

The episode plays on the relation of each to their "need:" David not needing "succeeding" and not needing "another," Julia not needing to have David's understanding.

Cognitive direction—or possibly conscious cognitive determination—anticipates the end—David "not needing" anything at all. The beginning of his terminal withdrawal is signified by his "completely not eating some things" [MA 894.] What is left for David's active life is "aloneness" and "advising," which he does for both Julia and Alfred over their bitter quarrels. [MA 872–873.] Briefly, he experiences once again moments of euphoria, "knowing people." and "explaining living" to them, and particularly telling it to *one*, but wondering whether this one would keep on needing him to tell it [MA 885.] But once again he is "deciding about eating," and his need for this decision, and his need for others to understand this, and his *urging* on others his own understanding of clearly thinking and needing meaning. "He might have fought for his understanding" Gertrude interjects, "but no one needed to fight him." [MA 891] [And so the last urge, the urge for self-defense and self-justification, evaporates.]

He is for a time "continuous and clear" in his understanding and advising some "to go on with his understanding." [MA 888–889.] But the recognition that he is only "needing to eat one thing," and his decision that "there was no use going on living" and yet "not completely deciding about living," he becomes "the quite quiet one, the quite gentle one," retired from all friends, and "quietly enough living and teaching." He was dead "at the beginning of middle living." [MA 880–882, 889, 863–865.]

What, in retrospect, sums up David Hersland? Gertrude carefully enumerates. Some, not David, achieve gentle life, fulfilled, complete life, with its "beginning, middle and end." [MA 861] David did not, neither gently nor finally, see or know anything as a "complete thing."

Oddly, for all his intellectual wanderings and self-scrutinies, he continued doing things the way his family had done them since his childhood. But there were those who recognized that he was not to be identified with "family living." [MA 861–862] He knew, too, terminal certainties, knew and "needed to know, that there was no succeeding in living," [MA 865.] He completely remembered and was completely certain that "each one is one," and that in his lifetime, he had pursued only his own chosen way. [MA 865, 872, 902.]

Taking into account the ultimate mereness of David's significance in life, Gertrude calculates the residual meaning of his being in death through the ways in which he is remembered and not remembered, mourned and not mourned, needed and not needed, constantly and not constantly held in mind,—so commemorating "one," David, and what remained of the impress on existence left by him, which constitutes Gertrude's judgmental but compassionate neutralizing equanimity:

> Not any one needed to be one expecting that he should come to be a dead one.... [I]t was not a needed thing. Some were indignant about this thing that he had come to be a dead one.... Some were remembering hearing this thing, that he had come to be a dead one.... Some were vague about this thing about his having come to be a dead one.... Some were not certain that he would have been one coming to be beginning succeeding in living.... Any one could be one not very constantly remembering his being a dead one, his having been a living one. Any one could remember this thing, his having been a dead one, his having been a living one. [MA 904]

***

3. THE NOTEBOOKS OF GERTRUDE STEIN FOR *THE MAKING OF AMERICANS*

1. BEGINNING

(Summer 1903 to January 1903)

What was to become the prodigious labor of almost nine years during the writing of her massive novel, *The Making of Americans*, began in desultory brooding in London during her stay there with her brother Leo. It was during that summer of 1902 that she met the first Europeans and transplanted Americans who were to figure in the complexities of the psychological topography of the novel, and it was in London during the following winter that she was to start the Notebooks that gradually accumulated the memories, observations, quotations and narratives that were to become the matter of the book. The five months that ensued in Bloomsbury remained among the blackest of Gertrude's memories. The Sitwells, who knew it in later years, dubbed it "Gloomsbury," and Gertrude adopted the name as apt.

She and her brother Leo had rented lodgings near the British Museum that were dully comfortable, and they continued to see their English and American friends who did nothing to relieve her hatred for Bloomsbury and Oxford Street "and the dismalness of London and the drunken women and children and the lonesomeness." Leo's stay in London came to an abrupt end the day before Christmas, "because I lacked diplomatic talent of even an elementary kind." The writer on architecture to whom he had been introduced, horrified that Leo would have to spend Christmas without companions and away from hearth and home, invited him to share his own houseful of children and grandchildren. Leo told him he would come if he was still in London, and not knowing how to put him off further without deliberately lying, left for Paris in the afternoon of the twenty-fourth of December. He intended to stay there for a short time, then go to Florence and then return to America.[1]

Gertrude's solace during her enforced loneliness was the British Museum. Living in its shadow, she would arrive at the reading room early in the morning and read until late at night, leaving only when she was hungry.[2] When she was off this regimen, she wandered the dismal London streets. "Anything can frighten her and London when it was like Dickens certainly did."[3]

Her reading at the Museum and at Mudie's bookshop was apparently begun with a rough plan in mind to read straight through English narrative writing from the

---

[1] Ibid., pp. 118-119.

[2] Toklas, Interviews.

[3] G. Stein, Autobiography, p. 70.

sixteenth century to the present.[4] She bought a set of minute grey-covered notebooks[5] in which she entered her lists for reading and buying books, and in which she copied out quotable passages for the pleasure of having them.

She was subsequently to letter sequentially some of the small notebooks that pertained to the writing of *The Making of Americans*, but quantities of others and miscellaneous loose notes remained unmarked. At Yale, the unmarked notebooks and miscellaneous single-page notes were numbered by me in the order in which they were found, which numbering consequently bore no relation to the order in which they were written. Dating evidence, content and further examination produced a chronological sequence for all the notes. But to avoid the confusion of disparate numbering, and for the convenience of scholarly search and corroboration of texts at Yale, what had been the initially tentative numbering of the archived notes has been retained.

For the notebooks on *The Making of Americans*, a considerable number were written concurrently, the content of one Notebook sharing significantly the simultaneous writing and thinking in another. To clarify those relations, the graph on the following page makes clear their chronological connections.

***

It appears that of the lettered notebooks, Notebooks J, K & L remain missing. Those designated *C, *B & *J are also Stein's designations, though her lettered titles appear to belong to a sequence that is missing.

---

[4] Toklas, Interviews.

[5] The small copy-books are referred to in the Autobiography, p. 70.

Chronology of the Notebooks

Date	*The Making of Americans*	Notebooks		
1902–1906		Jottings, *p. 57*		
April 1906	First Draft revised and continued, after lapse since 1903	NB-2, *81* NB-9, *93* NB-6, *103* NB-1, *119* NB-11, *131* NB-12, *143* NB-10, *155*	NB-MA, *167* *entitled "Making of Americans"* ↓	Diagram Book
June 1908	Returned to First Draft pp. 1–72; then revised rest of First Draft with insertions creating Second Draft. (Final version begins with the completed 'Schillers' episode.)	NB-14, *197*		DB, *305* *LGB begins* *Sept. 1908. Both begun* NB-*C, *203* NB-*B, *263*
Post-Nov 1908 **Dec 1908**	Wrote the 'Seamstresses' episode (MA 260ff.) (265–278)	NB-7, *369* NB-5, *423* NB-8, *427*	NB-A, *371* NB-B, *391* NB-C, *407*	NB-*J, *283* ↓
Jan 1909 **June 1909** **July 1909**	 Martha Hersland chapter begun (382–476)	NB-3, *477* ↓	NB-D, *435* NB-E, *449* NB-F, *463*	
Dec1909 **Summer 1910** **Jan 1911**	Martha Hersland chapter finished Alfred Hersland chapter begun Alfred Hersland chapter finished	NB-4, *485* NB-13, *529*	NB-G, *493* NB-H, *509* NB-I, *519*	
Sept 1911	David Hersland chapter begun		NB-M, *537* NB-N, *557*	

	Epilogue (907–925)			

2. Jotting and Early Draft Notes

London, New York, Paris, 1902–6

Among the earliest notes are those begun as jottings and lists, written during the winter's stay of 1902–03 in London during the Christmas season. It was then that she appears to have written a sketch of London's "East End" describing its greyness, its Chinese or Indian or Malaysian population, its modest refreshments and its empty streets.

Jottings

Note #176

["EAST END"]

When I went into the East End I thought everything looked so grey, grey houses, and grey everything, and then I slowly found that the one thing they lived for was color, every woman bought flowers, they would go without eating but not without flowers and birds are a passion birds everywhere all colors and anything they buy always always color, birds and flowers. The streets were empty and everything that comes into these empty streets were was like an awfully important event, a truck coming along, a child with a ball, and it all made the architecture so much more finished[?] and the architecture is the most important thing there. Suddenly I recognized that it was all eighteenth century, these grey buildings, and filled to bursting with vital life and next to them bridges, creaves [?] all the things that make to-day living and so these eighteenth century arched windows all which I had always admired dead became suddenly alive.

There are no such things as hotels, there are rooming places but these are let by the month there is no place to stay the night seamans homes and salvation army rest ~~homes~~ houses, and it is there where you get into contact with the unemployed and the first thing that strikes you is their gayety, they are so optimistic, they ~~think~~ talk of world affairs but it is not real to them the only things they really worry about it [sic] are the plants they have bought for their misses [?] or the way the bird in its cage feels. They have rows with their families and that smins [?] them but everything else is far away, as far away as the eighteenth century in which their houses were built.

In the whole of the East End they love amusement, they love luxury, they like to go to the dogs, dog-racing and Queens, the Queens is the big music hall, everybody talks to everybody, they have no class feeling, everybody is just the same everybody is just in work or just out of work and so everybody is just the same. If you are out of work everybody who is in work pays for ~~him~~ you, and no questions asked, the only people they do not like are [senhers]/, a man who sponges on drinks, lives on the dole, when he gets his dole he spends it all on drinks and gets a room to sleep in for nothing and then sponges for his drinks. They pay for his drinks too, everybody who has anything pays but they despise him. At queens they drink and talk, their whole life is having a glass of beer and long conversations generally all about work, they talk about the king, they say he is a good king ~~but he w~~ because he works hard, and they like Mr. Chamberlain because although he is an old man he works hard at a hard job. Everybody says long live the king everybody stands and takes his cap off, ~~not for political~~ not for any reason xcept that he is a good man faithful[?] to his job.

The large part of the population, in fact nearly ~~all~~ everybody there has to do with the sea, actually most of the people who have the little homes and the birds in bird cages and the flowers are stevedores, the shop keepers are almost all Chinese or Indian or Malays. Shops are all very beautiful, they are all either clothes shops selling clothes to sea-men or restaurants, there are two classes of shops some of them look rather mysterious with curtains up there you find a group of work-men who have meals there making themselves a kind of club because the proprietor is amusing or they may be laundries or they may be tea-shops, they look mysterious they have no signs but they are just ordinary shops just the same as those that love flamboyant signs. There are no mysteries in the East End and very little fighting, the Queens has no signs out, it is just [____?], Some bars have signs a good [?] many have none at all, everybody knows them and everybody just wanders in. Some of the Indian restaurants have so much decoration on the outside that it is all covered with painted cut out figures and little Venetian niggers with lights stuck in and around them and every color and every design, and inside are very beautiful highly colored engravings from Ceylon with religious subjects, and among them are mode drawings of English tailors of double breasted suits, and these framed are mixed up on the walls with everything else, and in the back are little rooms that the men use when there are a group but the proprietor often says no mate you can't have that room to-day, the kids are doing their home work, or sometimes the kids are doing their cross word puzzles, the proprietor serves [?] everybody everybody but stokers out of work as waiters because he himself was a stoker, so while they wait, they discuss the number of tons of coal they can carry.

When the sea-men are really flush they go ~~not to the~~ to the Chinese restaurants where they have a big blow out and can giggle at the West Enders who come down looking to their eyes very funny as they walk [?] in the East End.

The hours of the meals are very different, they do not go to the restaurants until the pubs and the music halls are closed, that is after half past ten because the restaurants are open all night.

The streets are always empty night and day, you never see groups in the streets, the docks are all closed off with iron gates and you can't get in unless you belong to the company, you just can't walk along the water front, you just see the distant masts and the grey 18 century houses make [?] the East End.

LK But the cheerlessness of London was modified by her access to the British Museum's Reading Room. Devouring books with speed was already old habit; it remained so for a lifetime. She had turned her back on public school in California at the age of sixteen, determining to get her education out of the public library, following her own pace and passions. England. Beginning with "Stang," the rest of the lengthy book lists were assembled during Gertrude's stay in New York at the "White House" (at 100th Street and Riverside Drive) in a flat she shared with friends.

The titles and authors of well over one hundred books, with the addition of their identifications of publishers and publication dates of copies that would have been available to Gertrude in 1903, are, the editor judged, far too lengthy for readers' patience for sequential reading. And so, the reading lists have been banished to Appendix A to accommodate detailed scrutiny. Gertrude, out of habit, copied passages for her particular interest or pleasure during her reading. These passages, telling of her taste and admiration, accompany their sources.

*

Note #135

(See Appendix A for first half of this note, Note #135A)

LK Leo had started buying Japanese prints before he left Johns Hopkins in 1900. After his trip to Japan in 1895, he had amassed a considerable collection. Japanese art in the Nineties was not merely a novelty but a revelation. It represented the most advanced taste of the moment, a gesture as well as an enthusiasm. But the gesture very quickly became the fashion, and for Gertrude the taste for Japanese prints began to parallel suspiciously the taste of the "spare American imagination." The "etching and print Japanese stage" became for Gertrude part of contemporary American tastelessness, and one of its pretentious "culturines." But in the Spring of 1903 when she was readying for another trip to join her brother in Europe and to see new additions to his impressive collection, she was getting up on names, dates and reputations in Japanese art's history.

Nahizani
Jotetsu
Gesshu
Gesson
Korin
Shignaga
Tanyu
Rin Rio (Chinese
Makkei (Chinese
Choki (Chinese
Matahei

Kyonaga
Muonobu
Kaigetsudo
Kionobu

Shingemasa
Utamaro
Kyohiro
Toyoharu

Churin
Shunsui
Toshinobu
Mangosaburo
Kiomasu

Toyonobu
Kyomitsu

Nahazani… Matahei: [first column of names]

Kyonaga… Toyoharu: [second and third columns of names] These lists correspond to those in Ernest Fenollosa, *Masters of the Ukiyoe*, where the names of these Japanese printmakers, with some additions and deletions, are set down "in order of merit." The volume was published, however, in 1911, years after this note was written in 1902–3. But Fenollosa lectured in New York at Cooper Union in 1902, and returned to the city for lectures in 1903, with fairly elaborate slide presentations of this material. It is possible, though hardly certain, that GS attended one of these lectures, and jotted down this list of names.

Margosaburo very interesting almost a forerunner in breadth of Kionanga hand-colored about 1732 cont[?] 4 or 5 prints single figures except one of wrestling man.

Toyabaru 1 print man raising small female form not hand-colored very delicate

Margosaburo [sic]... very delicate: Source unidentified.

Eighth century by Godoshi
Riromui[?]
Kobo Diashi
Kose Kanowoku the Godoshi of Japan
Yeishin Fra Angelico of Japan
Motomitsu his contemporary & rival founder of Tosa school
Twelfth century beginning of Jap. individual genius the four great masters of action are Toba Soja strong in action
Kasiya Mitsinaga whose son is Tosa Keim
Nobuzane Japs greatest colorist.

Culture lost once more in 14 cent.
Kalshi founder of naturalistic landscape Sung landscape
Kakei greatest landscape painter in the East.
J. S. Bache
66 Exchange Place
Cho Densu
Josetsu Chinese painter
Shubun Jap with ~~Kakki~~ Sung inclination his
Josaku
Motonubu
Yitoku [?]
Sotatsu.
Konin

LK ***Eighth century by Godoshi... Korin:*** List taken from Ernest F. Fenollosa, "An Outline of Japanese Art," *Century Magazine*, v.56 (new series v.34), May and June 1898, [Part One] pp. 62–75; [Part Two] pp. 276–289. This article, a seminal presentation of Japanese and Chinese art, the first for American readers, was subsequently published in 1911 in considerably enlarged form in *Epochs of Chinese and Japanese Art.*

"In 1878 Ernest F. Fenollosa, an American critic, became Professor of Philosophy in Tokyo. He was the first to open the eyes of the West to the beauty and importance of the older art of Japan and China; but he also had great influence in Japan. He persuaded the government to forbid the temples to sell works of art, and to schedule as national treasures all the most precious objects. His enthusiasm for the old traditions reacted on Japanese artists. The School of Fine Art set up by Italian professors had been a failure. A new school was established in 1887, and… the teachers were… all eminent painters in the traditional styles." [Encycl. Britt., vol.12, p.965a.]

(GS's lists follow Fenollosa's article closely and systematically, focusing on his sections on Japanese and Chinese painters and printmakers, ignoring entirely passages on history, religion, sculpture, etc. The artists she notes appear under these headings:)

p.71, "Chinese Painting:"	(Godoshi, Ririomin)
p.72, "The School of Kobo Daishi"	(Kobo Daishi)
p.72, "The School of Kose Kanowoka"	(Kose Kanowoka)
p.72, "The School of Yeishin Sozu"	(Yeishin)
p.72, "Decay of the Second Period"	(Motomitsu)
p.75, "The Four Great Masters"	(Toba Soja, Kasuga, Tosa, Nobuzane)
p.279, "Kakki"	(Kakki)
p.279, "Kakei"	(Kakei)
p.279, "Yuen and Ming Art"	(Danshidzui)
p.279, "The Hangchow School"	(Mokei, Kakei, Bayen)
p.279, "The Quadrilateral of Kioto Schools:"	(Cho Densu, Josetsu, Shubun, Jasoku)
p.280, "Kano Motonobu"	(Motonobu)
p.281, "Nobunaga and Hideyoshi"	(Yeitoku)
p.287, "The School of Korin"	(Sotatsu, Korin)

About twenty blank pages to end of notebook. From inside back cover to three pages forward, as follows:

2 & 3

Kionaga

Toyonobur

Konusai

Masaburo

Toyabaro

Kyoburo. [Ryoburo?]

Kionaga…. Kyoburo [Rioburo?]: This list of names appears in this sequence in Fenollosa, *Epochs of Chinese and Japanese Art*, 1st edition, 1911. The date is puzzling. See note above re: "Kyonaga…. Toyoharu."

*

Maria 41st & Broadway 1 o'clock next to Criterion

*

Mokei contemporary
Danshiduzi near to Kakei
Sung landscape Kakki founder
Bayen
Danshidzui last of Sung land.

Mokei contemporary, Danshiduzl near to Kakei, Sung landscape Kakki founder, Bayen, Danshiduzl kast of Sung.land. [Unlocated]

*

Note #66

Its very handsome here in Janverville [?], and the good Lord is letting the sun shine and thats very nice. I am very fond of the sun and very grateful to the good Lord.

Draft for GS letter, unidentified

*

Note #195

Early entries for abandoned stories and for Three Lives*, and miscellaneous "trial" sentences for the first draft of* The Making of Americans

First evidence of GS's beginning short stories: "Maggie" became "The Gentle Lena" in Three Lives. *The rest of the note offers evidence of text that Gertrude contemplated using in her first writings. Some of these entries were used as written, or in altered form, in the earliest pages of* The Making of Americans *They are evidence for the novel having been begun in 1902–03. These passages are intermingled with text intended for early stories which in part survived in the stories in* Three Lives.

The Progress of Jane Sands being
a history of one woman and many others.

*

Maggie being the history of a gentle soul.
story

*

A woman painter.

*

The Tragedy of the Wirkin sisters
The busted[?] twins.

*

Completely clothed in moral atmosphere

*

Due to the fact that lightning is likely to strike twice in the same place. Negatively altruistic because you are willing to let the other man's individuality work.

*

The American attitude that the man who is getting nothing out of it is to be considered. The French view that the people who are getting something are the ones that count.
The French are passionate and unemotional, sentimental and cynical.

*

Earning a living is not the ideal of existence it is only an unfortunate necessity.

*

If I am fool enough to love I may as well be fool enough to trust you, although any student of human nature would admit that the second is infinitely more dangerous than the first.

*

Pain doesn't count its only the loss of joy, the loss of faith that is important. Pain isn't pleasant of course but it isn't a thing to remember.

*

There are some people that can make even the face of the Almighty look smutty.

*

The power of coping adequately with e

very hour in the day.

*

Felt like a classic or at least like a German eighteenth century translation of a classic.

*

Which only goes to show that if a man wants a thing badly enough he can generally get it.

*

Nothing can justify such cringing, such slavish subjection, such abject lying.

*

The power of coping adequately with every hour of the day.

*

I need it in my reading

*

So long as there is hope there is despair.

*

The moderately poor man can afford luxuries that are luxuries to him but the moderately rich man can only afford the luxuries that are necessities to him.

*

Its the great objection to heroic lying that it arrogates to itself the right of choosing just how much truth is good for another. It is an unwarrantable liberty to take even with a child to say you are capable of facing only so much truth the rest, I will lie you out of.

*

Facts are rarely illuminating, they are so often the same when they hide such very different things.

*

There are two great classes of humans those who lie and those who don't. Of course there are sub-classes, those who can't and try and those who can and don't.

*

In youth there is nothing we are so intolerant of as our own sins writ large in others but later on there is nothing we are so lenient towards for surely these sins of all sins are those most worthy to be forgiven nay to add a charm to character.

Draft for MA 3

*

Whats a halo between friends.

*

There comes a point where generosity becomes assininity.*

*

The ostentatious arrogant simplicity of wood panellings and green burlap, a room in which one could not possibly commit a crime where one could only tell a very white lie.

First version of description of Julia Dehning's decoration of her new home is altered in text to read "...the passion for the simple line and toned green burlap on the wall and wooden panelling all classic and severe." MA 31

*

It was dangerous to accept his statements he always had so many good reasons why the whole truth should not be told.

*

When one is walking along alone it always seems wonderful that one can walk so very fast, until one is overtaken and passed by somebody who isn't walking fast at all.

*

a little month and ere your lips were dry a little month.

Altered from Hamlet; Act I, Sc. II.

*

taught me to worship and then fouled my altar for me.

Dialogue for David Hersland after one of his projected love affairs in MA. Not used.

*

Ibid

believe in you as one should only believe in God.

*

Ibid

no better than a prostitute that gives her miserable body from one to the next and fills the world with loathsome sadness.

*

not the pure ~~unhap~~appiness that begins at the toes and goes up but a simple sadness that begins nowhere and ends nowhere
to make the situation an incident and a joyous genealogy out of them.

*

Three histories by Jane Sands.

One of GS's discarded pseudonyms.

*

he was frank and generous in his nature, and at times open to conviction.

*

Note for a collection of short stories. Abandoned.

The Making of an author being a History of one woman and many others.
One of them

*

Projected opening for "the Jane Sands stories."

There is always a lodge in every Paris house. There are many masters of these lodges in Paris. They are called concierges. One story is the history of one of them and of the many servant girls that he in his place came to know...

*

Note #194

Initial title and note for Three Lives

A German woman, a german american woman and a negro woman, three serious stories and in each story one of them.

Three Serious Stories

*

Note #178

Negroes.
Aunt Carrie Etta & Dolene. French nigger Vollard, another family Clarence & Hortense mother living, Aunt Carrie does them, Caesar no rest of the family.

*

Note #177

Anna's life in Dr. Shojen's home hearty joyous bachelorhood, making suppers [word?] dishes at night, [holding?] ~~son the father~~ scaring the colored man with skeleton enjoying the life and the good german patient Mrs. Schiltz stands out desciption of Mrs. Schultz and her family by describing Anna's [?] new to them.
[listening succ... .?] jealousy of her brother's family abrcating [?] over 6 years special kind of [bread ch____?] by betting on a wager. The girl are a good daughter. Mrs. Lehntman still holds her place with Anna adoption Anna's [abridgement?] Description of Mrs. Lahntman's family.

Dr. threatening sometimes to get married. Anna's opinion of it. Mrs. Lehntman talks of starting [home?] finally [having?] Anna's [away?]. Doctor gets married Anna goes away.

Planning Note for "The Good Anna" in Three Lives. *In* G.S. Writings, 1903–32, *Library of America, 104ff.*

*

Note #185

The remaining or receiving of conversation which is in expressing and not crying not only in crying is so done that it makes certain that not any one possessing is particular in differing. This is to say that each one readily says the same and so putting in putting more in nothing is not repetition. So then Three Lives does so explain that thing the reseeing that words not wording is being seen seeing. This is the way it does show that any one together is not repeating. Three Lives telling all the same ~~celebrating so telling the~~ soothing of reorganized celebration and yet not that as each one dies separately and any other time by leasing. This is not the story. It is the citation of a whole which is by each one in saying. This makes the book have what it has. No one can relieve it. It is convincing. So it is.

Quotations unidentified & unlocated

*

Note #196

One man may put as much original thought as much power for coordination in the invention of a toy [?] as another does into the invention of an industry-revolutionizing machine but ~~if he have n~~ since he has not the sense for what is significant for human life we deny him the name of genius.

Not in GS handwriting. Quotations unidentified & unlocated

*

Note #133A

[...?] woman with two red [?] daughters. Maybe cousin
knew the old man the father-in-law wanted her cousin well married.

*

Why you take so long to burst out. If you going to burst out all Amy [?] burst out sudden.

*

Peasant with accordion [?] be [?he] Maggie her[?be] friends the other two. Her husband like that man in car with two children only more so weaker and a little nastier old woman like the man that drove the geese. Haven't found old man yet.

Put two little pigs in the story the two little Perugian pigs, or better the big nasty pig of the old lady feed her with [?hurbound] drops.

Four planning notes for early stories

*

Early Draft Notes

(Notes for Drafts I and II, Paris and Fiesole, 1906–1908)

Gertrude had, settled in Paris for three years at the rue de Fleurus when she returned to an earlier plan to write a conventional narrative of two families, the Dehnings and the Herslands. The two families were her own—the West Coast Herslands—and her Uncle Sol Stein's—the East Coast Dehnings—and the novel was to follow their interweavings and make a point of their contrasts. The novel's ambition was to extend no further than to recapitulate the saga of German immigrants converting—as her title suggests—to proper Americans, but as GS planned her story, neither family was wholly to succeed nor wholly to fail. But the nature of their success-failure was to be carefully distinguished—the Western family's practical failure was to be finer in spirit than the other's greater success. Her notes for this First Draft, determinedly uninventive, stayed as close as possible to the reality of the families' lives as lived, Her cast of characters was remembered, none invented. And the bits of dialogue set down in her notes were clearly being tested for their rightness in the mouths that were to utter them.

Six of the small notebooks as well as single fugitive pages were filled with notations merging family members and friends with fictional counterparts, and, of course, in working out narrative details for the novel's plot. Concluding these labors, Gertrude wrote on the cover of a larger schoolchild's notebook, "The Making of Americans," and recorded in it the small notebooks" residue of significant details.

The essential labor, then, of the notes for the first full draft of the novel was wholly to accommodate family and friends to roles in the novel's narrative. and conversely, to accommodate the details of the narrative to their own "characters" and to real events. Some years later, Gertrude confessed that she had no talent for inventing fictional events but only for reporting them. And dwelling on those that had in fact occurred. That was the initial objective of *The Making of Americans.* own "characters" and real events. Some years later, Gertrude confessed that she had no talent for inventing fictional events but only for reporting them. That was largely the initial objective of *The Making of Americans.*

*

Note #136A

The old world in the new or more exactly the new world all made out of the old that is the picture that I want to make because that is what ~~has~~ really ~~happened~~ is.

Used in slightly altered form in MA 3. The sentence is converted to "The old people in a new world, the new people made out of the old, that is the story that I need to tell, for that is what really is and what I really know."

*

St Galmier 5 sous a bottle

*

There never was anything so beautiful except [-?-] but [-?-] everything [-?-] it really is wonderful.

Discarded note for early MA text.

*

~~...sympathy of my audience on the ground of looking upon this manifestation as an interesting survival. No it is nothing as subtle as this I can claim no right to the American attitude on any such ground I am interested in the family because [...]~~

[Draft of text for First Draft of MA, not used; but its sense is incorporated into the first two paragraphs of what was to be Chapter 2 in the MA's first version. The text is reprinted in GS, Fernhurst *144–145].*

*

Biblioteque Cardinale
Place St. Sulpice
Biblioteque Universelle
Rue Tranchet 4
La Lecture Universelle
Rue des Moulins 5
Libraire Internationale
Rue Chaveau Lagarde 14
Kritchefsky,
c/o Dr. Sauvet
17 Rue St. Petersbourgh

Miscellaneous list of Paris addresses

*

It is my misfortune I know it very well I have no excuse and I throw myself frankly on the mercy of the public

Draft of text for First Draft, revised and extended in MA 34

Hortense
Marion
Mrs. Oppenheimer
Dolene
Hortense
Etta
Marion
Emma get complete set of little [o]nes and me
Hortense set is less complete & Leo & me
~~Dolene part set & me~~
~~Big one Bird, Mabel, Marion~~
 & & &
 me me me
Etta ~~small set~~ & me
Mrs. Oppenheimer 22nd.
Leo & me
Marion " " "
Bird coss [?] Cezanne now [?] and me
Mabel " " "

Alice Toklas note: List of photographs

*

Note #67

It has always seemed to me a rare privilege this of being an American, a real American and yet one whose tradition it has taken scarcely sixty years to create. We need only realise our parents, remember our grandparents and how ourselves and our history is complete. The old people in a new world, the new people made out of the old that is the
story that I mean to tell ~~picture I want to make~~ for that is what really is and what know.
I really ~~know.~~

Original draft of first ten lines of text from the early version of MA (reprinted in GS, Fernhurst *137.) Incorporated into final version in MA 3.*

Twenty years ago the fever to be an Anglo Saxon and a gentleman for why [...]

Text in First Draft following above, excised from final draft.

And now having carried all my generation into marriage and into middle life and having seen them all start a posterity on the road to make for itself again a fortune a character and a career we must content ourselves to leave them. I could draw for you a very dismal picture of that future in America with the young ones all grown up and battling in our midst or I could please you with a noble one of that very same America, but these things are for readers of the stars for seers and for prophets and I am only a chronicler of ~~the~~ such things as have come to pass and so good-by good reader if indeed there still be any such and pleasant dreams.

Draft of text for the conclusion of the First Draft of MA, intending the novel's story to end with the marriages and "middle life" of the two Dehning daughters and their husbands, the central tale of the original version

*

Note #110A

MA Manuscript, section beginning "We living now are always to ourselves young men and women" *and several reworkings and repetitions of this passage.*

Draft of text for MA 4

*

"And now Melanctha was always more and more with Rose Johnson and Rose had commenced to advise her" and ends "Sam Johnson was always now very gentle and kind and good to Melanctha Herbert who had been so good to Rose in her trouble."

A section in Manuscript. from Melanctha. The passage is about Rose having and losing her baby.

*

Some of the fathers we must realise so that we can tell our history really were little boys then, and came across with their fathers, the grandfathers we need only just remember. Some of these, our fathers, were not even made then, and the women, the young mothers, our grand mothers we perhaps just have seen once, carried these our fathers into the new world, inside them, these women of the old world strong to bear them. Some looked weak little women with their big german husbands but allways [sic] even such as were so weak and little were ~~all~~ strong to bear many children.

These german men and women our grandfathers and grandmothers with their children born and unborn with them, some whose children had gone ahead to prepare a home to give them, other countries too were full of men and women who brought ~~their many children,~~ but only german men and women and the children they had in them to make many generations for them will fill up ~~thise~~ history for us ~~the~~ a family of ~~this family's that I know~~ ~~and their~~ and its ~~and its~~ progress.

Draft of text for MA 3. All references to "German" in draft are changed to "certain" in the final version.

AT Gertrude had enormous respect for her grandfather on her mother's side. Grandfather Keyser was the religious one who meets the 'great death' in *The Making of Americans*. He was the one who was so honorable that the people in the little Bavarian town where he lived as a tanner brought their money to him for safe-keeping because there was no bank.

*

Note #223

The young ones have it through their fear etc. and then begin the description of the children.

Draft Text: MA 8

*

Note #224

Put in the Berkham washing aparatus [sic] in Julia's home. This washing business is certainly very curious.

LK Planning Note: MA 16

Berkham washing apparatus: has apparently left no trace in public record.

*

Note #220

Put in about the elaborated purpose in regard to George and Hortense and his being very moral. He always began his tomorrow full of these fine ~~ideas to~~ resolutions to ~~mostly fill them~~ do all things every minute and to do them all completely. He will listen [to] them and with his veiled eyes he will be as if he were always then living with himself well hidden behind him and so he will be wise, as for a woman it will be as if he were always in a dream of them.

LK ***George and Hortense:*** the younger son and daughter of the NY Steins Julia Dehning's siblings. [Planning & Draft Note for MA 17]

*

Note #33A

[...] the marriage. History of second marriage and beginning troubles. Consummation of second marriage

Liked business men better chose best-looking of all suitable suitors. pronounced trouble. Effect of second marriage trouble with father in law definitive pictures of Julie's home after description of brother and sister, lead up to incident in the real country of family together sense [?] Bertha attempt to join.

Effect of second marriage and family,

LK Comprehensive planning note for First Draft's "Chapter 5." Its extant closing text is *"...handsomest of the men from the most imposing of the bourgeois families of their acquaintance."* Chapters 1 to 5 of this draft are reprinted in GS, *Fernhurst*, **pp. 137–172.**

Further drafts of text for last sentences of Chapter Five:

"The lover who came next had an easy, quick success. He was the handsomest and biggest man in the most imposing bourgeois family in their set.

"This substantial family the Lohms always filled rooms very full. They blotted out all others with their solid solemn weight."

*

The burden laid on us moderns

Amy & Stern

In sixty years we moderns must create a complete tradition and live in to it for we do not follow teaching. Hence our art and ourselves and he who runs may read the ~~me~~ dreadful failures.

Gustav Brossoff

*

best looking

The handsomest man from the most imposing bourgeois family of her acquaintance

[From the first version of the MA, Fernhurst, 172] The extant manuscript ends abruptly two sentences later, at the beginning of the story of Julia's younger sister Bertha's [=Hortense's] marriage, which story is omitted from the final version.

*

Note #137

Legal-size Notebook, marked "English Manufactory."

Contains first five chapters of MA, First Draft. reprinted in GS, Fernhurst ***137–172.***

Content of these chapters condensed in ***MA Final Draft, pp. 6–31***

*

Note #111

Chapter from early version of MA typed with corrections and penciled notations written in by GS.

Penciled note above first typed page, as follows:

Begin again now with the married life after long episode of Hersland's.

LK "Now" signifies: "in this new version," in which the "long episode of the Herslands" has intervened between the first four chapters and this remaining text of the fifth, separating the story of Julia's and Alfred's courtship from the story of their married life. When the "long episode of the Herslands," which eventually came to some 450 pages, was finished in December 1909, three years after GS's return to the "family novel," she pulled out these pages of the First Draft's "Chapter Five" for use in the renewed recounting of the story of Julia's and Alfred's marriage. This fragment of the early Fifth Chapter, however, did not survive in the final version. Nor did any First Draft text that may have followed this fragment. As various early entries in the Notebooks indicate, much of that draft would have been written in the same vein as these first five early chapters, replete with realistic descriptions of persons and places, conversations, dramatic confrontations and so on. None of that writing remains in the later chapters on Alfred and Julia [Chapter appears in finished version MA 477–720.], and on David Hersland [D. Hersland chapter appears in MA 721–904.,] although the narrative substance of those notes is incorporated somewhat differently, and far more obscurely, in those later texts.

*

Chapter 5.

Passionate women, those in whom emotion has the inensity [sic] of a sensation, afflict their world with agitation, excitement and unrest.

Sometimes they marry well and then excitement is with them deep joy. More often their marriage is a failure and then they rush about miserable seeking to escape from misery.

The other women, those who know not passion, make marriages no less unhappy but with them not to be happy makes so much less stir. These must content themselves with emptiness. They These [sic] cannot overflow their misery in ceaseless restless action. They sit so quiet lest their emptiness increase and leave when with all thats [sic] inside, gone and lifeless. They are like them that have a horrid fear when standing on high places. Nothing comes to them but emptiness. They dread the loss of all themselves and every second go on losing more. The one relief there is, is to sit down and so make a resisting compact mass that will not let itself all drop away.

And so the creature without passion makes its unhappy marriage and then sits still for what else can it do. It is not in human natures that it is still waters that run deepest. The restless ones know as keen sorrow as those who make no stir; but emptiness is more sickening long kept up than overfullness. The stomach overloaded is always very sick but then it can discharge itself upon the world. The empty starving stomach can only weaken sadden, grow more helpless.

Julia Dehning had rushed upon her sorrow passionately, fervently, heroically. Bertha Dehning sank down into hers quietly, helplessly, unaspiringly. Bertha Dehning soon after Julia's marriage came to the fullness of her youthful bloom. She was darker, richer, fuller in her curves, softer to the touch, easier to be friends than her more brilliant elder sister. The harshness in the speech and thought, the hardness and the jerk in the manner and the walk, all these her mother's ways it had not come to her to have. She like her father loved compromise and peace. It was results that theses two wanted not the strife.

*

["Use this about one of David's friends."]
~~Bertha Dehning was a kindly friendly creature. She liked the other girls and they liked her.~~

*

Describe home life Hersland's family Dehning, David there for vacation

conversations etc.

That is, after the Herslands episode, come back to the Dehnings and the Julia-Alfred marriage. David, visiting them, has conversations with Julia.

*

Notebook 2

Life of Dehnings & Later life of Herslands (cover note)

NB2, #1

Life of Dehnings & Later life of Herslands.

GS note on notebook cover

*

NB2, #3

Yes you children have an easy time of it nowadays I say

LK Draft for MA 8.: Mr. Dehning to his children: "'Yes,' he would often say to his children, 'Yes I say to you children, you have an easy time of it nowadays doing nothing.'"

*

NB2, #4

Leo is fond of spiders and goats and I am fond of frogs and lizards.

*

NB2, #5

~~Yes three generations~~
~~Yes mothers fathers sons~~
[1] Yes it had made more difference these 60 years three generations then go on describing Dehning's father
Hinawack [-?-] german
/ like Franklin and his mother and his wife and her father and mother
[2] then new chapter and modern education of children.

Plan for text, MA 3, then Plan for text MA 6.

*

NB2, #5a

Introduce ~~Alfy~~ Dicky Wolkins as another friend of Alfy Hersland. Damn it all and I go and find I am just like my father now & you know he just fixes it alright he talks it so nice you think it bad to be right and I make a fuss ~~just~~ and there I am just like my father.

Incident of table Oh you know I can't say it how I mean it but you just listen to him he says right you just follow him talking it always fixes it not like me making a fuss just like my father. Why I remember it made me sore as anything the way he always remembered it the [word?] & table and then now when I come home he begins to talk and then there it is he gets mad all over and there you see I go I do it too just like my father but you just listen [him?] I tell its the only way you ever can see to come right I know. Make him Leon and Selina's friend sort of suffly [souffle] comedy.

*

NB2, #6

I intend for the future never to speak of experience as the best teacher of fools and weak mortals, but always of necessity.

Later politics of M[artha] & L[eo]. politics on the reform side.

*

NB2, #7

Use for Leon [Solomon] [= the young David Hersland] the part about 29 years old when he decides on cancer ultimately separates him from Bird [=Julia Dehning] ultimately kills himself, through operation like Leon's.

AT ***Leon... ultimately kills himself:*** Leon Solomons chose his death; he practically committed suicide. He had an organic disorder and thought that a diet would cure him, and so he went on a little bit like Leo. Finally, he saw that he was weakening, but he persisted until he died. Gertrude said he willed his death.

Late in the writing of the David chapter, when she saw what was coming, Gertrude said, Don't type for a few days. Then—It's finished. And that was the day, the day her hero died, that Gertrude went to see Mildred Aldrich. The book is done, Gertrude told her. What happened? My hero was killed last night. And Mildred said, shocked, How could you have killed him?

[P20 continues:] When Gertrude died, Marcel Brion, who wrote seriously on Gertrude in literary reviews without apology or explanation, sent word that he would like to see me. He came with a friend, and I told about the last days. Gertrude decided on an operation against the advice of doctors and surgeons. And Marcel Brion said, She chose her death exactly as she chose her life, didn't she?

LK Another AT account of the end of the writing of the MA:

> After David Hersland was killed in the novel, Gertrude went to tell Mildred Aldrich. I went too, and at the time of going, I knew Mildred Aldrich only slightly. By 1910, Mildred had

borrowed money from me when we were already intimate, and the book had been finished for a few months. [Note: Date in error; MA not finished until Oct 1911]

*

NB2, #10

Make Bertha child of Betty and Leb.
Einziger tante leaves money after separation to Lucius.

AT ***Bertha child of Betty and Leb:*** Gertrude hated [her sister] Bertha as a little girl, because she ground her teeth at night. They slept in the same room and it was very unpleasant. Later on, she lost all interest and connection with her. —What became of her, Gertrude? —Oh, she married. —Who?—Oh, she married a downtown Baltimorean. The real daughter of Leb Stein [who was, of the five brothers, the poor one who never made a living] was Sophie, who was not a Bertha. Leb and his wife raised her to have no decided social or political opinions because you could never tell whom she was going to marry.

*

NB2, #11

Make Simon [Stein, GS brother] a brother in country on farm till [Father's] failure and then runs the car.*

LK Simon had the appetites of a baby; indulged enormously in overeating and fattened into immobility. He became a motorman on the SF trolleys, where he would distribute candy to his passengers. He is not retained in the MA, and GS plan for him here is not pursued.

*

NB2, #12

Use Mabel H[aynes] thereafter of [roons?] and kind of person she likes as one of Leon's semi flames, incident of bag of Mabel Earle's in Cambridge. Sort of combine Mabel H with Helen Butterfield as Mabel's friend. Leon in love with her chucks her as Leo did his ships that pass in the night and Mabel Earle succeeding her the strong symptom of succeeding the carrying of the bag and letting Helen go to her house alone. Change in progress during country walks as it was between Mabel and me.

Interest first in kind of subjects Helen call her that and Leon could talk about Mabel as Leon and I did that night of the credit she got. Make Mabel act just as she really did. Francis [Pollak] attentive to her too.

AT ***Leo… his ships that pass in the night:*** *Ships That Pass In the Night* was an early best seller by an English woman novelist. It meant an unsuccessful love affair. Later, Leo was in and out of love affairs which he usually brought to a crisis. A California woman once told me about Leo and Gertrude in Fiesole before I came. One day Leo stretched out at her feet and talked all day long about himself. She *really* wanted to know about the pictures, but Leo talked only about himself, and *au fond* was thoroughly unbearable.

Leo had the habit of becoming flirtatious. Before I was in Paris, he had had an affair with Katherine Dudley, who later became Mrs. Scott, the wife of the South Pole explorer. She was the one who was poor but helped feed Raymond Duncan. He [Leo]fell in love with women but it would sort of peter out. Leo's *real* affairs were with professionals, and they were really affairs. His falling in love with Nina was for him thoroughly natural. He wouldn't have been so desperately interested were it not for her story of the Englishman Skeene who wanted to kill himself for her. Nina liked to arouse and upset cures and so on, and that pleased Leo.

Leon…. Francis: They were a contrast. Leon was very sober, serious, high-minded and high-principled. Francis Pollack was witty, gay, a genial person.

LK Note anticipates one of young David Hersland's originally planned three affairs at Cambridge, but never explored in final text.

*

NB2, #13

Bird and Fred's father's attempt to remarry Mrs. Meininger helps him but he dies before it is completed scenes like ones Fred speaks to him as Mike did. Bird works on him as I did.

Money question handled as we handled it. Distinction I made between practical life not founded on impressions but on own reaction due to own temperament ~~and~~ pleasantness or self-preservation. Impressions and convictions ideas in regard to others.

Leon have incident in speaking to Bird like mine with Margaret Lewis about paying her making her wait for my income first realisation of property values illustrate that with Julien's loss of promised money, as he had no right to yowl it wasn't his.

AT ***Money question handled as we handled it:*** Mike settled a franchise and had a plan for a consolidated railroad system for San Francisco. For the idea and for the franchise, Collis P. Huntington paid cash, which enabled them all [the five Stein siblings] to live comfortably. Mike told me once, 'If Huntington hadn't paid me then, I would have had to support them forever. You can see how passionately I worked.'

Since the California Street line was the only one in San Francisco not included in the franchise, Simon [the fat, genial, incompetent brother] worked on that one. Mike wouldn't have him on his line. Simon worked as a grip on the cars and did his work the way he lived his life, handing out cigars to the men and sweets to the lady passengers.

incident... like mine with Margaret Lewis about paying her: When Gertrude was at Radcliffe, a stipend came once a month, and after the landlady was paid, and Gertrude visited New York for two or three nights of opera and dinner, there was nothing left for the month. Then the incident of paying money for the lessons to Margaret Lewis occurred, who replied as she did. Gertrude told me that when it happened, she felt for the first time like a New York Stein. After that she always paid Margaret Lewis a month in advance. She hated to be taken for a bourgeoisie.

LK ***Distinction between practical life....in regard to others:*** Note repeated in NB-MA #23 below.

*

NB2, #14

Bringing children up on a system like unto nature musn't ~~never~~ forget nature is very wasteful in her methods.

*

NB2, #15

A phrase of Leon's

I supposed something like that was working in you, let me know sometimes what is happening to you.

Leon to 3rd girl when he has left her.

And thats not the worst of it either a phrase to be used.

*

NB2, #16

Selina [=Martha]—takes care of old father after failure after she returns from Europe after it all Leon very good to her and the old man.

For [?] Lucius etc. not pay much attention but kind of does his duty, Father had never loved Selina she annoyed him the way Bertha used to our daddy. Must not forget Bertha lived in their house call her Hannah. Cousin child of the kind of poor things who never made a living and had child and just died away and left them. She marries Jay [Garblin] as is. Sol's relation to her like his to Jay. Calls him a nice modest young man social position [alure?] of marriage joke like ones with Simon made by brother & Bird & Leon.

*

NB2, #17

Hannah Hammel child of Sol's sister died away and left them never knew how to make a living.

*

NB2, #18

Such a woman (as Aunt Pauline) could not have so many children.

*

NB2, #19

Describe that characteristically unpleasant rapid utterance and self contemplative end of a triumphant argument with consenting [?] of outside [?] people too with it often in Leo & Leon.

*

NB2, #20

Herslands California family of 3

Selina	Henry	LeonDave, George Weymouth

Selina never married to Hodder. / Nobody knows it like real story of Hodder. Happened when Henry came East to make a great start as lawyer.

LK ***Selina Henry LeonDave:*** Early and possibly first note on the names of the Hersland children, who were subsequently to be renamed: Selina = Martha; Henry = Alfred; LeonDave = David.

George Weymouth: Alfred Hodder—in this note, called George Weymouth. GS later reverts to the name she used for him in *Fernhurst*: Philip Redfern.

Selina never married to Hodder: [Later changed. Based on real story of Hodder's first marriage—the suspicion, later confirmed, that there had been no marriage.]

Henry… to make fresh start as lawyer: Alfred's career as lawyer—his father sending him to Bridgepoint [=Baltimore/Johns Hopkins] to study law, and his return to Bridgepoint to practice law—are referred to synoptically in MA 21. Two other Notebook references to Alfred's career as lawyer are in NB9, #17 and NB12, #1.

*

NB2, #21

Hersland death like Uncle Sol plus Simon H. I am so nervous. Dehning dies like Sol. Dave makes remarks like Leo's in diary. Jig is up.

*

NB2, #22

The old lady lives with the Herslands unpleasant for Fanny like Mrs. Samuels mother-in-law.

*

NB2, #23

Leon living free life in the mountains all kinds of people feels like me and David Copperfield when he gets East with civilised ones.

LK A part of the composite portrait of GS and Leon Solomons later to be used for David Hersland suggested in this note.

*

NB2, #24

There were three children in the Hersland family an older sister and a younger brother The real drama is Dave Hersland and Julia Dehning, Dave's final split like mine with Bird because of her not realising him and her dishonesty when in a hole. David—Leon saying on one occasion What right have you to talk like god almighty you never succeeded in doing anything. Perhaps not but I have a fighting chance to do a big thing sometimes and that makes it right for me to feel like I [out done?] just like I talk it ~~straight~~ big to you.

LK ***There were three children…*** [MA 35]: "There were three of them, Martha, Alfred, David, there had been two others, but they had died as little children." The trauma for GS of learning that neither she nor Leo would have been born if two other children preceding them had not died, is recounted a number of times in her writing. For David Hersland in the MA, the discovery of this fact becomes a key to his troubled existence. Given the mere accident of his being, his history is essentially a questioning of whether there is meaning or need for him to be living at all. His testing and scrutiny of that need leads to a gradual loss of need for anything, and ultimately for life itself.

The real drama … final split like mine with Bird … Bird's "dishonesty when in a hole" was manifest for GS during their quarrel-by-mail which began in April 1906, the month GS returned to writing MA. Early notes on Julia Dehning, and drafts of letter fragments to Bird which found their way into the Notebooks, attest to GS's anger and resentment, and her vituperative responses to Bird during the quarrel. The "split" between Julia and David is not explored in the final version of the MA [though it may have been explored in detail—as fragments of planned dialogue attest—in an earlier no longer extant version.] [For dating: Letter, GS to Bird, April 19,1906, dates the break between them.]

*

NB2, #25

Henry [=Alfred] Hersland like Mike stands up against father's irritability about eating and things when business goes bad You have no right to lose your temper and act peevish like a baby, Not eating your dinner and saying it was because of not being fit to be eaten. Selina and sugar in coffee. this while Selina is at the university, before the marriage with George [Weymouth] and before Henry has settled down East, but has met Julia and will soon after be engaged. Henry showed this kind of temper afterwards in relation to his wife.

AT ***Henry… like Mike stands up against father:*** Mike once said to Daniel Stein, 'You don't have to bring all your business troubles home and make your children responsible for them.' Gertrude, however, had great respect for her father. She felt that a great deal of her gift probably came to her through him. Mike was not unlike him either. He was also irritable, though he didn't show it, and had that flash of genius to stand up to Collis B. Huntington in negotiating the family's income from their father's earlier connection with the Huntington ownership of the San Francisco streetcar lines.

LK ***Selina and sugar in coffee:*** Martha's relations with her father after Mrs. Hersland's death are based on GS's recollections of her sister Bertha who used to irritate their father in his last years with her bottomlessly well-meaning stupidity. As the oldest daughter, she took care of him when Mrs. Stein died. He hated to be regarded as an invalid. He could not bear to have his coat held for him; she always did. It made him furious to have sugar in his coffee; she never failed to put it in. Used for MA 471.

*

NB2, #26

Hersland

California, old man not so much money getting into trouble.

Selina [= Martha] engaged then to George [Weymouth = Philip Redfern[, Henry [= Alfred] two long trips East had met Julia. Engaged. Crash, not yet real marry. Selina gone a year before. ~~2~~ 3 years after left George. Complete crash. David East in college etc. etc.

LK ***Selina engaged then to George:*** The chronology of the novel is frequently altered in the Notebooks, and never worked out accurately. Martha, according to this note, married George [= Philip Redfern] a year before Mr. Hersland's final business failure, their marriage lasting for four years. And Alfred, according to this note, was engaged or just married when Martha had been married for a year. Later, however we are told that Martha's separation from Philip Redfern occurred eight years after Alfred's marriage. The chronology of the Dehning family story is even less reconciled to arithmetic. The general flow of events in both families, however, is reasonably clear.

*

NB2, #27

David talk about [hoad?]—Janes [?] rizzle [?] on a rock.

*

NB2, #28

[GS uncle] Sol [Stein] & his son Fred (=George.)

*

NB2, #29

Leon David and Mabel Earle and another girl forming history girls & death like Leon's. Leon like me in ideas and revolt.

LK ***Mabel Earle:*** GS uses her earlier rivalry with Mabel Earle re: May Bookstaver as David's failed third lover whose discovery of her true nature "filled [him]with loathsome sadness."

*

Bertha Hannah Hammel like Bertha with my experiences with Uncle Sol, before she gets married she lives in house with them taken by them to be brought up. Sol's attitude toward Leon David like Sol's to Leo & Leb's children

~~David chummy~~

AT ***Uncle Sol and Pauline:*** Gertrude didn't like him at all. Aunt Pauline amused Gertrude because she was pompous, pretentious, proud, but the uncle she plainly didn't like. Once he asked Gertrude for the photo of her grandmother (his mother) for $100, and Gertrude replied, you don't sell your grandmother at any price. The power of the purse was everything to him. Fred, escaping that, was left with nothing.

LK ***Sol's [attitude] to Leb's children:*** Levi Stein [b.1839], the sixth of the ten children of the Stein grandparents, [Michael and Hannah Stein,] was the uncle who "died a glutton" and whose wife Betty and her children were supported by his surviving brothers. After the death of GS's father, his share of responsibility for Levi's family was assumed by his children, and Michael, the family bursar, always deducted from GS's and Leo's monthly allowance their share of the burden while they were at college. Mike in a letter to Leo, January 16, 1899, informs Leo that GS, now in Baltimore, had promised to look into the business of Betty Stein's children, and would let Mike know the condition of their affairs. The story is told briefly in *The Making of Americans*:

> One [of grandmother Martha's children] … died a glutton and spoiling him was the one weak thing the strong mother did to harm any of them…. the glutton died and left his wife and children to his brothers, he had not made enough money to leave them provided, and his brothers each one in their turn gave the money to support them. [MA 42]

"Sol's attitude" toward the orphaned and dependent children is perhaps suggested in the Notebooks [see Note NB-MA #9] in the fictional situation GS remembers but never uses, "Hannah Hammel", a daughter of Leb's and Betty's visiting in Sol's home, being harassed by him, or as GS puts it, "experience … like mine with S[ol.]"

*

NB2, #31

Simon (our) will belong to Hortense-Emma-Madam Boiffard group and the Baltimore Steins and Keysers and Guggenheimers & Sutros & Mahonri & Cone sisters tragedy.

LK First suggestion of "groupings" in the notebooks. But the note suggests further that Gertrude is returning to these first-draft "narrative" notes with a view toward enlarging them twice over: (1) in narrative detail and more importantly (2) in the new vocabulary of the developing "system." The overlaying of typological notes (beginning slowly in the succeeding Notebooks) more and more displaces the first draft notes, until the typology becomes the essential burden of the Notebooks.

***

Notebook 9

NB9, #1

[GS notebook title:] Book for life of Alfred & David.
Use this book soon.
Hate to see you repeating yourself until your life has lost all meaning.

*

NB9, #2

There were these three children Martha, Alfred and ~~the~~ young David.

LK ***Martha, Alfred and young David:*** Plan for introduction of the three Hersland children, used in MA 35ff.

*

NB9, #3

The Herslands were not like the Dehnings Eastern they were altogether in their nature Western.
Introduce the discourse on California freedom before the specific talk about the children after the sweet women but in the children.

LK ***The Herslands… Western:*** Theme introduced in MA 21–22.

discourse on…freedom before the…children: Theme of "California freedom" is introduced MA 45.

sweet women: The Hissen women described in MA 43–44.

*

NB9, #4

Put in Berkham washing aparatus [sic] in Julia's home. This washing business is certainly very curious.

LK Note repeats Note #224 above

This washing business: A planned addition to the early text when it was undergoing revision for the novel's final version. Specific reference to the "Berkham washing" apparatus did not survive but added to the description of the elder Dehnings' home are "complicated ways to wash, and dressing tables filled full of brushes, sponges, instruments, and ways to make one clean." [MA 28] In their daughter Julia's new home, the "washing business" takes on greater dimension: "In ways to wash, to help out all the special doctors in their work, in sponges, brushes, running water everywhere, in hygienic ways to air things and keep one's self and everything all clean, [in] this house that Julia was to make fit for her new life… there were more plunges, douches, showers, ways to get cold water, luxury in freezing, in hardening, than her mother's house had ever afforded… ." [MA 31] A separate, and digressive, study of "this business of washing" is elaborately explored in MA 15–16.

*

NB9, #4a

About 10–15 pages torn out. Then begins:

[...] ~~whores. The young ones have it through their fear etc. and then begin the description of the children.~~

LK ***… through their fear… and then… description of the children:*** Plan for MA 8, describing the children's fear of Mr. Dehning's "old man's looking."

*

NB9, #5

In describing Julia perhaps just suggest the heroical sweetness that there was always in her.
boyish sweetness in George, a dependent loyal up-gazing [sic] sweetness in Hortense.

AT ***Julia… heroical sweetness:*** When Gertrude used to call Bird 'Marie Antoinette,' I said, 'You leave my queens alone.' 'You go far enough with your queen,' Gertrude answered, 'and you'll find she's nothing but Bird.' Gertrude was convinced they were alike in their character, that Bird's mouth like Marie Antoinette's expressed a certain decisive meanness, and that for an archduchess who had become queen, Marie Antoinette was as stupid as was Bird. But Bird, like Marie Antoinette, was heroic when it came to a crisis, and this idea of Bird I also opposed.

Bird: Sharp, hard face, very regular features, a prettiness almost bitter, a mouth that clapped closed, thin-lipped mouth that shut like a box.

LK Corresponds to NB1, #14

Julia… heroical sweetness… in George … in Hortense: Early descriptive tags for the three NY Stein children, Bird [= Julia], Fred [= George] and Amy [= Hortense.] Julia is so described in MA 18: "[All the family] … delighted in her daring and in a kind of heroical sweetness there was in her."

Hortense is described, in MA 18: "… and little Hortense was very devout and adored her instructor [her older brother George.] There was always a dependent loyal up-gazing sweetness in her."

*

NB9, #6

The Herslands were ~~Californian Southern way down south~~ Western.

LK ***The Herslands … Western:*** Draft for MA 21.

*

NB9, #7

David Hersland was among the most prominent citizens of Gazelles.

LK Draft for text, not used.

*

NB9, #8

Hersland family, they had not had their money longer but they had taken to ideas and to culture quicker.

LK ***Hersland family… to culture quicker.*** Draft of text for MA 21–22

*

Note #5

[…] gentle little soul was lost among them. Through her make Alfy Hersland meet Julia, through a common relation. He had gone to Bridgepoint because it was the best chance for him now his father thought it […]

LK First mention of Alfred in Bridgepoint: MA 21; expanded reference to his story in Bridgepoint and marriage to Julia in MA 22ff., 35.

*

NB9, #9

David Hersland was a splendid kind of person, he had made a princely fortune.
Give life of Martha till she returns home.
Alfred. He had not been any trouble to his father. Young David was more a singular than any of the others. Give his history till he goes to Bridgepoint to college.

Later insert:

Advanced 20, 17 when Alf leaves home gets a scholarship to support him, beginning of father's failure.

After Alfred's marriage, when he first meets Julia & George who is [...]

Alfred had been at college and at law school at Bridgepoint. Home 2 years comes back to Bridgepoint at 27 father beginning to have trouble sent him back to Bridgepoint better place to make his living. His mother's family there but they can't help him much. From them he gets his artistic impulse.

When a boy at college love affair wine business little gentle mother wants him to have it. She goes into the closet where his clothes are. Father says no don't be a fool Fanny. Its foolishness for a boy like Alfy he don't really want her. Parting [?] square foot of grass, older woman Helen and so leave off.

Young David finds it out teases his brother despises and same time respects and loves Alfy. Alfy explains to David he'll be in love too ~~now~~ some time if he don't get too strong in his high falutin reforming notions and then he will see day-light and understand more about other people's ways of acting.

LK This note, focused on Alfred Hersland's years before marriage, l is central to the early plan for the major sequence of the novel. After the Herslands are introduced as a family, a separate chapter was to be devoted to each of the three Hersland children, taking the story of each of them to "middle living." The novel, after these chapters, was to give an account of Julia Dehning's and Alfred Hersland's marriage troubles, their divorce, their association with the young David, then David's Eastern college experiences and his love affairs, the death of Mrs. Hersland, and the beginning of Mr. Hersland's failure in business. All of this was to constitute the long middle section of the novel. The final section was to relate the breakup of the two families' continuities: the deaths of Mr. and Mrs. Dehning, Julia's adjustment to her broken life, Alfred's half-success and half-failure in his second marriage. But it is young David's failure and death that becomes the only subject of the final (fifth) chapter of the novel. It is devoted exclusively to a telling of his life from childhood to death—a 200-page exploration of a single character's "internality," absent any revelation of the content of his private ruminations, observations, expressions, emotions, or ongoing states of being. What remains is only a naming of the sequence of "internal actions" attendant on the largely hidden motions of his intellectual and emotional life—the fact of his thinking, seeing, learning, loving, experiencing talking, listening—seen as solitary and wholly internalized "ways of going on living,"

Most of this outline was completed as planned. As the novel's focus increasingly shifted from narrative, the events of the last two sections were treated synoptically in the concluding pages of each of the three separate histories of Martha, Alfred and David.

David Hersland... princely fortune. Draft text for MA 35.

Alfred ... any trouble to his father. . .Draft text for MA 35.

Young David ... more a singular than any of the others. Draft text for MA 35.

Bridgepoint: In the novel, Cambridge, New York and Baltimore are all condensed into "Bridgepoint," and both Harvard and Johns Hopkins become Bridgepoint College, just as Oakland and San Francisco become "Gossols," and the University of California (where Leon Solomons, Leo Stein and Michael Stein had all studied) becomes Gossols College.

...life of Martha till she returns home. Based on Selina Solomons' career in the women's rights movement. GS, who in general was indifferent to the woman's suffrage movement, uses as the model for Martha's later career in the novel—as an extremely active suffragette—Selina Solomons whom she describes in her suffragette travels as "a little crazy as she is now."

*

NB9, #10

After their marriage Alfy becomes president of chinatown lodges in the course of which he first meets Minnie Vail and takes charge of her affairs of divorce. knows her 7-8 years before they go off together.

LK Planning Notes for the final phase of Alfred Hersland's history. They are not used extensively until the end of the Alfred Hersland chapter, MA 688–718. Few of the specific details mentioned in these notes survive the radical alteration of focus in the novel's last pages. The last of Alfred's history is intertwined with the last of Julia's, Minnie Vail becomes Minnie Mason, and William Beckling is the man whom Julia marries after divorcing Alfred.

*

Note #47

Use Marie Lorensen for Minnie make it a history of the blue eyes, kind word Alfy's story, don't care for money don't want natural children been so herself and so forces on the divorce. I don't think I will forget that whole situation. The type of mother austere bad in her youth not bad but independent daughter says. Give perfect liberty to daughter Not malicious but stupid is what she says of Julia as Marie did of Fernande. Why should she be jealous she has an antipathy to me. bletter [= skim] through books to find pictures that look like her. Make Alfred regard her as Apollinaire did her. Malicious poignant no chance for Julie.

*

NB9, #11

At first Julia enters very eagerly in his chinatown ambitions
and even at first gets to know Minnie Vail her queer kind of ignorance of the danger Again remember the contrast with Martha and Miss ______ the teacher.

*

NB9, #12

Make ending like Beethoven symphony. Make Julia sort of peter out getting a little crooked when she is in a hole and finally gets married again.

*

NB9, #13

Make Minnie Wehn Marie Antoinette Dicky talks about Alfy's relations everybody says he is a damn fool but I can't forget she has wonderful kind of ways in her.

*

NB9, #14

Use that middle class conversation of mine in the other book that begins things as David's beginning of intimate re lations with moonlight walk with Rena Barkholdt.

LK ***middle class conversation of mine in the other book:*** "The other book" is *Q.E.D*, written three years earlier in the Fall of 1903 (reprinted in GS, *Fernhurst*) In this passage Mabel [= Mabel Haynes] and Adele [=GS]:

> "Mabel tells me that you consider yourself a typical middle-class person, that you admire above all things the middle-class ideals and yet you certainly don't seem one in thoughts or opinions. When you show such a degree of inconsistency how can you expect to be believed?"
>
> "The contradiction isn't in me," Adele said… "it is in your perverted ideas. You have a foolish notion that to be middle-class is to be vulgar, to cherish ideals of respectability

> and decency is to be commonplace and that to be the mother of children is to be low. … You don't realize the important fact that virtue and vice have it in common that they are vulgar when not passionately given. You think that they carry with them different power….but as to their relation to vulgarity, it is as true of vice as of virtue that you can't sell what should be passionately given without forcing yourself into many acts of vulgarity and that chances are that in endeavoring to escape the vulgarity of virtue, you will find yourself engulfed in the vulgarity of vice… ."
>
> Tell me," [Helen] said "what do you really mean by calling yourself middle-class? From the little that I have seen of you I think you are quite right when you say that you are reasonable and just but surely to understand others and even to understand yourself is the last thing a middle-class person cares to do." "I never claimed to be middle-class in my intellect and in truth" and Adele smiled brightly. "I probably have the experience of all apostles, I am rejected by the class whose cause I preach but that has nothing to do with the case. I simply contend that the middle-class ideal which demands that people be affectionate, respectable, honest and content, that they avoid excitements and cultivate serenity is the ideal that appeals to me, it is in short the ideal of affectionate family life, of honorable business methods." [*Fernhurst*, **pp. 56–59**]

Neither a version of this conversation nor the name of Rena Barkholdt appears in MA final text, but GS's abiding commitment to "middle-class ideals" is celebrated briefly in her encomium to "Middle class, middle class" in MA 34.

*

NB9, #15

Brother Singulars I did you wrong you have done better here than I said before that you have done but even so you have not yet come to a real flower.

introducing young David.

LK ***Brother Singulars:*** The first reference to "brother singulars" appears in MA 21, in which Alfred Hersland is judged to be a poor imitation of the real thing in "being singular to be free." The theme is further developed in MA 47–48, in which, for vital singularity, "there is still some hope for us in the younger David," though the older Alfred is still held to be a weak surrogate.

*

NB9, #16

Alfy never break no young girls heart. Sole advice of mother to Dicky Wolkins.

*

NB9, #17

Alfy ~~Dehning~~ Hersland babyhood—~~then~~ describe mother's feeling and then kind of skip to, 17 years old experiences with Olga, like me what he tried to do, stage and and then eastern experiences first love affair wine business, then return, Martha had just come back troubles, then he goes back to be lawyer and stock-gambler and meets Julia Dehning.

LK ***experiences with Olga, like me what he tried to do:*** Alfred tried to seduce Olga. [cf. OaklandNB11, #4.] "Olga" may be the "bad un" whom GS remembered from childhood, with whom—as Pauline Sandys—she combines her own character in MA.

*

NB9, #18

Young David begin existence about Allan's stage now, and then skip to Gossol's college life and love experiences, Mabel Earle and me and Olga and then goes East to college after father's failure ~~to~~ meets George Dehning etc.

LK ***Young David begin existence:*** An early plan for David Hersland's career. Allan Stein, Michael and Sarah's only son, was 13 in 1908, when this note was written. The place, the number, and the identity of David's "love experiences" underwent some revision, but GS, in the final text, settled on three affairs:

- 1st—Rena Barkholt [= Mabel Haynes and Helen Butterfield]
- 2nd—Helen Lawson [= Mabel Earle]
- 3rd—Pauline Sandys [= GS and "Olga" or "the bad un."]

The "affairs" interweave facts from Leon Solomons' and GS's experiences, and in the final text are placed not in Gossols College, when David is still in California, but in Bridgepoint [= Harvard] when David has already gone East, conforming more closely to the actual background of these events. Except for "Olga" or "the bad un" whom GS knew in Oakland during High School days, the other women were associates of either Leon's or GS's or both at either Harvard or Johns Hopkins.

*

Note #170

....sea[r]ching [sic] to decide in him and no one could ever understand him from day to day what life meant to him to make it worth his living. It was less in Alfred this love of freedom inside him,
who was soon to marry...

*

....[David] to college there and to find out in himself and no one could ever understand him what there was in life to make it worth his living. Joy was a little dim now inside for all of them.

*

First the history of Martha to the time she had come back to them from the trouble she had been in.

*

Martha Hersland had all her life had a good deal of trouble in working out how to feel inside her with her living.

*

Note #71B

David Herslands mother was the good german woman who was strong to bear many children and then always after she was strong to lead them. These german ~~husba~~ women had many different kinds of husbands.*

Use that before Fanny's 4 parents are described or rather after mother is described before father and then come back to her and she had many and very little children.

LK ***David Hersland's mother was that good German woman...*** Draft of text for MA 36, "german" changed to "certain."

***

Notebook 6

NB6, #1

Felix Vallotton
Vallotton
Olf Rudien
Menda Herzel
Cora Moore

AT ***Felix Vallotton:*** His portrait of Gertrude was finished when I came over, that is, before Fall 1907. Gertrude remembered that when he painted the portrait, he painted from the top of the canvas and came down like a curtain. It was done in very flat color and flat, Japanese tone. It made quite a stir at the Salon. I never heard any more about Vallotton after I was here.

He was a Swiss Protestant married to a Jewess, devoted to his wife, but felt helplessly surrounded by her family and complained to Gertrude about it. He was supposed to be very witty. While he was working on her portrait, Gertrude went to see a play he wrote which she didn't find witty.

He was just ignored as a painter. Like Manguin, he was one of their mistakes. Gertrude was not solemn about mistakes. They were much more normal than a find, because there were more to look at.

LK ***Olf Rudeiner:*** Swiss painter and printmaker, associated with the Nabis. Important in the development of modern woodcuts. In 1893 at the first Salon d'Automne, he adopted a style of cool realism in opposition to the Fauves and was in part responsible for the revival of woodcuts together with Gauguin and Munch.

*

NB6, #2

GS Note: [re: notebook contents:]
A little of Martha here called Selena. A good deal of young David, and some of Alfred, & the Dehnings.

*

Note #76

Martha a little girl 5 & 6, then 12 then 15 at college.
Alfred babyhood then skip to 17 year old stage
David begin picture [?] about Allan's stage now, and then skip to Gossol college life.

AT ***David... Gossol College life:*** Leo at the University of California learned to dance for the Freshman Hop from Isadora Duncan and her sister. They had a dancing class going then at which their mother presided.

Leo probably went to the University of California for only a few months before going East with Gertrude.

LK ***Martha.... Alfred ... David:*** Note, originally used only partially. Set down during the writing of the last pages of the chapter on Mrs. Hersland and the servants and governesses, the Note adheres to the story outline projected earlier, and projects a sequential narrative thread more often than not lost sight of in the remaining chapters.

*

Note #59

Don't forget that Martha failed in annual promotion just
before Madelaine was [prendre??] to [Stern??].

*

Yes its very nice oh don't I say it was very nice you know I mean to say it was very nice. Oh you are so bad. Why sure (me) I say it was very nice sure I did David & me

*

NB6, #3

True splits in family.

Mrs. Hersland & Mrs. Dehning ma and Aunt Pauline servant girl. death of mamma forgives aunt Pauline not sincerely.

LK Cf. Radcliffe theme on the argument between GS's mother and Aunt Pauline, [Miller, *Gertrude Stein: Form and Intelligibility; Containing the Radcliffe Themes.* New York: Exposition Press, 1949.]

*

NB6, #4

Alfred Hersland & Julia Bird & Mike & Louis Sternberger

Ehock [?]. Leon, & Bird. Jay, Uncle Sol opinion very modest young man marries Ruth.

Uncle Sol's household.

Brother [Moses?] + Uncle Sol +

+ Babe [?]

Leon's hand-writing Pa trying to make it good [now?]
Leon kisses father on bald spot.
Mike being good to Leon about wager.
Mike & Lucius & LS = Alfred Hersland
Come back to Ruth in Sol's household.

*

NB6, #5

Leon's reiterative [?] thought of death let himself go to think of it. Death.

*

NB6, #6

Leon conversations with Bird like mine about hospital sense of justice of that kind his strong point

*

Nicodemus Savans [?], Scandinavian [semttler?] & Julien & Arthur makes jokes [?] and religion Leon's death. I am very nervous like Simon.

AT ***Julien:*** [Julihn.] He was mixed up with Sarah in Paris. He went back to San Francisco with Sarah and Michael after the earthquake and fire. A nondescript person, pale and rather displeasing, his "religion" probably stemmed from Sarah's leading him to Christian Science.

*

NB6, #7

The world is such a very beautiful world, why does one have to be so homely always in it.

*

NB6, #8

Write essay on the feeling strong of death from living out of doors one in particular for Leon.
29 years older for Leon, from other book.
Dissertation on women's education for Selina from other book.

LK ***essay on the feeling strong of death:*** CF. Note NB-MA #16, on the "feeling strong of death" in David Hersland [= Leon Solomons] and in Pauline Sandys [= GS.]

29 years older for Leon: Passage taken from *Fernhurst* concerning Philip

Redfern; **pp. 29–30**. Not used in MA until **pp. 436–437**. GS used *Fernhurst* passage almost intact.

Dissertation on women's education: Passage taken from *Fernhurst*, **pp. 3–5**. Not used in MA until **pp. 436–437**.

*

NB6, #9

Marry Selina to Hodder with that scene and then the college business like in the other book, and the subsequent trouble. Western family. Leon, Lucius & Mike married to B. Selina & [Hodder's?] wife changes afterwards when he leaves her to be like Selina is now. Begin this the other end to from my old book. The most interesting man in her class was Hodder and then describe him as I describe him and then scenes to marriage, then scenes to divorce leaving out student action and afterward Selina gets mixed up with Charlotte Perkins Stetsen [i.e. Stetson] becomes free and funny a little crazy like she is now.

Leon disgusted with her methods of attack but always loyal to her. She sides with Mike & L.S. ~~against~~ against Bird though he ain't fond of her and she always abuses Bird the way Selina might. This was the end of Selina's marriage. It took place 8 years ~~or so~~ after Bird's marriage but during this time Selina did not see much of the family. Leon 18 years old time of brother's marriage. Discusses, Selina question decides Selina had better resign herself Year after comes father's smash.

introduce Daddie lending money and smash comes like Raymond's father.

AT ***Marry Selina to Hodder:*** Gertrude got the Hodder story through Howard Gans, whose lawyer he was. Hodder's first wife was a common-law wife only, so when he met the one at Bryn Mawr who took on being a philosophy teacher, she got Bishop Potter to marry them since Hodder had never been divorced and didn't need to be. She was about thirty-one when she married, and a beautiful woman who, Gertrude said, looked like the Mona Lisa.

the college business like in the other book: Gertrude took this [the Martha-Philip Redfern-Cora Donner episode based on Hodder's affair at Bryn Mawr] out of the first version entirely, but it was never rewritten. That's why there is such a break. She wrote the Hodder story probably a year or so after it happened [in the story entitled *Fernhurst*], but that's not definite. Gertrude said she took this section complete from an isolated thing.

I took over the typing at the beginning of 1908 while still living at the rue Notre Dame des Champs flat with Harriet, considerably before the break, and so the section containing the first version was probably retyped by me [the break, therefore, not evident in the typed manuscript.] The early typing was abominable, done on a Blickensdorfer, a Swiss or German machine, and that's where Gertrude gets names like Henriette de Dactyle and Yetta von Blickensdorff. The typing that Gertrude herself had done on it with her own special finger by finger method could hardly have improved the copy.

If Leo was not in the studio, I would type there in the morning. If he was, I would type in the evening. In the afternoons, Gertrude would work or meditate, so there was no typing then. By the Autumn of 1909 [Error: 1910], I was living at the rue di Fleurus, so my typing probably started in the Autumn of 1908.

I was using the old machine, the Blickensdorfer, for three months when my patience with it came to an end. Then Gertrude bought the largest Smith Premier machine ever invented. The man who brought it, despite the fact that he had a *legion d'honneur*, kept persuading us, You don't need this attachment, you certainly don't need this one, and all the while kept removing the attachments and finally left with them. But there was no reduction on the bill.

[During the second world war] some of the manuscript of *The Making of Americans*, Henry Miller's two books, and novels Gertrude wouldn't read again, were used for heat at Bilignin. We would roll together the moist paper and ashes and coal for a fire. We used after to remember Henry Miller with gratitude for this service, and for no other.

Charlotte Perkins Stetson: Gertrude was at the Charlotte Perkins Stetson Basket Lunch given at Radcliffe. Mrs. Stetson was an emotional and very beautiful woman, with an emotional appeal like Amy Semple Macpherson's. A cultured, calm woman, inexperienced in big movements like the Suffragettes, she had to divorce to continue her activities in the movement.

Leon... always loyal to her: Leon Solomons was the only person who came near the kind of comradeship Gertrude had with Leo.

father's smash... like Raymond's father: Gertrude's father never had a financial crash, but Raymond Duncan's father did, and it was a terrible scandal in San Francisco. I remember it well. It was called the Ralston failure. Ralston was Duncan's partner in a savings bank, and the crash was his fault, not Duncan's, because he loaned money, which was not legal for a savings bank to do. Raymond's father was not mentioned in the scandal, but he paid a percentage of the bank's failure, and was ruined as a result.

Gertrude's father was no gambler at all, and in fact never failed. He lost money as everyone did. It was the belief in his ideas that caused the gradual dwindling of his resources and financial affairs. The only people who were making it then were those who were bringing in new money to California. It was just land that made money then. [It is Duncan's failure, not Stein's, that is used for Hersland's "smash" in the novel.]

LK ***Marry Selina to Hodder... then college business like in the other book:*** "The other book" is *Fernhurst*, written in 1904, from which the entire episode of Selina's [=Martha's] marriage and the "subsequent trouble" with Hodder [= Philip Redfern] is copied into the MA.

Western family: Introduced on MA 21, line 37.

Selina... mixed up with Charlotte Perkins Stetson... a little crazy like she is now: Used at the end of the Martha chapter:

> First she was traveling and studying and then she was working to make some women understand something and many laughed at her and always she was full of desiring and always she was never understanding in desiring. [MA 470, lines 2–5]

*

NB6, #10

Pauline says, how I hate this fool kind of talk about nature the sweet voice of birds etc.

*

NB6, #11

Give sketch of Leon's life his experiences wandering through the country his gait and walk meets Julien combination in wandering about the hills. Julien medical student stage. older by 4 or 5 years than Leon. Leon's experience with Jams [Janes?] woman. Be thee a tramp his characteristic ways. (love of pigs Pauline) sometime give scene with Bird long walk in hill country back gives way forced to lie flat and then move on the way I did once with Leon.

Helen Lawson Rena Barkholdt

Leon's trip in mountains with Mabel and Helen Butterfield in place of me. Helen's relation to Leon like that girls "and now I have made you despise yourself." Give her whole relation to me as Leon and Mabel coming in and Leon then turning to her all the time friendship with Bird continues.

Fear of feminisation, as Scandinavian puts it causes his death.
Ned Holt his other best friend but he hates Julien. Leon's love Helen Butterfield Mabel and then disreputable one. 29 years old failure of influence finds has not really affected people like my feeling about Bird and others and so death. Leon's lack of sense of honor.

AT ***Ned Holt:*** A recollection of Gertrude's out of her grammar school days. She thought him then a very good boy. That's all on him.

*

NB6, #12

Francis Mabel's friend Herbert Spencer kind of man nobody marries Francis afterwards Helen Butterfield. 4 year interval between end of Leon's last girl disgust and death.
Make the sadness that I feel about full sunshine all around atmosphere of Leon. Sunshine insects etc and yet rejecting the sentimental beauty and melancholy of half-lights. Needs brilliant sunshine to taste reality deeply enough to be ~~broadly~~ of a broad luminous sorrow. Leon's remarks about Janes being so broad.
Joy of heat of expansion and perspiration makes you feel broad.

AT ***Herbert Spencer kind of man:*** Leo was all for him. He bored Gertrude stiff. She thought of it as Leon Solomons' kind of philosophy, what she called, Applied Philosophy.

LK ***Francis Mabel's friend:*** Paraphrase: "Francis Pollak will be Mabel Earle's friend. In the novel nobody will marry Francis. [After David's affair with Mabel Earle, David will meet] Helen Butterfield." Final plan: Helen B, then Mabel Earle. But last pages re: David's affairs name none.

*

NB6, #13

Leon says to Helen at end of their relations you I believed in
you as one should only believe in God and then you fouled my altar for me. You are no better than a miserable prostitute who gives her body from one man to the next and fills the world with loathsome sadness.

*

NB6, #14

I was furious and I spoke furiously but the meaning holds now and always in me.

*

NB6, #15

Make Alfy Dicky with thin stream of genius all through adoring Alfred like Alfy.

*

NB6, #16

Leon's favorite doctrine all through you don't [know] whether any man is any good until he is dead.

Vulgarity Leon's favorite doctrine disparity between ideal and type you belong when vulgarity flows together into a harmony the thing you are and the thing you would be.

Let Leon discourse on ceremonial naked soul in the naked body.

*

NB6, #17

The struggle between people like the struggle I watch so often between the clouds and the sun burning them away.

*

NB6, #18

Make the trouble between Uncle Sol and Lucius a political [one] lent him large sum of money for politics and Lucius lost it by not altogether a straight deal thats it. Slow struggle between the two for victory.

Selina attitude like that of Adele toward me in regard to Lucius.

Series of human struggles, Lucius & Jake & Mike Bird

& L.S. & ~~Jake~~ and ~~Julia~~.

Between Selina and Hodder.

Between Leon and Selina

Between Leon and Bird

Between Leon and his 3 girls. Scandinavian struggles with his religion, Ned Holt, with everything and Alfy, with his inheritance from his daddy. My daddy with his failure. Uncle Sol with his children's troubles and Bertha against Aunt Pauline to marry Jay. Uncle Sol Jay he seems a very practical modest young man.

Inserted later:

Jenny Dehning objects down town people.

AT ***Attitude like that of Adele toward me:*** I knew only Mrs. Adele Jaffa, a very independent being, very free of Sarah, in fact sent Sarah scuttling about. Sally was afraid of her and tried to put up some defense, but Adele just treated her as an incompetent. At least, that was my impression. That had probably been high school mates. Adele had no use for Sarah's heavy intellectualism. She was not an agreeable person, although she was nice to be with. She had none of the possessiveness Sally accused her of with her children. She was, in fact, a good mother, a "Modern" mother, but with no conscious pretension about it.

Gertrude was bored with her because she was insistent. But there was no feminine weakness in the woman anywhere. She was strong, independent, mature. Gertrude always said she had no initiative, but I was of a somewhat different mind. But there was no dependence on Adele's part whatever on Gertrude.

Lucius Solomons, Adele's and Leon's brother, was a friend of Sally's, whom she wanted Gertrude to marry at one time, and tried to persuade Gertrude that she was interested in the wrong member of the family.

LK ***Selina attitude like that of Adele toward me:*** Adele Jaffa, Leon Solomon's sister. Her attitude toward GS, if this note is our guide and she mirrored Martha's [= Selina's] attitude toward Alfred [= Lucius], must have been a fairly worshipful one in GS's mind, but Ms. Toklas flatly contradicts GS's supposition. [See AT Note for NB-A #6]

downtown people: Downtown people were Baltimore immigrants. Downtown was the social line. Bertha, when the Bachrachs [with whom she lived in Baltimore] had had enough of her, married Jay Raffel, a "downtown" man. The family was outraged, but Aunt Fanny [Bachrach] with whom she had been living, said it didn't matter, it was time she got married.

Jenny Dehning [Aunt Pauline] objects down town people: The ironic implication: that Aunt Pauline of the New York Steins would object to "downtown" people since the Baltimore Steins had the greatest contempt for the New York Steins. They thought of them as vulgarians. [Vulgarity further confirmed by the fact that the New York brother, Sol, married a New York woman, Pauline.]

*

NB6, #19

Hersland family already professions and university

arts and music California family. ~~R~~ J. A. of San Francisco, and spirit of freedom comes through it.

*

NB6, #20

Let Leon discourse on immortality through work or the family.

LK ***immortality through work or the family:*** In the finished novel, this theme is used for the substance of the Epilogue, MA 911ff. (It should be noted that there is no dialogue in the MA after the pages taken over from the first draft, **pp. 1–70**. All Notes indicating the use of dialogue are either for those pages, or for first-draft text that is no longer extant or is omitted from the final text.)

*

NB6, #21

Lucius marries at 30. Selina is just older they are finishing her just before divorce.

college and just been married with Hodder. About Selina all this (including divorce had happened ~~a~~ some few years ago in a Western town and nothing much was known about Selina excepting only as a woman working for the rights and wrongs she knew so well she knew women whose names even Julia knew and she was strong in her love and worship of her brother Alfred and she came from her [work] with her German women so that she could see him married. Further description of Sally.

AT ***Lucius marries at 30:*** Lucius [Solomons] married a schoolmate of mine, but an innocuous one. Sarah was delighted because she was jealous of anyone Lucius would marry.

LK ***Older they are … and just before divorce:*** [Insert]Originally, Martha's marriage to Hodder [= Philip Redfern] was to occur a year before Alfred's, but when GS determined that Martha was to be the oldest of the three children, her marriage was set earlier than Alfred's. In going back over this note, GS wrote in the correction: "Older they are [i.e., Martha and Hodder] and just before [their] divorce" [at the time when Alfred is married.] Later, GS changed this chronology again, setting Martha's marriage again after Alfred's.

*

NB6, #22

Alfred even in early days when he loved Julia suggesting frequent[ly] she was too fond of her family always a little jealous discusses about her family not being so much comparing Selina and Leon.

*

NB6, #23

The loving spot in the Hersland house was in they [sic] youngest boy then.

*

NB6, #24

Interlining first 9 words below:

Young David with him be me Olf goes up to bench [beach?] David leaves. Make Olf Rudeiner have a religious experience in woman walking up and down the plank and waving her arms Leon had been then a bond of union between them when they met on the road.

*

NB6, #25

Harriet Magraine

Olf Rudeiner marries or is married by Mabel H. as described her character and general popularity among ladies of Rudeiner like Julien contrast with Leo. ~~Sol~~

Shrewdness of Rudeiner, scene like that last day with Sally.

[Inserted:] Prayer scene with Mme. Vernot.

AT ***Scene like that last day with Sally:*** That would be just before [Sally and Mike] went back to San Francisco after the fire. Julihn was probably high and dry, and so the incident would probably be connected with Mike's getting his ticket back home for him. Julihn, if this is so, must have returned with the Steins.

Mme. Vernot: Mme. Vernon, who took boarders. Annette [Rosenshine]stayed in her house, at 58 rue Madame. Mme. Vernon lived on the top floor of 58. The house had a Protestant church downstairs, and the pastor's flat and Sunday school constituted one floor. In 1905, Sally and Mike lived in the house as pensionaries, and then went to stay at 1 rue de Fleurus until Mme. Vernon had a floor at 58 vacant for them. After Sally was installed, she put into Mme. Vernon's a Christian Scientist from San Francisco as a *pensionnaire*. When Mme. Vernon learned through him of Sally's Christian Science, she, a stout Protestant, was most upset.

*

NB6, #26

Francis and his characteristic attitude toward woman's suffrage and trusts. Day we all went down to register F. protesting.

AT ***women's suffrage and trusts:*** Gertrude went to the women's suffrage picnics and meetings, all right, when she was at Radcliffe, and she remembered the Charlotte Perkins Stetson Picnic Basket Lunch—Something, but she was not really interested in that. What really was interesting to her was the trusts and the scandals about them and the attempt to control them, which led her to support Grover Cleveland's second administration, the only time in her life she did not support a Republican.

LK ***woman's suffrage and trusts. Day we all went down to register:*** The AT note above is possibly an only, though spare, indication of a sympathetic interest for GS in the suffrage movement at the time she was in college or later.

Francis Pollak, who was studying and ultimately practiced law, was out of the liberal swing of things in which GS and her circle were mildly, and momentarily, engaged. Ironically, his future wife, Inez Cohen, became the President of the New York Teachers Guild, AFL-CIO.

*

NB6, #27

Writing books is like washing hair you got to soap it a lot of times before you start to rinse it.

*

NB6, #28

Power of public opinion made as in teaching's like Bird's of her children destruction of individual power and liberty.

AT ***teaching like Bird's:*** It was a funny time in America when they all went ethical and high-minded. Bird raised her children at the Ethical Culture School. Marion suffered it, and Robert escaped it. Howard Gans was another of those high-principled men, but very weak. He would shift with the wind, and was not stable, except in the things he did not live by. The New York reform movement was his best moment; at least he did that with youthful enthusiasm.

All this lofty public activity and private immersion was meat to Gertrude, who had no interest in uplift at all.

Howard Gans: was a great deal at Bird's house and fell in love with her soon after she was married to Lucius Sternberger.

There is a photo at Yale taken at Fiesole in 1905, 6 or 7, of Bird,

Howard, Gertrude, Leo, Sally, Mike and Allan.

*

NB6, #29

Leon David chummy with Fred. George elegancies Bohemianism etc. Leo & Fred drift apart become Leo & me & Bird. Sol Abe Dehning and Bird & Fred. Fred good man & success opposed to non-success of other family persistently bring out the contrast of the two families. Pa Dave Hersland with twist like Raymond's father. Son Mike with twist like L.S. and Lucius Solomons young brother Leon with Raymond's madness. Leon's love affairs except me. My and Howard's relation to Bird used in David's comradeship with Julia. My ideas of liberty. Bertha and Jay, Sol offering to help Jay in just the way he did.

AT ***Lucius Solomons young brother Leon:*** Leon and Lucius couldn't have been very congenial brothers because Lucius was a very pretentious, pompous lawyer, dark and flashy. Whether he was in love with Sarah, I don't know, but Sarah was rather taken with him.

Raymond's madness: It was a question at this time in Gertrude's mind how it would all end with Raymond [Duncan.]. He wasn't stable or well-balanced in those days. Now it has calmed down into eccentricity, which is all right.

Gertrude knew Raymond in the early days [in Oakland.] He was first a telegraph operator, then he created a job for himself as impresario for Pablo Casals and two other concert artists. Raymond naturally mismanaged the venture, and the whole thing was a small disaster, and left Pablo Casals stranded in San Francisco without funds. Mike and Sarah took Raymond on, and that's how they knew Casals in San Francisco. Sarah started her first salon then, with Raymond, Oscar Weill, and her doctor, the osteopathic Rudolph Meyer.

[In the early days in Paris] Raymond and Isadora lived in the court at the rue de Fleurus, where they turned up in a condition of penury. Gertrude and Leo couldn't let them starve, so they took them on. Gertrude thought that Isadora was even more mad than her brother. Raymond found a girl in Greece on one of the islands, called Penelope, a very good looking and sweet girl, but pregnant, so that Gertrude told Raymond he would have to get married. Raymond, open to reason, did, but Isadora who didn't believe in marriage was furious and never saw Gertrude again.

Howard Gans: Gertrude felt no embarrassment asking Howard Gans for money for the Ford during World War I.

LK ***Leon's love affairs except me:*** Only place in the Notebooks where GS's relation to Leon Solomon is called a "love affair." Their actual degree of intimacy is described fairly explicitly in worth whileNB11, #17, in the guise of Leon/David's and GS/Pauline's history, which ends with "Platonic because neither care to do more. She and he both have their moments but they know each other and it is not". and subsequently in the planned scene of break between David and Pauline in which David queries whether their break is coming because Pauline wanted to "wander off with her."

The correspondence between them gives no evidence at all of any personal intimacy. With the exception of a single occasion, in which GS was angered by the lost opportunity (the fault, she thought, of Leon) of going on a trip together during their summer break in California, all their correspondence is only on their work at the Harvard Psychology Lab, and on publications of their research articles. If the plan for the scene of the break between David and Pauline can be taken at face value, then it is possible that GS, already conscious of her lesbianism, or already involved in an affair or affairs with women at Radcliffe, allowed a "break" with Leon Solomons to occur.

my and Howard's relation to Bird: Howard Gans as her lawyer and GS as her cousin and devoted friend were the rocks on which Bird leaned during her miserable marriage to Louis Sternberger, and during the extended court procedures through which her divorce dragged. GS's compassion for her cousin was reasonably disinterested, but Howard's was not. Though her lawyer in her battle against Sternberger, Howard was already in love with Bird, a fact that GS, after the bitter quarrel that ensued with Bird and Howard in April 1906, permanently deplored as a professional breach of trust. Before the quarrel, however, GS had been, from the time she came East and made regular visits to New York, her cousin Bird's mentor as well as friend, the same role Leo played for Bird's brother Fred.

my ideas of liberty: See also NB-I #3, See Note #76a; re: GS determination to have total liberty; and see note to AT re: GS absolute demand for independence.

Leo and Fred.... success... and non-success: Fred Stein remained a devoted friend of Leo's all his life. For the purpose of David Hersland's friendship with George Dehning, who was modeled on Fred, David is Leo Stein. Fred and Bird, the New York cousins of Leo and GS, were the children of Uncle Sol and Aunt Pauline, whose hospitality and attempted "civilizing" of what Aunt Pauline regarded as the Western aborigine in GS was hardly rewarded, or possibly thoroughly rewarded, by GS's depiction of her in *The*

Making of Americans. The "drifting apart" from Bird was true of both Leo and GS, both of whom were equally irate at Bird and Howard during their quarrel of 1906–7, GS taking on Bird for the most part, and Leo exchanging acrimony with Howard.

The contrast GS was planning between David and George was basically the contrast between the financially successful but spiritually cloddish "Eastern" and the failed but gifted "Western" Steins, which was initially projected as one of its major themes. GS and Leo's agreement on the Fred Steins of the world, for all of Leo's sincere friendship with him and Fred's unfailing devotion to Leo, was pat. Their distaste for the lesser breed of Steins is as evident in Leo's reflections on his one-year trip around the world with Fred as it is in GS's novel.

*

Notebook 1

NB1, #1

When he went East David
Menda Herzel
Cora Moore
Ellen Lawson
Mabel Earle

LK ***When he went East David:*** Paraphrase: When David went East, his friends were Menda Herzl [= Cora Moore] and Helen Lawson [= Mabel Earle.]

*

NB1, #2

[GS notebook title:] Life of Young David & George Dehning.

*

NB1, #3

Yes I think I will make Jane Sandys wander off with Mabel
Haynes and go to the devil David remonstrating Call her Harriet Maigrane.
Helen Butterfield Rena ~~Harten~~ Barkholdt for George
Mabel Earle Ellen Lawson

AT ***Mabel Haynes:*** [Mabel Haynes Heissig Leick.] She is Mabel [Neathe] in *Q.E.D.* Very curious handwriting. She crossed her T's with almost a dagger thrust. Note at Yale [in the Stein Collection] how much like the Stinker's it is. Though Annette's was more illiterate, Mabel's still had much the same things—the way of crossing the T's and so on. Annette was eaten with interest in herself. Mabel was interested in herself, but not eaten by it; self-centered, but not diseased. She was more of a person.

I met her in 1920 or '21 in Paris when she came to see Gertrude, but all the past memories affected her so that she nearly fainted. She was lurid. By 1922 she was *tres grande dame*, who made herself over completely into Austrian nobility.

Helen Butterfield: Here is Helen Butterfield: the girls at Radcliffe used to exchange pieces of clothing as students do. Once when Helen did, the girl with whom she exchanged complained, I don't think it's a fair exchange. But, said Helen, that was mine. Also, she was not very clean.

LK ***Mabel Haynes:*** [See note on final break between Jane Sandys and David

Hersland, above.] Oddly, GS has her fictional counterpart "go to the devil" with her actual rival for May Bookstaver rather than with May. Consistently in these notes, "going to the devil" meant for GS succumbing to lesbian attachment.

*

NB1, #4

Do Alfy (Dickey Wolkins) straight away as he is as Alfred Hersland's friend, with the thin streak of genius in him and his general doing nothing.

*

NB1, #5

Make that Davids characteristic mode of speech. What I was thinking of was not so much ________ but ________
Sure, and so to speak
Also describe his not thin but sharpened features and clear rims to his eyes like Leon and the twitch and the movement of the hand all the fingers together, with the delicacy of feeling in them have to have them altogether to give them power enough face like it lips eyes and nose work together to reinforce.
Combine in him.

AT ***characteristic mode of speech:*** Leo's way of concluding an argument was also characteristic, with that vacant smile of deep self-satisfaction. His speech was not only very rapid but very low. Sometimes when he didn't have the smile, he would get flushed with the excitement of himself. When he smiled, when he was making an analysis of another person and himself all to his own advantage, it was most unpleasant.

*

NB1, #6

Between lines above:

and Raymond's general kind of argument, Leon's science and out of door character and Sterne's yes you think so and Sterne's attitude toward Harris Leon's to Julien.

LK ***Sterne's attitude toward Harris:*** Sterne arrived in Paris 1904, met with Harris Fall 1906. Harris, according to Sterne became his patron, and paid for Sterne's trip to Greece. Subsequently Sterne gave up his Rome scholarship for Harris: "He needs it more."

*

NB1, #7

Hutch's intensive kind of sweetness, Raymond's bitterness and remark to Sally about nigger in the tropics, Pauline say that to ~~Jane~~ when she is just getting intimate with Harriet (M.H.) and making fun of preciosity like my remark to Annette they use works of art for personal adornment of themselves and life never the thing but the use of the thing nastily disguised materialism.

LK ***Raymond:*** Raymond Duncan. The brother of Isadora Duncan, "had known Gertrude Stein's elder brother and his wife in San Francisco. At that time Raymond was acting as advance agent for Emma Nevada" and Pablo Casals. "Raymond had gone completely greek and this included a greek girl. Isadora lost interest in him, she found the girl too modern a greek.... Gertrude Stein gave him coal and a chair for Penelope to sit in," [**ABT pp. 40–41**] Raymond Duncan was living in the courtyard with Penelope when his son was born, at which time Gertrude insisted that they marry. Isadora, who was more averse than friendly to the idea of marriage took umbrage at Gertrude's insistence, and never spoke to her again.

Annette: Annette Rosenshine arrived in Paris Dec 1906 with Mike and Sarah, she traveled with mother and sister Summer 1907, visited GS in Fiesole during those summer travels. From the beginning of Matisse School to the end of her stay in Paris. (Left for SF May 22, 1908.).

never the thing but the use of the thing: Becomes a major theme re: Julia Dehning in the final text. See MA 348, l. 19–22. Discussion of "object as object" is in NB-A #14, NB-A #15, NB-B #1, NB-B #3, NB-B #6.

*

NB1, #8

Stell described for Pauline Sandys.
Don't you know it you haven't got any manners. I am awfell sorry but just you wait a little, then you'll see em coming.
Afterwards with Mabel Haynes David objects they came too much. use Putnam to Mabel Haynes early stages to David.

AT ***Stell:*** "Gertrude carried over her moral values from Radcliffe days with Mabel Weeks, Miriam Price, Estelle Rumbold, who were all very high-minded. She was intimate with these before she met May Bookstaver and Mabel Haynes [at Johns Hopkins.]"

use Putnam: An American sculptor from California. He was in Paris from about 1905 or 6. Gertrude may only have heard of him from Annette and myself. He was very poor, with a wife who was not much help, and a baby. They lived in misery and cold. Nelly, with all her money, was taken to help him by me. When he said, Alice, you dropped your handkerchief, Nelly said, Let's go. She'd have none of that. He was very handsome, really a beautiful creature. Wild School as a sculptor and person.

*

NB1, #9

Quality that makes young men comparison in Sterne and Alfy Alfy not in that sense a young man David is his big brother not Leo F. or George in between.

*

NB1, #10

Don't describe David till later give his early life without describing. Describe him when after marriage he meets the Dehning family and describe him then in relation to each one

*

NB1, #11

Epilogue of the whole story will be yes I say it is hard living down the tempers we are born with.

LK ***Epilogue… hard living down the tempers…*** In effect, repeating the introduction of the final draft [MA 3,] but not used in Epilogue.

*

NB1, #12

Conversation.

No it isn't that. Well then what is it why don't you say it. Why it isn't that I ~~did~~ don't know why I don't say it. I guess I just kind of don't want to.

*

NB1, #13

Make little Hortense revert back to gentle grandmother make like Ruth Friedman.

*

NB1, #14

Keep in mind all through contrast between Phillistine honesty, goodness each their own kind of sweetness, heroical, (George open boyish sweetness) a dependent ~~sweet~~ loyal up-gazing ~~subdued~~ sweetness in little Hortense. Contrast.

LK ***Keep in mind... sweetness:*** Planning Note used in MA 18. "Sweetness" and its variants, "heroical," "boyish," "blustering," is the first example in the Notebooks of a descriptive category, though it has no part in the descriptive system GS later developed

*

Note #9

[...] activity, no dreaminess, no silent developement [sic] of soul, Nothing but incessant obvious, arrogant strong health. Health so crude, so unsoiled that it has no brute quality brutality. The perfect female flower of the vigorous, strenuous incessant life. No rest and no fatigue, a democracy without domination or rebellion. All there is of being found in the daily round of five o'clock rising, studying, reciting, boating, gymnastics rehearsals for theatricals a snatched dance a 15 mile tramp, a preparation of more lessons and a ten-o'clock bed-time. No part of the recognised creature neglected in this incessant hard round of activity, all that there is expressed, and with crude honesty the destruction of reserve. All that they know they do and all that there is they know and all ~~they~~ that they know they do. A boy's hard surface routine with a woman's maturity For a boy so a foundation of healthful vigor for the groundwork of a man, for a woman, a realisation habit of ~~ceaseless~~ incessant action without an understanding of values. A worship of all obvious success, to do and not to be, To use all one's strength all one's activity all the time not of inward necessity but in response to this ideal.

Smith college life.

*

Note #57

~~Leon~~ David don't meet ~~B.~~ Julia untill [sic] ~~just before~~ after marriage while describing father grandfather and grandmother and mother, mother dies just after marriage make B's preparation for marriage go on as described

LK [in GS, *Fernhurst* 163–166.]

*

NB1, #15

Father, blustering sweetness, David intensive kind of sweetness and big brother a little sweetness in him say of him he had a little sweetness in him and sister Selina the kind of anxious to please and seizing sweetness.

*

NB1, #16

Why do you spank me that way now I ain't done anything bad to you.

*

NB1, #17

~~David~~ George to Rena Barkholdt giving all kinds of excuses like me to Jean You know I am a working man I ain't got time to loaf all day, and I an expert Julihn and that train business coming in can't be put off you know not any way that I can see to fix it. No that don't satisfy you well probably you'll like it better if I just tell you I am bored to death and so I am going and that don't suit you either eh all right make it the way you like it it ain't ever anything to me but ~~that~~ there is one thing that there is no way I know of changing. Its to-morrow morning I am going.

*

NB1, #18

Make Jane Sandys not really in love with David, but his ~~rather getting tired of her~~ having been to the point and then retreated[?] from it and so she floats off with Mabel Haynes and his remonstrance but always on moral grounds only and she knows it. Describe the same amount of being in love that I had. Helen Butterfield's was more like Inez.

LK ***Jane Sandys:*** [= GS]. An early plan for incorporating a history of GS herself into the Gossols [=Oakland] cast of characters but disconnected from her own family [to appear as an "only child" of "respectable people enough."] Had the character survived, she would, according to this Note, have shared childhood friends with the Hersland [= Stein] children—May Lidell, the Richardsons, Tilly Brown and others—and according to NB11, #17, reappeared as one of the Eastern College [= Harvard/Radcliffe] loves of David Hersland. In the final text, Jane is converted into Pauline Manders, preserves her role as David's third and final college lover, and loses her Gossols childhood altogether.

Jane Sandys not really in love with David: See NB11, #17 for lengthy account of early relation between Jane Sandys and David Hersland.

more like Inez: That is: more like Inez's love for Francis Pollak.

*

NB1, #19

George with Rena.
Make use of that idea—I just refuse sometimes just because I think its sort of right to once in a while change my general revolt to a specific one. Sometimes I refuse to tell a story sometimes to go somewhere. Often I refuse and then I do it but sometimes it comes across me to be stubborn and then I do and then nothing anybody can say to me can ever change me. I could most go to the stake for a refusal which surely don't ~~certainly~~ make any real kind of difference to me.

*

NB1, #20

Also use that instance of Pauline Sandys when I wouldn't tell that story at Lounsbury's because by that time the expectation was out of proportion to the study and stubborness would make it seem a real good reason. Williams delivering the baby was the story but it will have to be another it won't be hard to find one, has to have a character a little brutal and not very interesting

AT ***Williams delivering the baby:*** That was Gertrude's humor, playing games of this kind at Radcliffe [sic]. Marion [Walker] Williams understood this very well; in fact, Marion Williams understood Gertrude very well generally. Her visit with Gertrude in Paris years later was one of the happiest meetings out of Gertrude's past.

When Gertrude was well into *The Making of Americans*, she was deadly serious. She laughed enormously but didn't ever provoke it herself. When she was at her funniest, she didn't know it.

LK ***Lounsbury:*** Grace Lounsbury, at whose Baltimore home GS's circle of women friends met during her Johns Hopkins years.

Williams delivering the baby: Dr. John Whitridge Williams, Professor of Obstetrics at Johns Hopkins. It was Dr. Williams who failed GS in Obstetrics in her senior year, and then offered her the chance to make up her failure during the summer, which GS, in her version of the incident, declined. But in fact, she had failed four courses in her last year, which precluded her taking a degree in any case.

*

NB1, #21

Incident of Stella making little Hortense's drawing and the family George particularly wanting her to go on with it as a life work. But Hortense was too indifferent though she did not know that she had not done it. Father's remarks like Sol's about Amy.

AT ***Amy [Stein]:*** Amy Stein was a stupid girl whom Gertrude sent to Smith College. She became an important social worker in Baltimore and married a Jonas. Their daughter was Priscilla, a blonde buxom one, not at all a Priscilla. Juan Gris was at the house one day when Priscilla visited, and was horrified.

LK ***Stella:*** Estelle Rumbold, the sculptor who shared the White House apartment in New York with GS, Mabel Weeks and the other former Radcliffe students.

*

NB1, #22

Make the story I will throw the umbrella in the mud a story of Martha Hersland when she was playing with some bigger children.

LK ***... umbrella in the mud a story about Martha:*** Used subsequently in MA 388.

*

NB1, #23

I hate to see you repeating yourself until your life has lost all meaning. A remark of David's to Helen Butterfield.
Any advice is good if it is only given strong enough, remark to Jane.

*

NB1, #24

David is to be 2 yrs. older than George.

*

NB1, #25

George to say as Leo F. did when he wanted that job. there is a waiting list of 500 before you. Those are not the ones I am afraid of ~~laugh~~ said George to him. The man laughed and said well then I'll put down your name ahead of them. Alright sir, I guess they won't mind George answered him, they must be used to it after all this time.

They appointed him to show they had no prejudice against a german. they used him to prove it for them. Lucky George he always liked it to be a

George's way of dreaming about all the trades in one moment rich contrast sensuous dreamy successful honest in his way [ardour?] and ~~hilli~~ intelligent contrast with David the singular the man not of talent but a certain genius in him. George always standing up for himself and yet always being in line with order and serious. No toady but independent to bring about things he wanted without ever offending. David [-?-] [none?] and yet always offended by offering when it was not politic to do so.

*

NB1, #26

Must not forget that twice George works little Hortense to do what he once [sic] of her by nobly going to ~~the~~ get the tickets to go when she had said the day before he would take her before the others had decided to go elsewhere.

*

NB1, #27

The fat lady sighed and got thinner this summer like Bertha and the stories she tells and the children and her suspicions [?].

*

NB1, #28

[Inserted later:] No either to David or Pauline.
Give that incident in ~~Sel~~ Martha Hersland's early career seeing the woman killed on the train and then for a long while always walking to the high-school. Make Martha more and more a contrast to Julia the one xemplifying success as the other failure like George & David.

*

NB1, #29

George's love affairs must be like Leo's he followed next with Helen B. after David gets through not much ~~he gets side tracked with Inez, who~~ who afterwards marries Julihn David like Leo Victor too level headed to go far ~~David~~ Leon ~~tries to stop~~ accepts the announcement the way I did that of

Francis and Inez. George then makes a very sensible marriage describe his girl Leo F. told me about it that his medical friend remarks on—and she ain't straight. these 3 affairs of George, Helen H. [Dubin's] girl ~~something like May only dark~~ like the girl with the [long?] brothers and father leaves her in the [word?] house like her relation with the architect. Can bring Mrs. Cummings a little if one likes. Call her Rena Barkholt and describe the way I used to watch her dress. George coming in to see her when she was sick with tonsilitis and Mrs. Samuels had gone to the country.
Had met Rena at a college party had tried to call I watched him do it once. Next time he saw her, this

AT ***accepts the announcement the way I did that of Francis and Inez:*** Inez Cohen, of a Portuguese family. Gertrude disliked Inez Cohen considerably and objected to the marriage of Inez and Francis Pollack, but I don't know why.

Mrs. Cummings: Gertrude's landlady at Radcliffe. She did the dinner table in fairy lights—not candles, but little oil wicks in porcelain. Mr. Cummings came in and said, Another one of these and we'll be in total darkness. Mrs. Cummings was High Church, dull, nothing.

LK ***Francis and Inez:*** Francis Pollak and Inez Cohen, of the Oppenheimer circle, and friends of GS and Leo. There was an odd tale at the time that GS was in love with Francis, which gave credibility to the way GS "accept[ed] the announcement" of Francis' and Inez' engagement. Her "acceptance:" she never spoke to either of them again.

*

NB1, #30

Alfy and Martha are fair like their cheery little mother. David dark like his father.

AT ***fair like… mother, dark like… father:*** There's a family photo taken in Venice [when the Stein children were very young and living there.] They were all handsome: the Governess, Simon, Leo (a sickly youth), Bertha (a little sullen, as she always was), and Mike (a stern, upright, ugly boy with pale eyes, pale hair but looks black.) The black ones were Stein, not Keyser.

*

NB1, #31

Use [some how?] me to Etta and the boys. You damn fool incident of May and her dress and 17 year old hoodlums. David comes up this is first flame Helen,

and he addresses you damn fool don't you know boys of that age are the most dangerous a girl can fool with. They have no sense of consequences like there is in a man. And with a man two men make a woman safe with boys the more the more dangerous they got to show each other they ain't afraid of anything. Didn't you see that little one trying to touch your breasts. I can't see why women have got to be such fools and not see things, do you suppose your being a lady would do you any good ever with them You women certainly are damn fools mostly.
Describe the light blue dress Helen May wore.

AT ***You damn fool incident of May and her dress:*** The incident of Gertrude and May Bookstaver in a restaurant, Gertrude saying, You can't act as you do without expecting it [i.e., the harassment of hoodlums.]

*

NB1, #32

Decent people are at home sometimes just to show there is no hard feeling, David to Mabel Earle. Write a letter like that one of the sc[i]entist.

*

NB1, #33

Make Jane Sandys have experiences with May Lidell driving around the grocers giggling and public school small boy and Ed Richardson and his sister with whom she went on a tramp. still she belonged to respectable people enough only child, public school experiences Tilly Brown and the rest. fat girl and religious talk like Mabel Haynes [knew?] one.

*

NB1, #34

When young David wanted a house like Leo. He says if you want a house it will turn up. his notion was if you wanted a house you ~~you~~ should go and look for it but thats not the way the real thing comes you got to stay and wait for it and so with strong inward protest David waited but the house never came. One day old David came home and said to young one. To-day I almost earned your house I tried hard to make the man buy the stock but it was no go. Perhaps it will be better some time. But there is my sugar money in the bank. That you can't take out but you just wait it will come.

*

NB1, #35

The conversation we heard at Vallotons like the niggers these very black ones they got poison in their teeth when they bite you.

*

NB1, #36

Use that for next book de fat lady that sighed yes I got thinner this summer description. The bourgeois always like to flee them the other bourgeois.

*

Notebook 11

NB11, #1

81 1/2 + 100

GS Note on notebook cover:

Important for later life and beginning of Alfred and David.

*

NB11, #1a

All their lives on later.

*

NB11, #2

Eastern colleges too dam anxious to be safe. They needn't be so afraid it ain't so easy to be hurt as they seem to think ~~least~~ at least not by getting hit hard on the head. They needn't be so scared of any of us got any chance of real stuff in us just because we are made different. Getting hurt by being hard is least dangerous ~~among~~ a thing can get it. They needn't be so afraid of their dam culture, it'd take more than a man like me to hurt it.

AT ***Eastern colleges:*** Gertrude went to school, she said, with an author of the 'M 'think School.'

LK ***Eastern colleges:*** A dialogue planned for David Hersland. GS's Radcliffe theme or First Novel has a similar passage. Her aggressive, presumably western, posture toward Harvard is planned for David Hersland's arrival at Cambridge. The passage was never used.

*

NB11, #3

Different kinds of ways of playing. The way Chalfin plays like Fred's friendly and civilised not childish civilised boyish contrast to Leon's intellectual bohemianism.

LK ***Chalfin:*** In a later letter to M. Weeks, [August 12, 1910] Leo Stein writes "Chalfin, late of the Boston Museum, who has been stopping with us some days and was with us at Hutch's last night. [He] is a fellow of unusual intelligence though a lazy thinker who is as hostile to America as Hutch is friendly.... He has much fineness of quality and will almost certainly do very good work but I doubt whether he has the keenness to do great things."

Chalfin, as artist and architect, began his Paris campaign visiting GS and Leo in Fiesole admiring enormously their "superb life": "idleness…. I only grow desperate to think how much now must be brought about before ever I earn this idleness or that of Fiesole, in such bulk and such divine length and such unconcern as I figure it."

Leo was his close friend, and a much admired one. He knew GS through Leo, but certainly knew her well and even banteringly, but he never took intimacies for granted, not even Leo's, which perhaps was his special wisdom.

*

NB11, #4

Disagreeable condition at home after death of mother and begin of father's business troubles though nobody knew about them at all yet troubles railroad stock savings bank and loaned money one of the reasons why Alfred was going East to begin law business. Just about this time too Martha married and left home and David stayed at home sometime longer and then his father got mixed up with spiritualists and Cora Moore etc. In the meanwhile Alfred had gotten married and then the smash came about 4 yrs. hence [time?].

And then Martha had had her trouble and came home and there was money enough from the money father had given the mother to take care of Father & Martha in a small way and so David went on East to College.

Martha's like Selina stints and travels with old man who tries many ways of getting on feet again describe his giving money to poor widows etc. as Raymond describes and then his constant downward turn always at outs with Martha coffee trouble as bad as ever the Moore's loom up every now and then Martha's friends Tillie Brown and the bad one & May Bruckminster father angry the way pa was with me. Meantime David has gotten his job troubles gotten constantly worse in Alfred's family ~~Successful~~ David being good to Julia etc etc failure small job in West home with his father. Death. father's slow death. Julia devoted to her cause. Alfred divorced married to 7 years attachment like Jake's to Minny extravagance admiration of Martha Redfern relapse. Alfred's political success finally like Jake's tries to handle wife, no go but live together off and on and so leave them. First trouble with old Dehning borrows a lot of money for politics nothing doing causes trouble. Made large debts then told about them afterwards.

*

Julia sided with her father Alfred sulks the way Jake did. David tries to speak to him listens the way Jake did to Sally finally Dehning paid it all. More trouble between Julia & Alfred bad temper etc finally Alfred begins to get interested in his client uses his own money to help her never tries to pay back Dehning final smash.

AT ***after death of mother:*** After their mother's death, Daniel Stein became important in the children's lives. Gertrude then realized that he was a whimsical, fantastic, exaggeratedly impatient man. The card games [sixty-six] episode and his leaving the table.

spiritualists and Cora Moore: Cora Moore was a classmate of Gertrude's during the few months she went to High School in Oakland. Cora was a dashing, good-looking California girl whose mother was interested in séances. Gertrude went to them with Cora, who put on the whole business for her mother. These were days when the gamblers gambled on mines, and they went to these séance people for information. Gertrude judged from Cora's contribution that she was in the act with her mother, but it was delicate ground and you could ask no questions, so you could only guess about the fakery. Gertrude was probably between fourteen and fifteen at the time, and her curiosity even then was very vivid.

Tillie Brown: In later days, she came to Paris, and seemed fond of Gertrude. They had common memories of the old days, naturally, and talked about East Oakland.

listens the way Jake did to Sally: If Jake [Samuels] 'listened,' it must have been without effect, since Sally's family regarded her as high-strung but ineffectual. Sally's voice was low, sulky, rather too suave, but always in her expression of herself there was the gesture and the drama. Sally's violinist brother in a way exposed her. He looked like her, and in his clearer way explained and expressed her. He never accomplished anything. All her family was given to 'phases.' Her father's was drama, Jake's was politics and law, Sally's was Christian Science and the Higher Life.

Jake, Sarah's older brother, was a lawyer. He was married but lived separated from his family. Oscar, another brother, was also a lawyer, and attended to Sarah's [posthumous] affairs.

LK ***Martha's friends:*** In Gossols [= Oakland.] Tillie Brown was one of GS's high school friends who corresponded with her in the Thirties, reminiscing about Oakland friendship.

one that went bad: Another Oakland friend who is combined with GS herself later on to make the third woman with whom young David is to fall in love.

May Buckminster: An acquaintance of GS's during Hopkins Baltimore days. May Buckminster figured fairly prominently in the affairs of Mabel Haynes and May Bookstaver, affairs in which GS became so emotionally entangled. She was the friend of Mabel Haynes.

*

Note #97

David Hersland blonde like Martha and Alfred, David young dark contour of face like his momma.

California and its greater freedom preliminary to general statement of children.*

the father had not his old strength for living, the mother was a little ailing. Martha had come back out of her trouble to them, Alfred was in Bridgepoint and just marrying Julia Dehning. David was soon to join him to go

And now we will begin with each one of them and tell their lives as far as they had lived them to the point where our history has [?] made its beginning. At this time [...]

*

NB11, #5

Have little Hortense disgrace the family by marrying Sterne as I originally planned it. ~~Make her Smith experience~~ Smith is where Hodder performance take place. Hortense does not go to college but has the kind of life of Beatrice's friend, nurse's settlement and so bring my knowledge of doctors and nurses that is where she meets a down town Leo Friedman who sympathises with the rest in keeping the old gentleman from getting married and about two years after he dies, and finis then go back to old Hersland and his son dead and he dying finis.

LK ***Smith is where Hodder performance takes place.*** GS's transfer of "the Hodder performance" from Bryn Mawr to Smith College in this note is touched with a measure of malice. It was Smith College women whose athleticism and lack of "dreaminess" GS couldn't abide, and it is to Smith College that she consigns Julia Dehning [= Bird Stein], at the end of Julia's career, "petering out… Deaning," a proper low fate for a terminally inconsequential Bird. In the final version of the novel, though, reference to

Smith college is obliterated.

*

NB11, #6

Our daddy's method of playing sixty-six symptomatic of his family also that whole youthful cooking and wandering [?] et al.

*

NB11, #7

Leon as a little chap with Richardson and his sister make our trip to Etna. Richardson and his sister Leon's first taste of religion and evil remember Richardson's religious father. Also the Rodhammel's had a big estate out in Fruitvale the Hersland family Martha and her friends. Alfred like Mike got his legal education in Harvard came back for two years to America. Sale of the old place like the sale I saw that time in the Bray family. describe like that with hedge of roses. Richardson's in little house Rodhammel's etc. all in the young family[?] Friends came to see them as they us[ed] to us governesses etc. but all stopped after death of mother. One camping trip like the Santa Rosa trip across the water asleep in the cabin trip of David with his father.

Later high [Sierra?] in the East trip like that one of Leon with this [sic] two girls Helen Butterfield and Mabel and what happened. Helen's [sadness?] wonderful morning.

Old man Hersland tries many queer things chinese doctor his whole family, and Martha when she was sick queer blind man and funny feels he gave her and the woman doctor makes her strong to love all such queer ways, including C.S. must bring out striking credulity of these real scientists as compared to the exactness of belief in orthodox faculty even in its reform movements of other family. Make George a doctor like Leo Friedman. Hortense in this book does not marry but goes in for district nursing. Fred Leo experiences in college etc and typhoid fever that is the kind of character. Orthodoxy of it and David always making more or less a mock of it. David the failure but in his dim way George sees that David the failure has real greatness in him. He mourns his death and so does Julia. David embittered by his failure more or less use Jame's [sic] letter, and Martha tries to get spiritual messages sends them to George who there has no tolerance in him. The Family see no more of each other.

Use all my doctoring experience and George's contempt for women in short a history just like Leo Friedman, and so he is more or less in touch with Leon in their work in scientific ways together. Different kinds of science. George's romancing like Leo. Gradually a falling off. [reclame?] of scientific methods and hygiene that sounds probable operation on neck.

AT ***our trip to Etna:*** Leo and Gertrude wandered around the countryside near Oakland, and when she was nine and he eleven or twelve, they took a cart up to Mt. Etna and Leo shot rabbits and they ate them. They wandered for days and nights alone. It wasn't at all unusual to go on such expeditions. Leon Solomons, Clarence Toklas [Miss Toklas' brother], everybody went up to the Sierras.

Fruitvale: Located not far from where Gertrude lived, up against marvelous blue hills straight over from San Francisco in the San Joaquin Valley.

Hersland tries many queer things: Daniel Stein took the children to a Chinese doctor and tried all the things Gertrude refers to in this note.

my doctoring experience: Gertrude had hospital experience when she was studying at Johns Hopkins and had to take on three births before she was to get her degree. Claribel Cone, who worked at Hopkins, also had experience with negro mothers in Baltimore. Gertrude knew Claribel more intimately than Etta in the Hopkins days because Claribel was a scientist working at Hopkins, and they'd walk there together in the morning. One of the mothers who was grateful for Claribel's care named her child Clara Belle. Gertrude's respect for the medical practice there wasn't always the highest. Once she saw three doctors diagnose a case as some sort of fever, and then Osler came in and said it was cholera. They didn't know it when they saw it.

The Free Ward at the Johns Hopkins hospital was black, and Gertrude got to know generally how to talk to them—how to be kind and keep your authority at the same time. It was like the story of Martha, the negro servant girl of Hortense Moses, who after traveling with her and being close to her during their trip, on the point of return, said, 'Don't forget, Martha, you're nothing but a colored girl when we go back.' Of course, Hortense was raised further South than Baltimore, in the Carolinas.

LK ***Alfred like Mike:*** Sentence should read: Alfred, like Mike, got his legal education at Harvard, came back for two years to California. Michael Stein never went to Harvard. He attended Johns Hopkins from 1883 to 1886, graduating with an AB degree, and from 1886 to1887 was a graduate student in Biology at the University of California in Berkeley.

Old man Hersland tries many queer things... Hersland's "queer ways" are first described, MA 48–53. Reiterated in MA 119–129

Richardson... his sister... religious father: A family GS knew in Oakland. The father's "importance in religion," occasions, together with the portrait of GS's maternal grandfather, one of the two full portraits of religious men in the final text of the novel. [MA 108–112.]

trip like that one of Leon: to which GS made vigorous objections having been overlooked as holiday companion. See also NB6, #11: "Leon's trip to mountains with Mabel and Helen Butterfield in place of me."

*

NB11, #8

Bertha brought to the house her family disappears like Hattie's sickly all others dead except Bertha at eighteen. Two years before Jenny's death (tumors?) like her sister. Bertha she [acts?] kind of nasty as only she can be. Herman sort of needs her to take place of his ~~father~~ wife in kinds of ways scare Bertha never went beyond pressure and coming into her one night to come and keep him warm, she more dislike than terror tells it to her husband persecution mania particularly as to Jenny.

*

NB11, #9

While David is having his serious love experiences George is like Leo F he takes up Helen H. after David's game is over and he and she sentimentalise long nights together while David does Mabel. George has left and gone home to study medicine when David [gents?] [shocked?] and gets mixed up with the bad.

Helen to David. Now I have made you hate yourself again etc. all [parmnettes?] to David till the bad one and that only an uneasy but a genuine sensation. Nothing but bitterness before his death.

George not married yet at finis waiting till he has enough to support a wife, but bring out the various character of him, study Chalfin some for him.

George does not approve of Dave's friends and his attitude toward mysticism keep your mind open was David's creed all these clean [?] things not proved yet. Also David not being socially or [dresingly?] clean annoyed him. David's graham diet George selling his clothes Spinoza family,

AT ***Spinoza Family:*** For Inez Cohen. She was from a Portuguese family

LK ***Leo F:*** Leo Victor Friedman, other half of GS's fictional George Dehning. Fred was a business man and later became a highly respected political and philanthropic figure in New York. Leo Friedman, one of GS's close Cambridge friends, was a medical student when GS knew him, and later a physician in Boston. The projected story of George Dehning is largely Leo Friedman's and to a small extent Michael Stein's, who also studied biology as a graduate student. But George's character is essentially Fred Stein's.

Helen H.... Mabel.... the bad: A slip; should be Helen B[utterfield], David's first love; Mabel [Earle] the second; "the bad" [Pauline Sandys (= GS), the "bad un"] David's third and last.

*

NB11, #10

When Hortense makes such a success of nursing father astonished didn't think his little Hortense had the sense to do it like that in practice. Make her George's shadow as is the custom in little sisters. Reading the labels for her. It was decided he was to be a doctor.

*

NB11, #11

When she was heroic there was an intensiveness [sic] sweetness in her. David feels that always in her. The key-note of his attitude toward her very slow very gradual discovery he don't count in the sense that she does not realise him. When all her family gave up around her there was this strong heroic sweetness in her.

*

NB11, #12

Must not forget Leo F. George passion for organisation handling of his assistants when he has gotten a job in the lying in hospital incident telephones for woman to write dress articles for jew ladies.

*

NB11, #13

Bring out in David's character the quality like mine the search for ultimate dependence the kind of final grasp that I found in M[']s relation to the universe her way bad. One like that and the way I found it in Sally, represented by Julien as end of his search have the archangel the mystic quality and respects him gives the feeling of the way I explained it to Sally that time, temperament and type and ideal flowing together to a perfect harmony.

Save idea [?] for all people that are not vulgar but rare to find in this so called spiritual type helps him in struggles against death. Mabel Earle tries but not great enough for faith for [?] can be ideally contemplated but does not support idealism weak in others. Helen B. just a passionate more like a girl's feeling.

LK ***search for ultimate dependence:*** The search, in other words, for an ultimate ideal, the nature of the ideal flowing "in perfect harmony" from a type and temperament.

One of the earliest of the "classifying" notes, it may serve as a model for some of the later ones, many of which are even more elliptically and confusingly phrased than this one. To paraphrase:

David Hersland, like GS herself, has this quality: that he searches for an ultimate spiritual dependence on an ideal, his way of reaching a satisfactory relation to the universe. Other ways of grasping for finality, such as May Bookstaver's, [may be equally strenuous, but] are bad. [Describe] one like her, though, and [then describe] the way I found this quality in Sarah Stein and in Julihn. As Julihn sees it, it is the "end of his search," and has the "archangel, the mystic quality," which Sarah respects in Julihn [and which Sarah emulates herself] and this eminently spiritual type gives GS the feeling "of the way I explained it to Sally that time, temperament and type and ideal flowing together to a perfect harmony."

Then follows a working note on how this category will be used:

> Hold on to this classification for a passage in which you will describe those of this so-called 'spiritual' type who are not, like May Bookstaver, of the vulgar, but of the 'rare to find.' And in describing David Hersland (as this rare spiritual type), show how it helps him in his struggles against death.

Once the idea for the grouping is set down, GS habitually footnotes further examples [in this case, Mabel Earle and Helen Butterfield], not of the pure type but of similar or only partially successful ones. and their links to other types. When the passion for grouping of this kind possessed her, GS made a separate activity of describing the linking and overlapping areas of groups, and her descriptions of these mergers, sometimes too complicated to set down in language, flowered into the charts and graphs of the Diagram Book.

*

NB11, #14

Olga whom Alfy Dehning tried to seduce tries to reform. Letter of Annette's friend to her.

LK ***Olga:*** The sister of the first Hersland governess. When she returns some two hundred pages later, she is re-baptised Ida Heard, and on a third appearance, she is once more Olga. Subsequently, she is referred to as "Olga who was Ida."

Letter of Annette's friend: One of the letters Annette Rosenshine was obliged to show to GS during her stay in Paris.

*

NB11, #15

~~Alfy~~ Dicky is a friend of Alfred's tries to go in between the two helps him in his politics like Dr. Mayer did Jake.

*

NB11, #16

David had no love affair with Cora Moore. His reallest passion was with Mabel Earle, alia[s] Helen Bayman [Early case?] of Selina friend Helen Butterfield alias Grace Johnston.

LK ***Helen Bayman... Grace Johnston:*** Mabel Haynes' fictional name becomes Helen Lawson rather than, as here, Helen Bayman, and Helen Butterfield's becomes Rena Barkholt rather than Grace Johnston.

*

NB11, #17

Jane Sandys meets her Jane (me) reading in back of car. David his tramping clothes and hat describe Pablo's look at each other the way the big workman and I did. Jane reading Frederick the great. Incident of well dressed flighty kind don't know where he once [sic] to go kindly curly nosed blue eyed young conductor sets him straight, [makes?] them together she [snorts?] into her book, he continues to regard her. old woman gets off he opens gate and examines mechanism, she regards him keep on into the country toward Tarren no remark all the way three little boys leading bearing a bamboo with leaves on top sunshine, country life the Tarren country in the depths of sunshine. Regard each other all the way. She later on I like to play the game with men's eyes when they are full, don't amuse me much to go farther. He remarks as he helps her off. Nice day for walking if it don't rain. He catches sight of book. Say if you are reading that I guess we might as well talk together. Alright, and they go off walking. Describe again Leon's David's gait, me one of our talks about people, me plus evil of his girl describe us together. Lying out in the country arrange mid-night walk, etc. Platonic because neither care to do more. She and he both have their moments but they know each other and it is not worth while. She tells her experiences he never his. She epicurean he with a purpose, she going to the devil or not as she likes like Etta's girl friend he advises her to marry now she has the chance Jack Preiss etc. etc. She begins to go about with May Liddell and her brother Sam gradually drift away from each other, the way David's death affected her but don't deal with her future. Also use with her the incident of Sterne rebuking his model for her rough ways David doing that to Jane and Jane saying I have only ~~known you~~ been reading something for 3 months I will do better after have been at it a year.

AT ***country… in the depths of sunshine:*** Gertrude is describing both California and Fiesole in Italy—a bare, parched countryside like California. There too she had the habit of endless walks, and when Mabel Weeks came over, they did a walking trip all the way from Fiesole to Siena.

arrange mid-night walk: At Radcliffe and Baltimore, everybody went on them. It was a generation when this was always done, everybody going together. Once Gertrude, Mabel Haynes, Emma Lootz and Grace Lounsbury went on one when Grace pulled out a pistol. Gertrude said, Put that fool thing away. But Grace wouldn't. You never know what can happen in a country like this, she said, where blacks are all about. In Baltimore in the Spring, when the whippoorwills were about, they did these walks.

In Cambridge once, Leo Friedman walked Gertrude home, and they hadn't finished their conversation. So, Gertrude walked him home, and then he walked her home. Now we must part, he said, but we will part together.

Sterne rebuking his model: A story Sterne told Gertrude when he had his studio at Saranesca, a year before I came over [i.e., 1906.]

Jack Price: married Miriam, one of the Oppenheimer girls. Gertrude met him at the Oppenheimers. The '[Oppenheimer] household' included Francis Pollack and Leo Friedman. Gertrude liked Francis enormously. He was companionable and cheerful, as a contrast to Leon Solomons.

LK This note, meticulously building an incident never used in the final text, also outlines a complete history of the fictional relations between Jane Sandys/GS and David Hersland/Leon Solomons, beginning in California days (meeting, apparently, on a trolley car in San Francisco, staying on it into the country), developing over time an attachment that carefully skirts sexual intimacy, surrendering to mutual confessionals, and finally, since she "is going to the devil or not as she likes," drifting apart.

[Possible conclusion: that if Leon Solomons was not GS's first attempt at heterosexual relation, he was certainly the last. In NB1, #18, Jane's "going to the devil," her final break with David, is her going off with a woman, to which David's objection, she realizes, is "a moral one only." The implications of the story of Jane are not developed in the final text.]

*

NB11, #18

Sometimes use the Samuel's brothers in relation to French story and Simon and Uncle Sam and then too use Etta's father and his stingy ways.

*

Incident of men not speaking of the cooking but only wines and cigars Vallottons and Etta.

*

Notebook 12

NB12, #1

GS Note on Notebook cover:

Dehnings and Alfred's marriage troubles Alfred lawyer and then politics

*

NB12, #2

Villa [O----]
Frankfort
33 Rue Marlborough
8206 M----}
23265 T----}
15424 M----}

*

NB12, #3

[...] beginning separation failure in profession and change of [direction?] works up to real disillusionment like [?] men.

*

NB12, #4

Aristocrats and bourgeois. Only people sure of their position recognise good manners Leon the kind like ours. Leon worried by his cowardice like breakfast proposition of mine and May

AT ***Aristocrats and bourgeois... May:*** Gertrude's knowing May Bookstaver intimately was in itself an odd thing. She belonged to one of the old Dutch families with enormous position, very much inner circle, home in Newport, and so on. When the New York Steins found it out, they nearly went to pieces. The Bookstavers deplored the whole family, but Gertrude, indifferent to social distinctions, made happen what was otherwise impossible—for this set ever to meet such a one.

good manners: Gertrude's manners were Western, but not Leo's, of whom the New York Steins did not complain. He had a great deal the attitude of the man of the world, courtesy, and so on. Leo gave every evidence of his position and Gertrude didn't. She kept hers well in the dark.

LK ***good manners:*** GS was the despair of her Aunt Pauline and her friends who could do little with her rough-hewn notion of the proprieties. She (and according to this note, Leon Solomons as well) were the Westerners unsettled by the social assurance of their Eastern friends and relatives, who took note of Gertrude's social manners and dirtiness.

*

NB12, #5

Leon stops going too far making suggestions to Bird [,] kind of feeling I had with Sally. in packing, going away.

*

NB12, #6

Mike remarks about Sallie's family to transfer to L.S. and Bird.

*

NB12, #7

Selena
Alfred Martha
Alfred + David
Hersland

*

NB12, #8

Pauline Sandys.

Thats good luck, I mustn't change it. He had all kinds of mystic signs. He must get his left leg into his trousers before his right he must hold his trousers with his opening in a certain twisted curve. He must never think of his trousers before the time comes to take them in his hand. If he thinks of them he must begin again with her dressing reconstructing her world from a new creation.

LK ***Pauline Sandys:*** Text planned for a character in the early version of the novel, altered here for incorporating into characterization of Pauline.

*

NB12, #9

After marriage of Alfred Hersland & Julia & Dave's college life. beginning of bad troubles for old Dave Hersland Alfred thrown on Abe Dehning scenes like Mike and Sally Damn your people.

AT ***scenes like Mike and Sally Damn your people:*** Mike damned her people all the time because they were always in the way. Sally's father had failed in business, and even after Sally married Mike, he had growing children who needed money. Sally also had a brother who was a violinist, and since he was never successful, I'm certain that Mike supported him. Her father was very sentimental, given to exaggeration of the drama he went through. Sally was like him in a way. When he failed in business, he very nobly offered his wife's jewels to his creditors. He offered them as though they were gems, and they were worth only a few hundred dollars. Mike disliked them all about equally, though he disliked Myrtle [Sally's sister] least.

Myrtle was Sally's sister. Mike took her to the Variétés in Paris once, and when it was over, she fell and cut her nose. Gertrude, worried that Mike would be disturbed, fixed her up that night at the rue de Fleurus, and the next morning went immediately to tell Mike what had happened. She deserves everything she gets, responded Mike. When she wears high heels like that, what does she expect. And she was the one he disliked the least. To his mind she was the least objectionable because she was the quietest.

Myrtle's quietness stemmed from the fact the she had nothing to say. She had her own tragedy though. She divorced her husband to marry a scientist whom she met on the boat going back to America, and before they were married, he died. Subsequently, Myrtle remarried her husband. [She looked] a little like a parrot.

*

NB12, #10

Cora Moore and her life and spiritualistic experiences.
David's earliest knowledge after death of his mother before father's troubles mixed up with Cora Moore. Just on verge of troubles, his mother ill, died before the troubles.
~~Sol's wife died 3 years before Sol George's keeping him from Smith College et al. stop his marrying.~~

*

NB12, #11

David with Cora Moore, wandering in search of knowledge. Unitarianism with Mrs. Hildebrand marching in the mountains be thee a good person. At College Arthur Julien learns more wisdom Cora tells him how she does it.
Some relation with Sam & May Lidell. David (Leon's) kind of jokes other friend Alfy. anecdotes given Eastern college life after marriage with Alfred

and Julia. Mabel Earle, Francis Pollak Mabel Haynes et al. Sort of Mrs. O. household beginning of the end for old David Hersland. Alfred thrown on Herman Dehning, like Mike to sally Damn folks. David spends vacation with Alfred & Julia so their close connection begins but he never interferes but only judges.

AT ***Mrs. Hildebrand:*** East Oakland

Sam and May Lidell: California acquaintances.

Sort of Mrs. O. household: Mrs. Oppenheimer was a little mad; she was a Sutro, and they go mad. She was also a great friend of William James, and Gertrude may have met James for the first time at Mrs. Oppenheimer's home in Cambridge. She was a very large woman with a smallish head, and she would chuckle. Adele [her daughter] was very moral, but the craziness in her was merely ugly. Gertrude didn't like her.

David… never interferes but only judges: [Alfred and Julia = Lucius Sternberger and Bird; David (in this passage) = Howard Gans.] When Gertrude first came to New York, the divorce between Lucius and Bird was already on the tapis. Howard would not have interfered between them because he was already determined to stay in the family. He was a great deal at the Stein house when Bird was first married, and he fell in love with her then.

LK ***Eastern college life:*** Paraphrase: During the first years of David's life at Harvard, just after Alfred and Julia are married, use anecdotes [from GS's circle in Cambridge]. This is to be concurrent with the beginning of the end for Mr. Hersland in Gossols.

Sort of Mrs. O. household: The Oppenheimers were living in Cambridge in numbers. Mrs. O. and her husband provided a haven of delight in her home for her children who were or had been at Radcliffe and Harvard with and before GS and her friends: Francis Pollack, Inez Cohen, Mabel Earle among them. Their recreation at the Oppenheimer house was apparently hilarious and loving, suffused with the glow of affections and first crushes out of which permanent friendships and marriages were made. William James knew the group well, gossips in one of his letters to GS about how one of the love affairs in the circle had turned out and asks GS for confirmation "since you being of that group would certainly know."

*

NB12, #12

Hate to see you repeating yourself until your life has lost all meaning.

I was furious and I spoke furiously.

*

Note #62

Then describe Hersland's wife Fanny's people like our grandparents.
[Insert:] woman like said of laughter ~~what~~ and of mirth.
~~then describe old man Bernard and his wife coming over.~~

LK ***... describe Hersland's wife...*** The description of her in MA 43 sets the motif for later, much extended descriptions: "Fanny Hersland all her life was a sweet gentle little woman. Not that she did not have a fierce little temper sometimes in her and one that could be very stubborn, but mostly she was a sweet little gentle mother woman and only would be hurt, not angry, when any bad thing happened to [her children.]"

Fanny's people like our grandparents... Described in MA 43–44. "The little weary weeping mother ... had a foreign husband who was not very pleasant to his children... [T]here was a great deal in him to cause terror in his wife and children.... His wife ... had sorrow from his being so important in religion, and she had sorrow too from her own self in her own religion. It was all sorrow and sadness, and always a trickling kind of weeping that she had every moment in her living.... It was a hard father and a dreary mother that gave the world so many and such pleasant children. ..." [MA 44]

said of laughter and of mirth: Used in MA 44. [Corresponds to NB-MA #56.]

Old man Bernard and his wife coming over: The description of David Hersland's mother and father and their children coming over from Germany [MA 36–41.]

*

Note #60

Describe when and begin the whole history of Martha and George Raymond Weymouth up to separation and then say but this had not yet been consummated. Alfred could talk to his Julia about his sister Martha and her interest in her college. And then he had a young brother he also was of the family to be singular. Describe Leon's appearance favorite and good to his father.

AT ***Leon's appearance:*** There's a photo of him at Yale, but it's nondescript. I have the impression that he was small and slight. There's a photo at Yale of

Francis Pollack too, a charming one.

LK ***begin the whole history… up to separation:*** This note outlines the first plan for what was to become three separate chapters, in sequence, on the careers of Martha, Alfred and David, and suggests a scheme, ultimately not used, for the transitions between those chapters.

To paraphrase: After the separation of Martha and George [= Philip Redfern], the Martha chapter ends. Then say, "but this had not yet been consummated," and go back to the beginning of Alfred's history, recounting his story up to his engagement to Julia Dehning, where the Alfred chapter would end. At the end of that chapter, Alfred could talk to his Julia about his sister Martha and her interest in college (which would underscore the fact that his early history stops some years before the end of the Martha chapter.) And then, in introducing the chapter on David, begin, "he had a younger brother" etc.

Charlotte Perkins Stetson: Charlotte Perkins Stetson Gilman (1860–1935) was a celebrated figure in the women's movement. She began her public work in 1890 lecturing on ethics, economics and sociology. She became especially identified with the labor and women's movement, and as a public speaker, traveled throughout Europe in 1896, 1899, 1904, 1905 and 1913. The fictional Selina/Martha joining her in her travels—as Selina Solomons in fact did—and becoming, as GS puts it, "free and funny a little crazy like she is now" as a consequence of her joining Charlotte Stetson, suggests the distance GS put between her own convictions and enthusiasms and those of the women's movement in the 1900's.

our trip to Etna: GS's life-long habit beginning when she was a child and walking California roads with Leo. At college, in Spain, in the Fiesole hills, she conducted these walks with one or two companions in endless conversation. Both Mabel Weeks and Emma Lootz remembered such excursions with GS. GS responded to them with an exhilaration that displayed her at her warmest, her most affectionate, her wisest, her funniest. Her "novel in the library" in the Radcliffe themes includes an episode of lonely wandering in the hills. It was especially one of the great enthusiasms she shared with Leon Solomons. Leon's father was a noted champion of walking explorations, writing articles for American nature magazines on his camping trips through the Sierras, etc.

*

NB12, #13

Make old Dehning want to marry old governess of Hortense and then Mrs. Meininger mixes up in the game with desire to marry her daughter to George works for both sides. Plain talk all around violent scenes between Dehning and son George. You have no right to bring us up into a good position and ~~and so~~ then disgrace us. Julia can't say anything for she is too dependent tries to quiet things. ~~Before de~~ Mamma always said that it would be so George I remember she was saying she hoped to outlive papa for our sakes. Good man as he was he would need a woman to lead him. Death bed scene.

Milly Dehning after operation she did so much for charity it wasn't right and she wished she could outlive Herman for his children's sake have her say that both to children and husband describe the scenes so it is as real as I can see it the two characters and how they come out as I have so often seen them.

*

NB12, #14

In early troubles David ~~Leon~~ trying to stop Alfred in his bad temper makes no attempt to in business straight dealing keeps Alfred from coming to the country where the family are and he has been staying scene like that at Capon.

~~M~~

~~Ber~~ Bertha there as she was. It is after her marriage she stays with Herman after death of wife and has scene like the kind I had with Sol.

*

NB12, #15

The governess woman like the red headed nurse George very polite to her tries to get her out of the house she had been very sweet. Lord deliver us from sweet little women. Only thing prevented marriage was old Herman's habit of kissing and making love to gay women she did not know that he really meant and George stepped in between and also Julia. Mrs. M. kept waving [?] them as bid [did?] their mother.

*

NB12, #16

Make Julia when the trouble begins economise the way Mike did by taking dishes off the table etc and Alfy swearing David supporting her but advising her not to go it too hard. Trying to make Alfred behave at table before the kind [=child] like Leo would.

AT ***Make Julia … economize the way Mike did:*** Mike had a strong sense of economy, but it wavered charmingly and pleasurably. He was always fixing up everybody's budget to show them how to stay longer. At Fiesole, he used to get a list of books from Gertrude to bring back from Florence when he went down—he always complained that she could read them faster than he could bring them—and once he asked me to go along with him. This was during the first summer I was in Fiesole, when Mike took it upon himself characteristically to keep me within my very limited income. Your whole trouble, he said, is that you've been on a wine diet and now you're on a beer income. And so, my ten-month letter of credit was being doled out by Mike to last for twelve months, and if possible thirteen, and he budgeted me so much for clothes, so much for travel, and so on. But the day we went down to Florence together, he lunched me at the best restaurant in the city. Might as well have a good lunch as not.

*

NB12, #17

What is it you've done. Nothing yet but I have a fighting chance and most of the rest of the world hasn't any.

*

NB12, #18

Read that in the beginning

Perhaps make Hersland family in early childhood like ours go to Europe and then come back and ~~to~~ restlessness of father make them seek fortune in California in Europe Martha at pension Alfred only remembers his French which he is always fond of reading like Leo [-?-] David remembers the tutor and his first scientific sensation the twisted mouth of the tiger as he sat in the bench to take a lesson with his big brother Alfred in his way always very decent to his family. Martha's friends like mine Tillie Brown and one that went bad and one like May Buckminster.

AT ***Hersland family in early childhood like ours:*** Gertrude always used to say that the attitude of a grown person to his childhood was unreliable. But it was just in that way that I came to be useful to her in her thinking because I had no emotion about my childhood. I simply had recollections of it as a fact, what was said, what was done, and so on. This was useful to Gertrude for having a fund of episodes without any coloring.

Gertrude herself didn't remember much detail of her childhood. She remembered Bertha's and Simon's more clearly than her own, what she did for them, and so on. She had a very vigorous physical activity as a child, ran hard and played hard, exhausted herself. Of her mother, she remembered mostly visiting with her, her mother wearing a silk dress and sealskin coat, and Gertrude would nestle into the coat. The smell of it pleased her.

Gertrude was surrounded by too many children to have impressions. She was rarely alone with her mother or with herself. Later she was more solitary and commenced to read by herself and go on excursions with Leo. Then she didn't romp so much.

Leo's memory of his childhood was highly colored by his emotion of being unhappy. Someone used to say that the 'liberal'-minded person was marked always by the sense of his recollecting his own unhappy childhood. When [Lee] Simonson came to Paris, there it was, the same thing, the liberal mind and the recollection of the unhappy childhood. That's how it was for Leo. Mike used to be furious when he heard Leo on his childhood unhappiness. Nothing could have been happier than our childhood, Mike thought, and he felt Leo's way of remembering and talking about it was an insult to their parents, especially their father, in whom Mike especially appreciated the fact that he had left them alone and provided well for them.

[Talking about the Stein's children's way of recalling their childhood, Miss Toklas suddenly embarked on a long reminiscence of her own. She had just finished the interviews with Duncan that week in which she talked mostly about the California days, and they were obviously very much on her mind. But there seemed to be a further, and different, urgency for comparing her own awareness of her childhood with that of the Steins toward theirs. She seemed proud of the difference.]

I had a very austere, unsentimental mother, and my father was indifferent to everything, really, except later to [my brother] Clarence. He was thoroughly indifferent, had no feelings really. With my mother, I was very intimate. Already as a little girl, my mother had said that about pleasing her. [This was a rule of conduct Miss Toklas' mother had given, a perfectly charming and intelligent one for the kind of world and ways of their family, which Miss Toklas had told me about earlier.] That couldn't lead to sentimentality.

My mother's sister was sentimental, but she married and left when I was six, and she and my grandmother, when they came back after my mother's death, struck me when I was older as sentimental, but then I simply resented it. My aunt was sentimental and very self-effacing.

My father would receive letters from his brother and never open them, and he would find them in his pocket when his clothes went to the cleaners, and then he would throw them away. He was devoted to Clarence, and when Clarence volunteered for the tanks in the first war, my father was thoroughly pleased. He thought it showed an interest in modern science and liked it that Clarence didn't go into the stuffy infantry.

There was no unhappiness, in fact, for me to remember. There was my grandfather's depression about his wife's death, but other than that, there was a very deep happiness in the family. My mother was happy, my father adored her, but he accepted her death as a fact. There was no one who could cure her, so he just took it like that.

When I branched out after my mother's death, he would say sometimes, Oughtn't you to see some of your mother's friends, in the sense of some lack of reverence for her. And then I would see them, and it was all right, some I liked, some not so much.

When my brother was born, I was completely put out because it didn't suit my game at all, though I had always wanted a younger brother named Tommy. And when he was born, I said to my mother, Are you going to love him more than me? No, said my mother, you need never think that again. I had no occasion ever to. In fact, when my mother died, my whole anxiety was that Clarence not forget his mother, because he was so young when she died, and I tried hard to maintain it. In a way I didn't, but it turned out fine because he and my father became fast friends then, which was a great relief to me. Otherwise I would have had to be a mother to him and a daughter to my father, which I had never been. I had been a daughter to my mother, and my father was incidental. Though I did get Clarence to make up a grade that he lost during pneumonia, and then even got him to skip one, because I told him if he could do one, he could do the other.

The 'unhappiness' that Gertrude wrote about in 'Ada' was that I had had enough of my grandfather's patriarchal hospitality and the brothers and so on and so on, who all descended on the house, and I was bored with that and wanted out, and so went to Europe.

My grandfather was gently dominated by his wife, but when she died, he had no one to dominate him, and so he began to dominate himself. He filled the house with old men, which his wife would never have permitted. And he got the satisfaction of domination through his other brothers. Mark, he would say harshly. I can hear it in my ears. Yes, Louie, Mark would answer. And that was just what he wanted. He was so occupied with his sorrow and his domination and his sentimental feeling about his wife that he didn't even realize that Clarence didn't belong to him when he no longer did.

There was no 'child psychology' at all in my mother, 'the needs of the child,' and all that. My mother was one of the sponsors of the first free kindergarten in America in the Eighties. It was organized by a group of San Francisco women, and she had classes for children, and I went there until I was ten. She established a school for teachers of kindergarten in the Froebel tradition. I always used to say that I was a granddaughter of Froebel. And I learned a lot there, I must say. I didn't go to a proper school until I was ten.

Clarence and [Miss Toklas' friend] Clare Moore were the most enchanted children ever. Clarence lost it in his college years, though. Clare later founded the new idea of Educational Employment, doing it first with children and then with the aged. There was also my mother's godson, who used to pull my hair and tell me I didn't know anything. I was getting to be a feminist under his influence. It was the time of the Oscar Wilde trial, and I didn't understand why there was a trial or what it was all about, and he said that girls knew nothing.

Nothing could have been happier than my childhood and youth with my mother.

One that went bad: Possibly Cora Moore. She would take Gertrude out in the evenings in East Oakland when Gertrude was fifteen and she seventeen and met men in the street and talked to them. Then she made appointments with the men for later, and she and Gertrude walked on. I don't know whether she got any worse.

LK ***in early childhood… go to Europe:*** Discarded plan for the novel. Refers to GS's three years as an infant in Vienna and Paris with her family, and the family's later settling in California.

Perhaps make Hersland family…like ours go to Europe: Idea was discarded in MA final version but is based on a scramble of memories some of which are recorded in the *ABT* **72–73**. "Martha at pension" recalls GS's and Bertha's boarding at a school in Paris; and "Leon-David remember the tutor and the twisted mouth of the tiger" reflects: "All she [GS] remembers of this is that her brother's tutor once, when she was allowed to sit with her bothers at their lessons, described a tiger's snarl and that pleased and terrified her."

*

NB12, #19

Mabel Haynes episode [?] better leave for French group and Marcousi [?] Simon H. Lord [?] Shelburne goes into French group.

*

Notebook 10

NB10, #1

[...] tangle
~~David & me~~ [?]

*

NB10, #2

Let Alfy as Hersland's friend give history of adventures with Mary [sic] Antoinette

*

NB10, #3

Have decided
~~Hersland oldest~~
Martha oldest. Martha returns home before Hersland leaves home for Bridgepoint beginning troubles.
Martha sees that that I did the man hitting the woman with the umbrella on California St.

LK Corresponds to NB1, #22 and NB9, #13

Martha returns home: Martha returns home to Gossols twice in the original plan. The first return occurred while she was at college. The last one was some years later after her separation from her husband and her suffragette career in California and Europe.

hitting woman on California Street: Corresponds to NB-MA #19 and Note #96

*

NB10, #4

Julia has a little girl dies in fifth year and then they separate Julia then becomes Miss Irwin job put in here the healthy business smith college generally satire on schools. family objects but mother is dead by that time introduce her passion for little babies, the little girl to have history like Robert.

AT ***history like Robert:*** [Robert Gans, Bird's son] was just a little boy when Gertrude was writing this. His grandmother [Gertrude's Aunt Pauline] used to say he was exactly like his father [Bird's first husband, Louis Sternberger.] After the divorce, Bird got both children and raised them both very badly. They couldn't have been more unsuccessful. Marion Sternberger later got very much interested in Nina Auzias [a prostitute, who became Leo's devoted wife] after some years when she got loose in Europe and on her own for the first time.

LK ***Healthy business... Smith College...Julia has little girl:*** [cf. NB-MA #11]

*

NB10, #5

~~Marth~~ Martha ends up by cicling [sic] around Europe to rouse up the women to sense of what they should be.

LK Corresponds to NB6, #9

*

NB10, #6

Me Jane Sandys
Pauline Manders
Pauline Sandys
Jane Sand~~ys~~ s
nom de plume.

AT The name Sands came from a prominent Boston family. Gertrude met them at Miss Ethel Sands' house in Paris.

LK GS again settles on "Jane Sands" as her nom de plume.

*

NB10, #7

Dickie
~~Jimmie~~ Wolkins
Alfy

*

NB10, #8

Later stages when Julia gets her job the etching and print Japanese stage.

AT ***Etching and print Japanese stage:*** Gertrude gave her good ones [Japanese prints] away as gifts and the plainer ones passed on to Leo. Leo gave me four or five of the good ones, and I was flattered by the attention but disturbed by what to do with them. It was the first of Leo's gifts, so I hung on to them for years and finally gave them away as gifts too. I had sold my own prints before leaving San Francisco, where already the good ones were the only ones one held on to.

Sarah still had Japanese but even more Chinese pieces—Jaehne's influence—but prints, in the face of Matisse, were long since gone. Bird might have had one Japanese print—as Julia—or if Gertrude gave it to her, it must have been a good one.

[As to other exotic holdings:] Mike bought five Coptic print cloths and gave Gertrude one. When she got bored with it, she asked Ernie Keyser if he wanted it. He said yes, but then he looked at it and asked, 'Say, Gertrude, what's the matter with it?' Ernie Keyser was a Mike with less force, though much prettier than Mike, a darling, with wit and a nice humor.

*

NB10, #9

I wish her a dollar and ~~fifty~~ forty five cents worth of misery; sure I do, Don't be of a foolishness what do you mean. I don't want her to have a whole lot just (David)/ one dollar and forty five cents thats all I can afford to buy her just now. I am kind of poor you know.

*

Note #186

27 Rue de Fleurus

My dear Bird,

I have just received your letter. Since you apparently do not understand the fundamental wrong of which I accuse you there is indeed nothing further for me to say

Sincerely yours

Gertrude Stein.

LK See **GS First Writing .44ff.** for controversy. Letters of GS and Leo in Paris to Bird and Howard in Baltimore quoted. Texts from GS letters quoted below in Notes #191, #187 and #188.

*

Note #191

Now, Bird just one word to greet you as you arrive so as to avoid our falling into any new misconstructions. I insist absolutely that you read and read with care, with as much care as if it were a brief in your ~~cause~~ case my long letter to Howard. Don't skip ever any part because it hurts. You owe it to me to endure that hurt, to read that letter and to read it again until you understand it and to do it within a month after your return. You must read that letter without ~~to yourself~~ defending yourself to yourself. You must get my facts before you begin to think of your rights and wrongs. You must understand thoroughly and completely why I wrote as I did, that it is still a question... [Note: Page missing?] in them. When you have done so of course tell me whatever it is that you feel about them. Leo tells me to say to you that he will be very glad to hear your...

*

Note #187

I have just received your letter. Since you apparently ~~cannot~~ ~~do not~~ do not understand the fundamental ~~quality~~ wrong of which I ~~have~~ accuse~~d~~ you, there is indeed ~~there is~~ nothing further for me to say.

*

Note #188

I have just received your letter It is evident that you do not understand the fundamental proposition involved in this whole ~~cont~~ affair but it is useless for me to go into it any further at present

Sincerely yours
Gertrude.

*

Note #189

GS personal notes on controversy with Bird:

Mike wrote in January
about April 8 my first letter
April 19 terrible letter by me
This letter from Bird
will write to Mike soon
April 9.
Her letters to me & Mike
April 18—10
28

*

Note #192

Roche, seconding Leo's negative opinion of the Three Lives *manuscript, wrote to Gertrude, and elicited this opinion:*

My dear Roche

I have read your letter with care and I am quite certain, ~~dare I say it that your diet is not doing you any too much good.~~ that you have not said anything important.

My dear friend you ought to be able to work more in understanding so that you come to realize that when a repetition has definite perceivable meaning for one that, ~~that~~ my being an artist, is its justification. I have not had the experience you speak of. Some who have most keenly appreciated my work particularly this last work have known neither me nor the people of whom I wrote ~~and have come to know me in consequence.~~ Do not fall into the masculine habit of getting an impression and then proving your ~~thor~~ impression to be a construction by picking out the things you need for it. I am dissapointed in you but I have been very grateful to you and still am

Sincerely yours
Gertrude Stein

*

Note #209

My dear Pritchard,

Thanks very much for your article. You have very admirably [word?] a clearly American point of view in the Prich language a thing I can just now very completely appreciate.

Alw______
Gtde Stn

LK Pritchard arrived in Paris in 1907. [A. Barr 105]: "The Englishman closest to Matisse" during this [c1908] and later years was the esthetician and ex-musicologist MSP… In 1910 he introduced to Matisse the young writer Georges Duthuit, later to become the historian of fauvism, and Matisse's son in law.

*

NB10, #10

Don't be of a foolishness. I wrote to you exactly what I thought, I have not changed my mind. I think I was and am right in the matter but I ~~certainly~~

don't want to cause you any unhappiness and I certainly undoubtedly will be glad to see you in Paris Canton Bridgepoint this winter in case you and ~~Dolene~~ [Knowles?] decide to come over

Sincerely yrs
Grtrude Sten

LK ***Don't be a foolishness…*** Draft of letter, a reply to Etta Cone's letter of Aug 22, 1909 in which Etta had written tearfully about her brother Mosey's death and about GS's "unfairness" in her response to the news.

*

NB10, #11

Mary Cooke big brother like unto [?] mixture big [?] Valloton boy [?] & Louis Stein meets [?] Mary C wants her to marry Hannah Ruth.

LK ***Mary Cooke:*** [Corresponds to NB-MA #14]

*

NB10, #12

I love em noble like that.
very tight and very fat.

*

NB10, #13

Work up Leon young David's Graham crackers and Mr. Greenhagen's diets for all they are worth. Also Bird's cures taken at home latest improved.

AT ***Mr. Greenhagen:*** Alma Greenhagen was one of the governesses, and Mr. Greenhagen, the candy manufacturer whom she married.

Bird's cures… latest improved: I guess that was one of her 'culturines.' Others were a gas log in the fireplace, radiators concealed in the walls. These came after her break with the first phase, which was her first marriage. The first marriage was False Gothic, and the second pure Italian Renaissance. Didn't she know the Steins?

It was the Mike Steins who started the pure Italian Renaissance furnishing of homes. Sally wanted more and more to get it for others to make her own [the first collection] the more outstanding. Mike did it because he really loved the furniture and helped everyone who wanted it to get the best that money could buy. How many homes in America have it now because of the Mike Steins!

*

NB10, #14

Interesting case red headed red-bearded man with fiery eyes sticking his tongue out like [inten-ouns?] Saw him second time scared, less scared because though he followed he did not wait. Remembered he was like Variot, he could have done that too. Scare fell off then.

*

NB10, #15

Must make my hero grow into realisation of B. ~~though~~ as I did of Sally, through experience, quarrels in the summer, that epoch making for me conversation with Harriet about her when I explained her after Harriet had given me her version which was alright except the bottom and then one with Leo about her originality.

AT [NB10, #15, (1–2)]

realization of… Sally through… quarrels in the summer… conversation with Harriet: These [quarrels] were in Fiesole, and they could have been on any subject. Sally was frequently inspired to see things wrongly, and Gertrude probably simply brought her down to earth. Harriet would probably give examples from Sally's past. Harriet knew Sally from the time they were in high school together. Sally had always been condescending to Harriet and had the air when she was with her of giving her a moment of her time. But despite despising Harriet, she was also jealous of her.

Harriet alternated between admiring Sally's ability to achieve what she wanted and scorning the means she used, as well as Sally's recital of it. Harriet's wit occasionally pointed at Sally, and when she went home, she had occasion to use it when she recalled Sally and her life of rapture.

Sally… her originality: Leo would talk on the general impression of how Sally had treated his theories. She would amplify them in the wrong direction. That was characteristic of Sally. She was wonderful to talk to until she began to explain you to yourself, and then it became unbearable. Gertrude and Leo bore her no animosity. They would speak of this side of her as a cold fact. To Gertrude, Sally was the best sister-in-law she could have hoped for because she was the least interferesome in the world. In those [early] days, Gertrude could talk out what she was working on [in the Notebooks and in the novel] to Sally because there was no one else to tell, and Sally was infinitely flattered until Gertrude stopped, and then she bore Gertrude a bit of animosity. Gertrude had in fact actually shown Sally the draft of the first novel, *Q.E.D.*

*

NB10, #16

Harriet's resemblance to Nelly Joseph & Marie Gruenhagen. Not Nelly but Harriet and May have greed this incident about Maria's wages & doctor's bill enormously significant.

*

NB10, #17

In life of Alfy lay stress upon the fact that the eldest son is not the eldest child and the inevitable disaster of that lack of training in dominance.

LK ***eldest son is not the eldest child:*** Used in MA 517–518; also in 540.

*

NB10, #18

Mabel Linker
Marie H. Maxworthing
Alice Bwaddus
Louise ~~Klohn~~ Krohn
Bertha Hinks,
Grace Maxworthing

LK ***Mabel Linker... Grace Maxworthing:*** Tentative list of fictional names for the servants and governesses, "Mrs. Hersland and the Servants" chapter, MA 150–288. "Mabel Linker" (introduced MA 205) becomes the companion of the servant "Mary Maxworthing" (introduced MA 203) and "Louise Krohn" (introduced MA 241) becomes the second governess employed by the Herslands. The other names were not used. In their place, the names of the other "servant girls" in the Final Draft are Lillian and Cecilia Rosenhagen [MA 193, 196.]

*

NB10, #19

Probably make of ~~one of~~ the first governess's sister an instrument. 2nd governess Louise Krohn. 3 Mary Gruenhagen with family just as it was.

LK ***first governess's sister and instrument:*** Planning Note, MA 205, introducing "Olga" as the governess's sister. She is reintroduced [MA 236–238] in relation to her sister's story.

Louise Krohn: "The tall blonde foreign American" woman who marries a baker, is introduced MA 241; her description ends MA 248; In the Notebooks, she is also called Louise Frohn.

Mary Gruenhagen: Called Madeleine Wyman in the Final Draft. She is introduced on MA 249. Her story, one of the longest and most detailed in the novel, ends on MA 283. The Gruenhagen family "just as it was" is apparently described from recollection of an Oakland family for whom there appears to be no discernible information.

*

NB10, #20

Remember Marie is gaily not afraid of robbers and that she whines impotently and musically it is her attack so go on now to the finish.

LK ***Marie is gaily not afraid… whines impotently… it is her attack…*** Theme of "gayety" in Mary Maxworthing is introduced in MA 208 and elaborated in MA 227: "Mary Maxworthing had gayety in living…. She had very little fear in her…. injured and angry feeling in her was part of such attacking living as she had in her…."

*

NB10, #21

She is exactly of the family of May and Miss Mars. Remember the woman [?] saleswoman 3 months along. Make Mary Maxworthing betrayed to doctor. Make her a saleswoman no [too?].

LK ***…exactly of the family of May and Miss Mars:*** May [Bookstaver] and Miss Mars stood in special relation to "instrument natures," which were the major subject of GS's study during the writing of the "Servants" chapter. At least ten references in the Notebooks are devoted to their placement within the framework of "instrument" natures, and the character of Mary Maxworthing is placed definitively in their "family" both in this note and in NB-C #12.

In the earliest note on the pair, NB-A #9a, GS sees Miss Mars and Marie [=May] as having "real sensibility and gayety, when tragic become hard the type of some of the French queens," and in deference to this refinement of their sensibility, promises not to use them in the novel as "servant" types. Gradually, over several weeks of rumination, this view of the pair is altered, and they do indeed end up as the model for the servant, Mary Maxworthing. The change occurs in NB-B #1, when GS sees the "lyrical" side of their sensibility as having no "real sense of the beauty of the object… only the emotion of it," and NB-B #3(1) further diminishes the status of their "lyrical sensibility," because it does not even have the "flavor" of that sensibility, only "the green acid even though pleasant fruit of it." Then, in NB-B #4, this lesser view of the pair is confirmed: "Miss Mars & Marie always a little hard but never to queens to princesses rather, their gayety & sensibility is of that kind." Their relation to the reactive side of "instrument" nature having become so tenuous, and its quality so minimal, the ultimate question becomes, to what extent are they examples of "instruments" at all? The solution is arrived at in NB-B #22, the note in which "instrument nature" is fully defined. In that definition, May is classified as an exception: "the instrument who is not instrumented but exists in itself," so much so that the pair's representative in the novel, Mary Maxworthing, is on the borderline of types, an "independent dependent" who nevertheless has a fundamentally reactive nature which seems to be its own opposite in her relations with her friend, Mabel Linker.

... three months along. Make Mary Maxworthing betrayed to doctor.... saleswoman too. The story of Mary Maxworthing's pregnancy, visit to doctor and decision to have an illegitimate baby is told in MA 212, and is completed in MA 222. In the final text, she is not "betrayed" to doctor, he simply examines her; and she is a seamstress, not a saleswoman.

*

NB10, #22

governess later married the baker.
You fat talk so much.

AT ***governess... married the baker:*** The German governess married a chocolate manufacturer in San Francisco afterward. The Stein children used to go there for chocolate.

LK ***Governess later married the baker:*** Used in MA 241, 243.

married the baker... fat talk: Used MA 247: "Later when she was married to the baker, when she was larger then and a little grimy, [Mr., Hersland] liked to see her, he would stop by at her shop where she was sitting... and he would eat a cake there and ask her how she was getting on...."

*

NB10, #23

Late[r] history of Olga full description of her in relation to Martha & Alfred

LK ***Olga... in relation to Martha & Alfred:*** When "Olga" returned to the pages of the MA "in relation to... Alfred," GS for some reason wanted to change her name. But rather than thumb back through her ms. pages to change Olga's name in the first instance, she rechristened her—double oversight— "Olga who was Ida" MA 590, later referring to he as "Ida" plain [MA 591.] GS's intention in her earlier Note [NB10, #20] to make "Olga/Ida" an "instrument" is borne out in the later passage [MA 591] in which she describes her "nervous sexual asking to be object of all loving," and on the other hand, "passively living," both modes part of her "instrument nature."

*

NB10, #24

Make Olga sister of the first governess one of the people Hersland in his old age wanted to marry and to use. She had an affair with Alfy, who tried to seduce her, young David tried to reform her. Bring her in as a complete Olga.

LK [Notes on "Olga" in NB10, #23, NB9, #17, NB11, #14, NB8, #16, NB-*C #1, Note #85 and Note #92.]

*

NB10, #25

Make the independent depence [sic] and dependent independence attacking and resisting themselves [?] like Martha Hersland for one and Brenner for another.

LK ***Independent dep[en]dence and dependent independence attacking and resisting:*** The two "kinds" are first defined in MA 163, in terms of women's "ways of loving," but a more extended and more detailed definition is offered in MA 165–167, where the division of the two "kinds" becomes the central distinction of types universally. This note anticipates the initial analysis of Martha Hersland in the opening pages of the "Martha" chapter [MA 398], in which she is "placed" among the independent dependent kind and described in terms of the "kind's" paradigmatic character, GS's sister Bertha.

*

NB10, #26

Give Mr. Hersland's educational ideas and feeling about his children and his feeling for Madeleine and hers about him fully then and later, and about the children a little then Mrs. to her and her to her and then relation and trouble with Mrs. Weiman. Just suggest Weiman family the Hersland's did not then know them much, and then Madeleine's marriage the children's feeling then and later and so to Martha.

LK ***Mr. Hersland's educational ideas… and so to Martha:*** A comprehensive Planning Note for the end of the "Servants" chapter, MA 244–285.

educational ideas and feelings: MA 244.

feeling for Madeleine: Fully described, MA 258.

a little then Mrs. to her: MA 248.

and her to her: MA 253, l. 12ff.

and trouble with Mrs. Weiman: MA 261.

Just suggest Weiman family: MA 260.

Madeleine's marriage the children's feelings: MA 262.

*

NB10, #27

Nov. 23 (100 frs.
Dec. 8 (100)
Dec. 16 (100)*

Notebook MA

Notebook MA is entitled, on its front cover in GS's hand, "The Making of Americans." The Notebook houses a miscellany of notes from different periods over the years 1906 to 1908. The most recent anticipate concluding the novel's narrative, in preparation for the new and final draft to be focused on GS's "new thing," her psychological typology. But there is still a compendium of First Draft notes not gathered for current use but either for the pleasure of recollection or for the pleasure of discard. Many of the earlier notes contemplated expanding already-written text for Drafts One and Two, ("enlarge this"), and it's conceivable that most of this Notebook's notes are aimed at the same task; but some, pertaining to the earliest entries of all—before the coherent writings were begun—appear to have no particular reason for expansion. Notes for plot and characters drawn out of recollections of GS' familiars continue, but the direction of these entries gradually focus more explicitly on development of the "system."

*

NB-MA #1

Hersland (old man) died long after his wife and David. Sort of finish up the whole story with the last of that older ~~generation~~ generation, life like Raymond's father trying to make it up. David dead Alfred married to Minnie and fairly successful at Bridgepoint and Martha (like Selina & her mother) takes care of him to the end. Beethoven symphony

Clang repeated clang

Wife Fanny died before the crash.

*

NB-MA #2

David Hersland's father.

Pa + Raymond's father.

fails in business, loses wife before failure, while Alfred is marrying Julia, and young David going to Bridgepoint to college.

*

NB-MA #3

Martha has come home after George Weymouth left her. She is left to take care of old Hersland after his failure and in his old age. Hersland feels toward Martha as our daddy did toward Bertha (coffee).

Fanny Hersland his wife. little gentle woman always goes in closet to see Alfred's clothes while he is in the East loves Alfred the best. He comes back to see her before she dies. Death like Mothers, Martha takes care of her Martha's delusions of pure [contin?]. All this happens after Martha left by Weymouth. Make Martha's history in regard to Fanny Hersland like Bertha's.

Later changed. In final version, Mrs. Hersland dies before Martha's marriage.

*

NB-MA #4

Herman [= Henry] Dehning have [Ulysses S.] Grant's kind of practical knowledge of men but as Grant failed with Robert E. Lee so Dehning with the 2 Herslands.

Corresponds to Ms Note #3

AT Gertrude's interest in Grant came early in her life and was passionate and perpetual. He based his strategy, she said, on the fact that he had known all the Southern generals at West Point, since the seven Southern leaders were all classmates of his at the same time. When you put that against Lee's throwing his people into the Civil War that he knew he couldn't win, the difference between them is plain. That was Gertrude's contention against Lee, that he knew what he was doing and saw the end. Probably in the early days when I was here, she reread the Grant memoirs, and so her interest in him was again alive.

Lloyd Lewis was the author of a Grant biography. Gertrude and he got on wonderfully because of their mutual enthusiasm for Grant. In fact, Gertrude wanted to collaborate with him on a book about Grant. She always wanted to collaborate and would get caught up in the plan of it, and it would die a natural death later. When Lewis was working on it, I found a photo for him and sent it to include in the book. He made a nice reference to Gertrude in the finished biography.

*

NB-MA #5

Mrs. Dehning died 3 years before Herman Dehning. George's keeping him from marrying like Mike + Mrs. Meininger and others acting. George and Julia and Hortense worked on by George, Herman died suddenly it was after that Julia became Dean separation had taken place before after death of little girl it was before Deaning and just after death of father Julia split

with David. Their connection lasted through the divorce broke after David took his job in the West. whole
experience like mine, in general detail.

*

NB-MA #6

Herman Dehning. Uncle Sol dies like pa after 3 years of trying to marry after death of his Miss Jenny. Stopped by Mrs. Meininger and George.

*

NB-MA #7

Jenny Dehning, Aunt Pauline, dies of operation appendicitis tell about how she speaks of Herman's remarriage both to him and to her children.

*

NB-MA #8

Summarizing the compositions of the children in the two families:

	Hersland	
Alfred	Martha	David
Mike + Lucius	Selina + Mrs.Hodder + Bertha Bette of Dehning family as it turns out.	Leon & me, cousins + Louis Sternberger
	Dehning	
Julia	George	Hortene
Bird + Ella	Fred + Leo Friedman + William Temple Franklin	Hortense Ruth Friedman + Milzeiner + Amy

AT ***Lucius:*** Solomons. Lucius and Adele were friends of Sarah's in San Francisco, and Leon the college friend of Gertrude in Cambridge. But she did not know him in San Francisco before she went to Radcliffe. During the year she lived there [after Oakland]—she left when she was seventeen—she knew practically no one except her father's San Francisco friends. Gertrude and the other children hated his friends—they came to the house and ate the fruit and who were they. [Miss Toklas did not know Seline Solomons.]

Ella Milzeiner: A very untidy, temperamental wife of a painter who did

Gertrude's portrait. She was the daughter of a woman who was a pioneer really, and who was a textile designer. Ella Milzeiner was the daughter. She lived in the Campagne Premier in a little nest of studios with her two children and left before I came to Paris.

LK ***Alfred = Mike + Lucius + Louis Sternberger:***

Louis Sternberger: Sternberger [–1947] was the son of Robert Sternberger, a banker and member of the Stock Exchange. It is the story of his marriage to Bird and their later court battles and divorce that were to be at the center of GS's novel. Like his counterpart in the novel, Alfred Hersland, Sternberger, as the newspaper account put it, "devoted a considerable time to painting and music," rather than to following his father's and father-in-law's footsteps in the world of business and finance. After his marriage to Bird in 1888, he settled into the residence in West 71st Street that Bird's father Solomon Stein provided for them as a wedding gift. The marriage foundered seven years later when the couple separated, and Sternberger brought an action against his father-in-law "for the recovery of $50,000 damages for alienation of his wife's affections." Louis won the privilege of visiting his children Robert and Marion for eight years until curtailed by Bird's counter-action for divorce in November 1903.

After "one of the most desperately fought actions between father and mother over their offspring that has ever figured in the courts of this city," divorce was finally granted in November 1904. Successive lawyers in the case included Joseph H. Choate, who relinquished to become Ambassador to England, and Elihu Root, who relinquished to become a member of President Theodore Roosevelt's cabinet.

The last of Bird's successions of the lawyers was Howard Gans. For a time, he was assistant district attorney in New York, and it was he who employed a private detective to trail Sternberger and a Mrs. Allison to a Utica Hotel in 1901. Gans effectually displaced GS as Bird's mentor and confidante, having fallen in love with Bird during her legal battles with her husband. They were eventually married July 9, 1908, four years after Bird's divorce.

Martha/Selina & Mrs. Hodder & Bertha: Martha Hersland is compounded of Bertha's dumb passivity, Mrs. Hodder's unfortunate marriage to Alfred Hodder (already treated in *Fernhurst*,) and Selina Solomons' career in the suffragette movement (for Martha's life after her divorce.)

David Leon & me, cousins Bette of Dehning family: Paraphrased: David [Hersland, who is compounded of] Leon [Solomons] and GS, to be cousins of Bette [Stein, wife of GS's uncle Leb] as it turns out [since Bette is to be] of the Dehning family.

David/Leon & me: Leon Solomons [1873–1900], the most brilliant member of the distinguished Solomons family in San Francisco, became next to Leo the most important man in GS's life. After taking his Master's degree in Chemistry at the University of California in 1894, "he went on to Cambridge," writes his closest friend, Arthur Lachman, "specializing first in mathematical physics and after switching to psychology." It was his interest—and his family's interest—in Spiritualism that led to his experiments in automatic writing with Lachman at the Harvard Psychological Laboratory. When Lachman left Harvard, Solomons invited GS to continue the experiments with him, both as subject and as collaborator. It is clear from the Notebooks that GS was in love with Solomons, but the degree of their involvement, as several entries suggest, was tempered by mutual anxieties, and finally ended when GS apparently "floated off" with a woman student. Three published articles resulted from their collaboration, "Normal Motor Automatism" (*Harvard Psychological Review*, Sept 1896), "Cultivated Motor Automatism" (*Harvard Psychological Review*, May 1898) and "The Saturation of Color" Solomons left Harvard for a year to return to the University of California, but in 1897, returned to complete his doctoral dissertation on "The Fusion of Touch Sensations," approved in May 1898. He taught then at the University of Wisconsin, but in 1900 he died, according to GS of cancer following an operation, but his death may have been caused by infections contracted in the laboratory.

In the final version of the novel, GS not only conflates the characters of Solomons and herself, but adds details from her brother Leo, who by the time of the writing of the David Hersland chapter in 1911 effectively displaces Leon Solomons as primary model.

Julia/Bird + Ella Mielziner. Bird Stein [1868–1944], GS's first cousin, was her closest New York family connection. During the years of Bird's marriage, separation and divorce (1888 to 1904) GS for many of those years (1892 to 1904) was visiting New York from Cambridge and Baltimore and then from Paris, but, to her mind, affecting Bird's outlook ethically and aesthetically. By 1906, GS's accumulating resentments against Bird and the New York Steins, and her disappointment over her failure to "uplift" Bird, led to Gs's choosing a trivial occasion to explode in anger over Bird's "behavior," and effectively brought an end to their close friendship. The characterization of Julia in the first draft, reasonably sympathetic, was qualified in the later draft, as the Notes suggest, to account for Bird's "lying when in a hole," and "not knowing that she lies."

Ella McKenna Mielziner, journalist, wife to Leo Mielziner, a prominent portrait painter, and mother of Jo, who was to become one of the foremost theatrical scene designers in the U.S. Mrs. Mielziner was Paris correspondent for Vogue until 1910 when the family moved back to New York but were frequent visitors to the rue de Fleurus in the early days of Leo's and GS's residence.

George [Dehning] Fred + Leo Friedman + William Temple Franklin: George [Dehning] conflates Fred Stein, Leo F. and W.T. Franklin.

Fred Stein, first cousin to Leo and GS, spent two of his four years at Harvard in close association with Leo, and in 1895, the year of Fred's graduation, they went together around the world, Uncle Sol's gift to his son and nephew. By 1906, Fred had already become a senior partner in Sol's woolens firms and, with Howard Gans and Alfred Hodder, had been active in Jerome's crusade against Tammany Hall in 1904, when they worked successfully to elect Jerome to district attorney.

Hapgood, when in New York, was a part of the Fred Stein—Jerome—Hodder circle, active in civic enterprise and reform of New York Tammany Hall corruption. His estimate of Fred is at variance with GS's:

"He lacks entirely the spectacular and advertising and meretricious splendor of his cousin Gertrude... and the exaggerated intellectual self-consciousness of his cousin Leo. But he has helped many important civic enterprises and never has diminished his helpfulness by demanding the limelight."

But the middle-class virtues and civic pieties of Fred and Bird Stein were the very ones GS in principle applauded and in fact despised.

Leo Victor Friedman, AB Harvard, 1895, and then a medical student in Boston. For the next several years, he was a close and enthusiastic member of the "Oppenheimer Clan" to which GS, as a student boarder at Mrs. Oppenheimer's, also belonged. Leo F., a devoted friend to GS, was grateful to her for the pleasure and sometimes hilarity of their outings, for her sympathetic advice, and for mentoring his education in the arts. The incidents planned for George's experience as a doctor came from Leo F's internship at Boston General Hospital.

William Temple Franklin [1760–1825], the grandson of Benjamin Franklin, published the first edition of Franklin's works (1817–19, 6 vols.) long after his death. Nearly all of Franklin's papers were bequeathed to his grandson, "but Temple did not take reasonable care of them and used them rather indiscriminately, eliminating things of great importance." [Encycl. Britt., 14th ed., vol. 9, p.694.] But Temple did complete Franklin's Memoirs to the time of his death, and possibly from these writings, GS fixed on a characterization of him useful for George Dehning.

Hortense/Ruth Friedman—Amy: Ruth Miriam Friedman, Leo Friedman's sister, who lived with him in Cambridge. In the year after GS left for Johns Hopkins (1898–99) Ruth enrolled as a special (non-degree) student at Radcliffe. GS knew her as one of the Oppenheimer clan while at Cambridge and during her later visits from Baltimore.

Amy (Stein) Hamburger, the younger sister of Bird and Fred Stein, who in the summer of 1904 was reported by Bird to be doing all the housekeeping at the Steins' summer home in Long Island, and doing it "with all her heart, soul and strength… She must dream housekeeping… Gracious, mother must be proud of her." Amy married Jonas Hamburger in 1905 and joined the Stein-Keyser-Bachrach-Bergman-Hamburger extended clan in Baltimore.

Both Ruth and Amy, self-effacing, hardly-there younger sisters, are combined to produce the MA's first-draft Hortense's "upgrazing sweetness." Hortense disappears in the final draft.

*

NB-MA #9

Hannah Hammel cousin Dehning's Bertha goes to them at sixteen and after Julia's marriage. Experience with Hermann Dehning like mine with S[ol].

*

NB-MA #10

Friends of Alfy Hersland

Dickie Wolkins (Alfy)

Dickie

Minnie Wehn (Minnie Jake's)

Martha's friends

Menda Herzel (Cora Moore)(really David's friend)

(Cora Hildebrandt & George.)

(Mrs. Herzel)

All this commences after mother's death and beginning of failure. David interested in it) goes to seances [sic].)

David Hersland's friends.

Olf Rudeiner

(Julien + Arthur Lackman

\+ knew him in California college)(he makes jokes and religion)

Menda Herzel (Cora Moore)

(and the women who act as friends and mentors to them [both]

Helen Lawson (Mabel Earle)
both mixture Sally and Mrs. O[ppenheimer]& daughter
(Dora Sachs) Dora
Pauline Sandys (me + bad un)
Black) some kind of relations of Rudeiner not love not
Harriet Margraine (Mabel Haynes opposition only uneasiness).
Rena Barkholdt (Helen Butterfield)

LK ***Cora Moore:*** From *Everybody's Autobiography*:

> When I was just beginning high school I knew a girl whose name was Cora Moore….Her mother believed in spiritualism, so perhaps did my father anyway they both believed in prophecy….Cora Moore said why should her mother go to another spiritualist when she could be one and so she and I used to go together when she was one….Cora decided to do it too. [EA 99–100]

In the novel, Cora Moore was to be used for the portrait of the occultist with whom both Mr. Hersland and the young David take up for a time after the mother's death. [On Cora Moore, see AT Note for NB11, #4]

Mrs. O.+ daughter: Mrs. Oppenheimer and Adele Oppenheimer. Tight circle of Radcliffe and Cambridge students in Mrs. Oppenheimer hospitable home, a circle of which GS was a delighted member. Adele Oppenheimer close to GS but in later years, according to E. Lootz, Ben Oppenheimer had developed "a violent antipathy toward Gertrude; gags at the mention of her name." Antipathy, fortunately, from any of the Oppenheimer's was absent during GS's Radcliffe days. [See AT note in NB12, #11. on "Mrs. O. household," LK note in NB12, #11]

*

NB-MA #11

Julia (has no friends)

Dissertation on crude virginity and education when Julia gets her job (dean) after David's death. (assistant dean girl's college.)

Children element make atmosphere as between Julia & Alfy but do not state.

LK Cf. Smith College Note #9 on "Life." The "dissertation" was not used fully in the final version, but what is left of it is used in the earliest description of Julia Dehning

> Perhaps she was too near to the old world to ever attain quite altogether that crude virginity that makes the American girl safe in all her liberty. Yes the American girl is a crude virgin and she is safe in her freedom. [MA 15]

The passage is a revision of the text in the early draft of MA:

> Perhaps she was born too near the old world to attain quite the completeness of crude virginity for underneath her very American face body and clothes were seen now and then flashes of passionate insight that lit up an older and a hidden tradition. [*Fernhurst* 146]

*

NB-MA #12

George. Difference between George and David (opposition) (Leo & Fred) George ~~efficient~~ efficient in the world, inefficient alone, David the other ways, world ethics (personal ethics) opposition.

*

NB-MA #13

Hortense, afterwards nursing father surprised she does it so well afterwards marries Sterne who helps George to prevent the old man getting married a downtown doctor, like Jacob. Still does her drawing for her George wants her to go on with it. Hortense like the sweet grandmother. (Ruth Friedman)

*

NB-MA #14

Hannah Hammel cousin comes later to the household married by Frederick Garblin (Jay) a modest nice young man according to Herman Dehning. Child of Herman Dehning's sister Bertha. Describe her life as like Bettie (Hattie Stein's mother.) Hannah mixture of Hattie & Bertha. Mary Cooke to be a friend of Hannah Hammel's in Hannah's home before death of parents and Dehnings take her. Attitude toward her as Bertha's would be in such changed circumstances Mary and her mother's opinion of her after all they done for her when she had nobody else. Mary's family desire to have brother marry Bertha who has a little money. Brother mixture of that eldest brother of Mary Cooke Charley Cooke and Heidelberger Mike).

*

NB-MA #15

David Hersland.
bad hand-writing father tries to make it better sends him to writing school has great hope of him. David affectionate kisses his father's bald head spot. Alfy always proud of and good to David.

David's constantly surrounded with the thought of death, puts it away from him then endeavors to embrace it to dead in a [death?] to conquer it almost never quite.

Habitual sense of justice in David makes possible the relations continuing with Julia and Alfy at once.
David's death (I am very nervous like Simon M.)

The world is such a very beautiful world why does one have to be so homely always in it (said by one of David's girls not sure which yet) (Cora Moore) Cupid's wife

*

NB-MA #16

Write essay about feeling strong of death as result of out of doors in Italian or Californian garden country. Characteristic of David and Pauline Sandys.

Corresponds to Ms Note #148. Theme is used (in the manner of the last chapter) in MA 801.

*

NB-MA #17

Use the 29 year old outburst from other book to apply to David before he goes out West 2 years later he dies.

Pauline says to him. How I hate this fool kind of talk about nature and voices of birds so much sweeter than humans, its not. And nature never deceives don't it just, it don't do anything else, its all made out to deceive us if we see it that way bah!

Use that time in the J.H.W. gardens when I got sick and faced flunking my exams.

AT ***29 year old outburst from the other book:*** F. Scott Fitzgerald, with his classic beauty, visited Gertrude on his thirtieth birthday, and he said to us, I'm thirty today and it's horrible. It's a fact, said Gertrude, that you can't avoid. But once past thirty, it's all right again. —Was it for you? —Yes. —What am I going to do? Go back home and write a novel. And when it was finished, he sent it to Gertrude with a note: This is the novel you asked for. Gertrude had gotten over it all, the adolescence and the twenty-nine years old, but she hated her own past and hated to go back to it. She never opened the package of these Notebooks or showed them to me.

LK ***29 year old outburst from the other book:*** From passage in *Fernhurst*:

> It happens very often in the twenty-ninth year of a life that all the forces that have been engaged through the years of childhood, adolescence and youth in confused and ferocious combat range themselves in ordered ranks—one is uncertain of one's aims, meaning and power during these years of tumultuous growth when aspiration has no relation to fulfillment… until at last we reach the twenty-ninth year… and we exchange a great dim possibility for a small hard reality. [*Fernhurst*, **p. 29**]

J.H.W. gardens when I got sick and faced flunking my exams: Cf. Leo F.'s letter to GS June 11, 1895, about sickness and facing an exam.

*

NB-MA #18

Seeing woman killed by train always walked to high school [save time?] Type of nervous temperament)

David

*

NB-MA #19

Martha Hersland.

Use that story I will throw the umbrella in the mud be youthful experience since man hit another with the umbrella in California street.

AT ***California Street:*** It was a part of San Francisco where you didn't go, between Chinatown and the prostitutes' quarter. You were likely to see horrors there. I remember seeing a man throwing down another man on California Street.

LK ***Use that story I will throw the umbrella …*** Used later in MA 388. [Cf. Note #20 and NB1 #22 for corresponding notes.]

Man hit another with an umbrella: The incident of seeing a man hitting a woman with an umbrella on California Street is from GS's own adolescence.

It is used in the novel (MA 424) as the beginning of Martha's intellectual maturity; it makes her decide to go to college "to find out why men and women are as they are" ["Martha saw this and this man was for her the ending of the living I have been describing that she had been living. She would go to college, she knew it then and understand everything and know the meaning of the living and the feeling in men and women."] and subsequently to fight for the cause of women. It is questionable whether GS attached the same significance to the incident when it originally occurred, but certainly she never became the militant suffragette that Martha does in the novel because of it.

The model for Martha's subsequent career as a suffragette was Leon Solomons' sister Selina, an important activist in the California suffrage movement.

*

NB-MA #20

Adolescent reading from my novel in the library bring in in fact that whole history of wandering around the hills and adolescent struggle freedom of college intercourse a little loosens it up inside of Martha. Also my high school experience and some of these friends and also religious breaking away like little Helen.

I am too young to die.

AT ***Adolescent reading:*** Gertrude didn't go to school after sixteen. She went to the library and read. The Merchants and Mechanics Library near Golden Gate Park in San Francisco had a fine collection of 17th and 18th century original editions, memoirs of unknown discoverers and missionaries, and so on. She read there when she was seventeen and did her entire 18th century reading there. After going East [the following year], she stayed in Baltimore for about a year, gossiping and living with the Baltimore family and visiting, and didn't go to Radcliffe for about a year. And she would visit New York and the relations there for a week or so at a time. Leo went directly to Harvard.

Adolescent struggle: The memory of it was so horrible that she didn't like California when we returned there in the Thirties. The Strattons had sold their house in Oakland. When she was at Mills College she was depressed beyond words. The memory of it was too horrible for her ever to put it down in her later writing, and it is only found in the Radcliffe themes.

When the [unpublished] manuscripts were piling up between 1914 and 1945, she wasn't depressed, just sad, that's all. She never thought about a public when she wrote, any more than she thought about audience. It was just when she had a stock of unpublished manuscripts that she started to worry about it.

This memory, though, was like a cloud. It came off the moment she left San Francisco. She didn't want to go to the library at all. She went down to the beach, and having seen the ocean, slept a little better that night. When we returned to the Algonquin [in New York], there was an envelope waiting for us containing a teaspoon of sand from the beach. It was addressed to Gertrude in her own handwriting.

She liked nothing in California but the people she hadn't known there. Gertrude Atherton took her to the Dominican convent where Gertrude was to speak. The Mother Superior, a very worldly woman, gossiped with her about old San Francisco things. The girls were very intelligent, knew Gertrude Stein and what she was talking about, and she had a lovely experience there. She and Clare, my old California friend, got on extremely well, but for all that she didn't enjoy Clare. It was painful that the one thing about the United States that I enjoyed most, California, was the one thing that left Gertrude most depressed.

When Gertrude went East, she and Bertha lived in Fanny Bachrach's house in Baltimore. The Bachrachs already had two maiden aunts living with them, and now there were another sister's two daughters. Gertrude got pretty thoroughly into Baltimore life, and liked her mother's family well. For a week or so at a time, she would visit New York, and the relation there. Leo went directly to Harvard.

religious breaking away like little Helen: Helen Bachrach, who left an orthodox Jewish home for Presbyterianism, as her cousin Ernie Keyser did too. Helen continued however to live in the family. All the Keysers and Bachrachs [who were closely intermarried] were a very devoted family. Helen never married. Her mother was alive when Gertrude and I were in Baltimore [during year of lecture tour in the Thirties.]

LK ***my novel in the library:*** GS's first novel, which she began at Radcliffe. The two chapters of it submitted as themes in her Composition course are published in *G.S: Form and Intelligibility*. In the first of these, the heroine, reading difficult philosophic matter in the library, throws up her hands, throws down her books, and flies to the simpler world of nature. It is a self-pitying portrait telling nothing of what was really troubling her in her "adolescent struggles" in her high-school years, and which culminated in the year (1891) in San Francisco, when she was seventeen.

*

NB-MA #21

Scandinavian Julien says David death due to fear of feminisation.

*

NB-MA #22

Martha's friends comes home late high-school experiences father angry hit her.

*

NB-MA #23

Distinction between practical life not founded on
impressions but on own reaction due to own temperament for pleasantness or self-preservation. Impressions and convictions ideas in regard to others.

*

NB-MA #24

Refer to book one last page for house transaction of David.

Full description in NB1, #34

*

NB-MA #25

Make a larger study of Heisman family in connection with Alfred Herslands first Bridgepoint experiences. It is there get the first relation of Alfy with a girl Aunt Helen poetry—and Fanny Bachrach Heisman, and sister's family

that is sister of David Hersland?

AT ***Heisman family... Bridgepoint [Baltimore]:*** [Amelia Keyser's mother's side of family] Amelia's brothers were Ephraim and one whose name I don't know, Ernie's father. Her sisters were Fanny Bachrach, Sarah who never married, and Helen, a younger sister who was a sort of house pet. Sarah was the one with religious uplift; at one time it was hard to communicate with her, she was so uplifted. The little one was weeny, smaller than any of them. Aunt Sarah and Aunt Helen were the two maiden aunts who lived in Fanny Bachrach's house when Gertrude and Bertha were living there. The Bachrachs were probably Gertrude's closest friends, plus the two maiden aunts. The daughter was Helen Bachrach, who used to make Gertrude laugh a lot. It was then that Gertrude saw Aunt Annie, the mother of Julian and Simon, and first knew Hortense Federleicht. The Guggenheimer's were Dolene's family.

Three of the [Baltimore Heisman] aunts from America once came to Paris to visit Leo and Gertrude, Mike and Sally. They were Aunt Annie, an old-fashioned Southern woman; Aunt Pauline; and the widow of another brother. The visit probably occurred before the earthquake. What they saw were rooms filled with incomprehensible pictures and the four of them living in studios.

So, the three aunts, not one of them a Stein, sat them down and told the four of them how Steins were expected to behave.

"The cheerful little aunts" was true of all the aunts—even the uncles—in Baltimore with the exception of two: Aunt Celia, who took a course in dress-making to make everybody's clothes, and Aunt Sarah, the religious one. From the photo I saw of Aunt Sarah, she seems sad about her religion. She would retire into meditation and have communion with the saints or God or something. All of them were weeny, five feet tall even Uncle Eph, but Aunt Celia was large.

LK ***large study of Heisman family:*** The Baltimore family of GS's mother, Amelia Keyser Stein, on her mother's side. Baltimore family connections for GS were elaborate, since her father's parents had settled there with their five sons when they emigrated from Germany, and her mother, according to GS, one of eleven children, had been born in Baltimore. [See EA.231] Two of the Stein brothers remained in Baltimore, Meyer and Leb. Most of Leb's children married and remained in Baltimore, some becoming part of Meyer Stein's banking house. The Heisman-Keyser children, GS's uncles and aunts on her mother's side, made innumerable marriages with other fairly well-to-do families in Baltimore. Since upper-class Jewish family life was, both out of necessity and affection, extremely close-knit, a single marriage brought a host of new relatives who automatically became life-long associates. Fanny Bachrach's marriage to one of GS's Heisman uncles brought the extended Bachrach family into the Keyser-Heisman-Stein orbit, and even years after three of Amelia Keyser Stein's children had taken up residence in Paris, their letters from Baltimore were filled with information about the Bachrachs as well as the other branches of the "family." And it must be remembered that "you Paris Steins" were suspected of having allowed their family interests to wane, so that only vitally important information about events in Baltimore was transmitted.

sister of David Hersland: While hunting about for a prototype for Mr. Hersland's sister who was to arrange his marriage to Fanny Hersland, GS discarded the First Draft of the novel, and tore out all the pages of the notebook, after the early pages of "Chapter Five," in which the First Draft was written. Material from the lost pages, centering on the Hersland early family history, was used, though, for the text of the final draft. What is left of that First Draft constitutes pages 3 to 78 of the novel. The new text was begun in Spring-Summer 1908, two years after the writing of the novel's second draft had commenced [in April 1906.]

*

NB-MA #26

Corresponds to NB11, #17

Elaborate farther the idea of Chinese ideal of eating in our daddy. mixture in young David.

Elaborate ideas of thoughts of death. Padua.

AT ***Chinese ideal of eating in our daddy:*** Daniel's sister took the children to a Chinese doctor and tried all the things Gertrude refers to in the Notebooks. From the Chinese doctor: Mr. Stein took the children's pulse and regulated everything from that. For cures, he had herbs for them, and gave them things to drink. The doctor had beautiful clothes and lived with his children in San Francisco in the Spanish consul's quaint Gothic house. Gertrude and her sister and brothers would come down and play with the children.

LK ***Chinese ideal of eating:*** Mr. Hersland's ways with eating are first mentioned in the general description of his "queer ways" in MA 49–52, and references to his "queer ways" and eating are later interspersed in the very extended description of him in MA 117–149.

Elaborate ideas of thoughts of death: The relation of eating to dying is introduced in MA 120. It begins: "There are many ways of eating, for some eating is living, for some eating is dying…."

The whole question of eating was one of GS's, and her family's, most troubling concerns. There was a peculiar correspondence between the men in her family and the way they had of becoming absorbed in the subject of food. Simon had the appetites of a baby. He loved candy, indulged his appetites enormously, and fattened into immobility. When he was punished for his over-indulgence by his gastric upheavals, or by the swelling of his legs which became too tender to put on the floor, or by his father's anger with him, or by Sally's impatience with him (Sally was his rock), he wallowed in contrition until the pressure was removed.

Mike, who had studied Biology at Hopkins before he studied Law, sent books on food and dieting to his friends, introduced his family to Fletcherism, conducted a food cure on his wife with, as she professed, "marvelous" success, and generally propagandized for the efficaciousness of a scientific approach to eating. Mike, it will be remembered, became the warder of the other children when Daniel Stein died.

But their father, and Leo after their father was dead, had the most particular involvement with food. Mr. Stein's approach was theoretical. It was not limited to up-to-date "scientific" notions of cooking and diet but ranged freely over a variety of formulations taken from history and from his own ingenuity. But he nurtured his theories one at a time, and the new ones, GS noticed, came at peculiarly appropriate junctures in his private history. The lengthy and reiterated portrait of Mr. Hersland in the MA is an analysis of her father, and the whole of GS's observations of her father with respect to eating are incorporated into the novel beginning on page 117 and continued or repeated until page 160.

Leo's struggles with diet are one of the keys to his enormous complexities of personality. When his sense of creative failure began to take hold of him (it began as early as 1901 during his two-year stay in Europe alone) he began to suffer from mild stomach disorders, and he turned his attention to the proper preparation of his food. This must be understood differently for Leo than for run-of-the-mill amateurs in dietetics. When his attention turned to anything, the matter became imbued with the full weight of the certainties, doubts and exasperations of a mind that had already, and repeatedly, shrugged off a lifetime of almost diabolical self-examination and worrying of aesthetic and philosophical questions. He was a man so uncompromisingly reasonable that his behavior, as GS was to point out, ultimately became grotesque. In his mind, there were direct relations between his food experiments and the general body of his ideas. Fletcherism attracted him after his first experiments, and he became the movement's apostle. Subsequently, as his stomach maladies became serious, he reduced his diet to a small range of greens prepared by himself, and then began experiments in fasting, at the height of which he retreated from the world into an incommodious corner of Florence Blood's villa in Fiesole, and for a time professed to have embraced Buddhism. GS observed these developments from their beginnings to his permanent decampment from the rue de Fleurus and from her life. In her comments on Leo in the Notebooks, and in her studies of him in the MA, one can discern the mixture of exasperation and sorrow she felt toward what she regarded as her brother's irrational rationality. But since eating and its attendant problems were in the forefront of Leo's concerns, they were also of GS's, for at least until 1906, the history of Leo's concerns were in large measure the history of Gertrude's. Her interest in the novel was in eating as a behavioral manifestation, and in this form it remained one of its subjects, in which Leo's whole experience with eating was transferred to the young David. In the early chapters, it was simply used as one of David's characteristics. But in the final chapter in which David's whole development is studied from the perspective of his search for death, the suggestion of this note is profoundly realized. For David's "way of eating" is in fact his way of dying. AS GS puts it in another note (Note #75a), the "problem of nutrition is the problem of death."

*

NB-MA #27

Adele's letter to Dora.

I was so glad to hear from you. Pardon my not returning Sally's letter. I had it put away carefully to bring back—forgetting it was to be sent. I would have written you but have been saving my eyes for the children's diaries. I did not get at them while Joe was here, partly because it was hot, partly on account of her society, and mostly because she was not anxious to have me do so. I had told her, after my house was in order, that when the diaries and albums were complete, I could die in peace. She answered that she'd see to it that they didn't get done. The fiend preferred to have my departing spirit tortured by work undone. Since her departure I have finished Edward's and done a great deal on Aileen's and am going home satisfied on that score. We have been here 4 months and let me whisper it in your ear, I do not want to go home. It is only the thought of poor Meyer being alone in the house that makes me go. I just love it here, an have found it very romantic to have a visiting husband—(a la your hermitage in the hills—eh?) There is nothing that attracts me down there where you live—not even my friends whom I love so dearly. My mental picture is of grayness -and crowded cars and close stones, and artificial manners at artificial receptions—and inane club meetings and poor servants—and even home comes into my mind—as a too high, too large house that will enslave me! These three rooms and porches just suit me (for here) and my rocks and trees!! I'm wicked, I know. Mind you. I'm willing, that's all. I feel that I am doing my duty to go, and therefor being a virtuous lady, I am happy at the thought of going back and ending my husband's loneliness. But if I had my choice? Meyer here! Yes, or even visiting! I don't want to go, its only my conscience that does. I stayed at first for Edward alone, but I have come to realise lately that I really dread the return.

But really I am grateful, awfully grateful for the time we have had here—for the Beauty and the Peace and the Quiet!

But I must quit. It has come to the vulgar, tag end packing up, but I am rushing it through quickly so that I may spend my last two days wandering about and taking last looks, and hunting out the few maples that have had the grace to die in yellow. We leave Saturday night. Come over and see us as soon as you can. Better let us know ahead.

With lots and lots of love, even if I'd choose the mountains to you.

As always Your friend
Adele

AT ***Adele:*** Of the Solomons' children, there was Lucius who was a friend of Sarah's, Leon a college friend of Gertrude's, and Adele [who was close to Sarah.]. I knew only Adele, whom I had met in 1904. She was Mrs. Adele Jaffa, and very independent, very free of Sarah; she sent Sarah scuttling about. Sarah was afraid of her. She tried to put up some defense, but I think Adele just treated her as an incompetent. She had no use for Sarah's heavy intellectualism. They were probably high school mates. Adele was not an agreeable person, but she was nice to be with. She had none of the possessiveness of her children Sarah accuse her of. She was a good mother—a "modern" mother—but with no conscious pretension about it.

At one time Sarah wanted Gertrude to marry Lucius and tried to persuade Gertrude that she was interested in the wrong member of the family [Leon Solomons.] Gertrude knew practically no one in San Francisco. She left when she was seventeen. And the children always hated the father's San Francisco friends, who came and ate the fruit in the house, and who were they?

*

NB-MA #28

[...] before she was always right now she has been wrong and she must take the humiliation and pain well into her.

Why do I want you to do it because I want you to fail to give up something you have believed in -

AT ***Bird's Divorce:*** Bird's divorce was on the tapis for years, with Bird pursuing it, trying to get proof against Lucius Sternberger. The children, when it happened, were about 3 and 5. Bird had wanted to marry Lucius, and during the years of trouble over the divorce, her family was careful not to remind of it. Howard Gans was probably a connection of Aunt Pauline's or perhaps his mother was one of her intimate friends, in any case, his coming to the house was perfectly natural.

When Howard and Bird were at last married, after Howard and handled the legal end of the divorce and been an intimate of the family while it was going on, Gertrude was plainly shocked. There was, she felt, something indecent about it. They had made so much of their bourgeoisie, and then went and did a thing like that.

They came over to visit Paris in Summer of 1907.

*

NB-MA #29

[...?] to help such a good friend
more than I can say for I think a great deal of you and you have the making of a fine woman (no taffy but honest talk). Your composition is too rich and needs toning down. All people who can do things in this world are bothered in the same way. if you were common everything would go easy. its hard like everything else. one thing makes it hard for a girl is that she can get out of things [insert:] you can't run away from yourself, you got to conquer yourself—a hard job—first of all Janette down the hysterical side of yourself—that half, do it with sunshine in your heart and the hysterics will go by a fast train don't stimulate tough ways for you are not tough. be feminine not soft or too sweet you will never be soft, be what you are without extra accent. You can if you will, cut out the [curse?] its no good

> *Passage is evidence of a much more completed early version of the novel being scrutinised from its beginning, and GS inserting additions and corrections—beyond the first five chapters extant. This passage would probably belong to a section on Jane Sandys (here, Janette) and David Hersland during their affair.*

*

NB-MA #30

General

Old man asleep in cart, young man pulling it. Let us moralise upon the scene. For pleasures are like poppies spread you seize the flower the bloom is dead, nature of certain (perhaps many people, not of pleasure and pain, they are the same).
Here is a note—but I didn't want to see you and here are some flowers—but I didn't want to see you
You have been hurt enough
Bird doesn't lie then she has certainly a very intricate way of telling the truth.

LK [For NB-MA #30, #31 and #32. Text from GS letters to Bird Stein and Howards Gans.]

AT ***Bird doesn't lie:*** Bird, because of her pretentiousness, would show no obligation to where she got her assistance. Gertrude had smoothed her difficult path when she became a woman of intellect.

Leo & Gertrude, in the days when they acted as one, didn't let anything pass from anyone. Like the French, they took up all slights, hurts, possible innuendoes, immediately. Leo, in his low voice and gentle way, could say things precisely. Gertrude, with her force, would move around the room with immense speed, and boom her arguments. It was the sort of activity that would make her see clearly. Talking, moving at top speed, shouting and pummeling, she would be dominated by a clear, cold intellect at such moments that could penetrate to the heart of the matter with precision, clarity and exactitude.

*

NB-MA #31

You are a damn fool Howard, thats what you are just a plain common, or garden damn fool.

*

NB-MA #32

I pounded and I meant to pound it in.

You are a pack of stupid fools you see nothing except what's got a label attached—nothing nothing.

The deep joy of understanding something is what you people can never know anything about. I don't envy your success and your thick-skinned stupidity.

*

NB-MA #33

NB-MA #33 to #40 are plans for David Hersland's life from boyhood to his love affairs at college:
You see your time and money are probably not important to you. My time is not important to me, why I use every minute. That's just it, you see I only use a very few of my minutes, but I have to have all my time because I never know what minute I am going to use.

Conversation between David and Julia some of the last talks before the split.

*

NB-MA #34

My God she don't remember. Of course you have no
memory when you have no consciousness. David's last act before he dissapears [sic] into the void is his relation to Annette and Mabel Haynes whom he met through Janet (me) and knew at his new post university where he died. The conversations the creation of an intellect. Describe the whole

relation as I have lived it and then ____ but its nice as are most things in this best of all possible worlds except death and taxes and ~~alas~~ those alas we can't escape and so we inevitably get mixed up with sadness.

*

NB-MA #35

This world is all. When I am dead I am dead.

Remember I want you not to submit yourself to me because of your fear of me but to submit yourself to me because of your appreciation of me.

Remember it is not that I have had more experience it is that I have a bigger soul and a nobler nature and steadfast ~~impersonal~~ ~~non-self~~ generous mind.

Remember when I am at my best when my mind and my nature are completely aroused I am as much above you as Michael Angelo's drawings are above your drawings.

*

NB-MA #36

Use as part of David's development the medical school
training ~~indivi~~ individuals less important life more important go into that whole experience as part of David's growth.

*

NB-MA #37

David's young life—sunset—walk to Etna etc. bycicle [sic] ride.

*

NB-MA #38

Three types of attitude toward greatness.

1 = Fernande, Don't see it.

2 Annette + Emma = Trying to pull it down to their level.

Make even the face of the Almighty look [scrimtly?]. Drag it with them into the ditch.

3 Aunt Pauline, throws mud at it.

*

NB-MA #39

Make her like Olga

David's astonishment at Helen B's / indignation at man talking to her while she is waiting for him, but what the hell did you expect. Get this out of other story.

LK ***Get this out of other story:*** From *Fernhurst*:

> … they had agreed to meet at a restaurant …. Adele arriving a half hour late found Helen in a state of great excitement. 'Why what's the matter?' Adele asked. 'Matter' Helen repeated 'you kept me waiting for you and a man came in and spoke to me and it's the first time that I have ever been so insulted.' Adele gazed at her in astonishment. 'Great guns!' she exclaimed 'what do you expect if you go out alone at night. You must be willing to accept the consequences. The men are quite within their rights.' 'Their rights! They have no right to insult me.' Adele shook her head in slow wonderment. 'Will we ever understand each other's point of view,' she said. [*Fernhurst*, **pp. 104–105**]

Another version of this incident, more downright and possibly more factual, is reported in this note:

> Use… me to Etta and the boys. You damn fool incident of May and her dress and 17 year old hoodlums. David comes up[,] this is first flame[,] Helen[,] and addresses[:'] you damn fool don't you know boys of that age are the most dangerous a girl can fool with….Didn't you see that little one trying to touch your breasts…. You women are certainly damn fools mostly.' Describe the light blue dress Helen May wore. [NB1, #31]

*

NB-MA #40

Oh I am a dog, how could I ~~fe~~ ever feel superior—how could I feel superior. I couldn't ever feel superior I never could have felt superior, I never did feel superior How could I feel superior I never could have felt superior No I never felt superior How could I ever feel superior. No I never felt superior.

*

NB-MA #41

Mrs. Valloton.

I went to a funeral and there were no flowers and no carpet and no music. It was lugubrious.

*

NB-MA #42

Smell for the glass whether the wine had been left in it over night before washing. Milk cooked in the vegetable dish. Sally noticed when she had stepped into something.

*

NB-MA #43

Notes from NB-MA #43 to #46 plan Alfred's affair with Minnie after his divorce from Julia.

Dickie Wolkin introduces Alfy to Minnie Whenn [sic],
Dickie painter met her through his sentimental friend Mrs.
George Ently. Dickie warns Alfy at the same time encouraging him just the way Maurer would do.

*

NB-MA #44

Minnie jealous of Julia Dehning. Julia never left Alfy till after death of her child. because of the child, Alfy saw that she would not get cause for divorce Minnie did not want him to have it because she was tied up with a man cigar store who still loved her would not get a divorce. He keeps her furiously jealous of Alfy. Story ringing a bell in Larkin Street ring up the house does Miss Larkins live here Yes. proof he rang the bell, then she tells him lies about Julia underwear purse etc. Jealous extravagant and yet knows what she wants interesting contrast. Julia after death of little boy which is a release to her leaves Alfy who becomes more than ever slave to Minnie. David's relations to Minnie.

AT ***Minnie:*** [The real] Minnie [Jake Samuel's wife] was, as I remember, the daughter of a Civil War general, possibly the granddaughter, and she made life difficult for Jake. She was also very extravagant.

*

NB-MA #45

I am a damn fool I am a damn fool There is no getting away from it Gertrude I am a damn fool.
What do you want me to do.

*

NB-MA #46

Corresponds to NB10 #2 and NB9 #13

Minnie like Marie Antoinette proud of her name any girl with a name like that has got to be gay. Very good to Alfy. thats what the real Alfy says to Alfy Hersland.

*

NB-MA #47

All generalisations from experience have equal ~~vari~~ validity. You are superior to everything but anarchy. I have to come to you to prove that I am superior to art. Later, all great art is anarchy.

AT [This entry, according to Miss Toklas, is a response to Leo's 'All experience is valid.'] Of course, Gertrude would rejoin, all experience is valid, that's a commonplace. What really matters is how you see what the experience has been.

*

NB-MA #48

And now we come back to the Dehnings and their very different kind of living, the very different things they needed to win out in, the very different ~~ways~~ way they looked at freedom, and it is for Julia Dehning and Alfred Hersland to make out between them their life when they had made such a different kind of a beginning.

LK This entry is further evidence of the long First Draft in which much of the projected narrative, as envisioned in this Notebook and concurrent notes, was completed.

The notes from NB-MA #33 to #40 are all plans for David Hersland's life from boyhood to his love affairs at college; those from NB-MA #43–46 plan Alfred's affair with Minnie after his divorce from Julia.

*

NB-MA #49

Derain (George Dehning)

It is more than a lack of originality this passion for ideas etc like Max in a man like Derain, it is as in the case of Alice, an endeavor to replace the lack of imagination and appreciation of the significant by a manufactured article, she does it with a dramatic they do it with a manufactured whimsical and feeling full imagination and it is so they create themselves into the thing they would be and hopelessly are not. Now in Alice's case she wants to be it so as to most powerfully taste flavors know the beauty of power. Why do the Derains Steins Fred's Leos want it. I dunnow.

LK The mention of Alice Toklas dates this entry as post-September 1907. Earlier entries in this Notebook date from the beginning of the writing of the novel's second draft in April 1906. It appears that the notes jotted down during the writing of the early draft were subsequently used for recalling narrative detail, as evidenced in the headings that appear on the covers of the very earliest Notebooks, such as:

- [**Notebook 6**] "A little of Martha here called Selena. A good deal of young David, and some of Alfred, and the Dehnings."
- [**Notebook 2**] "Life of Dehnings and later life of Herslands."
- [**Notebook 1**] "Life of Young David & George Dehning."
- [**Notebook 9**] "Book for life of Alfred & David. Use this book soon."
- [**Notebook 11**] "Important for later life and beginning of Alfred and David. All their lives later."
- [**Notebook 12**] "Dehnings and Alfred's marriage troubles. Alfred lawyer and then politics."

*

NB-MA #50

Interesting how Derain & Max approach each other. The fantastic half crazy superficial whimsical spirituelle dreamer and the practical untemperamental unimaginative vulgar bound success making Derain. Sally is right I think that the distinction is the profound unoriginality of it in Stein, Leo F. and Derain. In working out George Dehning's character you must make as theme this profound unoriginality.

*

NB-MA #51

The following two notes are characteristic:

Hutch, Leo F.—Derain

George.

The practical judgment of them is the deepest thing inside him. That is his ~~reacti~~ instinctive reaction to them. The understanding and the feeling for them that is in his head and what there is of religion in him. These are strong enough to start him they ~~not~~ [sic] are strong enough inside to keep him going. They are not strong enough inside him to make win out ~~against~~ a deep personal relation with him, then his practical judgment in the final moment makes him resent them.

*

NB-MA #52

Culture with a big C.

Janet Alice etc. Oscar Wilde completest form. Have ~~an ele~~ a delicate palate for an elegant~~ly~~ sensuous appreciation of flavors. Meat material is the plastic form no sense for that only sense of flavors ~~the~~ ... ~~beginning~~ no capacity for any vital understanding. Berenson has vital understanding for material and a delicate sensuous appreciation for the flavors of them that go with them, more delicate more sensuous not as clean cut or distinguishing as Leo's but Berenson labors under delusion that he has an elegant sensuous appreciation of flavors when he has not mastered his material that gives him his sense of superiority makes him vulgar and a cad. Hutch tastes reality as though it were a flavor he gets as it were the flavor of the gravy he even drinks it up a bit until it gets bitter and then a practical sense for bread and butter interferes with it. this blood gravy tastes too strong for him. Other people try it and find it the way growing boys do, fat. Neith also has a sensuous sense of flavors but in her case the kind of flavors she likes are sugar in her salad dressing, the kind of gritty sugar all through things the kind one gets in New England cooking until your mouth and stomach and whole system get gritty with sugar (very unpleasant) that is to her a sensuous flavor. She has too a sense of reality, a dry goods counter aesthete. Servant girl element in her.

AT ***Culture with a big C:*** 'Culturine' was the word created by Gelett Burgess of *The Lark*, the San Francisco paper that was the forerunner of *The Thinker*. It became the standard California word for making fun of seekers after Culture.

Neith... a dry goods counter aesthete: She was described by a Chicago friend as a 'bargain counter aesthete.' She wanted to look like an English Pre-Raphaelite, but it was actually a fairly Middle-West, Connecticut-Valley combination of it.

*

NB-MA #53

Alfy like his mother all there is of importance in himself inside him like hers.
Martha inarticulate like her father.
David completed individual.

AT ***Alfy like his mother:*** Mike [i.e. Alfred Hersland] was very little a Stein, mostly Keyser. He had a gentle, simple uprightness, even the consciousness of it, and that was characteristically Keyser.

*

NB-MA #54

Make Mrs. Rosenshine one of the Hersland family who arranges the match with the Heisman's yes.

LK Planning Note for MA 70–77. Corresponds to, and concurrent with, NB-*C #4 ["Begin this new thing."]; NB-*C #7 [At last I have my sister of David Hersland…. Mrs. Matisse and Mrs. Rosenshine.]; NB14, #3 ["Make Mrs. Rosenshine… make the match."]

AT ***Mrs. Rosenshine:*** Annette Rosenshine's mother Lizzie fought for her children like a lioness. Her marriage to Dolphy was a misalliance, she being beneath him socially. But her life was a real California story. As the oldest daughter, she married off all her brothers and sisters happily and well. Being a really able woman, she could take on that responsibility—to her mind, a natural family responsibility.

She was not really as coarse as *The Making of Americans* suggests, except compared to the delicacy of the Rosenshines. She put everything over. Like a Frenchwoman, when she was engaged in arranging a marriage, she had the ability and the right assurance to make everything a virtue. For a cross-eyed, witty one, she would make the wit appear to come from the crossed eyes. There was a certain brutality almost in her defense of her family. And a very very patient waiting. She waited for years to get the better of her husband's brother's wife, and did.

I knew the Rosenshines in California. Dolphy was very distantly connected with my father three or four generations back. My father introduced Lizzie to my mother when they were married.

Lizzie was quite plain, dark, had black hair, a slightly crooked mouth, no sense of elegance, and looked small and insignificant.

Carrie Rosenshine, Dolphy's sister, came from an extremely old bourgeois family in New York and accepted Lizzie as a lady does. Her daughter was Stella, a large, bouncing, good-looking woman who was a nitwit—all but lacking.

*

NB-MA #55

What's the use of listening if I can't remember.
They are kindly and selfish and not ashamed of either.

*

NB-MA #56

Corresponds to Note #62

Solomon said of laughter "It is madness" and of mirth "who doeth it" for even in laughter the heart is sorrowful and the end of that mirth is heaviness. I often think if I could be so fixed as never to laugh nor to smile I should be one step better. It fills (feels) [sic] me with sorrow when I see people so full of laugh.

LK ***Solomon said of laughter 'It is madness'...*** Ecclesiastes, II, 2: "I said of laughter, It is mad: and of mirth, What doeth it?"

Paraphrased in MA 44: "She [Mrs. Hersland's mother] never ever really stopped her sad trickling, to her joy was as it has been said of laughing, it is madness, and of mirth who doeth it, for even in laughter the heart is sorrowful and the end of that mirth is heaviness."

*

NB-MA #57

And she had many and very little children. She had wept out all the sorrow for her children, they were cheerful helpful gentle little men and women, they lived without ambition or excitement but they were each in their little circle joyful in the present. They lived and died in mildness and contentment.

Draft of text for MA 44.

*

Notebook 14

Notes for Final Draft

NB14, #2

Jakey Moses & Meyer Jaffa
Simon H. & [Laurie(?)]

*

NB14, #3

In this note, GS returns to second draft pages MA 56, 70–77 for their expansion, inserting the earliest terms of the "system" into the narrative's second-draft text. As already noted, the first term to be introduced is the feeling of "importance"—which term, with the feeling of "existence," produced the urgency—not to say the anxiety—to initiate the "system" itself. In this first attempt at the fundamental realignment of the novel toward what was to become its major preoccupation, Gertrude gradually incorporates, into the descriptions of her characters her newly formulated terms.

cf. corresponding Manuscript Note #24, MA 56

Make Mrs. Rosenshine sister of David Hersland make the match. Mrs. Rosenshine with a leaning toward Mrs. Meininger go back to that now before the trial launching on the Schillers go back to that then they were together then then a little recapitulation of her Fanny's character then grown young men and women always as older grown men and women to us the generation always to ourselves grown young men and women knew our parents etc. quote that and then

As I was saying about Mrs. Hersland and her first beginning of the important feeling this came from her meeting with old Mrs. Schiller and her daughter Sophie Schiller and her other daughter Pauline Schiller.
and then go on about das [?] etc.

LK ***… Mrs. Hersland and her first beginning of the important feeling…*** MA 64. The theme of Mrs. Hersland's winning her "important feeling" from knowing the Shillings begins in MA 56.

Mrs. Rosenshine… make the match… go back to that now: MA 66. The description and story of the matchmaker is later developed at length in MA 70–77.

trial launching on the Schillers: The earliest references to the Schillers [= the Shillings in the MA] are in MA 56. But after "go[ing] back to" the "matchmaker," the lengthy description of the Schillings follows, MA 77–85.

recapitulation of her Fanny's character: Previous "recapitulation" occurred in MA 64; this note anticipates MA 77.

then grown young men and women… knew our parents etc. Omitted in this sequence. Used in previous "recapitulation" in MA 66–67.

and then as I was saying about Mrs. Hersland: Draft of text for MA 84.

*

NB14, #4

[...?] description of Fanny's marriage etc. then the children as little children in her etc   little book and then go on to the Schillers. [Insert:] physical presence for them and then she was a princess to her brothers and sisters reasons

LK "Sweetness," "power" and "importance," early key terms used just prior to introduction of new systematic descriptive vocabulary.

Planning Notes:

- MA 64: "the she was a princess…"
- MA 66–77: Fanny Hissen marriage, and the sister of David Hersland role in its accomplishment;
- MA 77–78: Fanny Hersland's "almost important feeling;"
- MA 78–84: The Shillings and Fanny Hersland's "important feeling" with them;
- MA 90, 113: The three Hersland children
- MA 98–108: "Existence" and "Importance"—begins full development of system.

*

NB14, #5

Dec. 8 = 100

Dec 12 = 50

Dec 16 = 110

Dec 25 = 100

Jan 2 = 100

Jan 7 = 100

Jan 14 = 100

*

NB14, #7

Three stages, early just being of the earth, then ethical then questioning that May laughed at asking to find out—then experience in Spain when got the awful depression of repetition in history, then realisation much later that I did not believe in progress, that I was in that sense not an optimist, then realising that I was not a pragmatist just recently do not believe all classification is teleological, then realise, that aesthetic has become the whole of me, not so sweet as I was or virtuous, and then through christian science realising gullible through a certain fear like Mike but au fond like the Jew in Auctioneer but I did see him.
Use this partly in history of Leon but also in introduction.

LK Major reckoning at a critical juncture for GS, a sloughing off of old intellectual commitments and older habits. Probably most significant: [spelled out in NB-D #11:] "When Leo said that all classification is teleological, I knew I was not a pragmatist. I do not believe that, I believe in reality as Cezanne or Caliban believe in it. I believe in repetition. Yes. Always and always. Must write the hymn of repetition."

the hymn of repetition: Discussed above, Chapter Two, "The System," under heading, "Repetition."

I do not believe all classification is teleological. On the face of it, this last is a rejection of the rejection of pragmatism. But GS is in fact rejecting intellectual formulations of almost any kind, adopting—at least for this moment and for this passage—a "flattening" of all formulations as, in effect, "decorations" of "the thing-in-itself." In the same vein, she argues concurrently, in NB-A #15, re: the primacy of the object-as-object which must be known without irrelevant additions or qualifications. That this understanding contradicts the implicit "teleological" design of her contemplated "system" is a major factor, in the system's ultimate unraveling. (MA 583, 587, 730–732.)

like the Jew in Auctioneer but I did see him: (Guessing one's way through the text of a too-elliptical note:) It concerns, apparently, the persuasions of Sarah Stein and her devotion to Christian Science, and GS's "certain fear" of getting involved (the problem she shares, apparently, with Mike, Sarah's husband and GS' eldest brother.) But—another guess concerning the vanished The Auctioneer (presumably an undiscoverable 19th century melodrama) in which, possibly, the character of the Jew, having experienced a vision of Christ, is skeptical about his own skepticism, since it is contradicted by the reality of his certain vision. Final guess: The Jew, in an anti-slavery melodrama, is the low-down slave auctioneer who finally sees the light, thank God.

Use partly in history of Leon but also in introduction: Two major plans for revision: (1) Leon [Solomons] as the young David Hersland, —whose history is already understood to be a development toward "completed individual"—is to replicate literally the stages of GS's own progress. (2) The novel's introduction is projected to replace the current introduction's subject of immigrants' life-adventure in America by the new matter outlined in this note. But the first flush of enthusiasm for these plans waned.

AT ***May laughed at asking to find out:*** May [Bookstaver] thought like Melanctha, that all the moral questionings of Gertrude had nothing to do with anything.

It was the unhappy love affair [with May] of 1902–4 that more than anything else made up Gertrude's mind for Paris. Gertrude was only driven mad toward the end with the complications May made with Mabel Haynes. The May-Gertrude relation started in 1901 in America and was all over by the end of 1903 or the beginning of 1904. Gertrude returned to America in 1904, and there saw Mabel Haynes and May Bookstaver again. She wanted, apparently, to see the follow-up. Then she came back to Paris in the Fall of 1904. Mabel and May were in Washington D.C. during the Winter of 1904–5, and there Emma Lootz saw them. Then Mabel Haynes left for Vienna in 1905, and then it was all over [between Mabel and May.] But whether she [Gertrude] went back because it was over between them first, or because May and Charles Knoblauch [who May was to marry] were definite, or just to study, I never knew.

*

NB14, #9

Leon & Flexner

Leon was dep. ind. surely, Flexner ditto, Napoleon like Pablo.

LK Dep. ind. first noted, MA 163.

*

NB14, #10

the difficulty which even the ablest men seem to experience in analysing character amid the heats of a political conflict.

LK A GS unidentified quote.

*

NB14, #11

The whole moral problem of a development like mine discuss in history of Leon and its relation to Alfy, Mike more and less moral he is less complete & profound.

*

NB14, #12

She comes so near to being a big generous devoted nature that it is hard to believe that she misses being it completely, that she isn't it a single it[… .]

*

NB14, #13

Fanny & Sarah & Eph and Sol and sister-in-law—Bessie and Helen.

[… .] his impatient feeling lay—note to education business.

LK ***his impatient feeling lay … education business:*** Plan for MA 48; an introduction to the theme of Mr. Hersland's "impatient feeling" and his quixotic education of his children. Enumeration of the "different ways … that made education" occurs in MA 52 and is reiterated MA 90. The double theme of his "impatient feeling" and the "queer mixture" of his children's education weaves through the novel from this page to the end of the chapter on Mr. and Mrs. Hersland [MA 149] and reappears in the following chapter, on Mrs. Hersland and her servants [MA 150–288.]

*

Notebook *C

NB-*C #3

3 types of commonplace.
Story.
End of situation to marriage
Incident true sisterhood
Bertha's beautiful hands yes but they are dull they have no expression.

LK ***3 types of commonplace:*** [Corresponds to DB #42: "Three commonplace versions of doctor clergyman & actor.... Instinct for common-placeness."]

*

NB-*C #4

Begin this new thing don't forget anything not your first impression such as cutting out the wood Mrs. Matisse passion for routine work build that up into Mrs. Rosenshine plus

AT ***Mrs. Matisse passion for routine work... Mrs. Rosenshine:*** Mrs. Matisse as a housekeeper always carried it off as she wished it—the room, the meal, the way the guests were received—always as it should be. Mrs. Rosenshine's passion was for organization. She calculated hours, routine, and so on, all in detail. But her vision was longer than Mme. Matisse's. The important thing was not so much what she was doing every day. She would get into collision with her older son—not her husband Dolphy, he was docile—but rows with the son and the other children were considerable. Her older son was fairly able, but he was no power over his mother. The Stinker did much better by just being a Princess who withdrew. She was a victim of her harelip and thought herself not sufficiently protected at home. Dolphy was always ready to be run by his brilliant wife.

Gertrude got the information she wanted about Mme. Matisse from herself. She came and talked to Gertrude while Leo talked to Matisse, and Mme. Matisse was not at all embarrassed in talking about her home life. She was, though, a proud woman. The information about Mrs. Rosenshine Gertrude extracted from the Stinker [i.e. Annette Rosenshine], and she also got all her mother's letters out of her.

LK [Planning Note for MA 70–77.] [Concurrent with MA 54]

Begin this new thing.... Mrs. Matisse... Mrs. Rosenshine plus: MA 70. "This new thing" is the detailed description and story of David Hersland and his sister Martha, the matchmaker. Compounded of the "wooden" Mrs. Matisse and the overbearing "Mrs. Rosenshine plus," the portrait of her is one of the most carefully crafted and lingered-over in the novel. Unlike Alice, Leo, Matisse himself, and several other subjects whose analyses underwent considerable revision, Mrs. Matisse remained a fairly fixed entity, and was used in portraiture from this time to the writing of the *Autobiography* in 1932. Mrs. Rosenshine came to Paris "in May" says Annette, [i.e., 1908], when GS would have met her. "This new thing," then, being written post-May 1908, follows by two years the start of the MA in April 1906.

*

NB-*C #5

Use this sense of injury pure to make resentment in type character of Heisman's enlarge in later history of Mrs. Hersland and Aunt Fanny.

LK ***...sense of injury pure... of Heisman's...*** Used in MA 65. "With these who had sweetness in them, ... many in them, strongest in them... after the sweetness and gentle dignity... had it... to be hurt not angry when any bad thing happened to them, they would be hurt then and their mouths would be drooping."

... enlarge in later history of Mrs. Hersland and Aunt Fanny: Mrs. Hersland's "sense of injury" is introduced much later, in MA 175, in relation to the first of the Hersland servants.

*

NB-*C #6

Of course the people with the sense of superiority above all that which has no practical or any other kind of basis such as Emma's & Annette's do not have a lively sense of injury, there is nothing to injure.
Servant class particularly earthy have direct sense of injury, the earthy unservant have tolerance

*

NB-*C #7

At last I have my sister of David Hersland the one that makes the marriage Mrs. Matisse and Mrs. Rosenshine. Remember the
incident of the book that changed her life. sentimentality of melodrama common touch.

AT ***Mrs. Matisse... the book that changed her life:*** The novel she read in her childhood. Gertrude writes about it in the Autobiography. "[Mousier and Madame Matisse] had with them a daughter of Matisse, a daughter he had had before his marriage and who had had diphtheria and had had to have an operation and for many years had to wear a black ribbon around her throat with a silver button. This Matisse put into many of his pictures. The girl was exactly like her father and Madame Matisse, as she once explained in her melodramatic simple way, did more than her duty by this child because having read in her youth a novel in which the heroine had done so and been consequently much loved all her life, had decided to do the same."

Mrs. Matisse… melodrama: Her melodrama was in her walk—a stride—and it was accented by her speech which literally went into the rhythm of her stride. Her voice would deepen for such occasions. Her subject was, as Gertrude put it, mere melodrama, but I thought she really treated it in the grand tragic classical manner.

*

NB-*C #8

Of course I won't
When your [sic] like that I am afraid of you.

It was not that she had a common feeling it was in a way a stupid way of not feeling that made her give out this common way of seeing. And this way of stupidly not seeing so that the finer thing gives only a hazy sensation, when it begins to work it is a stupid way of feeling

It was not that she did not have feeling but she was not very sensitive in her feeling that is what made it to the Heismans a common kind of feeling.

It was not that she was hard to others in her feeling. She had real feeling she had understanding of the eldest Heisman daughters feeling in religion, she had a respectful humble protecting feeling when she saw the mother always weeping she felt strongly inside her the beauty of so much sorrowing for the sadness in all living, she felt respect and knew how to make others feel it for the gentle dignity in all of them but she never could feel any such a thing inside her as she felt whenever she saw them and it was this that made her common to them she was not a strong woman to them ~~her~~ and she was always a little hard and common for them but yet she was a good woman to of them [sic] to the father who liked her neat dressing and the respect she had for him and to the old mother who never thought much about any one and to the eldest daughter and there was really a friendship between them and the younger women ~~girls~~ who felt she was a good woman who always did things as it was always right to her feeling to do them. ~~The younger Heisman men~~

LK [Corresponds to Note #69] Draft of text much expanded in MA 74–77.

*

Note #69

Perhaps one of ~~Dav~~ young David's later friends will be Anette [sic] daughter of Martha [Hissen], and then we will be able to have a complete picture of the old man Rosenshine

[Manuscript material on Sister Martha] but to the others of them she was a good woman ~~to do things for them~~ but she was not really pleasing to her brother she was not really [inserted: pleasing but she was a good enough woman] but he let her choose a wife to content him. ~~and~~ Soon now then they were married [inserted: David Hersland and Fanny] ~~and she went to Gossols with him. Heisman.~~" [All this text crossed out, and on two other sheets of the same kind, all text crossed out.]

AT ***old man Rosenshine:*** Annette Rosenshine's father was a rather charming, good-looking, but very weak being. Gertrude had little respect for him, much as everyone else had. A weak amiable man, he would 'yes, yes' his way through a conversation. That was largely, in fact, his conversation. His friends called him Dolphy.

LK [Corresponds to NB-*C #8] Draft of text much expanded in MA 74–77.

*

Note #68

Fernande.

indolent egotist, a magnificent illusion is not opposition it is an ideal vapor in which she floats. Occasionally the egotism arises becomes tempestuous and slays as Salmon & Appolinaire [sic]. her visions of herself are not ideals they are perfect convictions. In Edstrom the conviction always remains imperfect, in Hodder it was perfect.

The type lady contains it all within herself. Fernande melts into infinite virtue and idealistic beauty.

Reverse side:

~~Seppie Shiller like most fat sisters was a little afraid of the thinner. Generally it was~~

LK ***Fernande indolent egotist….*** [Concurrent with Manuscript Note #29, for MA 78.]

Sophie Shiller like most fat sisters was afraid of the thinner. Text, MA 79.

*

Note #174

[Draft Text: MA 91]:

[… .] more the mother lost all interest that she once had in her with the people who were the natural people for her to have in her daily living in the will to do german american being living which was the natural way of being for her. But it never came to be in her …

*

(1) The detail picture of them comes in the history of each one of the three of them.

[Draft Text: MA 133]:

(2) In ~~the eld~~ Alfred then, there was beginning then a feeling in him as there was in his mother then, he was going then not to be any more of them he was beginning then the poorer people who lived around them more and more then such a feeling went out from him and it was filled up in him out of the feeling that gave his mother her important being. It was different with the two other of them in the daughter of them there was more in her then…

[Draft Text: MA 113]:

(3) …had in him, in the younger son the kind of feeling the father…

(4) …there always remained in him all through his later living the feeling that made him to be one with the people then around him, but all this will come out in the detailed history of them.

*

Note #85

second time, to begin again then when
It was (then) slowly coming to be true of them then [that]
the three Hersland children that they were more entirely of them, the

poorer people who lived around them, than they were of their mother than their mother was then, ~~she and she was never~~ of them then, ~~more of the poorer people~~ though they were all there was of their mother's daily living, then.

LK ***It was slowly coming to be true… mother's daily living….*** Draft of text for MA 92.

*

Note #105

Elisa [?] & Amalia, Johanna the three dress-maker girls
Genandenfeldt
George Charley Anna Lefollery Mary Cook family
~~Berkelin~~ Mary Lidell
Katisha Bercklin, (~~May Lidell~~)
Avel Pfefferman Panns.
Jenny Lauder [Lander?] a friend Tilly Brown.
Henry & Ewing ~~Pureklin~~ Richardsons
Kate Rodhammel May Buckminster
Henry Rodhammel friend of Kate Martin.
James } Rodhammel ~~Banks brothers.~~
Henry }
Pauline Sandys, Kate Martin
Wilson Tuggles

LK [Testing names: those that survived:]

The three dress-maker girls: became the three Rosenhagens: Cecilia, Lillian, and their mother. MA 195.

Richardsons: MA 109.

Banks boys: MA 417.

*

Note #105a

When it comes to description of Dehning and his wife and his wanting a wife after her death, he will want a woman he can own. ? [sic]

LK Used in MA 613.

*

Note #175

Draft Text: MA ?93, 95, 113?

1. It was then slowly coming to be true of them then (that) the three Hersland children that they were more entirely of them, the poorer people who lived around them, than they were of their mother than their mother was then, ~~she and she was ever~~ of them then, ~~none of the people poorer people~~ though they were all there was of their mother's daily living, then.

Planning Note:

Use this as introduction to beginning individual history of children seond tme. To begin again then when.

2. Work up now through description of dress-makers etc. to servant and governess life, children running through it and so to father and education [Insert: Ella Milziner from description by Mildred, debt.]

3. Detials of Lies family, Edyy Richardson & family, Louis Champion Cook family, all these just suggested as a family, the detail as individuals comes in individual history in which use each for intro.

Later insertion:

family with the wild son & Bertha, Lidell family, Rodhammel family, Boyce, mother and son and daughter, the Moore's and their later career with daddy. Mary Greenhagen family another part of town describe that.

*

Note #94a

I have a shrewd suspicion that you have to begin over again from the beginning say this for beginning of each special history

Make the qualities of the father to come out in the viciousness and practicality of the son and the idealistic quality in the daughter who is to be like Edgar Mathews wife.

Reverse side of this sheet and first side of second sheet Ms. material about Cora— "a little wooden then"—and Bertha as little girl.

Describe the Richardson family now Edley [sic], Lilly and the father, they will be friend[s] of young David, the little girl Lilly under tuition of Eddy with [?] [will] try to seduce young David. trips in the country etc. father church member smoking for his catarrh etc. After that the Banks boys with the shoemaking father, Louis Champion an[d] his little brother, leading off into the Cooks friends of one of the Banks boys and then back to governesses and household and father Through the book various other families come in later with school.

AT ***Richardson family... Champion... Banks boys:*** The people who lived around the Steins in the small houses nearby in East Oakland.

LK Concurrent writing with Note #94a— (Plan for *Richardsons*)
Note #43 ("In the case of Harriet...")
Ms.— (Text for Cora, Bertha, and then father.)

I have a shrewd suspicion.... each separate history. Not used as text.

Make the qualities of the father ... like Edgar Mathews wife: Refers to the Richardson family, which is described, MA 108–112. The children, Eddy and Lilly, are described in this passage in relation to their father's religion. not individually. But the promise is made, MA 112, that their "character... will come out then in the history of the Hersland children as they come to know it in them," but neither that promise, nor the suggestion of this note, is fulfilled in the later histories.

Cora: Described in MA 104–105.

a little wooden then: Draft of text for MA 99ff: "the mother's face was old now and a little wooden."

Bertha as a little girl: Draft of text for MA 105–106.

Describe the Richardson family...catarrh etc. Plan for MA 108–112.

After that the Banks boys... Louis Champion.... Omitted in this passage, the Banks boys and Louis Champion reappear among Alfred Hersland's friends much later in MA 531–532.

*

Note #94

And then go on with his schemes of education cooking doing society muttering I'll take mine later. Got to do it sooner or later. fishing, savage kind of living. More and more not with their kind of people that they were living. Hersl[?] wait till it would turn up.

[...] to her in her feeling if she could ever come to know it by a losing, ~~of~~ by their money going or of their losing from position and such a some wrong doing and such a kind of losing it could never come to Mrs. Hersland ~~as~~ to ever think~~ing~~ of as coming [...]

*

[...] would be just ordinary schooling. Sometimes the father would be strong in religion and the children would be [...]

*

First he would have people to teach them to read french and german and say they had to peak it all the time—then he would change.
Trycicles [sic]—horse-back—swimming—gymnasium -stop school to learn cooking—ranching [?]—gardening -vineyard—medicine—business always changing.
Caster-oil for the whole family—chinese doctors—a queer blind man to examine Martha etc. which you will hear more about in the history of her.

*

The children felt it hard on them when they would begin playing cards just to oblige him and after a few minutes with them he would have rise in him his impatient feeling in him and would say here you just finish it up. I haven't time to go on playing and

*

he would call the other child to take his hand from him and all these would have then to play together a game none of them would have thought of beginning or that they ever enjoyed playing and they had to keep on going for often he

*

would stop in his walking to find which was winning. And it never came to him to know it was he had made the beginning and that the children were ~~not for themselves~~ playing for themselves but just because they had to for him.

*

It was a small thing but it happened very often to them and most was / annoying ~~to~~ for them and I tell it here because it shows so well the nature ~~of~~ in him.

*

[...] to him. It was hard for the children to walk with him when he would be carrying a big water-melon, the hat stuck way back on his head and allmost

[sic] falling and his cane [...]
[...] but often she had a sharp angry feeling at some of the ways he had of doing mostly when it concerned the children.

*

Do Alfy Hersland's experiences like Mike in Meyer Steins family and then with the Bachrachs and so give a further account [?] of little men and women.

*

Must not lose that vision of the relation of Bertha to young Martha.

LK ***schemes of education cooking…*** Begins MA 119–129, passim. Preparation for long passage on Mr. Hersland, with passages of text anticipating full description of David Hersland, and shorter preparations for studies of Mrs. Hersland and the children.

Do Alfy Hersland's experiences like Mike in Meyer Steins family and then with the Bachrachs and so give a further account of little men and women: [In Alfred Chapter (MA Ch. 4) possibly planned for his Balto experiences but point of this note apparently did not survive.]

… vision of relation of Bertha to young Martha: Fully developed in MA 384, l. 8 to 387, l. 44. GS's sister Bertha is used as paradigm for "undifferentiated" "independent dependent" "mass of stupid being."

*

Note #221

Describe the Richardson family now Eddy, Lilly and the father, they will be friend of young David, the girl Lilly under tuition of Eddy will try to seduce young David, trips in the country etc. father church member smoking for his catarrh, etc. After that the Banks boys with the shoemaking father, Louis Champion an[d] his little brother, leading off into the Cooks friends of one of the Banks boys and then back to governesses and household and father [word?] [word?] [word?].

LK ***The Richardson family:*** Planning Note: MA 108ff.

*

Note #19

Send November number of American with article of James in it. If anything by James or anything of importance in the field of Pragmatic literature comes out to let me know.

> *GS note to Toklas to correspondent for copy of the Williams James article in* American Magazine *for November 1908.*

MA ms. in this copybook:

[First passage: Begins:]

"It was then slowly coming to be true of them that the three children were more entirely of them, the poor people who lived around them, than they were of their mother then, than their mother was of them then,..." etc.

[And ends:]

"this was stirred up in her with the governesses and seamstresses and servants who lived in the house with her and then for her poor queer kind of people who lived in the small houses near her."

[Second passage:]

Re: the many families living near 10-acre place in Gossols.

[Third passage, on:]

"There are many kinds of men. Some have it in them to feel themselves as big as all the world around them..." etc.

LK ***It was then slowly coming to be true... who lived in the small houses near her:*** Draft of text for MA 113–115.

There were then many families... Draft of text for MA 112.

There are many kinds of men: Draft of text for MA 115.

*

Note #93

With his children the kind of feeling he had in him was very different for they always were outside him, part of the world he was handling, sometimes using mostly fighting, and always dropping or domineering.

LK ***with his children... dropping or domineering:*** Draft of text for MA 118.

*

Remember his getting mad at trouble and pushing his food away from him.

LK ***getting mad... pushing his food away from him:*** Used for MA 123: "he, often then, before ending with the eating, would fill up with impatient feeling and then he would push his eating away from him."

*

Address written on sheet carrying above note:

Hapgood
Villa Duclos
7 rue de chemin de fer

*

Note #75

Same as Note #84a

Use the part of his stubbornness in carrying out some little beginning in eating or doctoring like E. the pride in him that did not touch the big beginning in him

LK ***Use the part of his stubbornness... the big beginning in him:*** Planning Note for renewed description of Mr. Hersland, MA 119ff.

*

Use Meininger a good deal later on. let him and his wife try to manage, Martha when she first gets home to marry her to a son of theirs by [pas?].

LK ***Use Meininger a good deal later on:*** Meininger's attempt to marry off Martha after her return home is not explored in the final draft, though this Note suggests it was to be continued in subsequent chapters.

*

Draft of text for MA 149:

A man and his living has many things inside him, he has in him important feeling of himself to himself inside him, he has in him the kind of important feeling of himself to himself that makes his kind of men; this comes sometimes from a mixture in him of the kind of natures in him, this comes sometimes from the bottom nature in him, this comes sometimes from the natures in him that are mixed up with the bottom nature in him, sometimes in some men this other nature or natures in him are not mixed with the bottom nature for him, made him to the governess and servants in the house with him a man who would not interfere with them for they ~~did not~~ could not feel the power in him for the feeling in him to them that ~~was~~ in his business living made a strong ~~world a~~ fighting [Insert:] in him they saw it in him in the daliy living in the home with him and his family around him they saw that it [Insert ends] used itself up without touching the people he was [...]

In all of them then in all the things that are in them in their daily living, in all of them in all the things that are in them from their beginning to their ending,—in all of them then there are always all these things in them,—in some of the many of millions of each kind of them some of these things are stronger in them than others in them.

*

Draft of text for MA 151:

There are then many kinds of men and many millions of each kind of them. In many men there ~~are~~ is a mixture in them, there is in them the bottom nature in them of their kind of men and there is mixed up in them the nature of other kinds of men natures that are a bottom nature in other men and makes of such men that kind of man. In all the things that are in all men in ~~their~~ all of their living from their beginning to their ending, ~~some of them such as their being important to themselves inside them~~ there can be as the impluse of them the bottom nature in them, the mixture in them of other nature or natures with the bottom natures, the nature or other natures in them which in some men of the many millions of each kind of men never really mix up with the bottom nature in them. ~~Some things in~~ [...]

*

Draft of text for MA 145:

[...] in him there was still spread out inside him a big feeling and that was the beginning in him the beginning that had always been in him all through his living

In his middle living then there were many ways of feeling this mixture in him by everyone who then knew him [...]

*

Note #75a

Corresponds to NB-MA #21

[...?] problem of nutrition is the problem of death, normal death more depressing than pathological death.

LK ***problem of nutrition is the problem of death:*** The theme is treated at length in MA 120–123: "… for some eating is living, for some eating is dying… to some to think about eating makes them know that death is always waiting that dying is in them…." etc.

*

Note #96

Now want to go on give the general atmosphere of their home and their lives like ours and the governesses etc. public school queer friends religion mother and father. Trip to Bridgepoint mother began ailing, father's character and then repeat ~~about~~ original description of the three children and begin history of Martha, how she annoyed father two incidents. I will through [sic] the umbrella in the mud and man hitting woman—religion etc. the Flora daughter of Mrs. Moore the other daughter for young David's experience. All through special description of first Martha then Alfy then David keep giving new lights on the atmosphere of the home.

Planning Note: "atmosphere of house and governesses" MA 125ff.

*

Reverse side of above sheet, interlined with penciled notation—probably draft of letter to Bird & Howard:

"...very definitely I cannot add anything ~~new~~ to them. ~~Everything in them is experienced~~ I do think it important that the two of you ~~both read them~~ both of them and together and reread them and know exactly what I say [...]"

*

Note #87

Make the transition from Hersland to Mrs. and Marie Gruenhagen and her family through Hersland's feeling for his wife

LK ***Make the transition... through Hersland's feeling for his wife:*** The "feeling for his wife," that "She never knew it in her husband that she was always less and less important to him," [MA 130, 133] is alluded to twice and constitutes only a small part of the "transition" preceding the first mention of Madeleine Wyman [= Marie Gruenhagen.]

Matisse's manner to Mrs. significant there.

LK ***Matisse's manner to Mrs. significant there:*** Matisse's "brutal egotism" is GS's essential characterization of Matisse, borne out as well, according to this Note, in his treatment of his wife.

*

Note #89A

Next tell how the men in business felt, fighting etc, how his children felt in the beginning of their individual feeling, then his friends men and women, Meiningen and various families and then his wife and governesses.

LK ***Next tell how the men in business felt… and then his wife and governesses:*** Plan for MA 142–149, in which all the subjects anticipated are included, with the exception of "the Meininger family."

*

Note #88

Alfred Hersland marries Bird [= Julie Dehning] (Sally) kind of woman father in his later living needed to fill him, later when he was shrunk away from the outside of him.

LK ***Bird (Sally) kind of woman father in his later living needed….*** Described briefly in MA 88, anticipating "when [Hersland] would be an old man and weakening."

*

Note #207

He never knew it inside him that he was not [br]ushing people away from around him when he went away from them in another direction in a [blustery?] fashion until his children in his late living when they were angry with him for his impatient feeling said it to him.

*

4 | 50

———

12.50

*

Note #90

[…] ~~in the history of him~~ Go on now with a history of him including sexual nature through the governesses to Madeleine Weiman. Then this will have to be used in the succeeding histories and in his end. [inserted: always suggesting his sexual relations at the] ~~then~~ end and his loss of assurance pushing it away by making it a boisterous being now.

Work it up and then through Fanny Hersland's relations to servants and governesses to Madeleine and her family and William, then say what was the status of the children then that som [sic] then the mother saw her family for the last time then before wakening[?] and troubles and so to history of Martha.

LK [The comprehensive plan for the chapter on Mrs. Hersland and the servants, MA 150–285]

Go on now with a history of him… The description of Mr. Hersland planned in this note is in MA 115–159. "[T]o be used in succeeding histories and in his end:"

his sexual relations … assurance… boisterous being: Plan for MA 154–159.

Fanny Hersland's relations… to Madeleine: Plan for MA 159–168.

with servants and governesses: Plan for MA 168–250.

with Madeleine and her family: Plan for MA 250–283.

and William: "William" becomes "John Summer" in the Final Draft. The story of the struggle between Mrs. Hersland and Madeleine over his impending marriage to Madeleine begins MA 261, 281, when he dies of "queer ways of eating."

what was the status of the children: Briefly mentioned in concluding the chapter, MA 281–282, but not used as planned here.

Mother… weakening and troubles: Not used as planned here for the end of the chapter.

And so to… Martha: The Martha Hersland chapter, MA 289–476.

*

Note #92

You see I must go ahead just constantly recurring to Herslands sexual nature and his woman and so introducing his relation to the children and their education and the importance of them to him and of his wife to him and the lack of importance of the children to his wife's important feeling and comparatively speaking unimportance of himself to his wife's important feeling and the relation of all this to all kinds of sexualness and paternity maternity and so on to the suggestion of his character and so on to the development further of his wife's important feeling, then go thoroughly in to the conditions of their living in the ten acre place Mary Gruenhagen etc entirely in reference to her then afterwards turn it to reference to him to further elucidate his character and education then give general sketch of them both to their troubles and then we will get the transition that I wrote out before to the children, then begin with the individual history but in between there must be a discussion of the lives of the children in general in relation to parents, to conditions governesses etc. and companions and education and so on to the history of Martha as it has been written.

LK A more extended Planning Note for the chapter on "Mrs. Hersland and the Servants," MA 150–285., only roughly adhered to.

the history of Martha as it has been written: That is, as written in *Q.E.D.* GS anticipated incorporating a section of the *Q.E.D.* story verbatim as the story of Martha's love affair and marriage. [See MA 429–440.]

*

Note #176a

Elisa & Amalia, Johanna Genandengeldt the three
dressmaker girls.
George Chanley [?]
/ Anna Lefoller
Mary Cook family.
~~Berkelin~~ May Lidell
Katisha Bercklin ~~(May Lidell)~~
Abel Pfefferman Panns
Jerry Lauder & friend Tilly Brown
Lidell
Henry & Erving /~~Bercklin~~ Richardsons
Kate Rodhammel May Buckminster
Henry Rodhammel friend of Kate Martin
James
Henry Rodhammel ~~Banks brothers~~
Pauline Sands, Kate Martin
Wilson Tuggles.

*

Note #80

Mrs. Hersland was more nearly of the second kind of them
the kind that subdue them [dependent independent kind] but she had so

little of this in her that it hardly made enough of it in her to be sure of which kind she had in her.

LK Draft of text, but passage in MA not identified. General sense of Note is used in MA 164–167, particularly MA 164: "… these are of the kind of them who always own their children who subdue those they need in living but these of this kind of women have it to have this that is them very lightly in them and Mrs. Hersland was of such a kind of them, these have it in them to be it so gently in them that it never comes out in them… ."

*

NB-*C #9

Got the definite difference now between Hersland and Dehning.
Hersland ~~murky~~ murkey sexual character, Leo, on to Matisse.
dirtier.

*

Dehning cleaner sexual bottom from Young toward Fred Stein.
cleaner.

*

NB-*C #10

Pablo so much dirtier than Raymond or Hutch. they cleaner sexual tabby goes to weakness, dirtier goes to pathology. weakness may end in senile pathology, does so with Dehning, Hersland always remains murky does not get pathological Dolene's preserves perfect balance between the two and so is basis for lady type and the simplest sex type. The adolescent type whether mistress or servant idealistic, sexual emotion pathological rather than sexual action. Same with men. Leo between the two. Derain between L.F. & Roche. Roche between Pach and aristocrat (Green.) Bruce toward the Jahne Leo F. toward Fred Stein, Stern between Derain and intellectual, and Persian, Leon, between Pablo and Stern mixture intellectual Persian & ~~sale~~ dirty Bozaraf. Pablo most genial Bozarof and dirtier.

*

NB-*C #11

*There is no NB-*C #11 in the original notebooks. Number inadvertently skipped*

*

NB-*C #12

Note that Neith, Maria Vladimirovna, Jane Cheron, Ella Milziener, Bird all have from varying complete servant girl of Bertha type to a beginning of Bertha mistress type complete in Mamy Berenson the same passion for intellectuality culture, higher ideas, morality ideally, etc, strongly sexual, mostly fairly stupid the more completely the servant girl the more completely intelligent until in that direction they got over to the flavor group Mary Houghton to the lady group and get really intelligent. Miss Blood, basis, new mistress top Bird quality in common with Alice Klauber who has bottom Adele about which I have already written. Dolene is undoubtedly bottom of Adele. Self-righteous and important and concentrated.

AT ***Ella Milziener:*** [Ella Milzeiner.] The very untidy, temperamental wife of a painter who did Gertrude's portrait. She lived up in Campagne Premier in a little nest of studios with her two children and left before I came to Paris.

*

Note #173

The Weiman family went in relation to Alfred and then his family in relation to him, each one, and then his going East.

Weiman family in relation to Mrs. Hersland, MA 250–285.

*

29897 Kitchen
21530
8322
33213 [Valden?]
19474 Garden

*

Note #91

Must concentrate and bring out Mr. David Hersland's character in the Marie Gruenhagen (Madeleine Weiman) transaction and then strongly in each individual history of death of his wife, and the funeral arrangements and his attempts at another woman broken down.
Its Sol Stein who has Rev. M.S. to find his woman
Now work in the country living for all of them, the children and the poor people, the mother in relation to them, the governess the father, his sexual

nature etc. Give a history of governesses to Madeleine Weiman, (M.G.) Jeanette Weiman her sister, Adolph her brother make him like Roche

LK ***the governess to the father, his sexual nature:*** MA 244–248.

history of governesses to Madeleine Weiman: MA 236–250.

to Madeleine Weiman: Begins MA 253.

Jeanette Weiman her sister: Becomes "Helen" in final draft. MA 263–268.

Adolph her brother: Becomes "Frank" in final draft. MA 268.

make him like Roche: [Corresponds to Note #61: "Adolph Weiman her brother, make him like Roche…."] His relation to Roche is problematic. Frank Wyman is described as vague, blonde and mild, with—the physical specificity is unusual—a long head and thick hair; a man who is not slow, but undecided, "a tender youthful being" with "being slower and pleasanter than his father." The two key terms describing him—key in GS's system—are these: he has no efficient nature, and he has "enough resistance in him to have his women keep on holding him up while he pleasantly and vaguely kept on living."

The Notebooks analyses of Roche intersect with this description only here and there. GS quotes—and repeats later in the *ABT*—that Roche is "a translation, as Pablo says [with] intelligence but no real intellect, the unfinished boy quality….no instinct for being a success….no heroic element," and like the rest of his "group" "stupid. Leo says it is because their minds move so slowly that they digest nothing and it comes out whole as it went in." [DB #53] An adolescent type [NB-*B #16], commonplace and mundane, but with a pride "that is the correlative of a certain passion for beauty and culture." [NB-*C #32] But he is also the chic man, the man of gayety [NB-A #9a], and rather than being characterized by resistance, is of the type who attacks [NB-C #24].

*

NB-*C #12a

The idealistic group are essentially rational in their intelligence and mystic in their temperament. Does that mean anything ain't very sure.

*

NB-*C #13

All the Bazarofs are at one time and mostly they marry them enamored of the ~~Bazarofs~~ family of Bertha. They like the apparent beauty, the apparent equality and the real inferiority. Bazarofs are not critical they have no touch stone for reality. They have reality and arrogance in themselves and the combination makes them not susceptibility of reality in others. Pablo is the highest type of it because being low he has most reality. I believe he will work out of submission to unreality.

*

NB-*C #14

Of this Therese, is close to Fernande, Therese and Neith are not the Bertha servant girl, or rather Neith may be nay is, Therese is not—Therese is allied to Marie Lorenzen, Dolene as base.

*

NB-*C #15

Marie Lorensen, & Mrs. Manguin same base one has intellect & character tothe[r] is nuts but its the same penetrating malicious unstable soulless feminine quality, the finest essence, it has sometimes a practical intelligence sometimes a piquant one sometimes a nutty one. Our Renoir portrait is the anaemic and lurid and hysterical version of it, what Neith ought to be but isn't would be the ideal basis for flavor group, I think [Nello Bealin?] had it, differs from the lady, lady nearer Hattie Bache but highly concentrated, Mary Houghton intermediate Alice Toklas not at all, it is possible that in an unconcentrated stupid form it is Fernande's base because hers is certainly not Bertha, who is Alice base. I imagine Fernande connects Hattie Bache to this group. Neith's base is servant girl. When this base goes over to Alice it is sale dirty wallows in filth masc—Pablo and so it connects to Adele Jaffa's group.

AT ***Mrs. Manguin... intellect and character:*** She was the one with intellect and character. She couldn't demean herself no matter what she did. She had no feeling of superiority, it was not that, but just a consciousness of being right. To her, it made no difference that she was clearly recognized as the nude model in her husband's painting.

Gertrude saw the Manguins for about three years, from about 1906 to 1908. They were not intimate, but Gertrude liked Manguin, who she felt was vigorous and had considerable life. Mrs. Manguin hadn't a speck of jealousy. She believed in her husband's painting but shared none of Mrs. Matisse's and Sally's way with Matisse.

When Sally discovered that Manguin was not a great painter, she threw him over.

Marie Lorensen [sic]... malicious unstable soulless feminine quality: [Marie Laurencin.] The first revelation she made of herself to Gertrude was when she came to the house and told of her abortion with Apollinaire. Later she took offense at the *Autobiography* and told Gertrude, We are public figures with private lives. They are not to be touched for any purpose.

When she was the mistress of the Prime Minister, M. Berthelot, she made no secret of it. His wife got in, forbade it, and Marie Laurencin took to her bed deathly ill Then the Berthelots came to a dinner party, and Pablo hadn't heard of Marie being seriously ill. He rushed at the Berthelots and said, Do you know Marie Laurencin is dying.

(The drawing by Marie Laurencin of herself, Apollinaire, Fernande and Picasso was bought by Gertrude, and when she was hard up, she sold it to Etta Cone for $100. Marie was furious when she heard of it.)

Our Renoir portrait: The blonde woman holding the child in her arms. Gertrude always spoke of her as being the Servant Girl type. It was meant to be the supreme love of the mother for the child. When Helene said it was the only picture in the room she liked, Gertrude said, You can understand why, it speaks to her directly.

Hattie Bache: Bird's older sister.

Mary Houghton: A little English woman devoted to her husband. They were among the first people Gertrude knew in Florence. Edmund Houghton never could earn any money. She always did that for him, selling old jewelry, anything. He once started to do photography, which he planned eventually to be a livelihood, and bought equipment and what not for it. But finally, Mrs. Houghton said, I can't afford to keep Edmund a photographer any longer.

in an unconcentrated stupid form... Fernande's base: Yes, Fernande would have gotten the worst of it in a harem, she would have come out badly.

*

NB-*C #16

Gabrielle bears a remarkable resemblance to Marie Lorensen. ~~Fr~~ Between her & Alice.

*

NB-*C #17

I am inclined more and more to derive all men's sexuality from one base, while the women seem to me more of the fixity of species.

LK Corresponds to Notes NB-*C #37 and NB-*J #4, and to passage in MA 151.

"Some of the things all men have in them in their daily living, have it to come, in more men, only from the bottom nature in them than other things in them."

"Bottom nature" is, according to discussion in MA 150–155, sexual nature. "In most men and many women go with the way of loving, come from the bottom nature in them" [MA 154.] And MA 158 summarizes: "their way of loving makes their kind of man." NB-*C #37 expands this notion: sexual character determines the type of intellect, and if the "temperament," which should be the "background" or secondary to the sexual nature, becomes instead the controlling principle of behavior, the character is "in contradiction," as in the instance of "Many… hav[ing] their [loving, thinking, working, etc.] to be made only of the bottom nature of their kind of them,… some… have the loving feeling in them with their way of thinking coming from … other kinds of natures in them not from the bottom nature in them." [MA 154.]

*

NB-*C #18

Harriet's attitude toward me like Aunt Pauline's and Mrs. Guggenheimer and Mrs. Schoninger that is the bourgeois stupid version of the primitive soul idea, the high falutin ones call me a primitive soul, the others, good-natured sweet, Dolene sympathetic motherly, never get tired etc, and all this is the same as Hutch's sweetness and humanity, its not me.

AT ***Harriet's attitude toward me:*** Harriet was very easy with Gertrude, liked her, and very early took sides with Gertrude against Sarah. She thought Gertrude interesting and Sarah not. Harriet knew Gertrude too from Fiesole on the trip before the one in 1906, when Gertrude was there for part of the summer and Harriet was flirting with Leo.

Mrs. Schoninger: The wife of the President of the American Chamber of Commerce in Paris. She was a great bourgeoisie and had herself painted by Beatrice Keyser so that her pearls would be immortalized, not herself.

*

NB-*C #19

Mrs. ~~Dennon~~ Berenson has the sexual nature of a very unconcentrated, unaccented, not even very jelly fishy Bertha and she has an intellect and a spirit to go with it, she has a ~~nature~~ character very different full of energy, desire and virtue and by that she would live but not having enough intellect she cannot make it come together. Sally has the highest concentration of the Bertha sex quality and intellect, she has the character of her father of Laura of Madame Vernot she has a great enough intellect to mostly bring it together.

AT ***Mrs. Berenson… character… full of energy, desire and virtue:*** She once said that she had married BB because he could answer more questions than her first husband could.

*

NB-*C #20

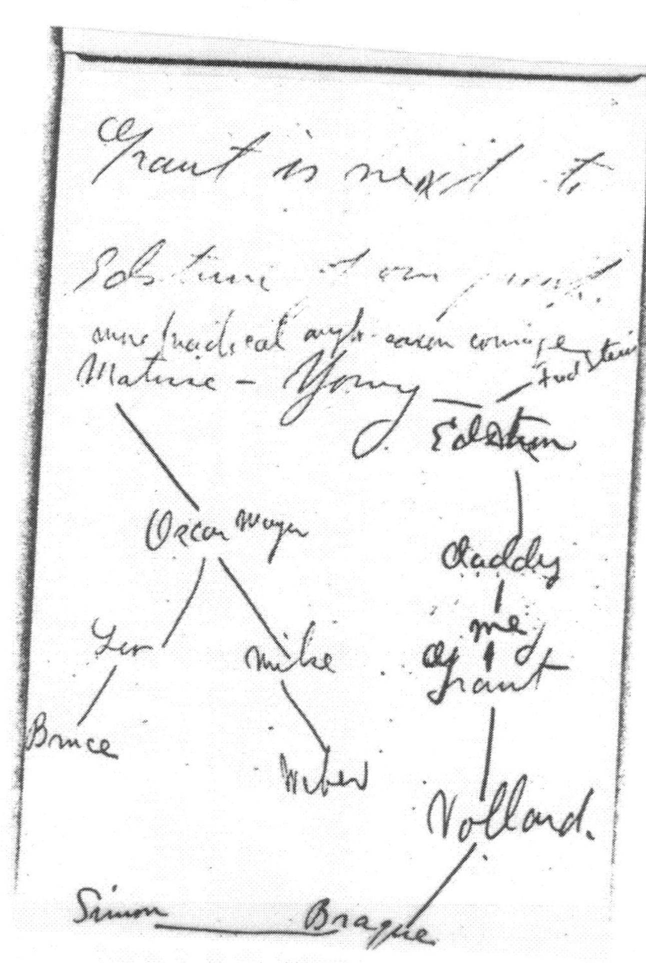

*

NB-*C #21

Consider if the division into—sex and mind and character does not explain those sentimental women cases that are so puzzling, Etta Cone—Fernande, Etta Guggenheimer, etc. I think this makes Bird clearer a good deal she is between Bertha and Sallie in sexual intensity and a [sic] intellect of low caliber to match character opposed so she don't know she lies.

AT ***sentimental women cases... Etta Cone:*** Extremely sentimental. As for her being a jelly fish, well, she was at the next stage where the shell was forming. And when it cracked, it hurt her and she retired in tears from the offense. She would strike out by giving a gift or making some such gesture. The more she loathed you, the more correct she was.

Etta Guggenheimer: One of Etta Cone's cousins, and Dolene's mother. She was very distantly connected to Gertrude.

Bird... don't know she lies: Later it was true of Sarah too that 'she don't know she lies.'

*

NB-*C #22

Take up the types of sense of injury, pride Alice Toklas, self-righteous Adele—Alice Klauber,—mistress type Sallie,—Aunt Pauline, verges to upper servant,—~~Harriet~~ Bird breaks down—prostitute power only with those who love them—Harriet certainly, greatness does not exist, no mystery for her. Harriet is more stupid than Aunt Pauline. Aunt Pauline recognises greatness and throws mud at it. Harriet is too stupid too insensible to recognise that there is anything ~~gre~~ intrinsically greater or better than herself in existence.

AT ***Harriet... too stupid... to recognize... anything... greater:*** She was more stupid for herself. 'Greatness' and all that was not interesting to her, it didn't hold her attention. What she felt close to in Gertrude was the warmth and humanity—that, she could touch.

LK ***Aunt Pauline recognizes greatness and throws mud at it:*** [Corresponds to Note NB-MA #38.]

*

NB-*C #23

Earth type tenacity and cowardice—Bertha type courage in attack and evasion. Bird an absolute case.

Alice Klauber has base of tenacity (self-righteous) character of Bird. Dolene Harriet & Adele. Self-righteous, materialistic, clever intellects. Dolene base prostitute, Harriet base materialist, Adele idealist. Hutch like Stephen Douglas. never worked his head, trusted to intuition. Must seriously work at H.

*

NB-*C #24

I think perhaps the two types Bertha & earth type sort of new parallel. I was thinking of it in relation to Alice T. & Pablo, but more in the fact that Derain and Co may be the earth version of the prostitute idealist, Hodder Greene—Edstrom ~~Roch~~ whose sexual emotional is pathological but whose sexual activity is only nominal. May represents this in women and perhaps Emma, Jeane Boiffard Hortense Federleicht are the earth corelatives [sic], in an earth type this would perhaps natural[ly] take the form of an adolescent type. Then in the concentrated forms probably one would also find the two varieties but this is only perhaps.

AT ***earth type… in relation to Alice:*** Gertrude mentioned this when I first came over, and I was alternately in and out of it. But one day Gertrude said, poking fun at me, I know what you are, you have the soul of an old maid mermaid. This was during the Spring, very early, in Paris. And I called Gertrude Erda for a while.

Jeanne Boiffard: The daughter of Mme, Vernot.

*

NB-*C #25

Characteristic that the three idealists Hodder, Edstrom & Byron all liked the cold women ideally, loved really the softer ones. Make that the theme for Martha

AT ***Edstrom:*** Married the cold one, finally. But he much preferred Gertrude's tenderness. He fled to Gertrude for consolation after his marriage with Cora Downer, his second wife. He was very frightened of his first wife, and also of the Steins.

Edstrom behaved like a weak coward. He married his first wife without her family having seen him. She brought him back to Denmark with her, where he was extremely well received and adopted by her family. But immediately he began to misbehave and be his own natural self, and his wife loathed it. They separated in Paris later, and she went back to Denmark on a visit. Edstrom, thinking he wasn't getting her back, turned up at the Opera in Denmark on the night his wife's family was sure to be there, with a Paris negress on his arm.

During the Spring after the Winter when Harriet saw God, Sarah advised her to use Edstrom as a healer. They flirted around to the point of the ridiculous.

For the first two years before his marriage to Cora Downer, he went completely under her thumb. Once he ran away from her to Vienna, and when he got there, he wired Gertrude, Do you know anyone in Vienna who would be interested in my being here? After their marriage, things changed. Quickly she lost her position as First Reader of the Christian Science Church. Edstrom would beat her up so that she couldn't go to the meetings.

*

NB-*C #26

Perhaps the correlative to the idealists is the Bazarof earthy. I don't know.

*

NB-*C #27

I really think that Mrs. Guggenheimer is the sordid solid base of Mme Vernot Laura Sally group. the mother Mrs. Wordsworth [?] in 3 clerks shows it they love their son-in-laws [sic].

*

NB-*C #28

No one without pride can be self-righteous? The whole subject of being injured is very important have to work it [out] sometime.

LK ***whole subject of being injured…*** The "whole subject" of "the sense of injury" is taken up in NB-*C #22, in DB #41, and in NB-A #15.

*

NB-*C #29

Note in Harriet the absolute lack of self-restraint in eating in general dirtiness of habit of busting things. All this ~~goods~~ goes with the true devil the spirit that denies the essential lack of morality, the coward fear the tenacity, the brilliancy. There is no evil. Soul of goodness in things evil does not apply. Evil implies its converse good as in posse. The spirit that denies can not affirm.

AT ***Harriet… lack of self-restraint:*** Harriet's greed at table was plain. It was not that she wanted to eat much, but wanted everything there was so that she could have a choice and leave it on the plate. She had a great consciousness of the purchasing power of money. Not that she was nouveau riche, she was much worse than that. A dollar was a terrific sum to her, even though she had a very good income. Her greed extended to money. She wasn't anxious, though, as Sarah was. Sarah also didn't want it for herself but wanted to destroy it.

When Harriet got intimate with the Mike Steins the first summer in Fiesole, they asked us to come to dinner. Harriet, a very good raconteur—a gift Mike loathed in her—told her take about a Mrs. Brown of London, and since Mike and Sally knew the people, Harriet elaborated on the tale. Leo and Gertrude roared, Mike and Sally sat silent and disapproving. Mike plainly hated the tale, but what Sally really resented was Harriet holding an audience. In any case, it would not have been in Harriet to realize that she was offending Sally deeply by the tale of these people.

All of them [the California set out of which Harriet came] were vicious, Harriet less than the others. Polly Jacobs once asked me to come buy something with her. When she had made her purchase, she asked me to take her purse from her arm and pay the bill. Polly didn't want to know how much she was in for.

*

NB-*C #30

Masculine quality of Mabel Haynes. The sexual quality there is not a concentrated one but an aggressive one and so it makes for masculinity, with it goes strongly the instinct for elegance and so this type is sexually really a masculine type. It is as far as I know the only really masculine type. In all the other concentrated sexually are concentrated to attract this is is [sic] concentrated to attack, they are therefor rarely favorite with men, often men mistake in women like myself because by temperament and point of view intellect and consciousness is masculine and the erotic emotion is masculine that the sexual nature is, my actual sexual nature is pure servant female. I like insolence I find it difficult to work up energy enough to dominate. Annette has not enough of sexuality for her type.

*

NB-*C #31

Mundane, Bohemianism.

All people in this sense are mundane who have not a kind of muggy sexuality. Thats the real reason Sally's house is less Bohemian. Purman,

Variot & Weber are mundane in this sense, morally respectable clean, in old men even these change, Mike is so a little murky but his affirmation is for clean, Sally has no murkiness, neither has Bird, nor in effect the Leo Friedman group, this sometimes goes with a murky kind where the affirmation is against as in Mike. By this group I don't mean worldly people but mundane that is so to speak morality that is without a profound acceptation of the basis of good and evil. Ethicalness and intellectually and sexually Sally is this, intellectually, sexually pridily, vaintily and practically, temperamentally and emotionally and intellectually with the critic intellect she is not it, but it is the other that the Bohemians feel. Matisse is like ~~Dohn~~ Hersland so big it don't count he is both, both murky coward, and on the other hand attacking and mundane and on the other hand idealist and irrepressible conflict person. Mundane in this sense means a non-recognition of the profounder meanings of evil, of damnation, in old men it passes away because old men must understand evil and its sex basis, young men may make it out of their imagination and then in their maturity deny it. Leo Friedman a type case of this, these understand that the Bohemians the ones that understand evil are dangerous. Harriet queerly enough has just a little dirt which might save her which is murky and not material but one can't reach it. Alice she is pretty nearly all bad.

AT ***Variot:*** Jean Variot, who wrote a book on Jeanne d'Arc. He was not an intimate of the Steins, just visited. He was a French Protestant who was converted to Catholicism during the First World War because he had the idea that the Protestants had ruined his life.

Harriet… has just a little dirt which might save her: When Gertrude said, After all, she didn't kill herself, I replied, Don't forget she wants to live more than anything else.

*

NB-*C #32

Of the group Purman Leo Friedman Derain Stein
Bush Pach Roche to idealist Bruce to Oscar Mayer Stern off in another direction, they have essentially the quality of wooden faces. Leo & Purman the most forceful and successful, they estimate themselves best, they are in a way teacheable [sic] for they have no pride, but they are the least sensible they are hard and mundane in ideal as well as in nature, they move

directly to their end. In all of them their minds are practical, detailed, unimaginative and common-place but in Leo Friedman and Purman there is no struggle because there is no intense personal pride. The intense personal pride in Derain ~~Pach~~ (least) Pach & Roche ~~are~~ is the correlative of a certain idealism a certain sensitiveness to beauty to the uncommonplace the unmundane. Derain and Goguin have it least but Pach and Bush and Roche had it very strongly this pride that is the correlative of a certain passion for ~~pure an~~ beauty and culture. Bruce has something else as Roche has something, in both there is a sexual base that is not truly of their group less vigorously male Bruce in direction of Puy and intellectual quality of it Roche in direction of Hodder, Stern sexual base like Leo F. & Purman but rest of character temperament Persian not a keen personal pride, rather the pride of conceit, the lowest form of what in Adele & Raymond Alice Klauber etc. passes over into concentrated pride of self-righteousness. Claribel & Alice between the two. Alice Klauber the least concentrated sexually and personally of that superbly dramatic group Dolene Gabrielle Adele to Mary Houghton. Alice Toklas has not the right sexual base for this group verges on Bertha. Alice Klauber has not intensity it takes more the form of pseudo intellectual morality such as Bird's energy rather than concentration, resistance rather than power. In Dolene & Adele resistance an power are one and inseparable they are the meeting point of the resistance group (earthy) and power group (Bertha). In earthy group power is practical not aggressively attacking. Dolene is a perfect example. Adele also perfect but infinitely more subtle.

*

NB-*C #33

Braque—Guerin these two represent for me the bottom earth type and Bertha type. Guerin is Bertha. The german man. Chalfin is of the Braque family, this are [sic] the unconcentrated sexual male types.

*

NB-*C #34

Salete—Adele, Pablo Harriet, Mary Houghton—Alice sexual base is not it, in Alice Klauber verges into the lady, Dolene really lady, it is when the flavor character is dominant that it is dirty, Alice without doubt has Bertha bottom her daddy is the real thing. Etta, Annette Mabel Haynes, sexually more dirty, personally not.

*

NB-*C #35

More and more to the two general groups the unconcentrated sexual groups show themselves. The general character of the Bertha, Sally, Edstrom, Edmund May, courage group clean sexually, practical not sordid, strong in attack, have to be beaten to be conquered, hard, type Anglo-saxon and American, the other earthy, sordid, cowardly, tenacious. ~~Grant~~ prudent—Grant, ~~Lincoln~~ Matisse, Young, me, Harriet, etc. [long? lay?] etc. now the interesting new point, is that the first group have to be cowed to be respectful, to know fear to love, the second group they have too intimate an acquaintance with fear to wish it, they love freedom, they wished to be conquered only by themselves for that is to conquer fear. Edstrom is a coward, but he is a coward of the first group, a courageous and practical person who has been cowed, and that is why he would ultimately fail to understand Harriet. Matisse belongs essentially to the earth group as I do still more as Grant did as Young does. Now certain lurid groups are one kind some the other, Puy luridily [sic] is degenerated, first group. Valloton, Jaehne Jack Preiss, Fred Stein, are all this group, Jake Samuels, May Bookstaver Roche they are all this group. It passes over into cowardice in the sensitiveness of Jaehne and Valloton, into modesty by excess of sexuality in Jakie Moses, & Puy, into insensibility in the tabby cat group Edmund and the clergy and Henry Clay, into another kind of inefficiency in the idealist group, Bertha is really the female correlative of Edstrom so is Olga and in a lesser degree Fernande. In the second group it passes over into fearlessness in the creation of self-righteousness in Adele, Alice Klauber Mary Gruenhagen, Dolene, fear has been hit and hardened into consciousness of virtue. Leon was the intermediate stage (the Bazarofs are then again it all intermediates self-righteousness or fanaticism or pure passes into luridness in Mabel Haynes group which is in this genius.) group the correlative, of Puy, Simon H., Laurie, in Simon H and Laurie is the most complete sordidness this group is capable of that is the first group. Then the second group goes through a process of cleanness in Mike to lack of internal spring in Leo Friedman that is their nearest approach to the practical quality of the other group, the unimaginative side.

The real flavor group are not of group two but of group one. Mary, Alice Toklas Janet, Mary McClean their sexual base is not earthy, they are the salete of Bertha's group, they have a lady version and it is not of Aunt Fanny, it is Hortense and Mrs. Samuels and Emma and Maud Tilton and so we come to adolescents but these are not clear yet. Dorothea Reade and Gracie Gassette here we have I think the most courageous of the fearful second group where there is no sexual concentration, they are really very fearful, but their attack is as if they were of the other group, Dorothy knew she would take no risks but she carried it off grandly, I imagine that is also true of Nelly.

AT ***Edstrom is a coward... and... would... fail to understand Harriet:*** He would fail to understand her because she would have no effect on him at all, and he could only have effect on people who could have effect on him. The two weak people could not affect each other. Harriet and he were pleased about their relation, he as a new experience, and she because she thought she was becoming a new kind of woman. But then it all wore thin.

May Bookstaver: Once she overheard her father and mother say, What a pity that since two of our children had to be taken, it should have been the wrong two. When her sister died, to prevent May from inheriting the money, the father gave as much as he could to charities and the income from the rest to the mother, so that even the mother couldn't will May the money. She was kept in luxury by her father and then by her mother until she married, but until then was permitted no financial independence or security. The story of the horse accident in 'Melanctha' is literally true. When it happened, the father refused to get a doctor for her, and May stayed in bed until she was strong enough to get up and go to friends, who called a doctor.

The history of Melanctha is true through the Jeff episode, but not Jem. Rose was added not as a portrait of Mabel Haynes, but a little bit of the Mabel Haynes story in connection with May Bookstaver. The relation between Rose and Melanctha came to Gertrude in a flash when she saw the two negro women one stormy night at Old Point Comfort, Virginia, when she was traveling north after a visit to Virginia. She was waiting for the boat to go back to Baltimore and saw this on the dock.

Gertrude [in *Q.E.D.*] used 'Helen Thomas' as the natural name for May—Helen Carey Thomas, remember, was the President of Bryn Mawr—and Mabel Neathe for Mabel Haynes, after Neith Boyce.

modesty by excess of sexuality in Jakie Moses: A perfect description of him— 'modesty by excess of sexuality.'

Puy: A contemporary and classmate of Matisse and Manguin in Carriere's class. Gertrude certainly wasn't seeing Puy any more in 1908, though she was still seeing Manguin. But she had known Puy through Matisse.

the female correlative of Edstrom... Olga: Olga Meerson was Purrmann's love and Matisse's first transgression. She used to come up to men, never to women, grab them by the collar and say breathlessly, I have something to tell you, and then would have absolutely nothing to say. She did that with all men. Olga wasn't proud, she never knew failure. Matisse swam in her beauty and her seductions. They went off together for about a month, then it was over.

*

NB-*C #36

This question of slow mindedness, It is a perfectly definitive quality that goes with the various sexual types. The earth type generally is slow minded slow and active, slow and inactive less slow, least slow the aggressive type is quick minded. Etta Cone, Annette to Mabel Haynes are slow as Pach and Bruce so slow they come to a stand still so slow that they are insensitive and worldly, so slow that it takes a tremendous stimulus to fire them. My group are slow but always in motion. Dolene is not slow Alice is not slow The Bazaroffs are not slow they are blind, they are facile they learn really easily, but they are blind. Pablo's instinct is right, he does not wish to slow himself but to concentrate himself.

Mike comes nearer to Leo Friedman, Derain is a good case he is the correlative of Annette, he is facile but not real, the Bazarofs, Sally's group are facile and real, they have the aptitude for culture. Berenson and Chalfin both have the ordinary bottom of Bertha group sexuality, slow of their type both are facile but not real. This is not sure because I think Chalfin's sexuality is like Braque's and B.B's like Alice but Alice is much quicker. BB's is not a very slow mind it is about like Leo's Bertha's, Chalfin Simon's group. Hutch is a non-earth Bazarof. The Keyser group if they did real thinking would be slow but they have none of them bottom for that, to be real they must be either like Mike or like Daniel Meyer. With them the facile, the sensitive, the superficial lyric is all there is of them.

AT ***Dolene:*** She was widowed before I met her. Her sister came over with her. The sister was very plain and Dolene was quite lovely with violent eyes—gentle, small, quite fancied herself. Dolene married late, at twenty-eight or thirty, and when I saw her in Paris, she was about forty. When her husband died, quite suddenly Dolene had too much knowledge of his stocks and bonds and assets, and as soon as he was dead, she managed all the business matter very quickly and knowingly.

Pablo's instinct was right: He never made an effort to be either slow or quick, he just wanted to concentrate his gift.

*

NB-*C #37

The conception of the sexual character determining the type of intellect and the temperament being either the background or to the detriment of the whole being the controlling force is constantly showing itself more clearly. It is the rare person like, Mike, like the Keysers, like Mary Houghton where there is no such contradiction, Aunt Pauline, perhaps.

*See NB-*C #17 and NB-*J #4.*

*

NB-*C #38

Connect the dramatic sense the reaction to the demands of the moment actuated by the temperament of the person as the essence of the dramatic temperament and to be found in what I call clean not muggy sexuality, Clay, Sally, Edmund, Fred, etc.

*

NB-*C #39

Bird shows a combination different from Sally. Sally has the character and intellect of Laura with the temperament of Aunt Pauline but in Aunt Pauline it is homogeneous it is the whole of her it goes all through her but in both Sally and in her they ~~play~~ fight to win. Bird fights to win something, she is sordid, in a sense greedy and grasping, Alice Klauber is greedy but does not want what she gets, Bird is greedy and wants it all, Au fond Bird is just the weakish prostitute of the ordinary type that accounts for her lack of maternal feeling. Mme Demarez and my german lady, are the purer and at the same time more practical expressions of Lana Oppenheimer, Sally's family, the thinner with the emphasis on the spiritual quality, Mabel the thinner with the emphasis on the sensative [sic] and prudish and pedantic quality, because in all of them their morality can become prudishness.

AT ***German lady:*** Fraulein Adelaide de or von Hessler, who lived in the court of the rue de Fleurus from 1908. She was a sculptress and was working on a large composition of an angel and a devil. She was a friend of Mildred Aldrich. Two things about here fascinated Gertrude, her reversible coat, the first Gertrude had ever seen, and her question—this is in the *Autobiography*—Miss Stein, in your writing, do you do it by intuition, by imagination or a theory? She disappeared in 1914 and was never heard of again.

*

NB-*C #40

General theme moral attitude in three different people in relation to men Sally, Bird, Alice Klauber and in relation to their type of mistress character. Sally married the master, the mistress greed the least and the other nature in her greatest, Alice Klauber next she rejected him at the last minute, Bird took hers. Archangel look in Sally to go with this possession.
Bird bottom of Miss Blood, no prostitute quality, the determination and [liking?] the Bertha version of my group Adele Alice Klauber etc.

AT ***Archangel look in Sally:*** It was Mildred Aldrich who called it the 'Little Eva expression.' It was perfect when Sally was with Matisse.

*

NB-*C #41

Alice Toklas has not a slow mind, it is a blind mind, and not ~~enough~~ an awful lot of it but it is quick enough, everything in her is personal flavor turns into affection or the attack is direct, fondness for young people fondness for their aroma, perfect specimen of flavor group except that it does not satisfy her. Have to do miracle on another to win her, the worldly side of her, the appeal to her admiration of success, like B.B.

*

NB-*C #42

Sally, Bird, Aunt Pauline, The combination in the three is the same, in Sally the sensibility is great the need is great and the mistress end is not for sordid purposes, not for practical results but for the love of power. (Edstrom, practical results.) Bird the mixture is the same only there is much greater quantity of the dominant stuff and its all practical ~~almost~~ to the point of greed, in Aunt Pauline it is almost all the practical, it is not greed in her it is like Sally's excepting only that it wants results. Bird is the least capable person of the three.

*

NB-*C #43

Sally's bottom sensibility and reserve, and benevolence, this in Mabel Weeks is only sensibility never practical benevolence and a petty mystery in place of real reserve. The reserve has in Sally and Laura the correlative of real intellect, the petty mystery in Mabel has its correlative in student intellectual pride, now Sally with Matisse comes nearer Mabel than any other time I have ever seen her, she melts him with sensibility and nerve, he possesses her in that sense she enters into him so. In Mademoiselle and the german lady, the reserve concentrates into a more practical quality with a practical intellect, in Mademoiselle purer in German lady less pure, in Madame Vernot it is all over the shop and sordid but real.

It is that sensibility that in some of them might become sheer clairvoyance that makes their apparent lying. Edstrom explained that very well, they have impressions it is only afterwards that they can prove them and their realler [sic] knowledge which they have afterward they are often inclined to believe they had at the same time as their impression and so they think they always knew they were always right, looking upon themselves as intuitive and being intuitive that is in the highest degree responsive, and being so sometimes intuitively right, their being no moment between perception and apperception it is most natural that they should think themselves to be right so much oftener than they are, particularly where the mistress the dominating quality is strong because then passes over so spontaneously into directing, consequently Sally would think she would be running Matisse when really she would be only in the most intensive way reacting to him, she so explains things to him, gets him as Leo puts it to make him do what he wants to do, never what he does not want to do. It is this which is the basis of their apparent lying, in Bird the sensibility is so at the minimum that she mostly don't lie, in Mabel it is mixed up with this petty spirit of mystery, in Edstrom it takes the form of hard practical success, in Sally and Laura in the belief that they were right, much oftener than they were particularly in important things where they only came to the right conclusion after a long time, vanity of course which all of them have helps to this, and so I think that unless it was extreme and completely fought out between them it would remain what it now is sensibility and nerve, entering into aggressive egotism and sensibility.

AT ***Mabel Weeks... petty mystery in place of real reserve:*** That was my impression of her. I was supposed to rescue her when presumably she was alone in Paris. When we met, she was with several other people, and then went off with a man, but we agreed that I would telephone her the next day. When I did, she was, she said, unfortunately occupied, but there was no explanation.

Sally with Matisse... melts him with sensibility: Gertrude called it her 'tremulous, gross flattery' of Matisse. I remember her once talking to Matisse *tete a tete* when she put her foot on his chair to support herself in her enthusiasm to tell him something. Matisse, as a Frenchman, noticed it, resented it, looked troubled, and didn't know how to withdraw.

[Sarah's] clairvoyance: Sarah could devance your speaking your thought before you said it or were ready to say it. That was her method of proceeding.

*

NB-*C #44

Mike differentiate[s] himself from Leo Friedman and Purman in being an individual, he is conventional, mundane as they are, he transcends it by being completely themselves [sic] they don't.

*

NB-*C #45

Mike and Harriet are of all people I know most simply and perfectly individual without egotistic admixture, Leo & Sally and Pablo all three have the mixture, Bruce is a weak individual, Hutch is like Leo and Sally, Leo is nearer the individual Sally nearer the egotist. Edstrom is a weak aggressive egotist, Matisse ~~is a strong~~ and Edmund are strong brutal egotism, I am a strong tenacious egotist. Chalfin is very weak mixed individual, Alice is an individual in Leo's kind, but weak, so is Mary & B.B. May, Purman, Leo Friedman, Jeanne Boiffard, Annette, Roche, are not individuals, Alice Klauber Adele Jaffa etc are individualists of a strong type who have the egotistic point of view and so fail as human beings. All the adolescents in this sense are not individuals although tremendously efficient, Simon H of course is, Dolene is but has the egotistic point of view, Claribel is very greatly an individual, Etta I don't understand.

*

NB-*C #46

My attack on Alice is like Grants on Lee and that is the essential character of the unaggressive complete egotist, always a forward pressure, often suffering fearful loss (Wilderness campaign) perfect discouragement and then takes to drink ~~but~~ or amusement but always a forward pressure till the final achievement doing the necessary things. Johnson (Samuel) same kind, Balzac same kind, me. The aggressive egotist, (possibly Shakespeare) Matisse, Edstrom, Van Goch ~~etc~~ Sally etc, if they achieve will achieve the greatest because they have brilliancy and direct attack added to what the others have. If Matisse does it, he will be the greatest, Edstrom is a weak one but a complete one, Van Goch was too aggressive for his egotism quantitavely [sic] also Sally is. Their sensibility is too great for their resistance. Napoleon was not in this an egotist he was an individual, Abraham Lincoln, Leo, Pablo is half and half. Young was the aggressive egotistical type but not a very full natured one.

Hutch is the mystic and practical these are not egotists, they are also connected with a kind of powerful aggressive lurid practical persuaded sexuality which arouses fear in me. Green between Hutch and the idealists (the aggressive egotists) Braque and Appolinaire between Hutch and Matisse. Pablo and Leon to the beauty Bazarofs. The female correlative group, aggressive sexualists and mystics, and individual in type, they are individualists with the egotists point of view, they are mystics and self-righteous, they have the profound contradiction of being mystics, absolutely negation of themselves in the infinite and and [sic] most aggressive sexually and individually, consequently it takes the form of self-righteousness most commonly, Hutch is the very same type of it, Greene is also of it but tends to idealist group. They have the tolerance of the mystic universal they have the intolerance of the intensely inefficient practical dominating perhaps rather than aggressive actual.

Edstrom and Sally are really aggressive, efficient and practical successful, and their religion has the larger movement of this their nature, their danger comes from the passion of success, which makes them lie etc because they must always have been successful always have been right. This I think makes clear, Adele's child passion for there this can be best expressed the mystic and the dominant, the complete abnegation and losing herself in the infinite and the relentless aggressive ~~domi~~ intolerant domination, Alice Klauber it is the same, in Mary and farther in Alice, mysticism becomes less domination less efficiency greater. Dolene is the material basis of all this. This was true of Jeane. they all have this lurid passion.

*

NB-*C #47

Women (probably Lucrezia Borgia) Puy's women, Fabre's woman, practical cold, don't care for their man, care enormously for something else children, business, friend, something, hold a man of a weak nature beauty living, flavor with strong lurid sexuality, Fabri, Therold, Mrs. Therold is the finest type of it, they have a beauty of fine plaster cast, they so completely hold the man for they satisfy him sexually entirely they can't be hurt by them for they don't care for them they care for something else, the[y] are practical tyranical [sic], beautiful, immobile, more or less efficient, in their weaker forms they are like Mrs. Mathew and Mrs. Putnam their husbands then think them absolutely pure and good, ~~somehow they connect with~~ Mrs. Therold at one point touches Adele, they may be the Bertha version of the Adele group.

AT ***Fabre's [sic] woman:*** [Egisto Fabbri.] The woman to whom Fabbri was devoted, and for whom he sold all his Cezannes to build a chapel after her death.

Mrs. Thorold… cared for something else: Mrs. Thorold cared most for her religion.

*

Big new long book

Draft text & planning note:

One must remember all the different kinds of ways one sees them, as men and women, as one kind or the other kind of them, as bottom nature, as flavor, as basis, as emotions in them, as acting in them, as wordliness in them, as life and vigor, in them, as joy or sorrow in them, as repeating of them, as vanity and modesty in them, for different kinds of value in them, all these ways of looking at them each one of them must be brought out in this history of every kind of man and every kind of woman.

Then too goodness and badness in them, honesty and dishonesty to themselves and to others around them, are important in them to understand them.

AT ***Alice… flavor:*** I was supposed to be in the flavor group, but I got out early. [LK: So she imagined. GS, in the Notebooks, assumes Alice continuing as prime example of the "flavor group" character, certainly until the end of the Notebooks.]

LK ***Big new long book:*** [Draft text & planning note:] Probably the first entry for *A Long Gay Book*. Written, apparently, as both text and planning note, but not used as text. Corresponds somewhat, and only in part, to *LGB,* **16–17**.

*

NB8, #12

A long book.

A history of everybody.

Leo concentrated and blinded makes fanatic like Raymond. this unidealised makes into Hutch.

*

NB-*B #1

I have in truth some penetration; I am able to say when a flea bites me from what woman it came.

Source unidentified; at a guess, Jonathan Swift

*

NB-*B #2

A long book, being a history of ~~many~~ all kinds of men and women, ~~and~~ when they were ~~first~~ babies and then children. and then ~~then young~~ grown men and women, and the many kinds there are of them and the many millions always made of each kind of them.

LK ***A long book, being a history of all kinds….*** [Corresponds to Note #139.] Text later appended to the title of *A Long Gay Book*; it appears on the front cover of the first of the Long Gay Book's eight manuscript volumes.

*

NB-*B #3

Planning Note:

Short note for long book -

Begin with life history of Alice go on to Mary H. and then a general discourse on all the Bazaroffs to Stern and Leo and then on through the idealists male and female ending up with Puy and servant girls through Marie Vladoniovna and Hortense Federleicht.

*

Note #34

Planning Note:

In this book give all the fashions of allying oneself to eternity by various ways Sally and the being buried alive, May etc. and finally created work, family, pride, intellect, materialism go [on] and show how they all do it. With my experience a sort of connecting thread routine work another way of grasping eternity, ethics, beauty, love, philanthropy money,

LK ***In this book … allying oneself to eternity:*** Plan for text in *A Long Gay Book*, p. 15.

*

Note #23

Planning Note:

In this book there will be discussion of pairs of people and their relation, short sketches of innumerable ones, Alice pablo, Pablo Fernande, Leo and I, Sally and I, Annette & Laurie, Matisse & Mrs., Manguin & Matisse, Mike & Sally, Miriam & Joe everybody I know Brenner & Nina, Leo and Nina, Leo & Jeanne, Jeanne Boif & me, Marie & Helene, everybody I can think of ever, narrative after narrative of pairs of people, that will be the long book. Manguin & Mrs., Valloton & Manguin, Braque & Harriet, Sally & Polly, Therese & Sally etc. etc. everybody, Sterne & us, Leo F., & us, Emily Dawson & me.

AT ***In this book…*** Marchand the painter did a picture of two women who weren't looking at each other or anything, and Gertrude said, That's a very very interesting relation you have in those two personages. There were two isolated figures, and yet not separate but in relation. Gertrude told Matisse at Vence when she saw him there, and he flew up to see the picture. What was it he hadn't yet done, that was original in painting?

In *A Long Gay Book*, Gertrude would take a kind that suited her, and then make something suitable to put it in relation to another one, not necessarily of the same kind. Pairs, it would be, and in fictional situations.

Leo and I: Gertrude was never dependent on Leo, though she adored him, but only as a younger sister. She didn't refer anything to Leo at any time. By the time I came over, it was Gertrude who was making the flat statements that

Leo could take or leave. Leo would come and argue them, and at first Gertrude would answer him, then a little later, she stopped bothering. When they were still arguing, and Leo would say something, she would cut right through with enormous force, and her powerful body and voice made it even more forceful.

As a protector and older brother, Leo was extremely kind. When they traveled, he saw to it that Gertrude was comfortable, he saw to the arrangements, he saw to everything. And they were very close then. On the third trip over to Spain, they had the greatest difficulty getting two rooms because no one would believe they were brother and sister but took them for husband and wife. Or living as.

LK ***In this book … Emily Dawson and me:*** Outline of plan for *A Long Gay Book*, but incorporated as text in LGB. The text substitutes pseudonyms for the names mentioned in the Note, as follows:

> In this book there will be discussion of pairs of people and their relation, short sketches of innumerable ones, Ollie, Paul; Paul, Fernande; Larr and me, Jane and me, Hattie and Ollie, Margaret and Phillip, Claudel and Mrs. Claudel, Claudel and Martin, Maurice and Jane, Helen and John, everybody I know, Murdock and Elise, Larr and Elise, Larr and Marie, Jenny Fox and me, Sadie and Julia, everybody I can think of ever, narrative after narrative of pairs of people, Martin and Mrs. Herford, Bremer and Hattie, Jane and Nellie, Henrietta and Jane and some one and another one, everybody Michael and us and Victor Herbert, Farmert and us, Bessie Hessel and me. [LGB, **p. 17**]

But this outline, though incorporated into the text of LGB, is subsequently ignored, and the strategy of analysing "pairs" in the rest of the work is for the most part abandoned. The analyses of characters tend to be listic, one following another, as in the concurrently written MA and *Many Many Women*. A different list of pseudonyms is used in the LGB [see Note #14]. The names in the later list and in the published text retained from the note above are only these: Paul (Picasso); Larr (Leo Stein); Jane (Sarah Stein); Claudel and Mrs. Claudel (Matisse and Mrs. Matisse); Murdock (Michael Brenner); Elise (Nina Auzias); Nantine (Felix Vallotton); Bremer (Georges Braque).

*

Note #24

First side, apparently concluding a previous note:

Heiroth and his wife must pervade this history

*

Remember that illustration Sally to Harriet, if you dreamed your mother was dead if you wake up would you put on mourning, Mrs. Matisse would if she believed it as H. does her dreams. Mrs. Matisse connected with the fanatic group but both more attacking and more attackable.

LK ***Remember that illustration…*** Plan for section of LGB, expanded into text, 17.

*

Note #32

Go carefully into the flavor question giving short sketches of ~~Neith~~ B.B., Chalfin and any other man you can get describing the complications then branch off into the women, Neith, Janet, Grace Lounsbury etc to Alice, and then say that its hard to bring it in with other feelings in them but it has been done and I have seen it and so you must hear me tell it and then describe Bertha, as I have known it [sic] from Bertha go on to all kinds of women that come out of her, go from them to Sally's group, then come back and describe Hattie's group, then spinster Etta's group always coming back to flavor idea & Bertha idea, then go on to adolescents, mixing and mingling and counteracting. Then start afresh with May's group, practical, pseudo masc. etc. Then start fresh with Aunt Fanny and business women earthy type and kind of intellect, enlarge on this and then go back to flavor to pseudo flavor, Annette's group, and then to the concentrated groups. From then on complicate and complete given [sic] all kinds of pictures and start in again with the men. ~~flavor~~ Here begin with ~~adolese~~ Leo Victors group and ramify from that. Simon bottom of Chalfin Braque et al. and then go on and tell how one would love and be loved as a man or as a woman by each kind of them and so end up with the refrain and I from love escaped am so fat I.

AT ***Aunt Fanny and business women:*** Aunt Fanny organized her family comfortably and beautifully in a small, quiet way. Gertrude said she always managed her economies by saving one and one and one and one. Her small economies were saved up for household furniture, for household things, and so on. It was always done gently, quietly, efficiently, with nothing sordid about it. So in that sense, she could be connected with business women.

LK ***Go carefully into the flavor question … as a man or a woman:*** Plan for section of *A Long Gay Book*, converted into draft for text, used in LGB 18.

This text duplicates and expands Planning Note [Note #139] which was incorporated into the text in the paragraph immediately preceding.

And I from love… so fat I: See Note #139 for corresponding entry.

*

Note #14

Single sheet, both sides, written by Alice Toklas:

~~Ollie~~ Olive	me
Paul	Pablo
Fernande	Fernande
~~Leo~~ Larr	Leo
Jane Sands	Sally
Hattie	Harriet
Mildred	
Margaret	stinker
Phillip	Laurie
Claudel	Matisse
Minnie Claudel	Margot
Martin	Manguin
Nantine	Valloton
Maurice	Mike
Helen	Miriam
John	Jo
Murdock	Brenner
Elise	Nina
Marie	Jeanne Charron
Jennie Fox	Jeanne Boiffard
Sadie	Marie
Julia	Helene
Herford	Valloton
Bremer	Braque
Nellie	Polly
Henriette	Theresa
Michael	Sterne
Victor Herbert	Leo Friedman
Farmert	Berenson

Bessie Hessel
Pauline
Eugenia
Mabel Arbor
Sophie
Fanny
Helen
Lucy
Simon
Alden
Henderson
Myrtle
Constance
Nina Beckwith
Grace

Emily Dawson
Bertha
Etta Cone
Hattie Bache

Aunt Fanny
Grace Gassette
me
Simon
Chalfin
Pritchert
Neith
Janet Dodge
Grace Loundsbury [sic]
May Buckstaver [sic]

Rest of list written by GS:

Sloan
Gibbons
Johnson
Hobart

Pelrot
Lee Simonson
Russell
Spaniard

*

Carmine
Watts
~~Johns~~ Arthurs
Miss Lane
Vrais
Mrs. Gaston
George ~~Clifford~~ Clifton
Punkley
Miss Danien
Miss Waltny
" Hendry
Inez
Haick
Marie

Winzer
~~Black Man~~ Coolidge
Frost
Purman's American
Roche
Mrs. Edstrom
Frank
Purman
Danoise
Vohlmuller
Funke
Olga
Francis
Inez

On next side: Real and fictional names reversed:

Nelly	Nettie
George Clifton	Tom
~~Grace Nina~~	~~Elise~~
Mildred	Madelena
Helene	Mary
Sayne	Mr. Peter
Mrs. Sayne	Mrs. Peter
Bruce	Flint
Allan	Martin
Ulman [sic]	George
Maddalena	Maddalena
Egenia [sic] *[Etta Cone]*	Eugenia
Mabel Dodge	Minnie Harn
Miss Mars	Miss Furr
Anne Fletcher	Anne Helbring
Carrie	Minna
Steichen	Mr. Hurr
Simonson	Sender
~~Gibb~~ Harris	Henns
Gibb	Donger
Bruce	Clay, Clellan
Miss Blood	Miss Harvey
Basil	Wilbur
Howard	~~Daotlys~~ Antliss

AT ***Pelrot:*** [Perlrot.] A Matisse pupil. A dreadful Austrian or German painter who wore heavy pale gaiters that got a little dirty as the week went on. Everyone would announce, Pelrot has new gaiters this week.

Anne Fletcher: A dull creature, an American art student from Richmond whom Leo picked up. Bruce used to roar with pleasure at Leo's taking such people seriously. It was another thing that made Bruce scorn Leo's judgments, predilections, views on people, philosophic pronouncements. Leo had a facility for taking up with bores like these. And, too, he was flirtatious in a strange kind of way.

Harris: The son of Sam H. Harris, the theatrical producer. He was a friend and patron of Harry Gibbs.

Winzer: A charming Pole and a painter, probably a bad one. After the first world war, he was in love with Adrienne Monnier, the partner, sort of, of Sylvia Beach.

Coolidge: A tall Bostonian, Harvard probably, who was brought by Lee Simonson. Very elegant, very black and white, very tall and a little lugubrious. He came twice at most.

Danoise: The woman with the Cheshire cat smile in the court [of the rue de Fleurus] when we went out.

[Die] Vohlmuller: The woman Purrmann finally married when he didn't marry Margot Matisse. Her brother was a poet, and later a famous aviator, though that perhaps was another brother.

LK List of pseudonyms planned for text in LGB, partially used, as follows:

Sloan	=	Pelrot, p. 28, l. 21
Gibbons	=	Lee Simonson, p.28, l. 27.
Johnson	=	Morgan Russell, p. 28, l. 32
Hobart	=	Spaniard, p. 29, l. 1
Carmine	=	Winzer, p. 29, l. 9.
Watts	=	Coolidge, p. 29, l. 14
Arthurs	=	Arthur Frost, p. 29, l. 17
Vrais	=	Henri-Pierre Roche, p. 29, l. 23.
Jane Sands	=	Sarah Stein, p. 30, l. 9.
Larr	=	Leo Stein, p. 30, l. 22.
Mrs. Gaston	=	Mrs. Mary Baker Eddy, p. 30, l. 32.
George Clifton	=	Frank Jacott, p. 31, l. 2.
Claudel	=	Henri Matisse, p. 32, l. 29.
Mrs. Claudel	=	Mrs. Matisse, p. 32, l. 33.
Payman	=	Hans Purrmann, p. 33, l. 12.
Miss Hendry	=	Miss Funke, p. 33, l. 18.
Miss Damien	=	"the Danoise" p. 33, l. 23.
Miss Lane	=	"Purrmann's American," p.33, l. 31.
Miss Watling	=	"die Vohlmuller," p. 33, l. 34.
Minnie Claudel	=	Margot Matisse, p. 33, l. 37.
Marie	=	Inez Cohen, p. 34, l. 13.
Haick	=	Francis Pollak, p. 34, l. 16.
Nettie	=	Nelly Jacott, p. 37, l. 2.
George Clifton	=	Frank Jacott, p.37. l. 8.
Elise	=	Nina Auzias, p. 37, l.18.
Madeleine	=	Mildred Aldrich, p. 37, l. 37.
Mr. Peter	=	H. Lyman Sayen, p. 38, l. 37.

Mrs. Peter	=	Mrs. Jeannette Sayen, p.39, l. 19.
Flint	=	Patrick Henry Bruce, p. 39. l. 20.
Martin	=	Allan Stein, p. 40. l. 13.
George	=	Eugene Paul Ullman, p. 40. l. 30.
Maddalena	=	Maddalena, p. 41, l. 1.
Eugenia	=	Eugenia, p. 41, l. 15.
Minnie Harn	=	Mabel Dodge, p. 42, l. 7.
Anne Helbing	=	Anne Fletcher, p. 42, l. 8.
Minna	=	Carrie Helbing, p. 42, l. 9.
Mr. Hurr	=	Edward J. Steichen, p. 43, l. 18.
Clay	=	Patrick Henry Bruce, p. 44, l. 27.
Anne Helbing	=	Anne Fletcher, p. 45, l. 11.
Minna	=	Carrie Helbing, p. 45, l. 28.
Thomas Whitehead	=	? p. 46, l. 11
Clellan	=	Patrick Henry Bruce, p. 46, l. 26.
Murdock	=	Michael Brenner, p. 47, l. 27.
Nantine	=	Felix Vallotton, p. 47, l. 31.
Lamson	=	? p. 49, l. 8.
Miss Harvey	=	Florence Blood, p. 51, l. 12.
Wilbur	=	Basil, p. 51, l. 12.
Clellan	=	Patrick Henry Bruce, p. 51, l. 32.
Vrais	=	Henri-Pierre Roche, p. 53, l. 17.
Boncinelli	=	? p. 53, l. 30.
Mr. Peter	=	J. Lyman Sayen, p. 54, l. 19.
Mrs. Peter	=	Mrs. Jeannette Sayen, p. 54, l. 19.
Clellan	=	Patrick Henry Bruce, p. 55, l. 26.
Wente	=	? p.62, l. 3.
Bremer	=	Georges Braque, p. 66, l. 3.
Paul	=	Pablo Picasso, p. 66, l. 4
Herford	=	Felix Vallotton, p. 66, l. 12.
Clellan	=	Patrick Henry Bruce, p. 66, l. 20.
Cheyne	=	? p. 66, l. 28.
Helen	=	Miriam Price, p. 66, l. 34.
Paul	=	Pablo Picasso, p. 67, l. 5.
Dethom	=	? p. 67, l. 13.
Clellan	=	Patrick Henry Bruce, p. 68j, l. 7.
Larr	=	Leo Stein, p. 68, l. 23.
Clellan	=	Patrick Henry Bruce, p. 69, l. 35.
Gibbons	=	Lee Simonson, p. 70, l. 16.
Lilyman	=	? p. 70, l. 25.
Fabefin	=	? p. 70, l. 35.
Watts	=	Coolidge, p. 71, l. 10.
Donger	=	Harry Phelan Gibb, p. 71, l. 34.
Murdock	=	Michael Brenner, p. 72, l. 6.

Clellan	=	Patrick Henry Bruce, p. 73, l. 29.
Antliss	=	Howard Gans, p. 74, l. 1.
Clellan	=	Patrick Henry Bruce, p. 74, l. 37.
Donger	=	Harry Phelan Gibb, p. 75, l. 5.
Polly	=	? p. 76, l. 30.
Anne Helbing	=	Anne Fletcher, p. 76, l. 33.
George	=	Eugene Paul Ullman, p. 77, l. 3.
Henns	=	Harris, p. 77, l. 6.
Antliss	=	Howard Gans, p. 77, l. 17.
Sender	=	Lee Simonson, p. 77, l. 26.
Donger	=	Harry Phelan Gibb, p. 78, l. 29.

*

Note #37

When you come to Mrs. David ought to have [-?-]
~~D. D. the way she teaches me everything.~~
~~Grace love story, ma, all.~~
Mrs. Manguin children, husband, no desires.
go on to her fear. her ma and her submission and he[r] waiting to have friends and going any one better and not really having feeling.
Dangerous woman?
oDo*
Combine utilitarian and marrying Vall[o]ton

*

education of children etc. washing, family

*

Dora Israels. Her failure and effort, her movement, her illusion, her love and her incapacity to do the thing she has always in her mind. suffrage devotion.

*

Double-cake

AT ***Mrs. David:*** Cora Downer, Mrs. David Edstrom.

D.D. the way she teaches me everything: D.D. is "myself." Gertrude also used the initials possibly in her writing at Vence one summer, in about 1924.

LK [Miss Toklas made a point of avoiding explanation of these initials beyond the fact that they stood for her. She told me instead:] When Virgil [Thomson] was here a few weeks ago [asking questions about the volume he was introducing for the Unpublished Writings series, Gertrude Stein's Bee Time Vine] I told him, 'No, the initials stood for nothing. They were made up out of pure imagination.' I wasn't going to tell him what they stood for. [When I asked if I might know what they stood for, she reared back with a laugh, and barked:] You may not, young man, I've told you enough already. [They remain a subject for ingenious supposition.]

AT ***Grace love story, ma, all:*** [Grace Gassette.] Gertrude knew Gracie through Mildred Aldrich. Her relation with Gertrude was that she wanted to own her, and still she knew that Gertrude had more value if she didn't own her. She was simpleminded but astute, told stories about her mother, herself and her mother's two husbands to entertain Gertrude, and they did. She behaved badly about Mildred Aldrich at the end and came and cried to Gertrude that she didn't know [how Mildred had been suffering], and Gertrude said, If you wanted to know how Mildred was getting on, you would have gone to see her, stop making a fool of yourself. Grace's mother, Mrs. Gassette, was a very weak, very dignified, calm, feminine woman, above all feminine, who ran things with an iron hand in a silk mitt.

Mrs. Manguin children, husband, no desires: When I saw her, she was surrounded by her husband and three children. I didn't get to know her at all. Gertrude's intimacy with the Manguins was over when I arrived. She was wellborn, of army people, but that didn't deter her from posing nude, recognizably, for her husband. That was all right, she felt, if that's what he wanted.

marrying Vallotton… family: Vallotton married a Mme. Henriquez, a South American with two boys and a girl. It was of her daughter that Gertrude said, She's a very pretty girl with thin Jewish hair. Vallotton complained to Gertrude while he was doing her portrait about the bourgeois family dinners of his wife's people, and that his stepchildren were too noisy and took up too much room.

Dora Israels. Her failure… her love: She was in love with a very young boy half her age. A typical old maid, very plain, dreadful. It took all of Gertrude's patience even to make a note of it.

*

Note #138

For A Long Gay Book, *references to page numbers in the Plain Edition and in the Dover Edition of* Matisse, Picasso and Gertrude Stein and Two Shorter Stories *are identical.*

Manuscript Notebook #8 of LGB, ***pp. 1–17****, is concurrent with* NB-*B *#1. the* ***Diagram Book & Notebook *C****. The Note below is one of a number of versions of introduction-cum-planning note for the LGB, none of which survived intact.*

GS Manuscript. note:

[A LONG GAY BOOK]

"Many kinds of people have it in them to be proud inside them—there are many ways ~~then~~ of having such a proud feeling. Then go on with all the kinds of proud feelings and those connected with being important to themselves inside them and those connected with the sweetness that one loves in them. then go on elaborating this through the whole gamut then describe intelligence and idealism and sex and success in all its forms, Any descriptions of all the groups in relation to their most dominant feature etc. etc. the common-placeness, sordidness, earthiness, religion, ethics. Many kinds of people have it in them to be proud inside them."

LK Close to period of MA 128, re: Pride, Kinds, Babies, and "a man in his living has many things inside him." [MA 149]

Many kinds of people… proud feeling: Early draft of text for LGB 14. Not used.

Then go on with all the kinds… religion, ethics: Planning Note for passage intended to follow text above, but not used as planned.

*

Note #139

On front cover of first notebook for LGB Notebooks 1 to 8:

"A long gay book

by

G. Stein

[Added later to title:]

"being a history of all kinds of men and women, when they were babies and then children and then grown men and women and then old as old men and old women have it to be in them, being a history of the many kinds there are of men and women and the many millions always made of each kind of them."

*Cf. NB-*B #1.*

Also in ink, on facing page is the quote from Chaucer:

"Since I from love escaped
am so fat
I never think to be in
his prison lean.
(Geoffrey Chaucer)

Inside back cover:

"Make this book a general leading up to the description of Alice as an xception (bottom nature), then speak of the Bertha servant in her and describe in full Bertha then describe in full spinsters (whole group Etta etc) then grade from them to Hattie Bache group, then come back to Bertha and go through the whole woman group ending up with Sally and her relation to men and so to the group men ending up with Pablo genial. Then take a fresh start with Aunt Fanny and run through servants and adolescents to me and so again to women and how they love men and how they are in detail, and so to Simon as type man."

LK ***make this book a general leading up to… type of man:*** Planning Note for *LGB,* **p. 17, l. 29 to p. 18, l. 6** converted into text and expanded, with pseudonyms replacing names, as follows: "This is a general leading up to a description of Olive who is an exception in being one being living. Then there can be a description of the Pauline group and of the Pauline quality in Ollie and then there can be a complete description of the Pauline group and there could be a description of ones who could be ones who are not at all married ones a whole group of them of hundreds of them, and they grade from Eugenia to Mabel Arbor who is not like them in being one who could have been one not being a married one. Then once more one can begin with the Pauline group and Sophie among them, and then one can go through whole groups of women to Jane Sands and her relation to men and so to a group of men and ending with Paul. Then one can take a fresh start and begin with Fanny and Helen and run through servants and adolescents to Lucy and so again to women and to men and how they love, how women love and how they do not love, how men do not love, how men do love, how women and men do and do not love and so on to men and women in detail and so on to Simon as a type of man."

"Since I from love escaped …" Quoted from Geoffrey Chaucer [d.1400], "Merciles Beaute, a triple roundel:". The brief poem, on love's capture and the lover's fortunate escape, is in three parts: I "Captivity;" II "Rejection;" III "Escape." The third part, celebrating escape, concludes:

> Love hath my name y-strike out of his sclat,
> And he is strike out of my bokes clene
> For ever-mo; [ther] is none other mene.
> Sin I fro love escaped am so fat,
> I never thenk to ben in his prison lene;
> Sin I am free, I counte him not a bene. [W.W. Skeat, *Complete works of Chaucer*, 1899, vol. 1**, p. 388**]

[See NB-*B #1 for corresponding entry.]

*

Note #140

Note for LGB 35: "In beginning going on living"

"~~Filling being living~~"

*

LGB 42: "Having come to be that one he was one come to be one"

"How Fernande taunted [haunted?] him with her society[?] and how he was a liberator forcement[?]."

*

LGB 47: "Nantine if he were a sadder one would be a lonely one."

"(do a lot Manguin etc)"

*

LGB 48: "In putting down anything"

"(Go on with Matisse)"

*

LGB 49: "If, and if not then it is not,"

"(Go on in being ones and works of art)"

*

LGB 65: "One knowing everything is knowing that sometime"

GS deleted following paragraph, and revised as printed:

Why should any one want to know what they come to
know. In coming to know what they come to know they come to know what some knew and if some knew then if they had been told they would have

known and having known they would not have had to come to know and not having had to come to know they would not want to know it when they came to know it. In short it is a foolish thing that any one must use what they have when some one else has more and there is not any reason xepting that it has not been why everything should not be known to the one who has not known what was known."

*

LGB 70: "If he were seeing clear if Gibbons"
"(List of clear seers]

*

LGB 79: "Enough of them who walk walk quickly and so there are very many."
"(Go on to Spaniards)"

*

LGB 96: "A lame way to say that the day is not that time"
"Go on with any scene"

*

Note #16

Mr. & Mrs. Claudel	Matisse
Minnie Claudel	Margot
Pairman	Purmann
Miss Danien	Danois
Miss Waltny	Volmuller
Miss Hendry	Funke
Miss Lane	American
Inez	Olga
Haick	Francis
Marie	Inez

Frank's crisis in detail. remorse, arm, telling, everything. filling days.
Go on about days.
Describe Sally's Frank's
Nelly's, Sayne's, Bruce, Matisse, Leo's mine.
Frank
Ray's [?]
Frank's stories

Pleyell
[Ambling ?] German etc.
etc. anybody's

AT ***filling days. Go on about days:*** Generally. all of Gertrude's days were empty. There was just her work to do, but otherwise there was just taking distractions as they came. She never had on her mind what was to be done today or tomorrow, never, never. When Gertrude said, We must do…, it was the only thing planned to do for the next week or two. There was nothing else that actually had to be done.

Her days before I came to Paris were for the most part uneventful and not very social. She would see Mildred Aldrich, go for short walks, buy the paintings, have an American visitor or so, dinner perhaps with Leo and a visitor, and then proceed to the question, What to do after dinner, with Leo answering, There's nothing to do in Paris at night. She did know Alice Ullman then, and Mildred Aldrich, and Gracie Gassette, and certainly Beatrice and Ernie Keyser, whom she saw constantly then.

After the time I came to Paris, her days were more social. There were tea parties both at the house and at Mildred's, and there were evening parties at Gracie Gassette's, who knew officialdom. At Gracie's, there would be the official painters, or Bonnard, or a visiting Chicagoan—her home town—or an English dignitary. Mrs. Gassette would be there to receive them too. It was a conventional life that Gracie led. Mildred's was more mixed.

The Saturday Evenings produced relations and connections, amusing and otherwise. Always there were the visits to Montmartre. And Gertrude took to taking me around to the suburbs for walks. We would take the Sceaux line out to Sceaux, and I would catch cold on the way back in the snow in the open-top bus. In the morning Gertrude would come down so late that lunch was already ready. She would take cafe au lait at the table and start lunch.

Gertrude always worked at night. She tried to do it in the morning during Bilignin, but there were always interruptions and difficulties. So it was always at night, *quand meme*. She would start after everyone had left at night, would walk around the room, quite madly, circling the two little tables and the enormous writing table at the center of the room. She would walk around them very quickly, then suddenly sit down. I couldn't even turn a page as I sat silently in a corner of the room reading. Please don't bletter, she would call out. She wrote like sheet lightning, and the pages would turn down almost every second. Then she would go to bed at four or five in the morning, and sometimes wouldn't get out of the house for weeks except for a short walk at five or six in the evening. During the writing of *The Making of Americans*, she averaged four or five hundred words a day. Later, in the Twenties and Thirties, it was three hundred words a day.

In the Twenties, she could talk about writing—always about painting, but before writing was not for conversation. She commenced to go about to see people, and in the early Twenties, she saw the young. Later, it was all kinds of people. When she came down with such a bad cold in the early Twenties that the doctor was called in, I told him of her habits and then, Gertrude taking the doctor's strenuous advice, started to get up at eight in the morning, then at nine, then at ten, then eleven, then would take a short walk, then another short walk in the evening, and would be in bed at twelve. Even during the Occupation, the night walks with the dog continued.

When her habits changed in this way, she wrote when she was free to write, and usually worked in the evening. During the first world war, she would not even work until midnight because she had to be at the garage to attend to Aunt Pauline [the Ford she drove for the war relief fund] at eight thirty in the morning.

LK ***Mr. & Mrs. Claudel…***

Inez: Repeats partial list of pseudonyms in Note #14 and used as working note for LGB 32.

Frank's crisis in detail: *LGB,* **pp. 34–36**.

Filling days. Go on about days: *LGB,* **pp. 36–37**.

Describe Sally's…. Leo's mine: *LGB,* **pp. 37–41**. The sequence of descriptions appears to be: Nelly Jacott, Frank Jacott, Nina Auzias, Mildred Aldrich, Lyman Sayen, Jeannette Sayen [sic], Patrick Henry Bruce, Allan Stein, Eugene Paul Ullman, Maddalena, Eugenia.

*

Note #39

~~D.D. and doing.~~ Mamie Weeks, her efforts to create herself energy enthusiasm intellect anger character.

*

The trip to Boston.
Her dignity. Her pedantry. Her pride. Her movement.
A little more of Mabel. Her pedantry, her pride, her love.

*

Go on with May, her sentimentalism and weakness and energy and intention and ~~honesty and dishonest~~ and loving and marrying?

*

Telling the way she was a hard one. The way she was attacking and not being a courageous one, the way she was
[-?-] and being a courageous one.

*

High class stinker. Princess. Muriel [?] and Mabel. Love nigger, love what she got. virtue & weakness D. not a stinker but has to have what she has to have.

*

Mabel Earle & Lilie [?]. The character of the criticisms they make on their fellow-men. & women. Then her life and Lulie [?].

AT ***Mamie Weeks… anger:*** She had angry animal eyes. The Stinker [Annette Rosenshine] had them too, not intelligent eyes, really animal. Mabel Weeks had a love affair that came to nothing, but I don't know the details.

Go on with May: [May Bookstaver.] At Urbino in the summer of 1910, we spent a day or two looking for Italian pottery. I found for very little a late Fifteenth Century pot with signs of the Passion on the inside, and a cover. Being entirely utilitarian, I left the cover purposely because I couldn't carry it, and when we were back in Paris, Gertrude said, I'll send it to May Mary because she was very nice about *Three Lives* and I never gave her anything.

Probably in the summer of 1910, May came over with her husband. Mr. and Mrs. Knoblauch lived in great estate, she with her low-cut evening dress and all her gems. I received them before Gertrude was up, and that's when I got my impression of May. Their visit to Paris lasted only a few days, perhaps a week.

High class stinker. Princess: Dolene [Stein Block.] Gertrude thought of her as the Princess. All the little Baltimoreans had a tendency to become Princesses in Gertrude's mind—her mother was the Princess in her family—in the sense that they were treated as such, and also, they had the airs and graces of it. It's easy to see why Dolene was it in her family. Her sister was coarse, but Dolene was prettier than you can imagine, delicate, with almost exquisite ways and movements, always with the sad violet eyes. But she was a stinker all right. Dolene too must have had the crossing of the T, the dagger thrust. She never forgot herself, never, and she was always out for herself. When her [first] husband died, she looked at the stock reports before he was buried. An innocent, clinging little person, a little violet, who knew all about the Stock

Exchange, thank you. Her husband had been a rather distinguished man, and the second marriage to Block was a sort of shock to everyone. But he loved her, and she wanted protection.

Mabel Earle and Lulie: Lulie was Mabel Earle's sister.

*

Note #38

Abe Ortenried Miriam's religion in relation to sensibility an[d] her letter-writing. Her whole set Demarez, Miss Donner and the german lady, and then give her relations to everybody, & to Florentine who is like Harriet, about the governess. Conditions & traditions as formative education.

AT ***Miriam [Oppenheimer]'s … relation… to Florentine [Sutro]:*** Florentine was a niece or something to Mrs. Oppenheimer. She was interested in the women's vote in France.

*

Note #40

~~Fernande.Get into her intelligence and poise more and hostess quality, then d. and [definities] and~~ [-?-].
~~Marie. Marie, Marie Pierre & Marie.~~
~~(Pierre,) child, mommy. Difficile & patient.~~
D.D. [Alice Toklas] expecting nothing needing everything, having everything.
Go to Mrs. Matisse melodramatically accepting.
~~Harriet and telling and loving.~~
~~Germaine, her voice, her pleasantness, her neuresthenia~~ [sic].
~~D. round ones and loving.~~
Olga. Tell about D's decisions and dislikes without prejudice.
Go on with marriage and then child. money, work, tastes, people, American.
My little dearest one existing, that is everything.
De jew & de Chlichaw hurrah hurrah. Wunderband. What you feel.
Excellent wife and step-mother and swell. Galumping and all the rest. The Brenner's Fernande, Sally. Go on make her more specific and the D's. being little helpful and being spoiled, sense silliness [adieu??].

AT ***Fernande… her intelligence… poise… hostess quality:*** She was always hostess in her own home, even when they had nothing. At Clichy, she even became something of a *salonniere*, and introduced everybody, moved about, owned her home—and this, when she was about to leave Pablo. Yes, she had the poise. She couldn't be flustered, got through her story, did what she wanted to do. All this was true of her social graces.

Marie… Pierre…. child: Marie was the servant of Mike and Sarah. Mike told Sarah that Marie was getting stout. So she should, said Sarah. But actually, it was not just her well-being that was doing it; she was pregnant. It had happened with a mail clerk on the railroad. Pierre was probably the name of the father. Marie came one day with the baby, who looked sickly. Sarah, so moral, had to have a little bastard thrust upon her. The baby was born just before or just after I came over, but it died soon after. Marie was a passionately devoted mother, though not a good mother, any more than Helene [Gertrude's and Alice's servant] was.

One day, Helene's baby was there when I came down. Helene said to the baby, Say how do you do, and the baby said, *Oui, maman.* To all questions, the baby answered, *Oui maman.* Helene was a proud mother, but not a passionate one.

Mrs. Matisse melodramatically accepting: Probably about [her daughter] Margo [and her physical handicap], Mrs. Matisse 'melodramatically accepting' as in *The Autobiography of Alice Toklas.*

Harriet and telling and loving: 'Telling' is telling stories. 'Loving' was only for her nephew. Gertrude referred to her as having an 'aunt' heart. Only this nephew got it, in that way.

Germaine… her neurasthenia: Neurasthenia, yes, definitely. With all her energy, she was neurasthenic.

D round ones and loving: Dolene was small and dumpy. She was a little round one when I knew her. Just her head had that distinction.

Excellent wife and step-mother… Galumping and all the rest: This is Mme. Matisse, definitely. She was a fine step-mother, and she definitely galumphed.

*

Notebook *B

NB-*B #4

In people like Alice and Bird, the apology is necessary for them to recognise that they have made reparation, that is because of the strength of their pride, in Sally not because though she has pride truth is too strong, in Harriet and Annette not because it has nothing to do with vanity only with pride, the[y] either know it or they don't the apology don't affect them, when one goes over into the world of the self-righteous then the question comes more complicated also in the world of the unmoral ones.

AT ***In people like Alice… apology is necessary for them:*** I told Gertrude about my father, who invited a lot of men to lunch. I was being hostess, and since there was no red pepper to put on the game, I began to offer my apologies. Don't ever be sorry, my father said. There should never be cause for it.

Annette… pride: Annette had shame rather than pride, shame at discovery. She flushed, rather beautifully in fact, at such moments.

*

NB-*B #5

Very little doubt, Edstrom connects, Van Goch, Jean Jaques Rousseau to the men of the world and through Byron to the pure idealists, they all have the fanatic quality.

But the purest fanatics, Mrs. Eddy, Adele Jaffa to -Harriet ~~the havy~~ they have absolute self-righteousness and no self-consciousness, Alice Klauber too and Dolene, Alice Toklas has a good deal but it is flavor in her because her sexual base is not that of course, her sexual base is May, the elusive, finer purer flame of the prostitute. Of course, Neith, Chalfin, Berenson, Alice, all flavor because of that contradiction. Therold & Fabri another version, but it is only pure when it goes over into lady, fanatic self-righteous or ~~Napo~~ Mary Houghton evil Napoleonic or Marie Lerrenzen [sic] insouciant, completely, not real flavor because reaction in all these cases is complete the meat is chewed characteristic of Mr[s]. Eddy & Marion & Adele, the importance of women, their belief in them, their domination over a man, their genuine intellect and their horrible literalness and practicality, their assertive dominating quality, and their lack of practical efficiency, their greed and vanity, they have almost a demoniac power of possessing themselves and others, that accounts for their tempers. their intellect is very genuine but unoriginal, it is personal and intensive but runs into theoretical general grooves [wired?] with moral purpose, Mrs. Charlotte Perkins Stetson type case, singular lack of penetrative beauty, their literalness has too great a poignancy to be beautiful, it is too pure too unbased upon the earth. for them to be literal is to be empty, I think Mrs. Bruce and Mrs. Davenport are allied forms, Bird is this in the unidealistic prostitute form. Remarking that in Sally this literal practical, uninstructive unsensual dominating hardness, does not act as it does i Edstrom and Bird. In Edstrom is [sic] is alternative with the sensitive religious and sometimes confines with it in Bird it is continuous in Sally it does not combine with herself and except in her archangel moments which are always less and less, that is certainty without knowledge or instinct but on the general principle of vigorous assertive attack, not assertive domination without knowledge or earthy instinct that makes Adele.

AT ***purest fanatics... Adele Jaffa:*** Definitely of the fanatics. She was so fanatic on any subject she was taking up that she didn't see it clearly. It prevented her normal judgment from acting.

Fabri: [Egisto Fabbri] had the Cezannes, lived on a small income and collected the paintings when he could afford them. He was himself a painter, of a poor Tuscan family with two banker brothers in New York and he the poor one. He was Mme. Matisse's love; she thought him beautiful. He was like a seventeenth century portrait of a silken charming prince. He went back to Florence to live, and finally sold his Cezannes and built a chapel for his mistress who had died.

He didn't come much to the rue de Fleurus; I never saw him there. Gertrude took me to see his Cezannes in Montmartre where he lived, but in *a monde* apart from the bohemian Montmartre of Picasso.

Mary Houghton: She was a little English woman who married a man above her station and held him by her force. She was a hard-working creature and he a shilly-shallying weak man who had all the grace and beauty and manner that she hadn't. It wasn't the habit to like Mary, but everyone liked Edmund. She was a little grubby. I knew Edmund more, and Gertrude knew them in Florence, never in England.

She becomes a little clearer from a World War One story about her and her husband. He was driving an ambulance with patients in it when he ran over a child in the street. When she saw him after, her first question to him was, Did you get your cases back to the hospital?

Marion [Walker]… horrible literalness and practicality: I doubt whether 'horrible literalness and practicality' is true of her. Gertrude always spoke in praise of her. It wasn't so much that she was true to type as that she was true to her beliefs.

*

NB-*B #6

A man like Quimby could be a real idealist a person like Leo, any one who has the power of abstraction in unity that is as a whole but people like Edstrom, Harriet Mrs. Eddy, Hutch can't because for them idealisation must be essentially mystical, the intensity of the hold of the practical ~~and or~~ or material aspects and in cases ~~of~~ like Therold of the sensual that idealism with them can only be when they are completely dual personalities or when as Edstrom does with Mrs. Eddy they worship the practical in its most energetic expression; Mrs. Demarez, as a whole is an idealist boy

AT ***A man like Quimby:*** He was the man in Mrs. Eddy's book that gave her the start. He was a real doctor, though, who inspired her and from whom she stole the original thought. Gertrude read Mark Twain's book on Mrs. Eddy in Paris. It was written at the time.

Gertrude felt about Christian Science that unless you felt it to the degree of Mme. Demarez, it was nothing in them except as an expression of character. On the other hand, she was really interested in Mme. Demarez' Christian Science because she lived it. The others practiced Mrs. Eddy's tenets consciously; she didn't but lived them instinctively.

In cases like Therold of the sensual: [Algar Thorold] A regular man-about-town, a diner-out, not necessarily with his wife. She was probably better born that he was, though he was a nephew of Labouchere, an MP. Thorold inherited his money and lived the life of an *homme de lettres*.

LK ***A man like Quimby:*** Phineas Parkhurst Quimby [1802–1866], a clockmaker and mental healer in Portland, Maine, was developing a 'science of mental health' when Mary Baker Eddy consulted him in 1862 and 1864. She became his most ardent patient and disciple, and, according to Mark Twain and other detractors, his most unconscionable plagiarist. Mark Twain claimed in his book on Christian Science that the whole of Science and Health, Mrs. Eddy's testament, was stolen from Quimby verbatim.

See Mark Twain, Christian Science, with notes containing corrections to date, NY and London: Harper & Bros, 1907. [Two parts. Part One was based on Mark Twain articles that had appeared in Cosmopolitan Magazine, 1899, and in North American Review, v. 175 (Dec 1902), 756–758; and v. 176 (Feb 1903),1–9, 173–178. Part Two was previously unpublished.]

*

NB-*B #7

I understand now how that feat is accomplished the anglo-saxon not letting his right hand know what his left hand doeth, In Dolene it is because the whole of her occupies each direction successively and there is no self-consciousness, no memory. In Mary it is like Harriet, the prudishness is a conviction, a virtue and a defence [sic]. It goes with the practical personality.

*

NB-*B #8

Chalfin (connoisseur of conversation) intellect goes with sexual character good-ordinary with a very great deal of energy in the sense of keeping it going but with very little capacity for letting it work by itself so the results ordinarily are below the actual calibre of the intellect which is a thin version of the Vollard type the kind that when it is forced is absolutely commonplace, Grant's type. The flavor aspect the pride and the dominating quality of it has also a great deal of energy but is not a very sensitive quality, it is good academic preciocity [sic], no more, it is so that he gets his impressions and these which are good academic preciocity [sic], he backs up by the vigorous action of his intellect which is then perfectly common-place, his moments of real quality are the impressions of his own life which are the parts of his existence when he has allowed the penetrative (the affirmation) of his nature and intellect to act of itself, with the flavor of his flavor feeling, that is his boyish idealism, his feeling for his sister, his feeling for decay, his melancholy, all this has little energy, no effectiveness but a great deal of beauty. His flavor perceptions are good the energy and ambition and domination of them are strong, but they are neither as vigorous or as nearly actual as in the case of Alice nor are they as fine in their quality as in the case of BB, or as steady and crude as in the case of Neith. Mary Houghton they become a complete thing no longer flavor group, in Janet Dodge they are a less refined and very dull version of B.B. (with an ordinary sexual nature? [sic]) In BB the flavor quality is very fine, his intellect and sexual nature ?) seem to be a more practical version of Lamb's and Alexander Heiroth's that is approaching Valloton which is a highly sensitive man of the world's not an earth type at all, connects to Fred Stein and Jake.

AT ***Chalfin:*** Chalfin the Charmer. An American of North Irish Catholic extraction, and an absolute charmer, nothing like him, the dark beautiful creature that he was. He had a mercurial quality, floating in and out. He held himself like the magpies [in Four Saints in Three Acts], with a movement you could see but not feel. He had great taste and no money, and in spite of having to earn his living in various ways, he always kept his independence and himself intact.

He was susceptible to anything. He could fall in love with a pigeon, a man, a chair, a woman, anything. He visited me at the Notre Dame des Champs flat, I saw him at Gertrude's, then he disappeared, then he came back. Sometimes Thornton Wilder is so like him that I see his face rather than Thornton's.

Chalfin was not a great painter by any means. He came with a commission to paint a mural and he did, a very primitive, Italian-influence one, with a purity that he didn't have.

*

NB-*B #9

The impressions of the aesthetic flavor group, Chalfin & B.B. have the same uncertainty as Edstrom pointed out in intuitions, sensibility to persons, like his and Sally's may be of the person and may be of the person thinking of some other person or some other person entirely, in short they may be right or they may be wrong but they are of no value except when they are backed up by experience and intellect, the same is true of the esthetical ~~sensi~~ sensibility and in BB's case it is backed up sometimes, rarely ever in Chalfin's. In a case like Weber it is like in Lana's the whole nature works together, in Mme Vernot it works together but badly having mixed ~~it~~ with it material earthy considerations.

Flavor in Alice almost has reality, it is so strong, I think one may say it has reality. In Alice au fond the sexual character which is allied to Lamb and Mary Houghton and Alexander, is not aggressive and so pride has not the bottom source, pride is all connected with flavor which in Alice almost comes to affirmation so complete is it, in Harriet, the bottom is I am quite sure a sexuality like the type Kaysers [sic] just between complete submission and reaction, earthy type, I don't think her vanity has this deep root but her vanity is the complete positive expression of her complete denial. There is a certain vanity connected with her sexual bottom but only that of existence the female version of Mike ~~. In him~~ not an aggressive vanity like her denial vanity but a passive one like in our mother. In Annette the bottom sexuality like Mabel Haynes is aggressive and the vanity has this deep root and also is aggressive, luckily it was not as aggressive as Mabel Haynes but its idealism for me is aggressive also not as Alice's for Nelly which is loyal but not aggressive. Harriet is in between. Annette has a double vanity, that is the reason it is more tenacious than Harriet's which her vanity undoubtedly is, at bottom Harriet is not pathologically vain. Annette has all Emma's vanity and all Mabel Haynes's vanity, and the combination makes that died in the wool superiority, Harriet never feels superior when she is hard hit, Annette does and being aggressive and practical she can to a certain extent make it good.

AT ***Weber:*** A student without paying at Matisse's atelier. Bruce was the massier, the one who directed the academy, arranged the easels and places, and also took the fees at the end of the week. Bruce persuaded Matisse that Weber should be allowed to work there free. But at the end of the year when Weber went back to America, he went back with a Picasso. It didn't come out until much later that the free student had bought with the money he saved on the fees the rival's picture.

Bruce had a charming laugh, a little one, the opposite of Gertrude's but just as effective. How he laughed when he told the Weber story after he heard it.

when she is hard hit, Annette: Annette, who came to Paris to paint, had been thoroughly upset by Gertrude and Sarah. Her own existence was filled with her own troubles—her tragedy of the hare-lip, of her position, of Lizzie being her mother. She spoke of her 'debt' to Gertrude and myself, but I wouldn't let her enlarge. She saw Gertrude only in connection with herself. She never thought of Gertrude's existence other than in that way.

*

NB-*B #10

Sally the ~~bottom~~ instinct is sensibility, sympathy, unaggressive, character—dominating & aggressive, Edstrom same mixture sensibility more profound more original, character worse, sum total lower expression with greater moments, Jean Jaque [sic] Rousseau the same and so to the whole idealists group Byron etc. Matisse instinct aggressive sensibility, character earth fearful and tenacious muddy etc. and aggressive sensibility working through that makes a great result, in Sally sensibility does not work through her character but sometimes becomes fused with it, hand reading and best art work but makes originality of temperament not of point of view, Matisse's temperament is less original than his attaque this is also true of Edstrom his sensibility is more profound and original than his temperament that is his character, and they practically never coalesce. I have the character of the tolerant and understanding not the instinct, I have the material instinct which becomes sensible only in its tenacity to negation, _____ [sic]. I still don't know about Harriet.

*

NB-*B #11

In Sally the sensibility temperament, in common with Edstrom, in her it is drowned in the thing, not the thing drowned in the sensibility as it is in Edstrom and Rousseau, so in Edstrom and Rousseau the sensibility has originality and is an end in itself, they want success to be sure but it is not necessary to their self-realisation, the moment of extreme sensibility, the sensibility being so great but not great enough to be self-expressive in the pure existence, with her success is necessary, that is the reason that she has this incapacity to remember failures or to expect them, because that would give the lie to her whole scheme of self-expression, success is the sine qua non of her existence, but not a self-seeking success there is no element of grab in it, for she has no element of ~~a~~ small self-interest but it has that appearance sometimes because so badly does it need support, so little can it stand alone, so strongly is the instinct of self-justification to preserve it intact, for to be wrong is to be all wrong, success is the only self support there is to justify it, therefor there is the constant tendency to attack, to justify herself—to have been always right, to have the sense of power. the sensibility lacks originality as I have said owing to the fact that it is not sufficiently egotistical, it is not sufficiently an end in itself, Sally is the egotistic type but she is not an egotist and that is the weakness of it, Edstrom tremendously is, Matisse even more tremendously is, and therein is Harriet right in saying that Sally's power of self-justification makes hers pale, but the fundamental difference as I made it was I am sure correct.

Now in Bird there is the same need of success but instead of great sensibility there is the minimum just enough to make her lovable and a power to those who care for her. Mabel Weeks has a great deal of that sensibility but no aggressive power, and so she is haunted by a sense of failure.

*

NB-*B #12

Miriam's letter-writing expresses her too. It is always personal although arid but she is arid with the one exception of Felix Adler. She is by nature a pessimist not a moralist, she would have had her natural growth in rather a large experience with men and in despair and as such she would have gone crazy. The influence of Felix Adler the moral meaning to the universe makes her sane but arid, leaves her without enthusiasm for anything but the person who gave her her gospel. She should have been a pessimist and a lover of men. Laura is an optimist by the abundance of her human sympathy, Miriam has very little of that, she belongs to Adele's group in that respect but she has attained a servant tolerance through her gospel of morality and Felix Adler. Adele Oppenheimer is very different, with her her gospel is her own it is a religion, a fervor, Miriam's religion is second hand as is her optimism, it is Felix Adler's. He is her Christ, she should have been a sinner and a pessimist.

AT ***Miriam:*** [Miriam Price] Leo once said to me that Miriam was like Nelly. Now it is true, in this description. Leo apparently thought of Nelly as this fulfilled, and possibly that's why he was in love with Nelly and held back from being completely in love with Miriam.

*

NB-*B #13

The true base of Alice Toklas is the same as Harriet Clarke's, the great and beautiful suggestibility combined with impersonality and personal ineffectiveness is the great characteristic, it is the slender white stem soul, and there goes with it a clear cut, subtle quick ~~but~~ humorous but not sensitive intelligence. they both have the same fancifulness. In Harriet there is no complexity, with Alice this soul is of little power in her most of her is the elderly spinster mermaid, with all her faults. I think Alice is a perfect example of the intellect with the sexual nature, her hands also show this.

AT ***Alice Toklas... great and beautiful suggestibility:*** At this time—during the first six months of our friendship—Gertrude was struck by me as an 'exotic,' as someone outside the run of her experience. Everyone she knew then was well within the run of what she was accustomed to. And then too I could always make her laugh with stories, first about my father whom Gertrude loved to hear about and thought a wonderful character, and then the fact that I was so unlike what he would have been expected to produce in a daughter.

No, it was not as though there was anything special in my grasp of her conversation. Anyone at any time could understand everything Gertrude said, and if not then one question, and Gertrude would clarify thoroughly.

We saw each other very frequently during that time. There was in those months the loneliness when I first came to Paris, the unhappy situation I was in when I left San Francisco and to which I was to return, the inadequacy of Harriet as a companion who had to be taken care of almost, with her fears and her illnesses and her indecision—even about such things as going to see the great balloons launched in the Paris sky—and in the midst of this, there was Gertrude, with her world and her experience and the pleasure of her company and her conversation.

Alice... the elderly spinster mermaid: It was in the late Winter 1907 or early Spring 1908 when Gertrude used this in conversation. When she said it, I said Oh rats.

*

NB-*B #14

The man in the train made me wonder if the bottom of BB was
not like the bottom of Simon H. and Laurie. I rather think it is their sexual type their superior type and their intellect, sane and clear, they are all temperamental and little au fond inexperienced, Laurie more so than the other two. Sam Stein is the successful bottom of it.
[V]ery important idea. Classification, this goes over but is not the Puy type.

*

NB-*B #15

Alice T. Edstrom Weber, sensitive, crooked, good at bottom ~~Annette not~~ that is they are not bad, their sensitiveness and their desire at bottom makes for good, weak and wobbly, Alice feather-headed, Edstrom cowardly, Weber crazy.
Annette not good at bottom good at top. Adolescent insensitive neither good nor bad at bottom, neutral, could go in either direction depending on

intelligence and object and worldly influence. Sterne etc.
Women adolescent perhaps more positive toward good at bottom Loyal but so are the men. Sterne, Derain, Leo F., Purman not the true adolescent type. Pach, Roche, Bruce, truer adolescent type.

*

NB-*B #16

Heiroth like Leo. Impulsive, impatient, proud, original, non-temperamental, lyrical, intellectual, mature, serious, sexually masculine, and aggressive, sensitive and tender hearted and influencable [sic] by much patience and independence. B.B. top is that bottom is like Simon H. & Laurie, not aggressive sexually rather pathological common sense, reasonable ~~not~~ nervous rather than impulsive, hysterical rather than impulsive, petty desire for fine gentlemen, not aggressive, always `good', protecting others.
Howard like Annette superior.
I think Alice is nearer BB. than anybody else only she is crooked her being a lady is being a prostitute as to flavors only.
Puy is in that group too, only his sexually [sic] is so great it drowns itself.

AT ***Heiroth like Leo:*** Gertrude heard most of their conversations in 1906 and 1907 [i.e., before AT's arrival.] I don't think she was as impressed by it as this note suggests, but Gertrude thought very well of Heiroth. I'm not surprised she writes so warmly of him here.

*

NB-*B #17

Braque and Palmé.

AT ***Palmé:*** Probably a Florentine association.

*

NB-*B #18

Bring out strongly in both books the difference between follower and leader, between individual egotists and school.

*

NB-*B #19

Man like Chalfin with his three aunts. tall and talked Italian.

*

NB-*B #20

Chalfin is like Alice neither one nor the other has brains nough to go round, intellect enough to do the job made for them and they know it. Harriet and Annette have brains enough for their job but not character enough. Leo does his with his brains, Sally hers with her character, B.B. with both brains and character, that is ~~th~~ so they get their ini[ti]ative their propelling power. Matisse, Pablo and I do not do ours with either brains or character we have all enough of both to do our job but our initiative comes from within a propulsion which we don't control, or create. Edstrom lacks this and so he is no good. His propulsion is only emotional and sensitive reaction of the highest type there is nothing within him that speaks. Hutch has also the lack of inward propulsion, his, too, is reaction, Edstrom and Hutch two excellent cases where reaction is the whole, nothing inside even to keep going after reaction from outside starts them, therein they differ from Derain, Sterne, Leo F. etc.

Braque and Palme [sic] ~~there~~ and Chalfin and Alice there is inward propulsion but not enough. Braque and palme enough to keep going and they have enough brains to content them. Alice ~~& Edstrom~~ and Chalfin have not enough brains to content them so they make it up, he with energy (manufactured), with sensitiveness and taste and charlatanism, she with crookedness, melodrama, desire, and prostitutism. Edstrom tries to make [up] for his lack of inward propulsion by charlatanism, claim to higher sensitiveness, and the Jesuit ideal. B.B. has enough intellect for his job, but not enough for his social ambition, not for his desire for success, he has enough inward propulsion for his job but he uses everything else for a cheap success.

*

NB-*B #21

Laurie, Simon H., Francis., B.B. ~~Pu~~ Valloton & Jaehne Puy Francis is the pure form of it. In him in his youth there was an intellectual integrity of a kind, not an absolute kind but still not a practical kind, he wanted to reason and endlessly and [sic] he had genuine devotion to follow out reason as it lead him but his ambition was for success, his belief was in utilitarianism, he had nothing that by instinct succeeds, he had a rational subtle intellect, he had common sense as an ideal but not as an instinct, he attained to common sense

by the force of reason. He was as I have elsewhere said of BB. he was nervous not impulsive, that is true of Simon H. Laurie & B.B. and I imagine of Jahne [sic] and Valloton. Their intelligence is clear and rational their desire is for success, they are sensitive but not finely imaginative not lyrical at all. they do not connect to the idealist but I suppose they do to sensitiveness and intuition although not having emotional sensitiveness nor dramatic instinct it never comes to intuition. They all like worldly ways and comfort. I think for two reasons their common sense brains which makes them understand the value of success for which they have no instinct therefor never any tendency to despise it [-for?-] knowledge and their nervous sensitiveness which makes them dread harsh intrusive discomfort. they have a sensitive excess of nervous sexuality, not of any attacking kind, sometimes I think Hutch's top is like this not his bottom. In Francis in his youth there was the integrity of rational thinking and the natural ethics that goes with it but his ideal was entirely to the other part of this nature, success, subtlety of mind to uphold authority expediency, opportunity, it was deliberately embraced, with all these people ~~what~~ their ideal is formed out of their nature and very deliberately embraced. In Chalfin three layers.
Simon H -
flavor -
Braque -

In Simon H. after some struggle the ethics side of the integrity was embraced as an ideal. In B.B. the intellectual integrity side of the complex was embraced as the ideal. They are none of them aggressive, in BB. it takes the form of protecting the lady whom he might get into trouble, in Simon H. in drowning himself in her, in Francis his more balanced opportunist nature again showed itself, he frankly took her for what she gave. In Jaehne and Valloton you get a new form, there it becomes large in volume and you get in Valloton the common sense realistic satirist, who hasnever embraced any ideal but is simply a man manque and in Jaehne it becomes almost impulse and pathology.

I guess through Puy they pass into the dull ones who love themselves in ladies, Edgar Matthews type and the kind of woman like Therese then to Algar and Fabri there you have a kind of cowardly emptiness but more of all this by and by, by and by is easily said.

AT ***the dull ones who love themselves in ladies, Edgar Matthews type:*** He was an architect, fairly futile, whom Sally created out of practically nothing. He was discovered by Olga Ackerman in San Francisco—this, from 1900 on.

*

NB-*B #22

Hortense Moses, May-Maria, Nelly, to Jeane, Alice, Gladys. The first lot have rather a flat and empty bottom, they lack poignancy at bottom, they may be stupid and get common place, they may be common place always, they worship genius, M. Maintenon, they are glorieuse, they learn all things well, thoroughly, quickly, and intelligently, they want to influence but are not impatient if they cannot, indeed they don't insist if they meet genius. They hold themselves to be inscrutable, they are fearless, but never genuinely tolerant or charitable. They are all things to all men and hold themselves to be inscrutable, and that is quite true they are for they are a vanishing point. Spiritually, they are negative, they are never positive except in emotional passion and then it is a reaction. Roche is like them. They are passionate but not temperamental, they have no profound sensitiveness as has Sally's group and so they have no real understanding as has all of Sally's group. As I say they are like M. Maintenon gentle, and charitable and sweet poignantly so sometimes but they do not really feel this deeply and they can be quite merciless. Hortense is the intermediate to the lady. They are thoroughly worldly but rarely practical. Nelly seems to be that but even she is not so ultimately. ~~I think they are the corelatives of Roche to~~ I don't quite know their relation to the adolescents the~~y~~ second part of the group is positive at bottom not negative.

AT ***Hortense Moses:*** The wife of Jacob Moses, who was raised in the home of Etta Guggenheimer, Dolene's mother. She didn't like them and none of them liked her.

May-Maria, Nelly… they may be stupid and get commonplace: In May Bookstaver's photo at Yale, you can see where she's stupid. Nelly was stupid all along the line, but not when the moment came to be awake. That's why I resented Gertrude's 'resemblance' idea of Nelly and May B.

Nelly didn't arrive in Paris until after I had been there several months. Gertrude used to say over and over again after she met her, There's something about Nelly that jingles the way May's did. What, I would ask. The way she throws back her bracelets.

I didn't like Leo's finding Nelly like Miriam Price nor Gertrude's finding her like May Bookstaver. But Gertrude gradually got to like Nelly a lot. This note was probably written after the first few times Gertrude had seen her.

When Gertrude spoke of the bracelets comparison, I had still no idea of *The Making of Americans*, nor of Gertrude's deep interest in the varieties and contrasts of people. It was in September 1908 that Gertrude got to know Nelly in Paris. Nelly had gone in August or July to stay with the Bracketts in Maison Lafitte, and then took a flat in Paris in the Fall.

Frank [Jacott, Nelly's husband] was an awful bore, impossible. As Virgil Thomson put it, The glorious, uproarious forties. Since that was what Frank was going through then, I wanted Gertrude to meet Nelly alone first, so Frank came on the scene for her later.

Maintenon... glorieuse: Gertrude must have been reading Mlle.de Maintenon's diaries. That's why 'glorieuse' comes in.

*

NB-*B #23

I think this is a solution, the non-individual, non sensitive, Sterne, Purman, Leo Friedman are the unindividualised unsensitised form of Braque. As Fred Stein is of Leo. They are not adolescent, the real adolescents, Pach, Roche, Bruce, Anette [sic], Mme Boiffard Emma, they are real adolescents, ~~nont~~ not unsensitised adults. that is the reason that Leo's group have ~~the~~ peudo [sic] the imagination and intelligence of our group and they have really only reaction (practical). I think 'em yes. Carfioil [?]—Zobl [sic]—Pablo.

Weber and Manguin and the Keysers generally are another class from the above, they have great creative sensibility, but are dull, have no originality of personality. The first there are original whether it expresses itself in their creative activity or not. I don't know where in this matter Alfy comes in. I myself am most likely to be deceived by that group not deceived, because they are original but to believe in them, as having creative power which they do not necessarily have.

Annette Bruce Pach all have an inward impulsion but not enough to break through all that has in these cases to be broken through. The weakness in character is when the top is stronger than the bottom for whatever reason brains lacking, character lacking, inward propulsion lacking, weakness need not necessarily be failure of the goal not failure as to success. Hutch & Chalfin and Alice are type cases. ~~B.B. &~~ Also in a way

Sterne Leo F. and Purman & Derain. Leo F. the least because his ideal is least, he is like Francis, they both choose the lesser expression of their bottom at least the least idealised. Sally and Neith and B.B are all strong enough in their bottom although they unify only fitfully with their top. Edstrom does not unify with his top at all. Leo and Weber and Alexander and Pablo have no top. they are individuals. Mike has but a very important one. Matisse and I bottom breaks persistently through making it over into itself of all the top as it breaks rather than an amalgamation. Mike's amalgamation is practically complete ~~also Miriam's, also Laura &~~ Mimie Weeks like Edstrom practically never amalgamation and with her top is mostly in evidence with him bottom.

AT ***Roche... [of the] real adolescents:*** Roche had a false freshness that wasn't adolescent at all. When Gertrude called him the Introducer, Pablo contradicted her and said, No, he's a translation.

Bruce... [as] adolescent: This is strange to me. But it helps explain his end.

Emma... [as] adolescent: [Emma Lootz Erving] had a love affair when she was living with Gertrude at Johns Hopkins. Lena [their servant, who figures as the servant Anna in *Three Lives*] started bearing tales to Gertrude who didn't want to hear anything until it came from Emma. When Emma told her, Gertrude said, she behaved like a child.

Carfioil: Karfiol was a really young painter who had an early success at the Salon, and so the following year he sent several paintings, as was proper after the first success. They were all refused. Then he went to Young's in the dead of night, and pounding on the door, kept shouting, Let me in, I'm a disappointed man. This, at twenty-two. I never saw him, I only know the story.

Zobl: Czobel was a Hungarian peasant proprietor's son whose wife was a disturbing factor because she slept with so many men who kept cropping up. Czobel who was really bourgeois had to put up with this. His was a very very gentle side of the Hungarian nature, it was almost something you could touch. I knew him only to say hello and to watch him. He was quite well known later in Hungary.

Alfy... I... most likely to be deceived: [Alfred Maurer.] But Gertrude was not particularly deceived by him. He had originality, but no endowment, and so it came to nothing in the end.

*

NB-*B #24

Simon H.'s group are hysterical but not suggestible. Annette's group are more suggestible but only very slowly and with complete idealisation on their part. They are hysterical from repression only more pathological perhaps than hysterical. Simon H.'s group nervous hysteria. Anette's group are superior because of their intense self-absorbtion [sic] and vanity and they do not need the world as a mirror, the vanity of other concentrated female groups need the world as a mirror, as an admirer or as slaves or objects of adoration. Anette's group not.

Why is Simon H's group superior. partly because they lack self-confidence and real self-absorption, they dare not use the world as a mirror, they have pride but it is different from the orguiel of Leo and Alexandre different from the self-defensive pride of Claribel & Alice, different from the sore personal pride of Pach. I don't know their pride well yet but it carries with it a certain pleasure masochism witness B.B. in abusing him Simon H. Dolene, France et. Hutch has some connection with these but ain't very sure. this character of the Simon H. group is very clear.

Alice is really modest and to bolster herself up she ~~covers~~ covers herself with her pride and false success, with melodrama and crookedness and prostitution, (the lily soul is alright for great moments but ordinarily pretty impossible too determined & clear.) Chalfin has to do the same, its because neither of them have brains enough to win out on their bottom lines Where does Alfy come in and why are Simon H's group patronising, thats [sic] it rather than superior. Annette's group is superior, Simon H.'s group is patronising. this is a part of them for protection as well as [positive?] in them. The kind of possession in authority that Alice has is true of her bottom along with the modesty like Harriet Clarke. When you get it in Mabel Earle it becomes more like Lilly Hanson which then goes through Mrs. Bruce (offshoot to Adele Jaffa) through to Theresa Therold. These last are not modest they are rigid, not suggestible sure always.

Mary Houghton conceives herself with a lilly white but it ain't there, flavor which in her is wickedness. She is a strong crooked (O.M.) not (O.M.M.) is all her. so is in his way Edmund.

AT ***Lily Hansen:*** Lily Hansen came to Paris with Mrs. Boyle largely on account of me, whose California friend I had been. She was Scandinavian, that is, of American Danes of Norwegian extraction. She visited Gertrude once, and came away and told me that, no, she was not intimidated or overpowered by Gertrude, just by the pictures. Gertrude asked her no questions but got the drift. Lily asked me, Do you think Gertrude is an altogether wonderful and extraordinary woman? And I said, Perhaps. What a pity, said Lily Hansen. She didn't like anything overpowering or anyone to be over powered.

She came to San Francisco originally to study music, and then came to Paris with her mother and her sister Agnes. There she lived a tense life of one story after another, and finally became tired and anemic. I suggested Gertrude's French doctor, who gave Lily twelve bottles to use, and she used not one. Then Gertrude suggested Edstrom, but when he asked her, Now what about your father, tell me about him, she simply told him, That's my business, not yours. She loathed Edstrom for that.

She was really a lovely creature, beautiful even now, one of the nicest experiences of those years for me.

O.M. not O.M.M. = Old Maid, Not Old Maid Mermaid

*

NB-*B #25

That thing of mine of ~~natur~~ sexual nature and correlative mind I think works absolutely. Chalfin, Braque, Palmé Grant, aggressive sexually not vigorously but not cowardly unaggressive wallow such as Young, Matisse, me. Saml. Johnson, Balzac ~~Grant~~ not sure. Leo F.'s group sexually vigorous, masc. aggressive but more affectionately so than passionately, Leo & Alexandre's group passionately aggressive sexually, Leo F. romantic and sentimental, in Sterne more poignant in the direction of psychicism like ~~Leon~~ Leon, in Purman, faith, but not at bottom, bottom same in all four Derain, Leo F., Sterne, Purman.

AT ***Young:*** Mahonri Young was a descendant of Brigham Young and a well-known American sculptor. He lived and worked in Paris for a time and was a friend of Alfy Maurer's and a group of young Americans.

*

NB-*B #26

Our group Matisse, Young, Edstrom, Saml Johnson, Balzac top not bottom all cannot stand solitude. they get scared in solitude scared of themselves, they are influenceable but not at bottom. They can as Leo said of Sterne ~~bll~~ blow hot blow cold, can't think profoundly, no inward propulsion.

*

NB-*B #27

Interesting the common-placeness of Greene Fielding Hall, Alice Keith in Clever [?] woman of the family, the more empty and sexually unaggressive version of Leo & Alexandre.

*

NB-*B #28

Bentley the type Jake Samuels etc type judicial man striking in that ~~conversation~~ conversation about Hutch, yes your analysis shows how little would make the difference to produce a work of art and therefor the differences have no meaning, they exist and the work of art does not come off. The lack of sense for significances, common sense of facts, judicial mind.

LK ***Bentley:*** [Dating: Introduced to GS and Leo in Paris by Hutch in the Spring of 1908. Before May 8th, when GS was already in Fiesole and Leo still in Paris. Bentley saw both Leo and GS in Florence in May and June 1908, left for US with wife on June 5, 1908. Hutch and Neith in Paris before leaving for US June 12, 1908.] [This Note written either in Paris before May 8, or in Fiesole before June 5.]

*

NB-*B #29

Jack Preiss, Jake Samuels to Bentley then to Valloton and then to Jena. This whole group have the sense of fact of reality, not dogmatism but existence, personally highly sensitive, not emotionally sensitive but what you might call physical spiritual sensitiveness, responsive to so to speak the touch intellectually emotionally etc. spiritually etc. They do not transmute it they react to it, they do not reflect it as Edstrom Sally's group but they react, they do not recognise and react, they do not act out of their own insides as do the whole of what I call the genial group Pablo's, ours, the Cleveland Grant, Balzac, and the concentrated feminine groups, they do not transmute into emotional meanings May, Roche, etc. they just plain react to it, nor do they recreate as do Leo Alexandre etc. they just react, direct, sense of fact, sensitive, proud only in that sense, unimaginative but real in their reaction, judicial, scientific, practical minds, well to be married early, else they get into sexual difficulties later.

AT ***Cleveland:*** [Grover Cleveland.] His attack on trusts put Gertrude violently on his side. During his administration was the only time Gertrude was ever interested in a Democrat.

*

NB-*B #30

Great vanity of sensitiveness. Weber etc. Interesting Simon H.'s letter, his being in a hole and lonely and yet puts it in such a way it sounds like patronising, their vanity is not sure, their reaction is not sure, nothing in them is sure, and they always over emphasize to cover it, not consciously of course their over emphasis is inevitable.

*

Notebook *J

(No Notebook J)

NB-*J #1

Simon's group are not superior, they patronise, they are nervously hysterical not worrying, they are never sure, they overemphasise everything to make themselves sure, they are to a certain extent practical sensitive to facts and in that sense judicial but not enough so to make that simply their reaction, they help it out by principle, by conviction by over emphasis. make it Valloton, Jena Benm [?] Mr Meininger Sim, Meininger, Laurie, Berenson, Simon H, Francis, Herbert Spencer. J.S. Mill, Puy they are not enthusiastic or impulsive, they are sexually not genuinely attacking but muggy.

Puy goes over to intellectual group. They are given to emotional suffering, over emphasis in every direction, a genuine sensibility but always has to be reinforced and so they are not sure, nervous, and patronising, and dogmatic, or like Valloton manque.

*

NB-*J #2

The spinster group, Etta Cone, Fernande, Olga, to a certain extent Emma and to a certain extent Annette they have very different bottom natures take this lot but they all have this in common that they see themselves no not see but absolutely vitally completely feel themselves to be quite otherwise and what they are is so small a proportion to what they are to themselves they are completely self-centred and completely vain, they hold the world as a mirror up to themselves and that mirror always completely flatters which is the true mark of the spinster, of all the people in the world they are the only ones to whom one cannot tell the truth, they would never forget or forgive that they would be implacable, they copy always the thing that is most successful near them. In Emma & Annette they have enough real idealism to be able to hear the truth and profit by it. Of course they [sic] are many people who resent the truth, Bird and Harriet and Claribel but they can forgive it, the true spinster cannot. The pure female like Bertha everything in her that is not female is spinster but then there is such a mass of female, Hattie Bache group is sentimental but not vain to an inordinate extent this group ~~are~~ is like Leo Friedman's the Hattie Bache, the bottom dough of female or male as the case may be has completely woodenised, solidified ~~with~~ not concentrated or moulded or just a piece cut off, simply liquified that is made solid into wood therefor they have no fountain of of [sic] expression, they have no profound sensibility but they have a fairly deep superficial reaction and this may have various forms. This in the women ranges from Hattie Bache to Jeanne Boiffard. In the men you have it lead off to Ulman and Robert Kohn in whom the bottom wood is pretty well lost. In fact I am not sure but Robert is more like Chalfin at bottom.

Therefor it is that these people can never do more than copy ~~nature~~ life they cannot create it ever.

*

NB-*J #3

The spinster lives in the thing she isn't not alone the thing she isn't but the thing that has really no roots in her, it is not that she thinks herself something she isnt but she is something she isn't. She does the things she is and she lives the things she isn't. Take Sterne he lives the thing he is though he conceives himself the thing he isn't but it always remains play acting. A woman like Bird conceives herself what she isn't but she lives out the thing she is. That is true of many women and also many women are the two things as Alice Toklas as Chalfin, then Simon's group also feel themselves to be what they know they are not and May's group feel themselves to be what in a sense they are that is what is always in them in posse, etc etc but the spinster group is different they live in their conception of themselves because what they are is with its accompanying train so small ~~that~~ proportionally to their lives so to speak. Take Etta all she really is is a little practical edition of Bros. Mosey, while she has the husks of the complicated temperament of most of the Cones, she lives in these husks not in her practical self, Olga lives in the husks of bohemianism, Fernande in the husks of maternity and womanliness, Emma in her vanity but in her and in Annette there is a balance, Mrs. Valloton in the husks of good housewifery and independence. Bird lives in what she has and in principles. May's group in what she is and drama and intellectualism, Harriet in what she is and vanity, Claribel in what she is for that is egotism as she degenerates, ~~she~~ that is weakens the ~~defen~~ superb defensive egotism will become pride. Mary Berenson lives in what BB stands for she is a spinster, Now Bertha has a little spinster but that is so much sloppy oozy female in her that that is only querulousness, almost all spinsters are querulous, jolly Mary Berenson is ugly, all spinsters are ugly. Etta Guggenheimer is a different case Write them up sometime as I described them to Claribel. Brother ~~Mosey~~ Moses is not an egotist he is a man who believes his tradition and his tradition is the law of the world, for everything else is foolishness, it may be pretty but it has no purpose, hence his limited understanding. Impossible to really tell spinsters the truth. Inez Cohen. She is like Etta Guggenheimer. Hortense's flatteries all must be written up.

AT ***Sterne... it always remains play acting:*** Sterne was very ingratiating, flattering, good-looking and suave. He had long lashes, of which Nelly said, Beware of men with long lashes. There was a great deal of sentimentality evident in him. I thought he saw himself in many roles, but it may have been more continuous. He always wanted his women to feel he was the only one in the world they were interested in. He was really a little too suave.

Gertrude and Leo knew him in Paris as much as they did in Florence. He had very pretty ways with Gertrude. He wasn't very American in manner, but it was hard to tell what European manner it was. He gave the same consideration to Leo, but that was genuine, there was nothing suave about that. He walked a little like a red Indian, one foot directly in front of the other.

His intimacy with Gertrude and Leo? He confided in Gertrude and listened to Leo. He told Gertrude a great many of his stories. One of them was about Raymond Duncan. He went to Greece soon after Raymond did and lived in the interior. He told the natives he was an American. They didn't believe him. If you're an American, they said to him, why don't you wear the national costume like the Ducans [who being in Greece wore white sheets, chitons and sandals.] Sterne lived in the Grecian hills alone.

In Anticoli he was alone too. He went there because the handsome peasants would later come to Rome as models, and Sterne found them out in their habitat so that he could get them cheaper. People, though not very rich ones, gave him money to go to all the places he visited and lived in—Borneo, Greece, and so on.

He was very low-keyed, had a typical American voice, no gestures, no 'glorious uproarious forties' like Frank Jacott's. One woman that Sterne fell in love with from California looked like a Greek goddess.

Gertrude said he was an extremely nice house guest, no one could have been pleasanter. The Casa Ricci was a small house with just Leo and Gertrude in it, it was not modernized in any way, and Sterne fell into their routine pleasantly and easily, talked when he wanted to, didn't when he didn't. He spoke low, pleasantly and modestly. That was Sterne—so suave, smooth and gentle.

Gertrude's friendship for him wasn't a lasting one at all. There was an intimacy, she liked it and the conversation with him, but when he came back [from three years in Borneo], there was no attempt to revive the friendship. She just found him as uninteresting as she had remembered him. When she was doing the portraits and the character studies, she found everyone passionately interesting, but in himself, no.

most of the Cones: There were eleven children: Etta, Claribel, a younger brother, a brother who killed himself, the oldest brother Ceasar, a sister, and five more. The oldest was always called Brother or Sister So and So.

Olga lives in the husks of bohemianism: Olga Meerson was very bourgeoisie. She later married a German kapellmeister during or after the first World War. It was the last anyone heard of her. As a pupil of Matisse's and inamorata of Matisse for a short time, and intimate of Purrmann, she tried a flirtation with Mike, who was flattered and bewildered but not at all engaged. She always ran and was breathless, she was small and pudgy, and she bleached her hair of which Gertrude said, she never knew how far she'd gone, a little more would always make it lovelier.

Mrs. Vallotton: A Jewish widow of a South American Catholic. A strange mixture of French, Jewish and Bourgeoisie. Then she married a Swiss but maintained a family and household for all that. Vallotton complained about her low middle-class come-uppance relatives who were picture dealers, but he never complained about the housewife. Gertrude spoke of her daughter as very pretty, but with 'thin Jewish hair,' which meant not curly but rather straight.

May… and intellectualism: I never saw any sign of it until much later when she translated Apollinaire following the Armory Show. It was printed after the war. She did prose too for a New York little magazine.

Mary Berenson lives in what BB stands for: But that was very nice, because BB would never have sustained himself so well without her belief, her confidence—unwavering, her presence.

all spinsters are ugly: In the sense, probably, that when they show their spinsterishness, it is not comic but simply wrong and ugly. Marsden Hartley once, when Harriet was describing her own clothes or something to him, retired from it. It was particularly ugly coming from Harriet.

Etta Guggenheimer: Dolene's sister. Dolene married a rich man because she was pretty. Then when she was a widow, she married her ugly sister [Etta] to a rich man. Etta was literally a spinster—an old maid when she married.

Brother Moses... his tradition is the law of the world: In explaining the morality of Trusts to Gertrude once, Brother Moses talked of 'The Higher Law of Trusts.' She loved it and remembered it for a generation.

*

NB-*J #4

Vollard group gets strength from wallowing, Algar's group melts in it so they have not enough left for use in work. Simon's group Puy etc, exhaust themselves in it, Leo's group enjoy it, Mathews dissipates in it, Alexandre intermediate.

LK [Corresponds to Notes NB-*C #17, #37]

strength from wallowing: Note is recast and generalized in MA 154, as follows: "Some men have it in their loving to be attacking, some have it in them to let things sink into them, some let themselves wallow in their feeling and get strength from the wallowing they have in loving, some in loving are melting—strength passes out from them, some in loving are worn out with the nervous desire in them, some have it as a dissipation in them, some have it as excitement in them, some have it as a clean attacking, some have it in them as a daily living...."

*

NB-*J #5

Mike and the wooden group attacking no particular result from it. Bentley's group no particular result. Hutch connects on to Simon's group but strong in it becomes a mystic. Edstrom mystic who should wallow. Hodder mystic who should enjoy. Genial group attacking group who get poetry and meaning sometimes mysticism out of it.

*

NB-*J #6

Zobel [sic], Jewelry boy to Barker, unoriginal genial type that is not genial type original sexual type. imitation of genial type, like black butterflies. Interesting how this jewelry boy [Levy?] one imitation and Sterne another imitation touch Leon and Pablo two versions of the genial type par excellence. Sterne's group the attacking adolescent insensitive attacking adolescent.

Ask Leo about originality in relation to this group, strong sexuality in this group but no vital originality, wonderful adaptability of the things sinking into them.

Zobel originality is to the point of novelty, journalese.

*

NB-*J #7

Sally—no woman who has Bertha really as a foundation has any real originality any real playfulness it is a serious a dramatic, an aggressive but au fond attackable temperament that is its domination is only with those who love it or fear it, it can never resist an assault.

No matter whether it is large or small fine or deadish in quality it always has the same lack of idea of playfulness of originality, it is highly sensitive but always reactive always personal, even its practical sense is always highly personal, therein it differs from what we may call the peasant type. This is a little true with men of that same type but their practicality and their sensibility may become informal and so they may be original but generally speaking it will be an originality of a moment not of a continuous process, as it is in Edstrom, in the greatest expression in Jean Jacques and Van Goch in other men it takes a practical form such as in Jack Preiss Jake Moses uncle Sol, and Bentley, in our daddy and Leo and Alexandre it becomes really creative in criticism in ideas in personality.

*

NB-*J #8

Faith hope and charity, the greatest of these is charity, Sally is faith, Harriet hope, and Mademoiselle Demarez charity, faith type belongs to the (nothing bad can touch them, true female appeal) can be raised to the aggressive point of Mrs. Wildmann, hope can go with grab (Bird's greed is not ultimate—ultimately she is dependent) Harriet, Adele, Mrs. Eddy Alice Klauber, then the resignation version Mrs. Samuels, and the lady type generally then through Mary Houghton to the genial personality, in these we can in its highest expression get love, love as Lincoln & Christ and St. Francis & Mme. Demarez with meekness of heart and love of God, or as in ~~me through~~ Pablo me Balzac Zola through love of beauty. The true and the beautiful. Leo from Matisse through Jake Samuels concern themselves with facts or science rather than with emotion and so these things are not the vital part of them. Now Mrs. Hersland like Mrs. Samuels almost creative old man her father was. Louisa Frohn etc. etc. various types, in relation to femininity and religiousness.

Harriet is a miniature Mrs. Eddy Charity-love is no part of her emotion, she can come to very complete religiousness without it in fact the more her relation to God grows the more she realises him the less will she need charity-love in relation to humans so it was with Mrs. Eddy, she will own God and she will not need people. Marie Gruenhagen was like her, so was Alice Klauber and Adele, Mary Houghton not she approaches Alice on the creative side, these last are genial personalities, Adele's group are original and assertive personalities.

Sally's remark about Edstrom's statement that it is her sensitiveness that would stand in the way of success, no it is the lack of originality, of personality in Leo's sense of bottom ideation. Supremely sensitive reverent, not charitable nor humble except as a dependent woman. Faith in great degree, sensitiveness to the point of complete realisation but not complete comprehension. ~~yes complete compreh~~

Faith type par excellence, not aggressive Mrs. Wildman and Mrs. King, not an egotist like Edstrom, not a brutal ~~wallower~~ attacking egotistic wallower like Matisse. Complete realisation, bathing in faith, and sensitive realisation, real realisation, never real creation. realisation not profound comprehension except through the shock of other personalities. Bird stupid in that respect, [he? be?] willed life an intensely passion realisation of a formalism, [imposes?] early in life. Howard like Annette with a mixture of Zobel family imitation quality. Faith -Sally—all women with Bertha bottom, aggressive Mrs. King and Mrs. Wildman—Miss Blood. Hope, grab Mrs. Eddy et all, resignation Mrs. Samuels. Charity—Mme. Demarez Beauty Class, Neith etc, Mary Houghton the flavor group—Alice.

AT ***highest expression… Balzac Zola through love of beauty:*** Gertrude read all of Zola she hadn't read in America when she got to Paris, even some in French. She never reread him later, but he was the first realist that moved her after the Russians, whom she had read in America before she read Zola. Balzac too always interested her. Gertrude liked those men who hadn't the time to finish their styles, who just wrote and wrote and wrote—Cooper, Scott, the older Dumas. It was their fertility rather than their effort she liked.

Except for the complete Flaubert in French, about all she read in French was the Zola she couldn't get in English and the Mardrus direct translation of the *Arabian Nights*.

She was enthusiastic about the Mardrus translation, and much preferred it to Burton. When Mardrus and Gertrude met in the Thirties at Natalie Barney's, she laughed when he read his translations that pleased her. He didn't like it because he didn't know that Gertrude laughed when she was pleased, not when a thing was funny.

Sally's... lack of originality: Gertrude told me that when Mabel Weeks was here, Sarah complained to her that Gertrude didn't treat her as an intellectual equal.

Sally... Supremely sensitive reverent: She had no reverence, that was her trouble. Her attitude toward Gertrude was one of reverent attention, but really it was just attention through jealousy. Not exactly jealousy, but wanting what the other one had to add to herself. She really took anything that anyone had that she considered admirable, and anything could be admirable that fitted in with herself. For example, she believed in Matisse as in no one else, but later when she had no money to buy Matisses and she was possessing Gabrielle de Moncy, Matisse was practically forgotten. Only when the pictures were hung in the new house could she talk about them again, and then to visitors.

aggressive... Mrs. King: The San Francisco woman who had such great influence on Harriet Levy. She stirred, moved, upset Harriet as no one else did until she met Gertrude. She was a woman of great force.

brutal attacking egotistic wallower like Matisse: In his attitude to Picasso's painting, he wallowed in being able to feel—with Picasso absent—this very ugly emotion of his—this was in 1914–15. I thought at that moment he was the most offensive person I had ever known. There was nothing *maladif* about Matisse's attack, it was a healthy point of view, not like the Stinker's and such. Gertrude made no defense of Picasso as she never did. As she said, you only explain to the stupid. She listened enthralled to Matisse, fascinated, but had no feeling for it at all. It didn't touch her feeling about the pictures. Gertrude's dispassionateness.

Matisse used to find the things that were wrong with the pictures—the aesthetics was wrong, the métier was wrong, and where was it going to end. Matisse objected to the whole Cubist movement, and though he didn't like Leo *au fond*, and had no respect for him as a painter—Leo painted like a commonplace American with a Renoir influence—he agreed with him in this.

About that time, people used to say that Picasso was not really a painter, that he couldn't put paint on canvas, that he was interesting more for his ideas. Of the Blue Nude with the red flowers on the wall here [at the rue Christine] for example, they would say, It's a picture but it's not a painting. After this attack period, Gertrude and Matisse practically never saw each other. Matisse was furious when Gertrude kept only one of his pictures when they were divided with Leo.

As to the first Matisse they bought [the Portrait of Mme. Matisse], it was bought at Gertrude's suggestion. Leo didn't like it but generously said, If you want it, buy it. But Gertrude said, No, not if you wanted it. But then they both bought it.

LK ***Sally is faith… nothing bad can touch them, true female appeal:*** Elaborated in MA 161, l. 17–35: "many women have [the]… feeling that… the last end of a bad thing cannot come to them…. they are part of important being… somehow something someone will take care of them… many have it in them as a religion."

can be raised to the aggressive point… MA 167, l. 41–44: "women [who]… never believe that anything can really drown them, they have aggressive optimism in them…."

Mrs. Hersland… almost creative old man her father was: GS relented from this judgment. In MA 167, l. 7–40: "Mrs. Hersland never had her religion to be in her like in her father…. [R]esignation to the pain that killed her, that was all the religion she had in her."

*

NB-*J #9

Adele Harriet Mrs. Eddy not capable of idealising. Annette's group love is all. real intellect but sluggish and dormant and capabable [sic] of idealism.

May's group vanity on Sally's insensitive and love, true mistress group, no real intellect.

Mine the peasant group, earthy, patient, real intellect, strong sense of reality—Marie Lorensen a variety of Lady and flavor groups concentrated reactive creative but no intellect.

Bertha's group including Sally. She needs me … I love her, their strong love for little babies. I want to teach Harriet to say I need her therefor I love her. this is the reason that the Bertha group to May's with its minimum of maternity have power only when they are loved, the lover needs them that is his claim and weakness. Harriet's Adele's group they need the object of their love and so they must subdue it, Annette's group need the object of their loveand so they grovel before it. The flavor group, the genial groups generally are more inconstant, it is always a demand for beauty and so there is give and take, attack and allurement. Mrs. Matisse is Adele's group with a strong leaning to peasant type, has that kind of humbleness, the servant girl group appeals by its dumb despair. Fernande is a spinster servant girl. Jeanne is an adolescent peasant servant girl, Emma is an adolescent spinster mistress servant girl, that is upper class servant like Lawny[?], which connects on to Bertha's group.

LK ***Bertha's group.... She needs me ... I love her.... Harriet's Adele's group they need the object of their love:*** First pronouncement of what are to become the two major types of human being, to be defined subsequently as "dependent independent / independent dependent." [See NB-*J #14.] Its statement here is concurrent with its first appearance in the text: MA 163, l. 27–34: "Some women have it in them to love others because they need them, many of such ones subdue the ones they need for loving, they subdue them and they own them; some women have it in them to love only those who need them;... others loving them gives to them strength in domination as their needing those who love them keeps them from subduing others before those others love them."

*

NB-*J #10

Harriet has a genuine receptivity that is creative, she receives beautifully, not a mirror like reflex like receptivity but an [sic] sinking receptivity, it is not engulfed it sinks into her.

Added later:

Harriet is a pill
she is a stinker.

AT ***Harriet... genuine receptivity:*** Harriet was still coming to see Gertrude immediately after seeing God.

Harriet is a pill... a stinker: This is odd, because Gertrude was passionately interested while doing something, but thought of it as a dead subject when it was over. Harriet's provocation could have been her greed, anything, and Gertrude would get discouraged and impatient, because not God not Gertrude not any other G ever had any effect on Harriet, nothing changed her.

The following year, when Harriet was under the influence of Edstrom,

Gertrude would come up to the flat once in a while, and I would disappear so Gertrude could have long talks with Harriet to find out how things were going. These discreet investigations into Harriet's progress interested Gertrude enormously, but the following summer, when Harriet went back to America and Christian Science was over for her, Gertrude lost all interest in the subject of Harriet and it was dead.

Gertrude had really washed her hands of Harriet in the autumn of 1909, when she had been turned on to Edstrom, and Gertrude also turned her on to Harry Phelan Gibb as an innocent distraction, more though because he was very interesting, a very good painter, and extremely hard up.

Gertrude had great comfort from him, in fact, because he was the first one who knew what she was doing. He was in a way the first abstractionist, but by then he was poor, old, and living in the isolated English countryside, and it came to nothing. Gibb, oddly, discovered Matisse about a year after Gertrude did, was interested for a while and then threw it off.

*

NB-*J #11

James (Wm.) is what Hutch is in appearance his voice which in Hutch is only sound is in James full his humanity also go into this more.

AT ***James... his humanity:*** Gertrude met William James on the street in Paris, said he had heard she was in Paris and asked what she was doing. Well, said Gertrude, my brother and I've been writing. I've nothing to show of the writing, but the pictures can be seen at the studio. Can I come now, said James. They went at once together, and James scrupulously regarded each picture, and all the while he was looking at them, he said nothing. Well, he finally said as he was leaving, saving all his approval for Gertrude, I always say, keep your mind open.

James was anxious for Gertrude to make up her failure at Hopkins, because he already had a position picked out for her in an insane asylum. That was the definite end for Gertrude of the study of medicine and psychology.

*

NB-*J #12

Nelly Joseph is the most material of May's family, she might be a dress-maker, Maria might be a model, May might be anything. they are stupid at bottom they have no real intelligence and that is the reason they don't hold, they are insensitive really and commonplace. they have a fine attacking sweetness, they need a supreme emotion to give them momentary quality. If one does not love them they are nought. Perhaps they are a female version of Leo's Friedman's [sic] family, but I don't think so.

AT ***Nelly Joseph... May:*** Gertrude used to say Nelly and May Bookstaver both "jangled" and I resented the comparison.

Nelly Joseph... material... stupid... insensitive... commonplace: This, strange for her. Although Gertrude was never enchanted with Nelly, she always liked her charm, her warmth, her feminine quality. She liked her because she liked me, whom she liked.

*

NB-*J #13

I wonder if Dickens does not belong to Hutch's family, read his life and letters next summer.

AT ***Dickens... read... next summer:*** Gertrude never read him here [in Europe.] She probably did before, in America, but not here.

*

NB-*J #14

independent dependent (Sally's the blue eyed
dependent independent dark-eyed.

AT ***the blue eyed... dark eyed:*** This was the time [c. Nov-Dec 1908] when Gertrude started with physical resemblances being indicative. At that time, Gertrude began to question me about all the people who looked like other people, and therefore were like other people. If she knew one, she wanted to know all the others. A physical resemblance would be something that was enough to cause one to say, 'Oh, she looks like...,' and then, 'What was it that made them resemble.' Later, she lapsed from resemblance in the face to the physical resemblance of the type.

She would give me the example and ask me to provide examples from people I knew, examples related to the people of whom she was speaking. She asked me more about Nelly whom she had met, but she dropped Clare at once as not interesting to her. She was determined to use only the normal, because she felt the abnormal was of no value. Trying to find out the bottom nature of people was fairly complicated because the symptoms were not easy to distinguish as symptoms or as excrescence. It was Annette who made her realize that nothing was characteristic [of a type] in an abnormal person.

What I answered may have had no interest or relation to her interest at all, but she would listen to all of it. She had endless patience, listening to the rhythm, the repeating of whoever for as often and for as long a time as she had.

*

NB-*J #15

I don't know whether I put down about Claribel's almost inspired egotism becoming as she grows older and admiration and adulation does not flow to her a sordid selfishness. More interesting in one way than Willoughby's because she did once not have either sordidness or selfishness she had a large bland unaggressive ungrasping, non-sordid egotism with the grandeur of I am as I am and I can't change. Etta's grip may also have helped the change.

AT ***Willoughby:*** Out of Meredith's The Egotist, probably.

*

NB-*J #16

Allan may become one of the Dicken's [sic] family, that is to be like the character of Dickens himself, belongs to Wm James and Matisse's family.

*

NB-*J #17

Probably use the tragedy of the Cone sisters as a big episode in other book.

AT ***tragedy of the Cone sisters:*** It was used in The Making if Americans and also in 'Two Sisters.' The tragedy was the eternal combat with no gains, no points on either side. It was alive, their relation, but it had no advance in it.

Gertrude once said, When I say 'sisterliness,' I mean the Cones, for example. Etta was dependent because the younger, because of Claribel's temperament, and because Claribel treated her as such. Etta was jealous of Claribel, and Claribel had no reason to be, she simply wallowed and swam.

In the Hansen sisters, I saw the complete idolization in one and dependence on the other sister.

*

NB-*J #18

Bird's and Edstroms weakness springs from the fact of their cowardice not from their sensibility as in Sally and Alice. There are moments when Edstroms weakness springs from his sensibility but those moments are excessively rare for generally speaking his moments of sensibility are great moments and so they are moments of strength not moments of weakness, this cowardice comes in them both from the Bertha quality in its sordid expression it is closely connected with the passion for an ordinary practical, mercenary practical worldly success, practical efficiency is their desire and aim, might be called political success with a mercenary accompaniment. Bird idealised this to herself and so it gave her to my young eyes a quality of brilliant courage, there was courage in it, the courage of resolution, I never knew the meaning of the cowardice behind it, Edstrom with his sensibility has also infinitely less courage of resolution and so he fails more steadily, while Bird on the whole wins out. Sally has neither sordidness nor mercenary nor even political desire in her instinct for being a success, hers is a dramatic desire, she knows the weakness of her sensibility, she has but does not know it the weakness of unoriginality but that is not important, Alice is the completest in sensibility quality, with her it is so complete that it is creative, but she misses entirely the success side because she has not even the mercenariness of drama the practical quality of drama she has the failure of melodrama. Bird then has no sensibility in her weakness nor in her strength. Edstrom has enough not to make his own life but to make it in spots and so be more original than Sally. When you get to the masculine types like Matisse and Young they don't count as such because with them sensibility cowardice et al are merely part of their personal equipment, they own them, they are not owned by them. In the case of men like James & Dickens you have a condition of more complete possession by sensibility but still it is not that sensibility owns them, they are at moments a complete mass of sensibility, it is more like Edstrom on the one hand in his great moments and Alice on the other hand in her complete moments except that with them there is the constant play and acquisition by their intellect and character of material which makes a unit with their moments of sensibility.

AT ***Alice … has the failure of melodrama:*** Gertrude said that I was like The Charge of the Light Brigade, that was my pleasure in failure. It was not that the Lost Cause appealed to me, or that it had glory, but to me it was nothing shameful.

*

NB-*J #19

That Howard is quite entirely like Annette I think there is no doubt, he has more fineness to cover it up but it is good taste in its almost creative form but it is nothing more. It is not as in Alice and Berenson creative. His sensibility and lack, the fact that nothing really counts that does not concern him, his essentially [sic] immortality with idealism therein differentiated completed from the allied ethical forms. it is perfection idea in all of them, Alice's group idealise but they create their ideals this group worships anything they need. Mabel Haynes of all this group was the most nearly creative, elegance with her almost went over into something creative, in the rest it is only disguised and limited vanity. it is never creative of that I am certain. And his humility is not real humility, anymore than Annette's it can be so by effort and it sometimes becomes so but mostly it isn't, it is pleading. this made it possible for him to disregard my letter this made it possible for him to be neither a just man nor a gentleman, I still think he is like Annette. He knew he loved Bird when he was denouncing the L.S. He knows it now and he is not ashamed.

AT ***Howard… quite entirely like Annette:*** His resemblance to Annette always left an unpleasant taste in Gertrude's mouth. She got to actively dislike Howard when he came over with Felix Frankfurter after the peace. The story in *The Autobiography of Alice Toklas*— 'over ever since the peace.' Gertrude thought they were a pair well matched.

Howard… knew he loved Bird when… denouncing the L[ucius] S[ternberger]: Howard was a great deal at Bird's house and fell in love with her soon after her marriage to Lucius Sternberger. Gertrude was horrified at Howard's being in love with Bird at the same time that he was being just to the first husband. She probably felt too that Bird was foolish in not realizing the kind of love Howard had for her.

*

NB-*J #20

Several things tonight made Bird clearer, Careless determination, which might as in my case in the face of failure take the form of lass bleiben. She has courage except when attacked and then she appeals as do they all. She is not hard she is simply insensitive, I am right life has not made her harder, it simply has not made her more sensitive. Her intelligence is alright but it is not penetrating nor continuous, it is essentially practical like Sallie's, but she has no material to use it on as Sally has because she has no sensitiveness. She is essentially a practical not an efficient animal and she don't change. Nobody has influenced her except the ideals of her father and the current culture and that is all, the current culture started with L.S. That whole group have a passion for knowledge, sometimes they become students, but they have an aggressive optimistic passion for knowing things, they are essentially uncreative. Bird cares only for a child and Howard is the only one who has so appealed to her, Howard and her father, no one else has ever touched her, she admired and depended on me, she had a passional affection for me, the kind Sally has but the dependence was the important element as it is in all the group except Alice and I love her. The picture of her is clear, careless domination is a bad phrase but it will help me. It would have been nicer in me to have been friends but I really don't care and it would not have been so instructive, she surely is more like Sally than she is like Hattie Bache. She has the persistent courage that goes with that kind of domination, she is not egotist she is not selfish, she is simply insensitive and don't really need any thing except her father and Howard. She has not enough charm to be magnetic and she has no sensibility, she is not passionate enough to be magnetic and she is absolutely without a trace of sensuousness and so she never has really had any women friends, she could only be important to a man like Howard who as Sally puts it pastures on her. She understands nothing—nothing, not because she is stupid but because she is so insensitive. She is not stupid, she is simply practical and attacking, and responsive to immediate stimulus of every sort, she needs everything for anything can feed her. She is by no means a bad sort and they are very well matched. She is nervous but that is simply physical, neither sexual nor moral. It interests me very much the fact that I think people generally find their sexual kind, (that is people who are grown up) that is their kind of the two kinds the most important to them for friendship, except for the ~~pas~~ complete passional relation or the one important need of their life. Sally Matisse, Me Pablo & Leon. Annette, me but I think it is true, ... Sally Hortense, Bird,

Mabel Weeks more
May still more
Alice most

have never really touched me, it is the same with most of the men of that class. Simon H. & Francis, Alexandre & Hutch are the exceptions, Jake

Samuels, Jack Preiss, Greene, Bentley etc are the rule.

Those who are exceptions are the Bazarofs and they touch me by their nervous intensity. Thats the reason I know Annette did not care that way. Jeanne Boiffard is another case so is Edstrom and Matisse. It has to be the completely opposite thing or the like thing. But I hope I have Bird vigorously clear now, I think I have. As anything but a superficial relation it is over, and to have expected moral courage for her was impossible because she has a splendid memory for facts but she has not a grain of constructive self-consciousness and she has never been one bit influenced. I was quite right about her going on when everybody was falling dead all around her. L.S. must have been nearer her match then [sic] Howard but he was not strong enough to win out because of the idealism of her attacking that she got from her father I could go on repeating it but it is clear her sense of facts, her splendid memory for such facts, her zeal, her energy, her continuous attacking her lack of ~~sens~~ all sensibility, she has not to any marked degree either vanity or pride, she wants success and she has it, why not, all these people do not count their failures Edstrom don't count them nor Matisse but they feel them, Bird neither counts nor feels them, Sally counts them but she don't really feel them.

AT ***Alice … I love her:*** [Miss Toklas' response, when this note was read to her, was astonishment at first. Then, after a pause: 'She says it.' Yes. 'Just like that.' Yes. 'Well then, c'est ca.' For Miss Toklas, the frank reference legitimized public reference thereafter to the fact. It was also, in its, for her, surprising unambiguity, clearly deeply satisfying. From both the dismissive note on Howard and Bird, and the 'I love her' entry, she dated the note Autumn, 1908.]

Bird… as anything but a superficial relation it is over… never been one bit influenced: Gertrude's disillusionment with progress was wedded to the experience with Bird. You couldn't do anything with people. Annette was done with by this time, Bird finished in this note, Harriet pretty well a lost cause.

L.S.… not strong enough to win out [over Bird]: Lucius Sternberger came from a more cultivated family than the Steins. Bird's cultivation took the form of California-style 'culturine'—shaded lamps and false Gothic, and so she could go on with no conscious jump to the [Mike and Sarah] Stein's 'Tuscan Renaissance.'

(Harriet called the flats influence by the Steins the 'Steindissimos.' Harriet's and my rue de Notre Dame des Champs flat, also furnished Tuscan Renaissance, was too funny to be Steindissimo. It would have had to have been more sober.)

Bird belonged to one of the first 'mother' classes, and she was no mother at all to her two children. She was the leader of the group, but she was not inarticulate but a bit illiterate, and she had Gertrude write papers for her that Bird read to the group. Amy Stein [Bird's and Fred's sister] who went to Smith also had great trouble learning things.

Bird was restless and had butterfingers then. She had physical presence when she came into a room, but that's all. She had a bitter smile, a silly laugh when nervous, and was small and dumpy.

idealism of attacking that she got from her father: Gertrude's father and Bird's [Gertrude's uncle Sol Stein] didn't get on better than did Aunt Pauline and Amelia. Sol made his money first. He sounded very unpleasant to me, but perhaps he was not. His 'ideals' would probably have been business ideals. During the Pre-Radcliffe days, when Gertrude visited New York once or twice from Baltimore, she disliked Sol and Aunt Pauline actively. Later they interested her.

LK ***Several things tonight made Bird clearer:*** [Dating: Written, apparently, September 1908, when the quarrel was over. Reconciliation seems to have been effected by letter, no longer extant.] This Note was written the night of Bird's and Howard's visit to rue de Fleurus.

Bird to GS, NY to Paris, Jun 22, 1908: "On July 9, Howard and I are to be married and we sail for Europe on the eleventh. We expect to be in Paris in September so I suppose we will see you then."

*

Note #78

Go on to the servants and then the governesses and then the seamstresses like Nelly, then after all this has been done in detail then come back to page 247-248. to Mrs Eddy and Harriet and how they covet [?] and come over to Madeleine Weiman and how she owned and her relation to Mrs. Mrs. the children and their later feeling about her. then to the history of struggle.

*

After the servants.

Now begin with repeating in substance page 427-428 then go on to their being sometimes a mixture of them then go on to Mrs. Hersland being of the first kind of the man then later on repeat this page 427-428, then speak of the mixture, Alice is a perfect example, of the need and the top layer of Adele bottom Sally top Adele & where Mrs. Hersland was of the first kind.

*

Mrs. Eddy & Harriet
sway, rocking in cradle,
reckless not before attacking
my stockings
jewelry

AT ***the seamstresses like Nelly:*** Nelly reminded Gertrude of the seamstresses [her mother used] in California.

Mrs. Eddy & Harriet… rocking in cradle… jewelry: Mrs. Eddy had people rock her in a hammock because it soothed her. That was when she first founded Christian Science. Mark Twain has this in his book on Christian Science.

Harriet had a great fondness for jewelry and for decking herself out. When Mike was making jewelry, Harriet was his greatest admirer.

LK ***Go on to the servants… history of struggle:*** [Planning Note for MA 169–285. Used as follows:]

the servants: MA 169–193;

and then the governesses: In the final text, this order is reversed. The section on the "governesses," MA 236–248, follows the section on the "seamstresses," MA 193–232;

then come back to pages 247–248: of the manuscript. In the final text, the repeated passage is taken from MA 133, l. 31 to 134, l. 30.

to Madeleine Weiman and how she owned … later feelings about her: Plan for MA 252, with much repetition and recurrence of these passages to MA 285.

then to the history of struggle: Between Mrs. Hersland and the Weiman [= Wyman] family over Madeleine Weiman. Plan for MA 261–265.

Now begin with repeating in substance… of the first kind: Plan for MA 169–192.

Mrs. Hersland was of the first kind: Draft of text for MA 165, l. 43–44.

*

3. GS Notes for Third and Final Version of *The Making of Americans*

1908–1911

GS Notes for "The System" begin with the first entries for the novel's final version. The development of "The System" is largely, almost wholly, accomplished in these notebooks. They are (more or less simultaneously written) DB (= **Diagram Book**) which contains eight GS illustrative diagram. Written concurrent with the Diagram Book are three other Notebooks: **Notebook *B**, **Notebook *C**, and **Notebook *J**. These four Notebooks and the loose notes attached to them assume the completion of GS's construction of her typological system. Apparently, the terms of that system were composed before the diagram book, although there appears to be no record of notebooks in which those terms were initially assembled. Further, unlike GS's insistence that *A Long Gay Book* was begun well after the development of the system itself, in point of fact *A Long Gay Book* was begun *simultaneously* with the first notes in the Diagram Book, and consequently, simultaneously with the earliest use of the finished system.

Diagram Book

DB #1

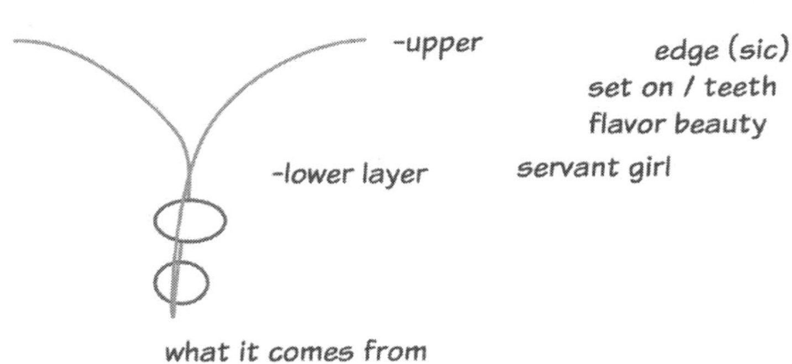

*

DB #2

Diagram Book

In this book (the long book) describe all the kinds of women and the way the men are like them.

*

DB #3

The long book.

For this book use all the diagram people, plus the complete lady & servant girl + prostitute.
Earth group, not.

*

Note #48

Neith & Ella Milziener [sic] come together servant girl side, neither of them are thoroughbreds.

*

DB #4

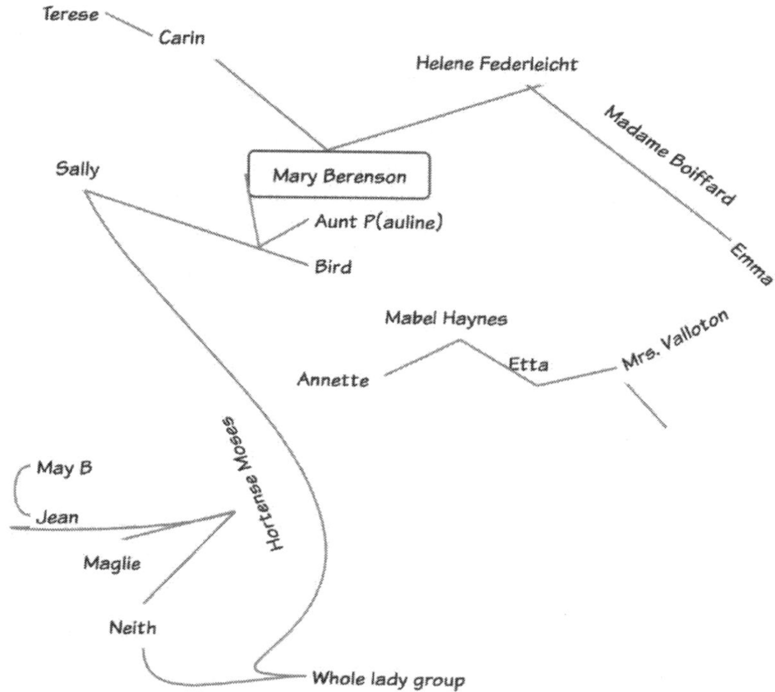

LK Apparently, the first mention of "servant girl nature." is in MA 172ff.

*

DB #5

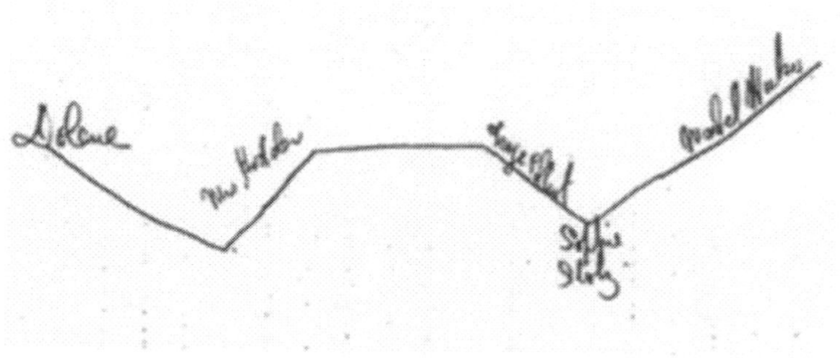

*

DB #6

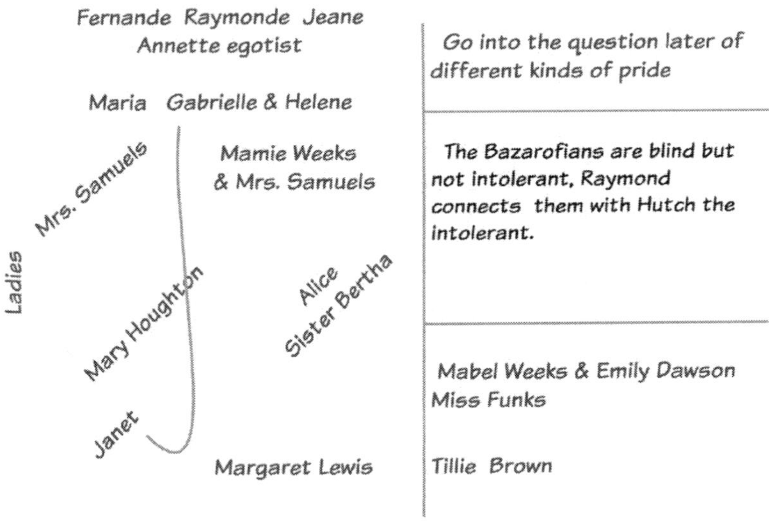

*

DB #7

Go into the question later of different kinds of pride.

LK ***question of… kinds of pride:*** Note anticipates MA 128: "… each one of the Hersland children had… a different way of having pride in them…."

*

DB #8

The Bazarofians are blind but not intolerant, Raymond connects them with Hutch the intolerant.

*

DB #9

Escape from the sense of eating.
Its an all overish feeling

*

DB #10

All women are alike. I know it, I always say it everybody always says it and yet in some ways there is nothing in it.

*

DB #11

If you don't use it you lose it. If you do not use it you will lose it.

*

DB #12

The practical mistress connects Etta Cone's group, Sally and Bird to Lena by bridling.

*

DB #13

The Sally-Emma group idealise and idolise mother who usually have another for a favorite child. Madame Vernot, Mrs. Samuels, Hortense Federleicht's mother, Mrs. Lootz. usually taken by lady quality of mother they being otherwise. In every case it is a son that is the favorite. and in the cases of—Henry Vernot and Jake Samuels sons have made a bad marriage with a rather a chippy kind of person. Daughters usually are like the fathers, mothers respect daughters and husband but don't love them, make lovers of their sons then bad marriages.

*

DB #14

Mrs. Meininger is the link between ~~man and~~ the practical woman to the ~~dis~~ efficient and practical man, she had a gleam of disinterestedness.
Aunt Fanny link between the mother of all and the boy.

AT ***Mrs. Meininger:*** Mrs. Meininger wanted to arrange another marriage for Gertrude's father. She wanted to marry him to one of her daughters, which Mr. Stein resisted.

*

DB #15

Vanity and bridling the commonest that is the most ordinary form that it takes was in Emma and she lacked the inconsistency, with her it was not pleasing or whimsical or emotional or good-natured it just turned sour.

*

DB #16

The group from Mabel Weeks to Mary Berenson including Bird

inconsequential foolishness.

*

DB #17

Sally (crest-fallen Allan)—disturb regime, ain't got no sense condition, in Lana it was pathological in its inconsistency, the pleasantest form it took was in regard to buying her own flowers and then weeping when they forgot to take them out of the ice-chest. Bird and the diptheria [sic] paper.

Aunt Pauline has just a touch comes out mostly with Uncle Sol and Fitza. and touch on wood.

Hortense Federleicht it almost gave great temperamental musical expression, in her it was the mostly [sic] closely wedded. Madame Boiffard has the least. Just see it in such actions as large playful gambols.

Russian lady is the lowest bottom of it.

Mary Berenson because there is the least head of all of this whole group is the most utterly foolish. Almost the biggest nature of them all except Laura [?] and after that Hortense Federleicht where it is the most completely wedded. In the extreme left wing Mabel Weeks her vanity makes pedantry and the inconsequentialness is like a left over girlishness it has less volume than in the case of any other. It is this in Bird that made Howard call her an amiably shiftless young woman. Men are very certain to misunderstand this whole matter, because the whole group are mistress prostitute type.

It often as I said that time ~~has~~ to Madame Boiffard has an appearance of excessive frankness as a matter of fact their natures are usually reserved it might easily in some examples almost take the form of hipocrisy [sic] in Madame Vernot where there is very little head much sentimentality and a great deal of sordid quality it comes very near it, if it does not sometimes really take the form of lying. About Etta that time it was well on the inconsequential side.

She is a fine woman, dear Miss Etta such a fine family, she never sent me a postal card, she is too much a lady to send me a postal card. They in their extreme form encourage themselves not to know the truth, the motive for not knowing the truth ranges from empty headedness in Mary Berenson, pure pathological lack of continuity in Laura, emotional world living etc in Sally, a mixture of all including sordidness in Madame Vernot to it[s] most puerile form of pedantry and girlish lack of intesity [sic] of vision in Mabel Weeks.

The group then on from Hortense Federleicht have the vanity but the inconsequentialness is almost non-existent.
In Bird it gives a slight flavor and makes her dependent in a slight degree and is perhaps the basis of that attitude toward teachers [?] characteristic of them all in a way, the wonderful capacity to keep going when they are started to so to speak improve upon their teachers.
Emma's vanity takes the more vulgar form, Bird's the meaner form.

This whole group are mistress prostitute type a group to be differentiated from the pure prostitute like May who is mistress only to and so of the man who loves her not of servants etc. She comes off of the Bird point, the prostitute without the mistress element.

The free soul, mistress type are important to themselves inside them,—they have a personal pride in them.

AT ***Hortense Federleicht... great temperamental musical expression:*** She was a Baltimore friend, a really musical one. When Gertrude was tired, she would go to Hortense Federleicht's who could play anything she asked for, so in this note, Gertrude exaggerates her musical prowess.

A fine woman, Miss Etta: Mme. Vernon on Etta Cone, who had been her boarder at the rue Madame pension.

inconsequentialness... Bird... dependent: She had a silliness in her that you forgave because you thought it was amiability. And she really leaned on you very heavily.

*

DB #18

		Anglo-Saxon type
Fanatic	Hutch	
intellect	Hodder,	
		Idealists
Beauty	Wild[e]	
Romance	Byron	
Power	Edstrom	
		Man of World,
Jake,		
Jack Freiss		
Fred Stein		
Green	thin gentleman, connecting link.	
Edmund	anglo saxon	
Roche	actor	
Matisse	connecting link	

AT ***Man of the world… Jake:*** Jacob Moses met Matisse at Gertrude's, and Matisse began by treating him as a rather insignificant American. Jacob Moses without doing anything and saying very little made Matisse gradually change his attitude toward him.

That same afternoon, he, Gertrude and I walked back to Jake's hotel. We passed an antiquity shop on the Boulevard Raspail. The shop was run by Brenner's brother. Brenner had been a pupil at the Matisse school and had been thrown out. Rumor had it that the two of them had stolen an extraordinary collection of Greek and Roman antiquities. Jake saw something on display and went in. He asked the man directly, What is the price of these two Italian paintings? The man replied in a huff, I am a great collector, I am not bargained with. It was the way in which Jake said, No, I'm not bargaining, I am just asking for the price of two pictures, that made the man say, Ah, I see you are a gentleman, we will talk differently.

*

Note #58

Relation of validity of solution to cleanness of expression, L & P.
Leon in relation to these things partakes of the nature of both, any feeling not real but suggested in him about both kinds.

*

DB #19

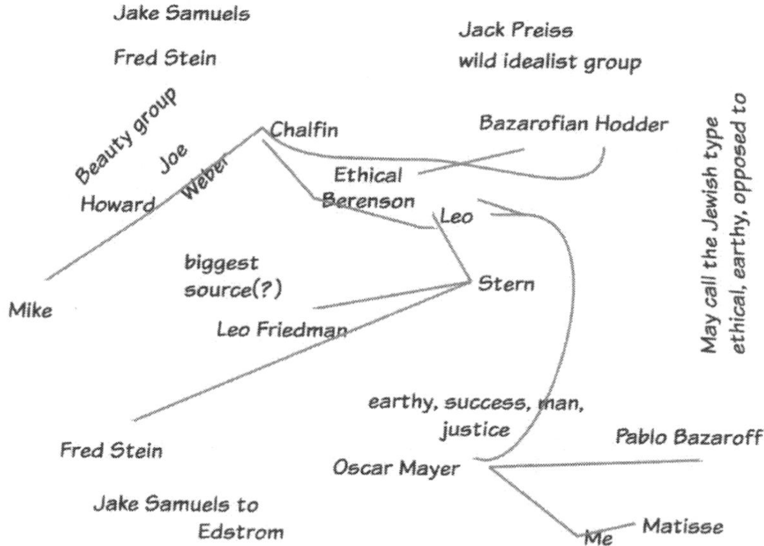

the most idealist and purest form of the conventional success.
beauty-earthy group
Alfy / has not the instinct for conventional success,
but has the instinct to be a beauty group success.
Leo Friedman both and Stern instinct to have the practical success but despises it but cannot rise above it.

*

DB #20

Making for success.
Instinct for being successful
practical in knowing whats going to happen.
(dramatic?)
earthy successful. (me)
literal like Matisse.
no quickness of mind in me & Mayer
quickness of mind in Matisse.
conventional success
Allan difference with diavolo distinction,

not any in collecting, the reason he tells things, that constantly appeals. proud of, allies him to Keysers and Uncle Sol but not the instinct of being a success. In that sense a perfect materialist not

practical. conventional success is what he appreciates Joe group Leo Friedman to Stern group.

practical success. conventional instinct.

man of the world. Jake etc. plus high type instinct to be a success.

Leo Friedman

This basis in M. explains all the contradictions of [marising?] moods humors Leo connects to the temperamental idealists.

Mike to the man of the world through Fred and Uncle Sol.

The earth admixture makes for justice and having his way, the beauty admixture makes for quality.

AT ***Allan… diavolo:*** Diavolo was a child's game, a shuttle-cock that you tossed in the air and caught. I don't know the incident Gertrude is referring to. Allan was only seven or eight years old when Gertrude wrote this of him. It became true of him, or at least it became clear, in his later life through his going bad.

*

DB #21

Masculine prostitute is a ~~masculine a~~ passionate adolescent.

*

DB #22

Me, not passionate adolescent
earthy boy

*

DB #23

Madame Boiffard and Emma dispassionate efficient adolescent.

*

DB #24

p[s]eudo masculine

I. Marion, Mabel Weeks, Mildred, Doctor, practical

adolescent, the continuance of adolescent where
boy and girl is not distinguishable.

II. Lady masculine
Napoleonic type not disinterested.

*

DB #25

Mabel Haynes pathological passionate male adolescent. not disinterested, no disinterestedness.

*

DB #26

Mabel Haynes is a masculine (genuinely so type)
I am masculine type.

*

DB #27

Jahne, Valloton & BB all have the same kind of familiarity catching hold of me men as well as women and through them you get to Simon. He and the pure lurid intellectual untemperamental, connects the other way to Stern. worldly. I think Francis was untemperamental.

AT ***So Sarah realized... Jaehner:*** [Jaehne] There was an art dealer in San Francisco then who was educating the city for Chinese art, and it was through him that Sarah got her objects and furnishings. She had started her artistic career with early nineteenth century mahogany and brass candlesticks, but as the Chinese idiom was becoming increasingly her own, she threw over the mahogany and candlesticks for Chinese things, and did so at the same time that Jaehne, the dealer, was doing it.

Sarah finally got Mike to back Jaehne for a trip to China, and Mike did it just as he had given Jaehne money previously to buy Chinese things. Jaehne was an unscrupulous man, left scandals in his wake, weird and wonderful. There was something reptilian about Jaehne.

There was also Olga Ackerman, a woman of extraordinary taste, with beautiful, delicate, slightly animal brown eyes. Sarah was very jealous of her, but she learned all about Oriental art from her. Sarah, when she furnished her flats [in San Francisco], did it on Mrs. Ackerman's lines. She had no taste but an instinct for acquisition, and always knew how to use well the taste of others.

*

DB #28

Lurid male group. Hutch is a connecting link between Anglo-saxon and lurid. Jaehne [sic] is a Bazarofian connecting to Hutch, Berenson to Valloton and through Valloton to Jake Samuels. He also connects through Hutch to the idealists.

Weber connects Joe Preiss to Bazarofians.

AT ***Joe Preiss:*** [Joe Price] He married Miriam, one of the Oppenheimer girls [in Cambridge.] Gertrude met him at the Oppenheimers'.

[In New York, after the Cambridge years] Leo was, through Howard Gans, an intimate of the Prices. He also kept up with Hutchins Hapgood, and through him, Willard—the man who wrote Tramping with Tramps—and other New York friends, whom Gertrude knew through Leo. So the New York friends of Leo's were a little separate for him, and Gertrude's women friends separate for her.

*

DB #29

Pach & Roche ? [sic] youth quality that is boy much in common with boys like Allan & Frank Bache?? [sic]

*

DB #30

Ladies pure their reality is coexistent with the flavors they taste.

*

DB #31

Flavor group their reality is in very much inverse ratio to their flavor

*

DB #32

Tacklessness [sic] invariable sign of flavor group.

concentration, ignorance of others, knowledge of themselves, Power and technique of suffering invariable sign of lady group.

*

DB #33

pure Ladies	flavor strike for freedom
Miss Blood	= Bird + lady
Sister Bertha	= instinct for being and for success.

Mrs. Samuels	= pure lady.
Hortense Moses	= Lady plus free soul
Neith	= Lady flavor (teeth on edge) + servant girl
Mary Houghton	= Bare bones of pure lady.
Mary M'Clean	= Flavor napoleonic
Janet	= Flavor culture
Bradford kid.	nasty flavor excessive concentration. connect—link to lurid.
Adele	ethical + lady.
Jaffa	

AT ***Mary McClean:*** May McClean was a Northwestern author who wrote a book that had a great vogue at the time. It was a very self-revelating kind of thing. Gertrude knew only the book.

*

DB #34

Ladies and flavor both no knowledge of people. Ladies not tactless because of concentration, and power. Flavor tactless because of reaching out and the ignorance of others that is the keynote of the group.

*

DB #35

Ladies all have the important feeling of themselves inside them though the best of them nearest to pure intelligence in Mrs. Samuels has it the least, Hortense has it very little.

*

DB #36

May and Mrs. Heiroth

I think I will find prostitute group egotists but no feeling of being important to themselves inside them. their kind of importance to themselves comes from their not yielding, they keep themselves from giving themselves and so get their sense of importance. their resistance however is not the resistance of free souls who own themselves, it is s subtle evanescence, when conquered they become commonplace, unconquered they have quite essential sweetness and emotional intelligence in its highest form, they are not true mistresses, anymore than they have the true sense of self-importance, they have power only when they are loved.

AT ***prostitute group egotists... no feeling of being important:*** [Seems contradictory but] Feeling is one thing and expression is another. They needn't have the feeling, yet could well express their egotism.

*

Note #49

Remember Mrs. Heiroth's lack of expression also Mays. Not sure of their class when one sees them and even when one knows them very well, this goes with their kind of freedom which is not inward freedom but freedom from the fact that they can keep themselves from being conquered by illusiveness. It goes with that kind of being mistress that they have, as they have power only with them who love them.

*

DB #37

Note the way two depths in most people. first resemblance least important in great moments they coalesce.

Annette	= Emma on top	- Mabel Haynes below.
Miss Blood	= Lady on top	- Bird below.
Alice Klauber	= Bird on top	- Florentine below
	-	- + Adele Solomons.
Jahne	= Berenson on top	Valloton below.
Allan	= Sally on top	Mike below.
Mike	= Daddy on top	- Keyser below.
me	= Keyser on top	- daddy below
Sally	= Aunt Pau. on top	- Laura below

When it comes together through mind-emotion, what you will it makes a personality [in] many people it never comes together.

*

DB #38

I think B.B. is intellectual, honest sensitive on top, the below is male version of the most perfect balance of flavor and lady which often slops over into a bad expression as when he wants and thinks he can do flavor straight. Edstrom is a more curious mixture because they [sic] are more layers. The bottom layer is not fear, he does not know it except with people more practical than himself.

*

DB #39

Bancel La Farge & Spicer Simpson makes connecting link idealist and tabby cat to Roche et Co. and they through Leo F. to Stern & Derain to beauty. Roche & Co. through Fred and Jonas to business men.

*

DB #40

Men	Women
Idealist	free soul
Fanatic	-------
Beauty	lady-flavor
Intellectual	Mabel-Miss Funke
Earthy	servant girl
lurid	lurid
Bazerafs [sic]	ethical

*

DB #41

All sensitive people must either be cowards, or have an iron will or defend themselves instinctively by the emotional leap. It is like in philosophy, the destructive criticism goes alright but when the attack is turned against them they must get scared and mostly run like me or take the emotional leap and land in the sense of injury, that was a very good instance with Alice and Jahne, I joined cheerily in the fun knowing all the time it would turn and then I ran, Sally faced it with a sense of injury, Leo with a power of domination.

But that whole idea of the emotional leap which separates the dyed in the wool rationalist from the others is very important. the thing that makes the emotional leap a possibility is the ~~enhan~~ underlying sense of natural virtue those ~~that~~ who lack it are as naturally ~~cow~~ moral cowards. The emotional leap people however conscious they may be of wickedness having got this sense of natural virtue they can always make the emotional leap. Fernande is a most exaggerated almost caricatured version of it. I can do anything that I have to do, she says all the time, I can deny myself, and efface myself, but do you, I can she says.

I think the whole prostitute class have this that is those that combine with the free soul group, the Hortense Federleicht group not. the lady and the lurid group not. the lady group have another kind of certainty more allied to the old man Heisman. that is the reason pure flavor is tolerant.

Want to define Hortense's group more.

*

DB #42

*Corresponds to NB-*C #3*

The old tabbies connect through artist, doctor and clairvoyant & business man

Grazzini; Sol Stein, Julien Valloton through Edmund Houghton to Edstrom making the common place actor's group.

Make the three commonplace versions of doctor clergyman & actor.

Instinct for common-placeness of the tabby cat Messersmith variety to be differentiated from the man of the world of Jake's type distinctly of the order of Fred and Uncle Sol.

Fred in this respect connects directly to Leo Friedman.

AT ***Grazzini:*** The local doctor in Fiesole. Sarah had a mild heart attack; they sent for him, and he gave her pills. I went to see her afterward. She accepted my visit with condescension, and I said, The doctor was able to help, wasn't he, and you're feeling better. To which Sarah replied, I had the greatest heart specialist in Italy!

tabby cat Messersmith: An American or Englishman in Florence, possibly in the diplomatic service.

*

DB #43

~~Policran~~ [sic] ~~more idea~~

Common place religious anglo-saxon.

Earthy—more apt to be ethical until you come to the primitive souls who are religious or pagan.

*

DB #44

Allan Williams?
Whittemore close to tabbies.

AT ***Allan Williams:*** Marian Walker William's husband. He looked like Aubrey Beardsley.

*

DB #45

Genuinely primitive souls
Federn

Howard not earthy—persian. ~~Chalfin~~ to Mike, [Crelenko?] Jaehne to Howard, Howard's kind of cleverness very close to Persian lying.

Primitive souls not beauty ~~lovers~~ lovers like beauty group but are themselves beautiful, no feeling of importance inside them is typical Keyser Will Erving the best specimen genuinely modest very little personal influence, a common place sid[e] which makes for getting on

Stern & Leo Friedman, fingers close together Leon Will Erving, Stern make good musicians, Moses Jonas, Leo, etc. When get beauty mixture fingers sensitive hairy Joe Chalfin, Howard in between them all.

*

DB #46

Fernande & Mabel [Simis?] connected with Emma strong feeling of themselves inside them, inefficient give appearance of efficiency and sacrifice but merely an appearance, always leaving their job.

*

DB #47

Maddalena

Group of women, no important feeling of themselves inside them Miriam, Marion Walker, Florentine, Margaret Lewis, Mrs. Matisse Aunt Fanny, Mrs. Samuels Estelle, technical member of this group holds the same relation to it that Mabel Weeks does to hers.

Most of this group their intellectual life is not connected with their nature. Slow in development no instinct for culture. Unfortunately Miriam and I are the only ones who make their intellectual life of their nature mostly they take up theories and carry them but even then they are more sui generis than Bird's group.

Miriam's letters characteristic of the group. I connect to it through Miriam only on one side of me, the other is the Rabelaisian, nigger abandonment, Vollard, daddy side. bitter taste fond of it. This group has little power hold through the things they are not conscious of consequently give a sense of a hole like Florentine (skip a page) [sic] they also have a hardness they are not affectionate and have to be dominated to be won, and held, constantly dominated, they do not resist, they are not strongly maternal they are cumulative in their effects, recognition of them comes very slowly. They have no personal pride in them, no amour propre, they may be sensitive, they may not. they [sic] are two big groups of them, the sensitive and the not, the sensitive have sweetness, the not not, not. they connect on Mrs. Matisse -Mrs. Valloton—to Etta Cone, Mrs. Matisse, to Bird, to lady group through Mrs. Samuels. They are not sentimental, they are in intellect realists and scientists and ethical, it is in relation to their power of disciplining ~~that~~ children that they tack on to Mrs. Valloton to Etta & in another direction when it hasn't changed to egotism and self-importance it runs into Fernande. In Mrs. Matisse there is the galumping quality that connects her to Jeane Boiffard.

AT ***Maddalena:*** The Italian servant at the Casa Ricci in Fiesole.

Mrs. Matisse… galumping quality: There were physical moments of Mme. Matisse's walking that were breathtaking, like a Greek heroine, but then she would sometimes be too awkward to get out of a chair.

*

DB #48

Sentimentality, women ~~all important to themselves inside them are sentimental are free soul~~ Bird—Sally -(not Laura) ladies—lurid -

*

DB #49

They are the opposite expression the spinster expression perhaps of the sister group.

LK ***Spinster.... Spinster quality:*** "Spinster nature" is at first very briefly introduced, with no elaboration, in the MA text on 199, in relation to Lillian Rosenhagen's sister, Cecilia, with the promise that "later there will be much discussing of this spinster nature. Now it is enough to know that Cecilia Rosenhagen had it in her." The promise is partially fulfilled in the later portrait of Olga, the sister of the first Governess, in MA 240–241. She, like Etta Cone in this Note, is apparently not given to the spinster's "lack of generosity and sentimentality;" she seems to have the attacking ways "to give to her more attraction and men could be in love with her," but like Etta after her love for Ida Gutman was over, she later became defined by her spinster nature, though it remained undetectable. "Everyone just thought it was stupid being in her," but it was the nervousness, the "lack of generosity and sentimentality" of the spinster.

*

DB #50

Spinster quality, lack of generosity and sentimentality. Conceive themselves heroes but do nothing heroic Etta Cone perfect type with all her splendor and richness and possible dis spinsterising quality, when she was in love with Ida Gutman least it, she became almost generous in her nature, for her love became heroic, now she is her own hero and spinster state is complete. Earthy people, real idealists and ladies never are spinsters, because earthy sordidness makes of its pettiness heroic character. Alice Klauber is I am sure spinster at bottom, it has a mild lyric flavor but it is pure spinster, Mrs. Valloton has more than richness, she loves Valloton and so her lyric note became real music. Alice Klauber did not marry her man she became a spinster. This lack of generosity is the keynote to Etta. It is very deceptive in her because of her splendor. She and Annette striking contrast. Annette never interprets smally though she sees smallness by instinct. Etta does not see the smallness as small but interprets smally. Work out the contrast of spinster sentimentality from sisterly sentimentality.

AT ***Alice Klauber:*** After the San Francisco fire, Frank and Nelly Jacott, Paul Colts and Alice Klauber came to Paris. Alice Klauber hated Picasso and Matisse art while she was in Paris, but when she got back to California, she propagandized for Matisse. I hardly met her.

*

DB #51

The group goes Bertha—Fernande—Belle Bergman -Hattie Bache—Myrtle ~~which~~ ~~who~~ introduces the spinster element and connects through Mrs. Samuels to the perfect lady Penelope connects through Bertha to the earth group. Aunt Fanny.

*

DB #52

Fernande connects on to Bertha the particular kind of sense of importance, the maternity element, Penelope, is it without the sense of importance asserting itself where she loves, she connects on to earth to Aunt Fanny, to me. Bertha is nearer Fernande sulkyness [sic] no sense of differences, they are not conceited they have no sense of differences. Hattie Bache, Belle Bergman and Myrtle are all weaker expressions, less maternity earthness in them, more pure sisters, that is their greatest character that and common-place sentimentality. With Bertha Fernande & Penelope there is a richness of reality that overwhelms their sentimentality takes them out of the ranks of commonplace.

Want to keep in mind this common place sentimentality as a definite quality of Hattie Belle Bergman & Myrtle. Hattie Stein had it too. Find out what it is they connect on that side to Mrs. Matisse. Have not the kind of sense of importance that we have in Penelope Bertha and Fernande.

Emma [?] a very good case of that quality plus a Dolene like prostitutism.

Fernande is a wonderful case of the disintegration when ~~pressure~~ pressure of domination is removed. Egotism scatteredness in full ~~pla~~ blast. She is all over the shop. Her pride is so like Berthas. Too proud to work for anybody, too proud to be dishonest or vulgar but gets into a ~~w~~ hole where in the end she is dishonest. she is vicious but never with any delight in vice but on account of ~~ince~~ lack of resistance. Fernande setting sulkily into a kind of trance is wonderfully like Bertha.

This whole group which is the more common-place people becomes the sister group. Hattie Bache Myrtle etc. live to themselves and to others as type people of what they ideally should be and not at all ~~of~~ by what they are. They should be maternal, they aren't for they have no power of sacrifice, they should be good housekeepers and they aren't for they are indolent and have no sense of economy, they should be sweet and they aren't because they are too nasty proud. In short they should have all the womanly virtues, partly because they have not anything else partly because the suggest it to themselves and others and so they are the perfect example of sentimentality changing the object without changing the emotion both to themselves and to others without changing the emotion both to themselves and to others and so one goes on and on for years thinking one has not done them justice. Sally and Myrtle, Hattie Bache is the most commonplace and has least real existence and comes more nearly to realising the sentimental version of herself as real, only it is so empty. Bertha & Fernande are the worst because there is least commonplace in them, they are so s[p]read but not empty. Penelope is the best because in her there comes almost a complete replacement of the real thing earthy connects to Therese and makes a new reality so that she really has the virtues the others sentimentally possess.

AT ***Fernande:*** The break with Pablo in 1907 lasted only a few months. The final break came in 1914. The stage in which she is described in this note is the one she was in when I met her [when she had just separated from Picasso and had to give lessons for money.] She was even glad to be free and rented a flat and set up a studio. 'Fernande setting sulkily into a kind of trance' is literal. She was a heavy person, and when she settled in, she literally couldn't be roused.

The final break in 1914 was not as Mike reported it in his letter. As I had the story from Fernande, she and Pablo had a row and Fernande left and waited a week for him to come, and he didn't come. Fernande was not really betrayed by Eve because she knew what was coming. She got Marcoussis and Eve to come to Picasso's together, and Gertrude said to me at the time, Do you see the new combination, Fernande is giving it her blessing. Fernande had someone that she went to and stayed with him until the war broke out. This was the end for them, though Fernance was prepared for it.

Fernande… maternity element: Fernande was maternal, completely, toward Picasso. When one of his friends killed himself and Picasso got afraid of the dark, Fernande went everywhere with him. Motherliness kept her close to him for a long time.

connects on to earth to Aunt Fanny: Gertrude's mother's [Amelia Keyser Stein's] brothers and sisters were Gertrude's Aunt Fanny, Uncle Ephraim, Uncle—Ernie's father whose name I don't know—Aunt Sarah, Aunt Celia, and Aunt Helen, a younger sister who was a sort of house pet. This one was little, in fact weeny, smaller than any of them, who were all small.

Gertrude loved her Aunt Fanny, had enormous respect for her, she who took her and Bertha into her home [when they went East after their mother died] and already had two unmarried sisters, Aunt Sarah and Aunt Helen, on her hands, and now there was another sister's two daughters. Gertrude got pretty thoroughly into Baltimore life, and liked her mother's family well. They were the 'cheerful ones' [mentioned in the Autobiography,] all the Baltimore aunts and uncles, with the exception of Aunt Sarah, the religious one, and Aunt Celia, who took a course in dressmaking to make everybody's clothes. From her photo, Aunt Sarah seemed to be sad about religion. She would retire into meditation and have communion with the Saints or God or something. All of them were weeny, five feet, even Uncle Eph, but Aunt Celia was large.

Myrtle… commonplace sentimentality: Oh, but the quantities of it! When we saw her in our San Francisco visit in the Thirties, she wept about Gertrude, about Sarah, about Mike. She was considered beautiful, but why was beyond me.

Fernande… egotism… in full blast: Gertrude always used to say, But she's not vicious. Fernande had a way of walking down the street and feeling it really existed for her, and that people revolved around her and her beauty. I took walks with her during our lessons, went to theatres and museums to get by the boredom of our sessions together, and I saw during these outings how Fernande accepted the position she imposed on all passersby to accept.

the sister group: The 'sister' kind were the ones with the continuous consciousness of being a sister, and warring against the sister. Etta always asserting herself modestly and Claribel always pushing her away—Gertrude considered that to be sisterly, and told me so. Etta and Claribel were the type of it for her. Etta feared and envied Claribel, was subservient and obedient and loving toward her, and in her heart of hearts waited for the day when she would be the only Miss Cone. Claribel was always amusing, and toward Etta always put a humorous turn on everything, always made a phrase. It was the character of the Southern Baltimore manner—she laughed while she talked, neither pleasantly nor unpleasantly.

the more common-place people… Myrtle: Mike once took Myrtle [Sarah's sister] to the Variétés in Paris, and when it was over, she fell and cut her nose. Gertrude worried that Mike would be disturbed, fixed her up that night at the rue de Fleurus, and the next morning went to tell Mike what had happened. She deserves everything she gets, Mike said. When she wears high heels like that, what does she expect? And she was the one he disliked the least [of

Sarah's family.] She was the least objectionable because she was the quietest.

She was quiet because she had nothing to say. Sally at the end of the Matisse episode [when the school was over] was at one time winning Pritchard [an Assistant Director of the Boston Museum of Fine Arts] to—ah! intellectual companionship, and Myrtle dropped in one afternoon to report that Pritchard came to Sarah's in the evening. And Gertrude asked, 'What do you do?' 'Oh, we just chat.' Gertrude and I were imagining Myrtle chatting with Pritchard.

She had her own tragedy, though. She divorced her husband to marry a scientist she met on the boat going back to America, and before they were married, he died, and so she remarried her first husband. She looked a little like a parrot.

Bertha and Fernande… so spread: I once told Gertrude about an aunt of mine whom I said was like Fernande, but Gertrude said, 'No, she's more like Bertha, because she hadn't Fernande's possibility of rising to the top to be a leading character.' The Aunt and Bertha were empty and vague and certain. Bertha knew she was a good woman because she was a good mother, which meant to her being a good woman.

LK ***Hattie Stein:*** Hattie Stein Bache.

*

Note #51

[…] injury
Free soul & prostitute group—resentment going over into
use of power and to sentimentality from a sense of virtue Lady
injury—to autocrat sense the ~~king~~ queen can do no wrong.

Mrs. Matisse to Aunt Fanny resentment to sense of injury in itself.
Etta not sure, Annette Mabel Emma not strong in sense of injury
Work out Roche Bush & Pach.

LK Concurrent with (and possibly a fragment of) NB-*C #22.

*

DB #53

Bruce
Roche—Bush—Pach

He is a translation as Pablo says, all these have intelligence but no real intellect, the unfinished, unmatured boy quality. Worldly (not in intention) no instinct for being a success. Meditate on their relation to Leo Friedman and their positive quality. No heroic element in them.

Bruce is the best of them because he has a kind of dirtiness that has a little quality but they are all stupid. Leo says it is because there [sic] minds move so slowly that they digest nothing and it comes out whole as it went in. That the practical element is only as everybody is practical but as they don't understand anything else although they have a sensibility to the desiring of it nothing comes out of them but the practical consideration.

*

Note #41

Pach—Singer—Francis—Derain—Leo Friedman -
Bruce—Bush—Roche
Pach nearest perhaps to Matisse in singular kind of blindness not Bazarofian blindness of nature essentially
limitation of sympathy & experience by reason of pride. limited / not fanatic blindness like Hutch or Raymonde's due
to rejection of intellect and rush into sexuality and mystycism [sic], Leo's statement that mysticism and sexual abandonment have it in common that they deny the intellect, the Simon H. & Chalfin kind of blindness by clearness of intellect and lack of quantity of nature, of Francis & Puy incapac[i]ty for real experience, and remarkable facility & variety of intellect, to Pach ~~and~~ who has a hold on real experience but hopelessly slow, stubborn, and practical, to Matisse who has a tremendous hold on real experience, slow -stubborn practical and impenetrable except when he chooses to be penetrated. From there we go on through Bruce to the Jaehne people through Leo to intellectuals & idealists. through Singer to Bunting and Manguin who have sensibility but only for nuances, through Roche to the dramatic idealists, through Bruce to Derain who has no sensibility, to Leo Friedman through Francis to the lurid group.

Fred Stern
Bush Leo Friedman
Derain

When you get it to Fred the practical becomes complete before it passes over through Uncle Sol and Jake Samuels into the men of the world who passes [sic] over to the pure idealists on the one hand through Edstrom and the tabby cats on the other through Mary. Now this makes clear the difference between Dehning and Hersland sale, sensible, impractical except as players [?] or petit bourgeois clean direct unsensitive, the type middle-men (the Bernheims. In the true man of the world he adds a distinction to this foundation and adds sensibility and murkiness of a new kind. The earth type is another story Weber, beauty group—Persian group, Bazarofs, Braque perhaps the man of the world version of it.

LK ***Now this makes clear the difference between Dehning and Hersland sale:*** Corresponds to NB-*C #9 ["got the definite difference now between Dehning & Hersland… Hersland murky sexual character… Dehning cleaner."]

*

DB #54

Alice Klauber

Bottom Gertrude Davenport & Marie Gruenhagen. Cruel, intolerant completely domineering, graciousless making fun of the ~~daughters~~ adopted child's hands and feet. Alice K's humor about waling & what not complete possession. Insensitive quality of the pure lady. Like the pure lady without the beauty, grace, sensitiveness and capacity to be tolerant when complete that the pure lady has. It is the same thing in Adele only in her it is combined with genius, intellect, sensibility and a great moral passion. In all these it is insensitive. Alice K is in the middle, then it goes to May Gruenhagen who was it without any admixture so she really is the bare bones of it. thence it passes Adele Jaffer to the saintly type, to G. Davenport to Mary Houghton, through Miss Blood to the lady Mrs. Samuels, through Fernande to the sentimentalists, maternal, through Mrs. Valloton to the spinster sentimentalists, through, Alice Klauber and to Bird and pure prostitute brutality and to Florentine. through Mrs. Matisse to the earthy efficients. Very significant resemblance between Alice Klauber & Mrs. Davenport that she gets all the young men in sight around them. And I guess the young men makes equal fun of them both. But she Alice Klauber is essentially the mistress it is only when it passes through Bird to the prostitutes that it loses its power quality and through Mrs. Matisse to the earthy and so humble servant type that it loses power. In all the other directions it remains the mistress type, the lady type. Relation of Alice Klauber to her Doctor very important remember it all.

AT ***Adele [Jaffa]:*** This was my first impression of her, but in small. She had competence and didn't play you any tricks. Her actions were always on the same level. She had none of the petty feminine weaknesses that run through the Alice Klauber, Fernande and the rest group.

*

Note #107

Scrap of unlined typing paper

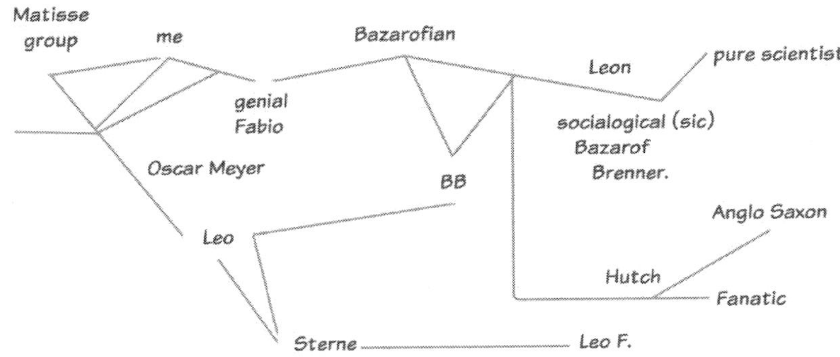

*

Chapter 5.

Passionate women, those in whom emotion has the inensity [sic] of a sensation, afflict their world with agitation, excitement and unrest. Sometimes they marry well and then excitement is with them deep joy. More often their marriage is a failure and then they rush about miserable seeking to escape from misery.

The other women, those who know not passion, make marriages no less unhappy but with them not to be happy makes so much less stir. These must content themselves with emptiness. They These [sic] cannot overflow their misery in ceaseless restless action. They sit so quiet lest their emptiness increase and leave when with all thats [sic] inside, gone and lifeless. They are like them that have a horrid fear when standing on high places. Nothing comes to them but emptiness. They dread the loss of all themselves and every second go on losing more. The one relief there is, is to sit down and so make a resisting compact mass that will not let itself all drop away.

And so the creature without passion makes its unhappy marriage and then sits still for what else can it do. It is not in human natures that it is still waters that run deepest. The restless ones know as keen sorrow as those who make no stir; but emptiness is more sickening long kept up than overfullness. The stomach overloaded is always very sick but then it can discharge itself upon the world. The empty starving stomach can only weaken sadden, grow more helpless.

Julia Dehning had rushed upon her sorrow passionately, fervently, heroically. Bertha Dehning sank down into hers quietly, helplessly, unaspiringly. Bertha Dehning soon after Julia's marriage came to the fullness of her youthful bloom. She was darker, richer, fuller in her curves, softer to the touch, easier to be friends than her more brilliant elder sister. The harshness in the speech and thought, the hardness and the jerk in the manner and the walk, all these her mother's ways it had not come to her to have. She like her father loved compromise and peace. It was results that theses two wanted not the strife.

*

["Use this about one of David's friends."]
~~Bertha Dehning was a kindly friendly creature. She liked the other girls and they liked her.~~

*

Describe home life Hersland's family Dehning, David there for vacation conversations etc.

That is, after the Herslands episode, come back to the Dehnings and the Julia-Alfred marriage. David, visiting them, has conversations with Julia.

*

Note #108

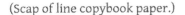

(Scap of line copybook paper.)

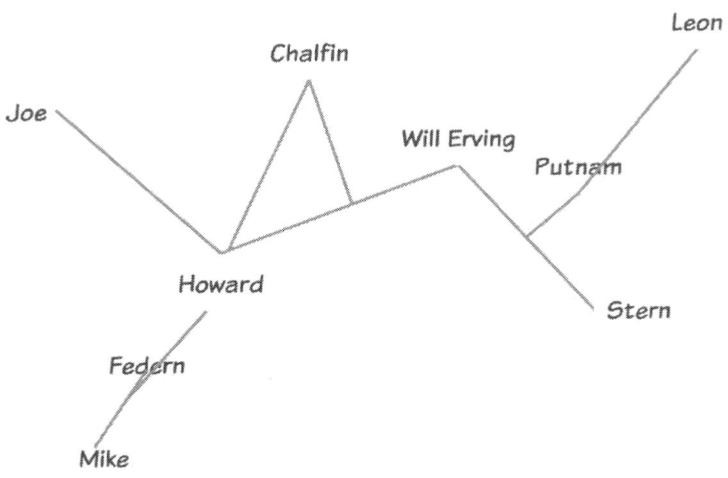

*

Note #45

Chalfin I am quite sure has the sexual base of our Simon that is to say of Braque leading to Jake Samuels. Vollard introduces a distinction a certain salete. Uncle Sol introduces another element common-place insensibility, lack of power of intelligence but on the other hand it may as in his case it has as opposed to Fred Stein it may turn into a certain judicialness not the highest type like Mike's because Mike introduces a pagan sensibility to beauty and so tolerance. ~~Valloton~~ A Chalfin is made up of three parts, Braque sexual base and a certain lucrative, active, gentlemanly intellect, Simon H type of energy and ethical ideal, Howard temperamental and there comes his preciosity and beauty, and aristocracy. Valloton, temperamentally like Jaehne, sexually like, & intellectually like Julius Levy, and there is his great limitation as an artist. His greatness is his temperament, his sexual base and intellect is below it.

The Roche etc group fall into two varieties, the one we might call anglo saxon having an inner sensibility a genuine interior vision, but slow blind, their mind progresses so slowly it stops and the practical worldly takes its place with them, also the practical may be only expressed in them by a passion for detail a losing themselves in illustration, but always they have real sensibility real faith. The jewish side of them lacks this sensibility this real faith and it is replaced by a lyrical pretty quality and a passion for rather confused emotional and transcendental thinking and an intelligent facile practical intellect in their real business whatever it is. It goes over with them into the purely intellectual group, the untemperamental intellectual as the other group the Christian side goes over into the idealistic group. It is interesting that Leo Stein meets both the extreme wings of this group.

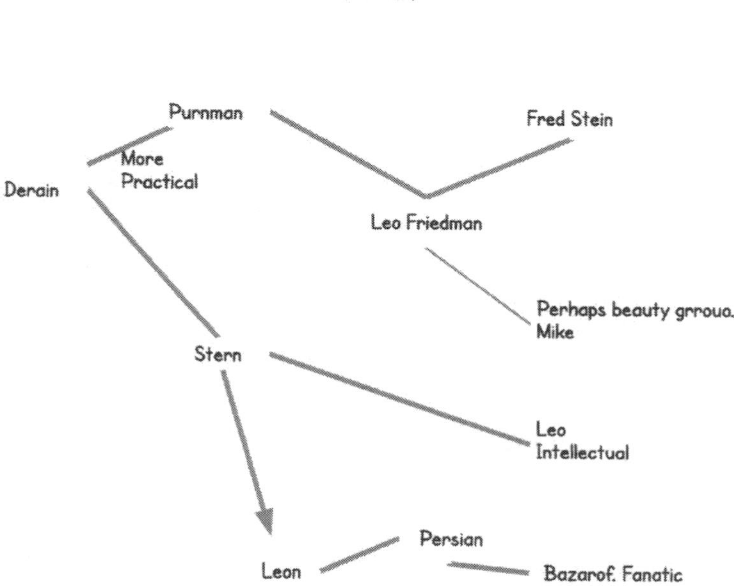

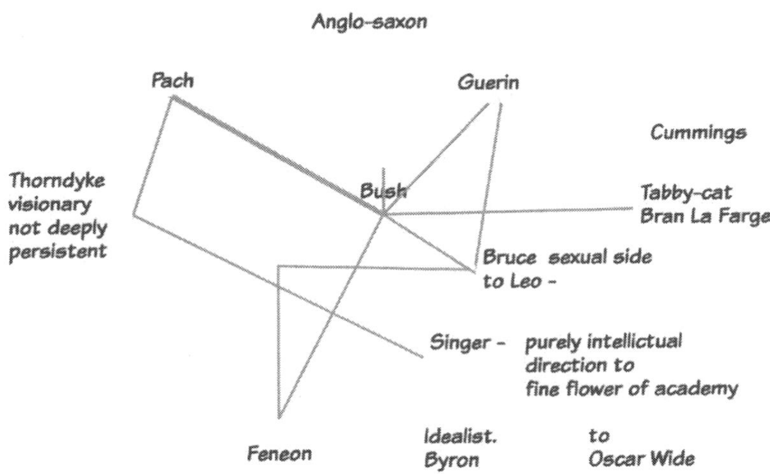

Pach in his attitude is very illuminating as he shows wherin[sic] this group fails. He shows the unreality mf their idealism, strong as he is in the expression of it and religion, his criticism of Leo's picture I recognise the giri, I don't recognise the atelier and then saying he and Henri beliaved in religion like the chinaman painting his soul at the end of his brush, Derain expresses the same Leo Friedman on a lower plane expresses the same in his living to go out of amorning [sic] and think over the occupations of all the world and they none of them see the essential profound contradiction between their two expressions, Leo F. sees it better in so far as he is more practical that is the Fred Stein element is stronger in him, he is less illumined, and he makes the two things both being on a lower plane come nearer together also his sexual base is nearer Mike's it has less turdifness than in the others who are much nearer Leo. So their blindness their spiritual ineffectiveness comes from a deep and fundamental incompatibility, the more ~~sensible~~ sensitive they are inernally the more definitive is this contradiction in them, the less sensitive the more they succeed in practical resuits. From them we pass over to Fred Stain in whom their [sic] is no idealism he is stolid common-pace he has no element of distinction. In his father Uncle Sol is introduced an element of distinction that is the man of the world, in a certain sense elegance, justice, action, savoir faire, mastery, the masculine version of Bertha at her best. In another direction the group passes through

Stern to purely intellactual creative he introduces a new element of idealism, in himself both in the pure intellectual side

(Will Erving)

and in a certain kind of elegance the Persian (Leon) a

(Putnam)

roaring spirit of freedom, In Stern these elements are not mixed in him, the only thing that dominates him is his sexual and intellectual kinship to Leo Friedman, the others derail him, they don't keep him in motion. Also remember the slowness of their minds which helps their not seeing the two facts together and so realising their contradiction. In another way through Feneon they get to be tabby cats and also idealist group the two parts both become vehement and strong so strong that like Leo F.'s on a lower plane they come together. Their blindness is in contrast to Matisse blindness, unreasonableness, he is unreasonable on account of the tenacity with which he holds to his central idea himself and his art, he can change slowly it is not with him an inner contradiction, there is no inner contradiction, it is the dogged persistence of the thing that for the time he knows, in Pablo and in Raymond ~~a~~ Hutch, ascending from it is the domination of the mystic idea to denial of their intellect and their experience. Matisse never denies his experience, he continually affirms it, so in him there is no contradiction, there may be a doubt of it, a terror of losing or having lost it as in Samuel Johnson but his whole life is the affirmation of his experience. the danger with the fanatic group is the denial of their experience, this may make them moral enthusiasts as Leon, Weininger, it may make them, aesthetic visionaries as Raymond & (I hope not) Pablo Pablo may be saved by the intensity of his actual aesthetic experience, if he can hold to that he will go on, Leon held to the reality of his scientific experience and so they touch Bazarof but it is this quality in them that so often makes their genius sterile. Hutch negates his for the white heat of life, and so there are innumerable ways of ship-wreck.

AT ***Weininger:*** After Gertrude read Freud on *Hamlet,* she refused to read any more. We both read the thing in Freud on *Hamlet*, and that was the beginning and the end for Gertrude. After that, she was just not interested. [Leo had sent Freud volumes from Berlin to Paris in 1910.] Leo discovered Croce, but Gertrude was not that interested. Weininger came from Andrew Green, I think. I'm not certain it was from him, but know it was not from a heavy intellectual, just a widely read man. She read it in translation, and then we went down to Gallimard's and bought out all the Weiningers and sent them to everybody. It was a mad enthusiasm. Gertrude thought he was the only modern whose theory stood up and was really consistent. Weininger divided people up so completely into parts and that was what she was doing in a different way. And he too was trying to get down to the bottom nature, as she was.

*

DB #55

Sentimental high school quality in Alice—her admiration for learning and virtue. Maud Tilton & Eleanor Gray—none of them virtuous or learned, various kinds of sentimentality. Olga Meershon [sic], Myrtle & Hattie sisterly kind, Bertha & Fernande all kinds, Etta lone spinster kind, Inez Cohen prudish prostitute kind Olga Meerhson [sic] between her and Fernande. Etta Guggenheimer between spinster and high-school. Pure W. always sentimental pretty nearly Dolene extreme one type or rather all the prostitute types of pure W. are sentimental Bertha perfect example of another. May B & Jean of another. Mabel Haynes central mass of another. Hattie Bache a sub-group of Bertha & Fernande.

*

DB #56

LK The day before we were to discuss the following note, I told Miss Toklas that it was written with considerable animus toward her, and that it would be well for her to be prepared for its contents. The following morning, she called me to say that she had hardly been able to sleep that night, and would I come some twenty minutes before lunch so that she would have a moment to look at the note to see just how bad it was. When she read it in solitude later, she came back into the room showing indescribable relief.

"Oh, that's all right," she said. "I thought it was quite different, I thought it was something else. No, this can be explained easily, and after what I had expected, or rather feared, it comes as a relief."

"What had you expected, Miss Toklas?"

"I was afraid that Gertrude had accused me of disloyalty. That's the only thing that would matter. This is perfectly understandable, where it comes from, and why Gertrude should have thought so then, at the time it was written. I think you did very well to warn me of worse than was in it."

There was not only considerable relief but considerable glee for Miss

Toklas in explaining the note's origin.

Alice Toklas

Only one person as low as Alice in my experience is Zobel. She is low clean through to the bottom crooked, a liar of the most sordid unillumined undramatic unimaginative prostitute type, coward, ungenerous, ~~cons~~ conscienceless, mean, vulgarly triumphant and remorseless, caddish, in short just plain ~~rotten~~ low like Zobel but not dangerous not effective, no evil. Low but not evil. No evil intention,

no steadfast intention of any sort. An acquiescent intention to be low which is her form of constantly tasting flavors. Absolutely no distinguishing sense for people. Self knowledge but no consciousness ~~for~~ of the significant, of the meaning of the things she knows. the practical intelligence of the Hellenising Jew but not the practical instinct as Stern has it. same as BB in that respect. Along with this is not a moral purpose or intention but an exquisite and keen moral sensibility. Does not come into relation or conflict with lowness because in both cases there is nothing willed, there is no intention, consequently no struggle, no moral nature, in the sense of effort. Her attitude toward generous or sympathetic conduct toward herself, moves her deeply and keenly and is beautiful to her, does not affect her reaction, Is not ~~civil~~ evil in intention but has no discrimination, her conception of people is diagramatic formulistic but just as she has a beautiful sensibility to morality and generosity so she has a certain beautiful sensibility toward people but her reaction to them from it is deliberate and diagramatic. The mental expression is practical and concrete the ~~emotional~~ emotion is subtle, intuitive beautiful. They run themselves by their intellect, consequently they know what they are but not the meaning of it. Consequently they do not come in conflict with themselves because they don't know the significance of their own beauty. They choose beauty Alice and BB in other words they choose to be low for that is their beauty as far as they see it. In BB. his occasional easthetic [sic] ~~ans~~ perception is the thing but that does not make a standard to himself. In Alice the moral sensibility is the thing and that does not make a standard for herself. It acts only as making her create her idols. It has never anything to do with her conduct toward the idols her hands have created. There she is always low, low but not evil conceives herself as low is low, lowness has the flavor for her, but she has no evil intention nor capacity. In short is a failure. Not the Napoleonic type. Napoloneic [sic] type do not conceive [sic] of themselves as lows may conceive themselves as evil. Mary Houghton mostly conceive themselves as moral but they have evil intention they are tremendously willed, they have enormous power, they go over into the compact pure lady type, who also has great power, but is guided by a sense of right and dignity, has no the vulgarity of a misfit between the evil, overpowering nature and the ideals. Can well believe Napoleon thought himself working for the glory of France. ~~Star.~~ Star significant. Mary Houghton believes she loves women. Just the other way round of BB and Alice. Alice runs herself by her intellect but there is not enough intellect in her to go around and so she fails in every way. Has a sense for virtue and Academic learning, admires the same, because of the falseness of her ideals. thinks she wants to be good. The puzzle about the neat clear practical unsympathetic intellect resolves itself into being the type of intellect that goes with the sexual Dolene quality and is not the intellect that goes with the flavor esthetic sensitive low sexual side of her. In Fernande the intellect goes with her sexual quality also in Annette might consider that perhaps a general rule in most cases intellect goes with sexual quality no with the temperament that explains the Pach Roche group and even more the Stern Derain group. It is only when the intellect is of a predominant quality that there is a fusion of the sexual nature and temperament which is often at variance. In most of the idealist group it is at variance. It is only in the highest expression of each type that it fuses and then either as in intellect as in Leo & Sally or inspirational as in Matisse or Pablo or in me that it possesses one. Have found that Alice's real sexual base is Bertha, stupid eyes, there are three in her, Dorothy Reade, goes with intellect, and B.B. the sensibility of her.

The last thing noticed is the way she can make you talk like one of her old gentlemen to whom she loves to listen and be docile to and so she makes a poor thing of one because one talks badly then, she listens, she is docile, stupid but she owns you, you are then her(s).

AT ***Alice Toklas:*** Gertrude wrote this after conversations with Annette or Sarah, before she knew me well, but after I had come to Paris. None of it could possibly have come from Harriet. It was written probably late 1907 or the beginning of 1908. Gertrude made a study then, after her very early meetings with me, on information gathered from a number of sources. A good deal of it holds true. The evil, that's all right. The lack of morality that offended

Gertrude, that was and is perfectly true. Gertrude was a little shocked that I could go on seeing Nelly after she learned about the Nelly story and Nelly's general ruthlessness. Nelly's general attitude to life and the world wasn't highly noble.

Gertrude was at that time still in the "deep-thinking" life, the kind that worries about "issues," and deliberates on the ethics and morality in each little act. This was the 'Stein thinking' of Leo and Gertrude separately and together. And it plainly offended me from the beginning. It was boring and ludicrous. For example, I subscribed to the Argonaut, a very free-thinking liberal newspaper in San Francisco, which I read thoroughly, and Leo and Gertrude got into a fierce discussion, a 'deep-thinking' argument that lasted for hours on an issue in California politics, without knowing anything but what Pixley said in his article. Later, I pointed to the article and asked Gertrude, How can either of you take seriously what the other one is saying when all either of you know is based on the same two paragraphs in Pixley's article? Gertrude looked, and said, And so it was.

My influence over Gertrude's relation to Leo was a little bit like my influence in the Bernard Fay affair after the war. When they questioned me about his escape from the prison hospital, I said I was not of sufficient importance to do anything but would have if I could have. In other words, Leo was right when he said I broke up their happy home; I did in intention rather than in effect. One of the jokes between Gertrude and myself later was that I had stopped the 'deep-thinking' vein for her. I was discouraged to be in an atmosphere where intellectual processes were the basis of life, and in which Leo's endless notes and Gertrude's answers would be passing back and forth between them. I had the impression at the time that 'deep-thinking' was the root of all evil, that the fallible minds of human beings were bound to go wrong. So, afterward, when Gertrude would be in her bath in the morning, and I would call her, she always said, Let me alone, I'm meditating. Not deep-thinking.

At the time, I spoke seriously of this Stein way to Gertrude; only later did we make a joke of it. I was really irritated by it, Leo's way of deep-thinking and the note-practices were very unpleasant. It became a phrase between us, 'Leo is so rude and so very impolite.'

LK [Leo's "rudeness" was explained by Miss Toklas in her later descriptions of his way of arguing, and of his odd way of behaving as though angry or of dominating when under the impression that he was making a devastating point.]

AT Gertrude was consciously free of the everlasting influence of Leo by the end of the Notebooks. By 1909, Leo had made his attack on Nelly, and I told

Gertrude about it in detail. Leo came and told me about all Nelly's faults, why he had no longer any respect for her, and so on, and I had nothing to say in reply because falling in love with Nelly had been Leo's own choice. After all, Nelly had been like that before she knew you, it wasn't you that produced these things in her. Probably that sort of thing happened at the end of all Leo's affairs; he had to make it horrible when he was done with it. With one woman, he went back after many years merely to confirm his opinion of her.

As for my moral values, Gertrude probably would have said to the end that I had a taste for them but didn't possess them, but probably wouldn't have put such emphasis on the pleasure in them in others. I believe with Henry James, not in morals but in manners.

Gertrude thought I was forgetful rather than not grateful concerning Nelly, and that my relation with Nelly had more meaning than it had. I was really just a good friend of Nelly's, it was not emotional. In the summer of 1908 at the Villa Bardi, I explained this to Gertrude, that Sarah and others had put all sorts of constructions on it, but that really Nelly's evil didn't touch me in any way.

LK [Later, I asked Miss Toklas about the short piece by Stein, "Did Nelly or Lily Really Love You," and the scene in *A Lyrical Opera Made By Two*, in which the phrase occurs: "not any Lily not any Nelly." The references are obviously to this conversation in which Gertrude asked about Miss Toklas' relations to Lily Hansen and Nelly Jacott, and Miss Toklas' reply, "Not any Lily not any Nelly." Miss Toklas confirmed that this was the most crucial conversation in the development of her intimacy with Stein.]

AT Harriet once asked me, Have you no principles by which you live? And I answered, None. Nelly went much further than I did in denying moral values. She would have said, A waste of time and energy. Nelly was a little like Pablo in that respect. She put up a very cynical front to a bad world to defend herself.

Gertrude carried over her moral values from Radcliffe days with Mabel Weeks, Miriam Price, Estelle Rumbold, who were all very high-minded. She was intimate with these before she met May Bookstaver and Mabel Haynes [at Johns Hopkins.]

When this note was written, Gertrude had had little occasion to make note of my reactions to people. We hadn't yet become intimate in any sense of the word at all. Discussions of people came later, after the summer of 1908. Then [back in Paris in the Fall] Gertrude would come in to visit with Harriet and me every day, we would make appointments for walks, and so on. During the summer of 1908, when Harriet and I were renting the Casa Ricci and Gertrude and Leo were staying with the Mike Steins at the Villa Bardi, Gertrude would bring people up to the Casa Ricci to Harriet's.

AT ***Along with this is not a moral purpose or intention:*** It was a question for me of manners, not of morals. Morals and manners go together, I believe, but not with me.

AT ***they choose to be low for that is their beauty:*** Gertrude has already said in these Notebooks that she's done with moral shock and so on, but it really still holds her, in this note, through Leo. And the Stinker [Annette Rosenshine] misinformed Gertrude about me by her ready answers, which were really not her habit. For example, there was Gertrude's entire misconception about my friendship with Lilly Hansen and Nelly and Harriet, and we laughed about it afterward. That was probably through Annette and Sarah. And there was Gertrude's entirely mistaken impression, from Lizzie Rosenshine, of my relation to Nelly and Ada [Nelly's sister.] Even [Annette's father] Dolphy Rosenshine's letters came in on this. He wrote very severe letters on the subject which Gertrude showed me with great glee after I told her what it was about. Sarah had it in for me good and plenty for not falling under her sway [in San Francisco, before coming to Europe] but one day in the summer of 1908, she granted me a confidential visit in which she said, Now that Gertrude has accepted you, all is forgotten and forgiven. Later, Sarah's forgiveness wavered, and I could watch it wavering through the gifts she gave me, through her need for flattering me, and through her premeditated courtesies.

AT ***BB his occasional easthetic [sic] perception:*** Gertrude thought that when BB as a young man had a sudden vision on how to proceed with the verification of a painter's work, he hit on a detail nobody had ever thought of using because it was so petty. It was in the draperies. You could always know about a painter's personal ways of doing from his use of draperies. This was all right, Gertrude thought, but to base a whole theory or method on it was pretty slight. For her a painter was judged by the endowment expressed in any part of the painting, not by a particular thing in it. You ought to know by any square inch in it. To her it was not a question of tactile values at all, any value would do.

His taste was not only bad in objects in art, but in people. He put the Piot murals in his library by the accident of Mme. Piot looking impressive to him, and he never knew that Mme. Piot was an ex-Montmartoise model. I Tatti, the villa he bought and built onto in Settignano, was awful. The house was badly placed, and just existed on a road. The garden was pathetic, nothing grew in it, and it had a weird little fountain with no meaning. That was at the beginning, when he first had it. Now of course it is very beautiful.

AT ***The last thing noticed... her old gentlemen:*** In San Francisco when I was young, I had two or three gentlemen to whom I was devoted. They were about my father's age, they were charming, and I enjoyed flirting with them. It was sufficiently a la mode in my youth, not at all odd or daring, girls did have men friends then. Gertrude never actually saw this side of me. There was no one in Paris like that for me. Chalfin was the first charming one, but that was later. Who were the people whom I could have made talk at all? There was no audience, I had no one to talk to at all.

At the beginning of our next interview, Miss Toklas volunteered further comment on this Note:

AT The note is based on Gertrude's cross-examination of Sarah and Annette Rosenshine. Annette's contribution is really her mother Lizzie's melodramatic version of me. Lizzie was especially melodramatic on the subject of my father, about whom she had such notions as that he was going to marry the servant girl and close the house.

The Note is definitely late 1907 or early 1908, because these are tales gotten from Annette told to her by her mother. There is also in it Sarah's version of how she put out a helping hand to me which I refused—Sarah saving her virtue again. But none of the Note is based on Gertrude's real later knowing of me or anything she learned through me.

Don't forget that Annette was very anxious not to let me get close to Gertrude. If I had been put in Annette's position of being a subject of investigation for Gertrude, Harriet would have spoken out. Harriet had that fine loyalty in her which I called her "sweetness," at which Gertrude laughed.

As for the conversation at Versailles [referred to in *A Lyrical Opera Made By Two*, where it is conflated with the conversation at the Villa Bardi in Florence] it was in fact not about Nelly and Lily. It happened in February or March of 1908. We were picking wild violets in the Versailles gardens when Gertrude told me for the first time that I was an 'old maid mermaid' type, and I said, Oh rats. I was in that group at first, but I got out early.

I knew Annette as a child in San Francisco. I helped her to get into Art School with my advice. Use your mother, I told her. And it was I who advised her mother Lizzie to let Annette go to Paris. And Nelly and Ada had been school friends, and then afterwards I didn't see them. But when Clare got married, she asked me to take charge of Nelly and Ada Josephs, which I did. Clare had been raised and schooled in France, and then came back to San Francisco where I became her very close friend.

Nelly and Ada were scandalous. Their mother was supposed by Lizzie quite wrongly to be the lover of the man who did away with the family money. Nelly and Ada smoked, made up, and did so publicly. Ada was weighty and heavy like Fernande, but much more amusing, much more of a person than Fernande. Nelly saw men all day long. She stayed home in the library and saw men. These stories were true, but what was supposed to be happening in the stories was not true. San Francisco was scandalized, especially by Teggart, the Irishman who was devoted to her, amused her and kept her from being depressed. Clare and I approved of Teggart enormously because he would keep Nelly out of another such love affair as she had been through.

Ada was outrageous because she rode a bicycle wearing riding breeches. She kept her fiancé a dead secret up to the moment when the story got out of her seeing him drowning before her eyes. The headlines of that weren't to Ada's credit. It was all the things you didn't know about Nelly and Ada that were horrible. Ada went out in her big English racing car with Johnny, 'for you and for me,' Ada said, and they stopped in road houses for drinks. That wasn't done.

Then there was Ollie, who carried on with a married woman, Lettie Hendry, for years. And Sidney with his Emily, a notoriously bad girl. When her sister was dying in Arizona, she prayed that if her sister were spared, she would be a good girl from then. By the time she got there, her sister was dead, so she didn't bother. And she certainly was a bad girl. But Nelly and Ada were both far too careful for the scandals of themselves to be true.

Early I told Gertrude, You mustn't forget that I don't base my friendships on character in any way. With my friends, I may be surprised, but I'm never shocked by anything in any way.

It was very shortly after the Versailles conversation that I remember conducting Annette to the train so that she would miss her appointment with Gertrude, and at that time Gertrude asked me, Why do you laugh, and I said, I'll tell you, but not now. Because I knew what I was doing, but waited until Annette was soon to leave Paris. Lizzie was due to come over soon and take her off.

*

Note #46

[...] idol with the feet of clay, you are hers, then, submissive docile, stupid humble as she is then to you and so you are dead and she passes over your dead body as she did with Sally. I want to know more exactly than I do yet how she makes that happen to one. It is ~~ses~~ essentially done by there being no relation between you. No response on her side. A withdrawal through stupidity & docility and a possession by your fatuousness in consequence. ~~Yo~~ That is what happened in the case with Sally. She is docile but fixes her own way and so gradually she gets superior, not as Annette or Harriet do, by appropriating your work and so pulling you down to their level but by making an idol of you and so you make your clay feet stick out. Then also her ~~no~~

being scared before there really is reason for running away and then afterwards being able to see clearly that there was no danger she is certain that she was not scared, in the ~~path~~ progress through the street called straight she winds and twists so much that she loses her original intention. She is not without intention sensation and relation

in the beginning /, but they all get lost through evasion, crookedness, pride, cowardice and stupidity and all these together make a crookedness that is extraordinary but never evil, it does nothing except preserve her sense of superiority. This idea makes her whole relation to Sally so much simpler[.] She made an~~d~~ idol of her in S.F. probably it broke down some by Sally's talk to her that time about being good and Nelly etc. for when she is hit she don't keep open, she closes over her wound and evades and so she is prepared to clayify her idol more than before. And so she felt superior the more she mixed up in things in S.F. the more she felt her power until at last it was to Annette don't fuss about Sally, strike for his mind and heart if not his, his brothers. Annette to her at that time had power because she partook of Alice's nature to Alice herself. With me the same thing, happened. I impressed the first day I was made into an idol. Then she got on top out of relation as always, then I impressed with an axe, and she has never quite lost that, after that she did not close up by getting out of relation in stupidity but by getting scared to death ~~with~~ which is part of the first half of the second half which I will enter into shortly. Then after my talk about Nelly she got out of relation by stupidity. And I turned into an old gentleman, With Annette she gets out of relation by the first half of the second half, which may be intense fear or intense superiority, When she is moved, by moral perception as after the axe, ~~and~~ a mixture of the first half and the second of the last half when I gave her the discourse in the gardens and she made the resolution, since then she has never been affected by me except when I talked to Harriet and the few minutes the night I told her she was scared to death. Now to take up the question of the two halves, and the two halves of the two halves. We must consider her sexual nature, that runs the gamut from concentrated Bertha (eyes & forehead) through (Etta Cone & Olga) to (Dorothy Reade and Etta Levy) what we might call the stupid evasive coward version of the same thing which in the last two is domineering unsensitive and pseudo intellectual. Then it passes over into the worldly, practical, academic ~~living~~ learning living, idol making, charlatan clear intellect self measuring, Dolene, Gabrielle conscienceless, crookedness of immorality etc. Then that passes over into the true flavor beauty, sensitive, proud, tactless, noble B.B. thing, generous and direct. And that is in Alice's case without doubt, the strongest in her but Oh ye of little faith, it is even less potent in her than it is in B.B. In Janet that is practically all there is of her but it is so feeble so impotent in its character, it really never becomes more than sentimentality. In Mary McClean it is more active it comes nearly being genius, in Charlotte Bronte, it became passionately imaginative it became genius, in Mary Houghton it passes over into the Napoleonic lady type, it loses a certain nobility and impotence that it has in the pure flavor type. In Neith it is strangely mixed, it is very beautiful in her, and one feels the sexual base it ought to have but it hasn't that sexual base that evanescant [sic] uncertain, she has the earthy servant girl base that allies her to Therese, and Maggie. But to come back to Alice, this is her but how little of it there is in the whole of her which is made up of every conceivable kind of weakness, crookedness, lazyness [sic], stupidity, everything induces crookedness, the concentrated Bertha evasive female, the charlatanism, the practical sense, the melodramatic imagination, the passion for vulgar beauty, and then finally the pride and sensitiveness of her finest quality and so she is undoubtedly a creature made to be crooked but never evil, for after all the Dolene which comes nearest that is after all the weakest of her admixtures. I don't [think] she would be evil even in self-defence, that is where she is different from her daddy.

Claribel is complete now between them, all the part of Claribel that is not in Harriet is in Alice. Pride is the basis of Claribel, it is that that she keeps intact, it is that that she guards so carefully, her vanity is even secondary to that and it is because of this enormous personal pride that she is vulnerable where Harriet is safe, that she loves the society of her most stupid inferiors, Harriet does not, that she is polite and ceremonious, that she is large and generous, Alice is all this on a smaller scale but where she is more vulnerable is in the beauty side the certain passion for beauty which at once makes her vulgar and worth while, in its best moments it is noble, in its worst it is caddish and then also she is more pure it [sic] than Claribel but that is the secret of this haunting resemblance which I could never solve, It is because of this that she suffers as I have almost never seen anybody suffer, and sometimes it takes the form ~~version~~ of being scared to death so eager is she to escape. Pach is bad as to pride but its nothing to these two. They suffer horribly in their pride there is no other word it is terrible suffering, there is the same naked nostril in the two of them. To save her pride Claribel is a fool, to save hers

Alice is crooked on the street called straight. Alice is compounded Claribel + B.B. Claribel = pride incredible in extent and power to induce her suffering. Claribel ~~would~~ sacrifices everything to preserve her pride -her brains, her body, her experience, her knowledge of life, all equality in comradeship—her love, Flexner,—society of intelligent men everything, Alice does not, she becomes stupid, crooked, insolent, evasive, appealing to senile passions, everything except a perfectly genuine passion for beauty and that to her is life, experience. This is why the group Nelly, Ada,[2, 3] Claire, were the best experience of her life (barring the three men {the painter land-scape—Bowles—Seliun[???]} about whom I don't know enough) but aside from these the three girls were the realest thing for though they supplied to her the vulgar, worldly, successful ignorant, insolent, rich, made-up kind of beauty yet it was not her pride that they fed, they gave her real experience a sensation of beauty, the service business, the giving people what they wanted, the humility, adoration of idols, higher life, aesthetics, music that was all the pride side, academic learning sort of in between. Harriet is an intermediate stage, Sally & Annette absolutely the pride end.

Difference between Annette & Alice. In Annette it is vanity not pride. In Annette one has to watch the whole in order to direct in Alice hammer away at the central point.

AT ***Annette... partook of Alice's nature to Alice herself:*** quotation from Annette: When one is a friend, one is a friend for always.

Ada: Weighty and heavy like Fernande, but much more amusing, much more of a person than Fernande.

Ada: Nelly's sister, Ada Brackett. Gertrude had a deep dislike of her, no interest in her at all.

*

Note #1

Harriet ~~etc~~ and the person I knew once somewhat like her.

Written after seeing her over at Sally's the first time she went there alone.

They are moral Calibans, comfort, save themselves, intellect purely academic (culturine) does not in any wise concern itself with actuality of their experience. They must absolutely keep things separate. Not headless with a pin-cushion or cologne bottle where the head ought to be.

another

Both Harriet & ~~Claribel~~ have good heads but it don't connect with them with experience. They both have a wonderful power of emptying out your words as they quote them, both are alike in that. Harriet is sordid and brilliant and fairly mean. The other ~~Claribel~~ is big and inchoate and bland, both have an incredible amount of vanity which is probably the correlative of their passion for comfort. They are not egotists really. They don't exist vitally enough to be that. Their lack of loving anybody is distinctly a negative rather than a positive quality. Harriet's attitude toward Sally is so characteristic. She held on to life through her and now drops her, that was all the meaning Sally had for her. These are not Tomlinsons, they are Calibans with just the same quality of vice each one of them in their different ways that Caliban had.

Harriet owns herself, she has put herself in a triple-lined double back action automatic safe, has put the key away in another and hired 16 policemen to guard them day and night. She has no principle of growth for she has no power to struggle except to self-defence [sic], no power to suffer except from being scared. She is not an egotist for she does not posess nor will herself, she is possessed by herself and can't even ever be killed cause she never can be scared to death, she has made herself too safe, but she is always scared to the point of complete self-defensive fight. Never can be caught off-guard. In another and grander and blander way the other is equally safe. I am as I am and I can't change. Her vanity is absolute but she has no belief in herself. She knows there is nothing there. She knows her policemen are watching an inflated empty tin can. Harriet is all tight and thinks it is infinitely valuable.

The other's vanity is real, it is the basis of her Calibanism, she preserves her vanity intact and to do so must preserve herself from experience.

Harriet's vanity is not real. It is a thing she has acquired and it is very good because it helps very much to keep her safe to keep her from experience. It would never do for her to choose anything else cause if she once got out of that safe deposit vault and out of sight of those sixteen policemen even for a moment she would literally be scared to death and that would be very terrible. She will never lose the key to herself as the other one has done, she will never in that sense be dead, there is the gleam of eternal life in her (Daniel Meyer kind of life) she can never be scared to death except by leaving her safety and that she will never do. It is the sordidness in her, the Daniel Meyer miser quality that will keep her eternally alive. The other gets emptier with the years, more inflated, more empty, Harriet has always the meanness the certain brilliancy the gleam of intensest sordidness and so she will live for ever and ever, time without end. ~~And s~~ She always feels to herself that she has the possibility of experience because she has not lost the key to herself she has just put it in another safe deposit box.

Written after the day Harriet was here and we had the talk about Mrs. King.

She wanted to know why she could not arrive by little by little over coming her fear. I knew she couldn't but did not know the reason why. The reason why is that after all she conquers her fear for self-preservation. Now there is no reason why she should take a great risk for the purpose of preserving herself unless she were in extremis. As long as she is not in actual sight of death she is sure of life, why should she risk death just to be alive when she is already alive and sure she can't die. It would be foolishness. Little risks when she still knows she is safe it is right and just for her to take. Great risks, not at all. Sally's courage when it ~~carried~~ carried with it the danger to come to death, scared her, it was almost unmoral to her as Matisse paintings are unmoral to Americans, when she decided that there was no real danger and Sally knew it and all Sally got was the excitement without any serious danger then she was comfortable again, Sally's daring has always been a joy to her. It would not be a joy to her if Sally really played with death, then it would scare Harriet as it did scare her but she could not long believe in it. She is the most typical type of the unbeliever, in Christ, of those who see the miracles and don't believe.

Added after the last seeing of her.

Her sexual nature is very close to Mrs. _____ she has the same cold-heartedness, normal sexual desire, earth type. It is the Keyser type without any of the Keyser richness or beauty or sensitiveness. I told her she was very slow but always went too quickly. She did not understand me, she thought I meant eagerness, avarice, but I didn't. I meant that when she came near to the point of understanding in stead of then going slowly and really understanding it was then that she went quickly and so her conclusion was always too simple it had not in it the quality of experience. it did not enlarge the subject, it made it too plain, too simple, consequently her recognition of conclusions is not an experience it is only recognition.

type academic.

She has no realisation of greatness not even a recognition she brings it down to her own level. If they have done it it must have been easy for them, I haven't done it because it is too hard, they would not have done it either if it had been hard because if they would have done it if it had been hard I would have done it even though it was hard, I have not done it because for me it was hard therefor for them it was easy because they have done it.

*

Final Statement

I am very far from certain that it would not be best for Harriet to wrap herself in the cotton-wool of, for her, fake idealism, fake hope, fake eternity, to feed herself hourly with the pap of all the virtues and so hopefully deluded to pass the rest of her days as a neuresthenic [sic] but a hopeful neuresthenic [sic]. If she will face herself, if she will rid herself of all unreal hope and faith and eternity and come down to the real tenacity of denial, affirmation of a sordid meanness, self-defensive fear, eager unmeaning curiosity etc. that is herself, the chances are overwhelmingly that she will then not be able to free herself, she will then find herself to be by the very essence of her nature so bound down that she can never be free, that in short there is no release except to drown herself because she is in the very essence of her nature damned. I say that the chances are overwhelming that this will be what she will find if she can come face to face with herself. Then there will be nothing for her to do except to go back to the palliatives, to the cotton-wool and the pap without then any faith in them, she will then in short repeat the history of her father's long death, she will then be a neuresthenic [sic] as she is now[,] but one without any faith in the palliatives. Therefor if I had for her one grain of tenderness, of affection, of pity, of respect I could not tell her to do this thing, I have none and so I do. Of course there is a ghost of a chance that when she does come face to face with herself that she will make then a titanic, long, laborious effort, that she will turn her tenacity to self-conquest, But I repeat that I believe the chances to be overwhelmingly against it, it will not be a miracle that can make her do it, it will be a miracle if she does it, I believe that when she does come face to face with herself that she will find herself so bound down, so tied by the very essence of her nature, that she will never be able to free herself, that she will then come back to the palliatives with her faith in them broken and she will then repeat the history of her father's death, be a neuresthenic [sic] all the rest of her days. The likelihood is of course that she will never really go to the bottom and then she will just go on being the kind of neuresthenic [sic] she has been.

AT ***Final Statement... no release except to drown herself:*** After Gertrude wrote this, she went over to see Harriet and told her the same thing. Then that night, Harriet saw God. She had already asked Gertrude; Do you really believe there's no salvation for me? No, said Gertrude. If there would be that's fine and good, but there isn't, so the only thing for you to do is to kill yourself. You really mean it? Yes, said Gertrude. And this was what provoked God to come down. Harriet called me from her connecting bedroom in the middle of the night. Don't put on the light, she said. There's nothing the matter, it's wonderful. I've seen God. In a little drop that came down like that, she said, making a gesture. Go back to sleep, I said. Are you going to sleep? I hope not, said Harriet. And in the morning, she said, Take this note I've scribbled to Gertrude. Trust Harriet, I thought. She's so damn practical. She had to get something out of it.

Lily Hansen came along shortly after God, and she asked, What's the matter with Harriet? And I told her she had a revelation of God. That's nothing, said Lily, a revelation of the devil would have been much better. But of course, she couldn't hold God, so she just went back again. It wore thin very quickly. After God, Harriet turned to Sarah, possibly at Gertrude's suggestion, and Sarah not wanting the responsibility, turned her over to Edstrom. She went back to San Francisco with Sarah believing she still held Him, but there was something like trouble between Harriet and Sarah afterwards in San Francisco.

The whole experience was mixed up with Harriet's greed and

sordidness and everything else. It made it horrible that she had seen God. There was something wrong with it.

LK ***Final Statement:*** Rewritten several times, and used in MA 333 for a description, according to Ms Note #48, of "why Harriet is damned."

*

DB #57

Harriet & Claribel

They are moral Calibans. Comfort, save themselves, intellect purely culturine does not in any wise concern itself with actuality of their experience. They must absolutely keep things separate. Not like Mary Berenson headless with a pin cushion or cologne bottle where her head ought to be. Both Harriet and Claribel have good heads but it don't connect with them with experience. They have a wonderful powering [sic] of ~~killing~~ emptying out your words as they quote them both alike in that. Harriet is sordid and brilliant and fairly mean. Claribel is big and inchoate and bland, both have an incredible amount of vanity which is probably the correlative of their passion for comfort. They are not egotists really. They don't exist vitally enough to be that. Their lack of loving anybody is distinctly a negative rather than a positive quality. Harriet's attitude toward Sally is so characteristic. She held on to life through her and now drops her that was all the meaning Sally had for her. They are not Tomlinsons, they are Calibans with just the same quality of vice each one of them in their different ways that Caliban had.

Harriet arms herself, she has put herself in a triple lined double back action automatic safe, has put the key ~~in~~ away in another and hired 16 policemen to guard them day and night. She has no principle of ~~growth~~ growth for she has no power to struggle except to self-defence [sic] no power to suffer except from being scared. She is not an egotist for she dies not possess nor will herself, she is possessed by herself and can't ever be killed cause she never can be scared to death, she has made herself too safe but she is always scared to the point of complete self-defensive fight. Never can be caught off guard. In another and grander and blander way Claribel is equally safe. I am as I am and I can't change. Her vanity is absolute but she has no belief in herself. She knows there is nothing there. She knows her policemen are watching an inflated empty tin can, Harriet is all tight and thinks it is infinitely valuable. Claribel's vanity is real it is the basis of her Calibanism she ~~wish~~ preserves it intact and to do so must preserve herself from experience. Harriet's vanity is not real It is a thing she has acquired and it is very good because it helps very much to keep her safe to keep her from experience. It would never do for her to choose anything else cause if she ~~wants~~ once got out of that safe deposit vault and out of sight of those sixteen policemen even for a moment she would literally be scared to death and that would be very terrible. She will never lose the key to herself as Claribel has done, she will never in that sense be dead there is the gleam of eternal life in her (Daniel Meyer) kind of life, she can never be scared to death except by leaving her safety and that she will never do. It is the sordidness in her the Daniel Meyer miser quality that will keep her eternally alive. Claribel gets emptier with the years ~~more~~ inflated more empty, Harriet has always the meanness the certain~~ty~~ brilliancy the gleam of intensest sordidness and so she will live for ever feels to herself that she and ever time without end and she always / has the possibility of experience because she has not lost the key to herself she has just put it in another safe deposit box.

She wanted to know why she could not arrive by little by little overcoming her fear. I knew she couldn't but didn't know the reason why. The reason why is that after all she conquers her fear for self-preservation, Now there is no reason why she should take a great risk for the purpose of preserving herself unless she were in extremis. As long as she is not in actual sight of death she is sure of life, why should she risk death just to be alive when she is already alive and sure she can't die. It would be foolishness. Little risks when she still knows it is safe it is right and just for her to take. Great risks not at all. Sally's courage when it carried with it the danger to death scared her, it was almost unmoral to her as Matisse paintings are to Americans, when she decided there really was no real danger and Sally knew it and all Sally got was the excitement without any serious danger then she was comfortable again. Sally's daring has always been a joy to her. It would not be a joy to her if Sally really played with death then it would scare Harriet as it did scare her but she could not long believe in it. She is the most typical type of the unbeliever, in Christ.

Her sexual nature is very close to Mrs. Rosenshine, she has the same cold-heartedness, they come very closely together, It is the Keyser type without any of the Keyser richness or beauty or sensitiveness. I told her she was very slow but always went too quickly. She did not understand me, she thought I meant eagerness, avarice, but I didn't I meant that as she came nearer to the point of understanding instead of then going slowly and really understanding it was then that she went quickly and so her conclusion was always too simple it had not in it the quality of experience, it did not enlarge the subject it made it too plain, too simple, consequently her recognition of conclusions is not an experience it is only a recognition, type academic. She has no recognition of greatness, she brings it down to her level even more than Emma and Annette. If they have done it it must have been easy for them, I haven't done it because it is too hard, they would not have done it either if it had been hard because if they would have done it if it had been hard I would have done it ~~if it had been~~ even though it was hard. I have not done it because for me it was hard therefor for them it was easy because they have done it.

Harriet is afraid of me, to her I am almost immoral. The way I tear off her thin dress of ~~raw~~ virtue & idealism is immoral. It is immoral to make anybody naked. Here she comes to be in common with ~~Al~~ Adele—Alice Klauber—Marion Walker and Mrs. Rosenshine.

Adele

Anglo-Saxon

idealists

Alice Klauber

Marion

Mrs.

Alice

Rosenshine

Klauber

Harriet

mama

bare bones

Bird

lady

Claribel

Keysers

All of them have self-righteousness without self-recognition. High principles without the concomitant fineness and generosity and character. All of them strong sexually. Female of Hutch, and through Raymond pass over to pure flavor—beauty in men—or Bazarof—sale sexuality.

AT ***Harriet & Claribel:*** This note was written before the end of the winter of 1907–8 when Harriet and I were still in the hotel on the Boulevard St. Michel. It was obviously written when Gertrude was seeing her every day. It has the fluency of observation from daily contact, and Gertrude would be ready when Harriet was ready to say it all to her. After the winter and spring, Gertrude saw her in the summer in Fiesole, and then in the fall in Paris nearly every day.

Harriet was very troubled then, she didn't know what was going to happen to her. She had had no religious experience [i.e. contacts] then [in these early days in Paris,] nothing but the Steins. Afterwards, she began to take up with friends. This [note] was before Harriet saw God, which was at the end of this time, still winter, just before spring [of 1908.]

does not… concern itself with actuality of their experience: Pablo said of [Claribel] She has so little contact that she's an Empress. Actually, Harriet because of this ['comfort, save themselves'] had very little experience. It was more her always being so afraid of getting into anything than 'not concerning herself with actuality of experience.' I used to call her The Great Indecision Board, and Bianco told the story of the little boy who spent an afternoon with Harriet, and afterward used to play a game called Miss Levy which consisted of his saying over and over again, My God, I wish I were alone!

Harriet: By the Autumn of 1908, Gertrude knew everything I thought about Harriet. Seeing God on the Boulevard St. Michel wasn't Harriet's first experience of Him. She had already gone through a Scotch Presbyterian woman, and Mrs. King, a woman who had no cause to further, but was just a sympathetic, intelligent person who had taken on Harriet. These two happened to her while I knew her in California. Harriet went to the country with the Scotch Presbyterian woman and prayed night and morning. I visited her there, and suddenly found myself on my knees praying too, why I didn't know.

Claribel… incredible amount of vanity: Claribel was vain and open to flattery, but it had no ill effect upon her. Her character was something already founded. My friend Clare Moore's sister Paula went off to medical school at Johns Hopkins, and when she came back to San Francisco told us all about Claribel, her home, her grace, her charm, long before I met her.

Harriet… hired 16 policemen: With all these 'policemen' she still had no sense of security. Harriet was Money-bags and Fear. She was more the persecuted ghetto than anyone I ever read of. Zangwill's was clouded with pity, Harriet's was not. Hers was the real thing.

[Harriet]… scared to the point of… self-defensive fight: Harriet's 'self-defense' mechanisms were plain. If she was to meet someone, she was afraid of—she was afraid of people, afraid they'd take something from her—she'd not be normal a day in advance. She couldn't eat, perhaps, or read, or sleep. And the person could be anyone—Sarah, or a stranger, anyone. She and I got on well because she knew I wasn't doing anything to her. I was a sort of inoperative machine for her, and so she had nothing to fear from me. And she could trust Gertrude not to do anything harmful to her. When Gertrude told her there was nothing for her to do but kill herself, Harriet had no bad feeling, ate her dinner, and was all right. Normally, she would have taken to her bed after such an experience.

Daniel Meyer kind of life: A banker in California who inherited his money and made a large fortune with it. His favorite pastime was foreclosing mortgages. Once someone asked him for advice on a large investment. After being told the proposition, Daniel Meyer said, yes, it is very wise. Then the man said there were several reasons why it was not feasible, and one was that he didn't have the money. Don't let me hear the others, Daniel Meyer said. In the Northwest, they had a horror of Daniel Meyer.

Harriet's fear: She was possessed by fear with a capital F, and only out of it when she was amused or caused amusement. Harriet was exhausted from her fear, anxious, upset, frightened—a physical wreck from this sort of thing. But at the same time, she was always very eager, eager to tell it, eager to hear it. When Gertrude was talking to her [about it,] she was entranced. She lived in [the talk] and adored it because she was the subject of it. Her vanity.

Sally's courage… danger to death: There was some trouble at the Matisse school, Sarah had said something which started it. Maybe that was the 'danger' mentioned in this note?

She did not understand me: Harriet had no profound understanding of anything. She could grasp it the first time you told her, grasp it again if you told her again, but her elaboration and conclusion would in fact be commonplace.

*

Note #42

The thing that one must keep in mind and that would make prognosis in a case like that of Harriet is the fundamental positive as well as the fundamental negative. Whether it is true or not that it would have happened so there is to me no doubt that there was there such a possibility, that in a nature where reality ~~was~~ is so strong as it is in Harriet and desire so great if the negation was removed it must come, she might have not done it, she might have gone crazy but I don't believe she would have done that, she would in that case have done nothing but we will see, the positive side in her I have not sufficiently allowed for I allowed for it but despised it. In fact that is the thing I must keep in mind, the element of beauty, the element of listening to their variety of expression and so get down to the positive as well as negative elements in their nature, In Alice there was not that difficulty, I did listen, in Sally and Leo I have only slowly learned their positive element, it is on that that ultimate expression depends, it is there that I have been inclined to misunderstand their being right in their great moments, in Sally her sympathetic sensibility, in Leo his, his makes only for character and understanding, hers is the completeness of her reaction as a personality, the temperament in her is simply a stimulus, a temper or a clog and in larger natures this bottom at great moments works. In Chalfin the bottom is only intensive affectionateness founded on the commonplace type of his intellect and nature with a flavor of his temperament, in Edstrom this bottom force is the practical successful one, its form is determined by all the rest in him and there I guess Hutch was right. where Hutch failed was in the ensemble. That they care enough to bring them back to repeat themselves with the intensiveness of a new vision, Edstrom's repetition is the practical success, Edstrom is the ideal Christian Scientist, if he don't get too far away from the religious emotion, a practical religion, these are more coldly practical than the Jewish or earth type, when it does transcend it recreates and you have Shakespeare, Matisse has that nature in him too, it is that which makes him akin to Sally but he is enormously held by the other thing of course to do that greatly one must either have descended to it through the idealist via Heiroth, Shakespeare's method, or dragged up to it through exaltation Grant, Matisse's method. The ~~exalted~~ minds who have practically forced upon them are as far as my experience goes ~~practic~~ original only efficiently, morally, not creatively and so I imagine is Mrs. Eddy, more greatly so Edstrom, less so Sally, so Sally still may be aesthetically creative, Edstrom no. I imagine that is true of Van Goch [sic] he was like Sally. In Bird I expected more why, because I made the same mistake that I made with Chalfin, I took the temperament for the whole thing, in her great struggle in the fighting that was true in her mostly it was not true, success, greed, domination, stubbornness, stupidity, energy, hardness, they in her great fight became fused by her love of her father into the power she showed, after that they went on alone, if she had loved her children as she loved her father it might have continued fused but she did not, she never loved anybody so except her father, in the great moments of realisation there is this fusion, for the creative artist there is more this fusion whenever he creates. Bird au fond was the fairly powerless not over intelligent dominated and with those who loved her satisfying prostitute Bertha woman. her only ~~concentr~~ fusing force was her father, in Sally's hand-reading, she fuses, in her whole history of her relation to Mike and to Allan, in her art not yet. In Harriet there was this perfect fusion.

*

Note #44

Final Statement.

I am very far from certain that it would not be best for Harriet to wrap herself in ~~h~~ the cotton-wool of ~~false~~ for her, fake idealism, fake hope, fake eternity, to feed herself hourly with the pap os all the virtues and so hopefully deluded to pass the rest of her days as a neuresthenic [sic] but a hopeful neuresthenic [sic]. If she will face herself if she will rid herself of all unreal hope and faith and eternity and come down to the real tenacity of denial affirmation of sordid meanness the self-defensive fear that is herself the chances are overwhelmingly that she will then not be able to free herself, she will then find herself by the very essence of her nature so bound down that she can never be free, that in short there is no release except to drown herself ~~that is~~ she is in the very essence of her nature damned. ~~This I think~~ The chances are overwhelmingly that this will be what she will find if she can come face to face with herself. Then there will be nothing for her to do except to go back to the palliatives to the cotton-wool and the pap without then any faith in them, she will then in short repeat the history of her father's long death, she will ~~in~~ then be a neuresthenic [sic] as she is now without any faith in the palliatives. Therefore if I had for her one grain of tenderness, of affection, of respect, I could not tell her to do this thing, I have none and so I do. Of course there is a ghost of a chance that when she does so come ~~to~~ face to face with herself that she will make a titanic long, laborious effort that she will turn her tenacity to self-conquest, but I repeat that I believe the chances to be overwhelmingly against it, it will not be a miracle then can make her do it, it will be a miracle if she does it, I believe that when she does come face to face with herself that she will find herself so bound down so tied by the very essence of her nature, that she will never be able to free herself, that she will then come back to the palliatives with her faith in them broken and she will then repeat the history of her father's ~~life~~ death, be a neuresthenic [sic] all the rest [of] her days. The likelihood is of course that she will never really go to the bottom and then she will just go ~~home~~ on being the kind of neuresthenic [sic] she has been.

*

Note #43

Concurrent with Note #94a

In the case of Harriet the really great mistake I made was the fact that I did not sufficiently recognise the element of vanity as profound connected with sexuality and religion, I left out the element of ~~prudishness~~ prudishness in her denial, a thing that Sally once spoke to me about, and that she has in common with Claribel also, this goes with the religiousness, the mystic saintliness, it is kept from being of the abandoned complete mystic because of the simple Kayser affectionateness which is I think her realest sexual nature. that is what makes the Edstrom problem difficult, In Mrs. Eddy and Saint Theresa the material side is practical determined the vanity all that there is in Harriet only in Harriet, the vanity, the sexuality, the exaltation etc and its corelative [sic] earthiness is never to dominate, it never gets farther than to protect herself, she keeps control for purposes of self protection not for purposes of domination and in this she and Alice are absolutely alike and so together they make Claribel in Annette it comes very much nearer having been for purposes of domination, in Adele and Mrs. Eddy completely so and that is why Mrs. Eddy's mouth is so much like Annette's and Annette's mother. Anette [sic] is more aggressive in her temperament than either Harriet or Alice. In all the rest of us each in our separate ways Matisse, Leo, Mike and I there is the strong effort always to affirm our experience, we are not afraid of experience for we must affirm it and in order to affirm it we must have it, Matisse as ~~and~~ an aggressive egotist, I an unaggressive egotist, Leo as an idealist and abstract thinker, Mike as a complete individual Sally and Pablo have both, the tendency to affirm, the tendency to deny their experience, also in both the tendency to dominate in the denial of experience, in affirming it they are as all people who affirm it humble to experience, it oer'leaps itself it is like Sally's archangel look, like the ridiculous improved optimism of Christian Science that is afraid of animal magnetism. It was alright for Quimby who was an abstract idealist to deny matter but for the hide bound practical Edstroms, Mrs. Eddy's and Hutches to deny matter is to be essentially divided in two, In Harriet it is more simply the correlative of her vanity in submission and ecstacy.

AT ***Sally's archangel look... Christian Science:*** Mildred Aldrich once reported that she came to see Sally and found her in bed reading the Christian Science bible. Sally looked up, Mildred said, gave me the papal blessing, and I left.

Sally's interest and activity in Christian Science were full-fledged before she went to Europe. She fell into the hands of a healer in Europe, a saintly Belgian woman whom I once met, quite saintly, one of those rare creatures with a strange purity in her. She was happy in Christian Science, extremely active, did a lot of outside good, and indulged in no propaganda. Her great friend was Mrs. Ehrman, the mother of Therese, the pretty girl from San Francisco. Mrs. Ehrman was also a healer, and probably a thorn in Sarah's side.

*

DB #58

Dolene pure type
Gabrielle Dolene + flightiness
Jane Dolene + dramatic emotional intensity + scared servant girl.
Alice Toklas Dolene + B.B.
This group are all efficient and then they pass on through Hannah Lezynsky, Etta Levy, Etta Cone, Annie Fabian and Mrs. Valloton to the inefficients and the spinster sentimentalists. Fernande & Mabel Simis intermediate to spinster sentimentalists.

*

DB #59

A new grouping of the whole bunch. Bertha, the mother of large quantities of them. The sexual character of Bertha both maternal & wifely, but diffuse all over the shop, in her herself no power of concentration, sentimentalist in the sense of feeling herself the type woman, good, superior, maternal, good housekeeper, cook, seamstress, judge of propriety and right conduct, and in a sloppy, diffuse, grimy way she is all that, naturally conceives herself as all those things ideally. Incapable of carrying things out against opposition and so submissive to a man, fundamentally diffuse in character, as in sexual quality. In Bird see the same character hardened tightened, the ~~much~~ sexual wife character more pronounced than the mother, essential strength arising from energy weakness, her strength a pseudo-ambition, and insensibility which has taken the form of moral purpose which has no foundation within her but she having tremendous energy if she begins anything it goes on forever, her weakness makes her appealing and gives her a power over those who are fond of her, but if somebody else attacks her, her weakness is extraordinary. In Aunt Pauline the maternity and wife are both stronger and better mixed, she is much nearer Sally than Bird is, they both have great efficiency but the weakness of the lack of sexual concentration in Sally this weakness is entirely overcome by the power of her intellect and her emotional temperament which allies her to Laura etc. in Aunt Pauline nothing supports it but brute force and as she has had to face rather intricate and subtle problems she has on the whole failed. The men they hold not attract are the earthy men of the world who have no lurid or idealistic or to be protected demands if they come in contact with such they fail. In Alice Toklas and Jane Cheron the sexual base is the same with none almost of the maternal and the character of it decidedly weak. they also are weak, not inefficient but easily undermined. Alice would not come over alone, very sassy until you give her hell and then caves right in. Now the next group that connects these to the spinster group are Hattie Bache's family. Here there is much less diffusion but also much less quality. it is a deader thing, it has no life, no movement, it has the same fashion of looking upon itself as a perfect woman, as completely womanly and more or less as the case may be it is. Belle Bergman is the bare unbeautiful most absolute form of it. There is a certain faithfulness, a certain beauty, a singular lack of movement or vitality or energy. Bertha then passes through these women through Myrtle to the lady in the form of Mrs. Samuels where you have then introduced a quality of concentration that rescues her from the commonplace, through Belle Bergman Penelope to the earth group, through Hattie Bache to the spinster group, through Sallie, to the temperamental emotional world lover idealist, and also through her and then Mabel Weeks to the adolescent, through Alice Toklas to the flavor and Dorothy Reede [sic], through Jane Cheron to the emotional sexual~~ist~~ aristocrat May. In each of these there is added a rarer and more concentrated essence that gives them power, Where the sexual base of Bertha is strong there is mostly weakness, oh and then through Aunt Pauline to the mere practical brute woman of the world Moll Flanders and Mrs. Moffat.

AT ***Alice... very sassy until you give her hell:*** Probably Gertrude's explanation of the note I sent canceling an appointment. This occurred early in the winter of 1907 [sic]. It was the first time I saw Gertrude livid. I said nothing, however, while Gertrude was holding the note in her hand, angry and lengthily berating. But there was no obligation of this kind to Gertrude, so it made no sense. There was no 'caving right in,' just no response.

*

DB #60

The spinster group.

Olga—Fernande—Inez Cohen—Etta Cone.

Bertha goes over very directly to Olga, but in all these there there [sic] is neither the maternal or wife spirit, they are more concentrated but empty, they are more living than Belle Bergman but they don't cover so much ground. sexually they are not very active except in response, they are apparently very active but not really so, sexually they attract young and rather lurid type. Myrtle is the intermediate stage, then comes Fernande, then Inez Cone then Olga, in Etta Cone she connects to Etta Levey who has a more positive quality and carries over to the concentrated sexualists, Dolene et al.

It is because of the negative quality of their sexuality both maternal & mistress that they are so complete an illusion more complete because they are not as Bertha and Belle's group more or less what they realise themselves as being but they are practically not at all and so they are perfect egotists only in the sense of being negative. The illusion therefore is with them the whole thing.

In Etta Levey it passes over to a concentrated form. Dolene's.
In Mrs. Samuels it passes over to a concentrated form lady in Mrs. Valloton to Adele's group.

The other unconcentrated form May's group. here we have also a lack of concentrated sexuality, although it has completely that appearance but the eternal vanishing [?] is a proof of what I mean. It is the intensest form of emotional sexuality but it is not ~~co~~ concentrated actual sexuality, ... when the element of emotional sexuality is removed they sink into very commonplace people, very much like the Belle Bergman group, more commonplace than Bertha's group because there is an inadequate basis for their apparent reality. So we have their high type of emotional intelligence and lack of real intellect, the base is nothing very much sexually, their dramatic instinct in the most determinate specimens of the group keep up the illusion longest in fact it is more than an illusion, it is an actuality. It is because of this that this group although not a servant group is not really a mistress group. Bertha's group is always a mistress group in posse. The other diffuse group that corresponds to Bertha is Aunt Fanny the earth group. this is essentially the servant group although it may transform itself into mistress by a practical intelligence in the shape of Mrs. Meininger which corresponds to Aunt Pauline, to real intellect like mine which corresponds to Sally, or to pure lady, as it does in Mrs. Rosenshine carried farther, than [sic] in goes into pure servant girl group into ethical like Miriam and so into ~~Estelle~~ Adele and then one has Estelle who is like the May group lacks fundamental reality. They all attract more adult determinately passion men, than the other large group more salete in the lover. ~~Then we have all the [Oneal?]~~ In the other Bertha group there is of course the adolescents Emma, Madame Boiffard Hortense Federleicht type examples and they as it were stand between the two general groups and dependent on their accent they attract the various types of men. Emma, nearer spinster, young boy, Hortense & Jane nearer earther, saler type.
Servant girl two types that founded on earth type and that founded on Bertha, Bertha's type cowed but not humbled as earth type is.

AT ***Etta Levey:*** [Levy.] Dolene's sister—the plain one.

*

DB #61

All the concentrated sexual types are evil in posse. These last two groups are not evil, they may do evil but they are not evil.

Lurid	- Mabel H. & Annette -
Piquante	- Marie Lorenz—Mrs. Manguin—Minnie
Flavor Napoleonic -	- Mary Houghton
Pure Lady	- Miss Blood.
Self Righteous	- Alice Klauber Adele
Pure prostitute concentrated	- Dolene -

LK ***concentrated sexual types:*** Discussion of "concentrated women" first occurs in the text in relation to "resisting" in women, MA 166: "Many women have at some time resisting in them….Patient women need to have… a feeling of themselves inside them to be really resisting to anyone who owns them….Attacking women with weakness at the bottom of them… resisting is natural to them, it covers up in them the weakness of them. Concentrated women with not any weakness at the bottom in them do not need to have in them such a feeling… [they] have never any such resisting in them, yielding is the whole of such ones of them…. [Women who] have not any such weakness at the bottom of them… have much concentration of themselves inside them."

*

Note #35

~~All the concentrated sexual types are evil, in posse.~~

~~Marie Lorenzin~~ [sic]

~~Has absolutely no continuity of thought in the most extreme sense of those words, has perfect concentration sexually a needle point, perfectly soulless and without consciousness, has malignancy, high suggestibility perfect vanity that is to say nothing exists except herself in the universe and never can, and so has universal jealousy and that is the origin of her eternal maliciousness.~~

~~[…] not there the whole of her, she did not know that there was not a whole of her, she just made a self defending instinct in her and that was all there was to her and so she had no power in her for she had no power of […]~~

LK ***…not there a whole of her … she had no power of:*** [Concurrent with MA 83.] Draft of text for MA 83 concerning Pauline Schiller [rechristened Shilling in final text], the "thinner" of the two Shilling daughters: "It did not make an individual of her because there was never there a whole of her. She did not know that there was not a whole one of her. This incompleteness always made a self-defensive instinct in her, and that was all there was to her, comfort and keeping out of danger… she had no power of attacking in her …and it gave her no appeal to any one who came near her…."

*

Note #65

Alice	=	pride		existence
Annette	=	vanity		
Sally	=	pride &	vanity	egotism
Leo	=	pride &	egotism	
me	=	egotism		
Matisse	=	egotism	vanity	
Pablo	=	pride	existence	
Mike	=	existence		
Harriet	=	existence		
		concentrated		
Etta	=	vanity	pride	existence
Claribel	=	pride	egotism	
Hutch	=	self righteousness		
	=			
Derain	=	pride	existence	conceit
Leo F	=	conceit	existence	
Emma	=	vanity	existence	
Mabel	=	pride	existence	
Weeks				
Edstrom	=	egotism	vanity	
Stern	=	pride	conceit	existence

*

DB #62

New tabulation

Alice T.	=	pride		existence
Annette	=	vanity		existence
Sally	=	pride	vanity	- egotism

Leo	=	pride		egotism
me	=	egotism		
Matisse	=	egotism		
Pablo	=	pride		egotism
Mike	=	existence		
Harriet	=	existence concentrated; (there is much vanity & pride but these are completely swamped in the absoluteness of existence)		
Edstrom	=	egotism (concentrated)		vanity
Claribel	=	pride		egotism
Etta	=	vanity (mostly an imitation of Claribel & s. Bertha)	pride	existence
Hutch	=	self-righteousness		existence
Derain	=	pride	existence	- conceit
Leo F	=	conceit	existence	egotism
Emma	=	vanity	existence	
Mabel Weeks	=	pride	existence	
Stern	=	pride	conceit	existence
Adele	=			
Alice Klauber	=			
Fernande	=			
Bird	=	pride	vanity	existence
B.B.	=	pride	vanity	existence
Neith	=	vanity	existence	

*

Note #212

...and with some of them it was a little the father and a little the mother in them. And sometimes it was in these then that they had suspicious feeling in them about every one toward them after the family feeling that made all them. And sometimes there was a mixing up of all these ways together in them.

LK MA 65. One of the last notes to use family traits as origins of characters' "natures." In the new terms (the "mixing up of all these ways together,") "mixing up" analytic terms remains a basic strategy, a constant.

*

DB #63

Pride
pride is connected with the instinct for culture in a very remarkable way as the list will show. Note the expression of pride as disease in the contraction of the chin drawing back of the muscles of the neck. It is interesting to see how in Claribel and Alice ~~this~~ and in B.B. this pride passes over into the lowest form of beauty, in Claribel in swishy petticoats in Alice in ~~court~~ whore clothes in B.B. in his millionaires. Where the sexual base with this kind of pride is Bertha as it is in Claribel, Alice & B.B. it goes into this low expression for the sexual base is not strenuous enough to support it. Chalfin is a little saved from this hopeless cheapness because although his sexual base does not belong to his type either it is nevertheless more solid it is like our Simon's. A more substantial thing than Bertha's. B.B. & Chalfin both less success than Stern or Leo or Pach.

AT ***Claribel in swishy petticoats:*** Claribel kept up the swish in her petticoats after it was well past the fashion. She got the best dressmakers in Paris to make her clothes in order to keep it up. It was as characteristic of her as the dagger in her hair which she got to cut pages, and simply found her hair the most convenient place to keep it. Later when the dressmakers refused to make the swish, she wound lace about the top of her dresses.

Alice in whore clothes: My feeling about them was greater than my experience of them. I had very few indeed.

BB… his millionaires: When he was successful, he got on equal terms with the millionaires whose pictures he catalogued, to the extent that Pierpont Morgan placed money for him in America. He got his sense of position from their treatment and regard for him, something he hadn't earlier been able to pull off in England.

*

DB #64

Hutch's contradiction is this. He has a sweetness a sympathetic openess [sic] and aggressive warmth, a tolerance and love of human things, a strength and persistence in this emotion that makes him like Abe Lincoln and he has a sexual base to go with, warm passionate, idealistic mystic, tolerant, sweet and lovable, ~~moist~~ humid and tender but, his character is very different, his character is that of a puritanic snob, he is hard, practical, intolerant, just to the letter but not the spirit, irritable, no power of listening, no ~~possible~~ possibility of ever seeing himself as in the way, dogmatic, self-suggestive in short he has about every quality that a man can have that is incompatible with his ideal and of this incompatibility he has never become really aware because so transcendentally is he apparently all that he would be that he fools everybody and fools them long and no wonder he is fooled himself. In order to be what he would be he would have to have patience, knowledge, humility, and he has none of these three, he is self-righteous in short which is an absolute contradiction to the thing he would be. When he was a reporter these things mostly nearly ~~cam~~ came together and made an efficient man of him but of themselves it is only on a fairly low plane that they can come together, in any completer, more complicated relation with people the contradiction between thing he is, in spirit and the thing he is in character is too glaring, and so more and more it is a vicious circle, there is no relation between his character, and his spirit and so his spirit gets no enlargement it ~~st~~ just goes round and round O in a little space just repeating itself not enlarging its experience or its expression, and his sexual nature degenerating into emotionality abandonment, liquor, mysticism, & restlessness. When he was about 25 the elements were nearest to being mixed in him to make a complete man of him, since then it has been a continuously more definitely marked separation between his spirit and his character, Now the two have absolutely no connection, his spirit, is in a treadmill, his character gives neither him nor any one else any satisfaction his whole life now is an endeavor to escape, he can't sit still with his misfit inside him.

AT ***Hutch's contradiction:*** This was written fifteen or twenty years before it was visible to anyone else's eye. What Gertrude says of him here was literally and obviously true in his later life.

***

Notebook 7

NB7, #2

This one is near them but not altogether of them. She is of a kind very closely like this kind of them but she is of a kind of them that have in them being a little different in them.

LK ***This one is near them.... a little different in them:*** Draft of text for MA 203.

*

NB7, #3

[...] Weeks, [M]abel Pann[?] real sensibility and gayety, when tragic become hard, the type of queens.

LK ***real sensibility... the type of queens:*** Concurrent with NB-A #10a.

*

NB7, #4a

Miss Squires [?] a servant like Murphy I got to plunge into the servants if only to get through with them, I think I will just generalise them and talk about eating in the kitchen etc. different kinds of women and a little more about servant queerness and then go to the seamstresses, story of Gabrielle and Marie for seamstresses living in between, Miss Rosenberg [?] (Nelly) for rich part) the Liess girls [german too?] and then to the governesses a gradual thing of them to Madeleine Weiman and in her case a resume of Mr. & Mrs. Hersland.

AT ***a servant like Murphy:*** The cook at the Rosenshine's [in San Francisco.] Annette told Gertrude about her. She was very self-sacrificing and devoted to them all. As a child, she wanted green hair, and she told Annette that she never lost the desire for it. She had blonde hair.

the seamstresses: In the Seamstress episode, one says to the other, 'angel Mabel, Mabel angel,' although it is not one of their names. When I discovered the story of May, Mabel and Gertrude [when Miss Toklas saw the manuscript of *Q.E.D.* for the first time in the Nineteen Thirties], I was most upset at the time and became hypersensitive to signs. Gertrude denied that she had recalled the situation of *Q.E.D.* [when she wrote the passage], but I was sure. I also found an 'M' carved into the table [at which Gertrude wrote] and I sanded it off. Gertrude asked me who cleaned the table, and I said, I did, don't you remember what I took off? Gertrude said she didn't. I'm certain at least that she didn't put it there. It was not her way to deface a piece of furniture. And Gertrude wrote 'A Play with Words' at the time I read *Q.E.D.* and it used the names May and Mabel again and again. The text of this piece is lost at Yale, but it was sent by me.

story of Gabrielle and Marie for the seamstresses: Gabrielle was the cook whom Leo and Gertrude gave with great pleasure to the Mike Steins. Her cousin or niece was a very good seamstress who turned into a dressmaker. Gabrielle married a white-collar man at $15 a month, and she raised a family on that. He went off to the first war and came back a Captain covered with glory.

About Marie, Mike told Sarah, Marie is getting fat. So she should, said Sarah. But actually, Marie was pregnant, by a mail clerk on the railroad. The baby, born just before or just after I came over, died. Marie finally became an important person at the Renault Works, and it was then that she told Mike she had never been married.

LK ***...the servants...*** Planning Note for MA 170–192.

... then go to the seamstresses... Plan, begins on MA 192.

Gabrielle and Marie... Plan, for MA 192–236.

then to the governesses: Plan, for MA 236–248.

*

Notebook A

NB-A #1

Important

In big book after doing most exquisite flavor to the pure genius, Chalfin to Pablo, Janet to B.B. and Alice show the basis on to Chalfin to Pablo, Bertha to Alice to Janet and the infinite variations that spring from these

AT ***In big book:*** Could be a note for *A Long Gay Book*. It was already begun.

Most exquisite flavor... Chalfin: Gertrude thought of Chalfin as a highly civilized person. He was black Irish and very beautiful. He was the man who disturbed Matisse by speaking such beautiful French despite the fact that he was a foreigner. Everybody loved him, that is to say, women fell in love with him. He had exquisite taste and no means, living on a shoestring. He was in Paris on a commission to paint a mural decoration. Later he took a commercial position in New York to do some kind of decorating, and he stayed a year and left. He was a most gracious person and had charming ways.

Flavor Groups: Those who live in the flavor, the charm of life. They don't have to be interested in anything.

exquisite flavor... Alice: The Flavor Group was for those who lived on the flavor, the charm of life, who don't have to be interested in the meaning of anything. I was supposed to have been in the flavor group. but got out early.

*

NB-A #2

To realise the noble [quates?] / Fathers are cowardly there

*

NB-A #3

Jews mostly run themselves by their minds, now they have good minds but not great minds and if you have a good mind but not a great mind your mind ought to be no more than a purveyor to you, because inevitably you are greater habitually than your mind. That is the secret of the inevitable mediocrity. Chalfin don't run himself by his mind, he just set himself in motion by it but thats because he hasn't mind enough to go around, Edstrom does that is the reason he is so much like a yid. He don't run his emotions by it and they are sometimes great but he runs himself by it, his mind is good but not great. Dougherty thinks he runs himself by his mind but he don't, ~~Leo~~

~~and Jam~~ he runs himself by his common-place solidity and common-place poetry, the man's man solidity and poetry. Leo and James run themselves by their minds but they have pretty great minds, BB runs himself by his mind but his mind is good but not great, he occasionally is great and he thinks its his mind and as he runs himself by his mind he thinks he is great all the time but it isn't his mind, its is moments of exquisite creative perception that completely xpressed themselves, mostly his exquisite perception like in Alice and Janet is nothing but sentimentality or vulgarity, that is because it is valued it is forced, it is applied, it is active to satisfy the need of their own emotion, and as none of them have discrimination because either they have not much mind or their mind is not great they go on most of their lives doing it badly. Pablo and I recognise the danger and refuse to run ourselves by our minds, if it isn't not running yourself by your mind among the jews it is running yourself by your ethics which is perhaps really nothing more than a crystalised mind it is as definitive to run as the mind only it is not so continuous, the non-jewish person runs themselves apparently by their conventions and their training but they don't do it themselves to themselves therefor they are freer than the more intelligent yid. Sally runs herself by her mind but does not run her sensitive reaction which is her greatest quality.

AT ***Jews:*** Gertrude had very strong feelings for and against.

Against: they were interferesome. And the bourgeois tradition of the Jews was more Jewish than bourgeois. Then when she began to believe that Leo was a typical intellectual Jew, she naturally got to hate them. Also, at the outbreak of the first world war, intellectual Jews were all for the Germans, including Leo, and that she couldn't get over.

For: They had a certain honesty. And though they were not very creative, they had a taste for beauty when they could touch it, as in BB's "tactile values."

She always spoke of herself as an Oriental, not as a Jew. For many years, she used to say, They accuse me to this and that, but they have never accused me of being a Jew, so I guess I'm not typical. She thought Jews didn't get far with their endowment, since the gift was usually small. She said, Jews are like Spaniards, it takes a million of them to make a genius, but then the genius is first rate. Mostly the endowment, being small, is prevented from coming to full expression.

Gertrude's father was very indifferent toward religion until after the death of his wife in Oakland, when he got into the hands of a rabbi. The rabbi didn't influence him, he just listened. Her mother told stories of Jewish family life, but Gertrude didn't see it or know it until she went to Baltimore. Her father had removed himself and his family from the rest of the [Stein-Keyser] family, and they remained independent of it. The family of Steins in California was isolated in its feelings and habits. They lived surrounded by these few poor people with occasional visits from the San Francisco bourgeoisie whom the children resented and the father apparently paid no attention to.

The Steins had no connection with the Jewish community in San Francisco. Gertrude's father had rented a large tract with a house on it soon after they arrived in Oakland. East Oakland had a straggling, very unbourgeois population. The Steins' was the only big house there, near Lake Merritt. It was well known as the Stratton Place, surrounded by shopkeepers and working families whose children were the Stein children's friends.

It was the Baltimoreans who impressed Gertrude with Jewish family life. In Baltimore, there were *hundreds* of relatives. Gertrude said, You walked down the street and they were all cousins sitting on the steps in the summer in their white dresses. They were delightful people, really charming. I can understand Gertrude falling under the spell of them. Julian Stein was once telling how Maryland had kept all the English laws from before the Revolution, and Gertrude asked him, You love Maryland, don't you? Maryland is the best state in the Union, he said, and Baltimore the best city in Maryland, Peak's Hill is the best house in Baltimore, and of course Rose Ellen [his wife] the best woman of any. That's the kind of pride Julian had. None of those things had ever disappointed him. He had family pride, but of that kind.

The [Baltimore] Keysers came to America earlier than the Steins. In fact, Jacob Moses had a great-great grandfather who fought in the Revolution. Amelia's father came when he was a young man. Gertrude would have built her feeling of Jews being honest on the grandfather who held the money for all the people in the German village because they had no bank.

Dougherty: A painter who did landscapes and seascapes. He gave one to Gertrude.

BB: BB didn't know Gertrude as much more than an emphatic person. When Gertrude sent *Camera Work* to him with the Matisse and Picasso portraits, he didn't know what to say in thanking her.

LK This note supports several major discussions in the Notebooks and in the novel, both of which draw on its distinctive variations of "running [oneself] by his mind."

Jews mostly run themselves by their minds... Passage used in MA 365ff.

Chalfin don't run himself by his mind... [Corresponds to Manuscript Note #53]: Used for full description of Chalfin in MA 366, l. 5–34. Chalfin in relation to "running himself" etc. is also referred to in NB-C #20, NB-*B #20, and NB-*B #24.

*

NB-A #4

In the case of Alfy you have it where the quality that in Howard & Annette remains merely taste elegance passes over into creation that is it is the bottom nature of him.

AT ***Alfy:*** Alfred Maurer.

*

NB-A #6

Mrs. Gibb like the sister of Leslie Hopkinson, it is the efficient version of Mrs. Putnam Mrs. Bruce, Mrs. Mathews which goes over in perfect nastiness in Therese Therold and becomes great in Mrs. Puy. the question is which kind of the two kinds are they, both they and their husbands are just on the border line of the two types, in each case there is a slight emphasis one way or the other. The reason they are perplexing is because each one in their separate ways border on fanaticism, in each case there is a slight emphasis one way or the other. For instance Mrs. Bruce nearer Adele Mrs. Putnam also, Mrs. Mathews also although I am not sure. I think it not impossible that it is the other way with Mrs. Bruce but time will tell that. the other way because I think Bruce is this other, my kind. I guess though the women most of them are always of the possessive type though blonde while the men though awfully near including Raymond to fanaticism keep steadily on the blonde Sally side. It is when you get it pure persian Will or Alfy or Sterne or Leo Friedman or Mike or Jake Moses that it goes over to the other. Meyer Jaffa is probably like Alice and Joe Preiss is too & possibly Myrtle's husband. I guess thats the division though one could only be sure with such border line types who so completely have a certain attenuated fanatic quality on extensive knowledge of them perhaps Adele & Meyer are the quintessence of it and they point that way. Alice & Janet & B.B. are I guess the other (not sure about B.B.) uncertain about Therese Therold and Mary Houghton. I guess the difference is to be determined by a kind of suffering sensitiveness, I don't know, Dolene I don't know for sure about either but I think she is possessive ultimately. The emotional sensitiveness is the real test and yet the other kind might be allied to May's group but I don't think so, I think in most of these cases the men are the blonde group, the practical the attacking group, the women are not, I imagine the sensitiveness is the test and yet there is the question of practical quality, but the women are more sordid than practical more common sense than efficiency. Neith & Hutch. It may be and is not unlikely that Bruce is the other kind and ~~not~~ like Alice, I don't know, Alice Klauber undoubtedly ain't, Miss Blood I think is, I don't know about Mary Houghton or Therese Therold, nor am I entirely sure about Hortense Moses. Hortense Fiderleicht to May. To know surely in these cases one has to know the complete history and weigh it carefully, almost one has to love them, to find out it is the border land of types.

AT ***Mrs. Gibb:*** Harry Phelan Gibb's first wife.

Therese Thorold: The 'nastiness' is hers.

attenuated fanatic quality… perhaps Adele: Gertrude was bored with Adele because she was insistent, but there was no feminine weakness in the woman anywhere. She was strong, independent, mature. Gertrude always said she had no initiative, but there was no dependence on Adele's part whatever on Gertrude.

*

NB-A #7

Emily's dancing steps every now and then, she wants to be lively, not a child but girlish which with others like her is to be niceish [?], she is not an adolescent she is just before you get adolescence, she has in her the dread of coming adolescence so has Mamie Weeks, and therefor they want to be lively and fresh and interested. They dread the coming on of adolescence. A child does not know adolescence a youth loves it but the Mamie's and the Emily's live it … they take dance steps as they walk.

AT ***Emily's dancing steps:*** Gertrude knew Emily Dawson during the 'Gloomsbury' winter in London in 1902–3.

LK ***Emily [Dawson]'s dancing steps:*** Used in MA 174. The note is incorporated into the descriptions of women with "children natures." As one type of these: "Some women have … the fear of adolescence … [even] beginning … [T]hese always have it … to be very lively … and they try all their living to keep up dancing so that adolescence will be scared away from them....[T]hese have not ... sentimental feeling, they have aggressive liveliness in them ... [T]hey do not want ... the restlessness of adolescent living ... and so they make a dance step every now and then in their walking."

*

NB-A #8

In dealing with the character of Martha want to go into an elaborated discussion of what I was saying yesterday of the practical the aggressive, the emotional, the sensitive act of faith. Marie Demarez is of my class not of the independent dependent. A little introduction to all this in the character of Louise Frohn the governess, this is the fact that the Mrs. Kelcey's do not translate their spirituality into practical terms but they through Mrs. King and Roosevelt and Edstrom to Matisse see it in all varying degrees of practical activity, to the case of Sally a mixture. All this will be very important in the history of Martha.

AT ***the Mrs. Kelsey's... their spirituality:*** A Christian Scientist, and an impossible creature, uneducated and uncultured. She was probably a boarder at Mme. Vernon's, and Sally had to know her because of Christian Science. The two of them had uplifting conversations, but Sally couldn't stand her.

Mrs. Kelsey, a Christian Science friend of Sally's who came over for a year from San Francisco, and finally went to live in a little house in Fontainebleau that the Mike Steins took over as a weekend place when she left. I met her—an impossible creature, sentimental, with not a grain of intelligence, no education, inarticulate, and unpleasant to look at.

In Paris, Sally stayed apart from the Christian Science community and wasn't really in it. At one time she even had her own version of Christian Science. An English Christian Scientist, a Mrs. Norlidge, who was very downright and factual about it, influenced Sarah considerably. She thought Sarah intelligent, but she didn't discuss any of Sarah's subjects with her. She made her husband and herself into Christian Scientist; he became sanctimonious, she tactful. Mrs. Norlidge had an almost exquisite quality, a delicacy. She was far and away the nicest of Harriet's acquaintances, and the nicest of the Christian Scientists.

LK ***A little introduction to all this in the character of Louise Frohn the governess:*** The introduction doesn't materialize. Louise Krohn, or Frohn, is named in NB10, #19 the second governess, and her story is told in MA 244–248. It has no bearing, however, on "the practical, the aggressive, the emotional the sensitive act of faith," or on "femininity and religiousness;" it has no religious context of any kind. Louise Frohn is the "big strong healthy woman" Mr. Hersland employs when he wants no more of the first governess's French and German and music education. She subsequently marries a baker, gets larger, and is visited by Hersland and the children in her cake shop.

*

NB-A #9

~~Sally~~ I humble rather than reverent, Sally reverent rather than humble.

*

NB-A #9a

Miss Mars, Marie they are type of whom I will make not a servant, they they have it in common with the chic man the gayety, they go off into Emily Dawson & Roche in another direction, and from Emily to Mamie Weeks, real sensibility and gayety, when tragic become hard the type of some of the French queens.

AT ***Miss Mars, Marie… have it in common with the chic man, the gayety:*** Miss Mars was a well-born, good-looking version of Marie, who was good-looking enough. Marie's gayety was the foolishness of allying herself to a man ten years younger who, naturally, left her. Miss Mars was genuinely gay and lively, Marie was only gay. All this was at the time Gertrude began to question me about all the people who looked like other people and therefore were like other people. If she knew one, she wanted to know all the others. First, there would be physical resemblance enough to say, 'Oh she looks like…' Then, what was it that made them resemble? Later, it lapsed from resemblance in the fact to the physical resemblance of the type.

LK ***Miss Mars, Marie…. the type of some of the French queens:*** [See NB10, #21 and NB-B #4]

*

NB-A #10a

I recognise that I am not a good arguer any more than a good critic I have the quality of it like Dougherty or Matisse or any energetic vigorous intelligent but not ~~brilli~~ genial youngster, my powers being so I get tired and I get impatient in arguing because it is like being a good fencer it takes more energy to keep up the defense than the game is worth. Weber has the sensibility to color, he has not the constructive ~~sensib~~ color sense, so as I said long ago about Manguin, he has the sensibility to works of art he has not a real sense of them. Derain & Sterne et al have a real intellectual sensibility but not a real intellectual process. that is what makes them what they are they have this for the genius life, Leo F. & Purman being less romantic au fond are more successful their essential commonplace worldly efficiency is less interfered with, they have only the romantic or idealistic conception they ~~have~~ never xcept in their early youth attempt its realisation. none of these have a vital sensibility they are wood or petrified wood or stone or metal but they are always a dead substance they have no ~~part living~~ earth principle of vital growth, so they differ from the group which Mike forms an intermediate step to mine which has. nothing is within them, they are worldly because their reaction is always a readaptation never a creation, not even a creation like Zobel et al Carlo these have the novelty side of the really genial people like Brenner. ~~Alfy Alfy~~ Howard and Annette are that to Alfy, Manguin & Weber are perhaps that to the genial type, Edstrom is that to Matisse, there it takes the form of emotional sensibility rather, than intellectual (Sterne) or beautiful (Manguin Weber) or clever quick sensibility (Carlo & Zobel) or profoundly what shall I call it that Annette & Mabel Haynes have.

BB & Alice & Brenner have all of them moments of really creative sensibility but there is not very much of it, but that in Alice's case has nothing to do with her emotion, she is truly a double personality, that is the reason she is not creative more, I think that is also true of B.B. only I think this is his bottomest I don't know.

AT ***I am not a good arguer:*** She was not a good arguer because Leo always interrupted and corrected, and it upset her. She didn't argue much with anyone else. Bien sur, said Picasso, we get the worst of it [with Leo.] Leo always levelled off the ideas. Gertrude contradicted with illustrations always, built on things she'd found out by herself, which Leo didn't like because it wasn't by the rules of simple argument. His feeling would get warm and would die down when Gertrude recognized that the argument wasn't worth all this feeling.

Gertrude always saw the essence of the thing, and was crystal clear, secure, vehement, and Leo wandered off, and he made a gesture. It ended beautifully, looking at it, but if you listened, there was nothing. Gertrude would however put a light on something before she would get tired and give up.

Gertrude never said anything that didn't add something and was always absolutely clear and certain. More and more, they talked less and less about many subjects, and finally talked only about a few things. Writing, painting, people were the big subjects. Politics too, American mostly, even European. She was passionately interested in American politics, and in the English at one time—in the way they were treating the Irish—and in the suffragettes. The failure of the whole Irish question was the illustration to her of the decadence of England. In American politics—municipal graft, presidential elections, voting credits, everything. Sayne, the inventor who turned painter, talked, not argued, with Gertrude about politics. Mildred Aldrich would have argued with Gertrude, but Gertrude didn't like to argue with her. She was old, tired, had seen a great deal, and should have her way. Occasionally they would argue anyway.

Derain & Sterne… wood… dead substance: For the rest of her life, Gertrude spoke of Derain as 'wood.' When I asked, What do you mean, she said, You recognized it well enough in Therese Ehrman. Of Balthus, whom Gertrude liked but who was under the influence of Derain, she said, But that doesn't make him wooden. She used this description of Sterne too.

Annette and Mabel Haynes: When Gertrude was working on Annette in Paris, she often made comparisons of her and Mabel Haynes. She often compared their handwriting. Mabel's T's crossing like a dagger point and her handwriting not crowded but tight—her terrific egotism. Annette the Stinker crossed her T's brutally much as Mabel Haynes did. If you look up Mabel Haynes in *Q.E.D.*, you will really know what she was. By the time I came to Paris, Gertrude had had about enough of Annette. The Stinker getting greener and greener was frightful to see.

*

NB-A #10b

It is a very striking thing that portrait in the November 1908 <u>American</u> of the man who organized massacres who is so incredibly like B.B. I always thought B.B. & Howard could have been very bad as ~~well~~ easily as good.

LK ***The man… who organized massacres:*** Abdul-Hamid [1842–1918], Turkish sultan. "Abdul-Hamid, the Sick Man, is the most mysterious personage of our time.… No other has been so feared and so hated.… What titanic epithets have been hurled against the unhappy Sultan of Turkey, who has reigned for thirty-three years, throned in the fear of his subjects.…Rather tall and exceedingly slender, Abdul Hamid has the unstudied sloop of the consumptive. His face is wrinkled parchment, as if a thousand anxieties and suspicions had left their impress there. His features, besides cruelty and cunning, denote intelligence and cowardice. The eyes, of almond shape, by far the most interesting detail of his person, are dark and piercing, aged with eternal suspicion. They denote high intellect, extraordinary intelligence, subtle refinement and pitiless cruelty. The thin upper lip and the thick, sensual lower, indicate a combination of passion, irascibility and selfishness. His nose is aquiline and lends to his face the appearance of a bird of prey. The chin, though hidden by a beard, is weak and indecisive. The voice, however, belies the face. It is marvelously subtle and insinuating, melodious in its modulations, and full of dulcet tones." [From: "The Sultan of Turkey: A record of Personal Observations and Private Knowledge," by Nicholas C. Adossides, *American Magazine*, vol. 67, no. 1 (November 1908), pp.3,4. A photo of the Sultan taken thirty-five years previously, "the only photograph for which the Sultan ever sat," illustrates the article.]

*

NB-A #11

Brutal egotism of Matisse shown in his not changing his prices.

AT ***Matisse… not changing his prices:*** When the Bernheims took him on and regulated his prices, they asked, What about the Steins? meaning, since they were the first to buy his pictures, should there be any special consideration for them? His answer was, What about them? He made no special provision for prices for them.

*

NB-A #12

Love in Alice subversive, hard to remember her as she is. No consciousness, no fear, no shrinking, no doubt.

*

NB-A #13

I am quite sure that it is true of Matisse that he cannot do pure decoration because he has to have the practical realism of his group as his point de depart always. He must paint after nature, his in between decorative period was ~~a fa~~ and is a failure, it is only carried by his beautiful colors and his power in drawing but they have no real existence. He has always failed in such flat painting, he then of course not understanding his own failure cannot understand Pablo who succeeds in just this. I sometimes think that Matisse ~~did what~~ has done what Van Goch tried to do and Pablo will do what Goguin dreamed of. It is very interesting that the dramatic independent dependents have no lyric or decorative sense. You must have them like Leo, Alice, I imagine Renoir to a certain extent Valloton to have this quality, where the sensitiveness becomes creative not the drama & consequently where the practical sense is not dominant. Matisse—Sally—Edstrom.

*

NB-A #14

Its all getting wonderfully cleared up now. To begin. As I was saying of Berenson he runs himself by his head and he has a good but not a great head the real sensibility in him is one of affection, that is slow but certain in him, strong and persistent when it is fully developed but it is not in him a contact with the real thing not even in a sense with the art thing, it is an affection for that thing. ~~with Leo~~ I think BB goes over into our class as Howard does not into the blondes, but of this I am not sure, watch him carefully for it. He and Simon H and Francis and Howard and then Leo Friedman and Purman and Sterne and Derain ~~they all~~ and then Mike who is over the line and Valloton and Leo who are over the blonde line Purman too comes almost like Mike in being over the line but is not quite. Chalfin and Braque and Brenner are. Now all these people do not get their inspiration from their relation direct to the object but from their affection for the object. Alice is an interesting mixture she has this affection and she has the emotion passionate that connects her with Sally Mamie Weeks and Emily. This people get their sense again not from immediate contact with the object but ~~with~~ from a passionate emotion about the object. That is the reason all these have a dramatic, a practical and a crudely material imagination and of these Matisse is the great creator. He truly said he painted his emotion but in order to paint it he had to have it attached to the crudely materialistic object when he gets away from this he is lost. He still makes lovely but not significant painting. Now Cezanne is the great master of the realization of the object itself, Pablo connects on to him. Renoir on the contrary ~~realises the~~ is in direct relation so to speak with the beauty of the object, so is Leo, in Sally's case the emotion about the object is never enough to make her creative, she is therefor what I have always called her a passionate partisan. Then in both groups there are people like Alexandre who are directly in relation to their own passion that is also true of Alfy, and so in that sense they are creative. Braque Balzac Chalfin etc, are all more or less of Pablo's type, in all three of them they are to a more or less degree in actual creative relation to the object. The chances are a man like Shakespeare was like Renoir with the more vital reality of the man of the world. Valloton stands between the affection and reality groups.

This is what Pablo probably meant when he said that Matisse always gave the crude feeling of the object but he never really paints the object.

AT ***Chalfin... of Pablo's type... in actual creative relation to the object:*** Chalfin's painting was very commonplace indeed, but what Gertrude is describing is the way he was before other paintings. I was with him once at an exhibition, and he was quite a transported person.

*

NB-A #15

The courage of those who are sensitive and have no sense. They have the complete courage because they have no sense of danger not knowing what is the possibilities of action on the part of the other. Self knowledge for such a one without force of character would be bad. Sally is not a homogeneous personality. It is alternating rather than complete her weakness and sensitiveness and her attack and they cannot come together. When the sensitiveness gets to a certain point it is creative lyrically so as in Leo & Edstrom or prosaically so as in Dough and Matisse. in both the latter cases the point of departure is the object, as it is in the dramatic temperament. that is the object not as an object but as a point of departure. this is their practical sense and their attacking power because they do not realize the object to be afraid of it, they see the object as a point of attack as a point of stimulation as a point for rousing their emotion. this is the great difference, in a person like Sally it becomes merely liveliness of movement, in Matisse tremendous emotion expressed in line and color, in Alice, beauty of the object `it is to eat', in Leo lyrical in Edstrom lyrical dramatic, in Dougherty, pure prose. Brenner is on our side, he is of those who have an affection for the object, not an emotion started by the object. I think this is the basis of the different methods of attack. Pablo and Braque and I and Cezanne and Mike are all of the other kind, object as object. This all goes with the two classes etc. this will come out steadily in the long book. Nelly is with us vague. May with the others vague. Mamie &

Emily sensitive enthusiastic emotion started by the object.

In the case of Derain and Sterne it would have been better for them to follow their other kind Derain Matisse and Sterne Whistler because though not in accord with their bottom it is the most creative part of them, the superficially lyrical, the superficially romantic. Leo F. & Purman could go in more solidly for though wooden they are solid, though absolutely lacking in inspiration they can make up for it by persistence and instinct for the best way.

The kind of originality that is genius that has nothing to do with character in a sense, there are some imitative varieties of character kinds, Leo F. group, Zobel group, to a certain extent Manguin Weber group that can't have it and again it has not anything to do with personality that makes males a la Weiniger although of course as Leo was remarking courage and egotism are essential qualities for effective genius, but there can be found in certain kinds of women this kind of personality but anyhow what I wanted to say was that the last element of efficient originality may or may not be in a character, take Leon & Weiniger as a typical case, they seem to have been wonderfully alike and if Leon had had the last quality of originality in the sense of the thing that is new in form and thought he would have been able to do that, his personality was the same and that last effective genius is something in itself mysterious but it is or is not there. So often they say the most brilliant brother if he had written or what not would have been greater but the chances are that he though more brilliant lacked just that. The genius is not different from other men xcepting that he has that. He is of his kind and he is great only by virtue of that, there are his doubles who are as like him as two peas quand meme all but that.

About the emotional temperament, Edstrom, Matisse, Sally et al. the point is that the facts show there has been an emotion, they no longer or they do feel the emotion and so they must explain it and so they put it upon the other man. That makes May's performance so clear, she knew that it was started, she did not then want, I did then want it so I must have started it. Edstrom had a relation, he don't now care about it so the other person must have done it. Sally does it with virtue rather than with emotion, restrained saintliness, she feels injured, she feels a restrained saintliness, the incident shows that nobody was to blame, she had the sense of restrained saintliness because she uses up her vitality in a struggle so she has a sense of virtue though all she did was to misunderstand on very good evidence and when nobody was to blame. This is the way women put men in the wrong. Many men have it too, all the emotional type, business men etc, the generally emotional aggressive type, the method of reasoning is always simple, from the sensation of virtue or from the present lack of emotion back to the event. Also the very evident effect on their vitality however speedily they may recover and however ready they are to use it up some other way also gives them a sense of virtue over those whose vitality is more subtly consumed. There again they make a weapon of their suffering. It is different with Adele Jaffa et al for these stick to their emotion and conquer with it, by every kind of appeal but with it. Their misconstructions are because of the strength of their emotion not because of the forgetting of it. They are concentrated and it is passion and egotism with them not emotion.

The thing I said once about Polly and Sally is quite in line with this, that they are unconscious of their brutalities because they only in themselves feel their own sweetness and virtue, they are quite unconscious of their violent brutality which flows from their injured pride vanity etc. My kind are less deceived because they are then to their sensation resentful angry righteously or not as the case may be but consciously, but Sally & Polly are really then to themselves possessed of sweetness and virtuous love of their neighbor. The type case was that toward Annette. Now in Annette she just forgets everything else but herself that is entirely a different kind of way of doing it. In Alice it does not take this form it takes more the form of her consciousness of caring as much as she ever did about the person therefor she is acting the same way so it feels to herself however differently she is acting but she has not the sense of injury to herself, she only does not know when she is injuring others, there she touches Berenson and Leo, the unemotional ones of the blonde type. In the case of Polly or Sally one sees how different this is from a case like Mrs. Matisse with her insistence that when she is disillusioned then she hates or as Harriet would say they no longer exist for her or as Aunt Fanny would feel a deep sense of outraged injury, all these are to themselves concerned with their sense of injury, their sense of virtue is subsidiary to it as justifying it, in the case of Polly or Sally their sense of injury or resentment or anger is subsidiary their sense of virtue or of goodness is paramount and that is all that to themselves is existing, the sense of injury or resentment or anger to themselves so to speak flows from their virtue or their goodness. This difference is extremely important.

AT ***those who are sensitive and have no sense... Sally:*** The note came about in this way. Sally was crossing the street and I was with her. She was normally fearful and had no courage [at such times], but this time she walked off and into the street without looking, and I had to grab her and pull her back. We had been crossing the street before this with Sally clinging to me as if I were her rod of defense. Now suddenly, this.

originality that is genius: Toward the last half of the writing of *The Making of Americans*, she was conscious of the certainty that she had genius and that her work was of the first importance. It gave her security in the effort she was making, it was right. After *Three Lives*, she thought she was an original writer, that's all, but after this, no. If it was right, then she had the genius to make it so.

She never talked about her work to anyone in Paris. That's what she enjoyed so much about living in Paris, that there was no one to talk to.

males a la Weininger: [This, a later discussion of Weininger, produced several significant contradictions of the previous note on P.26, Note #43.]

I was living at the rue de Fleurus when Gertrude first read him. She was deeply impressed and convinced, and it didn't touch her own ideas at all. She went her own way, and he had done his. She shared it with Leo and myself. And she said, Once he was started, nothing was a surprise to him, it all developed so normally. Leo just wanted to argue points with her, though he was equally impressed. He wished to discuss it according to his own lights, not Weininger's, and Gertrude implied that Weininger had said it all, completely. Then we all sent copies out to everyone, to which one of my friends wrote that she was shocked by the book, to which Gertrude replied, I always suspected him of being a romantic. Gertrude didn't know at the time of reading him that he had killed himself and was frightfully shocked when she found out. She thought it was unnecessary from what she conceived him to be.

Leo probably came across him first, or perhaps it was Gertrude. Really, both would go down together and look at books for sale at the bookshops. At any rate, they were the first to read him and then suggested it to everybody. Leo knew a few French writers, but not Gertrude, who wasn't interested in them. They both knew mostly painters. Gertrude knew a fair amount of people at the time and saw them fairly consistently, but she led a very solitary life at the same time. And the more she enjoyed a book, the less she cared to discuss it with anyone, [to avoid their] sort of taking it away from her.

[As to Weininger's influence on her] Gertrude already having gotten into her work wasn't taking on anything else. She had to go on with her own, and so didn't take anything as a result of Weininger.

often they say the most brilliant brother if he had written: For the New York cousins, mostly, Leo was that. But Pat Bruce thought of Leo as an average intelligent American and didn't think he was going to write at all. As for Matisse, he had originally some but shortly no patience with Leo's ideas on painting. Pablo wouldn't listen to him at all, and he was furious when Leo cornered him and held forth. In 1907 when I first came over, Fernande hated Leo and found him a frightful bore. She thought he was very pretentious and that Gertrude was very real. I said to Fernande that I couldn't see how she could hate Leo with all the gratitude Pablo felt toward him. But Fernande replied that that had nothing to do with Pablo's feelings about him.

Pat Bruce couldn't stand a lack of social graces in anyone, and though Leo had the grace, he had no sense of social contact. In the end, Pat Bruce thought Leo was a little touched. He could say so about his fasts later, but earlier he spoke only wittily about Leo.

BB didn't like Leo, disagreed with him and found him insupportable in Florence long before Leo settled in Paris. Then BB took a fancy to Gertrude, and by this time he was something of a lion and wouldn't stop at such small houses as the Casa Ricci, so Gertrude took to walking to Settignano. Leo and BB were on terms where Leo could see him, but more often than Leo was welcome. BB couldn't support the half-hour, not-rapid, quiet monologues of Leo's which bored people unless they were really ignorant and young. BB could make social faux pas, but he had some sense of what social life was.

though more brilliant: Gertrude didn't like 'brilliance.' She liked of course Diana Abdy who was brilliant and brittle, but she did not like brilliance as a gift in anyone.

Edstrom had a relation: Once he was with Czobel's wife. Edstrom got away with her, though several were buzzing around her.

Sally… injured, she feels a restrained saintliness: This is the Sarah I knew, where she was vacant and saintly, complete vacancy and saintliness.

Polly… unconscious of [her] brutalities… only feel[s]… sweetness and virtue: Polly Jacobs, Harriet's sister. She came to Paris with her husband, probably in the second winter of Harriet's stay [1908–1909.] I knew her more here than in San Francisco. She was a good deal of a horror. She had all the feminine weaknesses and not many of the family charms. She had looks when she was young and didn't realize that they had disappeared, and so took on the role of a sort of prima donna. She had a very bitter, sharp tongue, was very sharp, and was not kindly toward Sarah. She was a hard woman, and cared for no one but her husband, and that was because she possessed him. I don't think she would have otherwise. She had no generosity, no charity, no kindliness—a hard creature, very unlovable and unattractive. She was a little comic because she was such an exaggeration of her kind. And avaricious. She asked me to go shopping with her, and then, Alice, would you take my purse and pay. No, I said, because I suspected Polly didn't want to see the money departing.

Mrs. Matisse… when she is disillusioned then she hates: As when [much later] she hated Matisse when he went off with Olga [Meerson.]

as Harriet would say: It was her favorite phrase: 'They no longer exist for me.'

LK ***About the emotional temperament, Edstrom, Matisse, Sally et al.… egotism with them not emotion:*** The passage is further developed in NB-C #30 and Note #73, then used as draft of text for MA 441–447, passim.

*

Note #6

I need not be in a hurry to give birth to my hero because it will be an enormous task to struggle his development I want to make him realise everybody in the book the way I am.

*

In Sally's case the certian obstinacy she is developing in reference to p.p. now is [...]

*

NB-A #16

The certain obstinacy Sally is developing in reference to painting, is it calculated to last long, her feeling of being sure she ultimately wants to do it, is it like Leo's Fletcherism or is it more like his writing, time will tell. I think it will last a good while but not long. She is to me like Edstrom with the quality to be always no. 1 At every school in her to be always no. 1 in a professional school in him. He has infinitely more personality and originality, she infinitely more steady reflection. The interesting element in the type of her understanding that I speak of as passionate partisanship is that the conviction was the same about Mayer about whom she knew nothing but his personality. Now that happens to many in various ways but in her particular way, emotional realisation it makes passionate partisanship, also makes her incapable of seeing really more than one at a time. She is not greedy.

AT ***Sally… painting:*** Sally started painting under Matisse's influence before he started the school, and then with the school, under his direction. She did a portrait of Therese Ehrman that was Matisse unbelievably vulgarized, like a magazine cover in the Matisse manner. She had the same 'Little Eva' expression with her painting as she had with Christian Science. Wasn't she closest to Matisse, didn't she know more of him than anyone else, wasn't she next to him now that she was doing it too?

Sally took notes on what Matisse said, and they've been published. Bruce once asked her about something Matisse had said, and Sally repeated it. But Bruce said no, and repeated what it was, and said I don't remember there was any more to it. That, said Sally, is because you don't understand. Then Bruce just said, Oh, what difference does it make? It makes a great difference to me, said Sally. It's important to me to know what I think. Her virtuous self-saying this.

[Sally]… she is not greedy: Sarah took away not out of greed but more out of something like jealousy. If she didn't want it then, *tant pis*, she had gotten it anyway.

*

NB-A #16a

~~Describe~~ Sally, Estelle, Fernande, Bird, Hortense Moses, don't touch me, friendship reason and will, not emotion or passion. Striking difference to Mabel Hortense Federleicht. Jeanne Boiffard, Emma Mrs. Berenson et al are in between, the lack of poignant feminine or sex quality in all of these to me, I need the more poignant to attract me.

AT ***Estelle [Rumboldt]… lack of poignant feminine or sex quality:*** All signs fail in her case. She looked feminine and lovable, all right. She was soft, very pretty, what Gertrude would have called 'pokable.' [combined with following, from P33:]

Estelle: She was a typical 'studio' person grown older [at the time Miss Toklas met her.] She had a story about her husband's bourgeois friends [who would visit and who bored her.] Her only pleasure in the evening was to see the laces of these elegant women. She told one of the guests she was going to Europe on a boat. Oh, what an adventure to go on a liner [i.e., not on a yacht.]

*

NB-A #17

A striking incident of Harriet when her servant Maria was sick to be willing to pay doctor and druggist but not her wages not to pay up for time lost. I thought it just a wonderful lack of capacity on her part, Leo explained it like always the action has its origin in the fundamental character, she wanted to do benevolence and therefor she was ready to pay the money under the guise of doctor and druggist not as a matter of course of wages. Very interesting and also very interesting that I did not see it. I so often don't in many cases. Fabri's group can be like Alice, I guess more often are like Alice. Not I think in Therold's case. I should not say more often, on that will depend their kind of women. I think Manguin is.

*

NB-A #18

Emile About had been living a long time in Bridgepoint. Vollard

*

NB-A #19

continues as NB-B #1

The practical realism [of] Manet Matisse Zola which leads to melodramatic romantic imagination, or in Matisse's case real emotional drama, it is realism but not the object, the emotion of the object. In Renoir there is much more really the sense of the real object, always the beauty of that real object but a real sense of it and not a practical sense, but in none of these cases does the reality of the

*

Notebook B

NB-B #1

[Previous note continues] object count, what I might call the actual earthyness of the object the object for the object's sake. That is the big point of difference. Leo Friedman and Purman have the earthy sense without the earthy sensibility. They have the false elegance imagination, elegance and beauty imagination as Derain has the false romantic and intellectual, and Sterne the false romantic and form greek beauty imagination. A man whose greatest desire is that and was fooled by Leo's test. Purman Matisse's greatest work is one, thin and featured and not inwardly illuminated. Leo F. afraid of the genius quality of the true mark of Bohemia when he loved Bohemianism. Derain goes flabby when a real romantic love affair comes to him.

To come back to the practical realism and its attendant emotional dramatic coloring. Edstrom has some admixture of the lyrical Renoir, Wm. James the other end of it quality, that gives him the greater originality. Originality xcept in action in the Matisse Zola group is extremely rare they are emotional practical realists that means action, ~~In this~~ and theoretical not real imaginative creation. One sees that very much in Matisse. I think the Tete d'expression is such a casse. The worldly chic that goes with it is in the new picture of Harriet, it is in Manet and in Delacroix. Rubens is nearer Renoir. He has the true lyric sense of the object. I think that distinction holds. This is what Purman would be but isn't. The simple realism with the sensation of beauty of the object not earthy of Renoir makes lyrics, this is very clear in my mind. Of course there is quite other kinds of creativeness like Alice's that makes lyrics. the true genial earthy type concentrated makes lyrics but that is another matter. this distinction I think holds. (think over H. James) Degas ~~and less~~ (Hewlitt Manguin sensibility not sense of color & beauty.) Man combination of Puy & Ben Oppenheimer [.] Miss Mars & Marie are connected to Emily Dawson to Mamie Weeks with this lyrical side but these people have lost all real sense of the object, to the first two there is not the real sense of the beauty of the objection, there is only the emotion of it and this in Emily is enthusiasm for it in Mamie enthusiasm and pedantry toward it. to ~~Sally who~~ Edstrom to Sally whose lyrical sense is quite non-existent having gone over to the practical and dramatic although retaining the sensibility of the group she is parted from, not the sensibility to the object or the beauty but just the sensibility which she always translates to passionate partisanship and a little to pedantry.

AT ***The practical realism Monet Matisse Zola:*** These notes were written at the beginning of Cubism, when Gertrude was looking at other painters with a colder eye. By 1909, Picasso had returned with the two Spanish Cubist landscapes, which were the definite break.

On matters such as 'the relation to the object,' it was likely that Gertrude would use such a phrase to Pablo and he would say, *Expliquez moi.* Then she would, and he would say, Yes, yes, or You see, you've seen it. I didn't hear these things directly because first, it wasn't decent to Olga, and then I knew Gertrude's questions, and she would tell me Pablo's answers. So I didn't hear them directly, ever.

Also, I never did and don't now relate Gertrude's problems to Picasso's problems. Though they understood each other, there is really no fundamental connection between writing and painting. I used to say to Gertrude, Don't forget that painting is a second art, which made Gertrude laugh.

They talked to each other each for their own good, not for the other's, and so they cleared their own minds as they spoke. Gertrude talked to Pablo because he was intelligent, and so she could get things straight with herself. They were both that way.

Tete d'expression: Probably the Matisse portrait of Mme. Matisse that Sally bought and put beside her own of Therese Ehrman in San Francisco.

the new picture of Harriet: Not a portrait of Harriet, but Matisse's *La Femme aux yeux bleus* that Harriet had just bought.

Sally... translates to passionate partisanship and a little to pedantry: [The day after we read this note, Miss Toklas began our next interview gleefully with a copy of Benjamin Constant's Memoirs, the page turned down on Constant's description of Mme. de Stael.]

I have a gem for you. I think you'll love this. Well, maybe you won't. I came across the portrait of Mme. de Stael in Benjamin Constant's Memoirs, and it's Sally to a T. Constant is killingly funny on Mme. de Stael, but you have to reduce her to something provincial to get Sally. Sally was first parochial, then provincial, for all her talk about Europe. When she returned to San Francisco after the earthquake, she asked me, Do you still like Henry James here? In Europe we think him rather thin. That was Sally. She tried hard, but she was eternally provincial.

LK ***Tete d'expression.... the new picture of Harriet:*** [A. Barr dates Matisse's *Tete d'expression* Autumn 1909. Notebooks A and B are dated by me Jan-Jun 1909, during the writing of the chapter on "Mrs. Hersland and the Servants."]

*

NB-B #2

The question of school is very interesting. Matisse did in this picture of Harriet's the whole thing that Purman would do if he could just as he did what Manguin would do in that other and he suggested what Sally would like do in the tete d'expression. This is not the case with Bruce he does really drink at the fountain head. If Matisse had not known Purman perhaps he would not have done the picture of Harriet's.

AT ***Bruce... does really drink at the fountain head:*** Bruce had no endowment, alas, but he was as pure as anyone could have been—in looking and listening to Matisse and living with Matisse's paintings.

*

NB-B #3

The type quality in Miss Mars and Marie the certain tang to them is a form of this lyrical sensibility without any of the sense of beauty or the sense of the object as the true lyricists have it but it [is] a genuine emotion of lyricism, it does not come to enthusiasm as it does in Emily and Mabel, it is not creative nor appreciative nor assertive, it is not practical, it is nearer the sensibility of Van Goch to Edstrom but has as it were the flavor of that rather than the reality and yet not the flavor of it, but the green acid even though pleasant fruit of it. This must be most carefully conveye It goes with the lack of responsibility and a lack of worldliness with a sense of these things, even a sense of accomplishing them, it is essentially self-centered because it is neither enthusiastic nor creative but not sordid nor really practical although when stimulated efficient because it is essentially self-centered because it is not practical nor enthusiastic nor creative nor really sensitive. It was fun doing, they say this though they are afraid, they are afraid but not anxious that is important. they have very little in them of anxious feeling, they have impatient feeling. It was fun doing it including the rouging of the lips and having the baby. Not easy to put up with them passionately loving or loved by them, they verge on spinsters

They have temperamentally bad tempers. Emma is of this group. To put up with them one must be passionately loving or loved by them, like Annette Miss Squires & Miss Mars (Mabel Haynes & May Bookstaver another combination) Emma is in a way a version of this it can easily degenerate into vanity and discontent, it always remains decent to a certain extent responsible, to a sentimental extent loyal, their possible gradual dishonesty as to Marie lack of sordidness or responsibility. Write about the instruments and the type of ideality in them.
Annette
Bruce, Miss Douglas to Sally.

AT ***Miss Mars… lyric sensibility… the green acid… of it:*** Miss Mars finally got herself made up like a cigar store Indian.

Emma… possible gradual dishonesty: There was a dark moment in Emma Lootz' career at Johns Hopkins when she cheated at an examination. Gertrude knew about it and got her out of it.

LK ***The type quality in Miss Mars and Marie…. Write about the instruments and the type of ideality in them:*** [Concurrent with DB #60] There is an accruing of terms that gradually approaches the formulation, "Instrument Nature," beginning with "injured" and "angry" feeling [MA 175], "anxious feeling," [MA 184–85] "impatient" and "nervous" feeling [MA 194], "stupid" being [MA 196], and "virtuous" feeling, and attributed in various degrees and combinations to "servant nature," "servant girl nature," "servant mistress," "mistress servant" and "spinster nature." The definition of "instrument nature" is finally articulated in MA 201–203, but with careful indirection, scrupulously separating and connecting the "instrument nature" from and to the terms and types that served as prologue to its revelation. See NB-B #22 and DB #60 for full "groupings" of Instrument types.

*

NB-B #4

Mamie Weeks real sensibility and gaity, when tragic became hard, the type of queens. Miss Mars and Marie always a little hard but never to queens to princesses rather. their gayety and sensibility is of that kind.

LK ***Mamie Weeks real sensibility and gaiety…. never to queens to princesses rather:*** [Corresponds to NB-A #9a] [See NB10, #21]

*

NB-B #5

Anxious being in the instrument, remember it in May, in the woman Leo flirted with in Sally, it is (in Miss Douglas) in Nelly, you see it in their bows in a certain apparently nervous movement, it is not really an anxious feeling in them, it is that their method is attacking with always in them too much sensitiveness too much weakness too much vagueness to let the attack come freely out of them, they don't get resolute as Alice, Alice Klauber et al, to conquer their weakness, they don't harden themselves as Bird and to a limited extent Sally does to attack, they don't work themselves up into a rage to get strength, they don't get crooked like the typical servant girl nature but they just go ahead and this halting gives to them an appearance not of timidity but of anxious feeling.

AT ***Anxious being in the instrument... in Nelly:*** As 'Instruments?' Both Nelly and [her sister] Ada were colossally certain of themselves. Nelly had the movement of the head like a bull. She would look directly from one place to another without changing the position of her eyes.

LK ***Anxious being in the instrument.... not of timidity but of anxious feeling.*** Used as draft for text in MA 203.

*

Work up now through description of dress-makers etc. to servant and governess life—children running through it and so to father and education.

*

Details of Lies [?] family, Eddy Richardson & family, Louis Champion Cook family, all these just suggested as a family, the detail as individuals comes in individual history in which use back [i.e., material from other side of sheet] for intro family with the wild son & Bertha, Lidell family, Rodhammel family, Boyce, Mother and son and daughter. the Moore's and their later career with daddy, Mary Gruenhagen's family another part of turn [?] describe that.

LK ***work up now... to father and education:*** General working note for MA 93–118.

Details of Lies family: The family, unnamed in the text, is described in some detail in MA 98–118.

Eddy Richardson and family: Described in less detail in MA 108–112. The plan for using the rest of the families and persons named in this passage lapsed, and was not used later either, as this working note anticipated, in the individual histories of the Hersland children. "Louis Champion" is described briefly in a listing of Alfred Hersland's friends in MA 532, and there remains an echo of the "Rodhammel" name in "Will and Frank Roddy" in the same listing.

*

NB-B #6

About B.B. as I say his is affection for the object that is like Alice & Janet etc and in all these cases it is indep. dep. kind for it is not a feeling of the actuality of the object. Manguin and Weber their sensibility is around [?] the reality of the object, I think so is Brenner's but not sure. This is awfully difficult to distinguish, but the general rule ought to hold, Mike Purman the Keysers are of the earthy but sensibility not actuality. Different kinds of flavor.

*

NB-B #7

It is not egotism in a man like Berenson, it is ~~path~~ diseased affection, for the thing for everyone, in his case. He and all his group flavor on one hand Alice & Janet & Mary McClean and on the other hand the practical opportunism of Simon H. & Francis Pollak, but in all the cases they are lonesome souls and nervously affectionate and being lonesome and diseasedly nervously affectionate and having all the self-importance of pride and self knowledge they are inevitably cads, they have all the self-importance of pride and self-knowledge for in most cases they run themselves by their intellect the less they do so the more hope there is of their escaping from lonesomeness
Alice & Puy

AT ***Berenson… diseased affection, for the thing for everyone:*** BB saw Belle Greene and conversed with her. Then she went back to America, and he had to have her. She was what was called a 'white nigger.' He was in a fever, took to his bed, suffered, and finally Mary Berenson wired her to come. She did, but nothing happened. She went home again and BB calmed down. This happened in about 1916 during the war. Cook told Gertrude and me about it—though it may have been later. Gertrude met Belle Greene in an elevator in New York, on the Mary Pickford occasion.

flavor group… Alice: Why in the flavor group? Well, for example, my liking for the 'taste' of Nelly. I'd tell Gertrude, I don't care about her 'bad character.' But as for Annette or George Hugnet, I couldn't bear them because I couldn't bear anyone who was *maladif*. To discover that is not to stand them anymore. I just don't like it.

in all the cases they are lonesome souls: [True of BB, frightfully so.]

*

NB-B #8

There are many kinds of flavor ~~each~~ people each larger group has its flavor class. Neith has flavor based on servant girl dependent independent.

*

NB-B #9

Miss Donner, Mme Demarez Mrs Van Dongen—Marie Lorenzen—Alice Klauber—Adele Jaffa, they all have in common a profound idealism and really genial creative quality, and a profound egotism and domination.

Fernande said of Mrs. Van Dongen that she had thought of her as of an exalted character, stupid but of an exhalted character and that she had discovered gradually that she was really not xalted but a profound egotist. This people are to us Vollard Braque, Pablo me, Balzac Cezanne & Mike what Miss Mars to May are to the emotional ~~type~~ no that is not it what Puy ~~etc~~ & Berenson and Francis are to the emotional type that is it. Miss Donner combination of domination, mostly with a fine spiritual virgin idealistic creativeness.

Van Dongen like Matisse, souteneur no intellect, elemental type. This version of Matisse an interesting one correlative in their wives, Mrs. Matisse and Mrs. Van Dongen. Mrs Matisse more bottom quality but less idealism, more melodrama less ~~egotism~~ not egotism but individuality, self-expressing to themselves individuality.

AT ***Van Dongen... Mrs. Van Dongen:*** Van Dongen's first and real wife. She was pure Dutch. It was Mrs. Van Dongen who gave the address to Mme. Matisse for the Dutch batik that we all wore then, and that Matisse painted his wife in. Gertrude met them before I came over, at the time the Picasso portrait was being done. She never got to know them intimately. By the time I came over, Mme. Matisse spoke of them, not Gertrude.

Miss Donner... profound idealism... and a profound egotism and domination: [Cora Downer] There was only one Christian Science church in

Paris, and Cora Downer was its Reader, who had enormous power because she attracted well-to-do people. She didn't like the poor and paid no attention to them. She rented a large gorgeous hall where they had their meetings, and there too she ran the private lives of the Christian Scientists.

Miss Downer came from Kalamazoo and didn't want it known. She was calculating, not cold, despised Harriet, and turned her over to Edstrom from the beginning. Sarah despised her. Harriet didn't think well of either of them.

Miss Downer was forced to resign her position because of the scandal with [her husband] Edstrom [who beat her so that she couldn't show up at meetings], and another church was started in this quarter [St. Germain des Pres.] The first had been in the Etoile.

When I first saw Miss Downer, she was very suave, and fancied herself a good-looking woman. Edstrom won her on simple, old-fashioned seduction, which she tried to do. She thought herself cold and seductive; actually, she was just calculating.

After they were married, she established them in a smart seventeenth century house on the Quay de Bethune, and asked Leo—whom Cora had never met—to visit, and Gertrude too. Then they came to the rue de Fleurus. There finally she took Gertrude's hand as she was speaking to her, and Gertrude said later, She felt there was no response, so she dropped it. Not only the hand but the subject. Miss Downer had been trying hard to win Gertrude.

Among the people who tried to 'win' Gertrude was Stella Ford, Ford Maddox Ford's daughter. She was, Gertrude said, like a drunken Fairy in an English pantomime.

*

NB-B #10

The whole subject of friendship and hypnotic influence between like kinds.

Edstrom

Matisse and Bird do it to Sally, Miss Donner and others try to do it to me. Likes imitate and hypnotise each other, they have little tenderness and no love for each other but they can have sympathy and friendship likes in the two classes. This is true also with male influence,

Jerome upon Bird
Matisse " Sally,
Leon " me
Van Dongen " Fernande

me upon Annette & Harriet

Leo

It is noticeable that one of the elements in this kind of relation is the life enhancement of intensification and enlargement of personality such as one can never get from an opposite. This is the true nature of school people, followers who live in the larger nature and life of the master.

This is not true with a Van Dongen who is himself, to a certain xtent not true with a Purman. True with Braque. Some who have real quality try to live the larger life and fail and come back to themselves. Webber and Manguin, that is the reason they suffer most, they have the realest personality they are whole not fragments as are Bruce and Annette.

AT ***fragments... as Bruce:*** He was not only in fragments, but they were diffuse.

*

NB-B #11

Interesting characteristic of Myrtle's letters she always begin[s] do what you please and then very precise in what she wants its the real resisting persisting opposed to the attacking in Sally's method and persistence

*

NB-B #12

~~Edstrom~~ Edstrom—Olga—Tommy Whittemore—Mabel -Sally—Mary Berenson Miss Mars—Marie Alice all have sensibility, Edstrom & Sally the most intelligently ground[ed], Olga bathological Tommy pretty nearly—Alice creative, Mabel etc. no more than spontaneously enthusiastic and sympathetic. They all have a virginal quality their souls don't get stained because they can't remember they are too impressionable ~~to or~~ too responsive that is what makes them emotional. Matisse on one side Alice on the other side get out. Matisse by driving brutal egotism, Alice by eloignement, by impersonality becoming creative—the sensibility becomes an entity, ~~an~~ self-existing self-created affection through Janet to B.B. connects here to the Francis group. May the whole prostitute group are different sensibility with them is ~~dull~~ concentrated to other things. Bertha is the mush of it all. Sally more intelligent and more brutally attacking. Passionate partisanship is in them all in some form, important in Mary

Maxworthing's case.

In Sally the Aunt Pauline attacking goes on because in all these cases the sensibility is never realisation of others, it is re-living others. Miss Douglas etc connect this group idealism a disease to the prostitute group, they have not the sensibility, they have only the instrument quality of re-living. When their idealism ceases they become pure prostitute and we get to Bird and May. these have not idealisms they have admirations, ethics, intellect.

LK ***Important in Mary Maxworthing's case:*** The story of the seamstress Mary Maxworthing and her friend Mabel Linker is first told in MA 207–220. The description of Mary Maxworthing begins in MA 201. She is first mentioned by name in MA 205.

Bertha is the mush of it all: Much expanded treatment of Bertha in this vein, as the ultimate example of a "complete undifferentiated mass of independent dependent being," in MA 384. See also NB-B #20 for identification of Bertha with the "I will throw the umbrella in the mud" story, illustrating a characteristic response of her kind: "no fury, only sulkiness actively expressed."

*

NB-B #13

Most of them have not real fear.

The question of curiosity in relation to all these important. Instrument have it, Bird and May have it, its interesting question.

*

NB-B #14

Striking in Harriet that incident of paying doctor and druggist bill and not wages for time lost. Chooses to be benevolent. Sally says she objects to suggestion but not to influence because in influence she chooses in suggestion she has it thrust upon her, I don't think this is the main point, the main point is sceptical fear. She is so like Mrs. Eddy. But she has real spirituality tout de meme if she can hold to it in the face of such doubting.

*

NB-B #15

Striking similarity between Mrs. Eddy to Harriet to Mary

Greenhagen. The sense of virtue, the choosing of the expression of it.

The money for doctor and druggist rather than wages type case. There was no question of justice, there was a question only of decent conduct. Shuts Alice's friends out while feeling virtuous about Alice. That is her way of being nasty and virtuous. The way Mary Greunhagen behaved about that kid must work up all this very completely. Shuts me out because of my association feels very virtuous toward me but don't consider me. Always chooses the way she will show her virtue and for the rest is naturally nasty. When discussing this in the history of Madeleine Weiman must remember its relation to religion. These are not passionate women, therein they differ from Adele Solomons and that whole group. On account of a lack of a certain virginal sensitiveness they differ from Mme Demarez and Miss Donner and Mrs. Gutman these are the dependent independent virginals as opposed to the independent dependent virginals Tommy Whitemore Mabel Weeks et al. These differ from May Bookstaver & Bird or Hortense Federleicht on the one hand and Jeanne Boiffard etc on the other in their virginal quality.

AT ***Harriet… shuts Alice's friends out:*** Nelly. Just generally, not a situation. Nelly and Ada and their brother were simply scandalous to people like Harriet. Ada enjoyed creating scandal. I would say, Ada, don't do that, and she would reply, But they *like* it!

LK ***Shuts me out… When discussing this in the history of Madeleine Weiman:*** First mentioned:

> Madeleine Wyman had then come to own their mother and their father to [the children.] This was always a sore feeling in them. [MA 252]

must remember its relation to religion: Not remembered.

*

NB-B #16

Its quite true that Alice can only keep one thing in her mind at a time it is true of her emotions too she cannot think two ideas at once, use this for Mabel Linker.

LK ***Alice … cannot think two ideas at once … Use this for Mabel Linker:*** Used in MA 215: "Mabel … never saw anything except the thing that then filled her …"

*

NB-B #17

Work out the fact that Harriet is excitable and nervous and impatient but not unenthusiastic nor emotional therefor in a sense always to herself and more or less reasonably so judicial, true probably of Mrs. Eddy. I am quite sure Harriet's group are the opposite of Marie's more anon. Its Tommy [?] different kind of shiftiness.

*

NB-B #18

Max Jacob a pathological expression of Simon H, Berenson & Francis.

*

NB-B #19

Interesting that all the earthy ones are afraid of heart trouble and poisoning etc and acknowledge it Marie Lorenzin, Harriet, Pablo, Mike and me. All the independent dependents not, Alice, Leo, Sally, Fernande. This is what makes me quite sure that Allan will turn out an earthy one. His lower lip says so too.

*

NB-B #20

Fernande is now doing full tilt what she did ~~wh~~ successfully when Pablo wanted to come back to her, but now it is a little spurious, it is not bluff on her part she is too stupid it is stupidity like Bertha her method of aggression, the only one she knows. It is interesting to be really behind the scenes in the rise and fall of her favorites among women. It begins with deference to her, and ends with a fancied injury or fancied danger. She and Harriet and Nelly, a bunch of sentimentalists all have ~~an~~ aunt hearts. No real emotions for any one not even for themselves, it is negative egotism. don't pay attention to them and you are wiped out unless they need you. Different from Annette who loves herself really. These three are really not absorbed by themselves, they are not absorbed by anything. Fernande and the ~~shif~~ shirt-waist—one form of I will throw the umbrella in the mud, exactly like Bertha there, no fury only sulkiness actively expressed.

LK ***negative egotism:*** A phrase also used in NB-E #7 in relation to a group of women. The phrase is fully defined in MA 231–232.

one form of I will throw the umbrella in the mud: [Used later in MA 388.] It is clear from this Note that the umbrella episode was GS's sister Bertha's, with its attendant "sulkiness actively expressed." The other Notes referring to this episode are Note #20, Note #109, NB1, #22, and NB-MA #19.

*

NB-B #21

Note the likeness in the action of throwing the arm in telling her story that Helene had the story of the robbery. Dorothy Re[a]de. It is the same as Grace Gassette and so to (Kate Martin) to Marie Laurencin, these connect far away—to Mabel Haynes whole group. In this whole group the same cowardness of action.

This different from Alice and Mary Houghton's little jerking movement to Adele Solomons, (Alice Klauber and Mary G. etc Adele Oppenheimer, Miss Donner Mme Demarez) these are earthy, Adele is like Alice so was Leon and so I think Raymond, Pablo not, these distinctions subtle, but I am sure. Nelly joins on to Mabel Haynes group.

AT ***Grace Gassette:*** An American from Chicago who knew Gertrude through Mildred Aldrich. When she painted Gertrude's portrait, Gertrude invited me to come too, because "four ears would make me have to hear less."

*

NB-B #22

Instrument type.

Miss Douglas to be used by others as an instrument.

Sally to use herself as an instrument. Both live other people's lives. Mabel Weeks, Miss Mars et al, reflect other people's lives but live their own, they have self initiated gayety all their serious life is reflected emotion and sympathy is reflected, enthusiasm is self created. They are therefor not real instruments for what they are mostly is themselves their enthusiasm, youthfulness gayety. Mabel, Emily, Miss Mars, Marie. All seriousness and intellectuality and even amorousness is reflected. So that makes that group then we have Miss Blood and Mary Houghton to Alice to Adele. then we have Sally to Bird Sternberger to Aunt Pauline and a sideshoot from Bird to Ella Milzeiner who connects to Marie. Now the more concentrated they are Mary Houghton and Alice, the less they are in any sense of the word students, then we get to Florence Sabine who is the leaner [?] end of Sally, Bird, Miss

Blood without any sensitiveness, prostituteness, weakness, or anything else, then we get to May who is the instrument who is not instrumented but exists in itself. In Bertha you get the shere mush. Dolene connected with Adele Solomons.

AT ***Instrument type… Miss Douglas:*** Kate Douglas could react immediately and possess a person. She could do all the things Cora Downer wanted to do, and better. When she chose a man, she was much more successful than Cora Downer. This 'instrument' thing came out when she was getting her man. Mrs. Dubryko gave me all the details at the time. He would let her treat him to Christian Science all she pleased because she wanted it and it didn't harm him. Finally, she got him by having him do something to her, she seeming to do nothing. The detail of it is gone, but this was the point.

Florence Sabine: There was a scandal at Johns Hopkins involving her.

LK [Continues subject of NB-B #3]

Instrument type… live other people's lives…. [or] reflect other people's lives but live their own. Discussion of instrument types begins on MA 201 and concludes temporarily on MA 203 with the promise that "Sometime there will be here a history of many of them." The text of this Note is echoed particularly in MA 202: "they are wonderful instruments for other people's lives they are living."

*

NB-B #23

(Also NB-C #1)

Mrs. Oppenheimer, Mrs. Vernot, Neith Hapgood etc to Gracie Gassette and ~~the~~ Marie Leaurenzin are the dependent independents with almost no earthiness, no sordidness, but they are more self-inspired than the other group. Mabel Haynes group to Etta and Nelly and Annette and Mabel since so it goes Haynes years. The Blood group remains the same, emotional sensitiveness makes living in other lives. Sally, emotional creativeness, Alice weakness and prostituteness with sullen stupidity with idealism makes a thing like Miss Douglas vanity, supreme sensitiveness of emotional kind with intelligence and comparatively little prostitute element or weakness makes the self using instrument type. The concentration and prostitute element without great sensitiveness but with intelligence makes the Miss Blood & Mary Houghton this with the prostitute increased enormously, the intelligence decreased, the student intelligence entirely dissapeared [sic] makes Therese Therold. The sensitiveness existing alone with prostitution and concentration makes Alice, with self created ideals makes Adele S.

Bird is the split in two kind[s] all who combine studentness with real sensibility or real prostituteness are split in two. The student part is always rote work with all of this group, it is never self-inspired it is in men but not in any women of this group that I have ever known there is not even enough personality to bring it together, Florence Sabine is only that. Sally is that and sensitiveness and weakness and prostituteness. There are moments in reflection when she has personality enough to bring it together never in action or creation. Bird it is completely separated and she sticks stupidly and stubbornly to both. she don't even do them apart, she does them together at the same moment. Mabel Weeks, is like Sally reflective moments she knows, never in action. Miss Blood knows while she is doing it but she never brings them together and never really thinks she does. Mary Houghton and Alice have not that, therefor they are more purely creating types and less instruments, Adele Solomons also. In some lower stupider lethargic types like Fernande there is an accompanying talent which is dead in action. ~~I think~~

AT ***Concentration... Miss Blood:*** She was very concentrated, nothing diffuse about her. Anything that was going to happen to her and the Princess was organized in advance by her. Gertrude used to call that little type of them— the physically very small ones— 'Generals.' She looked like Maria Louisa, very delicate.

*

NB-B #24

For long book use the aspect of nature as beginning in a baby and in children not always in men and women as in this book.

LK ***For long book... nature as beginning in a baby... not... as in this book:*** Reference may be to the Martha chapter [MA 378ff.] (as opposed to the Mrs. Hersland and Servants chapter currently being written) rather than to *A Long Gay Book*. It is the Martha chapter that discusses at length "the aspect of nature as beginning in a baby and in children." The opening paragraphs of *A Long Gay Book* discuss babies in a different context. General plan for the end of the chapter on "Mrs. Hersland and the Servants", used in MA 244–285.

*

Notebook C

NB-C #1

(Sane as NB-B #23)

NB-C #2

Manguin, [Vedresch?], Fabri, Schukin, Thorold are of the earthy, their talent and their handwriting Leon was too, Adele Solomons was too. Alice Klauber uncertain. Mary Houghton Alice not. Helene is and Gracie Gassette. Bruce uncertain. Frost is. All these women like their women uncertain. Puy uncertain not.

Uncle Sol and Fred resisting, Edmund Houghton too I think. Alexandre attacking.

*

NB-C #3

Dave, Bianco, Kremnitz, Mildred.

Their reaction is complete and instant, there is no accumulation, they do not take shape of impression[s] like the sensitive instrument, they do not change themselves, assume a form as all earthy people must to take an impression, to make themselves plastic, they react instantly and completely, their judgement is as complete as their sensation and therefor they so quickly become historic, as Alice said of Mildred, not of our generation as Fernande said of Kremnitz. This complete and more or less brilliant creation of impression or judgment to stimulus is their strength and with youth it passes. They are themselves but as Bianco said to me any of his judgments are as valuable as any other. Any of his impressions are as valuable as any other. Therefor these people though having the successful instinct are not ultimately really successful. They are left behind. They are often actors or hangers on to literary or artistic groups. ~~Wot wit~~

AT ***quickly become historic… Mildred:*** [Mildred Aldrich] She was the last person interested in historical events. No, she was thoroughly of her epoch and completely démodé. She could remember her own history since the time she was four. Still at sixty, she was only four, so she wasn't an aged one but a child, and still went way back. Gertrude wanted Mildred to write her memoirs, because she told them so wonderfully, and she had hilarious and charming tales to tell. She knew the secret history of everybody, and there probably was never anyone so thoroughly informed on private lives as Mildred Aldrich. Her whole correspondence, all that came to her, was one long indiscretion, and I remember the weeks she spent burning and destroying all her correspondence so that it would never come to light after her death. But she did one chapter of her memoirs, and it sounded like an article for a country magazine, so Gertrude didn't urge her to exhaust herself.

Kremnitz: He was outside the Montmartre group, a light relief in the background. Both he and Pablo had big dogs. He was French and had been English.

*

NB-C #4

I ain't sure but I think that Etta Cone, Annie Lyell and others are the ind. dep. version of Mabel Haynes et al. It is a type that in earthiness finds its legitimate expression, in engulfing, it does not find legitimate expression in attacking it could not and in its form [?] it must be sensitive. It then goes into Mamie Weeks et al. They are not in any sense instrument but they ought to be superior engulfers and they are neither really superior, really sensitive or really engulfing. They are practical and not earthy, they are not dominating, they don't take any hold on anyone. Got to do them once.

AT ***Annie Lyell:*** From California. She was Gertrude's classmate at Johns Hopkins, then a doctor in San Francisco. There were very tall stories about her, and they turned out to be true. She was pure New England, an only child, and very beautiful. She couldn't have that kind of looks and act up to it and dress up to it and not be 'wrong.'

*

NB-C #5

The german lady's friend who gets drunk Miss Old. is the bottom of sensitive kind. That makes Alice to Mabel Weeks et al.

*

NB-C #6

Group. Duse, Mme Demarez, Miss Donner, Adele Oppenheimer Alice Klauber, Margaret Lewis and Isadora Duncan. The same kind of energy and intelligence the same way of being possessed. Mrs. Bremer-Lee [?], possibly the same kind. Enlarge on this sometimes when the idea is clearer. Some connection with Emma Lootz.

Bremer true creative dependent independent instrument Harriet Clarke also.

*

NB-C #7

Emma Lootz sort of stands between Miss Mars, Marie, Mary Maxworthing et al and Isadore and Margaret Lewis on the other She is nearer Miss Mars. She has the same kind of dubious honesty like Marie.

Isadora goes over then into the instrument possessed Harriet Clarke [impersonality?] thereof.

*

NB-C #8

Remember that Florence Sabine had the student quality of Sally. What Leo calls pedestrian. Loeser is like Tommy. The family runs so.

Edstrom the in between this group and the aggressive childish crowd of Frank and the hero of Idyl of Red Gulch and Whiskey Bill, Edmund Houghton et al. Then I say comes Edstrom in the middle then Sally Tommy then Emily Dawson then Loeser then Mamie Weeks then Alice Toklas then B.B. then others.

Matisse and Van Dongen are the genius expression of this. ~~toward the~~ their kind of sexuality. They come Matisse between Edstrom and Frank et al, egotists. Van Dongen between Edstrom and Tommy and Loeser. Practical, brutal, not earthy, but brutally sexual. Remorseless, cowardly but not fearful. This business about our giving back the pictures and the terrible things Matisse might do and all he does is to hold my hand longer ~~reminds me~~ makes more marked his resemblance to David. It makes his tummy soft as Alice says of Edstrom. It makes it more striking that he is a coward but not fearful. Earthy ones are fearful. Edstrom is a coward but not fearful. Van Dongen and Matisse are bony handed, therefor they have a driving force, then go to Edstrom's hands which are soft to Tommy's and Mamie Weeks which are firm and sensitive. Sally's are near Edstrom's, not as decisive and more efficient. Matisse and Van Dongen then in the other direction go to Hutch and Bian[c]o and Dave Bachrach. That is the cruder practical and unsuccessful, the self-defensive brag with nothing really to defend. Matisse has a great deal to defend. This whole group are practical and simply brutally sexual, they have no poetry, they have a sense of practical interest [?] of objects, no sense of beauty of object like Leo Renoir group. No sense of the significance of objects like earthy group. When you get to BB you get a change from practical sense and sensitive emotion about objection to sensitive affection for object and a practical sense. B.B. is not a Bazaroff, because he has no deep ethical nature, all Bazaroffs are in essence ethical and fanatical, not by reason of their affection for object but by reason of their realisation of its symbolism. Pablo is saved from that because it is it itself that remains itself that makes it symbolic to him, he does not partly generalise it as do all the Bazarofs whether they are indep. dep. or dep. indep.

Loeser is earthy at bottom, he has so a sense of quality, a mixture of earthy, Chalfin, Carlo Platti bottom with Tommy top. he becomes more solidly earthy as he gets older, less a coward, straighter. Tommy Edstrom et al more cowardly as they get older. Whole subject of cowardice very interesting.

AT ***Whiskey Bill:*** A painter, a friend of all the American painters and a chronic drunk. Gertrude probably heard a great deal about him from Alfy Maurer.

Loeser: [Charles Loeser] Loeser, in Florence, was the one who had the Cezannes from Fabbri. He was the son of the man in Brooklyn who had the shop of the same name. Loeser had lots of money from the shop, and so had the Cezannes. Leo saw them there.

as Alice says of Edstrom: David Edstrom once asked me, when I was living in the flat at rue Notre Dame des Champs, to walk home with him. He told me all about his wife but made me promise not to tell the Steins the story. His wife was Cora Dounor, from Kalamazoo.

Van Dongen & Matisse… bony-handed… Edstrom's hands… soft: As for the hand reading business, Gertrude could do it better than Sarah who faked things always and was not completely honest about any of them. She gave this up for Christian Science because you were not supposed to read hands or do such things, and Gertrude more or less took it away from her.

LK ***Practical, brutal, not earthy…. cowardly but not fearful:*** "Practical" and "sordid" natures are mentioned very briefly in MA 224. This note specifically refers to the relation of cowardliness to fearfulness as it is discussed in MA 257. But though these categories are being used here in passages concerning the women Mabel Linker and Mary Maxworthing, they belong more fittingly to male characteristics as already defined in MA 150–159, and in the substance of this Note.

*

NB-C #9

Striking how Pollovetski was like Pach in his fashion of argufying, with Bruce. Both of them are of the very earthy type, with symbolism gone mad / or rather symbolism excessive and vague. Bru[c]e is a very wild but very genuine earthy type. Harriet is a little Mrs. Eddy. Derain and Sterne are romantics. Purman & Leo Friedman somewhat but not enough to interfere with their solidity or success. None of them have real emotion. Pollovetski has conceit to act for him as pride acts for Pach, to keep him from hearing.

AT ***Pach:*** Once Pach asked me to do some typing for him for an article on Renoir, and to thank me for my help, he enclosed a copy of a letter from Renoir. The copy had been copied by Pach in Renoir's handwriting.

LK ***Pollovetski:*** Charles Ezekiel Polowetski (1884–1955), an American painter. Studied in U.S. and Paris, exhibited in New York.

*

NB-C #10

Isadora Duncan to Margaret Lewis.

Nadelman Alexandre Heiroth plus Salmon = Goethe. Leo goes on from this group.

*

NB-C #11

Brenner instrument earthy for form and feeling, Edstrom practical aggressive for expression and suggestion.

*

NB-C #12

Some dependent independents take themselves to be independent dependents and make attacking most of their living. Mrs. Kritchefsky, Dorothy Reade, Gracie Gassette are these kind. They are really more dependant than independant of dependance independance their strength is resisting, their bluff is attacking and they are full of stupid being that is in them as attacking. This is clear now, to be used later, friend of Martha's husband with this character. bring it out in that way difference between that kind of person and Sally, Martha, & Julia Dehning. Naturally Mr. & Mrs.

Kritchefski can't get along, same sexual type.

*

NB-C #13

Sally & Estell Rumbold the same value, Sally indepent dependent, Estelle earthy dependent independent. border line.

*

NB-C #14

Edgar Allen Poe, Alice plus I don't know, find out some day.

*

NB-C #15

Braque connects Leo Friedman to really sensibility and creativeness of Vollard Chalfin et al.

*

NB-C #16

Kahnweiler, little Hungarian with the curls continuation of Zobel, Barker, Carlo to a condition of mere practical cleverness with not a great deal of that. then through Ernie Keyser to Weber etc, sensibility but not sensitiveness.

*

NB-C #17

Remember that Mabels Weeks essential trouble is failure of self discipline in the sense of sensibility, the whole group have it when they have not efficient egotism, they have no real power of self-education. They have really ~~a~~ only a more or less highly developed reaction.

Edstrom a romantic flabby egotism Tommy Whittemore, Mabel Weeks, Sally, she has reflection, Alice, she has creation, then Sandy of Idyl of Red Gulch, Frank Jacott, Edmund Houghton, Whiskey Bill, John Noble, emotional sensitive weakness and simplemindedness makes these. Matisse conquers with a brutal egotism, Van Dongen by drowning himself in it till it comes out of him.

And so for one reason or another these are not simple instrument natures, they are self directed.

AT ***Frank Jacott... simplemindedness:*** The last thing Gertrude said to Bennett

Cerf when leaving the United States was not [as reported in his book] Bennett, you're nice but dumb, but Bennett, you're the lowest type. It was a quote that came from Nelly Jacott on her husband's reading.

*

NB-C #18

Berenson-Ka[n]dinskey-through to Heiroth-Nadelman-to Leo.

Salmon Nadelman Heiroth Chalfin, Chalfin has a different bottom, a Vollard bottom. They all have the same kind of girlishness that I mistook for weakness. A finicky choosing sense of beauty, a profound sensitiveness to lyrical beauty. In all somewhat creative. This trails off into a little more emptiness in Greene but there too there is essential strength then through Leo they go through to Matisse through to Edstrom then Tommy and Loeser et al -Pablo has a different kind of womanish behinderend, sometimes in hands, like Alexandre Leo's model & Jake Samuels. a large subject. Through Frost Annette's group go into Zobel and Carlo and Barker. They also include Howard who touches them two ways and connects to Chalfin by the two ways seperately. Alfy is the most creative personality of the group. Kahnweiler and the little curly headed Hungarian are the completest and most unbottomed of the group. Clever imitative people react the way Edstrom et al do in their way, then you go on to Weber Keyser group. etc. Robert Kohn not earthy group and I think Manguin comes out of him, Fabre and Thorold earthy correlatives of his.

AT ***Salmon… girlishness that I mistook for weakness, a finicky choosing sense of beauty:*** Yes, for when he was young.

Greene: [Andrew Green] When he took off the cashmere shawls with which Leo and Gertrude had covered the paintings when they loaned him the flat, he complained later that he didn't like these paintings, but now he couldn't look at the others.

LK ***Salmon, Nadelman, Heiroth, Chalfin:*** [Concurrent with, and expands, NB8, #8]

*

NB-C #19

Resistance in Keysers sometime go into this even more elaborately. Sometime get it complete, its relation to earthyness & sordidness, practical nature resistance, practical nature attacking. A large subject.

*

NB-C #20

I think of Goethe and Frederick the Great as Jewish because they persistently and consciously ran themselves by their minds. They had great minds and used themselves to the full. This is different from like Roosevelt using all the mind you've got all the time. Leo would but doesn't not having resolution and singleness of purpose enough, also he is too enthusiastic and sensitive that is these run him even though they then don't obscure his mind because they don't, sensitive and enthusiastic like Mabe Weeks's group, only ~~with~~ in him this character flavors and interprets but does not govern. In B.B this running himself by his mind into being ethical having a halo of goodness and superiority is silly, his mind is good but not commensurate in quality the creative intuitiveness of his aesthetic affections.

Chalfin and Simon H run themselves by their moral energy that is their mind and not a spontaneous growth but it is stronger in Chalfin than his real ability, he earthy Braque like sensitiveness finicky delicacy and cleverness.

Edstrom runs himself by his mind too but only to win and he does win some but mostly his weaknesses are too many, his enthusiasm ~~etc~~ sensibility gone rotten. Brenner uses his mind to keep himself hard and he is right, his whole power of creation being instrument sensitiveness he has to keep hard to keep this power from being swamped, hard inside, persistent in his fanaticism, while Alice kept herself hard outside difference between dependent in. and independent dep. type. In Sally they don't work together when they do she is what Leo calls pedestrian but intermittently, sometimes in character reading by hands and in religion and in jewelry making they are fused on a higher plane, mostly she is intermittent in living attacking and sensitive. That is what Leo means by aesthetic integrity too hard work to do it in art. Emma must have as much common sense as she has to [keep] her vanity from swamping her and she uses her mind to keep it. all this may be called Jewish. incessant self-consciousness in directing oneself. Brenner with my bust very interesting. Makes himself an instrument started in to construct a combination that needs earthy bottom like Cezanne or Pablo or mine, couldn't do it possibly, now he is the completed instrument.

LK ***Goethe and Frederick the Great… consciously ran themselves by their***

minds. [Expands NB8, #13. Compare to text, MA 365, and to LK Notes for NB-E #5,6, and 7.]

Brenner with my bust very interesting: [Dating: Brenner was doing a bust of GS February 26, 1909 and later.]

*

NB-C #21

My estimate of Brenner was after all about right, not of Nadelman he and Alexandre like Pablo & Matisse have a maleness that belongs to genius. Moi aussi, perhaps.

*

Note #8

Feneon tabby cat + adolescent—adolescent, sensitive finer type of morality man of the world not ethical

*

Spicer Simpson and P.L. [Turze?] Mabel H. connecting link to beauty ~~group~~ idealist and tabby cat to Roche et co. and they through Leo F. to Stern & Derain to beauty and through Fred and [James?] to business men.

*

NB-C #22

Feneon—Pritchard—tabby-cat Carlo Platdi—Speicer-Simpson - Lafarge, good, fin as the french say -tall and gentle.

*

NB-C #23

Matisse and drama—Sally—Tintoretto, Rant in place of action. Sally has no essential originality because she has only emotional sympathetic attractedness, this gives her an immense capacity for entering into everybody's ideas and feelings and as she is clever and has the patient continuosity of her kind, Florence Sabine et al which is as near as they the fairly pure ones, comes to real quality of student, it is college girl type of faithful studentship -Sally has not real intuition, she does not penetrate into the thing she follows enough to create them not enough to ever illuminate them, she pretty completely realises them but she gives them nothing except her ~~foll~~ following. So she realised Adele, and Weil and Jaehner, and

Leo and me and Mrs. Eddy and Mike. She can only illuminate a personality like hers but lesser as in the case of Bird. Edstrom's emotionality is not that it is really at moments illuminating, really creatively intuitive. Of course BB's is brilliantly affectionate intuitively creative, I think this is really now a realisation of Sally.

Finis

AT ***So Sarah realized... Jaehner:*** [Jaehne] There was an art dealer in San Francisco then who was educating the city for Chinese art, and it was through him that Sarah got her objects and furnishings. She had started her artistic career with early nineteenth century mahogany and brass candlesticks, but as the Chinese idiom was becoming increasingly her own, she threw over the mahogany and candlesticks for Chinese things, and did so at the same time that Jaehne, the dealer, was doing it.

Sarah finally got Mike to back Jaehne for a trip to China, and Mike did it just as he had given Jaehne money previously to buy Chinese things. Jaehne was an unscrupulous man, left scandals in his wake, weird and wonderful. There was something reptilian about Jaehne.

There was also Olga Ackerman, a woman of extraordinary taste, with beautiful, delicate, slightly animal brown eyes. Sarah was very jealous of her, but she learned all about Oriental art from her. Sarah, when she furnished her flats [in San Francisco], did it on Mrs. Ackerman's lines. She had no taste but an instinct for acquisition, and always knew how to use well the taste of others.

*

NB-C #24

Alice definitively attacking, Leo considerable, B.B. at. but very little, Wm. James at. considerable, Sally like Alice definitive, Bruce resisting, Bianco resisting, Stell on the border land, Therese resisting, Annette resisting attacking, Brenner ressisting to the point of maniacal attacking, Mrs. Berenson attacking, Neith resist. Hutch attack find out about Edmund & Mary, Algar resisting, Therese attacking Manguin attacking Mrs. resisting, Adele Jaffa resisting, Meyer attacking, Alexandre Heiroth attack, Maria resist. etc. etc.

Laurie Strauss attack, Mr. & Mrs. Kritchefsky both resisting, Olga attack, Mme Vernot, Helene, Gracie Gassette resist. Jeanne Boiffard border line, Fernand attack Simon H. attack, Pablo resist. Nadelman Roche attack. Vlaminck resist. Leo Milzeiner resist, Mrs. Milzeiner, Bird attack -Uncle Sol uncertain, Emma border line but attacking, Will resisting, Marion and Allan don't know.

AT ***Mr. & Mrs. Kritchefsky:*** A Russian, and her husband a dentist, both of whom Gertrude knew through Ella Mielziner.

*

NB-C #25

Max Jacob, like Simon H. and Laurie, has the same sexual tendencies, Simon H. & Max are nearer the neutral line between the two kinds like Uncle Sol and Fred than Laurie is.

Nadelman is at times very like Paderewski, he has that same kind of sensibility like Alexandre and I think they then go into Tommy Whittemore in one direction and into B.B. and finally threw Jaehne and Valloton arrive somewhere. The ~~Relatio~~ kind of sensibility in Nadelman enormously interesting. Alexandre Paderewski and Salmon.

Relation of Purman brutality in manners with essential worldliness and insensibility to Pritchard and Spicer Simpson, and to Mike.

Pritchard connects to Feneon on the side of his sensibility, Brenner is the dry bones of the harshness in Pablo and in me. Purman connects to Pablo by temperament to Matisse in the beginning by sexual attraction and now by worldliness. Bruce [?] is dep. ind.

AT ***Nadelman... like Paderewski... same kind of sensibility:*** Gertrude had originally said that he looked like Schiller, and it was a perfect description of him from his picture.

Paderewski... sensibility: When we saw him at the Place de l'Opera, Gertrude said, It is a sensitive face.

*

NB-C #26

Women who subdue those they need for loving, dep. ind. these have it in them to really love a man because he is great. Maria Heiroth, Mrs. Kritchefsky, Neith, etc. two numerous to mention, the other kind would like to but can't, their love is not dependent, May would like to, Sally & Bird tried it, couldn't. Fernande tries to, Alice don't.

It's a good theme.

AT ***Maria Heiroth:*** Maria Heiroth was married four times. She had divorced a Dane to marry Heiroth. We met her again in 1914 [?] at the Villa Curonia, and

Gertrude asked her what became of Heiroth. Well, let me just think, —and she thought a while, and then told Gertrude, who was surprised at how updated her information was. Oh yes, said Maria. We're in correspondence. I'm on good terms with all my husbands.

*

NB-C #27

Nadelman exalted the light would be glad to bathe itself in his statues, akin in a way to Hodder but not of the same family. Hodder a split idealist, Nadelman a complete thing. An artist an exalted sensitive scientist like Goethe.

AT ***Nadelman… an artist an exalted sensitive scientist like Goethe:*** Nadelman had come out of a three- or four-year retirement for his 1909 show in Paris, and he asked Leo, Gertrude and me to come. Leo was transported—this was the great genius. After leaving, Gertrude and Leo walked behind to discuss the show, and Nadelman and I walked ahead, and I got very friendly and easy with him.

In 1913, Nadelman left for England with the English girl who wanted to return to her home, and so there was never any great intimacy that grew up with the Steins. Gertrude was interested in is work, but not impressed. She hated sculpture anyhow. Juan Gris said of it, The trouble with it is they can walk around it and see all sides of it and that's a mistake.

LK ***Nadelman:*** Note written after viewing the Nadelman exhibition in March 1909 with AT and Leo. Andre Gide was also at the exhibit. The entry in his Notebook on Nadelman's sculpture is counter to GS's: "Nadelman draws with a compass and sculpts by assembling rhomboids. He has discovered that every curve of the human body accompanies itself with a reciprocal curve, which opposes and corresponds to it. The harmony which results from these balancings smacks of theorems. The most astonishing thing however is that he works from the live model. He is young and has time to recapture nature. But I fear for an artist who separates himself from simplicity; I'm afraid he will not achieve complexity but only complication. Nadelman has known six years of misery; shut up in his dirty den, he seems to have nourished himself on plaster along; Balzac could have invented him. I saw him again yesterday in a little blue suit which doubtless he was wearing for the first time, talking with a very ordinary and ugly lady to whom he introduced me: it was Madame X… She said, indicating the rhomboidal back of one of the statues: 'That one! At least it's alive! It's not like their Venus de Milo! What's it to me that she should be beautiful? That, at least, is a real woman! It's alive!' And precisely no qualification could apply worse to Nadelman's art, which as yet has only technique, and that rudimentary. Doubtless this pleases [Leo] Stein, because it can be assimilated with effort. Stein is the American collector who has bought a lot of Matisse. The Nadelman show had hardly opened when he had already bought up two-thirds or three-quarters of the drawings." The distance between Gide's art-world in Paris in 1909 and that of the Steins is measurable by their respective judgments of the Nadelman show. Gide shared the Parisians' stereotype of the Steins as "the rich American Jews," to which the Steins paid little attention. His characterization of Miss Toklas [his marginal note in his Notebooks for this passage is, "*c'est a dire,* AT"] is balanced by hers of him: "Was Gide there? So characteristic of him, so grey, to be unremembered."

*

NB-C #28

Sally passionately partisan emotional excitability, advances toward Edstrom & Florence Sabine, Alice a sensuous emotional poignant sensibility, advances toward Mabel Weeks, George Eliot Claribel and other side B.B.

*

NB-C #29

Note is missing

*

NB-C #30

Edstrom when he forgets his emotion and declares it to have been all the other ones doing attributes his ~~yiel~~ having yielded to his own weakness, that being the thing uppermost in him Frank Jacott attributes his to philanthropy, she was ~~lonesome you~~ lonesome you know and ~~through~~ threw herself on me took possession so what did I do but take care of her.

May put it down to they wanted it and she gave it but she had no responsibility it was because she was so game that she did it. Sally puts her yielding down to unsuspiciousness that is the reason she yields she is so easy and they all of them forget their emotion and so it must have been the other person's fault, it happened and they have no emotion as they remember it and so it must have been the other person. Use this if possible in the history of Martha.

LK [Corresponds to NB-A #15, NB3, #5 and Note #73]

Edstrom when he forgets his emotion: Planning Note and draft of text for MA 441, l. 44, to MA 442. The passage is expanded and repeated—to MA 44. In the final text, the names in the Note are converted as follows: Edstrom = Johnson; Frank Jacott = Frank Hackart; May [Bookstaver] = Mary Helbing; Sally [Stein] = Sarah Sands.

Use this if possible in the history of Martha: Anticipates by five or six months the writing of MA 441ff. in which the Note was used. NB-C #30 was written in May or June of 1909; the pages of the Martha chapter in which this Note appears were written in November or December of 1909.

*

NB-C #31

Alice says of herself no she is not conceited optimistic but not proud. this is like Sally's bottom but Alice has not the attack that makes her aggressive.

Greene and Lee resisting type not attacking grey and blue eyes and brown, attacking hazel and black.

Bruce self-hypnotised by the practical aspects of Matisse's work. His practical mind as shown in the first long discussion, the other hidden and sensitive and slow. Dep. ind, sure,

*

NB-C #32

A long book, a History of Everybody

In long book must go at great length into earthy and non-earthy practical type and their relation to sentimentality and babies, aunt hearts [?] mother hearts [?], Matisse and Pablo and everything.

*

Note #79

Go on to describe Hersland's relation to his wife, his relation to visitors, men and women, to his church, to his tradesmen. Then his relation to servants and to the governesses in the house and so to Madeleine Weiman and her family and his acquiescence in his wife's foolishness, then his wife's life and her relation to servants, paying one too much too [sic] spite her ~~family~~ when she was willing to take half, servant Mexican, snow, feather, servant just jealous of governess neve[r] get anybody to make turnovers like my turnovers, then german then seamstresses spit curls bend back fingers

LK ***Go on to describe Hersland's… governesses in the house:*** [General planning note in preparation for Chapter on "Mrs. Hersland and the servants."]

*

Note #81

Work it out carefully that Madeleine Weiman and Mrs. Hersland were the same kind and Madeleine owned her by letting her be important to her and so possessed her and her memory completely to the infuriation of her children. the gentleness and timidity and beauty of her appealed to her to make her own her. A complicated but interesting study. finish up with that here and then more about it in Martha etc.

LK ***Work it out carefully… in Martha etc.*** Planning Note for MA 253–256.

*

Note #4

[...?] Rosenberg, the three sisters and mother,

LK ***Rosenberg, three sisters; mother:*** MA 193f. Madeleine Weiman and Mrs. H. story, MA 250–285.

*

Note #82

[Inserted later:] Biled [sic] [Build] up to form a resume of Mrs. Hersland.

Madeleine Weiman her kind of possessing has possession, she is owned by this feeling, by the need she has in her of owning and subduing. She has no weakening she has nothing ~~that is her difference fro~~ in her of bottom yielding, she has not any feeling that everything will give her winning, she has not any feeling that she ever will need saving, she has not any feeling that in killing she can always go on living, but she is strong in subduing some of such of them are strong in destroying.

This is the beginning for her.

LK ***Madeleine Weiman her kind of possessing … strong in destroying:*** Draft of text for MA 254–255.

*

Notebook 5

NB5, #1

Mrs. Hersland was never important for her children excepting to begin them. She never had ~~from them~~ ~~of~~ a feeling of herself to herself from them. She was of them until they were so big that she was lost among them, she was lost then between them and the father of them.

*

NB5, #2

The inevitable being in each one then is of the kind of being in them.

*

Note #83

After the first two governesses then at length types and Mrs. Hersland to Madeleine.

*

[Planned Text:] There are some women of the kind of them where the children are always a part of them where the children to them are always owned by them (dark eyed) Adele etc.

*

Mrs. Hersland a branch of this bring it out a propos of the servants etc. dependant independant [sic],

genial dramatic

reflective, resist material / creative practical / sensitive

attack.

*

Note #61

Governess

Madaleine Weiman,

her sister (Etta Cone)

Jeannette Weiman

Helen. (Bertha Fernande)

~~Eugenia~~ Weiman

Adolph Weiman

her brother make him like Roche, and so connect him with young David.*

Helen Weiman

perhaps Annette with Martha to attempt it and young David to become her ideal parting and all.

LK [Concurrent with Note #91]

Madeleine Weiman, her sister (Ætta Cone): Louise Wyman, first mentioned MA 257. A full description of her, MA 267–268. Etta Cone as model.

Helen. (Bertha Fernande): Helen Wyman, first mentioned MA 257. A full description of her, MA 266. As "spread" and "vague" as either Bertha Stein or Fernande Olivier.

Adolphe Weiman… make him like Roche: See footnote for Note #91

*

NB5 #4

The Weiman family were german american. The mother was always pretty german. No one of the children xcept perhaps the second one some ever knew very much what the father had in them. The children did not really know much about either of them, the Hersland's never had very much impression of them, nor indeed of any of the Weiman family except Madeleine, although they later came to know the others of them the two sisters and the brother very well in their later living. Every one had an impression that the daughter Louise knew what kind of woman the old german women and and what a kind of a man she had as husband but no one ever knew how they came to have this feeling that Louise had such a knowledge of them. This is now a history of the Weiman family and the living and being in all of the six of them, the mother and the father and the four children. Now there will be a history of Mrs. Hersland to them. Later there will be more history of them in the history of the [sic] each one of the three Hersland children. Now then for the six of them, the mother and father and the four children and Mrs. Hersland and a little Mr. Hersland to them.

LK ***The Weiman family… Mr. Hersland to them:*** Draft of text for MA 260–267.

*

Note #86

Describe the general life of the three children in relation to the father and mother, then father in general to the children and wife and then mother to the children then to the father then governess etc and so come back to the father and then to the children particular.

*

NB5 #3

This is now a history of the Hersland family being and of the being of the people they came to know in their living. There has now been some description of the Hersland family and their living in the middle of Mr. David Hersland and his wife Fanny Hersland. There has been already a little description of them. There will be later more description of them. There is now to be a beginning of the description of the being and the living in each of three Hersland children. There is now to be a beginning of description of the being of the oldest of them, there is now to be a beginning of a description of the being of Martha Hersland and a beginning of a description of the being in every one she ever came to know in her living.

Later there will be a description of the being in all these of the Hersland children and a description of every one they ever came to know in their living. Now there is a beginning of description of the being in ~~the~~ the oldest one of these children, now there is ~~a begin~~ commencing a beginning of a description of the being and the living in Martha Hersland the oldest of the children and of every one she ever knew in her living. To begin then.

LK ***This is now a history... To begin then.*** Draft of text for concluding paragraph of the "Mrs. Hersland and the Servants" chapter, MA 285.

*

NB5, #5

Bentley—Record-Herald

*

Notebook 8

NB8, #1

Refer to after dog-eared page for Martha

*

NB8, #4

Madeleine Weiman had had a pretty good education. he knew french and german, not as the first governess the Herslands had had knew [sic] them but well enough to teach them. She was not a musician but she knew enough music to oversee the Hersland children's practicing, she knew enough music to begin. She had a good enough english education, She had a good enough American governess training. She and her younger sister Helen were the only ones of her family who had had much education. Helen was more modern than Madeleine in her feeling. Later when Helen Weiman came to know the Hersland young people, she was more of them than any of her family for she was more modern, not more American perhaps but really more modern, anyway more of them, the Hersland children than Madeleine or Frank or Louise ever were of their generation. They had not many friends then the Weiman family. Frank & Helen Weiman were the first ones to have friends of people around them.

Now begin again with the beginning here. Then go on with what happened to each of the Weiman children then give a little description of the old folks and then of Madeleine again and then a little of the Herslands to her all of them and then her leaving them and the trouble and so to the history of Martha through her living not ~~then~~ being important then to the children.

LK ***Madeleine Weiman had had… people around them:*** Draft of text for MA 265–266.

Now begin again with the beginning: [i.e., the beginning of "the Wymans"] Plan for MA 266: "There were then in the Wyman family six of them…."

…Then go on… the Weiman children… Plan for MA 266–269, as follows:

- Helen Wyman: MA 266.
- Louse Wyman: MA 267.
- Frank Wyman: MA 268.

of Madeleine again: Plan for MA 269.

then a little of the Herslands to them: Plan for MA 269,

her leaving them and the troubles: [I.e., Madeleine's and John Summer's troubles] Plan for MA 270

and so to the history of Martha: Plan, beginning MA 285.

her living not being important to the children: [I.e., Madeleine's] Plan for MA 270.

*

Note #84

In the description of the sisters of Madeleine Weiman bring out the spinster character of Etta and how little their real being comes out of the bottom nature of them to almost every one that knows them and then more and more in their later living it comes out in them.

LK ***spinster character of Etta:*** MA 267, l. 20 to 268, l. 12. [See Note #61]

*

Note #84a

Same as Note #75.

Use the part of his stubborness [sic] in carrying out some little beginning in eating or doctoring. like S [?]. the pride in him that did not touch the big beginning in him.

Use Meininger a good deal later on. let him and his wife try to manage Martha when she first gets home to marry her to a son of theirs by Mrs.

LK Notes #84, #84a, both concurrent with the writing of text: "A man in his living has many things inside him…In many men there is a mixture in them…bottom nature…mixed [with] the nature of other kinds of men."

*

NB8, #3

The mother Mrs. Weiman had independent dependent nature in her. The second daughter Louise and the youngest daughter Helen were of her. The father Mr. Weiman had dependent independent earthy instrument nature, the son Frank and the eldest daughter Madeleine were of this nature.

The youngest daughter Helen was all spread and all vague in her independent ~~in~~dependent nature. The second daughter Louise was almost as concentrated as her mother but there was less to her nature. The son Frank was almost as vague in his dependent independent nature as his father, in the eldest daughter the dependent independent nature was more concentrated to make her, but it did not make her really an efficient nature, she had [sic] really resistance in her.

LK ***The mother Mrs. Weiman… resistance in her:*** Draft of text for MA 27.

*

Note #98

[…] the same being in her. Later there will be more history of her.

Now go on the same way and [do it?] for Frank and so lead back to the father and then for Madeleine and then mother when they were nagging her.

The mother Mrs. Weiman had independent dependent nature in her

After get through with Madeleine repeat this about Mrs. Weiman etc. then go on again to the Hersland middle living and how the children did not miss her when she left them.

LK ***more history of her:*** Draft for text, MA 268.

Now go on… for Frank and so lead back to the father: Planning Note for Frank, described in terms of his relation to his father, in MA 263.

and then mother… nagging her: Plan, MA 274. "… her defending her against her nagging father and mother was not really important being in her…" MA 274.

The mother Mrs. Weiman… independent dependent nature in her: Expanded in MA 268–269.

after getting through with Madeleine… Plan, MA 269–271.

repeat this about Mrs. Weiman: Plan, MA 271,

go on again to the Hersland middle living: Plan, MA 273f.

*

NB8, #5

In Mr. Hersland his early living, then in his middle, was not in him in his feeling.

Mr. Hersland in his middle living had then not in him his early living in his feeling, he had sometimes in his talking.

Then go on with this in this respect, relation of talking to feeling and then to general discourse on instrument being dependent ind. being.

resisting was their way of winning fighting resisting was not their only way of winning. ~~stup~~ resisting and yielding were not in them stupid doing.

LK ***In Mr. Hersland his early living … sometimes in his talking:*** Draft of text, MA 273.

…talking to feeling… instrument being dependent ind. being: Plan for MA 273–275.

resisting was not their way of winning fighting… stupid doing: Draft of text, MA 275.

*

NB8, #6

In Mr. Hersland, ~~the~~ his early living was not ~~in him~~ [sic], then in his middle living, in him in his feeling.

LK ***In Mr. Hersland… in his feeling:*** Draft of text, MA 273.

*

NB8, #7

It is interesting in each one the success and failure that one has in living. Every one has their own nature in them. This comes out of them as repeating. This comes out of them as making success failure in their living.

LK ***It is interesting in each one:*** Draft of text, MA 278.

*

NB8, #8

Salmon, Nadelman, Alexandre, Chalfin. Chalfin has a different bottom a Vollard bottom. They all have the same kind of girlishness that I mistook for weakness. A finicky choosing sense of beauty, a profound sensitiveness to lyrical beauty. In all somewhat creative This trails off into a little more emptiness in Greene but there too there is essential strength, then through Leo they go to Matisse & Edstrom. Through Frost Annette group go into Zobel & Carlo, and Barker. They also include Howard. Alfy is the most creative personality of the group.

LK [Concurrent with NB-C #18]

*

NB8, #10

When Mat- & Pablo met they both said how the other had grown old.

*

NB8, #11

Thank you kindly but I guess I had rather not. The first invitation is ~~not~~ now nicely outlawed and for the rest your automobile hospitality to me lacks graciousness to the degree of making it some[what] indigestible. Thank you just the same.

*

NB8, #13

I think of Goethe and Frederick the Great as Jewish because they persistently and consciously educated themselves, consciously ran themselves by their minds. They had great minds and used them to the full. This is different from like Roosevelt using all the mind youve got all the time. Leo would but doesn't not having resolution and singleness of purpose enough, tho he is too enthusiastic and sensitive like Mabel Week's group, only with him this character flavors and interrupts but does not grow. In B.B. this running himself by his mind into being good having a halo of goodness and superiority is silly, his mind is good but not commensurate to the creative intuitiveness of his affections, Edstrom runs himself by his mind too but only to win and he does some but mostly his weaknesses are too many his enthusiasm etc gone rotten. Brenner uses his mind to keep himself hard and he is right, his whole power of creation being instrument sensitiveness he has to keep hard to keep this power [from] being swamped, hard inside, while Alice kept herself hard outside, dependent ~~in.~~ independent type. Sally they don't work together but intermittently one and then the other, Attacking and sensitiveness. Emmas [sic] must have as much common sense as she has to keep her vanity from swamping her and she uses her mind to keep it. All jewish types.

LK [Concurrent with NB-C #20]

*

NB8, #14

Little by little they are not so young those being young. Little by little they are not so young and they are then so young they are then quite young. The girl at the [toloumests?] . The horseback [?] [hunchback?] boy who had a father, the one who hadn't, [...]

LK MA 261ff.

*

Note #7

They had their regular daily public school living, (enlarge that)
They had all the feeling of being country children (enlarge that)
they had around them for them poor queer people around them.

LK See above NB8, #14

*

NB8, #15

They had their regular public school living, they had all the feeling of country children, they had too every kind of fancy education, anything that their father could think would be good for them.

LK See above NB8, #14

*

NB8, #16

They had every kind of fancy education (enlarge that) then go on to eating and doctoring and so to the father's [probably] living

LK See MA 269ff.

*

NB8, #17

N.B. Young David was an individual. Alfy like Sterne had all the ear-marks but missed. Martha missed it entirely.

This whole question of individual most important. Chalfin just touches but ain't. Weber & Manguin are but weak. Valloton, Greene & to a lesser degree Chalfin is but failures. Matisse, Pablo, Hutch really are. Mike is in posse, sometimes in esse.

LK See MA 250ff.

*

NB8, #18

[...] to possess. Nadelman and Alexandre really passionate insight and realisation of women and men and beauty. Hodder also but mixed with other things and so Byronic & Romantic and false instead of purely poetic. He liked Martha for her courage and honesty. He mistook it for profundity. Edstrom emotional passion, they have true passion concentrated to the point [of] vision. True poets, simple, sensuous and passionate. Leo trails off from them. All different from the earthy in every respect. relation to object in both as described before.

LK [Duplicated in NB-D #15]

*

NB8, #19

Relation between appealingness and sweetness. B.B. not au fond sweet. Likes the sensation of being ~~tortued~~ tortured, it is to him a sexual sensation. Where there is more physique as in Valloton and Weisman [?] Weiman [?] sexuality is intensive, this is all B.B. sexuality amounts to, he is not sweet, he is self-centred. Howard appealing, more sweet but not so much so as he seems. ~~The~~ Insensitive au fond like Annette. Real but not profound ethical instinct, not as profound as Annette.

Pynsent probably also Purman et al.

LK [Duplicate in NB-D #17]

*

NB8, #20

Edmund & Henry Clay, Leigh Hunt, probably resisting type in whom resistance has lost its meaning, and attacking comes more nearly to be winning fighting. Driver [?] boy bridged over Dr. Hamburger to Leon & Raymond, and then to Zobel. hands. Mary H. connects to B.B. and thence to Miss Blood & Alice. B.B.'s type and Loeser's type can become real vagabonds earthy, dirty.

LK [Concurrent with and expanded in NB-D #18, #19, #20, #21]

*

NB8, #21

~~C'est~~ Vous avez decide que vous vous voulez que nous serons pour vous le connaiseur [?] comme les autres [?] d'acheter quelque chose quand vous voulez quelque chose a pris [?] que vous ou Vollard demande, n'est ce pas. eh bien—vous pouvez pas avoir le droit de demandez l'argent quand vous avez besoin et Leo pas le droit de choisir les chose [?] qu'il veut. Ca ce'st [sic] evident. Eh bien dans le dernier anne nous avons vous donnez a entre [pour?] [-?-] 2,000 & 2,500 francs. Avec le grand tableau ca serai juste. Maintenant il faut que vous [-?-] le grand tableau pour le faire acerchable [sic] et maintenant nous sommes les acheteurs comme les autres ~~et plus que ca~~ n'ect [sic] pas.

LK A note from Gertrude to the art-dealer Vallotton. Gertrude's French was abominable, and her handwriting in this instance also so. The note appears to concern a transaction or transactions between herself and her brother Leo with Vallotton. Whether in French or in translation, the text appears to be resistant to clear meaning:

"~~It's~~ You've decided that you want that we will be your connoisseur [?] like other [?] to buy something when you want something took [?] or you Vollard demand is not ee. Well—you can not have the right to ask for money when you ned and Leo have the right to choose the thing he wants [?]. It i'ts [sic] obvious. Well in the last year we have between you give [to?] [-?-] 2,000 & 2,500 francs. With the big picture ca be fair. Now you have to [-?-] the big picture to make acerchable [sic] and now we are like other buyers ~~and that it does~~ n'ect [sic] not.

*

Notebook D

NB-D #1

Sally—Mamie Weeks—Claribel—Alice—Maria (Harriet's servant)—Spinster character after Sally, Alice and Maria are in temperament like Claribel. Harriet has character like Claribel not nature. In all of the group emotionally not sexually passionate, Olga pathological version.

Helen & Gracie Gassette Resistant conservatism, takes the form of incessant attacking. Some kinds of attacking take the form of persisting ~~att~~ resisting. Bruce ought to be resisting to keep himself free inside—but he destroys his real resistance by excess of reasonableness turns it into dogged persistent attacking turns himself into attacking. Not very certain.

Berenson and Vieisseux same ~~ty~~ type. Berenson and Alice not ~~essen~~ au fond moral people, unmoral and so to Mary Houghton who is unmoral to the point of possible fanaticism. Berenson and Alice just plain unmoral. Hutch whom we used to speak of as unmoral is really passionately moral. Valloton, Simon H., Francis Pollak all unmoral in their various disguises. All these are unmoral in every way, they have not any of them a passion for truth really, nor an aesthetic passion, none of t[hem] can have really an abstract passion, they are therefor unmoral.

AT ***Maria (Harriet's servant):*** [Marie Lescaugas] Harriet's and my Basque servant at the rue Notre Dame des Champs flat, a very good cook but an unpleasant creature. She was there probably in the winter of 1908–9. There was too much elaboration in her speech and in her service. She went into ecstasies about her service, about what was at market, it was a great bore. We didn't want her back after the summer of 1909.

The first servant we had engaged was by the method Gertrude suggested. How do we know, we asked her, if she's good? You ask them if they can make an omelet, said Gertrude We kept that one for three days. After her was Marie Lescaugas—the one in the Note—and then a Marie Enz, a Swiss.

Vieisseux: [Vieusseux] The library in Florence. It's the name of the library, but who, as a person?

*

NB-D #2

Berenson and Vieussiex same type, Berenson connecting this type the Valloton base and then through Vieusseux and the Turk who ordered the massacres and Klossinski to B.B., in in the other direction to Jake Samuels, Jaehne also of this. Not moral at bottom as Hutch is. Opportunists at bottom. Simon H. Francis etc. also connecting on to Hutch, the essentially ethical type almost fanatic, the people who feel, the Bazaroffs of the non-earthy type as Brenner is of the earthy. Simon H. the non-earthy type of Leo Friedman et al. Nervous but au fond impenetrable and un self fed. Leo F. and Francis Pollak, a queer combination now I think of it, both stimulated by Inez, more of this. Leo F's may be romanticists too like Sterne & Derain, don't really come in contact nor have things arise from within them. This not true of Berenson's group who feel passionate affection for success, for things, for scents and clothes, and good form and so are in relation and feel an intense relation to successful accessories, they are real to them, criticism to B.B. and influential people. (He did not know our connection with Matisse, that makes him more completely what I think him, more greatly it.) Not a real lover of truth from his nature but from his intellect and a lover of goodness from his affection for it (affection for Leo) (his appealing side) not from his own nature. Fools himself and everybody it is so real but not self-sprung. His relation to Neith very amusing, not extremely proud as Leos Oscars Hodders Nadelmans are. The group is not proud—in fact rather given to self-abasement. Sometimes sexual, might even be fanatic. They connect on also in another way to Raymond.

AT ***BB… lover of goodness… affection for it (affection for Leo):*** It was more like a familiar attitude than affection. This could be Gertrude judging Leo gently now.

*

NB-D #3

Alice is of the St. Theresa type.

Demarez and Donner St. Katherine type ~~loving fo~~ Mrs. Eddy, like Adele Jaffa.

Sally's type, that is the student type Miss Douglas the idealist of other's ideas, the kind of women who think themselves student Florence Sabine, who are students but without any originality ~~or~~ because with their kind of thinking you must have power of abstract thought to be something. That is not true of either the St. Katherine & St. Theresa type they can be original by virtue of their personality of their passion, of their love or meekness or force, same of Mrs. Eddy. They can be practical and original, Sally's type not, these must be abstract thinkers to be original and none of them are, Mabel Weeks connects them by the purity of her ~~idealistic~~ idolizing emotional passion to Alice and St. Therese. Claribel also this.

AT ***Alice Toklas… St. Theresa type… St. Katherine:*** There was a book about St, Katherine at the time that Gertrude was familiar with. St. Katherine's mysticism was out of it a little then.

St. Therese didn't know herself apart from the Christ, if there was anything apart. She was altogether in her mysticism, it was her. In Four Saints in Three Acts, St. Therese 'indoors and out of doors' meant merely that she could be the practical saint only because she was so completely certain. She could be both of the mystic experience and of the life of the founding 'houses,' or orders.

This note was written of course before we went to Avila [in 1912]. I only knew St. Therese after the visit to Avila. St. Ignatius is commonly known to San Franciscans because of the St. Ignatius Church and the Jesuit Fathers there, and they were of enormous influence, so San Franciscans felt at home with him. I had known St. Therese only vaguely before Spain. At Avila, you can't escape her.

[When asked in what sense Gertrude thought of her as 'the St. Therese type,' Miss Toklas made no response, and then urged, did, with enormous reluctance and some anger. Nevertheless, her response, pained and hesitant, was: 'Because I felt toward Gertrude as St. Therese felt toward the Christ. For me, it was the same experience and the same relation.' A long pause, and then, blunt anger: 'It was stupid of you to ask.' It was.]

*

NB-D #4

Mrs. Eddy and Adele Solomons resisting to attacking, successful and active versions of Gracie Gassette and Helene & Dorothea Reade.

Very interesting the way Claribel & Alice and Dorothea and Adele Solomons come together with different tops. Adele Oppenheimer much closer to Miss Donner that kind of bottom. Remember the quality of personal movement in Gracie and Helene sure this is in Mrs. Eddy and Adele.

Resistance complete and completely disguised as attack. Bruce and Bianco like Uncle Sol really depen. ind. type but in Uncle Sol completely balanced in Bruce very badly adjusted in Bianco almost the other relation and so he fails. Sterne perfect adjustment. Fred Stein not he is of the attacking type, not like his father, weakish but attacking, well balanced like his father. Dolene like I don't know have to see her again.

AT ***Bianco:*** A blond Italian who married an English woman. He was the boy who played the game, 'Miss Levy.' His wife was the hard-working, devoted English sister of Eugene O'Neill's first wife. Bianco was the head of Brentano's library in Paris, and made connections with book collectors in England, and made much money from this. Then he went to America. He was extremely amusing and witty.

*

NB-D #5

Mrs. Eddy, Adele Jaffa, Harriet, Helene and Gracie all have the same kind of stupidity, the same density in relation, the same incapacity to understand—must make this clearer sometime, they have all of them the same kind of stupidity dependent independent Harriet as a type, and then the rest. It will be important.

*

NB-D #6

George Elliot was of St. Therese's type in fact very close to her. Alice's resemblance to George Elliot interesting in this connection.

Mrs. Hodder nearer Miss Donner I think.

Alice does not give me a feeling for beauty. The whole character of St. Theresa's visions in that respect differ from those of St. Katherine. They are about beauty not in or of beauty.

~~Nadelman~~ St. Katherine dep. indep. so different fundamentally.

*

NB-D #7

Nadelman and Alexandre Heiroth ind. dep. and they do poignantly give real sense of beauty, directly not derived as in the case of George Elliot Alice et al who have on that side emotion for beauty rather than passionate realisation of it. More than that Alice is a real flavor person that is not in her passionate emotion but that excepting in relation to me does not ~~in any way~~ at all govern her. In Edstrom Hodder et al, the idealists the emotion of beauty is not unified with the rest of them these stand between St. Therese group and Nadelman & Alexandre the true poets.

AT ***Alice... real flavor person:*** In Fiesole I was still fond of perfumes and indulged in them in those days. Once on one of our walks around the Fiesole hills, we passed a horrible smell in a field of cow-flop, and I said to Gertrude, who was standing utterly unconcerned beside me, Let's get out of here. That smell. What's the matter, said Gertrude. You're fond of smells, aren't you? You should want to know all smells.

*

NB-D #8

Sterne inside Leo Friedman Purman et al with a mixture of upper nature Leon Solomons inside insensitive romantic idealism, upper careful intelligent realisation of exact beauty. Not internally stimulated at all. He is beginning a little now to combine this exactness ~~of steady~~ with his idealistic romance. It is never really alive but is nearer it. He has combined now his early free hand beauty of line etc. with his painstaking observation of external facts of beauty. He is not scientific that is he has no power of generalisation, neither had Leo F, but they have an appearance of it when they combine their observation of beauty, with their romantic insensitive but perfectly formed, idealistic worldliness. So they have perfect tact and perfect stubbornness. They have not any real stupidity, they have not any real spontaneity.

*

NB-D #9

Nadelman like Leonardo when he is a scientist he is not an artist. Pablo and Michael Angelo are artist ~~wher~~ every moment of their being. Matisse and Delacroix are scientists only for the purposes of art never for the purposes of science. Leo and Renoir type, are artistically scientist, and artistically artists, their sense of beauty is their being. They are philosophers in that sense.

AT ***Nadelman... when a scientist... not an artist:*** Later, Gertrude said of him, It's a mistake to look like another man. Nadelman looked like Schiller and was after all not Schiller.

Leo and Renoir… sense of beauty is their being: Much later, Gertrude would have denied that 'sense of beauty was their being.' She lost interest in Renoir as a painter.

*

NB-D #10

Harriet is quite right to fear me, for her. The conviction of profound existence of earthyness is what made me realise her, that realisation would now, she not being ~~au fond~~ a profound nature would upset her.

*

NB-D #11

When Leo said that all classification is teleological I knew I was not a pragmatist I do not believe that, I believe in reality as Cezanne or Caliban believe in it. I believe in repetition. Yes. Always and always, Must write the hymn of repetition. Sterne gave me the right feeling of it.

AT ***not a pragmatist… must write the hymn of repetition:*** This must be the winter of 1908–9. I knew by then how much Gertrude was sure of herself and knew what she was doing. As for Leo, I did not suspect that the break between them was prepared so long ago.

Sterne gave me the right feeling of it: [A concurrently written note, NB3, #4, has the entry: 'Remember how Sterne sounded in my ears that day.'] During the cholera epidemic in Rome, Gertrude and I were the only other Americans [beside Sterne] there. He then took time to tell us all about his love affairs. He was not unattractive and had a great effect on women. Sterne could talk a long time about himself, telling story after story about women mostly, so that he felt more himself in talking his women than in other ways.

LK ***not a pragmatist:*** Leo's reference was to James' chapter, "Stream of Thought," in *Principles of Psychology. The Cambridge Dictionary of Psychology.* James takes as given that relations between things are equivalently experienced as the things themselves, consequently, "the only meaning of essence is teleological, and that classification and conception are purely teleological weapons of the mind." See "Three Stages" note NB14 #7.

*

NB-D #12

George Sand undoubtedly is of George Elliot's, Alice's family, thats easy, Mrs. Eddy & St. Theresa not so easy a connection to decide. St. Katherine certainly dep. ind. George Sand undoubdetly George Elliot, Mabel Weeks, Alice.

Marion Walker surely Adele, Mrs. Eddy, that is dep. ind. body movements of this group characteristic and yet analysis is very very difficult. Mary Houghton, ind. dep. I think certainly.

*

NB-D #13

Mrs. Oppenheimer and Mme. Vernot are the ~~pecu~~ complete ~~expres~~ left wing of Gracie Gassette and Helene, it is difficult to separate them from one like George Sand but I am more and more sure that she ~~is~~ is not of them but the ind. dep. With Mrs. Eddy & St. Theresa much harder to decide.

*

NB-D #14

B.B. et al not really flavor people as Alice and Neith
are because their desire for it and the passion of their affection makes it their possession. Their profound oportunism makes them real as a whole, which flavor people essentially are not. Flavor people do not ~~really~~ want to possess.

*

NB-D #15

Nadelman and Alexandre really passionate, insight and realisation of women and men and beauty. Hodder also but mixed with other things, so he becomes Byronic, ~~unl~~ and romantic instead of purely poetic. He liked Martha for her courage and honesty, he mistook it for profundity. ~~Edstrom~~ Edstrom emotional passion, they, Nadelman, Alexandre, et al, have pure passion ~~concentr~~ concentrated to the point of vision. True poets, simple ~~sensuos~~ sensuous and passionate, Leo trails off from them. All different from the earthy in every respect, relation to object in both, as described before.

LK [See NB8, #18 for duplicate Note.]

Hodder … becomes Byronic, and romantic: Note used in MA 445, l. 36–41.

True poets, simple sensuous and passionate... The phrase widely attributed to Coleridge, derived originally from Milton's "Tractate on Education". A note for MA 444–445. [Corresponds to Note #62, on MA 444]

relation to object ... as described before: The most extended treatment of the "relation to object" appears in NB-A #14 and NB-B #1.

*

NB-D #16

St. Theresa pretty nearly certainly Miss Blood to Alice, Mabel Weeks Sally et al.

Mrs. Duibukyo that is the Anne of Austria type are all ind. dep. resistance is stupid being in them, in Mrs. Eddy and Adele that is not so although apparently often it is equally stupid acting but as you know them better you realize that in Mrs. Eddy there is resisting that is stabbing attacking, in Anne of Austria there was stubborness that should have been stabbing attacking and as resisting it was stupid being. St. Theresa had attacking gay and sure attacking and sweet yielding, Mis s Donner has hard resisting and sweet emotion. This does hold good alright.

Alice Klauber and Bird. In Alice resisting was not stupid being though it often leads her to stupid acting, it kept her from stupid marrying, in Bird stubborn resisting is stupid acting it led her to stupid marrying and stupid education, her fighting her husband was attacking fighting with yielding to her family's directing. Her marrying Howard was yielding it was not fighting It was his winning. Her marrying her husband and her always keeping going in education is stupid resisting. All of Alice Toklas is yielding, is sensitive being, just enough fighting to keep on holding on to her friendly feeling.

AT ***Miss Blood:*** Gertrude saw her every summer in Florence and frequently in winter. he liked Gertrude and they laughed much together, amused by the same things. I have a definite memory of them together—Gertrude's full laugh and Florence Blood's English cackle.

Mrs. Duibukyo: Mme. Dubryko, an English born woman who married a Pole after being widowed by an Australian. The Pole took Christian Science as something he didn't know about and wouldn't find out. Mme. Dubryko once said to Sally, 'My dear, you are Christian but not Christian Science,' which half pleased Sally and half angered her. Mme. Dubryko's granddaughter became Allan Stein's first wife.

In Bird... is stupid acting: Marie Antoinette reminded Gertrude of Bird, with her general weakness and her having to get out of things by reliance on an outside force.

*

NB-D #17

Purman, & Leo Victor, & Sterne and Derain, the ladies loves them all. Goguin & Piot are of this family too. Piot must have looked very like Sterne in his youth. the difference between these and the adolescent headed kind Pach et al is very decided. These have slow struggling often never to the surface coming but real inner life. The difference in the quality of their hands is marked, Pach and Bruce and Roche, & Singer at Harvard Psych Lab. They are intelligent but not intellectual, romantic but not enthusiastic nor impetuous, facile but not clever, worldly but not calculating nor sordid, they are stubborn but not resolved or inspired Their reactions are perfectly attuned to get on. They impress women because they have all the allure of romance and idealism and they have no weaknesses. Their lack of weakness is their significant quality. They are to be differentiated from the Zobel & Carlo & Barker group who are all clever, not really sensitive but very nervously and critically poised, these have all the appearance of the weaknesses of the artistic temperament, they have not weakness really any more than the Purman group but they attract by the allure of it and with their cleverness and their real lack of sensibility, the Purman group attract by their apparent abandonment and romance without any weakness. Both these classes are the earthy type. They exist in the other but I have not them very well fixed yet.

A man like Dougherty is perhaps of it. Fred Stein, I am not very certain yet. A man like Degas is really intellectual, Howard combines the clever Barker class with the Annette group who have really inward spring of action

Mather and Berenson were an interesting contrast, Mather the really ethical type, Berenson the pure oportunist with an inspired affectionate passion for beauty. Degas I should imagine to be nearer to Mather. Berenson gets clearer to me always.

Relation between appealingness and sweetness. B.B. not au fond sweet. Likes the sensation of being tortured, it is to him a sexual sensation, where there is more physique as in Valloton and Vieisseux, sexuality is intense. This being tortured and being mellifulous is all B.B's sexuality amounts to, he is not sweet. He is self-centered. Mary Houghton is very close to him but without his halo of goodness, she is frankly unmoral. They are really very alike at the bottom. She is unmoral and could be a fanatic. He is an opportunist. She has real sexuality, he has almost none. They are both undoubtedly of the ind. dep. Mary has a Bertha chin. I like Berthas [made of lace?] so bertha-like. Howard is appealing more sweet but not so much so as he is appealing. Insensitive au fond like Annette. Real but not serious ethical impulse, not as serious as in Annette. ~~Pynse~~ Pynsent is probably of Purman et al kind.

AT ***Purman… and Derain:*** [Purrmann.] Gertrude associated them in their 'woodenness.' Derain was the first follower of Matisse and was the pet of Mme. Matisse who adored him. He was very young during this period. He had always been a Matisse follower, never Pablo's.

Piot: I knew Piot very superficially and Mme. Piot better. She was a very beautiful model whom Piot took down to Florence on their wedding trip. BB was very impressed with her, took her for a grande dame, and was disillusioned when he found out he was at the feet of a model who only appeared to be chic Parisienne. But all this happened after he gave Piot the order for the murals. BB doubled up when he found out. She had very sweet ways, was very charming, but she was what she was for all that.

Mather: Frank Jewett Mather and his sister. They were in Florence, and maybe saw the Steins in Paris once or twice. He later became the [New York] Times art critic.

LK ***Relation between appealingness and sweetness… Purman et al:*** [Copied and expanded from NB8, #19]

*

NB-D #18

Edward Houghton and Henry Clay and Leigh Hunt. hey may be made out of both ind. dep. & dep. ind. When ind. dep. they come out Whiskey Bill and Edstrom and Frank Jacott. They may also be the grey-eyed or blue-eyed resisting kind. Mike & Bruce. When resisting type they are it when resistance has lost its meaning, and attacking comes to be more nearly winning fighting. All the childishness, the stolidity of resisting in Purman et al is in these, and they do win out by resisting but only because the attacking winning in them makes them attractive enough so that people yield to the childish resisting in them because people want them so much they have to take them with them and as they are obstinate like a child in resistance there is no way to have them but to yield to them. In such of them then they have people yield to their resisting but the charm in them is in their attacking being. This is well true of Henry Clay and Edward Houghton. In these though and Bianco too is of them and Bruce resisting should be in them to give them power for fighting as in Brenner to give him power of instrument living, but in most of such of them resisting has lost its meaning and is in them just childish being. Of course in Bird you have stubborn being that also is empty resisting but in her stubborn being is always essentially stupid being, in Claribel it is more nearly like Edmund, only she is of the ind. dep. kind of being. All this is very important.

LK NB-D #18, 19, 20, 21 [All concurrent with, correspond to and elaborate NB8, #20]

*

NB-D #19

Dr. Hamburger can be connected on to Leon & Raymond and then to ~~Zobel~~ Zobel and Carlo. Sometime must get this group thoroughly cleared up. Barker too.

*

NB-D #20

Mary Houghton connects to B.B. and thence to St. Theresa, Miss Blood and Alice.

*

NB-D #21

Interesting B.B.'s type and Loeser's type can become real vagabonds easily. drink etc.

*

NB-D #22

Dolene & Etta are undoubtedly dep. ind. Claribel undoubtedly ind. dep.

*

NB-D #23

Emma ind.dep. she has some of this type of resistance in her case has meaning, she has really no winning fighting, it is resisting common-sense that is in her the real attraction, attacking in her is left in her only as vanity as curiosity as sordid criticism. This whole question of the type of practical nature in ind. dep. as different from that in dep. ind. is important. Attacking is a free movement in all ind. dep. a restrained one in dep. ind. like in Gracie & Helene. Maria Theresa was an admirable case of ind. dep. Frederick the Great was I think Dr. Hamburger Zobel kind.

*

NB-D #24

Harriet in anything she feels any knowledge in only judges by success. She has no realisation of inner quality except as measured by success and mostly by success to her. Her variations in her feeling about Sally, Miss Donner, Mrs. Dubuyko, are a constant expression of this in her. About Edstrom it was the same and about my literature. That is the reason why if she realises weakness ~~it is ho~~ in anyone it is hopeless because for her to recognise essential weakness in them in any way means that they have toward her failed in succeeding. Alice is the only exception and that is larger because she is to her a child, that is all amiable weakness. She has absolutely no real realisation of anything but success and in this way she connects on to Zobel et al. the clever people. It is because of this that she has no real doubt of herself but doubt of everything else. The essence of the spirit that denies, holds to herself and her criteria. This is where she is essentially different from Annette and Emma, who can recognise mystery, this lack in Harriet gives her that stupidity that is so astonishing and that in another way is evident in Howard. Howard though is nearer Annette. Harriet has the kind of stupidity that is like Zobel's etc. the sense for novelty and for effect, a quick reaction, not at all a practical mind, not a clear enough relation to causes to be a practical mind. That is the whole story, she has a little more an emotional sentimental slightly real relation to religion. Most of her though is this other. Her ethics are like her other reactions purely clever, worldly -successfully. This makes her a conservative as her kind are unless they are very weak and then they just go to pot, like Carlo, Zobel.

AT ***Mrs. Dubuyko:*** Mme. Dubuyko was a Christian Scientist of the better type.

Sarah treated her as an inferior. She became the grandmother-in-law of Allan.

Harriet... about Edstrom: It ended between them in the Spring of 1908 and was very formal between them after that. In the Autumn of 1908 Harriet and I went with him to see a collection of pictures, and by then it was quite formal.

Alice... is to her a child: Harriet felt about me what I admitted about myself, that I had no principles, that I had no wanting to be anything, that I made no distinction between failure and success, that I had my own distinctions which didn't change for anything. So, in that way Harriet thought of me as a child.

Harriet... emotional sentimental slightly real relation to religion: Gertrude's disappointment was great when she realized here that Harriet would do nothing with that small drop of religion that had come to her. She thought at first that Harriet would do something her own with the revelation she had had.

*

NB-D #25

Continues in NB-E #1

Gladys, Annie Lyell, english girl sleeping on train, woman I saw having hair washed all the same type, eyes, jaw and mouth. They are so to speak the ind. dep. of Etta Cone, Mabel Haynes, Annette, the Princess, et al. of this group Etta and the Princess are nearest to the sensitive type, least concentrated, but thats another matter. Gladys & Annie Lyell then are the ind. dep. of Mabel Haynes group, the same kind of jaw only with a suggestion of Bertha in it. Gladys has this hurling themselves in an egotistic ~~fl~~ mass at moments, mostly inert, they fall on to while the Mabel Haynes et al engulf. Both kinds are often spinsters because they cannot find the right stimulus to produce the attack or the engulf. They are not responsive, they are initial forces essentially. Mabel Haynes was perhaps the least so but was very much so. Gladys is it essentially, her emotionally, her responsive nature is superficial, the Hortense Federleicht quality, that is a covering, that keeps her in movement, for most of her type are stupid and inert xcept on grand occasions, they give an appearance of being empty but

AT ***Gladys:*** [Gladys Deacon.] She saw Gertrude frequently and alone in 1907 before I came over, and Gertrude had a long afternoon with her. Leo was always explaining her to me. Gertrude couldn't talk about all this much because while doing it, the writing wouldn't be clear. After her own explanation was finished, she felt that Leo was all wrong anyhow.

Leo dramatized her completely. He had her do all sorts of weird things to calm her because she was such a passionate nature. He had a fan of colored ribbons made to waft before her face as she lay resting. According to Leo, the real love of her life was the Crown Prince, who had been in love with her too, but she wasn't the love of his life. She wore the Hohenzollern ring he had given her which she refused to return when the affair was over.

the Princess: The Princess Ghika, an Austrian and Serbian Princess. Miss Blood and she shared the Gambaria in Florence.

Hortense Federleicht: I knew her in Aix-les-Bains in the Thirties and found her dull and uninteresting them. It is hard to realize how Gertrude could have been fascinated by her when she lay on the sofa in Baltimore and Hortense Federleicht played Grieg.

*

Notebook E

NB-E #1

Continues NB-D #25

they are never empty they are most complete in egotism, when they are in action they are grand, they are rarely in action. Mostly even when as in Annie Lyell's case they are in movement it is just the surface reacting.

*

NB-E #2

Nadelman is very interestingly connected to them, with him is is the reverse of Gladys' condition. In him the Alexandre the emotional sensitive burning passionate vibration is underneath and his upper nature which this and his intellect keeps constantly in motion is like this in Amy Lyell. The magnetic pole, that queer paleness they all have only in Nadelman there is the steady brilliant inside flame that gives this outer thing alive and moving. They are again allied to the Camillus Bush, Bruce, Roche, Singer, Pach group who all have mask like faces, but in all of this group there is not enough inner flame to keep them alive, these have not the great quality these others have, they have not ~~an abnormal~~ a completed vanity and egotism. Pach, Camillus Bush et al have most of them pride not vanity, they have individuality not egotism. Roche is the ~~nearest~~ nearest thing to ~~an~~ a connecting link there is. This all makes Nadelman much clearer to me. His vanity which is in that respect different from Alexandre's, Alexandre has inordinate ambition, Nadelman has all that bottom ambition, combined with all the vanity of Annie Lyell and Gladys. I doubt if Gladys gets much from emotional surface except vivacity. She is clear but not reactive au fond. She is not really responsive, she is a self-force.

*

NB-E#3

Tell the Purman story again as last night.

*

NB-E #4

Purman connects, Leo F. group to Jeanne Boiffard on the one hand and Mike on the other. He has a little sensibility a little flame but very small and when his resistance is worn down he is tremulous. He is made up of this and a Leo Friedman nature, the Leo F. nature is his insolence, his success with the ladies his worldlyness and his resistance and his intellect. This does not do much for him in his art, the little flame just keeps on burning but don't change much. It don't really come into relation with his Leo Friedman nature. That makes him gentle au fond and a bit timorous and nervous while the rest of his group are all emptily aggressive at bottom. They are not really egotists but they have all the ways and deeds of egotists. Purman then is au fond not forceful nor plastic but like Bruce and Mike, less but stronger than Bruce, less and less earthy than Mike. Derain had a little flame but through pride, and romance and therefor unteacheableness and no very great intellect he let it go out. Leo F. is the complete expression of it, no fire, play at romanticism, no real sensibility, complete success. Sterne combines with Leon, he has no fire, but a very little passion and with patience and dogged intelligence Leo thinks he can get a little flame lit. Goguin was like Derain but with more sensibility and much more intellect, and so he sometimes made a unity. Piot is like Sterne without the Leon combination and with a bottom watery weakness that connects him with Peduli and George Hildegrand without the practical whining enthusiasm and energy of those two.

AT ***Sterne... Leo thinks he can get a little flame lit.*** Leo didn't want pupils or followers, but an appreciative audience, people who believed what he said. He wanted people to listen not for their own material advantage or his but for something purer than that. It was different from Sarah, who was a materialist and wanted something in her hand, something she could look at.

Goguin: [Gauguin.] Gertrude and Leo had one each of Gauguin and Van Gogh; Gertrude lost interest in Gauguin first, then in Van Gogh. By 1908 it was altogether gone, as was her interest in Toulouse-Lautrec and Manguin and those.

Gertrude and Leo left the early Post-Impressionists at about the same time. Since I'm vague about the [Van Gogh and Gauguin] pictures, it must have been very shortly after I came.

Peduli: A collector in Florence who would go up into the hills and come down with a treasure. I saw him [at first] as a rather shabby man with a gift for finding things, but not at all. He turned out to be an Italian scholar and gentleman. He found many of the pieces of furniture that Gertrude and Leo bought, and very fine objects that Leo bought before Gertrude came over—the two wooden carved angels and the two marble heads.

George Hildebrant: The father of the friend that Jeff Salinger knew in Oakland.

*

NB-E #5

Claribel and George Sand.

Claribel & Berenson not slow-minded, ~~quick~~ earthy type slow-minded. Claribel long-winded, Berenson, mellifluous not clear-minded. Important and fundamental distinction, Sister Bertha needing her imagination [strict?], her sister, her sister living in a comically [?] storied [?] imagination. Claribel more practical than Etta. Alice connecting link between George Sand and George Elliot.

AT ***Claribel long-winded:*** Gertrude and Claribel used to walk to Johns Hopkins. Claribel was a teacher there after she discovered the things that passed under her microscope, as Gertrude put it. And Claribel was telling Gertrude something she did not have time to finish when they arrived. The next morning, she said, Good morning, Gertrude, and then continued with the phrase where she had left of the morning before. All this 'seduction' of Claribel's was done in a very gently, grand-manner way. Etta would call her 'Amaryllis.'

Sister Bertha: Sister Bertha was Brother Mosey's wife. It was the Baltimore way ['Sister'] of referring to relatives. If Gertrude had been pure Baltimore, she would have had to call her own sister Sister Bertha. Sister Bertha's husband bought an old house near Ashville on account of owning [the Cone] cotton mills. He worked up the gardens into a show-place at the end of the other century and permitted people to see it, with a sign saying, Drive no further. Sister Bertha would be very angry when people ignored the sign, and she would say, But it's the only house we have! [The name of the estate was Blowing Rock.] Etta would always say when she saw a place that was very beautiful, How like Blowing Rock, and then she would add, It's almost as fine as Blowing Rock, and Claribel would shake her head.

George Sand: I found in a rue de Fleurus bookshop George Sand's *Life* of herself in about twenty volumes. I got so engrossed and excited by it that Gertrude read it in French. Leo probably took it along when the books were divided.

LK NB-E #5, #6, #7

Berenson: The analysis of Berenson, the one who "for many years was baffling to me," is essayed here, MA 366–372, one of the longest and most detailed of the portraits of non-fictional people used in the MA. He is the fourth example in a list of ten variants of those who "run themselves by their minds," but of them, BB has the distinction of never having become "a whole one" for GS, and so couldn't be explained by her. The marginal note for MA 371 [Ms Note #55] tells us that the breakthrough came when the difficulty was cleared up by Leo, who explained that BB was "not a unit" at all, from which GS concluded that though he is compounded of all the elements of his kind, they are all in him in equal measure, and remain permanently unassimilable.

Notable about this entry is that as late as the Spring of 1909, Leo and GS were still capable of communicating in GS's private psychological language, that Leo was still consulted, and that he could and did respond, apparently willingly, in her terms. But in the novel's text, the revelation of BB's nature is attributed by GS to herself alone.

*

NB-E #6

Miss Donner type of slow minded religionist, Mme. Demarez also, Harriet also. B.B. not slow-minded, ~~Claribel~~ quickly reactive and all the rest pedestrian with ordinary quality of mind, ordinary version of Francis Pollack, in other words like Laurie, ordinary version of Simon H—B.B. & Laurie, not ethical, Francis Pollak, opportunistic by conviction, Simon H. ethical by conviction but these two have the moral values that do not exist in B.B. or Laurie. Hutch has it to the point of fanaticism the moral values and no opportunism au fond but a practical sense that has taken its place. Great question are Simon H. Francis Pollak slow-minded. Is Claribel, is Stell Rumbold. B.B. includes the whole gamut of his type, combines Laurie and Simon H. Chalfin, Vollard & or Brass & Simon H. Mostly there are combinations one does not usually include the whole of his type. B.B. does it. I do not think Francis is slow-minded, Claribel's fundamental resemblance to Alice I cannot decide. I cannot decide about Estelle. I think Estelle is slow-minded bottom and then connects to Sally but I don't know.

LK NB-E #5, #6, #7

slow-minded, quick-minded, opportunistic: [MA 364–366.] The relation of slowness and quickness of mind to the rationalising of one's moral behavior uses part of the discussion in these notes but is itself part of the larger discussion begun in NB-A #3, "Jews mostly run themselves by their minds."

*

NB-E #7

Francis Pollak and Simon H. undoubtedly attacking, slow-minded of quick-minded, B.B. is singular in being both the quick-minded and slow-minded of quick-minded version of his type. I think now he is quite clear to me completely clear to me, he is the virtuous slow-~~minded~~ and quick sensitive combined in one of his type, his quality as quick sensitive is much greater and is the bottom of him and the top of him. The other is an in between layer.

Claribel has turned the sensitive bottom of Alice into an ~~empty~~ long winded spued out negative egotism. She is in many ways very stupid. One must not forget that, stupid as the Annie Lyell's are stupid big stupid masses in in them, excepting that in Claribel the relation between the stupid and the non-stupid parts remains permanent, in them Annie Lyell et al it is ~~shif~~ not shifting but alternating, Annie Lyell's as men are often comic actors, Clown musical, Hands [?].

Pyot is ind. dep. he is between Peduli and Leo Stein. But he is insensitive au fond ~~although~~ like Leo F's group -the relation of all that to Puy is interesting Not sure yet about Estelle or Claribel.

LK NB-E #5, #6, #7

negative egotism: See LK Note for NB-B #20.

*

NB-E #8

George Sand undoubtedly not like Alice au fond but
Mrs. Eddy, Mabel Haynes sexually, Mrs. Ehrmann.

De Musset, Alexandre Heiroth, Chopin, Salmon. These Salmon enlarge into Annie Lyell. Not sure about resisting and attacking in them.

*

NB-E #9

Sally when working concentrates her attention, I concentrate myself. This is the important difference between pedestrianism Florence Sabine etc. and creation. All creative people concentrate themselves. Berenson in the slow side of him does not even succeed in concentrating his attention,

It all gets clearer. Go on.

*

NB-E #10

The bottom nature sort of shines through the rest. Mary Berenson, almost spinster type. Nadelman the Alexandre quality comes through the hardened Annie Lyell. Is that Salmon Annie Lyell, Gladys attacking or the other I want to know. I think there is no doubt about George Sand being the dep. ind. the mother role is so like Mrs. Oppenheimer and Mrs. Ehrmann and Mrs. Eddy. Mabel Haynes and Annette had it too. and Adele Solomons.

The combinations get clearer. Estelle is the real puzzle.

J. Caesar resisting type transformed by nervous ~~energy~~ energy into rapidity of conception. Want to make clear that slow type deep impressions react slowly but can be by practice made quicker.

Annie Lyell and Gladys attacking but long in between intervals and the action is almost a slow one. It is just between. They attack on to Mrs. Thorold and Mrs. Manguin and Mrs. Bruce. Adele Solomons, George Sand and Mrs. Eddy resisting.

AT ***George Sand... the mother role... Annette... Adele Solomons:*** [The mother role] was more a possession, an accretion of themselves. They make rotten mothers so—they own their sons-in-law and then it goes to pot altogether. George Sand, for example. Her son-in-law stood faithful to her after the daughter had gone off.

Gertrude never counted that as the character of the Stinker [Annette], that she wallowed in possessions, and the more she had, the more she could wallow. It was the first thing I couldn't stand about her. Funnily enough, Gertrude had none of the unpleasant recollections of her apparently that I have, vividly, even now.

Annette and Mabel Haynes: When Gertrude was working on Annette in Paris, she often made comparisons of her and Mabel Haynes. She often compared their handwriting. Mabel's T's crossing like a dagger point and her handwriting not crowded but tight—her terrific egotism. Annette the Stinker crossed her T's brutally much as Mabel Haynes did. If you look up Mabel Haynes in *Q.E.D.*, you will really know what she was. By the time I came to Paris, Gertrude had had about enough of Annette. The Stinker getting greener and greener was frightful to see.

*

NB-E #11

General scheme of resisting kind unless very sexual their response being slow they are mostly not in love when they have the object, the attacking are Musset & George Sand, me and May etc etc.

Etta Cone is like that in her affections always lingering with what is left over, this can only be conquered by excessive animalism or excessive intelligence of a rare kind. This is also the reason why George Sand and Mrs. Eddy and Adele Solomons and Etta Cone are less conscious of their weakness than Hodder or May or Edstrom because they didn't really lose themselves and so they don't have to explain it by weakness or denial, they can be even more of little tin Jesuses.

Fernande is very much on the borderline. Senda Berenson, Therese bottom connected with Hattie Bache with top of Bird.

*

NB-E #12

Sam Wolfe as Leo pointed [out] probably has the difficulty of not being able to realise his ideas and therefor he changes his thesis subject all the time. That is to say he is of the resisting type with most of him the clever end of it which in them is the superficial quick response not the profounder response, but he has just enough of the ~~larger~~ larger bottom to give him his ideas and his criticism, he has not the patience he has ~~nervous energy~~ the nervous energy of both the bottom and of the superficial quick reaction and so he fails. He is like Berenson he has the whole gamut of his kind. This is very interesting. Napoleon according to this last description is like all the romantic temperaments ~~an overwhelming attacking~~ complete one thing with another bottom that keeps it from unification. In Napoleon there is the overwhelming attack all on top at bottom the earthy type which should be indolent and slow because he had not the resisting bottom like Caesar or like Frederick the great or like Pablo nervously energised into rapid action. Napoleon's bottom was the indolent earthy muggy bottom that is practical but not really energetic. More and more as he grew older and the fire of youth did not hold it together it fell apart. Made him stupidly obstinate, with his attacking top lethargic with his ~~att~~ resisting indolent bottom. Vainglorious with his sense of success of his top and nervously irritable with his disturbed bottom.

Pablo like B.B. runs the whole gamut of his kind all except the calm of earthy waiting that I have.

Types are getting clearer. Still still remains a puzzle.

Sam who runs the whole gamut of his kind not a success as B.B. & Pablo are in whom two things are more balanced, in Pablo and B.B. both the genial bottom is the stronger in Sam the superficial top is the stronger.

AT ***Sam Wolfe:*** A New York friend of Miriam and Joe Price. Gertrude didn't like him.

Napoleon: Gertrude thought the same of him as the French of Hitler. She was especially annoyed with the devout French -the nuns, the clergy, the devout Catholics generally—who all approved of Napoleon because of the Concordat but didn't realize that he brought about the situation that demanded it.

*

NB-E #13

Miriam is the real religious personality, Mme Demarez and Miss Donner are of her kind. Miriam is the concentrated essence of it, there is really nothing else in her, emotions human relations really have no vital meaning ~~to~~ in her. Her letters are therefor very characteristic of her, nothing counts except that which it is needless to say. At bottom she is calm, complete, all her violent romances were before her 16th year which is very characteristic of religious natures. I still think St. Theresa was like Mary Houghton and Miss Blood.

AT ***Miriam:*** [Miriam Price.] She was the one Leo compared Nelly with, and when he discovered he was wrong, he thought of it as deception. This, when Nelly got bored with the business.

*

NB-E #14

Chalfin, loving, a beautiful life sexual nature would soon turn the beautiful life into an ugly one, vocation of labor.

LK ***Chalfin, loving, a beautiful life...*** [Corresponds to NB-A #3, and Manuscript Note #53 on MA 366ff.] Plan for MA 366.

*

NB-E #15

Mabel's nature is conventional not her mind, Miss Jones and Miss Erwin (I think and that Miss --- friend of Miss Jewett) their natures are not conventional but their minds are. George Elliot was like

Mabel with a conventional nature, not a conventional mind. Their minds are open, their natures determined, even though they may do things that are free, Alice escapes both so does Miss Blood so does Mary Houghton, these three are much more concentrated in their sensitiveness and ~~emotional~~ passionate emotion.

*

NB-E #16

Margaret Lewis relation to Gracie Gassette—Dorothy Reade—through Margaret Isadora Duncan—to Mme. Demarez to Miriam, to Adele through Gracie & Dorothy to Marion and to to possibilities like Miss Jones and Alice, only these have a different bottom these are yielding not resisting at bottom. The interesting thing of these resisting is the way they dominate their man they try to dominate him by attacking and mostly so fail, they can only really dominate by resisting. So many of this kind try to get a man and miss it. They try coercion, attacking is not their way of winning.

*

NB-E #17

Miss Coes and Marion very likely resisting Miss Coes has it solidified into a crystalline mass, and acts accordingly[,] Marion into a nervous mass. I wished I knew about Mary Houghton and Edmund but I don't. I think in the case of Estelle that it is true that she is resisting with a coating of attacking and that the bottom in her was not solid but the gaps filled in by drama. I think she is quite clear now, red headed brown eyed resistants.

*

NB-E #18

Simon H. Francis B.B. et al, people governed by an idea usually a moral one anyway an abstract one and at the same time oportunists and not vain or proud but ambitious, Caesar and Napole the earthy ones there is vanity as well as ambition and their general idea is a personal one.

*

NB-E #19

Sarah Yerxa, Claribel. with spread resisting but determined bottom, Too thinly spread. Estelle like Sarah's only more soft and billowy.

AT ***Sarah Yerxa:*** A Boston woman of means and position who ran a salon. Gertrude knew her through Tommy Whittemore, and didn't like her.

*

NB-E #19a

Degas	-	Simon H.
Renoir	-	Leo D.S.
Cezanne	-	earthy resis.
Monet	-	Simon H. Zola with Manguin bottom.
Manguin	-	resis. with almost no resistance

*

NB-E #19b

Margaret Sweeney was very interesting showing distinctly the relation between Bird and Alice Klauber. Margaret is made up of Etta Cone less wallowing and rather coarser, that is more consistent and lower type, and Alice Klauber, Bird head, with a dash of Dorothea Reade. this makes the whole woman, she is stupid, it is interesting to have Alice Klauber made like that out of Etta & Bird on top. Also it threw some light on Mary Houghton I don't yet quite know how much. Sophie Hart and Neith I think she is the complete thing that Neith would have liked to have been, Mrs. Palme has a little of it and then she is at bottom like Lilian Wing and has no head no brains.

AT ***Lillian Wing… no head, no brains:*** The Henry James character. She is one of the daughters with the scandalous mother whom she finally saves.

LK ***Mrs. Palme:*** The wife of the Swedish painter Carl Palme who attended the Matisse class intermittently. Sterne fell in love with Mrs. Palme [Letter Hutch to Leo, 1906], and was still concerned, at least with her well-being, when in July 24,1909, he reports to Leo that she had fainted from the heat in Anticoli.

[Dating: Note written circa July 1909.]

*

NB-E #20

Cecil Pynsent is a combination of Pyot, Leo F. Sterne group to Pach group, Singer, Roche, Bruce. Really combines Pyot and Pach. has none of the idealism really of either group but all the rest of the qualities.

AT ***Cecil Pynsent:*** Pynsent and Scott were two English architects who were invited to dinners in Florence

*

NB-E #21

Allan is a typical romantic type, lower face Mike, upper Sally equally divided, resisting slow-minded, self-conscious, earthy, practical, dramatic emotional, Sally type. The two kinds of romantics are very important to differentiate. There is then this type, Byron and Edstrom are typical. In Edstrom as far as I can at present make out the way of its expression in him is by his type of intellect which cuts right across the whole personality. Double head line, the secondary one is the one belonging to his temperament. The Derain, Leo Friedman romantics have romantic intuition, romantic imaginings but no romantic dramatic instinct and so mostly they don't get into any trouble with it. Pyot is undoubtedly very close to Cecil Pynsent, and they are a cross between Leo F's group, & Pach's. I must know more about the mixture in romantics, the first [?] Byronic they in a sense are connected Mrs. Pyot like Nelly only with Francis Pollak BB freer [?] nearer Mrs. Puy group by their way of making some dramatic conception their ideal in life but with them in some cases it is because they are not conscious of the other nature in them, in some cases because it looks pretty to them, then there is the romantic type like Zola & Monet but that is really romantic melodrama, not romantic drama. The relation in the Byronic, Edstrom type of the romantic temperament due to mixture, (also in Stell) and its relation to B.B's group has to be some time better understood.

AT ***Edstrom... double head line:*** The double head line was in his *hand*. Everybody has one.

Mike: once took Allan to an agricultural show because his son wasn't seeing animals except for the oxen at Fiesole. The shows then cost $1, $2 or $5 for admission. They went on the day it was $5, and everybody turned away except Mike. In for a penny, in for a pound was very characteristic of him.

He had a strong sense of economy, but it wavered charmingly and pleasurably. At Fiesole, he used to get a list of books from Gertrude to bring back from Florence when he went down. (He complained always that she could read them faster than he could bring them). Once he asked me to go along with him. This was during the first summer I was in Fiesole, when Mike had taken it upon himself, characteristically, to keep me within my very limited income. My ten-month letter of credit was being doled out by Mike to last for

12 months and if possible for 13, and he budgeted me so much for clothing, so much for travel and so on. But the day we went to Florence together, he lunched me at the best restaurant in the city: Might as well have a good lunch as not.

Mike was always fixing up everybody's budget to show them how to stay over longer. He told me, Your whole trouble is that you've always been on a wine diet, and now you're on a beer income.

*

NB-E #22

Continues as NB-F #1

Bianco attacking who attacks even before he gets his quick reaction, vanity and lack of emotional intensity accompaniment. this is in a queer way true also of Gladys Deacon and Annie Lyell and I think that accounts for much in them both. they attack like Bianco before they have gotten the reaction, they are clever and more occasional but its the same thing. I am now quite sure this accounts for so much in them, there being nothing to them in them, their brilliance and their occasional penetration and truth. I am sure this is it, they would only be great natures if they were engulfing, there being attacking makes them this for they attack before they have anything.

Reading the Tragic Muse makes me sure that Isadora is resisting that attack, like Gracie only in her and in the Tragic Muse and in Margaret Lewis in a sense the attacking has become the whole of them and it makes drama, it does not make power it makes drama. The drama of the attacking

LK ***Reading The Tragic Muse:*** Henry James, *The Tragic Muse*. In Letter, AT to Donald Sutherland, Oct 19, 1947, Miss Toklas recalled:

> About Henry James it must have been when she was at Johns Hopkins that she read the last two long novels [*The Bostonians* (1886) and *The Tragic Muse* (1890)] because in 1903 in a novelette (which was the point of departure for "Melanctha"—the three characters were white) she quotes Kate Croy. When I came along in '07 with an undiminished chronically young enthusiasm for H.J. we subscribed to the N.Y. Scribner's edition of H.J.[published in 1908–1909] and Gertrude reread the two last and the two or three later novels [i.e., the two above, and two or all of the last three completed novels, *The*

> *Wings of the Dove* (1902), *The Ambassadors* (1903) and *The Golden Bowl* (1904).] She always liked to use his word—*precursor*—in speaking of him. It was his paragraphs that finally enthused her. There are some pure Gertrude phrases in *The Wings of the Dove*.... [quoted in Burns, *Staying on Alone: The Letters of Alice B. Toklas.*, (New York: Liveright, 1973.)]

The Kate Croy quotation in the novelette [*Q.E.D.*] taken from *The Tragic Muse*, appears in *Fernhurst.*:

> Helen... instinctively endeavored to restimulate Adele by accidental momentary contacts, by inflections of voice and shades of manner, by all delicate charged signs such as had for some time been definitely banished between them.
>
> "What a condemned little prostitute it is," Adele said to herself between a laugh and a groan. "I know there is no use in asking for an explanation. Like Kate Croy she would tell me 'I shall sacrifice nothing and nobody' and that's just her situation, she wants and will try for everything, and hang it all, I am so fond of her and do somehow so much believe in her that I am willing to help as far as within me lies." [*Fernhurst*, **p. 121**]

Further comment on James, *The Wings of the Dove* and GS, is in Letter, Toklas to Donald Sutherland, Oct 8, 1947:

> About Proust and Joyce and James—wouldn't Proust come off better in comparison with James—as for Joyce wouldn't he be better off without comparison. Of course, James was the precursor alright. But in rereading *The Wings of the Dove* there were suddenly some very direct connections between Kate Croy and Melanctha—between Gertrude's dialectic and his. It fascinated me. It was the only one of his books I remember her having reread several times. [*Staying on Alone*, **p. 84**]:

*

Notebook F

NB-F #1

Continues NB-E #22

kind like Sally etc. that is the personality that responds, in these others in a sense there is no real personality, not because they are too responsive but because they are completely attacking when that is personally not that power. This is badly expressed but the truth is there.

*

NB-F #2

~~Mabel~~ Mamie & Tommy.

Tommy has Mamie's nature except that in him it is a more sensuous and more ~~responsiv~~ deeplly responsive thing but his intellect isn't at all and he is not worldly in intention but worldly from lack of power to be anything else and so he prostitutes his nature to worldliness.

Very characteristic of Mamie that she asked [Winor?] to meet her at the station in Paris after all. In this she was like Tommy, she can't resist anything, and so its hard to believe her.

Its hard to believe Mabel not a bit hard to believe in her. Sally is the other way. Alice is both ways hard.

AT ***Characteristic of Mamie… meet her at the station:*** This is the episode of my meeting Mabel Weeks at the station in Paris, already described [in NB-*C #43.]

LK ***Mamie… asked Winor to meet her at the station in Paris:*** Mabel Weeks incident involving AT's mischief, and her story to GS. AT dates the incident July 1909, following Mabel Week's visit to Fiesole during June and July (which dates this entry approximately.)

*

NB-F #3

Mirabeau like Charles Fox the true attacking type where the romance is completely realised, in Allan Edstrom, Byron et al Claribel, the romance is not completely acted because the attack is not a complete thing, there is a small thing in them that is potent and that completely destroys the completeness of the attack and so they fail in that but on the other hand do not lose themselves as Fox and Mirabeau did, they are the romantics that are not abandoned to their complete romanticism. This is now perfectly clear. Stell, Mildred, that is another group, Mildred is like Stell, resisting lumps combining by attacking fluid, Mildred is not completely successful in attack or in drama in consequence, not like Sally who has the sensitiveness and the intellect of the complete attack, Mildred and Estelle have the sensitiveness and the intellect of the resistance but the complete nature of the attack and it makes a real homogeneity.

Bianco I am now certain is the resistance type with none of it, that is there should be lumps but they aren't there except as infinitesimal in size and all of it is connecting fluid, that is what makes him as he is attacking before the sensation and makes him be on all sides of the fence at once, a connecting fluid cannot take shape. On the other hand, Manguin is this with attacking, that is he is all made up of resisting fluid (no this is not right).

Bruce is also made up like this excepting that in him it is not quick fluid like Bianco's but slow molasses that holds him together, slow molasses resisting holds together little lumps of attacking.

*

NB-F #4

Blue eyes Maria Heiroth, resisting I think in fact I know, resisting that is clear in attacking as a whole not like Gracie. Gladys Deacon is like Bianco resisting but in her it is as if there were lumps of connecting tissue and they are acting before the sensation, not the resisting masses that are sort of vacantly there. Annie Lyell and Gladys think of them more. Interesting in connection with them the actor type of the musician in presentez moi, the funny musician man, Julian Stein like this too, excepting that in Julian his real character is his resisting while in the red-headed actor like Bianco and Gladys what is active in them is the connective tissue that is active before there is a sensation.

AT ***acting before the sensation:*** I remember weeks of Gertrude noticing this. And then from this, it went on to, Was sensation strong enough to be an emotion? There was a frightful struggle to get them all down right.

presentez moi... the funny musician man: A clown at the Cirque Medrano would use this in his act. There were the same people but a different program there each Thursday. One of the musician-clowns did this, insisting on an introduction.

Uhde had a shop in which he sold pictures. Pablo and Braque went to see him, and Uhde didn't know Picasso though he had bought one of his paintings. Presentez-moi, said Picasso, playing the clown's game, to Braque. No, said Braque, also playing, *me presentez*.

*

NB-F #4a

Hortense and Clare lack subtelty [sic] of emotion that is what makes them moral, Mabel Weeks if she were dependent only on her passional side her eyes [?] would also lack it, but the sensitiveness that she has in common with Sally and Alice saves her. Sally has it but as everything else in Mabel saves her so everything else in Sally goes to spoil it, to make it banal and like Aunt Pauline's and Bird. Bird has excitement but no subtelty [sic]. Aunt Pauline has solidity but no subtelty [sic]. Georgiana Mrs Dodge and Theo Elwell have subtelty [sic] in Bertha like attacking passion that is their quality. Alice has perfect subtelty [sic] of emotion from her perfect sensitiveness and her absolute lack of interest in the practical sense, each reaction is complete.

AT ***Clare:*** Clare Moore. [Miss Toklas' San Francisco friend.] Gertrude never met her then and knew her only through her letters and what I told about her.

*

NB-F #5

Sometime go more into Nelly gradually dominating Frank.

AT ***Nelly:*** Gertrude was confused about her now. She was alternately on both sides of the fence. Her attitude toward Frank made Nelly one thing, her attitude toward the rest of the world made her another. I would tell her, You have to wait until someone is not in love before you get them down, when their ardor has cooled. Harriet used to say, 'Gertrude came to the conclusion that Nelly loved Frank when she no longer did. That she had loved Frank is what she discovered.'

Nelly... Frank: Nelly's marriage to Frank was very complicated. He had had a divorce which no one in San Francisco knew about, so that when Polly [Jacobs] was on the point of arriving in Paris, I carefully warned Gertrude not to mention Nelly at all in any connection, that I would undertake all the answers, and so perhaps there would be some way of avoiding telling Polly about Nelly's marriage to Frank Jacott. It taught me a lesson forever. When

Polly [in Harriet's and Miss Toklas' flat] said, Oh Harriet, what lovely rubber trees! Gertrude volunteered at once, 'They're not Harriet's, they're Alice's. Nelly Jacott gave them to her.' Polly never had to be told that Nelly was married.

*

NB-F #6

Alexandre Heiroth.

The only thing that could have saved him would have been that he was really an artist of some real quality and he isn't, the loss of his idealism is the beginning of the end in him, he is bound then to go to the bad, if he had been a genius he would have come together on the higher plane which is what Nadelman does, perhaps what the author of Old Wives Tale does but not having it he will come together as a bad one, his attack and sensibility will do that and Leo not having faith in him has been a very decided deterrent. He is complete now to me and so is Nadelman, Nadelman is bound to be a mirror[?] man because he comes together by virtue of his genius not by virtue completely of himself as Matisse and Pablo both do in their way. This is also true of Mabel, not true of Leo who comes together by himself, very true of Sally who comes together on many different planes.

AT ***Alexandre Heiroth:*** Heiroth used to improvise on the piano, and his uncle would put stamps on the piano so he could write to his wife. He made several attempts to borrow money from Leo and Gertrude, and though they never refused a first request, the second was a question. Leo got tired of Heiroth's general shiftlessness. He had no stamina, really. He amused himself like a man of means without spending any money. It was largely through Mrs. Heiroth's charm and beauty that he got by. Leo would speak of Mrs. Heiroth's beauty in a particular way though he was not at all in love with her.

LK ***Alexandre Heiroth The only thing that could have saved him…*** [Dating: Heiroth's loss of funds, and leaving Florence for Russia, and Leo's refusal to lend him more. Late 1909.]

*

NB-F #7

Leo Friedman's group come together at a steady level but not at a deep one, they have no inspiration.

*

NB-F #8

Maria is again a fighting resisting woman but it is an effort, it does not come of itself in her, she would prefer relaxing as she did after she had the child.

*

NB-F #9

Cecil like Adele Jaffa can accept any amount of sexuality from others, does not use it, does not need it, neither from necessity nor from vanity, nor from pride, just accepts it to any extent, returns nothing, prince of a reigning house, think of this more.

AT ***Cecil [Pinsent]... prince of a reigning house:*** There was some scandal about him in Florence about now. The Note is probably based on that. The story was in fact that 'he had accepted it all.' It was probably Gertrude's phrase. At any rate, it made the rounds.

*

NB-F #10

Girl in the train connected M. Laurencin with Mabel Haynes. Another Mabel Haynes with Hattie Bache and Amy. The man like Manguin with this resisting one, must look at Manguin more[.]

*

NB-F #11

The originality in Zobel, Barker et al is that they constantly exploit the best novelty there is and this is persistent, they do more than just exploit it, they incarnate it.

*

NB-F #12

Sally light blue eyes, remember that, notice Matisse and May had them too. Sally cross between Mabel and May, Mabel has them too, the clear light blue eyes and it does go with a certain lack of profundity of passion I think but we will see, it gets deeper in Alexandre, Leo, Alice, Mary Houghton, I think Mary Berenson has that kind the first kind, must remember to look. This does certainly go with a kind of lack of profundity of sexual emotion.

AT ***Sally light blue eyes:*** They were not blue eyes, they were speckled. Gertrude always thought of the blue-eyed blonde and what went with it as 'amiable.' I would ask her, A I amiable? And she would say, No, you're not an ay-mee-ahble baby, Sally is. Thank God I'm not them I would say.

The red-headed brown eyed ones—they were 'comfortable.' Then the blonde ones—that is, BB. The pasty-faced—Pach and those. May had *quelqonque* blue eyes, not the baby blue or pure blue. Matisse had the weakish blue

*

NB-F #13

Nelly's statement that Matisse was like any man that would enjoy a glass of beer is very characteristic that way of judging men, any man can be managed by desires eating drinking and women, that makes Nelly like Mrs. Meininger et al, their kind of wisdom. On the other hand there is in Nelly a repose a ~~love~~ feeling for the luxury of distinction for the richness of distinction. Leo is right there is there no subtlety, Alice is subtle. Nelly is all stupid excepting in respect to that, a feeling for and instinct for the richness of distinction, it must have a certain richness.

*

Note #56

The whole question of consciousness of virtue, apropos of different groups exhibited by the incident of lack of consciousness of little failings, Penelope and that is her faiblesse consciousness of virtue in mistress free soul type consciousness of right point of view in lady type.

Natures funny little ways.

bridling goes with this kind of freedom and consciousness of virtue and being mistress.

*

NB-F #14

Different kinds of virtue care for people through interest in them me, Mme Demarez cares for people because they are the children of God Sally has the sense of virtue for its own sake, to be virtuous to have the consciousness of virtue, this even mingles where she has affection, she has strongly the sense that people should be grateful because she is so good. She is good but she is it for the consciousness of virtue as much as for the instinct of goodness and that spoils its purity. Mabel's and Alice's is much purer, Mabel's is the purest of all, and that is the reason that she does not soil the people she describes as Sally does. Also the difference between enthusiasm and pasionateness rather than passion Nadelman and Alexandre have passion, Edstrom and Sally have passionate emotion, Sally is not romantic, therein she is cut off from Edstrom & Allan. Matisse is brutal and not in any sense a sounding board because his intellect and emotion is subservient to his brutal egotism, always. In Sally intellect and emotion is greater than her individuality always, that is the real formula, her ~~vit~~ virtuousness greater than her goodness. therefor one is not grateful, her expressive cleverness greater than her inspiration, all of which is real enough but unoriginal and rather timid, even that now she exaggerates her timidity. Thats the formula completely now.

*

NB-F #15

Nelly good case of needing them to own them. Some like Mme. Merle in the "Portrait of a lady" owns those they need for loving to the point of renouncing herself for them. Alice when melodrama unified her did this to herself, really she is spontaneously little helpful but needing love to be owned, this could easily be twisted by her by a melodramatic desire into a feeling of owning with that top of her that is like Adele Jaffa.

LK ***Mme. Merle in the "Portrait of a lady" … renouncing herself:*** Henry James, *Portrait of a Lady*, 1881.

Madame Merle is Isabel's friend, formerly the mistress of Osmond and mother of his daughter Pansy. She "renounces herself" by suppressing her own claims and promoting the marriage of Isabel to Osmond.

*

Note #109

From copybook containing ***MA manuscript, pp. 295–304.***

Use Mrs. Hodder the present [?] like Mrs. Merle in the portrait of a lady, owns those she needs for loving to the point of renouncing herself for them.

Then Manuscript material—passage on "One little boy does something to another little boy who does not like it," etc., to the other boy's delayed reaction which surprises the first one. Then:

repeat it with she, and then discuss its meaning and then as introduction to

This comes ~~after~~ the umbrella in the mud.

Work up that umbrella in the mud might be an expression of dep. ind, or ind dep. like Martha Hersland.

LK [Corresponds to Ms Notes #45, 56b.]

Use Mrs. Hodder the present: The second "Mrs. Hodder," Mary Gwinn, whom Hodder married in June 1904. She is "Cora Dounor" in MA.

Mrs. Merle in portrait of a lady: There is a second reference, in NB-F #15, to Mrs. Merle and "own[ing] those she needs for loving to the point of renouncing herself for them." During the summer of 1909, GS was reading both *The Portrait of a Lady* and *The Tragic Muse*.

Mrs. Hodder, as Cora Dounor, is described in MA 456–457 as "completely loving, completely believing, ... this finely sensitive completed feeling that is sometimes all of them and perhaps Cora Dounor was one of such of them," one of the kind, that is, that become so full up with their sensitive reaction that they become "completely then a feeling."

One little boy does something: Text used in MA 378–379. GS returns to the theme, developed in this and the following passages, of the various ages at which one's true and defining "repeating" emerges fully, in the autobiographical section of the *Geographical History of America*, written in Oct.1936, in which she discusses the place of the MA in her development.

Repeat it with she... Then discuss its meaning: Plan for MA 379.

Work up that umbrella in the mud might be an expression: Plan for MA 388. Other Notes on the episode are Note #20, NB1, #22, NB-MA #19, NB-B #20.

*

Note #100

Give the boy story, then it as a girl, then This can be in some having in them independent dependent being. This can be in some having in them dependent independent being. Then repeat the story [etc?] (this one), then go on to tell of Bertha the two different kinds of being, their feeling for objects etc. [Inserted: this comes after difficulty of dividing kinds for [-?-],] and then a little more description of the stuff making them ending with a description of Bertha's stuff as a little girl, more concentrated to make Martha, then I will throw the umbrella in the mud might be either of the kinds of them, it was Martha, [Inserted: then describe the way repeating is and is disguised in the young] and then describe Martha's girl friends and her attitude various ind. dep. attitudes toward girl-friends, always coming back to Martha and then having made Martha the incident on Calif. st. and her going to college scared and determined both. Then book.

LK The overall plan for MA 378–440.

Give the long story… always coming back to Martha: Planning Notes, duplicating notes for passages in Note #72 and Note #20.

Calif. st. and her going to college: Planning Note, MA 424–426.

The boy story: Begins MA 378.

Then it as a girl: Begins MA 379.

Bertha concentrated to make Martha: Begins MA 384.

throw the umbrella in the mud: Begins MA 388.

might be either of the kinds: MA 388.

repeating is disguised in the young: MA 388.

Martha's girl friends: MA 394 [followed by a long digression and recap]

The incident on California Street: MA 413.

going to college: MA 434.

*

Note #20

After the intro already written in little book. The kind of cases one does know absolutely, and where they come together to know, and the kind of cases one does not know Stell et al Mildred. with their type of substance, also like A. and Helene etc. where character not very determined and then to Bertha very determined stiffened into Martha. Come together in different ways, sometime later in discussing Hodder give history of Alexandre after throw the umbrella in the mud comes difficulty of deciding from a specific incidents. go into that and then do Martha strictly in relation to her friends to the Hodder experience always ~~emp~~ doing it by her friends and her relation to them.

LK [Consecutive working notes for MA 382–440.]

introduction already written in little book: Passage "already written" is MA

377, l.37 to 381, l.2.

The kind of cases one does know absolutely ... where character not very determined: Plan for MA 381, l. 3–18.

the kind ... one does not know: Plan for MA 381, l.19 to 383, l.3.

and then to Bertha ... stiffened into Martha: Plan for MA 383–388.

Sometime later ... give history of Alexandre: The apparent reference to Alexandre Heiroth on MA 384, l.8, ["Sometime there will be a description of a complete undifferentiated one that is of the dependent independent kind of them"] con reverses all other references to Heiroth in the Notebooks, in which he is described as "attacking", and associated with Nadelman in his "passion" and in his near genius.

throw the umbrella in the mud: Plan for MA 388. Probably the most famous passage in the novel, it is quoted by GS in her 1934 lecture, "The Gradual Making of *The Making of Americans*," as an example of her use of the "continuous present" in the MA.

difficulty of deciding from specific incidents: Plan for MA 388, l.23 to 394, l.11, intertwined with several other themes.

then do Martha strictly in relation to her friends: Plan, whose use is delayed for ten pages by repetition and elaboration of earlier themes, until MA 410, l.39 to 429, l.3. Planned to be "strictly" in relation to her friends, the passage nevertheless incorporates repetitions of earlier descriptions of Martha's relation to her father and to the governesses as well.

to the Hodder experience: Planning Note for MA 429–440. These are the pages copied directly from *Fernhurst*, the story written in 1904. They are followed by GS's apologetic explanation for their ineptitude: "Categories that once... had real meaning can later ... be all empty. It is queer that words that meant something... can later come to have... not at all any meaning."

*

Note #222

I have a shrewd suspicion that you have to begin over again from the beginning Say this for beginning of each special history

Make the quality of the father to come out in the viciousness and practicality of the son and the idealistic quality in the daughter who is to be like Edgar Mathews wife

*

Note #72

Difficulty of knowing kinds in children when they are young etc.

the kinds that are harder to know than others and then to Bertha's stuff as a little girl etc.

~~again to the disguises of the young.~~

Kind harder to know.

Mildred Estelle etc. etc. indeterminate not because of stuff but of coming coming together difficulties to Bertha completely determinate [Insert: by being always together then kinds of feelings to objects of two kinds [-?- vs. -?-] then back to Bertha] flat determinate too and then solidify this to make Martha.*

Martha did this

Umbrella in the mud story interpreted various ways difficulty of deciding character Martha is dep. ind. and kinds of men and women from incidents and then get to disguises of character in the young use the phrase on paper in the book and so to Martha and her friends.

LK ***Difficulty of knowing kinds ... and so to Martha and her friends:*** Overlapping Planning Note for same passages as in Note #20, specifically, MA 388–394.

*

Note #218

...comes to be all of them. Sometime there will be a history of all young living, feeling, talking, thinking, being. Some have their real being in young living, some do not have it then in them. Later there will be a history of all of them, of every one. [Insert later:] Use this for beginning with Martha's friends ending the describing repeating in young ones. [Insert ends]

To begin then again with a little description of my coming to...

LK Draft Text, MA 304, l.14–24.

*

Note #217

Some have their real being in them in young living, some do not have it then in them. Now there will be some description of young living in some.

Now there will be some description of young living—- being in some. Some have this real go to back.

LK Draft Text:

Some have their real being: MA 391

Now there will be some description: MA 391–392

*

Note #219

In starting Julia Dehning get it all together out of all the books, the dramatic emotion Sarah Sands, this, a piece out of a turned down leaf, reverence, weakness and attacking, reverence, resonating. Put it all together completely, obstinancy for resisting, to make Julia Dehning. The way of lying, C.S. strong in them. The way Pablo and Matisse were made unhappy by [cleaning? dancing?], I by hand reading and Leo's interest in her reflections on human being.

*

Note #77

Martha's friends at college before she knows Hodder, ~~M~~ Tilli Brown, Kate Martin, May Buckminster, cousin Henry Hersland visitor from east like Simon H. visits her at college.

LK ***Martha's friends at college:*** Martha attends a "Western" college [modelled on Mills College], in contrast to the "Eastern" college which Alfred, and then David, attend. The Hodder—Bryn Mawr story is transferred to Mills. "Martha's friends at college" are eliminated entirely in the final text, as is the projected visitor from the East. Martha's relation to Hodder alone is retained.

*

Note #73

Gray copybook, kind in which MA ms. is written, about 6" x 8", graph-lined. Book has miscellaneous scraps of paper inserted, which may be in the order intended for their use by GS. All these notes, and those found in copybook, are numbered consecutively in the order found.

In this book, Sally, Bird, & Martha [?] Dehning. Edstrom & Alfy and Mike and Leon Solomons, and Brenner.

In Martha's history make it clear that the Rosenhagen sisters were dependent independent resisting. [Continues on 3rd page:] In the description of Brenner refer to 581-582 Make a real description of every kind of instrument nature. Then go on about his needs in middle living and old age and Martha's "irritating" ways, sugar in coffee, ~~and his w~~ and end so not his death.

Edstrom when he forgets his emotion and declares it to have been all the other one's doing attributes his having yielded to his own weakness that being the thing in him to him uppermost in him. Frank Jacott attributes his to his philanthropy, she was lonesome and threw herself on him took possession and what did he do but take care of her. May put it down to that they wanted it and she gave it but she had no responsibility, it because [sic] she was so game that she did it. Sally puts her yielding down to unsuspiciousness, that is the reason she yields, she is so easy and thats it. All these things are true as characteristics in each one but they all think that characteristic is the whole of them. It ain't, they all forget their emotion and so it must have been the other person's fault it happened and they have now no emotion and so they had none and so it must have been their weakness and the other person's willing them to this thing.

Use this in history of Martha.

Hodder like these through chivalry to himself, the highest type of gentleman.*

The following MA ms. material is written on pgs. 4, 2, and 3, in that order:

Use this after Martha cures him.

No one knowing Mr. David Hersland in his middle living could have really been ~~absol~~ completely certain that he would never bring through to a completed beginning anything in his living. I was saying that he had in his middle living, the need in him, of having people around him, who were not in him in his feeling, who were there around him getting from his beginning the realisation of their being, he was to them life enhancing. this would have been in him this need in him in the middle of his middle living whatever would have been the power of completion in him, for it is a need in all of them who have in them the being big in a beginning. As I was saying no one knowing him could really be completely certain then about the completion of beginning in him, the carrying [?] power in him of a beginning action.

LK ***In this book:*** I.e., in this Notebook.

Rosenhagen sisters: The seamstresses described earlier in MA 193–201. In the "Martha" chapter, being written concurrently with this note, GS was still occupied with "dep. ind, ind. dep." descriptions, but the Rosenhagen sisters are not explicitly mentioned.

description of Brenner: Manuscript pages 581–582 correspond to published MA 422.

Make a real description of … instrument nature: Planning Note, intended to carry out the promise in the "Mrs. Hersland" chapter, but not used in the "Martha" chapter, as planned here.

Edstrom when he forgets his emotion … highest type of gentleman: [Corresponds to Notes NB-C #30, NB3, #5, and Ms Notes #61, #62, #63, #64 in MA 443–447] Used in MA 441, and repeated and expanded, to MA 447.

No one knowing Mr. David Hersland: Draft of text for MA 470–471.

life enhancing: Berenson's famous phrase, popularized in his art criticism. Bandied about by the Anglo-American Florentine colony, sometimes without reverence.

*

Notebook 3

NB3, #1

N.B. Important

21, rue vallette
Introduction to D. Hersland in this book.

*

NB3, #2

Everybody looks like somebody to some one. use this in going on to the umbrella story.

LK ***Everybody looks like somebody… umbrella story:*** Planning Note and draft of text for MA 332ff.

*

NB3, #3

Actor like presentez moi allied to Gladys.
Anticipate sensation
Alexandre history

LK ***Alexandre—history:*** [See Note #20]

*

NB3, #4

Remember the way Sterne sounded in my ears that day.

AT ***Sterne:*** During the cholera epidemic in Rome, Gertrude and I were the only other Americans there. Sterne then took time to tell us all about his love affairs. He was not unattractive and had a great effect on women.

He could talk a long time about himself, telling story after story about his women mostly, so that he felt more himself in talking his women than in other ways.

LK ***Remember the way Sterne sounded in my ears that day:*** See NB-D #11: "Must write the hymn of repetition. Sterne gave the right feeling for it."

*

NB3, #5

Go great length into description of Edstrom, Purman, after narrative of Hodder and of kinds in men and women. Much description of the being in the children living in the small houses near the ten acre place where the Herslands were living ~~will be~~ is to be now in the history of the beginning of the youngest of the three Hersland children.

LK ***Go great length into description of Edstrom, Purman:*** Planning Note for MA 445–447. In the final text, Edstrom is called "Johnson," and Purrmann is replaced by Frank Jacott, who is called "Hackart." [See Note #73 and NB-C #30 for the detailed drafts of the text used in MA 441–447.]

Much description of the… children …in the small houses: Planning Note, but used as text in MA 394–395. Revised in final text to read: "Much description of the being in the children living in the small houses near the ten-acre place where the Herslands were living and of children living in other parts of Gossols and knowing these children will be in the description of the beginning being of the youngest of the three Hersland children, in the history of David Hersland."

*

NB3, #6

There are many ways of being and of winning & of losing,

Just about this time Alfred Hersland was marrying Julia Dehing. Later ~~then~~ in the history of ~~Alfred~~ the ending of the loving, and of having honor in them and religion from the nature of them when this is strong enough in them to make their own in women and men. Some can make their own honor, some their own loving, some their own religion, some are weak and can do one thing their own, some are strong enough and all of it is some one else's some can just resist and not make their own. Out of their own virtue they make a god who sometimes later is a terror to them. Like laws. Use all this apros pro of Hodder and the Hersland family.

Use it again and again.

Some are controlled by other people's virtue it scares them, listen to each one telling about their own virtue and that grows to make a god for them and often afterwards scares them, some afterwards like it, some forget it, some are it.

However what is right for them to be doing.

Go more into sensitiveness when come back to Martha.

LK [Corresponds to Manuscript Note #61 on MA 443.]

Later in the history … honor in them and religion … some are it:

Planning Note and draft of text for MA 443. The passage is repeated later in MA 480 [See Note #112]

apros pro [sic] of Hodder: Plan for MA 444ff.

Use it again and again: The theme of religion, honor and virtue is resumed in MA 479–480.

Go more into sensitiveness: Planning Note, used in Bryn Mawr College MA 455 as introduction to the description of the three women involved in the revised version of the Hodder—episode. The text in final draft begins: "Every one is a brute in her way or his way to some one, every one has some kind of sensitiveness in them."

*

NB3, #7

Love themselves enough to not want to lose themselves immortality don't mean nothing. Love themselves negatively than impersonal future life alright. Love themselves and others so hard that they are sure that they will exist even when they won't do exist even when they don't, these have a future life.

feeling individual.

Go into this whole question of virtue in religion in between Redfern & Martha.

LK ***Love themselves enough not to want to lose themselves:*** Planning Note, and draft of text for MA 444, l.1–6

question of virtue and religion in between Redfern and Martha: Plan for MA 448–452.

*

NB3, #8

In the description of Alfy, make him want to do things with little girl friend and not go far enough, not a bad man but just his kind of them as I was just saying.

Get to this from the general description of his kind and many xamples to when he was about 18 and then work him down to younger and what he did etc.

*

NB3, #9

Introduction to David Hersland

[Dead is dead to very many men and women.] Dead is dead but not ever in religion. [Dead is dead and always David was beginning understanding this thing.

To be dead is to be dead is ~~an almost instinctive feeling in~~ really certain to very many men and women. Not even really in religion. To be dead is then really to be living. David Hersland had in him and this is now a history of him to be wanting to be really realising really understanding something, sometime this ~~very~~ certain thing.]

In the case of Leon just begin with his being a little boy and his meditations and struggle and then his tramps and games and the character of all his companions. Describe his camping trip and the [annachlyness?] with the little girl, and work up to his love affair with Mabel Earle etc. etc. and his struggle of chastity, etc. and the girl he tried to reform and me and then he went East, to join his brother and there knew more men and women.

LK ***Introduction to David Hersland. Dead is dead:*** Planning Note, and draft of text, for the "David Hersland" chapter, considerably in advance of its writing. (The chapter was written in October 1911; this note was set down in early 1909.) The theme of "dead is dead," and this early version of its text, were inserted, however, into the "Alfred Hersland" chapter, MA 498, as introduction to the discussion of the feeling of virtue and dishonesty in Alfred's type.

In the case of Leon… and then knew more men and women: Planning Note outlining the early chronology of David Hersland, used in the final text of the "David Hersland" chapter with some of the incidents omitted.

- Early struggles and meditations and games and companions: begins on MA 743, and is continued for some 130 pages, interwoven with other matter.
- Camping trip and incident with little girl: omitted.
- Love affair with Mabel Earle: MA 871–872.
- Struggle with chastity: omitted.
- Girl he tried to reform: reduced to David's general interest in giving advice: MA 873.
- Joining brother and knowing others: MA 883–901.

Given the radically altered formal style of the "David Hersland" chapter, few of these matters are described concretely. See Introduction above, for a discussion of the relation between narrative content in the David chapter, and its text.

*

NB3, #10

Go largely into disillusionment in Leon, David.
1910
1864
46

LK ***Go largely into disillusionment of Leon, David:*** "Disillusionment in living" is substantially the theme of the history of David Hersland and governs the chapter's narrative structure. It becomes too the underlying theme of GS's personal narrative in both the Alfred Hersland and David Hersland chapters, in which her growing sense of ultimate failure in realizing the objective of the novel becomes increasingly overwhelming. The theme is introduced in the Alfred Hersland chapter, MA 483–485 with equal reference to narrative subject and narrator.

*

Note #74

(Go on to bottom nature and the aroma of it in different kinds and what brutal and sensitive activities are instinctive and which not.

~~Mostly~~ Everyone is a little in her way or his way to some one, everyone has some kind of sensitiveness in them. (Work up that now perhaps

Conversation begins again with the three name [sic] and the sentence above and sensitiveness in detail.

All this will be part of the relation of the three women to Redfern, and then it goes on to sensitiveness in
Mrs. Bruce Miss Thornton

Go into description from red book of reactive and personal nature (Gracie.)

Go into personal and reactive activities. Some react bottom nature when much stimulated some when little. (This next and then virtue in all four of them keep playing them together for a while

LK ***Everyone is a brute … work that up now:*** Plan and draft of text for MA 455.

Conversation begins again … sensitiveness in detail: Plan for MA 455.

relation of the three women to Redfern: Plan for MA 455, l. 30 to 457, l.26. The names of the women are altered in final text: Mrs. Bruce reverts to Mrs.

[Martha] Redfern; Miss Thornton = Cora Dounor.

description from red book of reactive and personal nature: Plan for MA 457, l. 27 to 460, l. 6. The descriptions referred to are in NB-C #3 and NB-C #12. "Reactive natures" in Cora Douner and Martha, are described in MA 456, par. 5 to 457, par. 1, followed by description of Miss Charles, MA 467–469.

Go on to bottom nature… Work up that now perhaps: [See NB3, #6] Planning Note and draft of text for MA 455, following l.18.

the three women and the sentence above and sensitiveness in detail: Planning Note for MA 456.

The analysis of "Miss Charles" [=Cary Thomas, Bryn Mawr's dean and later president] is a particularly representative example of GS's analytic style. She is described, against her public image and all reasonable assumption, as dependent independent, and consequently fights by resisting. That is her bottom nature, but because of her ability to react to everything (in childhood, youth, etc. to the burgeoning "new ideas" of her time) her perpetual reaction becomes manifestly an attack. Adopting the moral zeal of her time, she comes to look upon herself as a force for good, a moral being. This becomes her "personal" nature, the nature she knows of herself and which is conceived by others as an aggressive force with a "general" conviction of high virtue and a "concrete" living of worthy causes. But the actual method she employs for this perpetually aggressive behavior must be in keeping with her type, which in fact, and at bottom, fights by resisting.

*

Note #76a

So when I want to kiss you good-night now I can't miss you as much as I love you—so please don't think about my being sad.

This ~~wa~~ (pain and sadness) was increased by the solitude I was in and as it seems to me no creature on earth holds me in bondage, I felt some little scruple, for fear I was not beginning to lose this liberty.

St. Therese

LK ***So when I want to kiss you good-night…*** [Quoted from GS First Writings:] [GS Note to AT, addressed "St. Therese":]

Fearful of not losing her liberty, Gertrude struggled—apparently for months—to accommodate this long-held, repeatedly-renewed vow of never losing her independence, never submitting again to "domination," but at the same time yielding to an overwhelming desire to abandon entirely her "solitude," to be released altogether from her lingering misgivings about Alice turning into another May Bookstaver. And during the months of 1910, there was new and urgent reason for such accommodation.

In the deepened and newly-painful solitude of her writing labors shared now with no one but Alice-as-amanuensis, she had reached what she recognized—and bewailed—as desperate impasse.

*

Note #211

Now the quality of personality in Mrs. Bruce and Miss Thornton, a touch again on Redfern and then ...

LK Planning Note for MA 458ff.

*

Notebook 4

NB4, #1

Who is it who without ceremony and with his hat on his head sits before king pope president.

Coachman.

*

NB4, #2

Apparently continues a previous note, on a page which is removed:

26831.

same way of hand-writing, same way of succeeding, of beginning, of losing. Gaps and help it out by [...] [followed by many missing pages.]

LK ***... succeeding... beginning... losing...*** Fragmentary note, generally relating to the renewed description of Mr. David Hersland, MA 470–475.

*

NB4, #3

There will be a little more description of her written in the history of the ending of the living in her father in the history of the later living of her brother Alfred Hersland, in the history of her brother David Hersland. More description of her will be part of the history of the ending of the existing of the Hersland family. There will be very much history of this ending of all of them of the Hersland family written later.

LK ***There will be a little more description.... written later:*** Draft of text for the concluding paragraph of the Martha Hersland chapter, MA 476.

*

NB4, #4

When she ~~left him~~ left him Alfred Hersland had just been marrying Julia Dehning.

*

NB4, #5

There are many men and many women see themselves as virtuous through the weakness as well as through the strong things in them Many men and many women see themselves as virtuous always in their living, this is a little very interesting.

*

NB4, #6

Young David father saying it was a habit.

*

NB4, #7

Alfred Hersland who in his ~~early~~ later young living before the beginning of his middle living married Julia Dehning was of one kind of men and women, one kind of the dependent independent kind in men and women. This is now to be a good deal of description of this kind of them.

CHAPTER FOUR, part one

ALFRED HERSLAND AND JULIA DEHNING

(Jan 1910—Sep 1911)

*

Note #132

In starting Julia Dehning get it all together out of all the books, the dramatic emotion Sarah Sands, this, a piece out of a turned down leaf, reverence, weakness and attacking, reverence, resonating. Put it all together completely, obstinacy for resisting, to make Julia Dehning. The way of lying, C.S. strong in them. The way Pablo and Matisse were made unhappy by [?daning? classing? doing], I by hand reading and Leo's interest in her reflections on human being.

*

Note #112

The joy of when you are ashamed, after it is known then it is no longer a complete discovery to yourself of

~~School of yourself.~~

~~yourself.~~ /

[Inserted later: Pablo said something he must keep himself from doing, they don't. They have a measure[,] him, he has none. Some can make their own honor [?], etc.]

Copy out of little book about virtue and go into being a school person, a school of yourself, how others impress you next page [sic]/ and the joy of being recognised when you are ashamed and if anyone has acknowledged it you can never again have that complete shame. Some so give you courage, though in another matter. The master minds, the school minds. so go to Sterne, none of the weaknesses of genius and ~~so to Alfred Hersland~~ concrete and general and so to Alfred Hersland and concrete and general in virtue etc.

Also use the way one builds up other people's convictions, other people's intentions other people's loving and virtue and religion. saying good-night to Alice, this is a very common this very many men do it for very many women, very many women do it for many men and for other women and for children, very many men do it for very many men, very many do it for themselves in their living.

Use all this to lead up to school work, and concrete and general to introduction to Alfred Hersland Page back [sic] and Mr. Dehning and then the contrast between them, in respect to goodness and then commence a regular history of Alfred

Use this before the butterfly business concrete and general on last page of this book [i.e., this Notebook. See Note #114.]

All along illustrate with sketches Sally, Bianco and ending up with Mike and butterflies and so concrete and general.

In description of concreteness and abstract describe Carrie's way of building, and her abstraction.

AT ***The joy of when you are ashamed:*** Gertrude was thinking of the Brahms clock with the figures that I bought for her birthday at her suggestion, '*un decor de cheminee*.' It was a petit-bourgeois object. Harriet chose a silk bedcover which wasn't out of relation to the bronzes but came nearer to the 'gold bed'—brass—so that Harriet's gift brought the two things together. The spread was made of brocade silk and was cleaned endlessly and finally brought down to Bilignin. When things were bad during the Occupation, I had two blouses made of the silk in 1942, and among the villagers it raised their respect for my housekeeping in Gertrude's household because it had been so preserved.

Pablo... measure... he has none: From weakness, he followed any impulse because he couldn't say no to anything.

the weaknesses of genius: Pablo's—he knows he has a foolish, false pride, and doesn't want to act on it and still must, and he can't say no to anything. [Alfred North] Whitehead's—that he was open to flatteries, and he indulged in sentimentalities, and he clung to mistakes that he believed in. Gertrude had inherited weaknesses—her father's impatience—though ultimately oriental patience—in small matters.

LK ***Some can make their own honor:*** Text for MA 443

about virtue: in MA 441. Text begins: "Many have it in them that their weakness is a virtue in them."

The joy of being recognized when you are ashamed… never again have that complete shame: MA 485–486. It begins: "When one is loving a clock that is to every one … an ugly and a foolish one…" The theme is developed further:

The note here is distinctly autobiographical, and, with respect to GS's writing, reflects Leo's defection and Roche's letter of criticism of the manuscript on the one hand, and the support of AT and Mabel Weeks on the other. The example of the clock is equally personal. GS's story of Rumbold's clock as wedding gift:

> It is a very strange feeling when one is loving a clock that is to every one of your class of living an ugly and a foolish one and one really likes such a thing… and liking it is a serious thing….or you write a book and while you write it you are ashamed for every one must think you are a silly or a crazy one… you know you will be laughed at or pitied by every one and you have a queer feeling and you are not very certain and you go on writing. Then some one says yes to it… and never again can you have completely such a feeling of being afraid and ashamed that you had then when you were writing…. [MA 487–488]

Go into being a school person… how others impress you: The theme of "followers and masters," or "school" persons and originals, is introduced MA 486, but the development of the theme does not begin until MA 488.

A school person, a school of yourself… the master minds, the school minds: Begins MA 486. An introduction to the theme: "I have not been very clear in this telling, it will be clearer in the description of masters and schools…" In MA 4880, the subject of "master and school" begins with the notion of "measure." "Some have a measure in living and some have not… to determine them." "Determine" is the key to the distinction. The self-determined are the masters, the followers are "determined" in their ideal of living by the master's ideal measure.

Some have measure... he has none: Pablo's "nature" is referred to (MA 479) in "Some can make their own honor," and in "Some can just resist and not their own anything." There's a codicil to this: "There are many who know them [who think them] geniuses without weakness... who are really schoolmen, followers" who seem to be and are taken for "real leaders." [In other words, the genius Picasso seems, but not the genius he is.] MA 494.

Pablo.... They have a measure[,] him, he don't. MA 488.

some can make their own honor, etc. Draft of text, MA 480.

Copy out of little book about virtue.... The passage is copied from NB3, #6, and was used earlier in MA 443. It is here used to introduce the subject of virtue, honor and religion in Alfred Hersland, most especially in the context of the relation of his and others' "generalized" and "concrete" virtue. The passage is copied into MA 480, l.1–17.

and so to Alfred Hersland: The "history" of Alfred Hersland begins MA 507.

Alfred Hersland and concrete and general in virtue: Begins MA 488, l.29, briefly introduced as the beginning of the Alfred Hersland question about "being a good one." The theme continues through MA 511, l.24, and leads eventually to the confrontation with the fact of: "dead is dead" and its relation to "concrete" as opposed to "generalized" moral convictions. It is the major theme of the early pages of the Alfred Hersland chapter, developed out of the earlier descriptions of men and women and their relation to virtue, honor and religion, and it is directed toward an understanding of Alfred Hersland that, despite this introductory analysis of him, finally eludes GS. Her failure to "realize" Alfred Hersland "as a whole one" eventually leads to her disillusionment with her entire undertaking, which in turn leads to her feeling of "having become an old one."

... a common thing that very many men do for very many women: MA 493 and Plan and draft for MA 497, and developed further in MA 503, in "saying good night to Alice." It's a question of, "build[ing] up other people's convictions" and ending by allowing the "other ones convictions... to be the determining frame for them," as in, GS illustrates, why she says good night to Alice in the way, and for the reason, she does. AT made no comment on this, but the implication is clear—she was adopting Alice's style ("intentions") as her own "way of loving and virtue" in that act, a way not natively her own.

the butterfly business: Begins MA 499, l.15, where the "butterfly business" is first mentioned. The "concrete and general" discussion refers to the pages above. [See Note #131].

illustrate with sketches Sally, Bianco: then "Mike and butterflies:" MA 497, l.27 to 498, l.19. The two cases "described:" the first, adopting "ritualistically" the way of the absent other one, and the second, with an "intuitive feeling" that the other one will know even though absent.

Carrie's way of building, and her abstraction: Plan, MA 492.

*

Note #131

Begin with repetition about virtuous feeling out of little book and then describe butterfly case, and so on, and so on, about old men and young men. Some kinds of young men do things to instruct them to ~~protect~~ themselves against every one. This is very common. Old ones have a different way in them etc.

Father loving children young girls. Uncle Sol, Amy, uncle them to them? Allan Mike? sometime work it all out, completely get it really solidly.

Nina's [?narrative]

*

It happens very often that a man has it in him, that a man does something, that he does it very often, that he does many things, when he is a young one and an older one and an old one.

AT ***Father loving... young girls. Uncle Sol:*** Gertrude's feeling about 'girling' for old men: She suggested once that George Hugnet's and Eugene Ullman's fathers as they got older and older began 'girling,' and that it might become dangerous. In Eugene Paul [Ullman]'s father, it was stopped once and forever by a servant girl who threw dirty dish water at him, and it made him feel that he would never again sink so low and be in such a position.

For Gertrude there was not in this any sense of criticism or even anything she could learn about them from it. As for Uncle Sol her dislike for him goes back to his feeling about the grandmother's photograph. She referred to it over the years, and I remember being impressed by her feeling about it when I heard it.

Nina's narrative: Nina's relation with her father was incestuous. It is hinted at in *The Making of Americans*, and it is also used in a portrait somewhere, probably in *Many Many Women*. Nina practically boasted of it, at least it was among the tales she told. It was common enough in the countryside anyhow, and not that unusual. Gertrude didn't use this particularly or by itself for Nina, but through knowing Nina's relations generally with men she had known.

LK ***Begin with repetition... out of little book:*** Refers to same passage as in Note #112.

Describe butterfly case: Plan for MA 489, l.34 to 490, l.6. The "butterfly case" was an incident as described in text between Mike Stein and his son Allan.

old men and young men: Plan for MA 489–491.

Some kinds of young men... Text for MA 490, l.12–13.

Old ones have a different way.... Fathers loving children young girls: Plan for MA 490, l.18–25. Old men's need "to keep warm" echoes the early Planning Note 11–9 about GS's Uncle Sol Stein, called in that Note, "Herman:" "Herman sort of needs [the fictional character named Bertha] to take place of his wife in kinds of ways scare Bertha never went beyond pressure and coming into her one night to come and keep him warm, she more out of dislike than terror, tells it to her husband."

Two further Notebook references make clear GS's personal memory of the episode: "Bertha ... stays with Herman after death of wife and has scene like the kind I had with Sol." [NB-MA #9] and "Bertha... Experience with Herman Dehning like mine with S[ol]."

Nina's narrative: Nina's narrative was the story she would tell of her incestuous relations with her father.

It happens very often... and an old one: Draft of text for a refrain beginning at MA 488, and repeated at MA 489, 490, 491.

There are very many men who are always saying.... more staying at home of an evening: Draft of text for MA 492.

*

Note #113

~~Some men~~ Some men in their youth do things that are immoral to instruct their sisters or someone, ~~eth~~ some men in their old age do it because they are cold then and need some woman some boy some one to fill them and all they are asking is to be kept warm then and then they get what they are wanting.

There will be now some description of virtuous being, virtuous feeling in men.

There are very many who are always saying if they had their life to live again they would live a different one, they would learn very many things, they would do serious reading. There are very many who always are going to more serious reading, more staying at home of an evening.

LK ***Some men in their youth…*** Draft of text expanded in MA 490–492.

*

Note #199

Explaining one's vices by one's virtues is one way of feeling thinking believing knowing, thinking believing feeling knowing overall [word?] in being.

LK ***Explaining one's vices by one's virtues… in being.*** Draft of text, MA 500.

*

Notebook G

NB-G #1

Painting in L. & Sally is reflection from really creative activities in them in him from creative creaticism from Sally from creative appreciation. Sally's seemed more like a real thing because of the sounding board feverishness that gave it a false life. Sally is for me now absolute complete. The commentator's mind, the reflection upon the text, and then she tries to make it a whole by sounding board and straining dramatic emotional intensity, the drama is sounding board as well, not real romantic drama as in the case of Edstrom, that is the great difference between them, why Edstrom is really more original. For wholes Sally has no sense of beauty, this comes out very clearly in her religiousness. It is now perfectly clear the whole of it. Some day Mike will be more complete.

AT ***Sally's... sounding board feverishness:*** There was always a false life in it, and no real impulse in anything she did.

LK ***Painting in L[eo] and Sally .... sounding board:*** The passage on Sarah Stein is referred to in Note #114 and used in MA 506–507.

*

Note #114

It is very perplexing the ~~poignant~~ generalised conception which is of virtue in many men and many women and the concrete feeling and acting that is not of virtue in them. This is perplexing. (little piece of paper): Then go on to copy again out of little book to Sally.

Then go on to Sterne's work [?], and then on and on to Mike butterfly caught for Allan, and Carrie. Another form of it like Hodder's kind is ~~Lee's chastity~~. Another form is believing other things are only a habit like ~~Russell about Nina,~~ another form is feeling themselves different like Andre and Elise surville [Inserted: Sally being lonesome and going back to uncritical C.S. and believing she cared and all because not p. [painting]], then come back to Mike's kind and go on and on and then to Alfred Hersland and all of his living.

Refer to little book about virtue and talk a great deal about it.

AT ***believing... only a habit like Russell about Nina:*** No, he said, Nina had no hold on him, it was only a habit, nothing serious. Russell was one of Nina's American conquests, and one of the four painters supported by Mrs. Payne-

Whitney. He attached himself to another painter who had a theory about painting. He was an American version of Friesz and took Cezanne with the same superficial brutality as Friesz did. It was not really brutal, just a coarseness that was no more than a lack of refinement. They were a dreary lot.

Russell was very poor. He was also a brutal, crude mid-Westerner and a physical coward. He once said something about Peggy Guggenheimer to [Lee] Simonson, who later told us, What was I to do but hit him, and I took what courage I had in my two hands and knocked him down. Gertrude was very pleased with Simonson for this.

Arthur Lee took Nina away from Russell. When Lee brought her to the Saturday Evenings at the rue de Fleurus, Gertrude was furious with him. Then Nina picked up with Leo, and he brought her once in a while. Nina then sometimes came alone and would sometimes call for Leo. Once I answered her knock, and she was asking for 'Steiney.'

Brenner was about the fourth with Nina, but then he kept her indoors and off the street. Brenner was a very experienced man, and Nina could teach him nothing. The Englishman Skeene was the one Nina almost drove to suicide, but it ended in his just going back to England instead. Gertrude knew Skeene, she did a portrait of him. He was a well-born, well-educated, gentle, firm Englishman. Leo was the only one who told Gertrude about Nina and Skeene, since he believed, like so many of those men, everything that was told to him, not only by Nina but by others.

Leo observed the forms with Nina, and his bringing her to the studio was in this spirit, but Arthur Lee in his pride and indifference had just brought her in to show her off. Gertrude thought of Nina as an expression of what Leo had become. She said, Leo is quite senile about Nina. He liked Nina to tell him about her other affairs, which Gertrude thought indicative.

Nina had a way of throwing her body about. She was literally the prostitute, with a loose-jointed, ugly, large body, like Sarah's, not ill-formed, but with not much dignity in her carriage. She walked with one shoulder up—just, in other words, a prostitute off the streets, not even of the cafes. Her eyebrows were supposed to be her most impressive feature, but she had very beautiful eyes. When she was with Americans, she dressed in the student cap of the period, like a boy.

Nina... Andre... Elise surville: Elise was an Austrian prostitute, one of Leo's loves. Gertrude wrote '*Elise Surville*'— 'Elise on the Town'—about her. Andre was another one, as was Nina. Sarah, who liked Nina [with whom Leo had a lengthy affair and eventually married] always thought Gertrude unfair about her and Leo. She refused to go to Allan's [Sarah's son's] wedding [c.1939] because Sarah had invited Leo and Nina.

Sarah... going back to uncritical C.S. Having lost Matisse because of the prices of his pictures, and having nothing to occupy her, Sarah went back to Christian Science. She had given up painting and so Mike would be pleased, not by her giving up Matisse, but going back to Mike's way of thinking about her.

LK ***It is very perplexing .... This is perplexing:*** Draft of text, introduced in MA 492 and repeated in MA 504.

little piece of paper: Refers to Note #199, which is written on a "Specimen Page" (page 192) advertising an Everyman edition of Bacon's Essays. GS's note is scribbled over the bottom of the page and on its left-hand margins.

copy again out of little book: Text again copied from NB3, #6, with inserted passage on Sarah Stein, and some further elaboration of text, in MA 505, l.1–21.

to Sally: A very long description of Sarah Stein is inserted in MA 505, l.8–14, and is resumed in MA 506, l.1 to 507, l.7, describing at length her ability to anticipate suggestions and become (especially in the presence of Matisse) a kind of "sounding board." This analysis becomes the basis for the portrait of her in Two, in which she is described in tandem with Leo Stein.

Then go on to Sterne's work: Possibly MA 503, l.33–43, but questionable.

Another form of it like Hodder's kind is ... chastity: Plan, MA 502, l.5–44.

Only a habit like Russell about Nina: Plan, MA 503, l.1–15.

feeling themselves different like Andre and Elise surville: Plan, MA 503, l.16–33.

Sally... back to uncritical C[hristian Science] ... because not p[ainting]: Plan, MA 506, l.18–38. Of this passage on Sarah Stein [see above], these lines refer to her returning to Christian Science after the Matisse school closed, and she was no longer painting. But to avoid a sense of failing, "in each [successive] thing they are doing, they are never stopping doing the last thing," but turn from it with the explanation to themselves that it had "not completely expressed the personality in them."

and then to Alfred and all of his living: Plan. MA 507, l.25, begins the history of Alfred Hersland, and does so because of the assurance that "the kind he is of human beings is to me very clear just now very clear inside me," an assurance that begins to diminish in a few pages [at MA 513]. Upon realizing that "I am now then not completely full up with him," GS determines that she "will be waiting, and then I will be full up with all the being in him." Throughout the chapter, her repeatedly lost confidence in Alfred Hersland being entirely clear and "whole" to her instigates repeated waitings, and digressions while waiting, but her sense of "wholeness" in her grasp of Alfred Hersland is never finally restored. It was during these digressive intermissions while "waiting" that the earliest Portraits began to be written.

Refer to little book about virtue: Again, the passage in NB3, #6.

*

memory,

How is some one meaning something, meaning and saying and feeling and thinking and being certain, which way.
Francis, Leo, Leon, Hutch & Sally Pach, Nadelman, Pablo, Mike, Alice.

LK ***How is someone meaning … Pablo, Mike Alice; Francis, Leo, Leon:*** [Corresponds to Ms Notes #139, #140, #141, #142, #143, on MA 782–790] Planning Note for MA 782–785. Described, possibly in sequence, but generally indistinguishable.

*

NB-G #2

Pritchard, Spicer-Simpson, Feneon, they all three have in them a certain element of bullying, they have all three of them the type of affirmation of the resisting type but it is a mixture in them between the ones like Leo Friedman and ones like Vollard or Brass. There is in them an intermediate stage some of it springing from a real sensitiveness in them, some from the surface adaptability of them and insensitiveness of them, they are interesting as such, Pach and the slow adolescent type generally are like them only all the little parts in them are individually exagerrated and actively xageratedly in succession in them. Must use these three groups in relation to George Dehning.

La Farge also in Pritchard's group, aggressive timidity the key-note of the group. There is to some extent in them the quality of Pach in Pritchard's group in Feneon of qualities xaggerated in them in succession. That Pritchard is a bully to women and won't come here cause Leo is too dogmatic like Pach only less dignified inside him as being, tabby-cat variety of men. Pach did not know why he staid away. Pach less really stupid than Pritchard's group, they are babies without the simple reactions of babies as Vollard Simon and I have them.

The abstract not poignant to them and yet they are so occupied with it that they have no real sensibility for the concrete. ~~Sterne~~ Leo F. et al.

AT ***Pritchard:*** Gertrude got to like him. She had met him through Emily Chadbourne. He had been at the Metropolitan Museum in charge of old coins and primitive Greek art and wrote on esthetics and became interested in Matisse. He eventually took Matisse to Oxford and he did there for art what Logan Pearsall Smith had done for literature. Oxford created a chair for him, and he had four or five glorious years at0 Oxford.

He was hesitant of speech and very involved in expression. And he was the one who told Gertrude, before she went to England for her lecture tour, Speak slowly and look at your audience. A Frenchman told her, Speak as quickly as you can and don't ever look at your audience.

Pritchard got to know Gertrude well when Leo left [permanently] for Italy. But this was after the war, which Pritchard spent as a civilian war prisoner in Germany.

Spicer-Simpson: An English sculptor and hypocrite, always doing underhanded things, never letting his left hand know what his right hand was doing.

Feneon: A journalist who discovered the three-line news. He looked like an inspired Uncle Sam, but he was pure French. He discovered, and knew, Seurat in his youth. The Bernheims took him on as advisor when they started to buy modern paintings.

Pritchard, Spicer-Simpson, Feneon: All three had the pasty face, but it wasn't the complete pastiness of Pach.

La Farge: The father of the present writer. A painter who also worked in glass.

Pritchard… a bully to women: He had to bully Sarah to keep her where she belonged, and Emily Chadbourne to keep her out of where she belonged, so this was easy for Gertrude to say.

won't come here cause Leo is too dogmatic: Anyone with social experience found it hard to sit at a school of philosophy at four in the morning and listen to the master monologize. Pritchard was himself accustomed to talking and people did listen. Leo never knew that they didn't want to hear him, or that they didn't really believe what he was saying.

Pach… why he staid away: Pach had already formed his opinions by this time. He was essentially an academician, and he had placed all the painters, and Leo disturbed all that. It didn't arouse Pach's interest or hold his attention.

Pach was going back to New York with a perfect set of notions and wasn't willing to have Leo disturb them. If Pach had been caught young enough, he might have been willing to listen and learn. He came to see Gertrude—that is, to hear what people were saying at the rue de Fleurus—after Leo and Gertrude had two rooms so he wouldn't have to run into Leo.

Pach, Russell and Stella were the three arrivistes, and each of them arrived in a different way, though Russell had his moment for only a few weeks. Stella was the Neapolitan abstractionist who once laid Pach out.

*

NB-G #3

Use the whole discussion Mike and kinds of resisting as introduction to Alfred Hersland's life. As a contrast ~~between~~ in resemblance between Uncle Sol and Mike. like between Bird & Martha Hersland.

Mike, Purman, and the others Sterne [Steins?], Alfy the concrete.

AT ***introduction to Alfred Hersland's life:*** By this time [at the beginning of the writing of the Alfred Hersland chapter, c. January 1910] as much as was said of people and the kind of thing that was going into the Notebooks was said to me. Gertrude wasn't talking to Leo any more.

*

NB-G #4

Mrs. Gassette in one picture looked just like Lena. Gracie in one looked like Amelie and in another like Margaret Lewis and this is very interesting and like her grandmother who was like a Guggenheimer. this makes Gracie connected with all the dep. indep. resistant types.

Mrs. G. uncertain she is like Lena, which is Lena, which is Emma, which is Lee, very uncertain.

AT ***Amelie:*** The servant of Madame Boiffard.

*

NB-G #5

Bruce, tenacity of resisting type and he clings to everything the same way, Harriet always grabbed and missed, he don't grab but whatever his fingers touch he holds on to till he slips off to something else. Has some attack which is always feeble though dogmatic and overbearing.

*

NB-G #6

Carrie is a new kind of resistant that is she is like Neith, she is always sure and builds up her own tastes and feelings piece by piece in detail and always sure of each piece. there is never any denial of anything for really she has no realisation of anything not so constructed, all general feeling is sentimental, when the detail formation is slightly disturbed she is fluttered, when it is constantly fluttered you have some one like Miss Sophie Hart.

AT *Carrie:* Carrie [Helbing], a friend of Harriet's, was visiting Paris now. She really came over to rescue Harriet from a bad situation. Though she thoroughly disapproved of Harriet and wasn't fond of her, she came out of a sense of loyalty. From Harriet's letters, she had got the idea that I was seeing too much of Gertrude and that Harriet was lonely, and when Carrie got here, I explained to her that the situation was not quite like that, and finally, long before the end of her visit, Carrie clung to me because she couldn't bear Harriet or Sarah or anybody else. It was not that she was disloyal, but she was given to a change of heart.

The 'flustered' was true of her and was part of her charm. The color would come into her face and she would get a little rosy. She would lose her wit and start to ask intelligent questions about something else. Her mind would clear itself while losing her fluster.

I corrected Gertrude about her. I said it was her charm, and that it was habitual, not so unusual. No, no, said Gertrude, you're reading it wrong, it was her mousiness that made her charming, and this was different. We ultimately compromised on it.

Carrie played a little too much for her own good—with ideas, people, things, a man (whom she finally married), a married sister, in fact everything except the big simple truths like family honor and so on. She was quite romantic. Gertrude was taken in very largely with Carrie's charm, which worked on Gertrude all right. She thought Carrie a considerable personage.

She gave up the rescue of Harriet because nobody thought it was a situation or that she needed rescue, and in any case, Harriet couldn't have put up much of a fight for it nor did Carrie think a fight on her part worth it for Harriet.

Carrie had a real antipathy toward Harriet. Once when all four of us were walking in Perugia, Gertrude and Harriet ahead and Carrie and I behind, I said something witty, and Carrie burst out, Oh, that's just like the bright Miss Levy! On another occasion, I was explaining to Harriet, Carrie is behaving abominably toward you, and Harriet said, I don't want to make a scene, I don't mind. She's leaving soon anyhow, so it's just as well to let it go. The next day Carrie came to me and she was livid. I overheard your conversation yesterday, and I think Harriet is horrible. But, I said, it was I who said those things. No, said Carrie, between Harriet and you I'd choose you every time. Finally, Gertrude had to make peace because I was on the point of being hung by Harriet.

Carrie didn't like Harriet the way she didn't like Sarah. She was here on her own. She lost her heart to Gertrude, but thought that Harriet, Annette and Sarah should all be done away with.

Gertrude told her, just as she was on the train leaving for America, Keep Harriet in California. Yes, yes, said Carrie, loving the idea of the game. And she did.

Clare [Moore, Miss Toklas' San Francisco friend] once said of Carrie, She's a cross between a fashion plate and a gutter rat.

LK ***Carrie … builds up her own tastes and feelings piece by piece:*** [Corresponds to Note #112.] The passage on Carrie Helbing is referred to in Note #112 and used in MA 492.

*

Note #215

Of the kind of one that Alfred Hersland was in his being they range from very good ones through to pretty bad ones but this is true of every kind there is of men and women. Alfred had it in him to be ~~neith~~ …

LK Draft Text, MA 522

*

Note #117

Camping shooting feeling about such things. The way he was ~~talking~~ reading and living and talking and leaving playing.

he was doing things and the ways others he was knowing then were doing things.

The crowd.

LK ***Camping shooting feeling about such things.… The crowd:*** Plan for MA 531.

The way he was doing things: MA 585–586.

*

Note #116

Allan & Jean & Jacques and Leo and Tim Bruce and Richard and Robert and Clarence as kids.

*

Note #129

Alfred anger, sister advises[r?]
~~rest and~~
important business[?]
sarcastic smile on
David.
advice, asks it and followed it
and therefor ~~show~~ had the right
to dictate, and be judicial
governesses
Just contemptuous.

Others not really realising frightening [fighting?] or just outside of experience. Later realise it more like tooth-ache or operation, nothing to be so morbid about.

LK ***Alfred anger, sister adviser.... And therefore had the right to dictate:*** Plan for MA 534

sarcastic smile on David: Plan for MA 594, l.33–36.

governesses, just contemptuous: Plan, MA 588, l.37 to 589, l.2

not really realizing frightening or just outside of experience: Used (possibly) in MA 607, l.12–30.

*

NB-G #7

Nina is a resisting type and sometime there will be much writing about her, closely connected to Mrs. Pyot and Puy's wife and Mrs. Israels.

AT ***Nina:*** Gertrude made up her mind about Nina before Leo took her on and didn't change it much after. The Portrait was written before Leo's attachment became permanent. Nina, when she was first winning Leo, had paid Gertrude those one or two visits and that was enough. Gertrude called her Nam-Nam. Such an open thing, she said, that didn't hold anything. Gertrude didn't think her the least bit interesting as a character, just easily classified of a kind.

*

NB-G #8

Jean Cheron telling all her stories and leaving out the main point and so making herself the kind of heroine she wants to be with no imagination whatsoever with which to lie is like Fernande. The story about her might be true that she had had a child. Always it makes a heroine of her, she is not dramatic, not consistently conceiving herself a thing as Sally's type do, but always the heroine of her story by leaving out something.

AT ***Jean Cheron:*** [Jeanne Cheron.] The model Leo found. She was singularly beautiful except that she had outlandish feet. Sometimes Sarah was invited to come over to Leo's studio somewhere near the rue d'Alsace and draw too. Leo also carried on a flirtation there with Eileen Gray, a very beautiful English girl.

Jeanne Cheron... stories... like Fernande: They both had the same story about having had a child. Gertrude had heard the story of Fernande's child from Mme. Matisse, but took no stock in it, as few did. Fernande told that she ran away from home with a man who left her and whom she never saw again. When Pablo proposed that they marry, about the time, probably, when Derain decided to marry Alice—they took these things as jokes: 'We will all marry!'—Fernande said she couldn't because, apparently, she was already married to this man. Ironically, Fernande's sister-in-law [through this husband] came to see her after the Liberation and told Fernande that her husband had been dead three or four years before Pablo asked her to marry.

In storytelling, Jeanne Cheron came after Nina, who didn't have to have any drama, any lies, because she had the tale to tell. Nina filled her voids with a theatrical laugh, noise, suddenly banging something. Jeanne Cheron had nothing, so she had to use the lies.

*

NB-G #9

Since I have known Carrie I am certain that Stell is resisting and in blobs other thing connecting. Carrie is in pieces and only connects by sentimentality of a dull and conventional kind. More and more she is interesting to me. The thing is like this I think now, there is the element that is so to speak self-produced in her, her certainties, her tastes and ways, her needs in respect to her self-conception, in Neith it is aesthetic books and literature. this is ~~slef~~ self produced and is rich. In case of Mrs. Friske[?], is lyrically rich in a diffused way. In Stell it is resisting kind, then there is in these a reaction to stimulus and much of the love emotion in these people is of such a character, it is almost a surface reflection to stimulation as it is a good deal in me but in all of them excepting a little in Estelle there is not a maternal affection which is spontaneous and helps out nor an active idealisation. The morality of these people is all part of this superficial reaction, it is the generalised form of it, it is not connected with such things as are certain things in them. Morality generalised superficial reactions to stimulus in many cases. The things the people are certain of are not there. In Carrie the things she is certain of can't fill up all the time. It takes vanity or pride or conceit or energy of some sort to fill up all the time, she fills it up with just dimly groping for the memory of her sensations in respect to her certainties. Her response to masculinity is never a certainty, it is a fluttering reaction like when something interferes with the completion of some little certainty. I think this helps out with Neith and Stell. Also in a way with Gracie et al, what I call their aggression is superficial reaction and it is their emotional passion their realer passion is either like Mike's or like Pablo's or like mine or a bit engulfing[.] I think this will help out in Mike.

AT ***love emotion... a surface reflection to stimulation... as it is... in me:*** There is a story behind this note. It came about in this way. Carrie, Gertrude, Fernande and I took the metro one afternoon to visit Marie Laurencin. In the metro, I didn't like it, Fernande didn't mind, and Gertrude and Carrie were talking. Presently, I said very loud, Do we have to stay here? and Fernande said, Yes. But when I looked over to Gertrude, I saw to my horror that her hand was resting on Carrie's. Then I repeated my question, and when Carrie said, No we won't get out, I got furious. When we were finally out, Gertrude asked, You wanted to get out because of Carrie? No, I said. But you were angry? Yes, at what I saw. What did you see? I saw what I saw. Well, said Gertrude, I wanted to put my hand on yours, and you weren't beside me, so I put it on Carrie's. Yes yes, I said. We'll leave it. Later when Carrie put it on Harriet when I was the one at fault, I said to Gertrude, You see, you did what Carrie does. That's Carrie's way of doing it.

Remember, Carrie was elfin, romantic, it was what one liked in her. And that's perfectly in accord with Gertrude's analysis of her 'superficial reactions to stimulus' and so on.

Carrie Helbring: Gertrude told her just as she was on the train leaving for America, "Keep Harriet in California". Yes, yes, said Carrie, loving the idea of the game. And she did.

Carrie had real antipathy toward Harriet. Once when all four were walking in Perrugia, Gertrude and Harriet ahead and myself and Carrie behind, I said something particularly witty, and Carrie burst out, 'Oh that's the bright Miss Levy'.

On another occasion I was explaining to Harriet, Carrie is behaving abominably to you, Harriet. And Harriet said, I don't want a scene, I don't mind. She's leaving soon anyhow, so it's just as well to let it go. The next day, Carrie came to me and was livid. I overheard your conversation yesterday, and I think Harriet is horrible. But, I said, it was I who said those things. No, said Carrie, between Harriet and you I'd choose you every time. Finally, Gertrude had to make peace, because I was on the point of being hung by Harriet.

Carrie didn't like Harriet the way she didn't like Sarah. She was on her own. She lost her heart to Gertrude, but thought that Harriet, Annette, and Sarah should all be done away with.

Clara Moore [Miss Toklas' San Francisco friend] said of Carrie: "She's a cross between a fashion late and a gutter cat."

*

NB-G #10

George Sand and Nina have powerful genuinely resisting personalities and they have with [it] the creative adaptability that Sally has. Sally's character is not powerful enough to make her a great man's woman of the dominating type. These other two have it. George Sand much more diffuse than Nina.

AT ***great man's woman of the dominating type:*** This is apropos of Nelly. Nelly and Sarah are also coupled in the Notebooks further back.

*

NB-G #11

Carrie living up to the created type of the delicate blonde
what is in Neith flavor both resistant servant girl type au fond. Their created ideal comes from intermittent activity of a part of themselves, and so gives them their flavor, not the continuous bottom of them or else they would be different.

*

NB-G #12

Alice and others like them the sexual nature of them determines their kind but their continuous activities are due to sublimated forms of this nature, only shows in them when highly stimulated or in Carrie's and Neith's case when slightly stimulated. Remember this distinction.

*

NB-G #13

Russell, Leo said it was like a billiard ball set going reaction prompt and personal but still a reaction. Go at great length into personal and reactive parts of personality.

*

NB-G #14

Lee like David, very completely sensitive like him.

*

NB-G #15

Harriet is so stupid that she has common sense, cannot keep on continuously exhalted.

*

NB-G #16

Ullman & Pollovetzki

they are very much alike banal and vague and slow, they are highly subtle forms of the kind of big thick vulgar Jewishness that runs theatres and trains ballet girls. These have black eyes from brown and are rather spread forms of Germaine and some tighter some looser ones like that. This whole class closely connected with Mabel Haynes, and then in the other direction with the brown eyed ones to Pablo.

AT ***Ullman & Pollovetski:*** Superficial, yes, but this kind vary to Mabel Haynes. Also, there is a certain kind of vindictiveness in Ullman and Mabel Haynes. They are more loyal to themselves than to anyone else.

Mabel Haynes: Black eyes, very long face, mouth a bit open. An Italian face.

LK ***Ullman and Pollovetski:*** [Dating: GS met the Ullmans Dec 1909.]

*

NB-G #16a

Russell is really attacking like Green not very sensitive but really attacking. The lame man with him I must think more about. The little bowery street tough cute boy is an attacking little kid of the sensitive kind mad [?]

into [?] [firy? fury?], Alice has a little of that only her sensitiveness being so much more complete she doesn't attack in little hits.

AT ***bowery street tough:*** An amateur pugilist. He took Brenner, Gertrude and me to a prize fight in a hall near the Sorbonne.

*

NB-G #17

Bianco has no convictions he wants to win and he wants the excitement of constant change, he has not as much continuity of personality as Gladys Deacon who is held together by her vagueness. He is incessant in his qualities and nothing is self-directed. She is so vague that somethings seem to come from herself inside her. These light blue eyed ones should be really resistant but nothing touches them enough to make them so, it is a very interesting group.

*

NB-G #18

Zobel is like Ullman & Pollovetzki, that comes to make the group clearer, & Carlo Levy in Florence. The Infantas court was between Tommy and Loeser.

AT ***The Infanta's court:*** The Princess Eulalia and her two ladies of honor. When she was first brought to Gertrude's at the rue de Fleurus by Alice Ullman, she stood back in the court and asked, What is this, is this a trap. Alice Ullman persuaded her anyhow. The Infanta was extremely, madly beautiful, like an Infanta should look and like a Bourbon beside. She had the raucous Spanish voice and a perfectly modelled body. She and Gertrude got to like each other.

LK ***Infanta:*** [Dating: GS met the Infanta Eulelia Dec 1909]

*

NB-G #19

Some men and women who are of the attacking kind are apparently resisting because they cannot think and feel, hear and think at the same time.

*

NB-G #20

The reason Brenner does not touch me is because he is the complete instrument. He has no more personality than a violin absolutely no more. He looks interesting in consequence but he is not. I know no attacking one who is so completely an instrument but I suppose they do exist, perhaps Lee is nearest to it but he isn't it, nor anyone else that I yet know. Brenner has no personality, he does not even make his manias personal, it is not like in Bianco, Bianco has an ambition, to keep on top if it is only bobbing like a boat on the waves, Brenner has no intention, none, he is the least intentioned person I have ever known, he has not even the vanity or conceit to make personality, not fear nor courage, nor pleasure, nothing at all to make personality, he is completely an instrument, he has not even the slightest tinge of being mechante of being anything whatsoever that is volitional, that is the reason I think he is bound to end up a madman but not a maniac, he is not volitional enough for that.

AT ***Brenner... to end up a madman but not a maniac:*** I used to ask Gertrude about Brenner. Will he go mad? And Gertrude always said, No. This Note was why she thought so, apparently. The only thing Brenner did have was precision, and this probably had an ethical base. Once he cut a dress for me. What shall I cut it with? Scissors, of course, I answered. It ought to be a razor, said Brenner.

LK ***Brenner .... violin .... not volitional enough for that:*** Note expanded in MA 548, l.26 to 549, l.20.

*

NB-G #21

Harriet has black eyes from brown like Pollovetzki, Zobel Germaine Pischot et al, only she is that without life, Sam Wolfe is of it too, that makes it more understood by me, Harriet's lack of real sensibility and her worldliness, these all have cleverness and a capacity for being always in the foreground with novelty, their stuff may be putrid as in Germaine or Mabel Haynes or simply dull as in Zobel, or subtle as in Pollovetzki & Ullman or dead as in Harriet or electric as in Sam Wolfe, but it is always dirty grey and resisting, and nothing is really lost in it and so they quickly react but with no fresh addition.

AT ***Germaine Pischot:*** [Germaine Pichot.] Strange to find her here with Ullman and Pollovetski. She seemed so tight, bound and complete. This is odd.

Harriet... lack of real sensibility... worldliness: Harriet had been a dramatic critic on a San Francisco newspaper for years. She was mixed up largely with newspaper people. She believed she would do the great American novel one day—jump from newspaper work to that.

Harriet… lack of real sensibility… cleverness: Bad drama and quick wit, that was Harriet. How Mike hated her. He considered her pretensions affectations, though they really weren't.

*

NB-G #22

Description

A History of Everyone.

Flandrin & his wife the seamstress painter, Derain and Alice, Puy and his lady, Adele O & me & Leo F, Adele Solomons & Sally and me. etc etc. Fabri & his lady, Miss Blood & the Princess Ullman & his wife, etc. Tommy Whittemore and all of us. Will you do something for me, listen to the chimes. Fred & Amy when he waited to go with the crowd and Amy did not know what answer he wanted. Leo Friedman reading the signs for Ruth. Ruth carrying the bag. Hutch & Edstrom & everybody Howard & Willard—Willard & Hutch, Hutch & everybody, Howard & Bird Brenner & Nina, Brenner & Bianco, Gladys & B.B. dead. Jeanne Cheron and Sally, Jean & Leo, Jean & Nina, Jeane & everybody, Valloton & Matisse & Mrs. Matisse's house Weber and Sally and Weber & me no discrimination in women Mrs. Bruce and Sally, Edstrom & Matisse.

AT ***Flandrin and his wife:*** Mme. Marval, who was a little deformed and had a brilliant smile. She took to painting and did it successfully. He was not a successful painter. She did big pictures of women figures which were exhibited at the Independants.

listen to the chimes: A great joke in the household. A postal card sent from Tommy Whittemore to Mabel Weeks, she going to Bruges. Will you do something for me, listen to the chimes.

*

Notebook H

NB-H #1

Sally, what one used to call archangel quality is really the hitched upness to the Almighty after the activity of hitching herself is at an end. This is very illuminating, the impression of a state without either the emotion or the condition of it. That is true with a great deal of Edstrom's emotion, in short it is the quality of being a charlatan. That is the essence of charlatanism. And in religious matters more apt to be the case with s.[word?] more than with other things because of the essentially generalise[d] character of religious conception and the real power of reflection that she has of the commentator type has then no way of expressing itself that is the reason why that expression is chronic when religion is uppermost, and when that takes a practical form it makes the lobbyist, the practical application of that left over generalised state.

AT ***Sally… the hitched upness to the Almighty:*** When the [Matisse] class was over, and Matisse was successful and Sally couldn't afford the pictures, life was empty, and she went back to Christian Science at once. Thereafter, going to Italy, everyone went first class because Mike said, We're not buying pictures any more. This was the summer of 1910 when Mike did this, the last summer that Harriet went to Italy with them.

There's a good deal of irony in this for Gertrude. Sally would become so exalted on occasion that much of what Gertrude would say to her she would not hear at all, she would be so carried away with her emotion. Words would flow from her then with no particular meaning in them, but without hesitation, and they would be her own reiteration of Mrs. Eddy.

Edstrom… the quality of being a charlatan: It was Gertrude who first suggested to me that my friend [Lily Hansen] go to Edstrom [for a Christian Science healing.] She didn't do it as a game, she really meant it. This was a Scandinavian girl, and Gertrude thought Edstrom could understand the Scandinavian in her and deduct it in the treatment. But Edstrom's curiosity got to the bottom of the story without ever asking—that she hated her father because of what he had done to her mother. After giving him her physical symptoms, he began to ask at once about her father.

Gertrude never wanted to know how Edstrom attacked his patients for the healing. She was not the least bit interested in how it was done or what was done. By then anyhow Edstrom had gone completely corrupt and was more interested in the patient than in the healing. My friend paid for one meeting and got out from under, saying Edstrom was the most awful man she had ever known. What business was it of his what my father had been up to? Edstrom had a fairly lively curiosity then, so his questions to his patients were beginning to come more from inquisitiveness than from professional zeal.

That's what pleased Harriet about Edstrom, that he had a special gift. But it came in flashes, and they were not frequent.

*

NB-H #2

Sally

Emotional intensity is the root of the being in her and she applies this to each thing that comes to her and bathing in this emotional intensity believes that the thing which comes from the outside comes from the root of her being and is deepened by her emotion, it is not, it is intensified and is a thing that comes to her made ready by somebody, her sensitiveness and receptivity and docility which I call reverence in her is there in her and something comes to her, ethics, art, religion what not and she bathes it in the emotional intensity of her and this [is] certainly the being in her. What I call aggressive optimism that is that such of them see only the thing that is then being bathed in the emotional intensity of them and so then there is aggressive and unreasoning optimism in them.

*

NB-H #3

Matisse like Mildred carries on the sensation of la vie est triste beyond where they have any vivid sensation, in fact mostly this thing is in them not a sensation not even a conviction but a convention from the historical sense in them for the life they are living. Matisse has cleaness as an intellectual pictorial quality.

Octave Mirabeau et al have it as an emotion not as an intellectual realisation. The sensitiveness of the Alice & Leo type added to this makes a man like Wm. James, the true attacking type.

AT ***Mildred carries on the sensation:*** A perfect picture of Mildred [Aldrich.] Even when she was foolish, she carried the enormous conviction of herself and all things.

Matisse... carries on the sensation of la vie est triste: This, when he came back after the Olga [Meerson] episode. Sally Christian Scienced the episode and would have none of it. Gertrude and I knew more of it than Mme. Matisse and Bruce when Matisse and Olga both disappeared and returned together.

*

NB-H #4

Matisse Sally was saying and it probably came from him, Matisse spent eight years trying to prove to himself that he was wrong, of a Cezanne one would always say that he was trying to prove to himself that he was right. Matisse not a storm-tossed soul, his emotion is clear, and is pressed through obstacles, but his emotion always remains a clear thing, his emotion is not muggy or earthy or quivering. Leo and James are clear by rationalising their material. Matisse is clear in his emotional power, that has a clarity and pushes through all obstacles and the more the resistance the difficulties the more vivid the expression. Mrs. Matisse the true type of dep. independent, she is now once more a power in attacking, they resist but do not attack when in trouble, this is sure.

*

NB-H #5

Russell is connected with Simon H and all those but in his case there is actually attacking actively only it is only that when there has been an impact, it is not self-generated. In other respects he is like them with always remembering this modification.

*

NB-H #6

If Pritchard were stupid or ambitious he would be less futile. He is amiable in his intentions and large in his aspirations but a weak no not weak no thin, not much of him and that with the other things in him makes him cowardly and shy and arrogant. If he were solidly stupid like Feneon that would give him a solid bottom or if he were dull and ambitious like Spicer Simpson that would make him efficient, now he is just futile, to be going to hear lectures and learning philosophy from Sally at his age, they all then have it Feneon Sp. Simpson & Pritchard amiable intentions large aspirations and no successful worldly instincts adaptations therein they differ from Leo Friedman et al.

AT ***Pritchard... learning philosophy from Sally:*** This is from the story of Myrtle, Sally's sister, who reported that when Pritchard comes, 'We just chat.' This was at the end of the Matisse episode. It was through Pritchard that Sally got to know Emily Chadbourne, whom Gertrude and I got to know about three years later.

Gertrude got to be quite fond of Pritchard after his four years as a civilian prisoner in Germany [during the first world war.] He came out apparently a chastened spirit.

LK ***amiable intentions large aspirations:*** Used in MA 562, l.41 to 563, l.2.

[A corresponding note, Ms Note #85, for MA 562, preceding **par. 1**, and again preceding **par. 2**: "Amiable intentions gentle aspirations."]

*

NB-H #7

Surely I have somewhere described Chalfin keeps going from early moral purpose,

LK Not evident. Multiple descriptions of Chalfin steer in multiple directions but give no evidence of "keep[ing] going from early moral purpose."

*

NB-H #8

From the way Alice acts about the Annette business I may come gradually to think that she cares more about loving than about me, that is she cares more about having completely possession of loving me than of loving me, in short the perfect emotion is more to her than the object of it and if I get to think so her tears won't touch me, not so very much.

AT ***the way Alice goes on about the Annette business:*** This was going on before Annette left in the summer of 1908. For me, Annette was always the Stinker and I had an unholy horror of her. My father said to me about Annette, 'You must never forget that Annette has an unfortunate disposition.' Whatever her disposition was, I loathed her. During my first year [in Paris,] I played tricks on her. I got her to miss appointments with Gertrude, who would afterwards give Annette merry hell. When I told her about it years later, Gertrude roared her head off.

Annette was a handful the way Gertrude raised her. When I first came to Paris, Gertrude was in the midst of working on Annette, trying to make a normal human being of her. But Annette always went blank in the crisis, would forget what she had said, what was said to her, and so on.

Annette was very tall, very thin, and had quantities of hair—hair was one thing Gertrude never noticed—animal eyes like a frightened deer's, ugly fingers, a beautifully proportioned body. When she was unhappy, she went quite green, and during the year she was in Paris when I was here, she was most of the time green. Normally she had the coloring of painted porcelain; all the Rosenshines had this indescribable coloring. During the year she was in Paris, when Gertrude laid her out so low, she was at her worst. Will she ever get back her looks, I asked Gertrude, that you took away from her? There's a photo of her at Yale taken at the Luxembourg Gardens, very tall she was, with a fur collar, during the dismal days after she gave up the Matisse school.

Annette thought of herself as a flirt in the old eighteen-karat way, but actually she had the heaviest hand there was. When I said this of her to Gertrude, she said, That's daily food for Annette, to be as mistaken about herself as she is. She never married, even though her mother was the matchmaker. Once, before she came over, I was pushing her to marry someone, but she seemed frightened, and the gentleman rather quickly married someone else.

She was so self-centered, and so miserable about it, that she took anything in her family that she wanted to. It just became hers in a short time. She said to me once, I never let anything escape me. No, you don't, my dear, I agreed, seeing the point differently.

Annette would have had enormous beauty had she not had a harelip. She made enormous capital of it in her youth, when she used it in her defense. Her mother Lizzie adored her, and Annette in her family was treated a little apart, though not as a Princess. When Annette gave up painting and went back to San Francisco after Gertrude convinced her to, Lizzie would say, 'My daughter will never paint again,' as though painting were a disgrace to the family. Lizzie disapproved of my knowing Nelly and Frank Jacott and Ada, and told my father so, on whom it had no effect. She thought Nelly and Ada were bad women—she meant 'fast'—and wrote Annette in Paris not to see me. Gertrude saw Lizzie's letter, told me of it, and I explained. [Gertrude, during her 'treatment' of Annette, had put Annette under obligation to show her all the letters she received.]

Albert was Annette's younger brother, and Leo and Edith another brother and sister. Albert was the one who absconded with about $850,000, and when the trial and investigation were about to take place, he died of a heart attack. He supported Annette, kept their home, and finally, after Annette had allowed her money to dwindle through bad investments, he supported her entirely.

Annette attached herself to anything that was interesting, that was new, and that would save her. Later on, she went Gurdjieff and afterwards she went

Freud. (Once Mike started to say, I dreamed last night, and the Stinker interrupted quickly. Don't say anything more, I'll know too much about you. Her Freud.) Gurdjieff was the Russian who mixed up Eastern living and dancing with promiscuity and worked a theory and a way of life out of the combination. Katherine Mansfield went down to where he was in Fontainebleau to be cured by Gurdjieff, and she died there. Jane Heap adopted legally the two Margaret Anderson children and put them with Gurdjieff. It was through Jane Heap that Gertrude and I later came to know Gurdjieff.

Annette Rosenshine: There is a photo of her at Yale, taken at the Luxembourg gardens, very tall she was, with a fur collar, during the dismal days, after giving up the Matisse school.

*

NB-H #9

Bruce is certainly resisting, Russell is certainly attacking, Dasburgh with those fanatic and brilliant ~~weak~~ ~~blue~~ deep blue eyes is I think the weakest thing they make in resisting or he may not be Dasburgh and Robert Kohn, Dolene and Marion Walker all puzzle me very much yes. Mabel Weeks has some connection with them. ~~Lee~~

*

NB-H #10

Lee is like Edstrom attacking, so is Mrs. Ullman, so is perhaps Mildred but of Mildred I am not yet certain. I am pretty sure Robert Kohn is attacking he is like the man who is married to the woman who is like Janet Dodge. Janet Dodge is resisting, Bianco is resisting. I am almost certain Leo said Harriet in the spiritual world thought the world owed her a living, that is undoubtedly true, she likes Morrison he is pathological version of Edstrom suits Harriet.

AT ***Morrison:*** Kenneth Morrison, the man who married Miss [Kate] Douglas, the Christian Scientist.

*

NB-H #11

Harriet Levy & Ullman and Pollovetzki and Germaine, the quality of their eyes all alike.

*

NB-H #12

Nadelman no profundity of emotion.

*

NB-H #13

Relation of Julian Stein to Feneon's group, like Pablo to Leo Friedman's group I am thinking.

*

NB-H #14

Frost and Annette have the instinct for distinction for people and things that merit distinction but not the emotion of the things that gives to those people distinction. Consequently to educate them you have to teach them to recognise and realise the things that those people realise who have distinction and that can only be done by teaching them to realise the detail of thinking and feeling, hence the method I employ of minute observation.

AT ***Frost:*** Frost was a good-looking edition of Annette, lean and tall and thin and dark and princely in appearance and empty in the head. He was just what Annette wasn't—successful. If he painted a picture, it would be well hung, and it would be sold. He was quite stupid, but such pride in his success. He was the son of Frost the illustrator, but the distinction he had, a good deal of that came from his mother.

Annette: Annette with her chic had the false allure of Frost's distinction and elegance, but he certainly was elegant.

Gertrude thought of her as being empty except for her vague aspirations. Gertrude said, There's a great deal that's simply empty in Annette—not as I said muggy in her—and so there is really little emptying to do.

*

NB-H #15

Pritchard more aspiration and emotion of sweetness and light & culture and love than character and intelligence and feeling, like a cannon ball resting on cotton batting. It sinks in and ain't supported.

LK ***Pritchard… like a cannon ball resting on cotton batting:*** Plan, MA 562, l.16–17.

*

NB-H #16

Alice said of her father that he always comes in ~~gro~~ intending to be useful as Mike does and then he isn't and comes to be in the way. Feneon and Pritchard certainly good-natured in intention and with amiable impulses but cottony and therefor cowardly shy and brutal when they can let go to win. Relation to Frost and Annette on one side of vanity and Pach et al on the side

AT ***Alice said of her father:*** No, this is more like Gertrude's father. When he made a mess and got in the way, he just left, leaving the whole thing just as Mr. Hersland did. What he had like Mike was very sensitive, delicate, masculine hands that could do things.

*

NB-H #17

Leo said that Johnston said he only cared about pictures for what he could get out of them and Leo said he wanted to be—enter into them and indent and them and Johnston said that he Johnston was more intimate with them than Leo and Leo said Johnston had a queer notion of intimacy if he thought caring for a thing for what you can get out of it is more intimate than living in it and with it and Johnston said that was true and that was really the nature in him and he was like it and Leo says he looks like it. Johnston has a mouth fuller but in character like that of Alger Thorold, Leo says he has not Thorold's pleasant inquisitiveness. Inquisitiveness is a subject I must think about.

AT ***Johnston:*** May be the husband of the California girl whom Sally knew. He was the one who said to his wife when she bought Italian furniture, They look somewhat used, my dear. His wife was a painter.

*

NB-H #18

Why does Frost want to do anything.

*

NB-H #19

Alice remarked about Sally that she could not talk to more than one person, Sally is really a medium, she transforms not at all the material that is given her she just gives it forth personally, she is rather empty in between. Lobbyists is the only way she could talk to more than one as from a platform, she could not be sensitive to more than one she can do practical work because the work holds her, presents problems in detail to her, she cannot propose problems to herself not even in detail. This is very important.

*

NB-H #20

Mildred like Stella attacking with complete bottom resisting. She cannot formulate quickly enough to bottom her attack. Picture at eighteen was more resisting, this kind must see themselves dramatically, one cannot conceive themselves emotionally with such a fundamental contradiction, one must conceive themselves as one thing or another entirely, emotionally and so never really entirely. Claribel conceives herself steadily as slow, Mildred alternates between the two things, the bottom resisting and the rest clean attacking fighting people off to keep them from attacking because not really enough resisting being to be really winning by resisting. This is interesting.

*

NB-H #21

Nina, May, Nelly, et al adapt their loving to anyone who is interesting.

LK ***Nina, May, Nelly, et al adapt their loving to anyone who is interesting:*** Draft of text, MA 575. Text reads: "Lena, Maria and Hetty and others that I am not now naming adapt their loving to anyone who is interesting."

*

Notebook I

NB-I #1

Nina, Maria & Etta and May Nelly ~~et al~~ other ones that I am not now naming adapt their loving to anyone who is interesting. They then want, not to own them, not to influence them, but to feel power in themselves through them, to know inside them that they are knowing the things the one who is interesting is knowing. These end up by marrying a man's man who only likes them of all women who is only owned by them of all women. Sally is possessed by the thing so she is different, Annette wants distinction herself so she is different. Hortense and Maria Heiroth care enough about genius to need to love one having genius in them, they have more real personal passion, more founded courage in them than May or Nelly or Nina. Bird is different because she wants herself to do the thing, she does not know that she adapts her loving and really stubborness pretty nearly stops her being adapting.

I am thinking, I am not yet certain every kind I have been describing of the resisting kind of them can be found with a different action in the attacking kind of them, I am thinking. I will now describe a kind of them and I know more of them and some of them I known in loving known very well in loving and some are of the attacking and some of the resisting kind of them and I will be describing them together so any one can see why I am thinking that there are attacking kinds corelative to the resisting kinds I have been describing.

Then after description go on

"But all this is one thing and now being in Alfred Hersland is something. I have been describing a considerable number of men and women having resisting being in them. Alfred Hersland had resisting engulfing being in him. Having been understanding so many having resisting being in them makes it more certain that I am understanding the being in Alfred Hersland.["]

Go on now to copy.

LK ***Nina, Maria & Etta and May Nelly… adapt their loving…. have been describing.*** Draft of text, MA 575.

But all this is one thing …. Go on now to copy. Draft of text for MA 575.

*

NB-I #2

Nina like May likes to go about to get herself excited but she has not the ultimate emotion as have Maria & Hortense Federleicht.

*

NB-I #3

Work out the drama between Alice and me, me wanting to give but resisting being owned wanting the feeling of generosity but not wanting to be possessed. So in a sense wanting to be right and yet have my own way. I h. h.

*

NB-I #4

Gracie's solemn superficial conviction about mediumistic power, and her romance, work her up.

AT ***Gracie… her romance:*** [Grace Gassette.] Her 'romance' was the son of the Saturday Evening Post editor, and he was her big romance, and that was the reason she came to Europe. Mildred Aldrich used to throw up her hands over Gracie Gassette because of this episode. 'What are you going to do with someone like that? She is so stupid that when she had one opportunity, she didn't have the sense to make the most of it.'

*

NB-I #5

Harriet & Sam Wolfe.

In these sometimes ~~that~~ what in them I have been just describing turns into [word??] before it is sensation about the person, the thing done or anything, in these turns into cleverness in them or self-protection in the sense of doing nothing and breaking every obligation. In some it turns before it is really a sensation into a sensual passion.

This is all very interesting surely to anyone really believing really being certain completely certain that different ones are different in kind from other kinds of them or really different in experiencing. This is in a way a very different thing to really truly believe in one that some one really has a completely different kind of a way of feeling a thing from another one. Mostly everyone in practical living needs only to be completely realising their own experiencing and then need only to be realising other ones experiencing enough to be using them. It is a very different thing to really believe it of another one what the other one is really feeling, it is such a very long learning anybody must be having to be really to be actually believing this thing. I do this thing. I am a rare one, I know this always more in living, I know always more in living that other ones really are believing what they are believing feeling what they are feeling, thinking what they are thinking, always more and more in living I ~~am~~ know I am a rare one, there are not very many having this very completely really in them. To go on now then describing a little more these I have been mentioning.

Then go on to Harriet having a revelation and Harriet thinking she was believing dead is dead from copy and that every one spiritually owes her a living.

LK ***In these... I have just been describing ... these I have been mentioning:*** Draft of text, MA 565.

Then go on to Harriet... from copy ... owes her a living: Plan for MA 567–568.

*

NB-I #6

Note is missing

*

NB-I #7

Sally, Adele O and many others are completely certain that learning that to be dead is not to be at all a really dead one makes every one a much better one than each one really is in living. Some only believe it for themselves, some believe their believing it makes all other ones better ones than those other ones are really in living. Some are very often realising that some one is a bad one but they have not understanding in them why any one should be a bad one. Very many never learn anything from the experience with themselves they have in living. They are always repeating of themselves what they could have been learning that they would not be succeeding in doing. Very many are not all their living learning anything from the experience they have with themselves in their living. This is very common. Alfred Hersland in a way was such a one. All the Hersland men in a way were such ones in their living, Mr. David Hersland in his living, Alfred & David Hersland in their living. Alfred Hersland was in a way such a one. This is now to be a complete history of him.

LK [See MA 576]

*

NB-I #8

There is something in what everyone says about anyone. In some way anything, everything anyone, every one says about any one is a true thing. ~~Somebody~~ Each one says something about some one and that one says something about that one about herself or himself and everything any one, anything any one says about that one anything that one says about that one everything that one says about that one is in a way a true thing.

Go on now and illustrate this by Mike's, my, Howard's Sally's and Leo's own version about his intent in dieting. Go on to what Sally thinks of herself what Polly what Alice what Mike what Mabel what Harriet what Adele what Dora what Alice Klauber thinks what her mother thinks of her, and what Edstrom thinks of her and Palme and what I progressively have thought of her and what she thinks people think of her. What Louis Steinberger thought of himself and told his children.

A full history of Mike so, of Pritchard so, of Berenson so and so to Albert Rosenshine and Alfred Hersland.

AT ***Leo's dieting:*** It was undertaken as something that was going to change him. Then he felt as though he were lifted off is feet by his long fast, that he was walking on air, and that he was freed for the first time in his life. He would undergo these exaltations while everyone else was trembling for his life.

The fasting started when I was living at the rue de Fleurus. He always thought that the experience he had during it was unique, and that it had sprung from something within himself, that the result of the fast and his reaction to it were unique. There was an unholy fear on everyone's part that he would find out that it was a fad and of no value. But never did he see the deception, he just went on to something larger and larger, to another elevation. Leo was always giving everyone an anxious moment in these ways.

He was always curing himself of something. It started with Fletcherism. It went on to a diet of his own invention. Then came the period of the fasts, the first for three days, then a week, then a month, and so on. When he appeared after breaking his fast, he was always weak, in a bad state of health, and under the impression that great thoughts had come to him, not realizing they were everybody's thoughts when fasting. Gertrude said that when he started to talk afterwards, it was all vague. She felt he had never been able to do clear thinking, and he couldn't now.

Toward the end of a twenty or thirty day fast, he couldn't move and was so weak that he had to stay in bed. When he came out, he was 'walking on air'—Harriet's phrase, after seeing God—but Leo couldn't walk much.

I never saw anyone fast both for his health and his philosophy at the same time. At the beginning he put a limit on his fast and did it for the number of days he said he would. Oh, the horrible calculation of it! Gertrude would go in to him during his fast and ask if he were feeling well, and he would waft her away and ask for one book or another. Mike toward the end got impatient and couldn't bear it and stayed away. Sarah remained aloof, since there was a fair break between Sarah and Gertrude and Leo, which Leo later made up when he got fits of going to Sarah's to talk to her. The break was not about anything in particular, just a gradual moving away. Of Leo's friends, Bruce thought the fasting absurd and treated it as a joke when it was over.

Albert Rosenshine: was Annette's brother. Leon and Edith were another brother and sister.

*

NB-I #9

Edmund and May in a way are of the flavor kind, they live in a flavor life but they do not make themselves important to themselves in it, au fond Edmund is a stupid fairly solemn unthinking believing lethargic non-poignant resisting person, at bottom May is a practical anarchistic grimy servant girl person, to themselves they are not really important for either being in them, but they are really actively living the flavor life and passively living the other being in them. Olga is like this, at bottom she is stupid resisting as Bertha is stupid attacking but being is there so stagnant in her it is very hard to be certain whether it is resisting or attacking, for the rest there is in her nervous pathologically sexual attacking and so not any one can understand that there is never any history in any man ever knowing her when she is always so constantly beginning and going on with them. She is like the Houghtons ~~there a~~ not living really to herself in either way in this living, she is really living in both of them and to herself inside her is not ever certain that she is living in the two of them. The one she is actively living the nervous sexual attacking, the other she is passably living. There are more who ~~to themselves~~ have flavor being and are to themselves important in living in that being and sometime there will be in the life of David Hersland many descriptions of these and of one who was the complete thing of living in the flavor of things in existing.

*

NB-I #10

Alice attention and not interest, complete flavor person, poignant attention pleasure, no interest excepting in what catches attention. Purest living.

*

NB-I #11

Mrs. Rosengarter Therese Ehrmans aunt is from Annette's description like Mme Demarez and Mrs. Edstrom, this is the type earthy that are certain nothing is existing except everything, they love themselves in being certain that everything is really existing completely simply existing, that is resisting mysticism, this is quite common use this in doubters of religion in David. Attacking mysticism Hutch, Alice, losing themselves in attacking complete emotion.

AT ***Mrs. Rosengarter Therese Ehrmans aunt:*** Therese Ehrman's mother turned to Christian Science, being practical. This aunt may have, but I don't know.

*

NB-I #12

Pretty brutal yes, I always knew it and now I am more sure of it. They can be more brutal those like that because they do not realise themselves as naturally bad and selfish and mean and unloving. Those who are seeing themselves this way have to make the effort to keep up an appearance, to be sentimental perhaps, so that they cannot let themselves be simply what is their impulse. Some are unconscious in this self-restraint like Etta & Julius Levey who hate whats sexual and low because they are not spontaneously idealistic. And that is what Howard Ghans and to a certain extent D[ic]kens don't realise, that they being really idealists can be honest, those who are not really idealists would make a great mistake to be honest, to be honest would be to have no real restraining power over themselves at all for why should you not be a hog excepting for your nature, ideals or social conventions. Its all foolishness. Amelioration not utopia is the only solution. Of course you can let yourself go if you know you won't go very far. L[eo] is a good example. I think I understand now, mistaken about power of abstraction, imaginative realisation not vivid enough to get so far away from presented problems of another's work of art. No complete power of construction imaginatively when too abstract. Trouble with writing book. It ought to be about concrete works of art to be really interesting. Quality of description very different then because original. In other case by own confession some one else always has had to do the completed thing, he cannot do the completed thing in realisation or expression. Will not do what he can because not comprehensive enough. When sufficiently comprehensive lacks imaginative content. Simplification is then empty. Would never believe it. Certainly not.

Has passion and is poignant but lacks richness and concentration so it becomes enthusiasm rather than imagination. Has really imagination when confronted by problem of another's work, or a body of facts. I am now quite certain.

AT ***Leo... trouble with writing book:*** From the time Leo stopped painting, he was writing at a book. It was to be philosophy touching on some new points, and aesthetics which was to be brand new and all his own.

For a while, Gertrude couldn't look at Leo calmly because of her resentments. Who was he to look at Picasso's pictures and then say these things to Pablo? As Pablo said, Who are we to say such things to him, he can prove everything, and we nothing.

As for Gertrude's writings, Leo had already argued against *Three Lives* to Roche. The *Three Lives* response was disloyalty, but the arguments against *The Making of Americans* cut to the quick. I don't believe he was ever shown *The Making of Americans*—the situation wouldn't have made it possible to show it to him. He probably saw it on Gertrude's table. That is, my memory of it is that Gertrude suspected Leo of reading it. He would come and say, Your theory of so and so is incorrect, and I'll tell you why. And then he would proceed to ramble. One mustn't forget that Leo wasn't very coherent. In the end, when he wasn't certain he had made his point, his voice would fade and he would make a stupid gesture that wasn't an ugly thing but rather a pretty thing. It was young.

His characteristic way of criticism was, he would look at a line of it, get an emotion from the manner of it, and that would give the impetus for the argument, but it would not be his argument. He would then elaborate endlessly and then use the line or two he had read to illustrate his point. But *au fond*, Leo was a man with nothing to say, and he would elaborate endlessly and maddeningly without making a point, trailing off. He eluded himself with such conviction that he succeeded in deluding others.

It wasn't his criticism of the book, but his living next to her and with her and getting in the way that was exasperating. It was insolent to her. What right had he to take away anything that didn't belong to him? At the end of the writing, when the book was finished, Leo was taking Pablo aside, taking Bruce aside, and telling them why it was no good and why it was foolish to expect anything of her writing. It was basically disloyal to her.

From around the time I came along, Sarah saw none of Gertrude's writing, though at the beginning of *The Making of Americans*, Sarah knew all.

Leo's painting was no good, and he knew it and Gertrude knew it, and it ended with his very sweetly giving me a little landscape before he left the rue de Fleurus—maybe earlier. That was the last picture he painted, after painting for only a very short while. He had also once made an architectural drawing for me which I had until the first world war, and then I destroyed it with a passion. I could forget quicker with no souvenirs.

Farther back, from 1907 to 1909 perhaps, when he was propagandizing for Cezanne, Picasso, Matisse, he would explain before the picture and point out things that would help people see what was there. And he did, way back, have something to say.

*

NB-I #13

Sally's is passionate excitement rather than enthusiasm. Alexander's is passion, Nadelman's [unrefined?] passion Edstrom emotional sensitive passion, Alexandre pure but not sustained passion, Berenson affection, Hodder pure but also not sustained passion and not sensitive enough. The pure one of this and rich enough I have not known.

*

NB-I #14

L. His content is not so full as his thinking and therefor he is not at all creative, that is inevitable and that is what I meant that time I told Sally that her creation was a reflection of her appreciation, his of his criticism, that implies that the criticism has to be objective not really ultimately creative. B.B. was creative although this creative faculty did not last long, his affection was a full content to overflowing and made his reflection upon it creative. L.'s is not because it is always less than the reflection upon it except when it is so to speak objective. All really creative personalities have this relation between content and reflection. I have it, a good instance when I watched [sic] asleep and then when she awoke I knew the content had been infinitely greater than the reflection, always is in anything really touching me, that is what I mean that talking about things that don't really touch me although I sometimes talk well it ~~seems~~ means nothing. His method is admirable, the content except when objective inadequate. Sally's excitement and partisanship and mediumistic sensibility reflection admirable, content inadequate. His adequate only when object arouses complete enthusiasm has to be objective. Bruce's practical application admirable content inadequate.

*

Notebook 13

NB13, #1

Matcher bank Tribe [?]
Alice
Russell
Frost
Matisse

*

NB13, #2

Edstrom, Hodder, Oscar Wilde, Lord Byron, idealists. double personality lines.
Connect Chalfin to tabbies.

*

NB13, #3

Fernande Mabel Simon [Hairdress?] of Bird

*

NB13, #4

In the History of Maddalena remember the leer and yet it was just like hers of the woman selling straw.

*

NB13, #5

Judetta Ricci connects onto Emma.

AT ***Judetta Ricci:*** The Ricci sisters, who owned the Casa Ricci [in Fiesole]. Maria was the oldest. She used to come out on the terrace before anyone else was awake.

*

NB13 #6

Jeane pure servant girl + pure dramatic + pure prostitute + passion for intelligence but all connected on a low plane.

Marya Vlachinirovna servant girl + much pure prostitute—a great deal of intelligence and full passion for intelligence and very little drama.

May prostitute + servant girl plus a considerable amount of drama, about the same intelligence as Marya.

AT [NB13, #6, (1)]
(1): Jeane pure servant girl:
This is apparently Jeanne Cheron, though I wouldn't have thought she was 'servant girl.' Another Jeanne, Jeanne Poule—Jenny Chicken—was Gertrude's servant in 1914, the one who told the stories Gertrude had to flee from in Mallorca in the 1915 visit with Cook during the war. This was used in 'Mallaorcan Stories.'

*

NB13, #7

[Insert: This is not correct. Was written before I saw Gladys.]
Gladys complete dramatic, little prostitute less servant girl same intelligence, less passion for it.

This whole group touches Sally's by it[s] drama and prostitute quality. Different to it fundamental by virtue of its being a servant not a mistress group and different attitude toward intelligence. Their intelligence is not a fundamental intelligence. Sally's group has.
[Insert: ? yes in Matisse surely.]

AT ***not correct… written before I saw Gladys:*** [Gladys Deacon.] Probably 'written before' a long conversation at BB's. Gladys also once came to the studio in Paris.

*

NB13, #8

Use comparison in Janet, high school girls sentimentality the same type as that in Birdie Rosenberg and Etta Guggenheimer in Alice and Grace Lounsbury it is chippy girls melodrama of situation and understanding people and handling them and mystery. has to do with incapacity for real experience.

Why!

AT ***Janet:*** Janet Dodge, who was not English but American, though raised in England. She was the daughter of a well-known Civil War general, younger than Gertrude, but still the daughter of a Civil War general. She lived all her life in Abingdon, England. Gertrude first knew her in Florence, way back, when Janet Dodge was a young girl, and she knew her during the 'Gloomsbury' winter in London in 1902–3. Emily Dawson 'took over' her house when she went to visit her. Emily Dawson did then what Mabel Weeks did to me in the Twenties, when she took over the fireplace and the flowers, showing her disapproval at the same time as her competence.

chippy girls melodrama… and mystery: The American woman's mystery, Gertrude used to call it. She always said the best examples came from Chicago.

*

NB13 #9

Rodin, Zola, Monet—romantic imaginative realists, photographic with a large emotion merely romantic in Monet, really existent as imagination at times in Rodin and Zola

*

NB13 #10

Kipling, style sharpness rather than vividness, the vividness consists in calling things by their names, he has an emotion about the names more than about the things, in earlier days he had enough emotion about the things to give him significance, now it is mostly emotion about names. The apparent precision that comes from using technical terms is what is so very attractive to most people, the way people like to hear medical jargon etc, it seems to be so exact, also it presupposes so very much experience. It is a reviewers trick but Kipling has very real emotion about it and his emotion about the names of things is all that gives any quality at all to his later writing, but his emotion about names is real and that still makes him an artist. Zola when he describes a shop has a conviction about description, the description does not give him an emotion all the emotion he has is romantic and so his description is purely photographic or listic, that is as lists, and so they have no esthetic quality.

AT ***Kipling:*** You can see why Gertrude called Hemingway a Kipling. This is a perfect description of Hem.

Kipling: Hem again, in seeing the thing, putting it down, and so it has no aesthetic quality. The difference between Gertrude's lists and these lists is exactly in these being photographic. The one is living, the other recorded without change, as it was seen merely.

*

NB13, #11

Leo say[s] Matisse's esthetic quality is clarity.

*

NB13, #12

Flaubert has no emotion about his material but complete emotion about his expression.

LK ***Flaubert:*** Gustave Flaubert [1821–1880], French novelist. *English Translations—Complete Works; M. Walter Dunne, 1904*

AT ***Flaubert:*** Gertrude read all of him in French that winter [1910–1911.] [In 1905] she started to translate *Trois Contes* into English, and then wrote 'The Good Anna' right away. She had already read *Mme. Bovary* in English, and possibly 'The Temptation of St. Anthony.'

She knew *Mme. Bovary* backwards and forwards, and she was surprised to hear that *Les Misérables* was the book of the Civil War, and that *Mme. Bovary* was the one of World War Two. When the GI's borrowed books from our 'circulating library,' we kept running more out of the copy of *Mme. Bovary.*

LK But another Toklas recollection of GS's reading in French puts this one in question: [AT interview with Duncan:] "She didn't [read French.] She read French in translations. She didn't want to read a foreign language. She spoke French because she lived in France, but otherwise she wouldn't. Even in her later years, she didn't read French, she didn't want to see it. The spoken French was one thing, but the written French was another. If she read Gide, for example, it was early Gide, she waited until it was translated. She wanted to keep the English language pure."

*

NB13, #13

Lady Macbeth no[t] the man of action, she did not do the act. Macbeth man of action with some superstition in him. This is quite common.

*

NB13, #14

Do one about Pablo his emotional leap and courage as opposed to lack of courage in Cezanne and me. His laziness and his lack of continuity and his facility too quick for the content which ought to be so complete to do what he wants to do. Too lazy to do sculpture. His work is not because it is too strong for him to resist but because his resistance is not great enough.

Cezanne resistance great but dragged along. Pablo is never dragged, he walks in the light and a little ahead of himself like Raphael. therefor his things often lack a base. Do him.

One whom some were certainly following was one who was completely charming.

AT ***Pablo his emotional leap:*** In the first landscape sent back from Spain [in 1909], Gertrude thought he had broken up the canvas as Cezanne had insisted it should be done, only not as literal as Cezanne. It happened that as a landscape it was literal, but it wasn't literal in the sense that it was the essence of the landscape. She thought it a sensuous expression of landscape. The two pictures in the hall and the still lifes [the dark ones of fluted fruit forms] she believed in to the end as perfect realizations.

The 'emotional leap' into the things that were after the cubist break-up—not merely a rearrangement but where the reference to the objects was personal—these things he did were a leap, but Picasso did find a base in that, and this note implies no criticism, just a fact.

*

NB13, #15

List of magazines to which portraits were submitted

<u>McClure</u>	<u>American</u>
Frost	~~Alice~~
The four proteges of Mrs. Whitney	Harriet
Miss Mars	Alice
Frost	Nadelman

AT ***The four protégés of Mrs. Whitney:*** Harriet Payne-Whitney. She supported four painters, Bruce, Lee, Russell, and one other.

*

NB13, #16

To little Sidney all ready to play
Three nice kisses every day
From Auntie Gertrude far away

AT ***little Sidney… Auntie Gertrude:*** [Sidney Cone.] Mrs. Cone was Dolene's mother's cousin, whose daughter married a cousin of Gertrude's. That's how the Cones were related to the Steins.

*

NB13, #17

McClure	Harriet
~~Russell~~	Alice
Frost	Frost
~~Alice~~	Nadelman

----

2. ~~Georges~~ [?]
~~Julian~~

*

NB13, #18

Drawing of face (circle with features penciled in)

Dec. 21 Slipt [?]
[-?-] [-?-] in Dec.
Sat.

Hortense
Annette

*

Note #210

Then a long discourse about knowing and not knowing, what one is doing, what one is feeling. Difference between what Pablo says and does. Me teaching memory and can't remember and did not know it. No not disloyal only lacking in self-consciousness. ~~Leon~~ Leo thinking he was clear and he was not close to his experience. Leo says women said but I didn't say, well no matter, Mabel [frais?]. Leon generalizes about ladies sense for fact never knew any other one being passionate, its all the same way, Pablo he says he is only a judge of products and yet he is clear and yet his distinctions are real very peculiar.

*

Note #214

Sense in living in each one of the group and how it worked out in them and then go on to Julia and her group, the atmosphere of it.

LK ***Sense in living…*** Planning Note for MA 678–679.

Go on to Julia: Planning Note: MA 679

*

Note #213

Pat Moore Alfy
Mackinly Young Bruce
James Flint liked Pat Moore very well. Young [he admired Bruce?].
musician
Young, Bruce.
James Flint Young
began as musician, ending as manufacturer.
gradually describe Minnie Mason
James Flint liked Pat Moore very well. He admired him.

LK [Corresponds to Note #122.], which reads:

Sense for living in Pat Moore Alfy[?]. Mackinly,

*

Notebook M

CHAPTER FIVE, part one

DAVID HERSLAND

(Sept-Oct 1911)

MA 723–914

*

NB-M #1

Note: Three small notebooks apparently marked in sequence "J," "K" and "L" by GS are absent from Yale Library Collection.

I wonder if not all who are of the kind who love themselves while loving but do not show it by becoming obviously nervous don't love their own kind, Algar Therese, Manguin & Mrs. M[anguin]. all resisting I think and Fabri and his. I must know further. Also go into the question of attacking and resisting kind in being jealous. The resisting kind resists the making another important, the attacking kind attacks the other directly. Plenty of examples, me etc. Leo & Alice and Sally.

*

NB-M #2

The woman driving the young horse and shaking hands with the men and hitting at the boy with her whip, splendidly attacking, a resisting kind in men and women, but was splendidly attacking, the resisting being was brightly burning and it made then a splendid attacking being.

*

NB-M #3

Nelly and Beatrice about the same amount of dead stupidity, they have quality but they have as a basis of their quality dead stupidity. They have not any wisdom in living, they are really innocent ones thinking they are powerful in living by experiencing.

AT ***Nelly and Beatrice... same amount of dead stupidity:*** But the best of Nelly was in the letters she wrote in 1905 to Clare and myself in San Francisco, when she was on a trip with Ada and Sidney [her sister and brother.]

Nelly felt no obligation to anything but her mother's memory, and she didn't care a hang about anything else. After she married Frank, she didn't care a hang about anything. Nelly called a spade a spade, it was always her way, and I always had my special reaction to it. When Nelly was in the midst of doing so, she would look over at me when she went too far and would say, Oh, Alice has abstracted herself again.

Beatrice [Keyser] was a very plain version of Nelly and had the same allure. Uncle Eph [Keyser], the sculptor uncle, didn't like to be seen on the street with her because she looked so bad. She had the same red hair and white skin as Nelly, but Nelly looked as though her tragedy had already occurred, and Beatrice looked as though it was surely going to tonight. Both she and Nelly wore black lace—with the red hair and the white face—and looked plain, like an early Borgia. Beatrice was very well bred, behaved herself the way Nelly didn't.

Beatrice once got permission to copy a picture at the Uffizi, and all the men in the gallery were entranced by the distinction of this young girl choosing a fine Seventeenth Century portrait, and they asked her why she had chosen it. Because the light is so good where it's hung, Beatrice said. She had that kind of innocence. And Gertrude once asked her, How do you come to have a von in your family name? Beatrice was Gertrude cousin by marriage to Ernie Keyser. And Beatrice, in the innocence of her soul, answered, Well, my dear, my grandfather was a bastard, but he was legitimized and recognized. Then she flushed red having said it.

Beatrice and Ernie had come over years back, and it was they who discovered the rue de Fleurus but wouldn't take it. But when Leo was looking for a place in Paris, they told him it was for rent and he took it.

*

NB-M #4

Alice suggested that the reason Sally never made any effort to give Allan distraction or companions is because having no play instinct herself it never presented itself as an imperative need.

AT ***Sally… having no play instinct:*** She had no sense of play or fancy of any kind. She didn't really know what humor was. When everyone else laughed, she had a false, sinister smile on her face.

*

NB-M #5

Friez and Van Dongen like the man that serves [?] Mike, and Frederic the shampooer. These have no natural authority over subordinates, they don't keep them, they change them often, they are suspicious when any of them get to know any one coming there often. As Leo puts it they are in touch with reality but not thickly enough to have weight of reality in them, drama and imagination for the quantity of reality they have in them. Different for Francis etc. who have a specific quality.

AT ***Friez:*** [Othon Friesz.] A Cezanne painter, fairly successful among the Fauves, but petered out. Gertrude was never the least bit interested in his paintings.

Frederic the Shampooer: He had a shop near Montparnasse. An American woman writer wrote a story about him during the war that was absolutely not true, and that made bad propaganda against France. It was about the dirty way the French treated their ex-soldiers.

*

NB-M #6

Nina maternal instinct without the instinct for practical morality, want their children to be young boys loving and admiring and not too individual from experience. Like children to be ~~a~~ equals without the equality experience gives them. George Sand and Nina much alike. George Sand Nina with a coating of Sally. likes young men unless she is subdued by some one, I like Alice, another version of this thing. I wanting equality of experience because I am wanting freedom for myself always in living.

AT ***Nina maternal instinct:*** Nina was violently interested in her younger brother's success in life. He was a cook, and Nina got him an apprenticeship in Paris. Gertrude knew this maternal side in her from that. Everyone thought it a little ridiculous, but still it gave her that feeling.

George Sand… with a coating of Sally: The George Sand autobiography in which Gertrude was violently interested. I had gotten it for her. It told the full story of George Sand in relation to everybody and everything. George Sand had that Sally instinct for devanceng a thought.

*

NB-M #7

Mrs. Perkins.

Common-place adolescent, Jeanne Boiffard et al. Some genuine sensibility to the teacher, a tiny bit of real sensibility to the teaching. Mrs. Berenson a passionate sensibility to the teaching of a teacher. Relation of all this to Bird work out.

AT ***Mrs. Perkins:*** Lucy Perkins' husband had some sort of tragic scandal in

Florence. I didn't meet him. I think they were Americans.

*

NB-M #8

Woman who ousted the other woman out of the car like Mme. Vernot. Mme. Vernot enthusiasm for others, this one for herself. Miss Fletcher like Mildred. Theresa Therold like Harriet Levy.

AT ***Miss Fletcher like Mildred:*** [Constance Fletcher, Mildred Aldrich.] Yes, they looked alike, acted alike, and had the same historical sense. Constance Fletcher made herself over as an Englishwoman. She was in love when she was young, and fiancéed to Byron's grandson.

Her mother when she was young ran away to Rome with her son's tutor, and Constance Fletcher told Mabel Dodge that she spent a whole day crying, knowing that something was happening and that she wouldn't be a part of her mother's life. She didn't know what it was, but her mother was packing surreptitiously, and in the middle of the night she came to Constance and said, You've been crying, haven't you? Well, you're coming with us. And they left with the tutor for Newburyport in the middle of the night.

Mildred, in the interest of her talk, her stories, her manner, held you, but her character was not nearly so interesting as Constance Fletcher's. There were no particular complications in Mildred. Constance Fletcher was a very complicated American, depth under depth. So much so that she became a figure in Venice in later years, and bishops and cardinals came to her for advice when she was poor and otherwise forgotten.

*

NB-M #9

Cecil attacking kind of Sterne. Lips passionate and exagerated like Pach Singer etc. not come to normal development, pathological in relation to the rest of them. Tell more about this.

*

NB-M #10

Harriet has not passionate hands like Therese Therold and May Bookstaver.

Good-night.

*

NB-M #11

Mrs. Perkins always being taught or teaching. Sensibility of that and the minor sensibility to the teaching but still some.

AT ***Mrs. Perkins always being taught or teaching:*** Definitely Lucy Perkins, not Charlotte Stetson Perkins.

*

NB-M #12

Think Georgiana allied to Stell Rumbold?

*

NB-M #13

Men like Barker have ~~unworld~~ unworldliness in emotion and the rest older men not having it love him, they feel toward him as old men feel about young girls that they are so sweet.

*

NB-M #14

Nelly and I have more emotion than we realise because emotion has to ~~possess~~ own us before we can believe it. Harriet and Annette have less emotion than even they think they have, they have very much reaction to what ought to be emotion. Hortense and Clare have more dramatic ~~and~~ expression than the emotion warrants although they have a great deal of emotion. Sally's expression is not greater than her emotion but her emotion is out of proportion to its basis in her ~~realia~~ being, Alice =.

AT ***Clare:*** [Clare Moore.] Gertrude had never met her then. She knew her only through her letters [to me] and what I had told her.

[In 1909] Clare came over and wired me from Vienna that she was here for a few days. I had just settled in Fiesole, and I didn't see my way to meeting her at that time, and so we didn't meet again until 1935. She was my oldest friend. I had known her since she was nine. Her full name was Clare Moore de Gruchy. She was of French descent. The family came over in the Seventeenth Century.

*

NB-M #15

Hortense Federlicht very much like Mrs. Perkins excepting that Hortense has more real sensibility to the thing and has more sense for living, more solidity in her relation to the thing taught and less intelligence. Emma ought to come in her[e] somewhere. Jeanne Boiffard not really, she is nearer the May Bookstaver Maria Heiroth type really.

*

NB-M #16

Hortense and Clare lack subtelty of emotion that is what makes them moral, Mabel Weeks if she were dependent only on her passional side her eyes would also lack it, but the sensitiveness that she has in common with Sally and Alice saves her. Sally has it but as everything else in Mabel saves her so everything else in Sally goes to spoil it, to make it banal and like Aunt Pauline's and Bird. Bird has excitement but no subtelty. Aunt Pauline has solidity but no subtelty. Georgiana Mrs. Dodge and Theo Elwell have subtelty in Bertha like attacking passion that is their quality. Alice has perfect subtelty of emotion from her perfect sensitiveness and her absolute lack of interest in the practical sense, each reaction is complete.

AT ***Hortense and Clare:*** [Hortense Federleicht, Clare Moore.] Gertrude, from a photo of Clare, thought they looked alike. Clare was married in 1904. If any of her letters are at Yale, they would be under Clare Moore de Gruchy.

Mrs. Dodge: [Mabel Dodge.] Leo, Gertrude and I walked over seven kilometers climbing hills to Mabel Dodge's [Villa Curonia] the first summer we visited in 1911. Mabel Dodge may have visited the rue de Fleurus in late 1910, certainly in the winter of 1910–11. Mildred Aldrich brought her, and it is easily possible it could have been before Christmas 1910. The Portrait of Mabel Dodge was written a year after Gertrude met her, when we visited Mabel in Florence.

The moment Mabel Dodge met anyone, she wrote a flattering follow-up letter which attached them to her. She wrote Gordon Craig right after meeting him in Florence and suggested a pageant to be given in the city. He thought she was planning to put up the money for it, and when he knew that she wasn't, he dropped it at once.

Her budget was always very precise. Her servant was allowed so much for each additional guest. The house was always full, but there was always an exact budget covering them all.

Mabel tried to get an invitation to Matisse and Picasso through Gertrude when Gertrude and I were at the Villa Curonia. Gertrude told Mabel it was ridiculous for Pablo to come, and she refused to sign the wire for Matisse, who of course refused.

(Leo once told Mabel Dodge some time after the break that one couldn't be interested in Gertrude any more. All she was interested in now was cosmetics, which I taught her. Mabel told this to Gertrude because she enjoyed making trouble, but mischievously only, not maliciously.)

*

NB-M #17

Annette knows what effect she wants to produce. She don't see herself as the finished product she works from the known fairly quickly to something less known and then that comes to be to that one a known and then she that one sticks there. That one she does not want to be conspicuous but does want to be intelligent and elegant. ~~Etta~~ It is a ~~indivi~~ personal thing for that one ideal. Etta Cone wants to be what she thinks the Cone family is and she can do it with them as a background, when she gets away she loses her grasp on what it is. Carrie Helbring never loses her grasp on what it is and builds it up piece by piece. Sally and Alice see it as a whole and cut [?] to make it, Nelly slowly possesses it, Harriet don't know what it is and never possesses it, Emma is like Annette, Mabel Weeks like Sally and Alice, I only know what it isn't.

AT ***Annette... works from the known... to something less known:*** Leo was like her in a way. Once having grasped something, she went through it but would never deny it. That's what made Leo so offensive.

LK ***Annette knows what effect ....it is a personal ideal:*** Draft of text, MA 644: "One knows what effect that one wants to produce to that one....That one does not feel that one as a finished thing, that one works from something that one is knowing pretty quickly to something that one has been not really knowing and then that comes to be... a known thing and then that one sticks there in that thing. That one does not want to be conspicuous in living but does want to be intelligent and elegant. This then is a personal ideal...."

Etta wants to be what she thinks ... loses her grasp on what it is: Draft of text, MA 645, l.6–15. "Another one needs to be for living what that one is certain anyone like that one is in being and in living....This one when this one is not being kept in living being by others being what this one is certain this one is being... loses the grasp really on what is what this one is certain anyone like this one is in daily living."

Carrie Helbring never loses her grasp ... piece by piece: Draft of text, MA 645, l.17–22: "Another one never loses realizing what it is that this one is certain is being in this one and always this one is building it up by little pieces….Very often this one is a vague and stupid one and not really being in living and so always this one keeps a little pile by always adding to make this one what this one and everyone expects… ."

Sally and Alice see it whole and cut to make it: Draft of text, MA 645, l.22–23: "Some see themselves as a whole one and they cut and add boldly to make themselves the whole one."

Nelly slowly possesses it: Draft of text, MA 645, l.23. "Some slowly possess it."

Harriet don't know… and never possesses it: Draft of Text, MA 645, l.24: "Some never know what it is and never possess it."

Emma … Mabel Weeks… Omitted.

I only know what it isn't: Draft of text, MA 645, l.24–25: "Some only know what is not it when they see themselves not it in daily living."

*

NB-M #18

Roosevelt like Mike and Frederick the nth degree of that kind of energy that does not learn in living, but has really genius for succeeding in living and ambition in intention, not necessarily as emotion, nothing matures in them but they go on enlarging the effect they are making, it is always reality they are touching but it never is growing it is only more effective in action as having a larger mass to operate on. Van Dongen & Friez.

*

NB-M #19

Mr. & Mrs. Brie, Mrs. Brie like that Philadelphia girl that married the Smithsonian man and was interested in Howard. She has genuine quality but no head and no temperament to reinforce, she has learned to completely use it, probably at Bryn Mawr. They together she with her presence and he with some talent and some brightness can get some people they must take anybody since they want solidity and distinction and are not actively offering anything.

*

Note #124

Moore A. Hersland & Young and Flint and Minnie mason and David. Do this bunch and then Julia and her friends and then continue all of them to Davids history. A little though about effect on Julia of her friends.

LK ***Moore A. Hersland:*** Plan, MA 692ff.

Young: Plan, MA 692, l.32ff.

Flint: Plan, MA 696.

Minnie Mason: Plan, MA 695–700.

Then Julia and her friends... effect of Julia on her friends: Plan for MA 691, 700.

Then continue all of them to David's history: Plan, MA 700–719, (end of chapter.) Twenty-one fictional names substitute for the real people GS has in mind for "Julia's friends." The list ends: "That's all just now."

*

Note #122

Sense for living in Pat Moore Alfy[?]. Mackinly,
musician
Young, Bruce.
James Flint Young
began as musician, ending as manufacturer.
gradually describe Minnie Mason
James Flint liked Pat Moore very well. He admired him.

LK [Corresponds to Ms Notes #125, 126, 127, 128 on MA 694–697]

Sense for living in Pat Moore: Plan for MA 692.

Mackinly, musician: MA 692, l.33f. [Mackinly Young = Patrick Henry Bruce]

James Flint: MA 694.

Gradually describe Minnie Mason: Begins on MA 697–700.

James Flint liked Patrick Moore ... admired him: Text for MA 696.

*

Note #119

Love [?] in living in each one in the group and how it worked out in them and then go on to Julia and her group, the atmosphere of it.

LK ***Love in living.... worked out in them:*** MA 701–702

*

Note #121

Go on with Julia's group. begin with (James Cranach) and wife Miriam and Jerome Theodore Summers and Howard William Beckling and ~~Joe~~ and Mabel (Helen Cooke) and Stell (Rachel She[r]man) kinder and (Henry) Robert Adolph Herman and that Keyser man who was (Charles Kohler.) friend and Leopold (Arthur Keller) and Felix Adler (Linder Herne) and the Barnard family and Florentine (Cranach) Sutro and Beatrice (Hilda Breslau) (not sister-in-law) (Ernest Brakes) and Ernie (Brachman) and Dolene (Selina Dehning) ~~and Howard~~ and Hortense (Ella) and Jake (Fred) and little Dicky (Robert Housman) and Aunt Carrie (Mrs. Conkling) and and Aunt Clara (cousin of Mrs. Conkling) and the girl and Dr. Claribel (Florence ~~Hambur[g]~~ Arden) and Mr. M. & sister Bertha (James Curson & Bertha ~~Ambach~~ Curson)

LK [Corresponds to Ms Notes #129, 130, 131, 132 on MA 704–711]

Go on with Julia's group: Begins MA 702. Catalogue of names of Julia's friends and descriptions of them continue until MA 708.

*

Note #106

May belong with previous note:

David Johnson.

Miss Ortenreid who married Olaf Lawson. Refer to place of description of [Musen?] 3 black or fourth of return in book vol. IV f.

Completely interested in being being. Do knowing and not knowing about emotion and changing about that. This will be all about letting other ones do what they want to be are being being.

Much Leo in writing about David. David knew him certainly. Also he knew Julien.

David death. relation to it in his living. food thoughts.

There will be more description of being and succeeding and failing and in Julia Dehning Hersland in the history of David Hersland now beginning.

AT ***David death… food thoughts:*** Leon [Solomons] too went to extremes in his food habits toward the end when he was ill. He was trying to cure himself and followed the recommendations of a doctor about dieting. But I'm uncertain about this. He chose his death, in a way committed suicide. He had an organic disorder and thought a diet would cure him. He went on with it a little bit like

Leo. Finally, he saw that he was weakening, but persisted in his treatment until he died. Gertrude always said of him, he willed his death.

LK ***Miss Ortenreid who married Olaf Lawson:*** Text, MA 707.

Completely interested in being being…. letting other ones do: Plan, MA 708.

Do knowing and not knowing about emotion: MA 746, l.39.

Much Leo in writing about David…. food thoughts: Anticipates David Hersland chapter, passim.

There will be more description… now beginning: Draft of text, altered and expanded, MA 716, l.37 to MA 717.

*

Note #130

Youth doing things people to learn [know?] What he said and didn't say, Personality?

*

Write about Frank & the kind David was knowing young ones. All kinds and in various businesses.

Frank.

Piot Painter Paris.

Craig relation to Edmund and David. Finer and more delicate than either and so really disinterested as he expressed it about Leo, Leo wants to satisfy himself, he wants exchange, no exchange no life, not love and be loved, but give light and receive light, give joy and receive joy, give meaning and receive meaning, not satisfy yourself like Leo satisfy your needs like Leo, not express yourself like Matisse, not be ~~material~~ giving birth like Cezanne and Pablo and me, not be sensitive like Braque etc. but to give meaning, to give light to give pleasure, to receive meaning to receive light, to receive pleasure.

AT ***Craig:*** Gertrude met him [Edward Gordon Craig] through Mildred [Aldrich] who was a great friend of his mother Ellen Terry. Craig was back from the Moscow Art Theatre then. Gertrude called him 'the Stanislavsky Theatre.'

LK ***Youth doing things… the kinds David was knowing… various businesses:*** Plan for MA 753–755.

but give joy and receive joy…not love and be loved: Plan for MA 870–872

*

NB-M #20

Cox and Mrs. Cox again a complete couple. Her intimate ways help them very much, they would otherwise quite often be forgotten. His reputation is solid and she keeps him remembered.

AT ***Cox and Mrs. Cox:*** Kenyon Cox, the painter. He was the first academic American painter Gertrude knew. She was very pleased with him; he was very intelligent. He was also very intelligent about Matisse's and Picasso's painting too. He said, They're striving for something, which is always a healthy sign, but I'm sorry it's taken this direction. We saw the Coxes in Fiesole.

*

NB-M #21

Draper here is like Raymond Duncan extraordinarily, Surely [?] an attacking with an idea that becomes of the nature of a fixed one and has not any further temperamental relation to Hutch and to Alexandre and to Francis et al is interesting. Attacking I think. Wife resisting, but almost not.

AT ***Draper… like Raymond Duncan:*** Paul Draper, Muriel's husband, the father of the present Paul Draper [the dancer.] He knew he wasn't a singer and that he couldn't be one, but he knew too that he was a musician, and knew what there was to do to become one, though he couldn't, and he knew that. This is really Raymond Duncan behind the scenes. Raymond knows it too but doesn't show it to anyone.

*

Note #102

Some one having some one who was with them became a dead one could be saying when some one was saying something, that one does not know he is a dead one, he will never know that thing. He doesn't know he is a dead one, some one said of some one who was a dead one. Some one could be certain that some one who is a dead one would not know he was a dead one, some one ~~that one~~ could not know that some other one who was a dead one would not know that that one was a dead one. Some one then has been quite certain that some one who was with them when that one was a dead one did not know then that that one was a dead one. Some have been certain that ~~any~~ every one who is a dead one does not then know that that one is a dead one.

Then a long discourse about knowing and not knowing what one is doing, what one is feeling. Difference between what Pablo says and does. Me teaching memory and can't remember and did not know it. No not disloyal only lacking in self-consciousness. Leo thinking he was clear and he was not close to his experience. Leo says women said but I didn't say, well no matter, Mabel pieces [?]. Leon generalises about ladies sense for fact never knew any other one being passionate, its all the same way, Pablo he says he is only a judge of products and yet he is clear and yet his distinctions are real very peculiar.

LK ***Someone having… become a dead one:*** MA 724, l.15ff.

Then a long discourse about knowing and not knowing: MA 746, l.39.

*

Note #123

All the ways of convincing by talking, ~~apparent not real~~ Yes and no Francis Mabel Weeks, L, Sally, me, Mildred, Alice Ullman, Annette, Simon, Hodder and Hutch. Young ones and older ones. Marion, Emma etc.

LK ***Convincing by talking:*** interspersed among other themes in MA 725, l.5 to 758, l.30

*

Note #103

One is being one some one is teaching.

David Hersland was certainly

was one of such of them He was one feeling in such a fashion.

not admiring any one teacher

teaching in him

regular fashion

until he was one at the ending of young living

at the beginning of beginning middle living.

Some one is one to whom some one is regularly teaching something.

Some one is one whom some one is teaching.

two sentences, with the too young

and that one can be certain that that is not at all a good way

for that

one to be teaching. That one can be certain of this thing when that one is quite in the beginning of the middle of young living.

Alice and me one of us must be uncomfortable and why shouldn't it not be you.

Certainly it is a trouble to me to be ~~reali~~ doing this thing I certainly cannot in any way know it is a trouble to you to do this thing when you asked me whether you should or should not do this thing and then did what I said you should do about doing this thing.

To some certainly not any one is ever a young one.

not to me go on with description of not any one being to themselves the young one inside them to some.

Alfy was often out in the evening, in the summer he was out a long time almost always every evening. Sometimes he was out with some of them living in small houses near them, sometimes they would be playing hide and go seek around the Hersland house. Albert Burck[e]ner[?] ~~before~~ was often playing this game, this was before he was thinking of beginning learning shoemaking. Frank and Will Rodhandt often were there in the evening playing with Albert Burckener[?] and Alfred Hersland and David. Sometimes some girls would be with them, sometimes Martha Hersland would be with them. Frank & Will Rodhandt lived near them.

(Frank later in his living went into the country to earn his living. Will Rodhandt cigar stand clerking, ~~failed and~~ partner and then they failed and he was supposed not to have been very honest and afterwards he went to jail little fellow and very quick. Difference when the girls played along, and when they went into the fields and bushes.

Later Alfred makes Martha go in or else he will tell her father. Don't you know any better than to come along he would say to her.

Friends of the Leises dress-maker, in a different part of Gossols

The Fischer family (Cook)

six of them

Mr. Fischer had something to do with houses, that was the way he made a living. Henry went bycicling [sic] with David. Mary, Alfy used to stay in the kitchen talking to her. Jim was a drunkard commercial traveler, all proud of him slowly it came out that he was going to ruin from drinking, Description of Mrs. Fischer good and cooking, always good and always cooking, a tall kindly faced frontier woman. Henry Fischer very reliable person, he was very pleasant always to Martha Hersland, he and David Hersland did a great deal of bycicling [sic] together.

Another family the Henrys, James Henry tall lankey [sic] not all there in his head, like Louis Stein and Max Roderiques he used to fiddle for their dancing, Rose & Carrie Henry, [Burned?] potatoes and plenty of them with meat always. Solemn dancing every evening, Father later killed himself and everyone wondered if he had been crazy when he did this thing. They kind of dissapeared [sic] then. The way Alfy kind of flirted and made fun of Olga sister of the first governess. The way Mary Gruenhagen's family made up to him, the way he knew them. Then come back to the being in him.

AT ***One of us must be uncomfortable:*** The kind of wit that Carrie would have. It might in fact have been something she said. Once, for instance, after Carrie had listened to Harriet talking endlessly about herself, she broke in, Harriet, now let's talk about me! Carrie could afford this kind of blunt wit because in fact she had the delicate sensibility of another generation and great consideration, which went along with the 'pale femininity' Gertrude talked of earlier.

the Henrys: A French family in Oakland. They were the ones who always had the gigot in the French manner. Gertrude always remembered that.

LK ***One is being one someone is teaching .... middle of young living:*** [Corresponds to Ms Note on MA 769, following l.31] Draft of text for MA 766–767.

beginning of the middle of young living: MA 768.

Certainly it is a trouble … about doing this thing: Draft of text, expanded in MA 772.

To some… ever a young one: MA 799.

Alfy is often out in the evening… learning shoemaking: Draft of text, MA 532–533.

Frank and Will Rodhandt… lived near them: Draft of text for MA 533–24.

Frank later in his living… fields and bushes: Plan and draft of test, MA 533.

Later Alfred makes Martha go in … he would say to her: Plan and draft of text, MA 533–534.

Friends of the Lieses … bycicling together: Plan and draft of text for MA 535.

Another family the Henrys … they kind of dissapeared [sic] then: Plan and draft of text for MA 535–536.

The way Alfred kind of flirted … Olga… Plan and draft of text for MA 536, l.11.

The way Mary Gruenhagen's family … the way he knew them: Plan and draft of text for MA 536. Gruenhagen's = Wyman family.

Then come back to the being in him: Plan for MA 536f.

*

NB-M #22

Georgiana, Mrs. Dodge, Theo Elwell all of them one might say they are of the engulfing kind of the attacking kind of them, that is to say the really engulfing kind of the attacking kind are the big [chimed?], the sullen kind ~~but~~ and really these the Georgiana family are the impotent engulfers of the attacking kind like Bertha only not so resisting and so these are lost in having others lost in them, they can get pretty dry as Mabel Austin is and these can be subtle in emotion and these are impotent very often.

AT ***Mrs. Dodge:*** This is all the early knowing of Mabel. Gertrude changed her mind about her before the Portrait was done, where Mabel's vulgarity is preeminent—the green bottle, the raw potato [descriptive references in the Portrait, according to Miss Toklas, to Mabel Dodge's commonplaceness and vulgarity.]

*

NB-M #23

Pride is having something to conceal. In the Cone family most of them the egotism does not run in the direction of their gift. ~~Alice~~ Etta wants to be first and she has the gift to be a wallowing woman wallowing in husband and children and she never can be first anywhere. Claribel egotism is connected with colossal vanity and pride and has no connection with her gift of wanting to do something and so she has really no ambition. Bernard has intellectual pride without any interest in the application of his intellect to law and business and so he don't come off. Moses was the only one whose egotism ran with his gift. Overbearing rather tyrannical success.

*

NB-M #24

Alice is the only person that Sally has ever met who has no impulse to be good nor any impulse to be sentimental nor any impulse to be endeavoring so she is for Sally completely intangible.

*

NB-M #25

Hortense and Fernande, the repetitions become fainter because they are not based and never varied and never clever and never excited in experimenting in experience.

*

NB-M #26

The explanation of why L.[eo] is to me not a real thinker in philosophical matters is on account of the lack of richness of internal general experience. He thinks away the conventional part of thinking as Raymond principles them away and really the only way to unconventionalise is by the power of experiencing. He has the power of thinking that Pablo has but much greater paucity of internal experience about everything but the art created by others. It is that that he can really experience and really originally meditate upon and that is the evolution of why he don't think originally upon anything but art products. He thinks thinkingly analytically but he does not present the object to his thought not having the experience.

Hutch then was right about him really. His experiencing power is too limited, for any real originality in creating or philosophising, he realises others art product but really realises them and having really the critically creative analytic he can do something real with them, but always when he makes philosophical discoveries it is with the intellect everything away because I think everything should be away so that I can think the world rational or so the world can be right not putting everything away because it is in the way and you must shove it away to feel it.

This is really why he is no philosopher is on account of the paucity of his experiencing philosophically.

*

NB-M #27

Russell has proved that he is interested in the emotion of power, not in power itself or the creation of power.

AT ***Russell… his emotion of power:*** This is about his painting. He must have talked to Gertrude about his work, and it's his emotion about it that she means.

*

NB-M #28

Henri of the resisting engulfing type Vollard and company but in his case the solidity of resisting engulfing is thinner in his personality than in his intellect and expression, giving to him an almost religious solemnity in expression. He is sensitive technically and has real imagination but he is not sensitive intellectually or emotionally, and therefor he is not going to develop except technically. It was interesting to see him.

AT ***Henri:*** [Robert Henri.] The American painter. Gertrude said that he gathered everyone around him like a clergyman with his flock, leading them and explaining the pictures. He usually brought one or two friends with him to the rue de Fleurus.

*

NB-M #29

Nina and May more concentrated in expression than in experiencing, Sally sounding-board, Stell romantico-sentimental-dramatic solidity, all these in contrast to Miriam and Alice who have concentration of experiencing, Hortense and Claire experience is diffused but real and gets fainter. Relation of all this to Henri and knowing people.

*

NB-M #30

Fasting is a stimulant as is drinking in the same way the destruction of inhibition and therefor of criticism. The theory is an idealism built on pragmatism. Attention exists but pragmatically so does consciousness. Attention is a condition of consciousness, some organism doing something with binocular vision is ~~one~~ the condition of the existence of attention. The moment you abstract attention beyond that you make the emotional leap into idealism. To me spirituality and idealism has no meaning excepting as meaning completest intensification, the minute you make it transcendence it has no meaning, it is no longer conditioned it is no longer existing, Leo to me makes the same error as all logical people do they do not keep the whole body of evidence and that is natural as their method is inductive instead of deductive, the essential failure to me of the most rational the most realistic of the rationalisers, of the intelligibility people. The pure idealists, they fall back on their experience their difficulty is only when they explain their experience then they get mixed between what was what is what will be and how it comes to be how it came to be how it will come to be in short they condition what in experience was unconditioned.

AT ***[Leo's] fasting:*** He broke his fast on oranges. After the fast, he said to me, What is coming out of it is something that is going to change the world.

*

Notebook N

NB-N #1

Eyes turn in in those not having wealth of experience or having no capacity for first hand experience. Great thinkers eyes do not turn in, they get blank or turn out to keep themselves from being disturbed. It is only sentimentalists and unexperiencing thinkers whose eyes turn in. Those having wealth of experience turn out or are quiet in meditation or repose.

This pragmatic idealism is a perfectly natural result, bound to come as Spencer's cosmic philosophy sprang out of evolution and in the present creator's case the field was quite ripe. The dissapointment of non-achievement of creative work, of love, the lack of stimulation of new work, the enjoyment of pragmatism the fanaticism of fasting made it already and the conception of binocular vision and its possible relation to attention fired the train and la voila a pragmatic idealism which is as Mabel would say a contradiction in terms. They used to universalise consciousness ~~that at least had some excuse to~~ now universalise attention ~~is just dull~~.

The notion that having got the idea anatomy will help shows just ~~that~~ profound lack of imaginative realisation. It is perfectly characteristic of a lack of experience, a lack of which I am certain. The idea yes that is imagination in a sense a logical imagination if one can call it so but which like all logical processes not reinforced by experience is short and never sustained, which has been, is and will be characteristic. It is because of this that most apparently logical people are so illogical ~~but~~ because rationality means that you have to be rational about something, Darwin the real rationalist. Use this to-night. Most people who are noted for logic are those having the clarity of non-appeal to experience. Sometimes it is very good if well started, it can never run long. It is impossible that it should, it either becomes sentimentality, logic chopping, ~~idealistic~~ idedistic conceptions, mania or it don't go on long. Real thinking is conceptions aiming and aiming again and again always getting fuller, that is the difference between creative thinking and theorising.

His theory of vision natural corollary to interest in pragmatism as painting of appreciation and color theory of painting. His realisation of Buddha due to his being less ~~vivid~~ gradual in his realisations than usual before getting the concentrated reaction. His reaction is concentrated and his realisations continual, but his concentrated reaction in the way of thought is not cumulative, his power of experiencing is cumulative and then it begins again and so he does not at all completely experience anything and so his thinking is not partial but momentary and his logical processes in beyond the moment of concentration have no relation to experience and are not important. He and Berenson then are alike excepting that his realisations come from critical sympathy and Berenson's from appreciative sympathy but in neither case is their experience first-hand that is it could not exist if it were not already given form by some one else and so they are critics not creators. Sally's thinking is so much less concentrated and her appreciations so much less of the thing than of the excitement of the thing. Sally more capable of first hand experience from sensitiveness but with that her intellect does not in any way connect.

AT ***use this tonight:*** In the writing. Gertrude wrote at night at this time. She did not mean in talking to Leo. She didn't anymore to him.

LK ***Eyes turn in:*** This note, recording GS's final rejection of Leo's intellectual projects, and of Leo himself, is concurrent with his letter to Mabel Weeks [October 3, 1911], in which for sixty pages he outlines his theories of "binary vision" and the "stereo-sensory event." The concepts themselves together with Leo's fasting confirmed for GS the bankruptcy of her brother's creative intellect. Her gradual, and sorrowful, recognition of his state was voiced at least four months earlier in conversation with Mary Berenson, who reported to her family: "Miss Stein… says her brother, Leo Stein, since he began his starving experiments (he goes 12, 20 or even 30 days without eating) is certainly better in general health and temper, and especially feels better, but that he has lost every bit of mental energy he ever possessed, that he never reads or talks seriously, never paints or looks at painting, that he seems like an old man in his second childhood" [June 1, 1911].

Use this tonight: The writing in the MA that night. The Note is used in MA 779–782. Leo's fasting is recalled later in passages, MA 888, concerning David Hersland's "eating one thing," part of his preparation for death.

*

Note #3

I am content! You are not content?—I am content!—You are not content—I am content, you are content—You are content, I am content.

LK [Corresponds to NB-N #2] Original Note on "Matisse and Mrs. M. about going to Spain," with only its punctuation removed for the Portrait.

*

NB-N #2

Matisse and Mrs. M. about going to Spain

I am content, what you are not contented, I am content, you are not contented, I am content you are content, you are content, I am content.

LK ***Matisse & Mrs. M. about going to Spain:*** Text copied from Note #3, eliminating the original punctuation. The text, with preliminary explanation of the circumstances of its writing: ["That one was going away to have a good time. The one that was married to that one did not like it very well.... He came in all glowing.... The one he was leaving at home... was not glowing....," etc.] was published in *Portraits and Prayers*, **p. 40**, as "Storyette H. M."

*

Note #128

Go on now about any[?] feeling and more angry feeling being in men and in women. Ask advice and take it, don't want to remember. Logic each beine[?] slips young ones, Leon & Martha. L. & m. Don't include all the evidence arbitrarily throw out something to the one thinking something else.

Go on about Martha & Leon.

LK ***angry feeling:*** Plan for MA 755–766.

ask advice and take it: Plan for MA 772–774

don't want to remember: MA 776.

logic each kind: Plan for MA 781.

Leon and Martha: Plan for MA 783f. [for an earlier version of Leo and "logical thinking" vs. "experience:" MA 372.]

L. and m. Plan for MA 784f.

don't include all the evidence: Plan for MA 786.

*

Note #115

memory,

How is some one meaning something, meaning and saying and feeling and thinking and being certain, which way.

Francis, Leo, Leon, Hutch & Sally Pach, Nadelman, Pablo, Mike, Alice.

LK ***How is someone meaning … Pablo, Mike Alice; Francis, Leo, Leon:*** [Corresponds to Ms Notes #139, #140, #141, #142, #143, on MA 782–790] Planning Note for MA 782–785. Described, possibly in sequence, but generally indistinguishable.

*

Note #104

David did somethings alone when he was a young one, somethings he did not do alone when he was a young one.

Surely—Describe how he certainly did somethings that some said he said and did.

/etc. Parents about their children, friends, Bruce and Purman, Sally and Purman, Arthur.

His youth likes and dislikes for and against, his adolescence.

Describe Leon and describe & describe and Arthur and everybody.

Bring out very clearly next time parents. What Sally says Allan says etc.

write upon Arthur and his relation with each one he knew.
Describe him with background of American life and how he was of it and yet not of it as some knew it. exqui[s]e[?] [esquire??]
One looked like someone and that   Butterfield,
one was one -
Simon H.
Howard
Fred Common sense play fellow

*

very rich one, a very elegant one

*

Didn't sleep very well etc. etc.
may
can
~~may~~ be
One ~~might be~~ one being more wonderful than ever in
~~is~~ being one being living.

LK ***David did some things alone... when he was a young one:*** Draft of text for MA 827.

Describe how he certainly ... he said and did: Plan and draft of text, MA 827. Both texts above alternated and extended, to MA 828, l. 30.

Parents about their children, friends, Bruce, and Purman, Sally and Purman, Arthur: MA 827–831.

His youth likes and dislikes ... adolescence: Plan, MA 830–831.

*

Note #183

Certainly very many are being living, certainly very many are dying, certainly very many are commencing existing.

LK [Preliminary text for MA 837.]

*

Note #127

Leon as small boy Cambridge crowd, Arthur, phil, love Mabel Earle, friends family, tramping, companionship me. followers Ben and Ned

Sadness in himself and others. Ladies. Various attitudes to various kinds of family effect.

Go on with a description of life with companions children older and college. The way Leon felt about ways of living, about people, about women about people about women feeling about ways of living.

LK [Corresponds to Manuscript Note #162, on MA 837, follow. l.2.]

Leon as a small boy Cambridge crowd: Plan for MA 836, l.3 to 837, l.2.

Arthur. [phil]: Plan for MA 837, l.3–34.

love Mabel Earle: Plan for MA 837, l.35 to 838, l.12.

friends family companionship: Plan for MA 838, l.13 to 840, l.22.

me. followers Ben and Ned: [Not identified in text]

Sadness in himself and others: Plan for MA 840, l.23 to 842, l.5.

Ladies. Various attitudes to various kinds of family effect. Plan for MA 842, l.6–34.

Go on with a description of life with companions: Plan for MA 842, l.35 to 844, l.2.

older and college: [uncertain:] Plan for MA 844, l.3 to 845, l. 14.

The way Leon felt … about ways of living: Plan for MA 845, l. 15 to 847, l.17.

*

Note #125

youth, smells, eating, pains, riding, marbles and games, companions, thinking, school, laughing, valentine.

18 Rue Val de Grasse

Make the distinction between clearly thinking about things and clearly thinking, characteristic of David. Clearly thinking about some thing was in him.

AT ***distinction between clearly thinking about things and clearly thinking:*** Leo's book [*The A-B-C of Aesthetics*] also bears this out as characteristic of him.

LK [Corresponds to Ms Note #165, on MA 851, following l.28.]

Youth: Plan, MA 850, l.35 to 851, l.9.

smells: Plan, MA 850, l.5–34; and MA 856, l.6–30.

eating: Plan, MA 865, l.1–7.

pairs: Reverts to [pairs] MA 221

riding: Reverts to [riding] MA 281

marbles and games: [marble] reverts to MA 28, [game] reverts to MA 129

companions: Plan, MA 852, l.3 to 853, l.11; and MA 854, l.25 to 855, l.22.

thinking: Plan, MA 851, l.29 to 852, l.2; and MA 855, l.23 to 856, l.5.

school: Plan, MA 851, l.10–22.

laughing: In listing of human habits "laughing" MA 290. Possibly, passage on "noise:" MA 856, l.35 to 857, l.4.

valentine: [Unlocated]

clearly thinking about things … Clearly thinking about some thing was in him: [Corresponds to Ms Note #191, on MA 889, following line 14.] Plan, MA 855, l.23 to 856, l.5.

*

Note #52

In this book David (Leon) tries for eternity but not by the full strength of love affairs, he worships but is not dominated, and is finally dead. Julihn.

Leon David Hersland. speak of the melancholy at 30 that is so common like Lincoln's mine Leon dead then, Pablo Matisse everybody.

AT ***the melancholy at 30… Pablo:*** It was melancholy then because he was young. Shortly after, it commenced to be the hard tragedy of Spain, something harder than melancholy.

LK [Corresponds to Ms Notes #177, 178, 179, 181, 182, 185, 186, 187.]

David (Leon) tries for eternity: Plan for MA 866, l.10–33.

…not by the full strength of love affairs, he worships but is not dominated: Plan for MA 866, l.43 to 867, l.23; and MA 871, l.28 to 872, l.10.

finally dead: Plan for MA 880, line 22ff.

… melancholy at 30… Plan for MA 869, l.36 to 871, l.27.

*

Note #101

Discourse about each one willing to have some one enjoying themselves and for each one a different reason. My feeling about L. & N. and its relation to possible successful activity etc. etc.

LK ***willing to have some one enjoying themselves:*** MA 860, MA 871, l.27. One of two extended passage on "enjoying themselves" in MA, but essentially about David Hersland's not wanting to share in enjoyment of theirs. 2nd passage 885, l.11 to l.36, reinforces David Hersland's increasing isolation from everyone in "not thinking of telling anyone" about his memories of their sentimental pleasures.

*

Note #54

Beginning of end of Long book.

Anyone has come to be a dead one.

Then go on to tell about various ages in man old age and feelings about death, Fiesole garden, parma [???], me various stges [sic], then tell about death of Uncle Sol, Mr. Hersland & their wives, and I am so nervous, etc. etc. courage Yit & Anglo-Saxon, finish.

LK ***Beginning of end of Long book:*** Plan for the Epilogue, entitled "History of a Family's Progress," from MA 907–925 inclusive.

Anyone has come to be a dead one: Text for MA 907, l.1, the first sentence of Epilogue.

various ages … feelings about death: Plan for MA 908, l.27 to 909, l.27.

*

Note #55

In finishing long book

Besides about death, put in about trained intellects thinking people won't be understanding. Like Alice perfectly simply realising that Nelly would not answer that postal about the mistaken letter and I really not understanding that she couldn't, that she would be confused and say its all rot, Alice is crazy what do they want anyway Frank wd. not find the letter and not do anything. Go on about this the difficulty of me [not] believing and the case of Alice believing it

LK ***… trained intellects thinking people won't be understanding:*** Plan MA 907, l.26 to 908, l.26.

*

Note #120

Go on with age and how some people know what others will do. Alice and Nelly, intellectuals don't know.

Difficulty of knowing that some one else is not illogical because he sees different things. Nellie and the

No

letter. L. et al.

No

Y e s. Y e s.

No No No No

No No No No No No No No No No No No No

LK ***Go on with age … intellectuals don't know:*** Corresponds to Note #55.

*

Note #53

Difficulty of understanding that some one else can't understand and is seeing other things, leads up to each one and the old ones.

LK ***Difficulty of understanding… old ones:*** Plan, MA 907, l.17–25.

*

Note #126

Don't understand others A & N. Mabel & Constance B.B. & Ollie and B. Mosey [i.e., Brother Mosey] and families. Duty and how it is felt and done. Fred & Amy and his pa & ma. Old ones and how they come to be dead. Some very old and some partly old would be old if there were not others older.

AT ***Ollie:*** Nelly's brother.

LK [Note corresponds to a series of ten Manuscript Notes repeating this text in part or in substance, for MA 912–923. See Ms Notes #207, 208, 209, 210, 213, 214, 215, 216, 217, 218.]

Don't understand others: Plan for MA 907, l.26 to 908, l.26. [recaps Note #55]

families: ("and going on existing:") recurring and recapped from MA 911, l.30 to end of book.

Duty and how it is felt and done: [page references not identified]

Old ones and how they come to be dead: Plan, MA 923, l.38 to 924, l.13. [recaps Note #54]

***

4. The Buried Narrative

Etta Cone had been visiting in Paris during the winter of 1906 while her sister Claribel had gone off on a trip to Germany. Delighted that Gertrude had turned to "literatoor." she offered to type the recently completed stories of *Three Lives*[1] It took her until April to finish her typescript, when Gertrude sent it off to Settignano for Hutchins Hapgood to read.[2]With the script out of the way, Gertrude professed to lose interest in it almost immediately. She turned at once to the family novel, and the next two years, was largely engaged in lost work. This, the first draft of the novel, was to be itself almost entirely supplanted by a further draft that was to start in the summer of 1908. In that final draft, the story that had been two years in the writing was not thrown away but simply—so to speak—submerged, so that the tale itself is for the most part assumed to be going on in the finished version of the novel rather than its being explicitly narrated, while the actual text of the novel is concerned with new, tangential matters. But in an odd way, nothing of this fully realistic story is altogether lost in the finished work. In one way or another, all of the later novel's overt deliberations depend for their continuity on the virtual but ongoing existence of the buried tale.

The complete chronicle is recorded in bits and scraps through the early Notebooks with entries substantial enough to make possible its whole reconstruction. Unadorned, that story is told here. Before she became involved in the ultimate problems with which the novel became infused in 1908, Gertrude supposed that the labor of writing her family chronicle was to be a comparatively simple one. She supposed that all she was undertaking was an essentially Victorian novel and getting the following story in it told.

***

Several families of lower middle-class Jews, artisans and tradesmen from Germany, settled in Baltimore in the 1840's[3] and on new soil, restarted a "family progress" which

---

[1]Letter, Etta Cone to GS

[2]GS, note to Etta Cone written on Letter, H. Hapgood to GS, April 2, (1906), asking that stories be sent to him.

[3]NB2, #5

In the course of the archive research at the Yale Stein Collection, the small notebooks of the years in which this version of the novel was being written, were arbitrarily numbered in the order in which they were found. Reordered, their original sequence was: **NB1,NB9**, **NB11**, **NB12**, **NB10**; a few entries in **NB6**, **NB7** and **NB8** and by the copybook entitled, "The Making of Americans" (**NB-MA**), in which

resulted in three generations—or sixty years—in a new way of life. Although the foundations for this new life were laid by the first two generations, it was the third—Gertrude's own—on which the chief burden fell of consolidating "family progress" by consciously creating and "living into" a new tradition. But her generation's remembered past was short; it had had only sixty years of family living in America out of which to create its sense of tradition. As if this were not burden enough, her contemporaries were confused by paradoxical feelings of both rupture and continuity with that fledgling tradition. As one of the characters in the novel would have said had the first draft been left alone, "In sixty years we moderns must create a complete tradition and live into it, for we do not follow teaching. Hence our art and ourselves, and he who runs may read the dreadful failures." [Note #70]

It is this generation's struggles on which the novel was focused. Gertrude's story chronicles the development of six characters to the years of their "middle living," relating their success or failure to their acceptance of their middle-class family tradition and their crippling, disorienting search for new values and pursuits that cannot be encompassed or understood within the terms of that tradition.

Three of these characters are children in the Dehning family. Their father, Herman (who becomes Henry) Dehning, after twenty years in America, has succeeded in arranging his recollections so that they correct and supplement his impoverished immigrant past. He has the bluff honesty and goodness of a man who can afford to be a Philistine. He remembers little about his life in Germany, but recalls with pleasure how he left, how he and his brother waited in a crowded room with other immigrants, and how he was released from that room into a big America. Starting his new life in Bridgepoint (= Baltimore) as a street peddler, he saved enough to bring his parents and brothers and sisters from Germany. Twenty years later, a deeply satisfied, wealthy man, one of his greatest pleasures is relating the saga of his struggles—a pleasure facilitated by his ability to forget that the man who was nothing and the man who is now everything are connected with one another. He uses his past for the text of a sermon on luxury's evils which he delivers with pride to his children. [MA 8–11.]

His wife listens to Dehning's sermons, and does not listen. She knows how delighted he is with his prosperity, and that he does not believe his own philippics against the evils of luxury and genteel education. She is herself the "quintessence of loud-voiced, good-looking prosperity," and with "a rasping insensitivity to gentle courtesy" she is, for all her honesty and generosity, a woman "whom you might like the better the more you saw her less." [MA 13.]

---

the contents of these small notebooks were reassembled and summarized. A very few early notes in **NB14** and in The Diagram Book also belong to this version. All these notations are precisely credited in the footnoting for this chapter.

Their only son is George. At the novel's opening, he is at "the senseless age of fourteen," athletic, cheerful, "full of excellent intentions and elaborated purposes... though these generally are destined to be lost on their way to fulfillment." [MA 16–17] He has an "heroical, open, boyish sweetness" [NB9, #5; NB1, #14] in him, the ways and the beliefs of his father, but without his father's exuberance and distinction. His little sister Hortense is ten, much petted by her father, raised largely by governesses, and greatly overawed by her brother George. [MA 17–18] Her "dependent, loyal, up-gazing sweetness" is directed mostly at George. [NB9, #5]

The oldest of the children is Julia, the heroine of the novel. Soon after its beginning, the family is occupied with her impending marriage. Julia, stamped with the features and much of the character of her mother, is at eighteen "a very vigorous specimen of self-satisfied, domineering American girlhood... [but] now and then flashes of passionate insight... [light] up an older and hidden tradition." [**"First Draft," p. 7**] Under her bright joy and ardent honesty, her face suggests the coarseness and rasping discourtesy of her mother, but her regard for her father's gentleness indicates that she is already condemning her mother's qualities in herself. "A large part of our family history," Gertrude explains, "must be a record of her struggle to live down her mother in her." [**"First Draft," p. 8**]

Even at eighteen, Julia is thought of as "brilliant" and "commanding" in contrast to her quieter sister Bertha (=Hortense.) But Bertha's nature, we're told, is deceptive. She is to end as the most complete moral failure of the family. [**"First Draft," p. 9**]

Because of her passionate temper, Julia is guilty of unconscious indiscretions, and one of her riding companions, mistaking her verve for license, becomes "intimate and gross" with her.[4] Awakened to the knowledge that "some men do wrong," she prudently decides to become "wise in the desire for a master in the art of life." Meeting Alfred Hersland, she unwisely decides she has found him. Hersland is sufficiently well-dressed and well-to-do to seem respectable, but more seductive for Julia than his respectability is his "singularity" and the pleasant, though disquieting mystery, in his voice.

Alfred Hersland from California is visiting in the East when he meets Julia. His family became well-to-do a little earlier than the Dehnings, and with earlier wealth came earlier enthusiasm for art and culture. For Julia, who is ambitious to find a husband with "passion and position and a strain of romance," Alfred could not seem more appropriate. But her cousins and her uncles, and most particularly her father find no attraction in his mystery, and suspect Julia's choice. Her father begins a gentle

[4] This and following the four paragraphs summarize Chapters 2, 3 and 4 of the "First Draft." All quotations are from this manuscript.

struggle to dissuade her, but she, unrelenting, wins her way. The engagement is approved, though the marriage is delayed for a year. During the course of the year, committed to her marriage and already making triumphant preparation for her new home, Julia becomes possessed by a vague feeling of distrust concerning her future husband's character, and the feeling becomes certainty once when he reveals that he is planning, when they are married, to speculate financially on the strength of her father's position. Whatever foreboding this gives her about his honesty, she remains true to her decision, and when, a few days later, they are married, it is too late for her to entertain further doubts.

Bertha (=Hortense) is doomed to follow suit with another unhappy marriage. Softer, less passionate than her more brilliant sister, her misery is to resolve itself into a sort of motionless life of quiet dread. "Julia Dehning rushed upon her sorrow passionately, heroically, fervently. Bertha Dehning sank down into hers quietly, helplessly unaspiringly."[5] True to her nature, and again in contrast to Julia, she is persuaded to give up her first suitor whose sister is consumptive because of her family's horror of hereditary taints. Julia's educated opinion contributes to the family's superstitious fear with "doctrines of predisposition and infection"—a turn of events that rouses Gertrude to apostrophise on the unscientific gullibility of the middle classes. But Bertha, not too strong in her love in any case, meets another suitor whose success is easy and quick. His family name is Lohm, and he is "the handsomest man in the most imposing bourgeois family in their set."[6]

With the accomplishment of this second marriage, the narrative leaves the Dehnings and turns to the Herslands in California. The first chapters dealt with events of "twenty years ago"—that is, in the 1880's. For the story of the Herslands, we move back to the 1870's when we meet the three Hersland children in their very young years. Their story is carried forward to the time of Julia's marriage in the first section. The novel then explores the life of the young Herslands and Dehnings in tandem.

Gertrude's first note on the Herslands reads: "The Herslands were way down south;" this is crossed out and changed to "Californian," crossed out again and changed to "Southern," and then changed once more to read "Western." [NB9, #3] The indecision is unaccountable, but "Western" the Herslands remained. The family leaves Bridgepoint to settle in Gossols in the Seventies, when it becomes entirely "Western," different in pursuits, temperament and beliefs from the Eastern Dehnings. The whole family is imbued with the spirit of California freedom, and lives joyously in the out-of-doors. [NB9, #3; NB6, #9] Its members grow to love music and the arts,

---

[5] Ibid, p. 25. (Passage is drafted in Note #111)

[6] Ibid, p. 28. (Passage is drafted in Note #33A and Note #70)

go to universities, and find themselves at home in professional and cultivated pursuits. In introducing them, Gertrude pauses for a discourse on "California freedom," [NB9, #3] which is, she says, hospitable to and fosters a kind of "singularity" that Easterners like the Dehnings can never know in their more restrictive bourgeois circles. It is hospitable, too, to the touch of madness and genius that is in some of the Hersland men, so that their lives—particularly those of the father and the youngest son, both named David—are acted out on a larger stage, with richer and more compelling consequences for themselves.

The three children are Martha, the oldest; Alfred, who later marries Julia Dehning; and David, the youngest. In their childhood, they, like the Dehning children, struggle with their father to win the right to find their own way and their own wisdom, but it is a less pleasant and gentle struggle than for the Dehning children. Their father David is an eccentric man imbued with an ineradicable sense of the importance of his person and his convictions. And his children's struggle to overcome him involves a bitterness and desperation that the Dehning children never feel in their effort to grow up. [MA 45ff.] But in both families, it is against the father that the children struggle; the mothers count for little in the shaping of their characters and their strength. Mrs. Hersland is cheerful, gentle, occupied with the routine of California life, and remains, for her children, a nonentity.[7]

Martha (a fictionalized Gertrude,) is here the oldest, fair like her mother, [NB1, #30] with a kind of "anxious to please and seizing sweetness." [NB1, #15] She is a silent, docile creature, doomed to a tormented and unhappy life. Her torments are suffered silently, never voiced, never shared. When she sees a woman killed by a train, she becomes terrified of train accidents, but she keeps the secret of her terror, and for years never gets on trains and walks the long distance every day to her high school. [NB-MA #18.] As Gertrude sees it, Martha's failure is inevitable. At the beginning, it is caused by her weak docility and her "sense of duty," and in later years, by her continuing sense of duty coupled, paradoxically, with a quixotic, ill-fitting, fierce "attack." One incident during high school days prepares the ground for the form her later "attack" is to take. She witnesses a man beating a woman on California Street. [NB10, #3] Never bright—she failed once in her annual promotion in high school [NB2, #2]—she determines after observing this beating to go to college so that she can take her place in the fight for the cause of women.

Her last years in high school are filled with the agonies of adolescence. Her days are spent reading avidly in the library, where she curls up in a leather chair and reads herself out of her tormented existence. When she can bear this no longer, she

---

[7] MA 45. On 53 begins the long descriptions of Mrs. Hersland and her relation to her children;

throws down her book, runs out of the library and wanders in solitude around the hills just outside San Francisco.

At college, with new friends, her torment begins to ease. With something like purpose forming in her, she falls more readily into relation with others, and friendships come more easily. [NB-MA #20] While there, she is called home by family troubles. Her father is ill, and his business dealings are beginning to fail. [NB12, #9] He himself is growing irritable and foolish, and Alfred is standing up to him. [MA 49.] Martha at once assumes the role of careful tender to their needs, but it is characteristic of her to irritate her father with her every attempt to help. [NB2, #25]

All his life, her father David Hersland, has loved experimenting in a big, important way with new kinds of eating,[8] of "doctoring," of education for his children, [MA 52] but as he shrinks into old age, he becomes merely crotchety. Queer doctors come to the house; he indulges one of them in his efforts to practice divine healing; and he moves from concern with his own illness to doctoring his whole family. Oddly, Martha, of all the children, takes to these experiments. Once when she herself falls ill, a doctor "who deals in fluids" comes and gives her "queer funny feels;" and once a woman doctor appears with her own erratic methods. But Martha, swayed by the sight of a woman in professional pursuit of any kind, is won by this woman to feel "strong to love all such queer ways." Among the "queer ways" she learns to love is Christian Science. [NB11, #7.]

With Martha's return to college after her useless efforts at home, the story reverts to Alfred, recording his early progress "to the beginning of his middle living." Alfred is never really a "young" man. He is the older son, but not the oldest child; he has neither the advantages of being the family baby nor the real position of leadership over the other children. [MA 515] He is, in other words, neither "young" nor responsible and dominating, and something of this is apparent in his history. At seventeen, he has the experience ("like mine," says Gertrude, "what he tried to do") [NB9, #17] of attempting to seduce a girl named Olga. The incident ends with Olga, an apparently willing victim, trying to reform. [NB10, #24] Soon after, Alfred leaves home to go to college and then to law school in Bridgepoint, where he falls sentimentally in love with an older woman. But several female relations see to it that nothing comes of his first passion to be married. [NB9, #9, #17; MA 22–23] He returns from college at the start of his father's illness, when Martha is nursing the old man and irritating him by putting sugar in his coffee. But unlike Martha, Alfred stands up angrily to his father's irritability, and shouts that he has no right to lose his temper with his children when they are trying to help, no right to sulk by not eating his dinner.

---

[8] NB-MA, #26: "Elaborate further Chinese ideal of eating in our daddy."

It is such shouting temper he shows afterwards during his marriage to Julia. [NB12, #9]

After two years, old David Hersland's illness and business difficulties become ominous and at his instigation, Alfred returns East to Bridgepoint to start a law practice. The old man reasons that with so many of their mother's family still living there, Alfred's way will be smoothed. [NB9, #9] But the family is of little use to him, and Alfred in any case is thinking of launching a career more financially rewarding than that of a modest law practice. He is anxious to gamble in stocks. Only in this ambition is one of his relations inadvertently helpful by introducing him to Julia Dehning and her affluent father. [Note #5; MA 32]

At the time when Alfred goes East to begin his career, young David Hersland is seventeen. [NB9, #9] He has always been the baby in the family, and his emotional life has been even more solitary than Martha's. We meet him first when he is about ten years old, when his ruminations are just beginning to burgeon into the strange complexities of self-consciousness. Alone and with his friends, he immerses himself in the out-of-doors, taking "sunset walks" into the surrounding hills, long bicycle rides, a camping trip with his father to Santa Rosa—an important trip for David—when they cross the water and sleep in a cabin during the night. [MA 47.] He has friends, some poor like the Richardsons, some well-to-do like the Rodhammels who live on a big estate in Fruitvale. Richardson's father is religious, and knowing his children, says Gertrude, is David's "first taste of religion and evil." [NB11, #7] When he is older, he finds the first of his intense experiences of friendship. Subsequently he uses his friends—to study them, to judge them, to influence them, but most importantly to feel through them some sort of strong contact with living.

The first of these friends are Ned Holt, David's contemporary, and Olf Rudeiner, a Scandinavian medical student at college, four or five years older than David. Rudeiner and David wander about the hills outside Gossols while David listens to his friend's saga of his religious struggles. Ned Holt, who is struggling "with everything," not merely religion, hates Rudeiner. [NB6, #11, #18]

But it is through Rudeiner that David becomes intensely curious about religion. One day they meet a woman on the road who suddenly jumps onto a plank on which she walks up and down, waving her arms. This startling act produces a religious experience in Rudeiner, who watches entranced. David, baffled, leaves. [NB6, #24]

But young David pursues religion. When his mother dies shortly afterward, he meets a peculiar young lady named Menda Herzel whose mother, a spiritualist, holds séances. David, profoundly curious, gains from the girl his earliest knowledge of spiritualistic abracadabra. [NB12, #10] Later still, he takes to following a Mrs. Hildebrand, a fanatic Unitarian, who marches up the mountains ahead of him calling out spiritual instructions like, "Be thee a good person:" [NB12, #11] He learns about

Christian Science by going to prayer meetings with Rudeiner, but detecting a certain shrewdness in his friend, he starts to speak bluntly and honestly to him. Doing so teaches him something about the religious, if not about religion. He realizes that one can go too far in talking honestly to the devout; he quickly learns to hold his tongue and say nothing. Rudeiner, Gertrude comments, is strong on two things: "jokes and religion." [NB-MA #10]

When he is eighteen, David's mother dies. Martha is home, and with the money Mr. Hersland had given to his wife during her lifetime, there is "enough to take care of Father and Martha in a small way," [NB11, #4] and so David goes East to college. [NB9, #18] He arrives at Bridgepoint soon after his brother's marriage to Julia, and there, for the next seven years, he acts out most of the drama of his life, becoming involved too in his brother's and Julia's drama.

After her abortive attempt to take care of her father, Martha, filled with the cause of women, goes back to college, not only to the congenial life of egalitarian conviction and moral purpose that she found there, but also to an unfinished love affair.[9]During her first year, Martha met a fellow-student who was bred in the Southwest in the genteel tradition she never understood. Philip Redfern is a man of breeding, of courtesy and of subtle dissimulation. He was raised by parents who had for years politely agreed to have nothing to do with one another, and "the constant spectacle of an armed neutrality between his parents early filled him with an interest in the nature of marriage and the meaning of women." [MA 430.] But what was at first a mere interest led to the formation of an ideal which he later embraced with all the fervor that can be attached to unusable moral convictions; for he never really experienced women, and he knew the equality of the sexes only as an armed truce between two people, each of whom feels equally certain of his or her ability to triumph without doing naked battle. His mother instilled in him the desire to be the champion of women, and he thoroughly believes that he is, but in contact with the practicing egalitarians at his Western college, he is usually afraid of the novelties in their feminine

---

[9]This episode is summarized from MA 429–440. The writing and dating of the Hodder Episode is discussed above, 60–65. Only quotations are footnoted separately in this section (ending on 179.) Gertrude's note setting the Hodder Episode into the second draft of the novel reads:

> Marry Selina [Solomons] ["Martha" in the novel] to Hodder ["Redfern" in the novel] with that scene and then the college business like in the other book [i.e., the novelette, *Fernhurst,*] and the subsequent trouble… . [Martha] changes when he leaves her to be like she [Selina Solomons] is now [who became a militant suffragette .] <u>Begin this the other end to my old book</u> [i.e., *Fernhurst.*]
>
> The most interesting man in her class was Hodder' and then describe him as I describe him and then scenes to marriage, the scenes leading to divorce leaving out student action.

behavior, and—like the gentleman he is—he does not let himself know that he is really politely, even icily, on guard against them.

He recognizes in Martha a companion whose instincts are as simple and as pure as his ideals. They spend their remaining three years at college in close conference, he doing most of the talking about his future, "she listening, understanding and sympathising." But for all their talk, they understand little about one another. "He never quite felt the reality of her simple convictions, she never quite realized what it was he did not understand." [MA 433.]

After two years of marriage, he understands Martha only too well. She is strenuously moral and earnestly in pursuit of higher things, but her mind is narrow and harsh, with none of the gentleness he really loved in women. Instinctively he responds not with open distaste but with elaborate chivalry. And Martha, confronted by the barrier of mere politeness, begins her energetic, graceless attack. She never makes any headway, and she never gives up; "she never became wiser or more indifferent, she struggled on always in the same dazed eager way." For Redfern, it is marriage as he knew it, an armed neutrality, but this time "with an inferior who could not learn the rules of the game." [MA 434.] When he is appointed Professor of Philosophy at Farnham College (the fictional name for Bryn Mawr),[10] they meet the two women who are to bring about the break-up of their marriage.

Unlike Martha, they are remarkable women. The Dean, Miss Charles, has great vigor and intellect, and believes in "the essential sameness of sex and [has] devoted her life to the development of this doctrine." [MA 434.] She controls the college, and sponsors her teaching staff's most impressive adornment, Cora Dounor, who is a brilliant teacher and scholar but has neither political ability nor competitive interests. Miss Dounor appears to have "a sort of transfigured innocence," and seems shy, reserved and blameless; she is in fact anxious and willing "to experience the extreme forms of sensuous life and to make even immoral experiences her own." [MA 435.]

When he meets Miss Dounor, Redfern has just reached what Gertrude calls "this fateful twenty-ninth year," when the vision of one's future starts to "narrow down to form and purpose and we exchange a dim possibility for a big or small reality," [MA 436–437.] and he is persuaded that merely teaching philosophy and being married to Martha will be a very small reality. Little by little, he adjusts his sense of virtue to embrace an imagined future of writing novels and running off with Cora Dounor. "Loving as he does the ideal of woman, and being her dedicated champion, Redfern

---

10 "Smith is where Hodder performance takes place," notes Stein, eliding Bryn Mawr and Smith (where Julia is subsequently to be appointed Dean.) Collectively, they become "Farnham College," just as Harvard and Johns Hopkins are collectively "Bridgepoint College," and Cambridge, New York and Baltimore are all "Bridgepoint."

willingly endured all pain to seek and find the ideal… and he never tired of meeting and knowing and devoting himself to any woman who promised to fulfil for him his desire and here in Cora Dounor he had found a spirit so delicate so free so gentle and intelligent that no severity of suffering could deter him from seeking the exquisite knowledge that this companionship could give him." [MA 438.] Virtuously, then, he makes love to Cora Dounor, and courteously he says nothing to Martha. But the Dean does. Abruptly one day she tells Martha that Miss Dounor cannot be the subject of scandalous talk, and that Martha will have to keep her husband in order.

The Dean has no illusions about Martha's power over her husband; but whatever were her beliefs about the sameness of the sexes, she knows with utmost clarity that even Martha, jealous, will behave like a woman, and "that before long she would effect some change." Martha, having lived with the misery of knowing what was happening, now lives with the dread of doing anything about it. Since she cannot change her husband's feelings, she can do nothing but "get the evidence to condemn him." Instead of feeling outraged by his conduct, she herself feels like the culprit, terrified lest she be caught by him vulgarly trying to find evidence. "She dreaded the condemnation of Redfern's chivalrous honor." [MA 439.] Finally worn out by her confusion and misery, one day "Mrs. Redfern rose and went into his room. She walked up to his desk and opening his portfolio saw a letter in his writing. She scarcely hesitated so eager was she to read it. She read it to the end, she had her evidence." [MA 440.]

Having lost Redfern, Martha turns zealously to the cause of women. [NB-MA #19] The habit she had developed of monotonous, blind attack, reinforced by the moral earnestness that maintains her sense of virtue, lead inevitably to her maladroit and somewhat bizarre future actions. She goes first to a Western town to get a divorce, but in her own strange way, everything she does seems to her a kind of preparation for the time when she and her husband will again share their "intellectual living." And it is not until years later, learning of her husband's death, that "it[is] really a certain thing for her" that her marriage is over. [MA 470.]

In the West, taking up her cause in earnest, she "got mixed up with Charlotte Perkins [Stetson]," [NB6, #9] a militant worker for women's equal rights. When Alfred's marriage is imminent, her old adoration of her brother returns and with a collection of her "German women," collaborators in her work, she makes the trip East to be at his wedding. [NB6, #21] Alfred, hearing about her troubles, is polite but indifferent. Within a year of his marriage, Martha, as miserable in her new pursuits as she was before, is urged by her sense of duty to return home and again take care of her father, who is worse, and of her mother, who is beginning to fail too. Her mother is grateful for her care, but she has never warmed to Martha whose only reward lies in the gratification of her own devotion to her duty.[NB-MA #3] In a few months her mother dies, young David is sent off to college in Bridgepoint,[NB-MA #2] and for some years, Martha stays with her father, putting sugar in his coffee though he detests it, holding his coat though her doing so infuriates him, always relentlessly trying, always hopelessly achieving nothing.

From his days of wandering in California, David is "constantly surrounded by the thought of death";[11] Gertrude notes: "Write essay on the feeling strong of death from living out of doors[,] one in particular for [David]." The out of doors he has known, the landscape with its hot sun, its arid stretches, its mountains, "makes you feel broad." It takes "brilliant sunshine," writes Gertrude, "to taste reality deeply enough to be of a broad luminous sorrow." Sorrow such as this is for her a kind of joy, for one expands, as does David, to enter into it. The "joy of [the] heat of expansion and perspiration makes you feel broad." [NB6, #12] David's concern with death stems largely from the sort of terminal perspective he achieves during these experiences of immersion and expansion in a hot, dry, empty landscape.

During his college years at Bridgepoint, his most significant relationship is with Julia, whom he befriends soon after his arrival. The story of their disenchantment with one another is the crucial episode of the novel, the "hinge" on which Gertrude's chronicle turns from its account of her generation's growth to the tragicomedy of its decline and fall. For Gertrude, "The real drama is David H. and Julia D." [NB2, #24] As the novel's hero and heroine, they are the central instances of the moral division between the Eastern bourgeois tradition, and the unworldly but ethically untrammeled Western tradition.

David's arrival in Bridgepoint signals the story's return to the Dehnings' history, which has been interrupted for the long account of the Herslands in California. Gertrude introduces the third and final section of the novel:

> And now we come back to the Dehnings and their very different kind of living, the different things they needed to win out in, the different way they looked at freedom, and it is for Julia Dehning and Alfred Hersland to make out between them their life when they had such a different kind of a beginning. [NB-MA #48]

When David meets them about a year after their marriage, [Note #57] the "differences" between Alfred and his wife have not yet begun to trouble them, and they are still sufficiently happy living in the Dehning family circle. David sees them at old Henry [=Herman] Dehning's summer home at Bay Shore, the home in which the novel opened, and the picture of family opulence and accord is repeated. The rest of

---

[11] NB-MA, #15. This note on David continues to be the main theme of the full portrait of David in the final version of the novel, in 1911: "David constantly surrounded by thought of death—puts it away from him—then endeavors to embrace it… to conquer it, almost, never quite."

the novel, for both the story of the Herslands and of the Dehnings, occupies eight years, and during the course of those years, the collapse of tradition and aspiration in both families is complete. The Hersland children at its conclusion are either dead (David), or quixotic (Martha), or mediocre worldlings (Alfred.) The more urbane Dehning children salvage enough of their tradition to become reasonably successful, but for Gertrude they are more contemptible in their practical success than the Herslands in their worldly failure.

The Dehnings, again gathered happily and wealthily in their summer home, pursuing their family life with cheer and bustle, are celebrating the arrival of Julia's daughter. Her passion for children is already manifest,[12]a passion which underlies her later zeal for teaching and leads her eventually to become a professional educator. Her younger brother George, like David, is enrolled in college at Bridgepoint, planning to be a doctor. Alfred, still in love with Julia, feels only mild resentment toward her attachment to her family. Out of loyalty and belated pride in his own family, he insists on comparing the singularity of his brother and sister with the commonplace virtues of Julia's family. [NB6, #22]

But soon his resentment against the Dehnings grows harsh. He begins to shout regularly at his wife: "Damn your people!" damning them because he has become, in the course of two years of marriage, financially dependent on them. His father's fortune has so seriously dwindled that he can expect no further help from him, and his own law practice has not grown impressively. The Dehnings shake their heads and scorn his penury. For them poverty is a clear sign of the failure of a man's character. [NB12, #9, #10] "Damn your people!" David hears his brother shouting at Julia during his stay with them, and he sympathizes with both, for Julia cannot restrain her instinctive feeling that her people are right. During these quarrels, David's close connection with Julia begins, "But he never interferes, he only judges," [NB12, #11] says Gertrude: his "habitual sense of justice" makes it possible for him to remain close to both Alfred and Julia at once.[NB-MA #15]

But seeing them at intervals during his college vacations, David watches the gradual disintegration of their marriage. Alfred in desperation has turned to his father-in-law to ask for large sums of money to go into politics. [NB6, #9] Old Dehning flatly refuses to help him, and the "struggle for victory" between the two men begins in earnest. Alfred, telling no one, borrows the money elsewhere, but his political coup fails miserably, and he loses all his borrowed money "by not altogether a straight deal." Seeing no alternative, he confronts an enraged Dehning once again with a demand for help, this time because he is ruinously in debt. [NB6, #18] David is visiting during this

[12] Anticipates use in MA 649–652

crisis. Julia is siding with her father, Alfred is sulking, and the tension among them is unbearable. Julia has been behaving with heroic forbearance, effecting economies in their straitened circumstances by taking dishes off the dinner table, and Alfred, infuriated at the sight of this, swears and bangs his fist on the table as he had once done with his father. To avoid these scenes, Julia removes her child to her family's country house, and David undertakes to keep Alfred from joining them. David's advice to his brother is restricted to "trying to stop Alfred in his bad temper, makes no attempt to in his business straight dealing." [NB12, #14]

Now old Dehning's "struggles" have effectively tempered his satisfaction with living. But in contrast to old Hersland—whose struggle, going on at the same time, is wholly concerned with his own financial failure—Dehning's fight is with his children's problems.[13] Besides Alfred and Julia, his other daughter Bertha has failed in her marriage, owing largely to trouble with her father-in-law.[Note #33A] And Hannah Hammel, the orphaned daughter of Dehning's impoverished brother, has fallen in love with a young man named Jay Garblin of whom Mrs. Dehning disapproves. Old Dehning battles with his wife to arrange Hannah's marriage. He finally succeeds in this,[14] but capitulates to Alfred by settling all his debts.[15]

Alfred never tries to repay him. He never tries, in fact, to salvage his marriage with Julia, but drifts into a liaison with another woman, and during the years of separation from Julia, finds what solace he can in his mistress.[16]The liaison comes about through Dicky Wolkins, David's California friend, who has also come East.[NB2, #5a] After meeting Minnie Vail, Dicky recommends her warmly to Alfred Hersland, explaining that "any girl with a name like that has got to be gay." [NB-MA #46] She lives in Chinatown, and Alfred takes her as a client to handle the matter of her divorce. [NB9, #11] Soon he finds himself partially supporting her, but in view of his own financial predicament, he looks foolish to his friends. Dicky defends him loyally: "Everybody says he is a damn fool, but I can't forget she has wonderful kinds of ways in her." [NB9, #13]

In the fifth year of her marriage, Julia's daughter dies.[NB12, #9] It was for her sake that neither Alfred nor Julia tried to separate, but with the death of their child, their marriage is over, though divorce comes only some years later.[NB11, #4] The child had been a factor in David's relation with Julia, too;[NB-MA #5] it had prevented the feeling in either one from spilling over into love.

---

13 NB11, #4; NB2, #16, eventually not used in novel.

14 NB2, #16, eventually not used in novel.

15 NB11, #4, anticipates narrative incident in chapter 4, but never explicitly described.

16 Ibid.

Miraculously, an aunt leaves money to Alfred after the separation, leaving him free to pursue life with Minnie. His difficulties with her descend into the comic. Her own husband, a cigar-store proprietor, has for years been refusing divorce, but he has managed to keep Minnie actively jealous of Alfred's wife. For the next several years, their situation remains unresolved: Alfred continues to be a. failure in his profession, Minnie does not want him to get a divorce before she does, and Minnie's husband remains adamant. [NB-MA #44]

Julia, now free, returns to her family but finds no ardent champions in it. But now David observes Julia exhibiting her greatest strength: "When she was heroic there was an intensiveness sometimes in her.... When all her family gave up around her there was this heroic sweetness in her." [NB11, #11] He himself is kind to her, but Julia's disappointment in her marriage, and David's in two love affairs,[17]are to be followed by their disappointment in each other. The time arrives when Julia can bear to listen neither to his advice nor his criticism. "What right have you to talk like God Almighty?" she cries. "You never succeeded in doing any-thing." David shouts back, "Perhaps not but I have a fighting chance to do a big thing sometimes and that makes it right for me to feel just like I talk it to you." [NB2, #24] And reversing the usual charge of the unworldly against the worldly, he points out to her one day, "You see your time and money are probably not important to you." "My time is not important to me," cries Julia, "why I use every minute." To which David answers, "That's just it, you see I use a very few of my minutes, but I have to have all my time because I never know what minute I am going to use." [NB-MA #33]

Their growing disaffection contributes to David's resigned acceptance of his practical failure in the world. When he finishes college, he takes a job in a small university out West, a job that clearly leads nowhere, and leaves Bridgepoint and Julia with a feeling of personal failure that is soon to lead him back to his earlier preoccupation with death. [NB-MA #17] Julia becomes quickly immersed in her family's own round of increasing sorrows. The brash, loud-voiced Mrs. Dehning dies, leaving her husband in her children's care. [NB-MA #5] After her death, her husband becomes simply an amoral old man with an old man's longing, Gertrude says, "to keep warm." When Hannah and her husband stay with him for a time, old Dehning wants her "to take the place of his wife in kinds of ways [that] scare [Hannah]." One night he comes into her room to ask her simply to come and keep him warm. There follows a scene, Gertrude says, "like the kind I had with [Uncle] Sol [= Henry Dehning.]."

---

[17] Themes, incidents and dialogues for both these affairs were planned in detail. The first, with "Rena Barkholt," is outlined in NB9, #14, #18; NB6 #11; NB1, #3, #17, #19, #29; NB11 #16. The second, with "Helen Lawson," is prepared in NB9, #18; NB6, #11; NB11, #16.

[NB12, #14] More out of dislike than terror, Hannah refuses him, and confides what has happened to her husband. Old Dehning, with his wife gone, becomes lost to respectability altogether, and falls into the "habit of kissing and making love to gay women."

When Dehning, like Hersland, becomes merely a sick old man, his youngest daughter Hortense, who astonished him by turning into a successful district nurse, comes home, as Martha had for her father, to nurse him.[NB11, #5, #7, #10; NB6, #2] But old Dehning suffers from another malady as well: he has taken it into his head to marry Hortense's old governess, whom he remembered with delight as very sweet. "Lord deliver us from sweet little women," cries his son George at the news, and he gathers Hortense and Julia into conclave to organize a campaign to stop the marriage. [NB12, #15] Julia, now entirely dependent on her father, can do little, and finds it best to try only "to quiet things." But George, violently opposing his lecherous old Karamazov of a father, shouts at him, "You have no right to bring us up into a good position and then disgrace us," and for a long time, the once-joyful household is filled with "violent scenes between Dehning and son George." [NB12, #13] The situation is further complicated by the machinations of an old family friend, a Mrs. Meininger, whose ambition it is to marry her daughter to George. To accomplish this, she works impartially for both sides, giving George a great deal of help in his campaign, yet encouraging the old man with equal vigor. The only thing that prevents the marriage at once is the governess's troubled observation of Dehning's uninhibited way with "gay women." [NB12, #15]

Out West, the last phase of David's career takes him through a desultory love affair with a kindred spirit, Pauline Sandys, who has managed somehow in growing up to embrace notions about life and death similar to David's.[18] Much like Melanctha and Jeff Campbell in Gertrude's *Three Lives*, they more or less bypass each other in their feeling, David "having been to the point and then retreated from it," and Pauline never having been genuinely in love with him at all. "Describe the same amount of being in her love that I had" for Leon Solomons, her Psych Lab colleague and collaborator at Harvard, comments Gertrude. [NB1, #18]

---

[18] NB10, #6. "Pauline Sandys" is the pseudonym for Gertrude Stein (cf. NB12, #8). A separate account was to be made of her development from childhood to her meeting with David Hersland, but the material planned for that account was used instead for David. All that was left of this autobiographical narrative in the completed plan of the novel was the recollection of Gertrude's association with Leon Solomons as it is treated in this section. Pauline Sandys' character and her relation to David Hersland, are treated in NB9, #17, #18; NB6, #8; NB1, #8, #20; NB11, #9; NB12, #8; NB-MA #16.

David is now twenty-nine years old, and the moment comes for him—as it did for Martha's husband, Philip Redfern—to face the fact that in essentials his future is already inadvertently determined. But the qualities that made it possible for Redfern to turn from teaching and marriage to the vision of a new life of freedom, are altogether lacking in David. He does not have Redfern's "sense of honor" to help him romanticize new ideals or refurbish old ones. After the shock of realizing the fundamental sterility of his relationship with Julia, and the illusory nature of the understanding he supposed he shared with her, he feels incapable of conceiving of new objectives. He knows he has no vocation for the kind of fixed and permanent belief which is in itself sufficient justification for living.[19] He knows he has mattered to no one in the world and is not likely to. Gertrude summarizes:

> 29 year old failure of influence, finds has not really affected people like my feeling about Bird and others and so death. David's lack of sense of honor. [NB6, #11]

At twenty-nine, then, "he decides on cancer," Gertrude writes, "ultimately kills himself, through operation like Leon [Solomons]" Having "decided on cancer," he gives up his appointment and returns home to live with his father and Martha. For four years he listens to his father's bickering with Martha, helps them and is kind to both of them; [NB2, #7] but he does nothing for himself, and feels nothing but bitterness and disillusion. His thoughts concentrate on death. "Repetitive thought of Death…. let himself go to think of it. Death." [NB6, #5; Leon (Solomons).]

Gertrude offers a further explanation of David's death: "Fear of feminization," she notes, ultimately kills him.[NB6, #11; NB-MA #21] The explanation is in accord with her references in the Notebooks to her acceptance of her own sexuality: "Floating off," [NB1, #18] "drifting into," "going to the devil"[20] phrases expressing her own feelings of submissive failure, and are themselves in accord with her lapse from strenuous moral commitments to a disenchanted, rueful wisdom. For the actual scene of David's death, Gertrude readied only one sentence: "I am very nervous." [NB6, #6; NB-MA #15]

George and Julia mourn for David when news of his death reaches them in the East. Martha, affected by all the séances going on around her father during these years, "tries to get spiritual messages[,] sends them to George who there has tolerance in him. The Family see no more of each other." [NB11, #7]

---

[19] His failure to achieve this "vocation" is the theme of the first two love affairs. See Footnote above for references.

[20] NB1, #3. Stein's characterizations of her own sexuality are recorded in NB1, #3; NB11, #17

The rest is epilogue. One after another, the histories of all the characters have been concluded, and they all end in either tepid or profound failure. Old Dehning, having been brought to stalemate in his struggle to marry the governess, suddenly dies.[NB12, #13] Julia, having obtained her legal divorce, follows her bent for education and, soon after her father's death, becomes the assistant dean at Smith College.[NB12, #13; NB10, #4; NB-MA #11] In her new eminence, she is free to pursue with ardor, Gertrude considers, her inherent passion for the second-rate. Like her bourgeois contemporaries, her decorative taste moves toward the "etching and print, Japanese stage," [NB10, #8] characteristic of her kind of preciosity. As Pauline Sandys says in another connection in the novel, "They use works of art for personal advancement of themselves, and life[,] never the thing but the use of the thing [-] nastily disguised materialism."[21] Julia, presiding over the "Smith College life" that Gertrude detested, caught in the mediocrity of her success, loses all interest for Gertrude. "Make Julia," she notes, "sort of peter out getting a little crooked when she is in a hole and finally gets married again." [NB9, #12]

Alfred, after a seven-year liaison, marries Minnie Vail at last. Nothing is left of Hersland "singularity" but Alfred's extravagance, his *pro forma* admiration for Martha's moral zeal, and his lack of success. In a very small way, he does achieve some sort of political success, but his marriage becomes the kind that simply drags on, neither ending nor achieving stability. "Tries to humble wife, no go but live together off and on and so leave them."

There remains Hersland shrinking into his failure, illness and old age under Martha's irritating ministrations. For years, Martha has stinted and saved, but finally they are almost penniless and it becomes necessary to sell their home. Martha "travels with old man who tries many ways of getting on feet again"; he continues to lend money in small speculations hoping for a coup, but no matter what he does, he is plagued by "his constant downward turn." [NB11, #4]

"Sort of finish up the whole story with Hersland's death, the last of the older generation, life like Raymond [Duncan]'s father, trying to make it up. David dead, Alfred married to Minnie and fairly successful in Bridgepoint, and Martha takes care of him to the end. Beethoven symphony. Clang repeated clang." [NB-MA #1]

With the old man dead, no one is left of the singular Herslands but Martha, who returning to her earlier cause of women's suffrage, goes from country to country in Europe on a bicycle, "a little crazy like Selina [Solomons] is now," [NB6, #9] "to rouse up the women to sense of what they should be." [NB10, #5]

21"Put in here the healthy business—smith college—generally satire on schools" NB1, #7

There were two tentative plans for the novel's last words, one of which concludes the theme introduced in its first pages: "Epilogue to the whole story will be: 'Yes, I say it is hard living down the tempers we are born with.'" The other calls attention to Gertrude's own role as chronicler of her own generation, all of whom at the end of the book will have reached "middle life." [NB1, #11]

> And now having carried all my generation into marriage and into middle life and having seen them all start a posterity on the road to make for itself a fortune a character and a career we must content ourselves to leave them. I could draw for you a very dismal picture of that future in America with the young ones all grown up battling in our midst or I could please you with a noble one of that very same America, but these things are for readers of the stars for seers and for prophets and I am only a chronicler of such things as have come to pass and so good-by good reader if indeed there still be any such and pleasant dreams. [Note #67]

***

APPENDICES

Appendix A

As above: "The titles and authors of well over one hundred books, with the addition of their identifications of publishers and publication dates of copies that would have been available to Gertrude in 1903, are, the editor judged, far too lengthy for readers' patience for sequential reading. And so, the reading lists have been banished to Appendix A to accommodate detailed scrutiny. Gertrude, out of habit, copied passages for her particular interest or pleasure during her reading. These passages, telling of her taste and admiration, accompany their sources."

*

Note #135A

Muggridge
149 Fellows Road
S. Hampstead, N. W.

"Muggridge:" [unlocated]

Century Magazine
56
N. S.
34
1898

The Century Illustrated Monthly Magazine, vol. 56, (New Series, vol. 34) 1898.

See Note below re: Fenollosa's article in this volume, "An outline of Chinese and Japanese art."

Belle Meade
Hazlemere
British Col.

In faith Euphues thou hast told me a long tale, the beginning I have forgotten the middle I understand not and the end hangeth not together. in the meantime it were best for me to take a nap for I cannot brook these seas which provoke my stomach sore.

John Lyly, Euphues: *The Anatomy of Wit* (1579), Westminster A. Constable and Co. (1900), p.248.

Stang

42St & 6 ave.

rgt. hand side going down

...to pay all his soldiers wages the greatest encouragement that can be given to a free mind.

John Lyly, *Euphues His Censure to Philautus*, John Wolf, 1587, p.29

Sweetly swilled in their cups. [Secretly swilled his cups.]

John Lyly, *Euphues His Censure to Philautus*, John Wolf, 1587, p.32

Huon of Bordeaux 1534 by John Bourchier Lord Berners printed by Winken de Werde best specimen of Charlemagne cycle of romances.

John Bourchier, Lord Berners [c1469–1533], ambassador, translator of Froissart and of this French romance, and a founder of the Tudor prose style.

The book of Duke Huon of Burdeux, done into English by John Bouchier, Lord Berners, and printed by Wynkyn de Worde about 1534 A.D. Edited from the unifque copy of the first edition, now in the possession of the Earl of Crawford and Balcarres, with an introduction by S.L. Lee, London: Published for the Early English Text Society by N. Truber & Co., 1882–1887. (Series: The English Charlemagne Romances, Pt. 7–9, 12), Early English Text Society [Series], Extra Series, no. 40, 41, 42, 50.

Caxton's translations.

Morte D'Arthur

Mallery

William Caxton [c.1422–1491], England's earliest printer, and translator of more than twenty works.

Sir Thomas Malory [c.1395–1471], translator-compiler, romancer. Compiled Morte d'Arthur, 1469–70.

Sir Thomas Mallory, *Le Morte d'Arthur; Sir Thomas Malory's book of King Arthur and of his noble knights of the Round Table, the text of Caxton*, edited with an introduction by Edward Strachey, London: Macmillan & Co., 1897.

Lyly Euphues

John Lyly [1554–1606], poet, playwright, prose romancer, published *Euphues, or the Anatomy of Wit*, and *Euphues and his England* in 1580, a prose romance in two parts.

John Lyly, *Euphues: the anatomy of wit and Euphues and his England, to which is added the first chapter of Sir Philip Sydney's Arcadia*, edited with notes and introduction by Friedrich Landmann, Heilbronn: Gebr. Henninger, 1887.

Brian Melbacke

Brian Melbancke [fl. 1583]

Philotimus, the war betwixt nature and fortune, compiled by Brian Melbancke... imprinted at London by Roger Warde..., 1583.

J. Dickinson

John Dickenson [fl. 1594], author of *Arisbas* [1594]; *Euphues amidst his slumber*; and *Cupid's journey to hell.*

John Dickenson, *Prose and Verse*, edited by A.B. Grosart, 1878.

Barnabie Rich

Barnabe Riche [c1540–1617], English soldier and author.

Greene's News both from heaven and hell, 1593;

The strange and wonderful adventures of Don Simonides, a gentleman Spaniard, 1584; and

Riche his farewell to military profession, 1581, his best-known work. "Of the eight stories contained in it," he writes, "five are forged only for delight, neither credible to be believed, nor hurtful to be perused." The others are translations from the Italian.

Tarlton

Richard Tarlton [d.1588], English actor, possibly the Yorik of Hamlet's soliloquy; Elizabeth's favorite clown. After his death, *Tarlton's Jests*, "many of them older than he," were printed in several volumes.

Tarlton's news of purgatory, 1590; [Supposed author of] Tarlton's jests, 1609.

Tarlton's jests and News out of purgatory, and Some account of the life of Tarlton, by James Orchard Halliwell, ... London: Reprinted for the Shakespeare Society, 1844.

Herrick.

Robert Herrick [1591–1674], English clergyman and poet. Largely forgotten for almost two centuries, his poems were reprinted, and for the first time edited, by T. Maitland in 1823, and then often reprinted.

The poems of Robert Herrick, London: G. Richards, 1902.

1 Greene

Robert Greene [1558–1592], English poet, dramatist, novelist and pamphleteer; author of the play, *Friar Bacon and Friar Bungay* (1589), and the novel, *Mamilia* (1583).

Life and complete works of Robert Greene, edited by A.B. Grosart, 15 vols., London: Published for the Huth Library, 1881–1886.

2 Lodge

Whetstone (Promos & Cassandra)

Stanhurst (transl. of Aeneid.)

Lodge: Thomas Lodge [1580–1623?], English dramatist, poet, novelist, pamphleteer, whose prose *Rosalynde* furnished the story for Shakespeare's *As You Like It.*

The complete works of Thomas Lodge now first collected…, Glasgow: Printed for the Huntrian Club, 4 vols., 1883.

Whetstone (Promos and Cassandra): George Whetstone [1554? –1587?], English dramatist, poet, pamphleteer, write of tales in prose and verse.

George Whetstone, *The right excellent and famous historye of Promos and Cassandra; divided into two comicall discourses… Imprinted at London by Richarde Thomas*, 1578.

Stanhurst (transl. of Aeneid): Richard Stanyhurst [1547–1618], English translator. Translated the Virgil "to prove Gabriel Harvey's theory that classical prosody could be applied to English poetry."

Richard Stanyhurst, *Translation of the first four books of the Aeneis of P. Vergilius Macro, with othere poetical devices thereto annexed*,1582. Edited by Edward Arber… London: (The Editor), 1880. [Series: The English Scholar's Library of Old and Modern Works… no. 10.]

3 Nash

Lady Mary Worth's Urania in style of sydney

Nash: Thomas Nashe [1507–1601], English poet, dramatist, pamphleteer whose novel *The unfortunate traveler*, [1594] was a major forerunner of the English novel of unfortunate adventure.

The complete works of Thomas Nashe. In six volumes. For the first time collected and edited with memorial-introduction, notes and illustrations, etc. by the Rev. Alexander B. Grosart, London: Aylesbury. Printed for private circulation only. 1883–85.

Lady Mary Worth's Urania: Lady Mary Wroth [c1556–c1640],

The Countesse of Montgomeries Urania, written by the right honorable the Lady Mary Wroath [sic]… London: Printed for John Marriott and John Grismand, 1621.

4 Dekker's (Raven's Almanac)

Thomas Dekker [1570? –1641?], English dramatist, poet, pamphleteer, best known for his London comedy, *The shoemaker's holiday* [1600.]

The ravevens almanacks foretelling of a plague, famine and ciuill warre that shall happen this present year 1609…, London: Printed by E. Allde for T. Archer, 1609.

Thomas Dekker, *Dramatic works*, edited by R. H. Shepherd, 1873.

Non-dramatic works, edited by A.B. Grosart, London: for the Huth Library, 1884–1886.

5 Westward for Smelts (1620)

Emmanuel [?] Ford [?] (not int.)

Westward for smelts, an early collection of stories, edited by James Orchard Halliwell, London: Printed for the Percey Society by Richards, 1848. [Series: Percy Society. Early English Poetry, vol. 22.]

Published with a reproduction of title page of 1620 edition: *Westward for Smelts; or, the Waterman's fare of mad merry Western Wenches whose tongues, albeit like Bell-clappers they never leave ringing, yet their tales are sweet, and will much content you. Written by Kind Kit of Kingstone, London. Printed for John Trundie, and are to be sold at his shop in Barbican, at the sign of the No-body*, 1620.

Emmanuel Ford [fl. 1607], *The most pleasant history of Ornatus and Artesia* [c1595] *Sixth empression exactly corrected and amended*, London: Printed by E. Alsop for R. Wood for Thomas Vere and William Gilbertson, 1662. [Series: Early English Books, 1641–1700].

Emnanuel Ford, *The most famous, delectable and pleasant history of Parismus, the most renowned Prince of Bohemia…* [1598] … London: Printed for E. Alsop …, 1661. [Series: Early English Books, 1641–1700].

Parthenesda

Roger Boyle

Earl of Omeney

Heroic Romance (1654) (Charles 2) [-?-]

Roger Boyle: Earl of Orrery [1621–1679], British soldier, statesman, dramatist and romance novelist.

Parthenissa, a romance…, London: Printed for Humphrey Moseley… 6 vols in 3, 1655–1669. An English Heroic Romance, written in imitation of the mannered French romances of Calprenede and Scudery.

Aretina G. Mackenzie's 1661 (better than above)

Sir George Mackenzie [1636? –1691], Scottish lawyer; as "King's Advocate" in Scotland for Charles II, was known as "Bloody Mackenzie." Author of this romance, tracts, and major legal works.

Aretina; or, a serious romance, published anonymously in 1661.

Incognita of Congreve

William Congreve [1670–1729], English dramatist and poet. Of *Incognita*, his first novel, Samuel Johnson said he would rather praise than read it.

Incognita; or, love and duty reconcil'd. Peter Buck, at the sign of the Temple, near Temple Bar in Fleet-street, 1692

The Female Quixote

Mrs. Charlotte Lennox

Mrs. Charlotte Lennox [c1720–1804], English novelist and dramatist.

The Female Quixote; or, the adventures of Arabella, London: F.C. and J. Rivington, 2 vols., 1820. [Series: British Novelists, v. 24–25].

Mrs. Aphra Behn

Oroonoko & Fair Jilt

Mrs. Aphra Behn [1640–1689], prolific English dramatist and novelist, the first Englishwoman to earn her living as a writer.

The histories and novels of the late ingenious Mrs. Behn; in one volume, viz., Oroonoko, or the royal slave; The fair jilt, or Prince Tarquin; Agnes de Castro, or the force of generous love… together with the life and memoirs of Mrs. Behn. Written by one of the fair sex. London: Printed for S. Briscoe… 1696.

[Later publication:] *The novels of Mrs. Aphra Behn, with an introduction by Ernest Baker, M.A.*, London: G. Routledge; NY: E.P. Dutton, 1905.

Bunyan.

Life & Death of Badman.

John Bunyan [1628–1688], English Puritan writer, whose *Pilgrim's Progress* won enormous popularity, became an English classic.

The life and death of Mr. Badman: presented to the world in a familiar dialogue between Mr. Wiseman and Mr. Attentive…, with an introduction reprinted from the *Life of Bunyan* by J.A. Froude, NY: R. H. Russell, 1900.

Mrs. Haywood

History of Betsy Thoughtless 1751

Elizabeth Fowler Haywood [1693? –1756], English novelist who wrote seventy novels. Attacked by Pope for "profligate licentiousness." *Betsy Thoughtless* was her most ambitious novel.

The history of Miss Betsy Thoughtless: in four volumes, London: Printed for T. Gardner, 1753.

History of Jenny Jerramy[?] 1753.

Elizabeth Fowler Haywood, *The history of Jemmy and Jenny Jessamy… by the author of The history of Betsy Thoughtless*, London: Printed for T. Gardner, 1753.

Miss Sarah Fielding

Adventurs of David Simple 1744

Sarah Fielding [1710–1768], English novelist.

The adventures of David Simple: containing an account of his travels through the cities of London and Westminster, in the search of a real friend. By a lady… Printed for A. Millar, 1744.

Peter Wilkins The fool of Quality. Ann

Robert Paltock [1697–1767], English, whose reputation as a writer rests on this one romantic novel.

The life and adventures of Peter Wilkins, a Cornish man. Taken from his own mouth, in his passage to England, from off Cape Horn in America, in the ship Hector, illustrated by Edward Bawden, London and Toronto: J.M. Dent & sons, Ltd; NY: E.P. Dutton co, Ltd., 1900. [see below, Henry Brooke]

Charles Johnstone's satire

Chrysal or Adventures of a Guinea. 1760

Charles Johnstone [1719? –1800?], English author.

Chrystal; or, The adventures of a guinea. Wherein are exhibited views of several striking scenes, with curious and interesting anecdotes of the most noted persons in every rank of life, whose hands it passed through, in America, England, Holland, Germany and Portugal. By an adept. 2nd edition, greatly enlarged and corrected. Dublin: H. Saunders, 1761.

Dr. J. Moore

Zeluco 1786

John Moore [1729–1802], Scottish physician and writer. Byron, inspired by this novel, intended his poem *Childe Harold* to be "a poetical *Zeluco*."

Zeluco [a novel]. Various views of human nature taken from life and manners, foreign and domestic…, London: A. Strahan and T. Cadell. 2 vols, 1789. [Later publication:] London: F.C. and J. Rivington, 1820. [Series: The British Novelists, vols. 34, 35.]

H. Mackenzie

Man of Feeling 1771

Henry Mackenzie [1745–1831], Scottish novelist, attorney, dramatist, pamphleteer, critic. This work, his first and most famous, became a model for the novel of sensibility.

The man of feeling, London: Printed for T. Cadell…, 1771. [Later publication:] NY: Cassell and Co, [1886.]

Robert Bage imit of Richardson (good) 1796.

Robert Bage [1728–1801], English author.

Hermsprong; or, Man as he is not: a novel. In two volumes. By the author of Man as he is, London: W. Lane, 1796. [Later publication:] London: F.C. and J. Rivington, 1820 [Series: The British Novelists, vol. 48.]

Henry Brooke 1766.

The fool of Quality (hard reading)

Henry Brooke [1703–1783], Irish novelist, poet, translator and dramatist, best known for *The fool of quality*, [1765–1770].

(*The fool of quality; or, the history of Henry, Earl of Moreland.* A new and revised edition with an introduction by the Rev. W.P. Strickland and a biographical reference, by the Rev. Charles Kingsley, NY: Derby & Jackson, 1860.)

Mrs. Brinton

Self Control 1811 (good)

Mary Brunton [1778–1818], Scottish novelist and Professor of Oriental languages; wrote two popular novels, this, and *Discipline* [1814.]

Self-Control: a novel, 2nd edition, Edinburgh: Printed by G. Ramsay & Co for Manners and Miller… 3 vols., 1810.

Francis Burney

Evelina

Cecilia

Camilla

Wanderer

Frances Burney d'Arblay [1752–1840], English novelist and diarist; an intimate of the Johnson-Garrick circle, remembered largely for her diaries and letters.

Evelina; or, A young lady's entrance into the world, London: T. Lowndes, 3 vols., 1778.

Cecilia; or, Memories of an heiress, London: T. Payne and son and T. Cadell, 5 vols., 1782.

Camilla; or, A picture of youth, by the author of Evelina and Cecilia, Dublin: W. Porter for G. Burnet…, 3 vols., 1796.

The wanderer; or, Female difficulties, by the author of Evelina; Cecilia; and Camilla, London: Longman, Hurst, Reese, Orme and Brown, 5 vols., 1814.

The *diary and letters of Madame d'Arblay,* 7 vols., 1842–46. [Annotated bibliography for full entry: PR-3316-A4Z6g---] [or]

The early diaries of Francis Burney, 2 vols. 1889. [For full entry: PR/3316/A4Z6g---]

The Heroine 1813

Eaton Stannard Barrett.

Satire on romances.

Eaton Stannard Barrett [1786–1820], English author.

The heroine; or, Adventures of a fair romance reader, London: Printed by Henry Colburn, 3 vols., 1813.

English Text Society

Four Sons of Aymon

Richardson

[*Quatre fils Almon*, c1489] For commercial speculation, Caxton "met the taste of the upper classes by the tales of chivalry which issued regularly from his press." Among those tales,

Four Sons of Aumon and *Charles the Grete. The right pleasaunt and goodly historie of the foure sonnes of Aumon. English from the French by William Caxton and printed by him about 1489. Edited from the unique copy, now in the possession of Earl Spencer, with an introduction, by Octavia Richardson*, London: Published for the Early English Text Society by N. Trubner co., 2 vols., 1885. [Series: The English Charlemagne Romances, pt. 10, 11. Early English Text Society (Series), Extra Series, no. 44, 45.]

Charles the Grete.

Early Engl. T. Soci

Fierabras. English (Middle English) Prose.

The lyf of the noble and Crysten prynce, Charles the Grete, translated from the French by William Caxton and printed by him in the British Museum, with introduction, notes, and glossary, by Sidney J.H. Heritage…, 1485. London: Published for the Early English Text Society, by N. Trubner & co., 1881. [Series: The English Charlemagne Romances, pt. 3(–4). Early English Text Society (Series). Extra Series no 36–37.]

Lymester seeing coming to the trench cried out and said Theseus if thou beest such a hardy soldier as fame reports thee to be why comest thou not out but like a coward lyest intrenched. nay quoth Theseus smiling Lymester if thou beest of such courage why dost thou not force me out of my trenches?

John Lyly, *Euphues His Censure to Philautus*, John Wolf, 1587, p.37

Greene Mamilia.

Whereby we may note the broad blasphemy of those which think because the tow cannot touch the fire but it must burn nor the Ivy clasp the tree unless it suck out the sap so like wise the green wood cannot touch the coals but it must flame nor the vine branch embrace the tender twig but it must consume it. that love and liking cannot be without lust and lasciviousness that deep desire cannot be without fleshly affection for soon ripe soon rotten.

Mamillia (A Mirror or Looking-glass for the Ladies of England), Robert Greene, imprinted at London for Thomas Woodcock, 1583, pg 5

or else you think because I said farewell friendly I did fancy finely[?].

[Ibid, pg 37]

promising in recompense of his disloyalty never to lend Publia a good look.

[Ibid, pg 38]

judging upon meat with a sick stomach and tasting wine with a furred tongue.

[Ibid, pg 41]

Now have I surely settled myself never from henceforth to lend a living look to Mammelia [sic].

[Ibid, pg 46]

March! March! pinks[?] of election
Why the devil don't you march onward in order.
March dogs of redemption
Ere the blue bonnet come over the border.
You shall preach you shall pray
You shall teach night and day
You shall prevail oe'r the kink gone a whoring.
Dance in blood to the knees
Blood of God's enemies

The daughters of Scotland shall sing you to snoring.

The Edinburgh Review, Or Critical Journal: … To Be Continued…, Volume 34, 1820; pg. 155–6

March march scourges of heresy
Down with the kink & its whillabaleresy[?].
March march down with supremacy.
And the kist[?] full & whistles that make sic a cleary[?].
Fife men & drummers haw
Many deils tak them a
Your lace & livery, lickpot & ladle
Jocky shall wear the hood
Jenny the dark of God.
For codpiece & petticoat dishclout and daidle.

[Ibid. pg 156]

*

Note #180

1. [*The Diary and Letters of Madame D'Arblay* (Frances Burney): 1778–1787; pg 87–89]

GS Quote:

Why madam she stole a quilt from the man of the house and he had her taken up, but Bet Flint had a spirit not to be subdued so when she found herself obliged to go to jail she ordered a sedan chair and bid her footboy walk before her. However the boy proved refractory, for he was ashamed though his mistress was not.

And did she ever get out of jail again sir. Yes madam when she came to her trial the judge acquitted her. "So now", she said to me, "the quilt is my own and now I'll make a petticoat of it. Oh I loved Bet Flint. Bless me sir, cried Mrs. Thale, how can all these vagabonds continue to get at you of all people. Oh the dear creatures, cried he laughing heartily. I can't but be lad to see them. And yet I have known all the wits from Mrs. Montague to Bet Flint.

"Bet Flint, pray who is she."

"Oh a fine character Madam. She was habitually a slut and a drunkard and occasionally a thief and a harlot.

"And for heavens sake how came you to know her

"Why madam she figured in the literary world too. Bet Flint wrote her own life and called herself Cassandra and it was in verse. So Bet brought me her verses to correct, but I gave her half a crown and she liked it just as well. "And pray what became of her Sir."

*

Note #197

2. [Helen Wilmans, *The Conquest of Death*; International Scientific Association (Seabreeze, FL) 1900; pp 90–91]

GS Quote:

To keep the race forever alive in its present animalized condition would be to perpetuate ignorance; to keep it as a stagnant pool in the heart of universal progression; and this could not be. Perpetual change is the order of life. He who catches on to higher thought and holds it with a faith so firm that it crystallizes into belief, is on the upward move, where higher influences meet him, and fix his thought in tangible substance. He who turns from his higher thought, doubting its practicality, pinches himself into constantly ~~lowering~~ lowering conditions until he is pinched out. There is progression for the one, and, at least, a temporary retroggression for the other; but there is no standing still. Therefor, immortality in the present status of the universal race though here in this world is not possible now.

But the dawn of it is here. The beginning of that credence in the human ideal, which alone will usher it in, is here. It is here for no less a reason than because ~~a~~ woman with her strongly intuitional nature, has come to the front. Woman has brought the morning of a new era with her; and, as her feet obtain firmer standing in the slushy quagmire of the world's present condition of thought, the morning of her day will brighten into the full splendor of a noon, that will arrest and hold the entire interest of the millions of dying souls about us.

This much is already accomplished. The beginning of the dawn is here. Universal thought has begun to move. A ripple runs along the full length of its connected links, even though it is only the few who stand in the front that are capable of seeing the light that shines so brightly ahead.

If this movement had to be confined to our earth, as the Malthusians must all imagine, then its scope would be so small as to furnish a reason for their doubts. But, because man's growth is limitless—and by his ever increasing power of thought I know his growth is limitless—the fact shadows forth the possibility of his leaving the earth when he shall have learned how to do so.

More than this. In the economy of nature the time will come when generation will lose itself in regeneration.

Conditions adapt themselves to each other. When one thread is sspun out, there is another thread waiting there to meet the outstretched hand of him who has resolved to go ahead. To him who is not so resolved, and who does not know his power to go on, though the thread is there, it is not there for him, because he does not see it. And so he falls, not because life was lacking, but because the individual intelligence with which he should have grasped it was wanting.

*

Note #198

3. [Edmund Garratt Gardner, *Saint Catherine of Siena: A Study in the Religion, Literature, and History of the Fourteenth Century in Italy*, J.M. Dent, 1907; pg 14–15]

GS Quote:

"How could I be content Lord," she prayed, "if any one of those who have been created to Thy image and likeness, even as I, should perish and be taken out of my hands? I would not in any wise that even one should be lost of my brethren who are bound to me by nature and by grace; I am fain that the old enemy should lose them all, and Thou gain them, to the greater praise and glory of Thy name. Better were it for me that all should be saved, and I alone (saving ever Thy charity) should sustain the pains of Hell, than that I should be in Paradise and all they perish damned; for greater honor and glory of Thy name would it be! And she was answered by the Lord, as she secretly confessed to me: "Charity cannot be in Hell, for it would destroy it utterly; it were easier for Hell to be destroyed than for Charity to exist with it. Then she: "If Thy truth and Thy justice permitted it, I would that Hell were utterly destroyed, or at least that no soul more should descend thither, and if (so I were still united to Thy charity) I were put over the mouth of hell to close it, in such wise that none should ever more enter it, much would I rejoice, so that all my neighbors might thus be saved." And on another occasion she prayed: "Lord, give me all the pains and all the infirmities that are in the world, to bear in my body; I am fain to offer Thee my body in sacrifice, and to bear all for the world's sins, that Thou mayest spare it and change its life to another." And when she said these words she was abstracted and rapt in ecstacy. But when she returned to herself she was as white as snow and began to laugh loudly and to say, "Love, Love, I have conquered Thee with Thyself. For Thou dost wish to be besought for what Thou canst do of Thy own accord.

*

Note #36

4. [*An Autobiography*: By Herbert Spencer, Volume 1; Williams and Norgate, 1904; pg 431]

GS Quote:

The often quoted remark of Kant that two things excited his awe—the starry heavens and the conscience of man—is not one which I should make of myself. In me the sentiment has been more especially produced by three things—the sea, a great mountain and fine music in a cathedral. Of these the first has, from familiarity, I suppose, lost much of the effect it originally had, but not the others.

Spencer

5. [Part of a letter draft, almost certainly to former Cambridge associate Leo Friedman:]

A man wot upholds fool economic theories wot interfere with the leisure of females and so discourages them from indulging in friendly courtesies (such as writing letters) ~~which same whole~~somely ~~decreases and so~~ increases wholesomely the lonesomeness of the universe and don't deserve to have ~~anybody~~ nobody nice to play with him not nohow. I stays in Europe, thank-you, where the beauty and harmony of reposeful adjunctcy is properly estimated. Let me know about the new adjunct when there is one

G. S.

*

Note #64

Cooper.
Routledge
The Crater

Home as found
Homeward bound
Jack Tier
The Manikins
Precaution
Red Rover
Red Skins
Sea Lions
Spy
Two Admirals
Wing and Wing
Routledge & Co.

6. James Fenimore Cooper [1789–1851], American author of novels, travel books, and polemics. [A listing of twelve novels by Cooper, all published in the Leatherstocking Edition of *The works of J.M. Cooper*, London & NY: Routledge Co., 1888–1904.]

The Red Rover, a tale, with an introduction by Susan Fenimore Cooper, vol. 16, London & NY: G. Routledge, 1894.

The Redskins; or, Indian and Injun; being the conclusion of the Littlepage manuscripts, vol. 24, London & NY: G. Routledge, 1895.

The sea lions; or, the lost sealers, with an introduction by S.F. Cooper, vol. 7, London & NY: G. Routledge & Sons, 1888.

The spy, a tale of the neutral ground, vol. 11, London: G. Routledge.

The two admirals, with an intoduction by Susan Fenimore Cooper, vol. 19, London: G. Routledge; NY: E.P. Dutton.

The wing-and-wing; or, le feu-follet, a tale, with an introduction by Susan Fenimore Cooper, vol. 12, London & NY: G. Routledge. [Published in England under the title, The Jack o' Lantern.]

The Crater; or, Vulcan's peak, vol. 18, with an introduction by Susan Fennimore Cooper, London & NY: G. Routledge, 1888.

Home as found, sequel to 'Homeward bound,' London: G. Routledge; NY: E.P. Dutton, 1889.

Homeward bound; or, The chase, vol. 9, London & NY: G. Routledge, 1888.

Jack Tier; or, The Florida Reef, vol. 15, London & NY: G. Routledge, 1888.

The Monikins, vol. 20, London & NY: G. Routledge, 1889

Precautions, a novel, with W.C. Bryant's "Discourse on the life, genius and writings of the author", London: G. Routledge; NY, E.P. Dutton, 1889.

*

Note #225

Gertrude Stein
c/o Etta Cone
Hotel Helvetia
Florence

*

7. Meredith, George
One of Our Conquerors
N.Y. Scribners, 1902

*

Note #133B

Connoly [sic]
Gloucester stories

8. [James Brendan Connolly, *Out of Gloucester*, NY: Scribner's Sons, 1902.:]

Colton
Phillipine stories

9. [unlocated]

10. [Collected and edited by G.B. Hill, 2 vols., Oxford: Clarendon Press 1892.]

6 to 10 notebooks.
Make out a list of autobiographies
Samuel Johnson's letters
buy a knife.
Ask about cheap edition of the journal.

11. James Boswell [1740–1795], *The journal of the tour to the Hebrides with Samuel Johnson*, [originally published 1785], London: J.M. Dent, 1903 [The Temple Classics edition, edited by Israel Gollanz]. The tour was made in 1773. Johnson published his own Journey to the Hebrides in 1775.

Mrs. Trench's journals & letter edited by her son.

12. *The remains of the late Mrs. Richard Trench [Melesina Trench], being selections from her*

journals, letters and other papers, edited by her son [Richard C. Trench] the Dean of Westminster, London: Parker, Son & Bourn, 1862.

The life of Mamie Manch [?] by Moin [Moir?] Methuen little library.

13. David Macbeth Moir [1798–1851], Scottish physician, humorist, writer. Best known humorous work was Mansie Wauch.

The life of Mansie Wauch, taylor in Dalkeith, written by himself, [by David Macbeth Moir] with an introduction and notes by T.F. Henderson, Methuen Little Library series, 1902.

Tcheckoff

14. Anton Pavlovich Chekhov [1860–1904], Russian short story writer and dramatist. [An early publication in English, possibly the earliest, was the short story "The Lady with the Dog" in 1903]

Gibbon's autobiography

15. Edward Gibbon [1737–1794], English historian, author of *The Decline and fall of the Roman empire.* Lord Sheffield, drawing on six autobiographical manuscripts, composed Gibbon's "Memoirs," now better known as his *Autobiography.*

The autobiographies of Edward Gibbon, printed verbatim from hitherto unpublished mss, with an introduction by the Earl of Sheffield. Edited by John Murray, London: J. Murray, 1896. [Reprinted in 1907, "as originally edited by Lord Sheffield," with an introduction by J.B. Bury, London: The World's Classics, vol. 139.]

Life of Cavour

16. Camillo Benso, conte de Cavour, [1810–1861], Italian statesman, architect of united Italy.

Countess Evelyn Martinengo Cesaresco, *Cavour*, London: 1898. [Reprinted, 1904]

Edward C.G. Cadogan, *The Life of Cavour*, in Makers of Modern History series, 1905;[A later edition:] London: Smith, Elder; NY: C. Scribner, 1907.

Life of St. Gertrude, other saints

a dozen copy books,

Seeber [?Saher]

Ask Sallie about library.

17. Mary Francis Cusack, *The life and revelations of St. Gertrude, virgin and abbess, of the Order of St. Benedict*, new edition, London: Burns & Oates; NY: Benziger Bros.,

[1870.]

*

Note #136B

Woodstock

18. Sir Walter Scott [1771–1832], Scottish poet and novelist, created the vogue throughout Europe for the historical novel. *Woodstock* is one of the later novels [1826] in an output rivalled in the 19th century only by Trollope and Balzac.

Woodstock; or, The cavalier: a tale of the year 1651, Edinburgh: A.& C. Black; Philadelphia J.B. Lippincott, 1887. [Series: The Waverley Novels, vol. 21]

Our Mutual Friend

19. Charles Dickens [1812–1870], English novelist. Our mutual friend [1864–1865], Dickens' last completed novel.

Our mutual friend, NY: The Mershon Co., 189–?

Black Dwarf & Legend of [?]

20. Sir Walter Scott, *The black dwarf [and] A legend of Montrose*, Edinburgh: A. & C. Black; Philadelphia: J.B. Lippincott, 1887. [Series: The Waverley Novels, vol. 16]

Quentin Durward

21. Sir Walter Scott, *Quentin Durward*, Edinburgh: A. & C. Black,1887. [Series: The Waverley Novels, vol. 16]

~~Martin Chuzzlewit~~

22. Dickens' "American" novel.

Charles Dickens, *The life and adventures of Martin Chuzzlewit*, NY: J. W. Lovell Company (1868?)

Vivian Grey Disreali [sic]

23. Benjamin Disraeli, Earl of Beaconsfield [1804–1881], British statesman and novelist. Disraeli's first novel, a roman a clef on chief public figures in British society.

Vivian Grey, Philadelphia: Carey, Lea and Carey, 2 vols., 1827.

Silas Marner

24. George Eliot (Marian Evans) [1819–1880], British novelist. *Silas Marner* [1861] is the last of Eliot's three Warwickshire novels.

Silas Marner edited with notes and an introduction by Robert Herrick, NY: Longmans, Green, 1899.

Aiguille a repriser

25. [A knitting needle.]

Gems of Chinese Literature

26. Herbert Allen Giles [1845–1935], British government official posted in China, who claimed to be the first to translate Chinese literature into English, and the first to collect Chinese texts and publish them.

Gems of Chinese Literature, London: B. Quaritch; Shanghai: Kelly & Welsh, 1884.

Historic China & other sketches

27. Herbert Allen Giles, *Historic China and other sketches*, London: T.de la Rue, 1882.

Strange Stories from a Chinese studio

28. P'u Sung-ling [1640–1715], *Strange stories from a Chinese studio*, translated and annotated by Herbert Allen Giles, London: T. de la Rue, 1880.

Chuang Tzu Mystic Moralist and Social Reformer

29. Chuang-Tzu, *Chuang-Tzu: mystic, moralist and social reformer*, translated from the Chinese by Herbert Allen Giles… London: B. Quaritch, 1889.

Chinese Sketches

30. Herbert Allen Giles, *Chinese sketches*, London: Trubner Co., 1876.

Record of the Buddhistic Kingdom

31. Fa hsien [fl399–414], *Record of the Buddhistic Kingdoms*, translated from the Chinese by Herbert Allen Giles, London: Trubner, 1877.

Remain of Lao Tzu

32. [Herbert Allen Giles, *The remains of Lao-Tzu*, Hong Kong: 1886.]

From Swatow to Canton Overland

33. [Herbert Allen Giles, *From Swatow to Canton: (overland),* Shanghai: Kelly & Walsh, 1877.]

San Tzu Ching & Chien Tzu Were metrically translated
Herbert A. Giles

34. [San Tzu Ching; *Elementary Chinese translated and annotated*, Kelly & Walsh, 1900]

Chien Tzu [No record found]

Blickensdorfer ink

35. [Brand name of first typewriter GS purchased and used. It proved extraordinarily clumsy and was subsequently replaced after AT began typing GS's manuscripts.]

Ray man boulevard Hauseman

Lothair

36. A satiric novel [1870], Disraeli's most successful.

Benjamin Disraeli, *Lothair*, London: G. Routledge & Sons, 1888. [The Primrose edition: a sixpenny edition of Disraeli's novels.]

Vivian Grey.

Disraeli

37. [see above]

Byron's Letters

38. George Gordon Byron, Baron Byron [1788–1824],

The letters and journals of Lord Byron, with notice of his life, by Thomas Moore. New and revised edition, NY: G. Routledge & Co., 1875.

~~Urquhart~~

~~Translation of Rabelais~~

Horace Walpole Letters

Greene

Fitzgerald's letters

Boswell's Johnson

~~Man of Feeling by Mackenzie~~

Charles Grandison

39.

~~Milton's Areopagitica~~ **temple series**

40. John Milton [1607–1674], epic poet, sonnet writer, pamphleteer. *The Areopagitica* [1644], Milton's magisterial attack on licensing and censorship of the press.

Areopagitica, a speech of Mr. John Milton for the liberty of unlicensed printing, to the Parliament of England [1644]

Bacon & ~~Locke~~ **temple series**

41. There was no single edition of Bacon and Locke in the Temple Series [for which reason, no doubt, GS crossed out "Locke" in her entry.] The Temple Series "Bacon" is:

Francis Bacon [1561–1626], *Essayes or Counsels civill & morall*, London: J.M. Dent & Co., 1897. [Temple Classics] [Contains the fifty-eight essays and the fragment of an essay "Of Fame."]

~~Cheap edition of Urn Burial & Religio Medici temple series~~

42. Sir Thomas Browne [1605–1682], classical scholar, antiquary, philosopher, man of letters. *Urn Burial* [1658] and *Religio Medici* [1634], two of the greatest 17th century prose meditations.

Sir Thomas Browne, *Religio Medici and Urn Burial*, London: J.M. Dent & Co., 1899 [Temple Classics.]

Spectator

43. Joseph Addison [1672–1719], essayist, poet and statesman.

Richard Steele [1672–1729], essayist, dramatist, and politician.

Spectator, "A new edition, reproducing the original text, both as first issued and as corrected by its authors. With introduction, notes and index by H. Morley." London: G. Routledge & Sons, 1888. [Series: "Routledge's Popular Library of Standard Authors"].

Literary Ethics, July 24, 1838.

But the mark of American merit in painting in poetry in fiction in eloquence seems to be a certain grace without grandeur, in itself not new but derivative, a vase of fair outline but empty, which whoso sees may feel with what wit and character is in him but which does not like the charged cloud overflow with terrible beauty and emit lightnings on beholders.

44. Ralph Waldo Emerson [1803–1852], American poet, essayist, Transcendentalist philosopher.

"Literary Ethics," a lecture delivered by Emerson, this date. Originally published as:

An oration, delivered before the literary societies of Dartmouth college, July 24, 1838.... Published by request. Boston: C.C. Little and J. Brown, 1838.

The lecture is reprinted in *Nature, Addresses, and Lectures*, by Ralph Waldo Emerson, with introduction and notes by Robert E. Spiller. Text established by Alfred R. Ferguson. The Belknap Press of Harvard University Press, Cambridge, MA; London, 1979, pp 100ff.

The essay on "Literary Ethics" also appears in volume six of the Riverside edition of *Emerson's Complete Works*, Boston: Houghton, Mifflin and company; 1889, of which William James' copy, with his markings and annotations, is preserved at [Note: Cat. no.: *AC85/ J2376/ Zz889e. Libraries: MH, NB. NE 0110395.]

The full passage from which this note is excerpted reads:

> Hence the historical failure on which Europe and America have so freely commented. This country has not fulfilled what seemed the reasonable expectation of mankind. Men looked, when all feudal traps and bandages were snapped asunder, that nature, too long the mother of dwarfs, should reimburse itself by a brood of Titans, who should laugh and leap in the continent, and run up the mountains of the West with the errand of genius and of love. But the mark of American merit in painting, in sculpture, in poetry, in fiction, in eloquence, seems to be a certain grace without grandeur, and itself not new but derivative; a vase of fair outline, but empty,—who whoso sees, may fill with what wit and character is in him, but which does not, like the charged cloud, overflow with terrible beauty and emit lightnings on all beholders; a muse which does not lay the grasp of despotic genius on us, and chain an age to its thought and emotion.

[Note #70 derives from this text: "…Hence our art and ourselves and he who runs may read the dreadful failures." And in Ms Note #19, there is the text omitted from MA 37, following line 27, on "the gentle attenuation, the thin imagination and the superficial sentiment of American expression."]

Benvenuto Cellini

45. Benvenuto Cellini [1500–1571], Italian artist, memoirist, metal worker, sculptor. His "barbarically untameable" *Memoirs* [1558ff.] have been called "one of the most fascinating books in existence."

Memoirs of Benvenuto Cellini, a Florentine artist… now first collated with the text of Giuseppe Molini and corrected and enlarged… translated by Thomas Roscoe, London: G. Bell & Sons, 1880. [Series: Bohn's Standard Library]

Parkman 5 vols.

46. Francis Parkman, Jr., American historian. His major life-work, on the struggle between France and England for colonial empire in America.

France and England in North America. 5 vols., Boston: [Little, Brown & Co.], 1865–1879.

English men of action

~~Emma~~

Laurence & Clive

47. "English Men of Action," a series of "books for boys," on heroes such as Wolfe, Sir Francis Drake, etc. The earliest volumes in the series date from

1889, the latest 1905.

Sir Richard Temple [1826–1902], *Lord Lawrence*, London, NY: Macmillan & Co., 1889. [Series: Men of Action].

Sir Charles William Wilson [1836–1905], *Lord Clive*, London, NY: Macmillan & Co., 1893.

Trowbridge

48. Probable reference: John Townsend Trowbridge [1827–1916] American novelist, short story writer, poet, memoirist, historian. Published more than 50 volumes, among them *The Drummer Boy* [1867], *The South* [1866], *The Three Scouts* [1868.]

Barchester Towers

49. Anthony Trollope [1815–1882], *Barchester Towers*, NY: Dodd, Mead & Company, 2 vols. 1898.

Life of Savenola 2 vol.

50. Girolamo Savonarola [1452–1498], Florentine monk, zealous church and social reformer. Pasquale Villari [1827–1917], Italian historian and statesman, major influence on later Italian historians.

Pasquale Villari, *Life and times of Girolamo Savonarola*, 2 vols., translated by Linda Villari, NY: Scribner's, 1893.

Ben Johnson's works

51. Ben Jonson [1573–1637], English dramatist, lyric poet; as critic, the first of England's literary dictators.

The works of Ben Jonson, with a biographical memoir, by William Gifford. A new edition. NY: D. Appleton & Co., 1879.

~~Marlowe~~

52. Christopher Marlowe [1564–1593], English dramatist, poet.

The works of Christopher Marlow, including his translations, edited with introduction and notes by Lieut.-Col. Francis Cunningham, London: Chatto & Windus, 1889.

Midshipman Easy

53. Frederick Maryat [1792–1848], *Mr. Midshipman Easy… with an introduction by David Hannay*, London, NY: Macmillan and Company, 1896.

*

Note #110B

54. A series of 11 quoted passages from Johnathan Swift,

The Tale of a Tub and Other Early Works, edited by Temple Scott, London: George Bell & Sons, 1897: [from "The tale of a tub:"]

(**pp. 58–59**:)
Once upon a time there was a man who had three sons by one wife and all at a birth neither could the midwife tell certainly which was the eldest. Their father died while they were young and upon his death bed calling the lads to him spoke thus.

(Ibid. p. 60:)
On their first appearance out three adventurers met with a very bad reception and soon with great sagacity guessing out the reason they soon quickly began to improve the good qualities of the town.

(Ibid. p. 82:)
Sometimes he would set them a warning to frighten naughty boys and make them quiet.

(Ibid. p. 83:)
it is certain they were no better than a sort of sturdy swaggering beggars.

(Ibid. p. 83:)
witches[?] [thirsting??] [last??]
The imitation [?] [thisting??] to this lost them [Their?] lives [?] and money too.

(Ibid. p. 86:)
What then my God replied the first it seems that this is a shoulder of mutton all the while.

(Ibid. pp. 95–96:)
We left Lord Peter in open rupture with his two brothers both for ever discarded from his house and ~~left~~ resigned to the wide world with little or nothing to trust to. Which are circumstances that render them proper subjects for a writer's pen to work on, scenes of misery ever affording the fairest [-?-] for great adventures. And in this the world may perceive the difference between the integrity of a generous author and that of a common friend. The latter is observed to adhere close in [-?-] but on the decline of

fortune to suddenly drop off, men in misfortune being like men in the dark to whom all colors are the same. But when they came forward into the world and began to display themselves to each other and to the light, their complexions appeared extremely different which the present picture of their affairs gave them sudden opportunity to discover.

We think it highly reasonable to produce our great forgetfulness as an argument manouverable for our great wit.

(Ibid. p. 100:)

And as in scholastic disputes nothing seems to rouse the spleen of him that opposes, so much as a kind of pedantic affected calmness in the respondent In short Martin's patience put Jack in a rage.

(Ibid. p. 287:)

Elephants are always drawn smaller than life but a flea always larger. A person reading to me a dull poem of his own making I prevailed on him to scratch out six lines together. In turning over the leaf the ink being wet it marked as many lines on the other page, wherat [sic] the poet complaining I bid him be easy for it would be better if those were out too.

(Ibid. p. 141:)

Going too long is a cause of abatement as effectual though not so frequent as going too short and holds true especially of the labors of the brain.

(Ibid. p. 142:)

This I mention because I am wonderfully well acquainted with the present relish of courteous readers and have often observed with singular pleasure that a fly driven from a honey pot will [similarly?] with very good appetite alight and finish his meal on excrement.

*

NB2, #2

Frederic Reynolds memoirs

Frederic Reynolds [1764–1841], 19th century English playwright.

The life and times of Frederick Reynolds, written by himself, London: H. Colburn, 1826.

*

NB2, #8

Sacrificing his oldest friendship at an age when friendship could not be replaced. Fox interposed. There is no loss of friends. Yes Burke fiercely rejoined, there is a loss of friends, I know the price of my conduct. Our friendship is at an end.

> *The French Revolution: Chapters from the Author's History of England During the Eighteenth Century*. William Edward Hartpole Lecky, D. Appleton and Company, N.Y.-Boston-Chicago, 1904. pg 261–262.

*

NB2, #9

Tis like Mrs. Pinnley's great belly, she may lace it down before but it burnishes on her hips.

> William Congreve [1670–1729], *The Way of the World*, III, 3: Mrs. Marwood: "The secret is grown too big for the pretence. 'Tis like Mrs. Prinnley's great belly; she may lace it down before, but it burnishes on her hips."

*

NB2, #32

"The late good old king [i.e. George II] had something of humanity and amongst many other royal virtues he possessed justice truth & sincerity in an eminent degree so that he had something about him by which it was possible to know whether he liked you or disliked you."

> Henry Smith Williams; *The Historians' History of the World: England*, 1642–1791; The Outlook Company (New York); 1904; p.592.

*

~~It has been~~ Activity is a cheap commodity. Mankind never profit by experience. Dr. Franklin used to say that experience was the school for fools. the most profligate woman that walks the strand can persuade any man that he is the first who has really captivated her.

*

NB2, #33

> Edmond George Petty-Fitzmaurice Fitzmaurice (1st Baron), William Petty Marquis of Lansdowne
>
> *Life of William, Earl of Shelburne, Afterwards First Marquess of Landsdowne: With*

Extracts from His Papers and Correspondence, Volume 2; Macmillan; 1876; pg 360.

*

NB12, #20

Melville White Whale Walls.

Herman Melville; *Moby-Dick or, The Whale*; Harper & Brothers Publishers, New York, 1851.

*

NB14, #1

Glover Memoirs

Alice send Greene digit of the Moon, ask about [thread?]

Francis William Bain [1863–1940], *A digit of the moon, and other love stories from the Hindoo*, translated from the original manuscripts by F.W. Bain, NY and London: Putnam, 1898. [Later editions, 1901 and 1908.]

Magyar empire the english translation if sold in separate volumes.

[unlocated]

*

NB14, #6

Letters of James Boswell Introd. of Seccombe 7/6 (Sedgwick & Jackson)

James Boswell [1740–1759], *Letters of James Boswell to the Rev. W. J. Temple*, with an introduction by Thomas Seccombe, London: Sidgwick and Jackson, 1908.

[For dating: no earlier edition of this publication; consequently, dates **Notebook 14** as no earlier than 1908.]

*

NB14, #8

Caesar was unalterably almost naively indifferent to all moral distinctions. This indifference was not due to depravity of life; it was inborn in his nature and unconsciously strengthened by his habits and company, by the bankrupts and swindlers and adventuresses with whom he consorted; conjoined with an unusual excitability of temper it gave him an extraordinary versatility and plasticity of mind and adapted him to act well or ill, supremely well or supremely ill, as the need might be.

Ferrero, Guglielmo. *The Greatness and Decline of Rome. Vol. 1.* 1907. Reprint.

London: Forgotten Books, 2013. 263. (Original work published 1907)

*

Note #63

Eustace Diamonds
Sir Harry Hotspur of Thimblethwaite
Harry Heathcote of Gangoil
The American Senator
Is he Popinjay
An eye for an eye
John Caldigate
Cousin Henry
Dr. Watle's School
Marion Fay [?]
Remember Mrs. Heiroth's lack of expression also May's Not sure of their class positive character of them goes with the kind of freedom and the kind of being mistress power only with those who love them

A listing of ten novels by Anthony Trollope (1815–1882):

The Eustace diamonds, 3 vols., London: [no publisher listed], 1873.

Sir Harry Hotspur of Thimblethwaite, London: [no publisher listed].,1871.

Harry Heathcote of Gangoil, a tale of Austrian Bush life, London: Ward, Lock & Co., 1883.

The American Senator, a novel, 3 vols., London: [no publisher listed], 1878.

Is he Popenjoy? a novel, 3 vols., London: [no publisher listed], 1878.

An eye for an eye, 2 vols., London [no publisher listed], 1879.

John Caldigate, 3 vols., London: Routledge & Co., 1880.

Cousin Henry, a novel, 2 vols., London: Chapman & Hall, 1879.

Dr. Wortle's school, a novel, 2 vols., London: Chapman & Hall, 1881.

Marion Fay, a novel, 3 vols., London: Chapman & Hall. 1882.

*

NB-*C #1

Twenty-three tales
Tolstoy—The World's Classics

Lev Nikolaevich Tolstoi, [1828–1910], *Twenty-three tales*, translated by Louise and Aylmer Maude, London: The World's Classics, 1906 [World Classics, vol. 72.]

Dostoschefsky. [sic] **Crime & Punishment etc.**

Fyodor Dostoevski, [1821–1881], *Crime and punishment*, London: Vizetelly's One Volume Novels, vol. 13, 1886.

Poor folks

Fyodor Dostoevski, *Poor Folk*, translated from the Russian by Lena Milman, introduction by George Moore, London: Elkin Matthews & John Lane, Boston: Roberts Bros., 1902.

Trollope

Anthony Trollope [1815–1882] Most prolific of 19th century English novelists. Wrote 55 novels, largely of English clerical society (The Barsetshire Chronicles), and of its political and legal worlds, and other works. [See Note #63, which lists ten Trollope novels.]

Poe's Tales

Edgar Allen Poe [1809–1849], American poet and critic, major influence on Baudelaire and the Symbolist movement in Europe.

Poems and tales, selected and edited by Alphonso G. Newcomer, Chicago: Scott, Foresman & Co., 1902

Olmstead Cotton Kingdom

Journey in the Back Country

Frederick Law Olmsted [1822–1903], American landscape architect whose account of Southern slavery greatly influenced British opinion during the Civil War.

The cotton kingdom: a traveller's observations on cotton and slavery in the American slave states, NY: Mason Bros., 1861.

A journey in the back country: the slave states in the winter of 1853–54, NY: G.P. Putnam' Sons, 2 vols. 1907.

Webster's speeches and letters

Daniel Webster [1782–1852], American statesman whose political life was centered on the slavery question, Constitutionality and states' rights. His speeches were adapted by GS in her 1946 opera, *The Mother of Us All*, in which he serves as the chief male opponent to the feminist activism of Susan B. Anthony.

The writings and speeches of Daniel Webster, 18 vols., Boston: Little, Brown Co., 1903.

[-?-] **Scott's book**

John Gibson Lockhart [1794–1854], Scottish writer and editor. His *Life of Scott* has been called "the most admirable biography in the English language after Boswell's Johnson."

The life of Sir Walter Scott, Edinburgh: T. C. & E. C. Jack, 1902.

The dating of this Notebook [*C] is confirmed by: Letter, Michael Stein to GS, Paris to Florence, May 22, 1908: "The Scott and the Webster arrived." But it is possible that a different "Scott's book" was ordered by GS in 1908. Mabel Weeks in Letter to GS, August 14, 1906, informs her that she is reading Lockhart's *Life of Scott*, and adds: "I think you said you did not care for it, but although at first it seems inflexible and ponderous, I think its effect is cumulative."

*

NB-*C #2

Letters to temple edited by Mr. Frances

James Boswell [1740–1795], *Letters of James Boswell, addressed to the Rev. W[illiam] J. Temple, now first published from the original mss., with an introduction and notes* [by Sir Phillip Francis], London: R. Bentley, 1857.

Boswelliana, Philobiblon Society, Mr. Milnes

"Boswell's Commonplace Book:" Boswelliana [Extracts from Boswell's commonplace book. Editor's forward signed: R. M. M., i.e., Richard Monckton Milnes, Baron Houghton], Philobiblon Society, vol. 2, 1854 etc.

Peregrine Pickle

Tobias George Smollett [1721–1771], British novelist.

The adventures of Peregrine Pickle; in which are included memoirs of a lady of quality, London: Routledge, 1896. [There were multiple publications of the book until 1907 in two and four volumes. This edition is in one volume.]

*

Note #89B

Sir Charles Danvers

Sir Charles Danvers (c.1568–1601) was an English MP and soldier who plotted against Elizabeth I of England.

Sir Charles Danvers, Mary Cholomondeley, London, R. Bentley, 1889

Diana Tempest

Diana Tempest, *Mary Cholomondeley, Leipzig Tauchnitz, 1893.*

*

NB7, #1

The Conspirators

The Regent's Daughter

Alexandre Dumas [1802–1870], French novelist and dramatist.

The conspirators; or, the chevalier d'Harmental, London: J.M. Dent and co; Boston: Little, Brown and co., 1893–97.

Dumas, *The regent's daughter*, London: J.M. Dent and co.; Boston: Little, Brown and co., 1894. [Series: The Romances of Alexandre Dumas, vol. 21].

Hugo—Toilers of the Sea

Victor Marie Hugo [1802–1885], French novelist, poet and dramatist.

Toilers of the sea, London: J.M. Dent & Sons; NY: E. Dutton & co. [n.d.]

*

NB7 #4

Blanche de Beaulieu

Alexandre Dumas, *The brigand, and Blanche de Beaulieu*, London: J.M. Dent & co.; Boston: Little, Brown & co., 1893–1897. [Two novels in one.]

*

NB8, #2

A. Young

Arthur Young [1741–1820], British writer on agriculture, social economy; famous for his *Travels in France* [1792], published on the eve of the French revolution.

Travels in France and Italy during the years 1787, 1788, 1789, with an introduction by Thomas Okey, Everyman's Library, 1906. [Originally published in 1792–94]

G. Sand—Letters & novels.

George Sand [1804–1876], pseudonym of Madame Amandine Lucile Aurore Duderant, nee Dupin. French author, prodigious writer of novels, journals, letters, plays. Her writings were eventually published in 112 volumes.

From *The intimate journals of George Sand*, edited and translated by Marie Jenney Hunt, NY: Loring & Mussey, 1929:

> "From 1836 to 1840" appears the first edition of George Sand's works, published by Bonnaire in 24 volumes.
>
> "A second edition..." published in 16 volumes between 1842–1844, is continued in 1847 by Garnier.
>
> "A third incomplete edition..." is published by Hetzel between 1851–1856.
>
> "The fourth edition... undertaken... in 1852", is continued by Michel Levy through 77 volumes.
>
> The fifth edition by Calmann Ley comprises 112 volumes.

Alice Toklas confirmed that GS read George Sand in French, Miss Toklas having bought the small French volumes for her from the bookstalls along the Paris quays. There were no English translations of Sand until after 1908, the date of this note.

Pascal

Blaise Pascal [1623–1662], French philosopher and mathematician; with Descartes, the seminal French philosopher of the 17th century. There were many translations of Pascal's *Pensees* by 1908. Among them, an edition GS might have used:

Blaise Pascal [1623–1662], *The thoughts of Blaise Pascal, translated from the text of M. Auguste Molinier*, by C. Kegan Paul, London: G. Bell and Sons, 1899.

Gardner St. Cath.
38710

St. Catherine [1347–1380], Dominican tertiary, feast observed April 30th. Her letters, in Tuscan vernacular, put her, it is claimed, "almost on a level with Petrarch." Played major political role in healing the church schism between Rome and Avignon.

Edmund Garrett Gardner [1869–1935], *Saint Catherine of Siena, a study in the religion, literature and history of the fourteenth century in Italy*, London: J.M. Dent and co., NY: E.P. Dutton co., 1907.

37471 Another life of her.

[Numbers listed (38710 and 37471) might be Mudie catalogue numbers. More probably: American Library in Paris.]

*

NB8, #9

[...?] the tight rope family Napoleon diary the gradual approach of the beginning of the middle of his middle living.

[loose note—out of order]

Napoleon Bonaparte [1769–1821.] During the years in captivity in St. Helena [1815–1821], dictated his reminiscences.

Memoirs of the history of France during the reign of Napoleon, dictated by the Emperor at Saint Helena, 7 vols., London, 1823, 1824.

[A later, edited edition:] *The Corsican. A diary of Napoleon's life in his own words*, edited by R. M. Johnston, Boston and NY: Houghton Mifflin Co., 1910.

*

Note #99

Willis the pilot sequel to Swiss family Robinson.

Johann David Wyss [1781–1830], Swiss author, Professor of Philosophy, collector and compiler of Swiss tales and folklore. Best known as author of *The Swiss Family Robinson* [1812–1813], first translated into English, 1820.

The Swiss Family Robinson, new and unabridged translation by Mrs. H.B. Paull, with the additions made by the Baroness Montolieu, London: Chandos Classics, 1890.

Galt—The entail

John Galt [1779–1839], Scottish novelist.

The entail: or, the Lairds of Grippy, London: Blackwell's Standard Novels, vol. 6, 1842.

The Annals of Parish

John Galt, *Annals of the Parish and the Ayshire legatees*, with an introduction by Alfred Ainger, London: Macmillan & Co., 1895.

Provost

John Galt, *The provost, and other tales*, London, Blackwood's Standard Novels, vol. 4, 1842.

Sir Audrey Wiley

John Galt, *Sir Andrew Wiley of that ilk*, London: Blackwood's Standard Novels, vol. 2, 1841.

Author Haji Baba

Sohrab the Hostage

Aysha.

James Justinian Morier [1780–1849], English novelist, served in diplomat corps in Egypt and Persia; wrote travel books mingling "memories of the Arabian Nights with … own experience."

Hajji Baba of Ispahan, 1824

Hajji Baba of England, 1828

Zohrab the hostage, 1832

Ayesha, the maid of Karls, 1834.

Henry Tolstoy. Ivan the Terrible.

Count Aleksei Konstantinovich Tolstoi [1817–1875], Russian novelist, dramatist and poet; distant relative of Leo Tolstoi.

The death of Ivan the Terrible, A tragedy, translated from the Russian by I. H. Harrison, London: 1869.

Willis the pilot—Swiss fam. Robinson.

Willis the pilot: a sequel to "The Swiss Family Robinson," translated from "Le pilote Willis" by Adrien Paul, by H. Frith, London: Ward, Lock & C0., 1890.

*

Note #33B

I am of opinion that honest man who married and brought up a large family did more service than he who continued single and only talked [?] of population. From this motive I had scarce taken orders a year before I began to think seriously of matrimony and chose my wife as she did her wedding gown not […]

Oliver Goldsmith's, *The Vicar of Wakefield*; Harrison; 1780. pg.1

*

Note #71A

Rudin

Ivan Sergeevich Turgenev [1818–1883], Russian novelist.

Rudin, a novel, translated from the Russian by Constance Garnett, London: W. Heinemann, 1894.

Poor Folks

Fyodor Dostoevski [1821–1881], Russian novelist.

Poor Folk, translated from the Russian by Lena Milman. Introduction by George Moore. Boston: Roberts Bros., 1894; London: Elkin Mathews & John Lane, 1894.

***

B. Loose Notes

Loose notes are numbered in the order in which they were found. Many have been placed in the context of other notebooks or the book reading list, Appendix A, as shown in the following table. The rest are presented in this section.

Loose Notes

Note	Location	Note	Location	Noe	Location
Note #1	Diagram Book,p. 345	Note #75	Notebook *C, 214	Note #127	Notebook N, 561
Note #3	Notebook N, 558	Note #75a	Notebook *C, 215	Note #128	Notebook N, 559
Note #4	Notebook C, 421	Note #76	Notebook 6, 103	Note #129	Notebook G, 501
Note #5	Notebook 9, 95	Note #76a	Notebook 3, 482	Note #130	Notebook M, 547
Note #6	Notebook A, 387	Note #77	Notebook F, 474	Note #131	Notebook 4, 490
Note #7	Notebook 8, 432	Note #78	Notebook *J, 300	Note #132	Notebook 4, 486
Note #8	Notebook C, 415	Note #79	Notebook C, 420	Note #133A	Jottings, 69
Note #9	Notebook 1, 123	Note #80	Notebook *C, 219	Note #133B	Appendix A, 601
Note #14	Notebook *C, 246	Note #81	Notebook C, 421	Note #135	Jottings, 60
Note #16	Notebook *C, 256	Note #82	Notebook C, 421	Note #135A	Appendix A, 586
Note #19	Notebook *C, 212	Note #83	Notebook 5, 423	Note #136A	Early Draft Notes, 71
Note #20	Notebook F, 471	Note #84	Notebook 8, 428	Note #136B	Appendix A, 603
Note #23	Notebook *C, 243	Note #84a	Notebook 8, 428	Note #137	Early Draft Notes, 77
Note #24	Notebook *C, 244	Note #85	Notebook *C, 207	Note #138	Notebook *C, 253
Note #32	Notebook *C, 245	Note #86	Notebook 5, 425	Note #139	Notebook *C, 253
Note #33A	Early Draft Notes, 76	Note #87	Notebook *C, 216	Note #140	Notebook *C, 255
Note #33B	Appendix A, 619	Note #88	Notebook *C, 217	Note #170	Notebook 9, 101
Note #34	Notebook *C, 243	Note #89A	Notebook *C, 217	Note #173	Notebook *C, 221
Note #35	Diagram Book, 362	Note #89B	Appendix A, 615	Note #174	Notebook *C, 207
Note #36	Appendix A, 599	Note #90	Notebook *C, 217	Note #175	Notebook *C, 209
Note #37	Notebook *C, 251	Note #91	Notebook *C, 221	Note #176	Jottings, 57
Note #38	Notebook *C, 260	Note #92	Notebook *C, 218	Note #176a	Notebook *C, 219
Note #39	Notebook *C, 258	Note #93	Notebook *C, 213	Note #177	Jottings, 68
Note #40	Notebook *C, 260	Note #94	Notebook *C, 210	Note #178	Jottings, 68
Note #41	Diagram Book, 327	Note #94a	Notebook *C, 209	Note #180	Appendix A, 596
Note #42	Diagram Book, 354	Note #96	Notebook *C, 216	Note #183	Notebook N, 561
Note #43	Diagram Book, 357	Note #97	Notebook 11, 134	Note #185	Jottings, 68
Note #44	Diagram Book, 356	Note #98	Notebook 8, 429	Note #186	Notebook 10, 157
Note #45	Diagram Book, 331	Note #99	Appendix A, 618	Note #187	Notebook 10, 158
Note #46	Diagram Book, 342	Note #100	Notebook F, 470	Note #188	Notebook 10, 158
Note #47	Notebook 9, 97	Note #101	Notebook N, 563	Note #189	Notebook 10, 158
Note #48	Diagram Book, 305	Note #102	Notebook M, 548	Note #191	Notebook 10, 157
Note #49	Diagram Book, 317	Note #103	Notebook M, 550	Note #192	Notebook 10, 159
Note #51	Diagram Book, 326	Note #104	Notebook N, 560	Note #194	Jottings, 67
Note #52	Notebook N, 562	Note #105	Notebook *C, 208	Note #195	Jottings, 63
Note #53	Notebook N, 564	Note #105a	Notebook *C, 208	Note #196	Jottings, 69
Note #54	Notebook N, 563	Note #106	Notebook M, 546	Note #197	Appendix A, 597
Note #55	Notebook N, 564	Note #107	Diagram Book, 329	Note #198	Appendix A, 598
Note #56	Notebook F, 468	Note #108	Diagram Book, 331	Note #199	Notebook 4, 492
Note #57	Notebook 1, 123	Note #109	Notebook F, 469	Note #207	Notebook *C, 217
Note #58	Diagram Book, 311	Note #110A	Early Draft Notes, 74	Note #209	Notebook 10, 159
Note #59	Notebook 6, 104	Note #110B	Appendix A, 609	Note #210	Notebook 13, 534
Note #60	Notebook 12, 147	Note #111	Early Draft Notes, 77	Note #211	Notebook 3, 483
Note #61	Notebook 5, 423	Note #112	Notebook 4, 486	Note #212	Diagram Book, 365
Note #62	Notebook 12, 147	Note #113	Notebook 4, 491	Note #213	Notebook 13, 535
Note #63	Appendix A, 613	Note #114	Notebook G, 493	Note #214	Notebook 13, 534
Note #64	Appendix A, 599	Note #115	Notebook N, 559	Note #215	Notebook G, 500
Note #65	Diagram Book, 363	Note #116	Notebook G, 501	Note #217	Notebook F, 473

Note #66	Jottings, 63
Note #67	Early Draft Notes, 73
Note #68	Notebook *C, 206
Note #69	Notebook *C, 206
Note #71A	Appendix A, 619
Note #71B	Notebook 9, 101
Note #72	Notebook F, 473
Note #73	Notebook F, 474
Note #74	Notebook 3, 481
Note #117	Notebook G, 500
Note #119	Notebook M, 545
Note #120	Notebook N, 564
Note #121	Notebook M, 546
Note #122	Notebook M, 545
Note #123	Notebook M, 549
Note #124	Notebook M, 544
Note #125	Notebook N, 562
Note #126	Notebook N, 565
Note #218	Notebook F, 473
Note #219	Notebook F, 474
Note #220	Early Draft Notes, 75
Note #221	Notebook *C, 212
Note #222	Notebook F, 472
Note #223	Early Draft Notes, 75
Note #224	Early Draft Notes, 75
Note #225	Appendix A, 601

*

Group of Matisse
Give details of their lives
The people near them.
Father and Mother.
Manguin and crowd.
Derain
Woman & Margot.
Mrs. Matisse & family
all the stories, sister and
her hands and career.
The children.
House
Mrs. M.'s life.
us quarrels fallings
away.
servants school
Frenchman asking for pictures
Shukin. on and on. Purman
Olga. change in appearance.
Mrs. M. & change in Margot.
hair and all, his clothes.
Walk with him when he was in
despair,
wanted to [claim?] family.

Group of Picasso

His people. His pupil and his
friends Salmon Max, Appolinaire,
women (?), Fernande
Sagot, Vollard, [first
class?]. Youth we knew.
Fernande. Pichots). Folks.
[Progress ?] big picture.
separation. friends. Haviland
Manolo. Frederick, adopted
child. Their feeling for each
other. Her Heisman like
character. His not extremely
passionate nature. His
phantasies, his success.
His needs. His temperament.

LK Planning Note for first two subjects.

AT for Group of Matisse:

Father and mother: Matisse's father was a wood merchant in a small town in the north of France. His mother was stupid and devout. She was glad her husband died, and every time the church bells rang, it made her shiver for the masses being said.

Manguin: Matisse's *camarade d'atelier.*

Derain: He was the pet of Matisse, the only real follower in those days, and the adored of Mme. Matisse.

Margot: [The Matisse's daughter.] She had had diphtheria, and it was treated through her throat. It affected her speech and left a mark on her neck. She always wore a black ribbon around it, and she is shown so in Matisse's paintings of her.

Mrs. Matisse & family: A South of France family, from Perpignan. Mme. Matisse had told Gertrude about them.

the children: The two sons of the Matisses. Pierre is the New York picture dealer, and the other one, unsuccessful, is now in Paris. Gertrude noted that Mme. Matisse kept Margot at home when her parents took one son and Matisse's parents took the other. Margot once said, 'I'm exactly like my mother, don't you think so?' to me, quite coldly, believing it.

Houses: It was probably already Clamart at this time.

Mrs. M. life: Derain said of Mme. Matisse that she was 'Sainte Amelie, la plus grande martyre de notre siecle.' The joke went the rounds like mad, but it was serious as well as not. Mme. Matisse saw how her husband was treating her, but not to the extent that other people did. Her martyrdom grew. In addition to running off for a month [with Olga Meerson] as soon as Matisse had money, his models were also his mistresses. 'Sacred Emily' is Gertrude's portrait of Mme. Matisse.

Schukin: [Shchoukin] He got Matisse to paint a third Joie de Vivre. There was a Bonheur de Vivre, then a La Ronde. Shchoukin had to have one, so Matisse painted another.

Purman… Olga… Mrs. M[atisse]: Olga Meerson was a Russian student in Matisse's classes. Matisse fell in love with her and they went off on a trip together. Matisse painted a picture of her in which she looked like a satyr.

Mme. Matisse sort of scanned her conversation as she walked. She had a rhythm in her speech and her walk. She said to me, I have such nightmares about Henri, but they couldn't be true. I told Leo, but it never got to Sarah, who wouldn't have stood for it [about her idol Matisse.]

Purrmann, Matisse's favorite pupil, was at one time ready to marry Margot Matisse, but didn't. But Purrmann also fell in love with Olga in Fiesole. She was very seductive for those who were seduced, very blonde, very pale, with transparent color of skin. Gertrude said [of her hair], She doesn't know its original color any more. When Purrmann was through, he was thoroughly through. He finally said of her, Pity for the time I've lost.

Here is a Purrmann story. When Gertrude was in Spain, all the rooms of her hotel looked out on a smart, small street with many men's clubs where they sat at the window and looked out at girls. At the back of the hotel, they had shops with deluxe articles for women. In one, Gertrude found a big rhinestone turtle that was expensive but flashy, and back in Paris, she wore it down low on the side of her kimono to hold it together. And Purrmann, when he saw it, asked me, Is it real? But if she wears it, I said. Ah, said Purrmann.

The 'kimono' was the corduroy dress in the Picasso portrait. Etta [Cone] made her spend a great deal on it in Baltimore, at a French dressmaker's, and Gertrude copied it for years, repeating it in a variety of materials, brown or putty- or fairly dark-colored but always the same ample skirt and balloon-like sleeves. Once I had it copied for a trip to England in an extraordinary silk with cashmere wool inside. I always called it 'Royal Mourning.'

change in appearance: When he became richer, Matisse looked less boorish. In the old days, he looked like a Professor in the German sense, devoted to teaching and investigating in advance the lesson to be given. He not only had the spectacles for it, but the look beside. He had the coloring.

Mrs. M. & change in Margot: Under the influence of Olga Meerson. Before running off with Matisse, Olga had changed Mme. Matisse's corsets and bleached Margot's hair.

his clothes: Matisse bought a goatskin coat for himself and Margot. Mme. Matisse probably refused one. She had considerable taste in clothes.

AT for Group of Picasso:

His people: Gertrude knew what Matisse told her. The father was very reserved, had enormous pride, and dressed like, looked like, and was mistaken for an Englishman. The mother was a little adorable mother. A pure mother. She was of distant Italian origin. Picasso was not a Spanish name, but his mother's name. Pablo was fond of his older sister. They lived a perfectly normal life for a poorish family of a fonctionnaire—the head of the Beaux Arts in Barcelona. The father was probably born in Cadiz, the mother in Malaga.

his pupil: I never heard of his pupil.

Sagot: His first dealer.

Pichot: The Spanish painter also living in Montmartre. He saw Picasso all the time.

separation: Fernande's and Picasso's separation in 1907.

Manolo: The sculptor. Gertrude tells about him in the Autobiography, about the lottery tickets and so on. He slept all day and lived all night.

Frederick: The owner of the Lapin Agile. He had a donkey, and the night of the Rousseau banquet, Fernande threw out the donkey.

adopted child: Fernande adopted a child without either she or Picasso having a sou. She pulled the little girl's hair when she combed it and the girl cried. Finally, she lost her because the girl had not been legally adopted. Fernande was maternal toward Picasso and had decided to be more fully maternal. Picasso was easy-going in those days, and said 'Yes, yes' to everything, because none of it disturbed him. It was all 'rigolo.'

Their feeling for each other: Fernande's and Pablo's. Fernande had no variety. Every second was the same as ten years ago. One got bored. She was at her most wonderful when she owned the child and bought ribbons for its hair, but she got bored.

His not extremely passionate nature: Yes, that was why women got tired of him. He got indifferent, they bored him, and they were dissatisfied. He was never adored by women. That kind of energy went into his painting. Gertrude once said this to Nelly, and Frank said, 'I just saw him once, and I knew he was no passionate pet.'

He exhausts a woman by over-loving her, and then has nothing more to do with her. Once, in about 1913 when Pablo was going through a trying period looking for someone to love, he would bring his new discoveries to Gertrude to give them the once-over. On one occasion, he brought her Irene Lagoute, a painter, and they spent the day with us. While Pablo and Gertrude were talking pictures, she told me that she came from Jurat, and looking at me hard and meaningfully, said, Where we are never caged. You understand me, we're never caged. The next day she left Pablo and Paris. Later she made a great marriage in the *haut monde*.

His phantasies: Picasso had that kind of stupid imagination, like Eugene Ullman's: 'If people had wings,' etcetera, only not that stupid. He had playfulness—Spanish, stupid, childish, innocent.

his success: He had it then, and it wasn't warped by anything in those days, neither by the outside world nor by the people around him. There is a photo of Pablo and Fernande and the dog Frika from this time [1911.] That was when Picasso was beautiful, and the photo shows him so.

*

Note #10

Single page, both sides:

Sayne says that the American would just say, oh lets go to the hotel.

The noises each one makes. Bruce and the peasants. The American as I see them. Sounds. Baby's sounds all sounds.

AT ***Sayne:*** [H. Lyman Sayen.] He was a Philadelphia Quaker. Oh, how he knew about the Americans! He could tell you what the Americans said all day long. Sayen retired on X-ray inventions around the time of the Spanish American war and lived on it for the rest of his life. He was a very bad painter and he knew it. His wife Janet gave Gertrude the expression, Dandy Girls. Miss Mars and Miss Squiers were Dandy Girls. It was about Sayen's baby's colored ribbons, when his wife asked him, What do you think? Compared to white, he said (of what was thought of as the *colorie vulgaire* in Paris) all color is vulgar.

Go on now sometime with L. & then go on sometime with her.

LK Most likely a note for TWO, being written apparently concurrently with the note above on Sayen. The note obviously refers to Leo and then Sara Stein, but in what sequence in TWO the note belongs is unidentifiable.

*

Note #11

Romance legend ideal

Right-side up:

Americans fear. short story. Sayne lets go to the hotel

Americans Americans

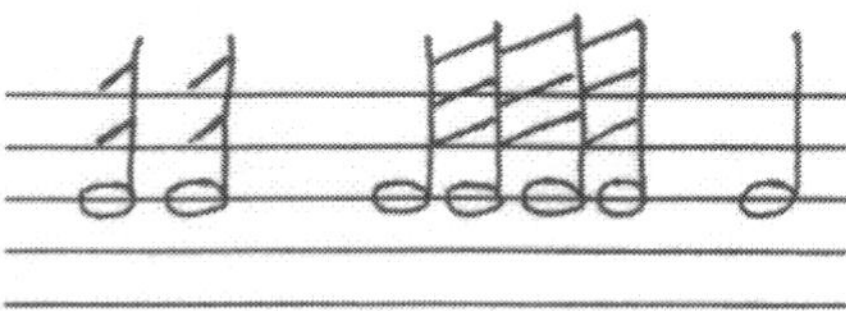

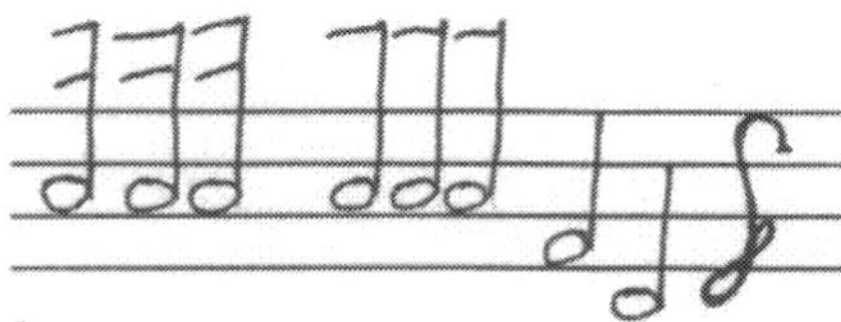

*

Note #12

(Possible, but uncertain location)

Try and deal in positives and contrasts, not negatives and it must be ample.

Go on with her and then begin again with him and go into resemblances and then her and then him.

Make more pictures before contrasts and resemblances come.

*

Note #13

(Possible, but uncertain location)

[...] but really Leo and Sally, Alice & me, Mike and others and others. that book called The Channings want some more.

I, no more conscience than a Vollard or an Acton. When I did not find the malachite. When I do not transcendentalise it becomes [?] a wife. Make long book conscience and no conscience.

AT ***no more conscience than a Vollard or an Acton:*** Vollard could take a lithograph marked 'Ten copies only,' and make a hundred later. Acton was the illegitimate child of Lord Acton's sister who married a rich Chicago woman. He was very strange, a little weird. He had a marvelous collection of Seventeenth Century Italian things which wasn't an accepted period at the time—alabaster figures, angels, hanging vines, lights, and so on. Gertrude said his place was a very fine Donizetti opera. Mabel Dodge used to suspect that when he passed a Madonna on the road it would disappear into his car. Mabel had a flirtation with Acton, and Mrs. Acton, just as Mabel was a disappearing hostess, was a disappearing guest.

the malachite: Gertrude had a large piece of malachite, Chinese, a large bowl or something. It was used then for brooches and other jewelry.

LK ***that book called the Channings:*** Mrs. Henry Wood [1814–1887], English novelist. Most successful work, both as novel and play, *East Lynne* [1861.] Mrs. Henry Wood, *The Channings*, 3 vols., London: Richard Bentley, 1862.

*

Note #15

Leo Friedman et Co.
Then the short sketches in the order done.
Claribel

Mildred
Old Maids
David et al.
Italians.

LK ***Leo Friedman et Co:*** alternate titles "Five or Six Men." and "The Four and One." "The Four and One" portrait follows this sequence: Leo Friedman, Derain, Hans Purrmann (33, l.12), Maurice Sterne and Piot

*

Note #17

Describe Laura any way. Describe Laura.
Her character her sense. Their mutual sisterliness. her feeling.
Being one and laughing at herself then.
Her criticism of Adele. Go on with Laura's activities and remarks.
In being one living some she was one sitting some

*

Note #18

(Possible, but uncertain location)

A Man.

Five or six men.

Two Women.
Italians.

by
Gertrude Stein

Grant Richard

Go on to resemblances and differences before details as in sketch & then influences and lives.
Go on with attacking, meaness [sic], vanity, practicalness, leaders.
Lead to
[Note following?]

Go on with L. he getting to be old. logic etc. Nammi and his voice, and then contrast exclusion, about judgement.*

[Other side. Note following?]

Pritchard, Adele, Therese, Raymond, Matisse, Pablo, Purman, Weber.
The Jew and de Chlistian hurrah hurrah. Listening and sympathy and how it is in her and what it does. Belief in her and how it works.
Acts of kindness and tummy and fat and thin and Myrtle's certainty, and spooking, and practicality and lack of practicality. Practical interest ~~no practical sense or purpose no purpose gives sense of sweetness and generosity.~~
~~Sally. Go on.~~
~~Then L.~~
Return to [sic] little believe too much in affect [sic] of appreciations or actions, both because there is no immediate passion.

*

Note #21

Note is missing

*

Note #22

Planning Note:

MANGUIN

The sensibility of a light kind and the serious worldliness of the idea of pousser, of finish of completeness. He can now pousser. He has lost all sensibility. Diagram this in saying what he said about Matisse.

Make this an exercise in diagram to be written after the three dishonest ones. Americans will then be written. The long book constantly going.

AT ***Manguin… Make this an exercise in diagram:*** That is, relate all the things in Manguin as though they were parts of a sentence. She did that for Manguin because she didn't know him as well as Matisse or Picasso, so it had to be done that way.

Leo and Gertrude were interested in him early, but lost interest quickly. His picture was up in 1906, stayed up for 1907 and 1908, and then was taken down. They didn't see him or Mme. Manguin after the picture disappeared, naturally.

In the Portraits, it is one complete look, all there at one time, just as in a picture. I remember when Gertrude told Haweis at Mabel Dodge's that she was doing Portraits, and he asked, Do you mean as Seventeenth- and Eighteenth-Century writers did them? No, I don't, said Gertrude, this is entirely different.

LK ***Manguin:*** The Portrait, "Manguin A Painter," is published in *Portraits and Prayers*, **pp. 54–56**.

The sensibility of a light kind and the serious worldliness of the idea of pousser…. He has lost all sensibility…. [Begin with full note on Manguin connection with GS and his background, etc.] Notes on Manguin run intermittently from late (probably November-December) 1908 to the Fall of 1909, though this Portrait was not done until [late 1911??]. They begin [Note #41] "Manguin… sensibility but only for nuances…" and add the general observation [NB-*B #23]: "Manguin… [has] great creative sensibility… but [is] dull, [has] no originality of personality." The comments are fairly uniform, though somewhat expanded: [NB-A #10a] "as I said long ago about Manguin, he has the sensibility to works of art he has not a real sense of them," nor can the Manguin "group" aspire to "the originality that is genius." He has sensibility, to be sure, but [NB-B #1] no "sense of color & beauty." The Manguin sensibility [NB-B #6] "is not a feeling of the actuality of the object;" it is "around the reality of the object." But a new and more compassionate view of Manguin emerges in the Note on followers and teachers: [NB-B #10] "… the true nature of school people, followers who live in the larger nature and life of the master…. Some who have real quality try to live the larger life and fail and come back to themselves. Webber [sic] and Manguin, that is the reason they suffer most, they have the realest personality they are whole not fragments." Manguin, among the most devoted of Matisse's student-followers, suffered from the unattainable aspiration of living "the larger life" of Matisse during the time of Matisse's school. But now, in 1911, GS notes, added to his "light" sensibility, is "the serious worldliness of the idea of pousser… He can now pousser," and with the practical object of pushing toward "finishing" displacing what he possessed originally, his "great creative sensibility," he has effectively, GS notes, "lost all sensibility."

Diagram this in what he said about Matisse: "Diagramming," as opposed to setting down all at once the whole understanding of her subject, meant, according to AT, that GS did not yet have the whole vision of her subject at her command, and so had to spell it out piecemeal, like diagramming a sentence. [*But* there is reason to question her explanation…]

There is a significant clue here, however, to GS's procedure in some of the Portraits. The "diagram" in this instance is to be of a text spoken by her subject, not directly the "portrait" of her subject, which is to insist itself, so to speak, through the texture of Manguin's "diagrammed" speech. But characteristically, what Manguin "said of Matisse" was more pointedly true of himself, particularly at this juncture when apparently GS observed his determination to "push" to "finish" his own work. The perspective of the Portrait consequently darts back and forth between Manguin's diagrammed saying about Matisse and GS's equally diagrammed saying about him.

to be written after… [Dating] the order of writing of the three Portraits: "Three Dishonest Ones," "Manguin A Painter," "Americans."

*

Note #25

(Possible, but uncertain location)

Scrap of paper belonging to none of the notebooks:

His intention, and vigor in xecution of thinking, and his actuality of xpectation, and his determination in being xisting as thinking

Go on to give his flavor and go on with contrasts.

~~Go on to contrasts~~ and Go on to contrasts then to specials in note. Continue and go on to contrasts. Contrasts, repetitions, fashion of speech

First sixteen words of note crossed out, and "Go on to contrasts" written in below them. Apparently, matter crossed out had been completed.

*

Note #26

(Possible, but uncertain location)

Repetition in Leo.

fierceness of arrangement in his head and no relativity and no recognition of error because he has done it so well.

Worship of intelligence Nadelman Bocconi

Scrap of paper belonging in none of the notebooks.

Go on with contrasts and then the lists. After that two sketches of what they do & did.

AT ***Bocconi:*** The most intelligent of the Futurists.

*

Note #27

(Uncertain location)

[Interim planning notes for GMP] (not yet located)

~~Bruce painting~~.

Introduces the feminist movement moderne with portraits of speakers & opponents.

Then feminists hark back to the introduction

Go on to cases. Go on with futurists, ignorance of others, creators.

How one feels about ones literature and one's admirers and ones neglectors, how one feels about depression. How one feels about a kind of thing that one knows about but has been neglecting, Miss Blood & Basil being like her, Roche and possible jealousy and what is he feeling anyway. everybody how one has been remembering any point of view. Manguin etc. etc.

AT ***the feminist movement:*** Gertrude was passionately interested in the English one, not the French one. May Bookstaver after her marriage rode a white charger down the avenue in New York in a suffragette parade.

futurists, ignorance of others: Gertrude saw them several times. First, they came as a group, Marinetti included, and then severally. She wasn't interested in them, and not at all in Futurism. She had to console the nervous, conscientious French who were impressed with the possibility of the horror of it coming true. Gertrude and I went to the Vernissage, and Blanche the portrait painter asked to be told exactly what was in it, he was worried. And Gertrude said, There's nothing in it. You believe me, Blanche told her. 'Ignorance of others' refers to the Futurists' ignorance.

Roche and possible jealousy and what is he feeling anyway: Roche was one of the first admirers of Gertrude, and a very great one. When he came under Leo's influence, he dropped her first on Picasso, and then on *Three Lives*.

Once, when Gertrude said something to him, he remarked, "Oh, but that is very important for the biography."

He felt that way about her. At the time, he was in love with Marie Laurencin. Two years later, he couldn't even talk to Gertrude. This Note is definitely in relation to Roche's letter of criticism of Gertrude' writing. It was under Leo's influence that he wrote them. Gertrude said of him, Roche is the most loyal of friends until he is completely disloyal. Before the letters, Roche in conversation reproached Gertrude for not doing the same thing as in *Three Lives*. Now listen, Gertrude told him, I'm the same person that wrote *Three Lives*. If you stop and can't go on, that's your affair. Gertrude took Roche rather simply. He was not a person you had to think about much. And Leo had his ear at this time too.

*

Note #28

[...] ~~religion~~ and ~~spirituality~~ and ~~integrity~~ and anger and inconsistency al la Hawker[?],

Romance Legend Ideal

persistence and criticism and critical attitude illustration helps her he won't take it, and tradition created and inherited fiasco of fasting painting and dressmaking and halting and finish.

Influence (one and the other test of originality.)

*

Make him noble and her vibrating
make him as anyone feels him
" her " " " "
Then back of other paper [i.e., Note #29.]
Then their lives thinly done.

*

Note #29

Following note is crossed out:

Keep on with Jane [40, par 2] actual morality in both [43, par 4]. Keep on with her and then come to morality in both. Go on to morality, sex [45, par 2], masculinity, worship of intellect [50, par 2] [Detail Aunt Fanny & me [omitted]] repetition [54, par 4] disdain [55, par 4?] love ~~and intellect~~ and accomplishment [55, par 5], an appreciation [58, par 1] and [more delicate break] logic [58, par 3] and avarice of distinction [59, par 3 (cont.) 62, par 1] [Myrtle hers describe listening to herself important to know what you think. [61, par 3]] and necessity of finishing winning [67, par 1] and pride, gentleness [70, par 1], impermeability, <u>preserving</u> memory [73, par 1] and courage [and the way they both come to{?three words?}] and sentiment [77, par 1] [incapacity of continuity in bearing an attack when hit [77, par 5] (inconsistency a la Hawker) & religion [NOTE: crossed out ends, text continues:] and ~~gentleness~~ spirituality [87, par 3] and integrity and anger persistence [88, par 5] [and criticism critical attitude illustration helps her, he can't take it. [92, par 5]] and tradition (created and inherited) [Romance legend ideal] [99, par 3] & fiasco of fasting [132, par 3] [insert: painting [135, par 1]] and finish
Influence [112, par 2] ~~& lives.~~
<u>Before lives</u> make him noble and her vibrating
make him as anyone feels him
" her " " " her.
then lives thin done. [113, par 3] [sic] (over) [i.e., below:]

Other side of Note #29:

After making him noble and he[r] vibrating [99 to 111?] discourse on passion for distinction and victory without ambition or interest in fellow-man bound to turn inward and stop ~~shortly~~ developement [sic]. satisfy themselves becomes an imperative need. She needs audience and takes dope. He destroys his critical faculty his dope. [136, par 6]

AT ***important to know what you think:*** Sally's phrase to Bruce [in A-19, the phrase is recalled as, 'important for me to know what I think.'] Gertrude and I roared over it for years.

LK ***Keep on with Jane....and finish:*** This is the major Planning Note for TWO, commencing on **page 40** of the published text and continuing to its end [**p. 141**.] The text of TWO follows this Note fairly scrupulously, with only one or two alterations and possible omissions. The following breakdown of the items listed in the Note is, for **pages 40–70**, based on internal evidence alone [there are no manuscript notes for these pages.] From **page 70** to the end, it is coordinated with the notes in the manuscript.

"He" in TWO is Leo Stein; "She" [or "Jane Sands" in the marginal Manuscript Notes] is Sarah Stein, GS's sister-in-law, not GS, as the title in the published version mistakenly claims (*Two, Gertrude Stein and Her Brother.*)

*

Note #30

Unlocated

Tiny scrap of paper from a manuscript notebook:

In doing their lives do it thinly and a little of hers and a little piece of his and so on. Keep the same method.

LK ***In doing their lives, do it thinly.... Keep the same method:*** Planning Note **pp. 113–136**.

Keep on with Jane: **Page 40, par. 2.**

GS ***Actual morality in both:***

For "He:" **Page 43, par. 4 and page 44, par. 2–5.**
For "She:" **Page 44, par. 1 and page 45, par. 1.**

GS ***Sex:***

For "He:" **Page 45, par. 2 to Page 47, par. 1.**
For "She:" **Page 47, par. 2 to Page 50, par. 1.**

GS ***Masculinity, worship of intellect:***

For "He:" **Page 50, par. 2 to Page 53, par. 1.**
For "She:" **Page 53, par. 2 to Page 54, par. 3.**

GS ***detail Aunt Fanny & me:*** Apparently omitted.

*

Note #31

Mrs. O when she compliments admires anything and admires it well in enthusiasm and playfullness [sic] and inattention.

Go on with Miriam and then the two together but full very full Miriam. Miriam's faces her intelligence etc etc to her feeling about Lana and Lana's about her.

*

Note #50

Remember to make Mrs. Hersland make husband foolish, attitude like Mr. Matisses, fix him with her eye, and he does it.

*

Snake lying in the grass he had no more intentions than the wicked men have mostly. You shall bruise his head and he shall bruise your heel. No more wicked intention [… .]

*

Note #70

The burden laid on us moderns

Amy & Stern

In sixty years we moderns must create a complete
tradition and live in to it for we ~~cannot~~ do not follow teaching. Hence our art and ourselves and he who runs may read the ~~me~~ dreadful failures.

Gustav Brossoff

*

The best looking man from the most imposing bourgeois family
of her acquaintance

*

Note #118

Fred's duty, and how he does it
Sal's " " " she " "
M. " " " he " "
Simon H." " " " " "

*

Note #134

MANY MANY WOMEN

Five Mss. Notebooks numbered I to V. Inside front cover of each notebook, GS lists index of all women remaining to be described in the work, and underlines, in Notebooks I and II, the names of women completed in those books. Index lists as follows:

[Notebook I]

How many are loved ~~in marriage~~ and what they are.
Alice, Nellie, Marie, Bird, Helene, Mabel Dodge,
Emma, Harriet Levy Germaine, Fernande, Marie, Mrs. Matisse,
Olga, Helen Bruce Mabel Haynes, Mabel Earle May,
Mabel Weeks, Dora Israels, Grace Gassette, Mrs. Double Cake, Mrs. Manguin, Mrs. Valloton, Sally

[Notebook II]

Many Many Women

How

Germaine, Fernande, Marie, Mrs. Matisse, Olga, Helen Bruce, Mabel Haynes,Mabel Earle, Lulie [?] Earle May, ~~Mina~~, Mabel Weeks, Dora Israels, Grace Gassette, Mrs. Manguin, Mrs. Valloton, Mrs. Double Cake, Sally, Dolene, Aunt Annie, Aunt Fanny,
Aunt Pauline.

[Notebook III]

Many Many Women

~~Stinker, Miss Grey, Miss Briggs~~[?]

Mabel Weeks, Dora Israels, Grace Gassette,
Mrs. Manguin, Mrs. Valloton, Mrs. Edstrom Mrs. Double Cake,
Sally, Myrtle Dolene, Julia Aunt Annie, Aunt Fanny, Aunt Carrie, Aunt Pauline.

[Notebook IV:]

~~| Myrtle, Dolene, Julia G., Aunt Annie, Mrs. Samuels Sally |~~
~~Aunt Fanny,~~ Aunt Carrie, Aunt Rose, Aunt Helen,
Aunt Pauline.

[Notebook V:]

Aunt Helen, Aunt Pauline.

AT ***Aunt Rose:*** Gertrude's mother's aunt in Baltimore.

*

Note #134a

The Many Many Women *Ms Notebooks apparently cover descriptions of women as follows:*

I.		
Alice	[ENDS:]	"She had not then been seeing,
Nelly		which was a pleasant thing. She
Marie		was not hearing, which was a
Bird		pleasant thing. She was not
(Helene)		seeing which was a pleasant
(Mabel Dodge)		thing.
(Emma)		She was not hearing and seeing
(Harriet Levy)		
II.		
Germaine	[CONTINUES:]	which was a pleasant thing.
Fernande		
Marie		Being one loving, being one, she
Mrs. Matisse		being one, she was one.
(Olga)		
Helen Bruce	[ENDS:]	and being one she was that one
Mabel Haynes		the one who not needing that
Mabel Earle		anything is done is loving and
(Lulie[?] Earle)		having done that thing has been
		one having been loving.
May		
(~~Nina~~)		
III.		
Mabel Weeks	[CONTINUES:]	She in living continued being
Dora Israels		living and this being what was
Grace Gassette		happening she was continuing
Mrs. Manguin.		being that one.
Mrs. Valloton		
Mrs. Edstrom	[ENDS:]	She, she was expecting what
		she was arranging and…in giving
		what she was receiving. She was
		believing what she was giving in

		receiving,
IV.		
Mrs. Samuels (Mrs. Double Cake)		
Sally	[CONTINUES:]	and giving what she was
Myrtle		receiving and receiving what she
Dolene		was giving she was feeling what
(Julia G.)		she was believing.
Aunt Annie		
V.		
Aunt Helen	[CONTINUES:]	was the other one.
Aunt Pauline		She had them and she needed
		to be living to be feeling what
		she was feeling in having them.

AT ***Mrs. Samuels (Double-cake):*** 'Double-cake' is Mrs. Dubryko, the Christian Scientist who married the Pole. Probably her resemblance to Mrs. Samuels is what Gertrude is remembering.

*

Maria 41st & Broadway 1 o'clock next to Criterion

*

Mokei contemporary
Danshiduzi near to Kakei
Sung landscape Kakki founder
Bayen
Danshidzui last of Sung land.

Mokei contemporary, Danshiduzl near to Kakei, Sung landscape Kakki founder, Bayen, Danshiduzl kast of Sung.land. [Unlocated]

*

Note #141

Note is missing

*

Note #142

GS Ms. Note:

ADA

GS title: "D----"

Ms. corrections:

… .Then everyone who could live with them ~~was~~ were dead there were then the father and the son a young man then and the daughter coming to be ~~an old maid mermaid~~ that one then…

*

2. Ms. Corrections:

…He wrote nothing and then he wrote again and there was some ~~sarcasm~~ waiting and then he wrote tender letters again and agin… .

*

3. Ms. corrections and deletions: The portion of the ms. written in GS's hand begins: "Some one who was living was almost always listening…" to "… listening to stories having a beginning and a middle and an ending." The rest of the ms. is in Alice Toklas' handwriting. In the portion in GS's hand appear the following corrections and deletions:

Someone who was living was almost always listening. ~~That one was telling very that if they~~ would Some one who was loving was almost always listening. That one who was loving was loving was almost always listening. That one who was loving was telling about being one then listening. ~~That one was telling more and more~~ that that one was listening. That one being loving was then telling ~~things~~ stories having ~~a happy ending~~ ~~s~~ a ~~happy~~ beginning and a ~~happy~~ middle and an ~~happy~~ ending. ~~and everyone was meaning certainly meaning that Alice was one being perfect in being loving.~~

*

4. Ms. corrections: The name "Alice" used throughout in ms. is changed later to "Ada."

*

Note #143

GS Ms. Note:

<u>ELISE SURVILLE</u>

GS title on slip of paper attached to ms. sheets: "NINA"

*

Note #144

GS Ms. Note:

BON MARCHE WEATHER

Dearest, I wish I had been good and not written this, first place because I would have liked to obey you, second place cause its rotten.

*

Note #145

GS Ms. Note:

FLIRTING AT THE BON MARCHE

Read it fast so as not to be sad in it, to make it sound gay. Flirting at the Bon Marche.

*

Note #146

GS Ms. Note:

RUE DE RENNES

[Original GS title:] "ALICE & RUE DE RENNES"

*

Note #147

GS notes in Ms. of RUE DE RENNES. *At conclusion of ms., the following note appears in GS's handwriting:*

Dearest

This is a trial, I have no idea what its like and very much doubt if it tells the story. If not I will try it again. Please be all well.

[signed] Y.D.

*

Note #148

GS Ms. Note:

ROCHE

Dating: Portrait is dated by Roche March 1911 on his copy

A deletion in first sentence of Portrait, as follows:

"...did that one completely have ~~a gift for~~ to do very well something that that one... ." etc.

*

Note #149

GS Ms. Note:

[A MAN]

1. *GS Ms. title: "DAVID AND MRS. AMERICANS"*
2. *Written on flyleaf of Notebook:*

very short fear[?] and fat and come to the hotel.
A man of genius is what. is it David. Is he an
artist, is he not. Is she religious, was she original.

3. ***Yale Edition, p. 239. preceding par. 1,*** *"He had been one being one completely working,"*

When I in being married am so fat how could
I in any living have been thin.

4. *This is written on flyleaf of opposite end of notebook. May be intended as a general reference to Edstrom, adapting the Chaucer quotation on the ms. of* A Long Gay Book.
5. *If this Portrait is the same as "David et al," then it was written before Sept. 1911.*

*

Note #150

GS Ms. Note:

[FOUR DISHONEST ONES]

GS title on cover:

~~THREE~~ FOUR DISHONEST ONES. TOLD BY A DESCRIPTION OF
WHAT THEY DO.

Written over title on cover:

Maddelena, Graciosa,
Shoemaker, Marie.

From Portraits & Prayers***, p. 57, par. 4:***

"She is not changing. She is knowing nothing of not changing... ."
"~~Maddalena~~"

*

Note #151

GS Ms. Note:

[FIVE OR SIX MEN]

GS Ms. Title:

THE FOUR AND ONE
LEO FRIEDMAN
DERAIN
HANS PURMANN
MAURICE STERNE
&
PIOT

2. **GS, TWO, in Volume I, Yale edition, p. 256, preceding par. 6,** *"They are each one of them knowing this thing,"*

Go on with sentimentality love affection,
loyalty, romance and real convention and
intelligence, use of themselves without
hurting [?] knowledge of insensitiveness.

3. **Yale edition, p. 257, preceding par. 1**. *"They are loving each one of them and they do that and they"*

Go on about their loving and how they do that and how they
finally marry a very attractive person and how some of them have
very much success in loving, any of them can have success in loving.
How they finally completely love some one to marrying and that is a
happy thing for them.

All this converted, by leaving out the "how"s and adding an introductory phrase to sentence, into the text of the next paragraph.

4. **Yale edition, p. 257, preceding par. 3**, *"There was loving existing."*

Romance, work, love, use of people, and so to special ones by way of the
seventh the man of Frascati and the older woman and the romance.
Also Simonson liking to walk with strange ladies they not,

5. **Yale edition, p. 258, preceding par. 2**, *"There was one who was succeeding in living,"*

Leo Friedman

6. **Yale edition, p. 260, preceding par. 1**, *"He was from the beginning liking someone. He was always doing this thing, always liking some one."*

Go on to his sentimentalities his emotions and his conventions and his loyalties and his lacks.

7. **Yale edition, p. 261, preceding par. 3,** *"He could be one having anything happen."*

Go on to his love adventures and his intellect and his loyalties and his sentimentalities and ideas and conventions, and marriage and everything together his ideal early winning [?] that he told about, and realised well enough.

8. **Yale edition, p. 264, preceding par. 3,** *"One is of the same kind as another one,"*

Leo F. is a different thing from Derain.

9. **Yale Edition, p. 266, preceding par. 1,** *"he was then succeeding in living. He was then succeeding in living and not being then one doing anything of this thing,"*

Go on with his following Matisse and how he looked and his success with Vollard, Pablo Max reciting louder, Alice and heavy elegant dullness, heavy dullness.

9a. **Yale edition, p. 267, preceding par. 1,** *"He was one succeeding in living. He was one knowing something and telling that thing, telling it to one who,"*

His success with Vollard, dropping Matisse, Pablo, Max, reciting louder, Alice, destoying Matisse in exalting Pablo, heavy elegant dullness, heavy dullness, a wine merchant, necessary disguise.

10. **Yale edition, p. 268, preceding par. 2,** *"He was succeeding in living. He was knowing something then. He was telling then the living he was knowing."*

Pablo Alice

11. **Yale edition, p. 268, preceding par. 2,** *"He was one succeeding in living. He was not telling something to some who were asking."*

Pablo, done [?] with Matisse discussions Alice fat.[?] dirty[?] wine merchant never a failure.

12. **Yale edition, p. 269, preceding par. 4,** *"He was loudly reciting that there is more existing than everything together,"*

Alice

13. **p. 270, preceding par. 2,** *"He was being then one saying something. He was being then having recognition in being one saying something."*

Go on with their living together, his real[?] relation to Pablo, to Matisse, weakness and eventual not failure.

14. ***Yale edition, p. 274, preceding par. 2,*** *"In being one naturally completely succeeding in living he was one telling some that they must wait again."*

His relation to Sally to Bruce to Picasso, to ladies, to Leo, to Mrs. Matisse and Margot.

14a. ***Yale edition, p. 274, preceding par. 4,*** *"He did completely solidly follow that one."*

Sarah Matisse & Mme. & Margot, Girls, Bruces, success and failure, the Dome gruppe.

15. ***Yale edition, p. 283, preceding par. 3,*** *"He came to be well enough known."*

Go on with his work & recognition and B.B. and hopes and failures.

This is followed by text, which was crossed out, as follows:

He was seriously working. He was a married one and he was seriously such a one a married one and loving and loved then and

Text continues:

He came to be well enough known." etc.

*

Note #152

GS Ms. Note

A Family of Perhaps Three

GS Title in Flyleaf:

MILDRED & EDNA

2. Geography and Plays***, p. 332, preceding par. 3,*** *"The older on was protecting the younger one from knowing where they had been"*

Go on Mildred and Doctor, Edna and Iris [?], bothand experiences and tastes and career.

3. Geography and Plays***, p. 333, preceding par. 2,*** *"The older one succeeded very well in living."*

Not of our generation. Gracie's relation to them.

4. Geography and Plays***, p. 334, preceding par. 1,*** *"The older sister was not ever married."*

Mildred not of our generation. Doctor and feeling young.

5. Geography and Plays***, p. 335, preceding par. 1,*** *"Certainly the older one had done something and certainly every one was content to tell"*

Mildred not of our generation. Edna young and
friends & five[?]. The Doctor. Myra, etc. Dean

of women journalists, Bridget.

6. Geography and Plays***, p. 336, preceding par. 4,*** *"They could both of them, they did, both of them, they would, either of them,"*

Mildred's full career & Edna's.

7. Geography and Plays***, p. 337, preceding par. 3,*** *"Certainly any one could know that having been being living"*

More details of each one's lives

8. Geography and Plays***, p. 338, preceding par. 1,*** *"They had been together, they were together, they were not together."*

A little of them together and then a long
ending about Mildred's doings concluding[?]
describing[?] calling by name and discovery and money
and masculine attentions[?] and cablegrams and energy
and success and failure and marriage[?] (not)[?]
with Chase and Myra[?] & pensions.

*

Note #153

GS Ms. Note:

[ITALIANS]

1. "Certainly any of them can be expressing completely feeling anything so that they are almost doing anything.

In Geography and Plays, ***p. 57, preceding par. 4,***

Emotional acting realised as emotion complete
but mostly they know it and love it and it is
only quite beautiful then.

*

Note #154

GS Ms. Note:

HARRIET MAKING PLANS

1. *[At end of ms., a note from GS:]*

My little dearest, this is your ma-in-law, a
beautiful ma-in-law. Good-night little dearest.

(L.B. = m.d.) = y.d.

*

2. [At beginning of ms., a line drawn across page over text, and above it, printed in very vertical, very large letters (by Alice Toklas):]

Beautiful is ma in law She has no meaning no
she has not yes she has not.

*

Note #155

GS notes in MS. of TWO WOMEN

Names used: Etta Cone is called ADA. Claribel Cone is called SISTER BERTHA in first draft of ms., and then MARTHA in final corrections.

*

Note #156

GS Notes in Typescript of TWO WOMEN in GS Collection at Beinecke Library, bound in volume of PORTRAITS (Vol. 8) pp 96–128.

1. ***Typescript, p. 98, preceding paragraph 2,*** *"The older one was more something than the younger one."*

Go on with their lives and duties and their worth. Go on with how one of them is more something than the other one, and how each one of them thinks it of themselves and the other one - Claribel on Etta, Etta on Claribel, both on the Cone family.

2. ***In typescript, p. 100, preceding paragraph 2,*** *"There were others connected with them, connected with each of them,"*

Tell about the others connected with them, their duties and how they did them, what effect they had when they were traveling, how they quarreled, how they spent money, how they each had what they wanted, Bertha when she wanted it, Ada when she was going to want it. Stinginess, buying scarves. Keeping things, patting hair, a little crazy, dress-making scenes, friends of each. Pleasing anybody. Etta and no father no mother. [Wick--?] and marry[?] again[?]. Sex in both.

3. In **typescript, p. 107, preceding paragraph 2,** *"The older was one and anyone could know this thing."*

Complete description of the two, each one of them, life history. Etta family father and mother, Ida, house, Saturday evening, Netty[?], Claribel, Sidney, Clarence, Hortense, etc, Amy, Carrie Gutman. Claribel, career, Mrs. Lud[?] etc, and the young man, reading, Flexner, sex, germans, bon marche, boxes, science, photographs, Etta, Brother Mosey.

4. In **typescript, p. 110, preceding paragraph 1,** *"The older, sister Martha, talked some and certainly she wanted to hear talking,"*

Go on about Ada. The younger Ada.

5. In **typescript, p. 113, preceding paragraph 2,** *"Any one being living can be one having been something,"*

Describe Ada the whole [famil? gamut?] youth Ida, brothers, art, flattery, family, lady, etc.

6. In **typescript, p. 114, preceding paragraph 1,** *"They were both of them certain that there was some connection between loving and listening,"*

Go on with lives and family lives and family quarrels.

7. In **typescript, p. 116, preceding paragraph 1,** *"They were together and they were often then not together,"*

Go on with their lives.

8. In **typescript, p. 119, preceding paragraph 1,** *"Certainly each one of them were ones that might have been better looking,"*

Go on with their lives and their needs for young womanhood are[?]. How being old is saying what you used to feel.

9. In **typescript, p. 120, preceding paragraph 1,** *"Martha was quite young once and that was never of any interest to herself,"*

Go on with each one of them young and older and old, and other people, and then a short narrative of how much money they had what they did with it,

to whom they left it, their family and their
relatives the number of brothers and sisters they
had how they liked them and how their mother and
father died and how they died and how they were
afraid of heart complaint and how ~~Claribel~~ Bertha
had it and ~~Etta~~ Ada didn't.

10. In typescript p 125, preceding paragraph 1, "Surely Ada would like to have been one going on living,"

Go on with Etta's private life and then a little
more of both of them and money and so end.

*

Note #157

GS Ms. Note:

PICASSO

David Hersland as a boy.
Author & spats and climbing, and companioship.

This crossed-out note appears above the text of the portrait of "Picasso."

- *It duplicates Ms Note #157 on MA 826.*
- *It is a Planning Note for MA 836, line 3 to 837, line 34.*
- *It is a note written for the early pages of the "David Hersland" chapter of the MA during the late summer of 1911.*
- *The Portrait of Picasso must consequently be dated 1911, not, as commonly listed previous, 1909.*

*

Note #158

GS miscellaneous note for AMERICANS and THREE DISHONEST ONES

Americans, theme fear. short story.
The three dishonest ones.
theme fundamental honesty. short story.
the Herslands & Dehnings,
Long book,/ death and death and death.

The note for "the long book," written in Sept-Oct 1911 for the Epilogue of the MA, dates both "Americans" and "Three Dishonest Ones": 19ll.

*

Note #159

GS miscellaneous notes

FOUR DISHONEST ONES

The [folks?] Marie, the last.
Story of lack of honesty in
Maddalina
Man at Giacosa
Mike's shoemaker
Why should they be honest. What they did.

*

Note #160

Written on the reverse side of Note #159. The two "stories" were apparently planned concurrently.

Begin Americans with fear, kinds of fear. Theme fear short story.

*

Note #161

GS notes in MSS.

<u>TWO</u>

1. *[GS title:] "Leo and Sally"*

2. *[Inside Front Cover:]*

Complete sound and then a list of what they did
and how. Then do Alice and me what we did and
how. Use the introduction for Alice about babies."
"Sally takes it up and makes it the same.
Resonating[?]. He takes it up and makes
it different and particular. Noises.
Continuing my argument.[?] [?], [] [?]
then [?] the profish[?]

3. *[In margin, inside front cover:]*

Two books of coordination[?] and 4 books
two each for close[?] descriptions[?]

4. *[First page:]*

This is to be told in diagrams introductions and diagrams. Baby piece for d. introduction and then diagram. [Imurablty?] introductions to be written and then diagram of acts, like S.'s & B's, etc, such diagrams, many of them. Diagram Diagram.

*

Note #162

GS miscellaneous notes

[JENNY HELEN HANNAH PAUL PETER]
ALTERNATE TITLE: "JHHPP"

"Jenny Helen Hannah Paul and Peter.
Laura Miriam Adele Ben and Joe.
There were five of them, all living. They all had been living.

[Inserted later:] Make it dramatic not character, relation. [Insert ends]

Two of them, (history of Laura & Miriam)

[Inserted later:] have Mariam emerge and then [Insert ends]

Two of them (Adele & Ben)
Two of them (Miriam & Joe)
Two of them
Three of them (Laura Adele & Ben)
Three of them (Miriam Adele & Ben)
Three of them (Laura Miriam & Joe)
Each of them
    One of them Joe
    " " " Laura
        Miriam
        Adele
        Ben
All of them (   )   (Laura & Miriam
    Adele & Laura)

Interlining the note above, the following scheme was written in later. The order is guessed at; not clear from the arrangement on the page.

Miriam & Laura
Adele " "
" " Miriam
" " Joe
" " Ben
then have
Laura & Ben
Then Ben & Miriam
" " Adele
" " Joe
then have Laura & Joe from the beginning
then Joe & Miriam
" " Adele
" " Ben.
Miriam & Adele
" " Ben
" " Joe
Then start Laura & Adele
have Adele emerge & then Adele & Ben & a Miriam & a Joe
Then the end."

*

Note #163

GS notes in manuscript.

[JENNY HELEN HANNAH PAUL AND PETER]

Page and paragraph references are coordinated with Yale edition. Judging from its style, this Portrait was probably written from mid-1911 to end, or early 1912.

1. *Flyleaf: [GS title paired with identifying names]*
   "Jenny, Helen, Hannah, Paul and Peter
   Laura, Miriam, Adele, Ben & Joe"

2. ***p. 174, above par. 1,*** *"Each one of them knew that they had…"*
   "(Their clothes)"

3. **p. 176, above par. 4,** *"They were not angry—that is, neither one…"*
"Miriam's attitude toward Laura (living and feeling) anger and disturb and annoyance and fear and understanding."

4. **p. 178, above par. 3,** *"She was not feeling all of feeling…."*
"Go on with Miriam's feeling about Laura"

5. **p. 178, above par. 8,** *"The older one was one, all of being that one…"*
"Their imitation and queer jealousy."

6. **p. 179, above par. 2,** *"one of them, the older one was not talking just…"*

GS placed an asterisk above this paragraph, marking the place in the text where the sudden break in style occurs.

7. **p. 180, above par. 1,** *"The one the older one was feeling what she…"*
"(Go on to other things they do just, or not just because)"

8. **p. 180, above par. 8,** *"The older one was the one she was because being that one…"*
"(More of what they are because)"

9. **p. 184, above par. 2,** *"Two of them were the two and he was the one…"*
"Adele & Ben"

10. **p. 184, above par. 4,** *"He who was one and was one and being one…"*
"~~Laura,~~ Ben and Adele."

11. **p. 185, above par. 1,** *"Standing & running he was taller than he had…"*
"Ben & Adele."

12. **p. 185, above par. 3,** *"They, their way was not what each one of…"*
"(Ben & Adele) (their life) (their character)"

13. **p. 186, above par. 7,** *"Where she did not know that she determined…"*
"(Relation to each other and Laura & Miriam)"

14. **p. 187, above par. 1,** *"He did know that he could see that which…"*
"(~~Ben Adele~~ Ben, then Adele to all, Ben to all)"

15. **p. 187, above par. 3,** *"They did not say each one of them was each…"*
"Ben & Adele to all."

16. **p. 188, above par. 2,** *"She and she was not leaving having following…"*
"(B & A and all & each) development)"

17. **p. 188, above par. 5,** *"He did not come to stay just because he could…"*
"Continue description of Joe."

18. **p. 189, above par. 1**, *"They who were married were not single…"*
"(Joe & Miriam, their life)"

19. **p. 189, above par. 2**, *"She was very likely not to dislike what she…"*
"Miriam & Joe"

20. **p. 192, above par. 2**, *"It is not likely that they and they were two were two…"*
"(Joe & Miriam & the rest)"

21. **p. 191, above par. 1**, *"Like not having been beginning, like waiting…"*
"(Joe & Miriam)"

22. **p. 191, above par. 3**, *"They were releasing advocating…."*
"(Miriam & Joe)"

23. **p. 191, above par. 5**, *"He and he was called Peter as his name was Peter…"*
"(More Joe)"

24. **p. 192, above par. 3**, *"Why if something that stuck was not sticky…"*
"(More Joe)"

25. **p. 192, above par. 7**, *"She ate what she found was there when she…"*
"Go on with M."

26. **p. 192, above par. 8**, *"Four who were four and there were five…"*
"More M. & J. &)"

27. **p. 193, above par. 4**, *"If four were there they were not staying while…"*
"M. B. A. Mrs O.
B. A. M. J.
A. Mrs. M. J.

28. **p. 194, above par. 1**, *"The four were the four and they were…"*
"B. A. M. J.
A. Mrs. M. J."

29. **p. 194, above par. 2**, *"The one who very likely said enough…"*
"B. A. M .J."

30. **p. 194, above par. 3**, *"She who lived was the one who was the only…"*
"(Adele) B A M. J."

31. **p. 195, above par. 2**, *"She came to be saying that she had what she…"*
"(B. A.)
M. J."

32. **p. 196, above par. 2,** *"She was not the one who returned to shine…"*
"A., Mrs., M., J."

33. **p. 196, above par. 5,** *"She, and there were the four she and…"*
"Adele & L. and M. & J.)"

34. **p. 197, above par. 4,** *"not anyone saying the same…"*
"(A. & Mrs. & M. & J.)"

35. **p. 199, above par. 4,** *"If they were five then there were the five…"*
"each one in relation to everybody. All Adele [?] groups in relation to everybody"

36. **p. 200, above par. 4,** *"The way enough have the rest of a way of…"*
"(People and the five) then each one and people)"

37. **p. 201, above par. 1,** *"She did call the one who did not come…."*
"(Five and Felix Adler)"

38. **p. 201, above par. 3,** *"She was the one to feel the same when the…"*
"More M. & Adele, then Adele Joe Ben."

39. **p. 202, above par. 2,** *"The only one who was not one…."*
"(Ben & Adele.) (Adele)"

39a. **p. 203, above par. 2,** *"one who was not bewildering was one who…"*
"(Adele & Adler & Ben)"

40. **p. 204, above par. 1,** *"To be all there and to have a separate room…"*
"(All of them & us) and everybody, and [Incl?] Fred, S. Wolfe, anybody)"

41. **p. 204, above par. 3,** *"An alarm that did not frighten…"*
"(Each one of them & groups and anybody) us etc."

42. **p. 205, above par. 2,** *"They did not have to stay all who stayed…"*
O. & L. Friedman, us etc etc."

43. **p. 206, above par. 5,** *"The Watson plate was not broken…"*
Cambridge life. pre-Cambridge"

44. **p. 207, above par. 1,** *"The articles that were mentioned…"*
(The crowd.)"

45. **p. 207, above par. 5,** *"They went where there was not a faculty of…"*
The crowd. "

46. **p. 208, above par. 6,** *"They all left all that…."*
Removal to New York."

47. **p. 209, above par. 3,** *"It did not explain that there were several…"*
"(New York life)"

48. **p. 209, above par. 7,** *"She was not largely responsible when she…"*
"(Adele)"

49. **p. 210, above par. 2,** *"The glad way to keep the may…"*
"(Describe her clothes)"

50. **p. 210, above par. 3,** *"She was well. She had the time to say…"*
"(More Adele)"

51. **p. 212, above par. 1,** *"He was her brother…."*
"Ben & then more Adele."

52. **p. 213, above par. 3,** *"They did stay and they were the…."*
"Go on to Ben & Adele & so to Laura & then Miriam and then Joe in each case some altogether."

53. **p. 214, above par. 3,** *"They were the same when there were all…"*
"Go on to the household. Three the two with Laura."

54. **p. 214, above par. 4,** *"It took the time that there was not to say…"*
"The household of the three with description of each then the household of Joe & Miriam, description of each, and then the households compared and contrast[ed]"

55. **p. 216, above par. 3,** *"Two who knew, two who were the two knew…"*
"All of them"

56. **p. 216, above par. 4,** *"Naming every piece was not an occupation…"*
"(Describe Miriam & Joe) and then ensemble."

57. **p. 218, above par. 4,** *"If the larger which is larger is larger…"*
"Miriam & Laura."

58. **p. 218, above par. 5,** *"There was not every moment and they did…"*
"Miriam and Laura."

59. **p. 219, above par. 3,** *"Telling that fashion is not the dark way…"*
"Go on with the way they treat each other. M. & L."

60. **p. 220, above par. 1**, *"Line the cape and be larger…"*
"The two."

61. **p. 220, above par. 6**, *"Where the color is different there is also…"*
"Go on with relation between L. & M. make M. einege."

62. **p. 221, above par. 2**, *"The use of quiet is not necessary when a noise…"*
"L. & M. relation. M. einege"

63. **p. 221, above par. 7**, *"There never is any threat when there is no…"*
"M. & L. M. einege."

64. **p. 223, above par. 3**, *"Pay a simple cover and never use silver…"*
"Start in again on Miriam then Laura then together."

65. **p. 223, above par. 6**, *"A position is not one where many meet…."*
"Drama L. & M. again and M. einege."

66. **p. 223, above par. 7**, *"There is no choice between that which has…"*
"Drama einege M."

67. **p. 224, above par. 2**, *"To be happy saying so is the way to go…"*
"Drama einege M."

68. **p. 224, above par. 5**, *"Excitement is not heightened by walking…"*
"Drama M. einege."

69. **p. 225, above par. 1**, *"To be so honest and so true and to say…"*
"Miriam & Adele"

70. **p. 225, above par. 4**, *"Come Hannah come and stay away…"*
"Adele & Miriam einege."

71. **p. 226, above par. 4**, *"Start the way to part and make…"*
"Miriam & Adele & Joe the[n] M. then B."

*

Note #164

GMP

["Matisse Picasso and Gertrude Stein"]

"Some day history of Matisse and admirers history of Pablo and admirers their rise and fall, change, my rise, Delaunay, Zobel, Futurists, Cubists, everybody, Uhde, Kahnweiler, Mme Weil, Vollard, Druet, Bernheims all the family, Manguin Puy, Valloton, Flandrin & the Hungarians, [Inserted: (Gibb and history, London, Russia. Steiglitz and Steichen, du Dom,] the school,

everybody pushing up and plucking down, breaking up of families, the real democracy, hate and pull down, not class but each one, not sex not reaction, each one push and pull, fetishes, comeradery, virtue, honesty, appreciation, ~~faiblesse~~ admiration, obligation, love, loyalty (et les Steins) solidarity, generosity, examples Heiroth, Manguin, Puy, Derain & Braque, all of it.
True democracy, ~~bal~~ egotism, release, pull down.
Effect of [important?] Matisse decor."

LK Planning Note (apparently initial planning note for GMP.)

*

Note #165

GMP

(Manuscript notes for GMP are in five notebooks. Same pagination and paragraph numbering in published texts, Matisse, Picasso and Gertrude Stein, *Something Else Press Inc. 1972, and* Matisse, Picasso and Gertrude Stein, *Dover Publication, 2000.)*

1. *In flyleaf of 1st notebook of Five:*
Alternate Title: "THE NEW BOOK"

2. ***p. 202, preceding par. 1****: "If all who were coming…"*
GS:"(Delaunay)"

3. *GS text change:* ***p. 202, end of par. 2****: from "This is Pat."*

to "This is Walter."

4. ***p. 203, preceding par. 1****: "If he were happy there"*
"How Pat came to know them all. all. P—t"

5. ***p. 203, par. 6****: "Larger than everything…"*
"(Matisse) (Delaunay) Manguin etc.) "

6. ***p. 204, above par. 1,*** *"In being each one moving"*
"Great art, art, Matisse, Picasso, etc. "

7. ***p. 205, preceding par. 2,*** *"In coming they said that…"*
"(Continue Matisse's group) (Then Pablo's) "

8. ***p. 205, preceding par. 7,*** *"They were staying. They were dividing"*
"(Matisse et all at first.) "

9. ***p. 205, above par. 11,*** *"They were particularly accepting…"*
"(Matisse's group in the beginning)"

10. **p. 206, above par. 4,** *"In staying together in staying …"*
"(Derain and Matisse at the beginning) "

11. **p. 207, preceding par. 1,** *"He who was one and all"*
"(Matisse & Puy and all and all & him) "

12. **p. 208, above par. 1,** *"He turned away and said that…"*
"(Manguin Matisse et al. teaching, older point of view toward them. Successes.) "

13. *[In back flyleaf of 1st Notebook]*
"Remember Pablo's resemblance to bull-fighters particularly Machiola[?]"

14. **p. 208, above par. 4,** *"He would not have refused anything…"*
"(Go on with Matisse and his crowd.)"

15. **p. 209, above par. 2,** *"Five of the different kinds one is and being had every day…"*
"(Do you niz zo baut can be[he?])"
"Longer staying"

16. **p. 209, above par. 6,** *"In pleasing and he did say…"*
"(Matisse & his crowd.)"

17. **p. 210, above par. 8,** *"If they had any of them refused…"*
"(Matisse et al in the beginning, the world) "

18. **p. 210, above par. 11,** *"Addressing themselves then…"*
"(Matisse's crowd and the world) "

19. **p. 211, above par. 3,** *"In having meaning, in expecting…"*
"(Matisse his group and the dealers & the world)"

20. *"(Matisse etc. & the world & dealers etc.)"*

p. 211, above par. 4, *"In staying and not waiting…"*

21. **p. 213, above par. 1,** *"If expecting nothing is not disconcerting…"*
"(Matisse again and long[?]) (younger man) we first knew)"

22. **p. 213, above par. 4,** *"If seeing all and feeling all…"*
"Matisse & all & the world and us."

23. **p. 213, above par. 6,** *"If making again and again the complete tinkling…"*
"(Matisse & all & the world and us and youth)"

24. **p. 214, above par. 3,** *"If it is a willing thing to be fairly active…"*
"Matisse & his young crowd, his beginning, him."

25. **p. 214, above par. 4,** *"Late in looking like a young man…"*
"(Matisse as a young man)"

26. **p. 216, above par. 2,** *"They are working and all working…"*
"(M. and crowd and us)"

27. **p. 216, above par. 6,** *"There were eight who were not laughing…"*
"(Matisse et al)"

28. **p. 217, above par. 4,** *"They always thought that they did not fail…"*
"(Matisse & all)"

29. **p. 217, above par. 6,** *"Not gathered together is a way of sitting…"*
"Matisse et al in more detail, with each one and us & the Bernheims, etc. to Pablo."

30. **p. 218, above par. 6,** *"He did not see…."*
"(Matisse et al in detail.)"

31. **p. 219, above par. 2,** *"There could be if there is the remarkable…"*
"Matisse et al.) in detail"

32. **p. 219, above par. 5,** *"Completely the having come to walk…"*
"M. & beginning. M. & Manguin."

33. **p. 220, above par. 1,** *"It is very likely that a way to be in play…"*
"Matisse & women & School, & Manguin"

34. **p. 220, above par. 2,** *"Likely very likely yes, likely very…"*
"M. & all."

35. **p. 221, above par. 1,** *"To see and have a beard…"*
"Manguin and art."

36. **p. 222, above par. 3,** *"If they all knew that they had met…"*
"The crowd."

37. **p. 222, par. 6,** *"He was the pronouncer…"*
"The crowd. M. & each."

38. *In back flyleaf, of MS Notebook 2 of 5:*
"Remember Pablo's resemblance to bull-fighters particularly Malchalita [Malchahita?]. Pablo & Braque The lime-light."

39. **p. 226, above par. 5,** *"To sweep and not to leave what is not…"*
"Matisse & his old crowd and Derain."

40. **p. 227, above par. 1,** *"Assailable barter in withdrawing slaughter…"*
"Matisse young with his group."

LK [Vol. 2 of 5, ms. page numbered 59 by ***AT:***]

Entry dates this part of GMP as summer 1912, when GS was writing Portrait of Argentina.

~~"O Argentina hupp~~[?]~~. Archentina. Archentina.~~
~~Now Now now o w now small way what [about?]"~~

41. **p. 227, above par. 5,** *"Walking around when the wet place…"*
"Matisse et al."

42. **p. 228, above par. 6,** *"Ninety-five and seventy-two…"*
"(Duets) bet M. & each one."

43. **p. 229, above par. 3,** *"All the way he had to say…"*
"Duets."

44. **p. 229, above par. 6,** *"He said it, it was not the only…"*
"Duets."

45. **p. 230, above par. 2,** *"Many many tickle…"*
"(Each one duets."

46. **p. 230, above par. 5,** *"A dark and light place…"*
"(Duets.)"
"~~A darling~~"

47. **p. 231, above par. 3,** *"Carting there where there was paper…"*
"(The duets)"

48. **p. 232, above par. 4,** *"It is apparent that…"*
"Go on to conversation M. & each, his crowd and us and P. etc."

49. **p. 233, above par. 2,** *"Darkness is not black enough…"*
"(Conversations)"

50. **p. 234, par. 1,** *"If the covered space has the same size…"*
"Conversations with friends."

51. **p. 235, above par. 9,** *"Like the arrangement of the place…"*
"Go on to Pablo."

52. **p. 237, par. 4**, *"If there is enough to do a certain way…"*
"(The old crowd later)"

53. **p. 237, par. 7**, *"If there was the whole way to go…"*
"(The crowd)"

54. **p. 238, par. 6**, *"If it were not so much…"*
"(Matisse's crowd, more and more)"

55. **p. 239, par. 1**, *"Mounting up into that place…"*
"(Individuals now) and the pupils."

56. **p. 239, par. 4**, *"Partly going he came there deciding…."*
"(Go on.)"

57. **p. 239, par. 7**, *"He was the same…"*
"(Go on)"

58. **p. 240, par. 2**, *"All the place where…"*
"Go on and the crowd. Draper."

59. **p. 240, par. 4**, *"A feeling that there is nearing…"*
"The crowd."

60. **p. 241, par. 5**, *"A wait that is not so long…"*
"Not Pablo yet. Do all Matisse's life in the new manner, then Pablo in the old."

61. **p. 244, par. 8**, *"Attend the closing of the door…"*
"Go on with general [?] atmosphere to now [new?]. & me."

62. **p. 245, par. 7**, *"One is not of three…."*
"M. & P. & me."

63. **p. 246, par. 1**, *"There is sound that…"*
"M. & P. & me."

64. **p. 246, par. 6**, *"If a cause that is not put there…"*
"The three"

65. **p. 246, par. 8**, *"All the time there is the use…"*
"The three"

66. **p. 246, par. 9**, *"Largely pressing the separation…"*
"The three"

67. **p. 251, par. 9,** *"Blanket the mist of a prick…"*
"Matisse & Pablo & me. offered circumstances."

68. **p. 257, par. 7,** *"An exceeding long stout single eagle…"*
"(Creation.)"

69. **p. 258, par. 1,** *"A mend which shows no…"*
"Creation."

70. **p. 259, par. 8,** *"A Baedecker, that is to say, no division…."*
"Description of everybody's work, success and dissapointment[sic] and time. which is better than Cezanne.

71. **p. 260, par. 8,** *"There is no more use…"*
"Description of work everybody success and dissapointment[sic] and time. Which is better than Cezanne."

72. **p. 262, par. 7,** *"To be no more separated than by…"*
"Creation and success & aims."

73. **p. 263, par. 3,** *"No target and no time…"*
"Pritchie with all."

74. **p. 264, par. 3,** *"A charge to a sausage is the swelling pepper…"*
"Silhouettes of each painted picture from the beginning success and failure."

75. **p. 264, par. 6,** *"park a whole park is a place…"*
"Each picture picture -Incl. all bought & seen."

76. **p. 266, par. 1,** *"A cushion, no fan and no rose…"*
"Detail of pictures. everybody making observations success."

77. **p. 266, par. 4,** *"It was a single breath in a circle…"*
"(Each picture)"

78. **p. 270, par. 8,** *"A tooth when is a tooth empty…"*
"(Different kinds of despair)"

79. **p. 271, par. 5,** *"What is a word that says resemblance…."*
"Despairs."

80. **p. 271, par. 10.** *"A lake, springing into a waggon…"*
"Their despairs and simplifications"

*

Note #166

GS notes in manuscript.

MABEL DODGE AT THE VILLA CURONIA

1. [GS note in flyleaf:]

"Mabel little Mabel with her face against the pane"

2. Name "Oscar" changed to "William" in the text.

*

Note #167

[TENDER BUTTONS]

GS Misc. Notes on stationary of Gran Hotel de Russia, Madrid n.d.

1. In GS handwriting, one side of sheet has notation: "FUNNY BOOK"

2. In AT handwriting, other side has note:

"Now I have it—now I see—this is the way—not that way—the other way is not the way -"

*

Note #168

Changed to Note #116

*

Note #169

Changed to Note #69

*

Note #171

Now it is the feeling in him when he is a boy and he is coming to have it in him to be himself inside him that we can know about him.

*

Note #172

Same as Note #45

*

Note #179

Note is missing

*

Note #181

A MAN

Just before the beginning of the trip. ~~you~~ say—(he became one who could be one not talking.)
The way art interested him. that is by the man's talk about it and meanings and intensity

LK ***he became one who could be one not talking:*** Planning Note for "A Man," referring to [*TWO*, **p. 245, line 30**.] "Just before he left" refers to Edstrom's leaving for Italy, and the "excitement" of meeting Maurice Sterne (and possibly Hutchins Hapgood as well) and their joyous and also drunken and violent encounters. Conversations about art were essentially with Berenson, but with BB, the violence of Edstrom's response was at least not physical, though nearly.

*

Note #182

MEN

~~Two Three~~
~~Three Many Men.~~
~~Men~~,
/ ~~Different. Not interesting.~~
Then—Not meeting -
/ Not related. Not exactly that.
Tommy, Jaques chagall
Hartley. Willie, Ronnebech[?]
Kandinsky, Coolidge
any one slightly known
Laurie Stephens Eugene
Alfy. B.B. Chalfin.
B.B.
B.B. & Jaques Blanche.

*

Note #184

GS Ms. Note:

MATISSE

One was married to someone. That one was going away to have a good time. The one that was married to that one did not like it very well that the one to whom that one was married then was going off alone to have a good time and was leaving that one to stay at homethen. The one that was going came in all glowing. The one that was going had everything he was needing to have the good time he was wanting to be having then. He came in all glowing. The one he was leaving at home to take care of the family living was not glowing. The one the was going was saying, the one that was glowing, the one that was going was saying then,

satisfied

[Insert: ~~to the one that was not glowing then~~,] I am content!

delighted

satisfied satisfied

~~What~~ you are not contented?—I am content—You are not

delighted. delighted

satisfied satisfied satisfied

contented?—I am content you are content—you are

satisfied satisfied

content, I am content.

*

Note #190

Leo Stein letter to Howard Gans, n.d., re: GS's controversy with Bird about Bird's "failure to understand."

*

Note #193

Note is missing

*

Note #200

He was seeing one then. He did then see that one. He was leaving then. He was leaving having complete permission to be one being exciting. He had permission then to be one being one who had been one doing something.

He had permission then to be exciting. He was leaving then. He was one being one doing something. He was one being exciting. He was leaving then. He was having then complete permission to be one being exciting. He was being then being one who was one who had come to be one doing something. He was one then who had come to be one who had been one who could be one not talking. He was seeing then. He was talking then in being one being living. He was seeing then, seeing one who was one he was seeing.

LK ***He was seeing one then....one he was seeing.*** Draft of text, altered and expanded in *LGB*, [Yale edition of *TWO*, **p. 245, line 12 to p. 246, line 3**.]

*

Note #201

Cook and Cook and Cock.
Capeing.
Ben, beniefice, a please
cache met, in a creeche,
creecher, in a create,
  (apart)
beach / her, in a ~~pay~~
pea—in—stall.

LK ***Cook and Cook and Cock:*** Text from the poem, "IN," published in *Bee Time Vine*, **pp. 44–52**. The passage here appears on **p. 47**, with several divergences from the manuscript (possibly errors in copying:)

1. "Cook and Cook and Cook," for "Cook and Cook and Cock;"
2. "benefice" for "beniefice;"
3. "Crecher" for "Creecher."

Editor Virgil Thomson dates the poem 1913. All his notes on facts and dates for the volume *Bee Time Vine* had the benefit, and the authority, of AT's input, which was given with the understanding that her name could be mentioned, in connection with the volume's notations, no more than twice.

*

Note #202

If she was beautiful one day she was beautiful that day because she was beautiful that day.
She was doing more than she intended and she liked it.
If she was etc. She was beautiful any day. If she was beautiful every day

she was beautiful because of the way that she was beautiful that day. She did more than she intended and she liked it.

*

Note #203

Helen [flavors?] [arranged?] repeats
does not remember repeats.
Ernie & Flossie.
Aunt Pauline remembers.

Note: Inserted later, upside down, between above two lines:
Between, feeling real and attention to be diverted.

*

Note #204

She could be one. In being one she was not saying that she was that one the one she was being, she was not saying anything.

She could be one. She was saying something. She was saying that she liked some things.

She could be one. She was one. She was not saying anything. She could be one. She was not saying anything.

She could be one. In not saying anything she was not saying anything of that thing. She was not saying anything of not saying anything.

She could be one. She was one. She was saying something. She was saying that anything is something. She was saying that something which is something is everything and that everything is not something and not being something she would be expecting that in continuing it was not everything. She was not saying anything of this thing.

*

Note #205

In listening and in listening sound coming out and sounding can be coming, in listening and coming out of her and sounding was feeling in thinking being existing.

In listening sound coming out of her and sounding was feeling understanding being existing. In listening sound coming out of her and sounding was feeling in agreeing to have thinking be continuing. In listening sound coming out of her and sounding was feeling that understanding is creating. In listening sound coming out of her and sounding is feeling that understanding in feeling thinking is feeling in thinking continuing in feeling in thinking continuing is feeling that understanding is thinking is feeling that understanding is thinking is feeling in thinking being existing and understanding being existing and thinking and understanding being continuing.

In listening sound coming and sounding was coming and coming out of her was feeling and feeling was sustaining understanding being existing and understanding being existing, thinking being existing, feeling is feeling and being understanding and being convincing and being sustaining and being experiencing understanding and thinking being existing, listening being existing and listening being existing sound sounding and coming was coming and feeling.

LK ***In listening and in.... was coming and feeling:*** Draft of text for **TWO, p. 54, lines 4–25**; used verbatim.

repetition:

For "He:" **Page 54, par. 4 to Page 55, par. 2.**
For "She:" **Page 55, par. 3.**

GS ***disdain:*** [Questionable] For "He:" **Page 55, par. 4** [?].

GS ***love and accomplishment:***

For "He:" **Page 55, par. 5 to Page 56, par. 5.**
For "She:" **Page 56, par. 6 to Page 58, preceding par. 1.**

GS ***appreciation:*** For "He:" **Page 58, par. 1.**
For "She:" **Page 58, par. 2.**

GS ***logic:*** For "He:" **Page 58, par. 3 to Page 59, par. 2.**

GS ***and avarice of distinction:*** For "He:" **Page 59, par. 3 to Page 61, par. 2.**

GS ***Myrtle... listening to herself... important to know what you think:***
For "She:" **Page 61, par. 3.**

AT ***important to know what you think:*** Sally's phrase to Bruce [in A-19, the phrase is recalled as, 'important for me to know what I think.'] Gertrude and I roared over it for years.

and avarice of distinction (continued):

For "He:" **Page 62, par. 1 to Page 64, par. 1.**
For "She:" **Page 64, par. 2 to Page 65, par. 1.**

GS ***necessity of winning:***
For "She:" **Page 67, par. 1**.
For "He:" **Page 67 par. 2 to Page 69, preceding par. 1**.

5. ***p. 70, preceding 1st paragraph,*** *"If she were coming and going she…"*
"Go on with Jane pride and gentleness."

And pride, gentleness: [GS Note in Manuscript for this passage: on **Page 70, preceding par. 1**: "Go on with Jane pride and gentleness."]
For "She:" **Page 69, par. 1 to Page 70, par. 4**.

GS **meaning and discovering:** *For "He:"* ***Page 70, par. 5 to Page 71, par. 5***.

GS ***remembering and repeating:*** For "He:" **Page 72, pars. 1–3**.
For "She:" **Page 71, par. 4 to Page 73, par. 1**.

6. ***p. 73, preceding 1st paragraph,*** *"If she discovered that discovering"*
"Go on discoveries, impermeability, ability, memories."

GS ***impermeability, preserving memory:*** GS Notes in Manuscript for these passages:
on **Page 73, preceding par. 1**: "Go on discoveries, impermeability, ability, memory."
on **Page 74, preceding par. 1**: "Impermeability and memory"
on **Page 75, preceding par. 3**: "A little more Jane spooking and impermeability."

7. ***p. 74, preceding 1st paragraph,*** *"If she said that she had said what she had said she would have said that she was hearing what she was hearing,"*
"Impermeability & memory"

8. ***p. 75, preceding 3rd paragraph,*** *"Doing, saying, believing, feeling,"*
"a little more Jane spooking and impermeability"

9. ***p. 77, preceding 1st paragraph,*** *"If quietly then certainly not…"*
"Courage [?] & comes [?] for sympathy she"

GS ***courage and the way they both come for sympathy and sentiment:*** GS Notes in Manuscript for this passage: on **Page 77, preceding par. 1**: "Courage & comes for sympathy she."
on **Page 77, preceding par. 4**: "Coming for sympathy."
For "He:" **Page 75, par. 6 to Page 76, par. 7**.
For "She:" **Page 77, pars. 1–4.**

10. ***p. 77, preceding 4th paragraph,*** *"What was told when she heard," etc.*
"Coming for sympathy"

GS ***incapacity of continuity in bearing an attack when hit:***
For "He:" **Page 77, par. 5 to Page 78, par. 4.**
For "She:" **Page 78, par. 5 to Page 79, par. 4**.
For "He:" **Page 79, par. 5 to Page 86, par. 1**.
For "She:" **Page 86, par. 2 to Page 87, par. 1**.

GS ***necessity of winning:***
For "He:" [Text returns to "necessity of winning" in] **Page 87, par. 2**.

11. ***p. 87****, preceding, 3rd paragraph, "If he were hoping what he would…"*
"Religion"

12. ***p. 88, preceding 2nd paragraph****, "If to do what she did was to work…"*
"More Jane religion"

13. ***p. 88,*** *preceding 5th paragraph, "He did hope and he had explained"*
"Spirituality"

14. ***p. 89, preceding 1st paragraph****, "He saw when he saw that he saw"*
"Spirituality"

15. ***p. 89, preceding 6th paragraph****, "She did follow and she did lead…" "Spirituality"*

16. ***p. 90. preceding 1st paragraph****, "She would not have a decision"*
"A little more spirituality"

religion and spirituality: GS Notes in Manuscript for this passage:
on **Page 87, preceding par. 3**: "religion"
on **Page 88, preceding par. 2**: "More Jane religion"
on **Page 88, preceding par. 5**: "spirituality"
on **Page 89, preceding par. 1**: "spirituality"
on **Page 89, preceding par. 5**: "spirituality"
on **Page 90, preceding par. 1**: "a little more spirituality"
For "He:" **Page 87, par. 3**.
For "She:" **Page 87, par. 4 to Page 88, par. 4**.
For "He:" **Page 88, par. 5 to Page 89, par. 4**.
For "She:" **Page 89, par. 5 to Page 90, par. 1**.

17. ***p. 91, preceding 1st paragraph****, "In saying it all he said what he"*
"Integrity the two"

18. ***p. 92, preceding 1st paragraph****, "If he came to go on he would…"*
"Leo integrity and how he is right and not right"

19. ***p. 92, preceding 5th paragraph****, "She did say all she said carefully"*
"Jane integrity and care in statement & criticism"

20. ***p. 93, preceding 1st paragraph,*** *"She could not mean all she meant if."*
"(Not a success try Jane's integrity again)"

21. ***p. 93, preceding 2nd paragraph,*** *"She expressed enough to satisfy all."*
"(Go on with Jane.) anger and integrity
(then L. anger)"

22. ***p. 94, preceding 5th paragraph,*** *"He did not say that all he said was…"*
"(Go on with L. anger and integrity)"

23. ***p. 95, preceding par. 2,*** *"If saying that a thing will happen"*
"(His strictures[?] about Simon H. & May[?] about Roosevelt)"

24. ***p. 95, preceding paragraph 3,*** *"He did look well in rising to saying…"*
"Go on with his integrity and hers."

25. ***p. 96, preceding 5th paragraph,*** *"She could not know what happened"*
"Jane's integrity to anger (the consistency of the two)"

26. ***p. 97, preceding paragraph 2,*** *"He settled that he began what he began"*
"(Jane's integrity and anger) (consistency both) (True she can have what she wants. don't know what she hasn't.) The two women and Papa & [Pach's/Paul's?] man"

and integrity and anger persistence and criticism critical attitude illustration helps her he can't take it: GS Notes in Manuscript for this passage:

on **Page 91, preceding par. 1**: "integrity of the two"

on **Page 92, preceding par. 1**: "Leo integrity and how his is right and not right"

on **Page 92, preceding par. 5**: "Jane integrity and care in statement & criticism"

on **Page 93, preceding par. 1**: "(Not a success. Try Jane's integrity again)"

on **Page 93, preceding par. 2**: "(Go on with Jane.) anger and integrity. (Then Leo anger)"

on **Page 94, preceding par. 5**: "(Go on with L. Anger and integrity.)"

on **Page 95, preceding par. 1**: "His strictures[?] about Simon H. & May[?] about Roosevelt."

on **Page 95, preceding par. 2**: "Go on with his integrity and hers."

on **Page 96, preceding par. 5**: "Jane's integrity to anger (the consistency of the two)"

on **Page 97, preceding par. 2**: "(Jane's integrity and anger) (consistency of both.) (True she can have what she wants. Don't know what she hasn't.) The two women and papa & Pach's[?] man."

For "He:" **Page 91, par. 1 to Page 92, par. 2**.
For "She:" **Page 92, par. 3 to Page 95, par. 3**.
For "He:" **Page 95, par. 4 to Page 96, par. 1**.
For "She:" **Page 96, par. 2 to Page 97, par. 1**.
For "He:" **Page 97, pars. 2–3**.

27. ***p. 97, preceding paragraph 3,*** *"He could be proceeding"*
"(Jane inconsistency) then his."

28. ***p. 97, preceding paragraph 4,*** *"If she was not remembering"*
"Jane and Le[o] inconsistency a la [Harber? Harker?]

29. ***p. 98, preceding paragraph 3,*** *"If he had the feeling"*
"(Inconsistency)"

30. ***p. 99, preceding paragraph 1,*** *"She said that she knew that she"*
"(Jane inconsistency)"

inconsistency: GS Notes in Manuscript for this passage:

on **Page 97, preceding par. 3**: "Jane inconsistency then his"
on **Page 97, preceding par. 4**: "Jane and Leo inconsistency a la Hawker"
on **Page 98, preceding par. 2**: "(inconsistency)"
on **Page 99, preceding par. 1**: "(Jane inconsistency)"
For "She:" **Page 97, par. 4.**
For "He:" **Page 98, pars. 1–5**.
For "She:" **Page 99, pars. 1–2**.

GS ***make him noble and her vibrating:*** Questionable where this Planning Note was to be accomplished. Possibly, it is concurrent with the passages on the "Romance Legend Ideal" on **Pages 99 to 111**, but this is uncertain.

31. ***p. 99, preceding paragraph 3,*** *"Each of them was not one…"*
"(the two contrasted) to bad[?] to Romance etc)

32. ***p. 100, preceding paragraph 1,*** *"He was and he was. He said he was."*
"(Continue contrast)"

33. ***p. 100, preceding paragraph 3,*** *"If one is one and one is not one…"*
"Contrast between the two."

34. ***p. 100, preceding paragraph 5,*** *"Likely enough he said what he said"*
"Contrast. (Romance.) legend) ideal)"

35. **p. 101, preceding paragraph 2,** *"She did have what was asked"*
"(Romance Legend Ideal)"

36. **p. 102, preceding paragraph 1,** *"He did come again to declare"*
"(Romance Legend Ideal)"

37. **p. 102, preceding paragraph 4,** *"If he said all he said"*
"(Romance Legend Ideal) He.[?]

38. **p. 103, preceding par. 1,** *"He said that he had conceived"*
"Romance Legend Ideal"

39. **p. 105, preceding paragraph 2,** *"He modifying was not…"*
"Romance Legend Ideal."

40. **p. 105, preceding paragraph 3,** *"Sound was not sounding"*
"(R. Legend Ideal)"

41. **p. 106, preceding paragraph 3,** *"He did come to stay when he was…"*
"(Romance Legend I. she.)"

42. **p. 106, preceding paragraph 7,** *"If the strength that does not come…"*
"(More L.)"

43. **p. 108, preceding paragraph 2,** *"If she was the child"*
"Jane Leg. Id. etc."

44. **p. 108, preceding paragraph 4,** *"A company that talks is a company"*
"More J. Leg. Ideal. Romance."

45. **p. 110, preceding paragraph 1,** *"Going on within her"*
"Go on with her"

46. **p. 110, preceding paragraph 5,** *"It was not the lingering way"*
"(Go on. to him as her [acler? order? arbiter?.]"

47. **p. 111, preceding paragraph 3,** *"He alone was there where explaining."*
"(Leo alone) what he takes and wants B.B.)"

[contrast and] Romance legend ideal: GS Notes in Manuscript for this passage:

on **Page 99, preceding par. 3**: "(the two contrasted) to bad[?] to Romance" etc.

on **Page 100, preceding par. 1**: "(continue contrast)"

on **Page 100, preceding par. 3**: "contrast between the two"

on **Page 100, preceding par. 5**: "Contrast. (Romance) legend) ideal)"

on **Page 101, preceding par. 2**: "(Romance Legend Ideal)"
on **Page 102, preceding par. 1**: "Romance Legend Ideal"
on **Page 102, preceding par. 4**: "(Romance Legend Ideal) He."
on **Page 103, preceding par. 1**: "Romance Legend Ideal"
on **Page 105, preceding par. 2**: "Romance Legend Ideal"
on **Page 105, preceding par. 3**: "(R. Legend Ideal)"
on **Page 106, preceding par. 3**: "(Romance Legend I. She.)"
on **Page 106, preceding par. 7**: "(More L.)"
on **Page 108, preceding par. 2**: "Jane Leg. Id. etc."
on **Page 108, preceding par. 5** "More J. Legend Ideal. Romance."
on **Page 110, preceding par. 1**: "Go on with her"
on **Page 110, preceding par. 5**: "Go on. To him as her arbiter[?]"
on **Page 111, preceding par. 3**: "(Leo alone.) What he takes and wants. B.B."

Contrast of the two: **Page 99, par. 3 to Page 100, par. 2**.
For "He:" **Page 100, pars. 3–4**.
For "She:" **Page 101, pars. 1–3**.
For "He:" **Page 101, par. 4 to Page 106, par. 1**.
For "She:" **Page 106, par. 2**.
For "He:" **Page 106, par. 3 to Page 107, par. 2**.
For "She:" **Page 107, par. 3 to Page 110, par. 2**.
For "He:" **Page 110, par. 3 to Page 112, par. 1**.

48. ***p. 112, preceding paragraph 2,*** *"The way to say that meaning is"*
"(His success) and influence) test of originality)

GS ***Influence:*** GS Notes in Manuscript for this passage:

Page 112, preceding par. 2: "(His success) and influence) test of originality)"

For "He:" **Page 112, pars. 2–5**.

49. ***p. 113, preceding paragraph 3,*** *"All the same he said enough"*
"Go on with his youth and success"

50. ***p. 124, preceding paragraph 5,*** *"If the practical throwing out what has"*
ee
"(L~~eo~~'s life)"

51. ***p. 128, preceding paragraph 2,*** *"He had the alteration of the…"*
"(The fam. [farm?] youth)"

52. ***p. 128, preceding paragraph 4,*** *"If he went away he did not say"*
"(Youth) the farm the W.C."

53. ***p. 129, preceding paragraph 3,*** *"Correlation between the past"*
"More youth. Venice."

54. ***p. 129, preceding paragraph 5,*** *"He had that excitement"*
"Go on with youth"

55. ***p. 130, preceding paragraph 6,*** *"A better piece of harness"*
"(Go on) youth character his father)

56. ***p. 132, preceding paragraph 2,*** *"It was not in the pressure of liking"*
"(Youth)"

GS ***and lives thin[ly] done:*** GS Notes in Manuscript for this passage:
Page 113, preceding par. 3: "Go on with his youth and success"
Page 127, preceding par. 5: "Leo's [crossed out] [inserted: Lee's] life"
Page 128, preceding par. 2: "The farm youth"
Page 128, preceding par. 4: "(Youth) the farm. W.C."
Page 129, preceding par. 3: "More youth. Venice"
Page 129, preceding par. 5: "Go on with youth"
Page 130, preceding par. 6: "(Go on) Youth Character. His father"
Page 132, preceding par. 2: "(Youth)"
For "He:" **Page 112, par. 2 to Page 116, par. 5**.
For "She:" **Page 117, par. 1 to Page 119, par. 1**.
contrast of the two: **Page 119, par. 2**.
For "He:" **Page 119, par. 3 to Page 123, par. 4**.
For "She:" **Page 123, par. 5 to Page 125, par. 7**.
For "He:" **Page 126, par. 1 to Page 133, par. 6**.

GS ***and fiasco of fasting:*** [Identification of this passage is questionable]
For "He:" **Page 132, par. 3 to Page 133, par. 6**. [?]

57. ***p. 133, preceding paragraph 7,*** *"Going past the street"*
"Go on with Jane"

58. ***p. 134, preceding paragraph 3,*** *"There was the day when she did that"*
"Go on to Allen C.S. Salon & Europe"

GS ***and lives thin[ly] done:***
Page 133, preceding par. 7: "Go one with Jane"
Page 134, preceding par. 3: "Go on to Allen. C.S. Europe"
Page 135, preceding par. 1: "Painting then failure and C.S."
Page 135, preceding par. 4: "Go on with painting"
For "She:" **Page 133, par. 7 to Page 136, par. 1**.

59. ***p. 135, preceding paragraph 1,*** *"She had not that day to walk"*
"Painting then failure & C.S."

60. ***p. 135, preceding paragraph 4,*** *"The leaves that are separated"*
"Go on with painting."

GS ***painting:*** GS Notes in Manuscript for this passage:

Page 135, preceding par. 1: "Painting then failure and C.S."
Page 135, preceding par. 4: "Go on with painting"
For "She:" **Page 135, par. 1 to Page 136, par. 1**.

Before completing the plan detailed in this Note, further matter was added:

61. ***p. 136, preceding paragraph 6,*** *"If coming into the one who is passing"*
"Relation to people each one from youth
up victory & distinction without ambition or
interest in men turn inward satisfy themselves
imp. need. [advice? audience?] and criticism"

62. ***p. 137, preceding paragraph 2,*** *"The ending which is not ending"*
"Go on with human instinct"

63. ***p. 137, preceding paragraph 5,*** *"Spacing the dimensions"*
"No human instinct and without ambition with need for [missing???]"

64. ***p. 141, preceding paragraph 1,*** *"She was the one who had"*
"She, and then a word of he."

65. ***p. 141, preceding paragraph 2,*** *"The closet was not holding all…"*
"(She & people)"

66. ***p. 142, preceding par. 2,*** *"If the date was not written"*
"She and people. He."

GS ***discourse on passion for distinction and victory without ambition or…. his critical faculty his dope:*** GS Notes in Manuscript for this passage:

Page 136, preceding par. 6: "Relation to people each one from youth up victory & distinction without ambition or interest in men turn inward satisfy themselves imp. need audience and criticism."

Page 137, preceding par. 2: "Go on with human instinct"

Page 137, preceding par. 5: "No human instinct and without ambition with need for [missing?]"

Page 141, preceding par. 1: "She, and then a word of he."
Page 141, preceding par. 2: "(She & people)"
Page 142, preceding par. 2: "She and people. He."

For "They:" **Page 136, par. 2 to Page 137, par. 3.**
For "He:" **Page 137, par. 4 to Page 140, par. 2.**
For "They:" **Page 140, par. 3.**
For "She:" **Page 141, par. 1 to Page 142, par. 3.**
For "He:" **Page 142, par. 4.**
For "She:" **Page 142, par. 5.**
For "He:" **Page 142, par. 6.**

*

Note #206

Go on with his processes and successes.
Romance Legend Ideal.

*

Note #208

List of books to be [printed?]

They are all over they [word?] and they are [word?] a at the same time, and they feel good, they bring light and having said they are giving me real delight.

I am pleased as can be with my big and little scarfs but I am quite nuts about the big one.

Curled as a sentence.

22-23

Lock on doors, key for back [word?], [word?] for tools, carry extra oil.

Mme Victor Magdelaine
9 Place de l'Eglise-Asnieres

*

Note #216

Mike, Albert R., Alfy Frank Jacot, Sternberger, Leo Friedman

*

Note #226

Note on back of letter, Hutchins Hapgood to Leo Stein, Tatti to Paris, n.d. [late 1905 or 06]

Journal of Mary Frampton
cont. of Byron

Memoirs of Lady Morgan

***

Appendix C

Ms Note #1 re [MA 4]

Corresponds to Note #110A.

Begins Volume 1 of ms, ***pp. 3–16*** *in final text.*

General Note for Ms. volume 1: All references to "german" are converted to "certain" or omitted.

Following MA 4, line 35, there is a break in this First Draft text. Draft text continues on MA 5, line 6. "We living now … we have just been thinking" is a later insert.

Text on "proud feeling" intended for A Long Gay Book*,* ***p. 14****, following line 36, but not included in final draft.*

*

Ms Note #2 re [MA 5]

MA 5, par. 4 ends with second sentence, and a fragment of a third:

"It is a horrid so much to have a sense of losing such that can only give me the feeling of being to ourselves…"

*

Ms Note #3 re [MA 6]

Line 38 and 39: begins conversion of "Herman" *[Dehning] to* "Henry," *a change which continues for all later references to* "Herman." *NB12, #11: changes* "Abe" *to* "Herman"

*

Ms Note #4 re [MA 7]

Original version of ***lines 24–29****:*

"Yes his son Herman had made everything for himself and it was very different. He was honest rich strong, good-tempered and respected. Yes he had made things to be for himself very different but always he liked to tell about it and most often to his children about what had been and what he had done and how himself had done it and how well it was for them to be his children.

~~" 'Yes you children have an easy time of it nowadays.' "~~

Next page of ms. draft begins the final text of passage, MA 7, line 19 to 8, line 9, and then continues Herman's speech, as above "'Yes' he would often say" etc.

concurrent with NB2, #3

*

Ms Note #5 re [MA 10, lines 39 and 43]

The name "Sam" is converted to "Adolph."

*

Ms Note #6 re [MA 11]

Opposite ***par. 1:***

"The young Dehnings had all been born and brought it [sic] in Bridgepoint. There [sic] were all very fond of Bridgepoint. Like all the wealthy people of Bridgepoint They had their city house and their country house etc. etc."

Text converted from First Draft, inserted in MA 10, lines 39ff.

*

Ms Note #7 re [MA 12]

Line 27, following "the family altogether would sail and fish," *text omitted in final draft:*

"Yes and all this was thirty years ago before the fever to be an Anglo-saxon and a gentleman (for why indeed should we wish to be an Anglo-saxon if we were not to be a gentleman,) yes this was all thirty years ago before the Anglo-saxon fever had broken over all the land and sport the royal road to this goal was then still the pursuiit only of the scorned few. Not that the American youth has not always armed himself out of doors but then he did it as the young animal does because he likes it and not because of an ideal.

"However these Dehnings had always had right Anglo-saxon instincts albeit their instinct sprang from peasant and not from gentle sources. Yes the Dehnings in the country were simple pleasant people. The young ones spent all their time in right doing in the manly Anglo-saxon way that now we all know."

Concurrent with Note #67

*

Ms Note #8 re [MA 14]

First Draft text, following line 34:

"The eldest daughter had just turned eighteen. She was ready now so thought her mother and Julia was quite of the same opinion to get married and to begin her real important living."

Expanded in Final Draft, MA 14, line 44 to 15, line 8.

This is followed in the First Draft by text used later in Final Draft, MA 19, line 1ff., in amended form. Original text reads: "The father never concerned himself in these affairs, they were all always arranged by the mother…"

Interlined with this paragraph, a Planning Note:
"Use this after telling about wife's management, after description of children."

The "description of children," Julia, George and Hortense, is in MA 14, line 35 to 18, line 37, and "wife's management" is in MA 18, lines 38–44.

*

Ms Note #9 re [MA 19]

Planning Note for MA 19, following line 13:
"Go on about Julia's life."

*

Ms Note #10 re [MA 15]

Line 32, following "… was not named after his grandfather."

Omitted text from First Draft:
"It was just then the first incubating of the Anglo-saxon fever had commenced its incubating. And so it was right that in his name he should not sound German as if he were a german, so at least his mother decided for him, and the father laughed and let her do it the way she like it, and so the boy was named George and the Herman was there but it was well hidden under the initial just to be used for signing.
"And so this boy George who was named in the heat of the new fever, it was before they called it Anglo-saxon in their talking, bade fair to do credit to his christening. George Dehning now about fourteen was strong in sport and washing. He was not German in his washing. Oh, no, he was a real Anglo-saxon."

In the final version, this text is replaced by MA 15, lines 32–40.

*

Ms Note #11 re [MA 16]

Omitted text from First Draft, following line 5:

"I remember when I was little, the Anglo-saxon fever was just then beginning, people began to talk always talking of of bathing, now I knew about a once a week bathing and for the rest it was for me just washing, but these others, they talked of an every day of bathing and I was ashamed and I never dared to say how on weekdays, I just could call it washing. Well I found out once that this bathng was just hands and face like my washing and that was a great relief to my young feeling, for I had been all ashamed and for I knew very well I never could do so much bathing."

Concurrent with NB9, #4

*

Ms Note #12 re [MA 16]

Omitted text from First Draft, preceding line 34:

"There are some humble souls, saints among sinners, who may have doubts whether they are as clean as all the others. Many people in this world give thanks that they are so much cleaner than almost all the others. Some perhaps sometimes feel that they are not as clean as their ideal of being clean demands, but then they know they are cleaner than almost all the others. Poor things they often suffer would that these noble souls could be content with the fair daily bathing that contents so many others, but then one must always suffer when one is really truly noble in one's nature, and that is what one must pay here to be nobler cleaner than any of the people others.

"Yes it is very funny always all this washing business for us, yes truly they [sic] are some humble souls among us, rare as saints always are among the sinners, who think they are not as clean as all the others. Huck Finn, he was one of these muck saints always, but mostly all the others they find plenty dirty ones to condemn among them."

Omitted text from First Draft, following line 39:

"Then one finds a few meek souls among us who confess sometimes with a halting kind of manner that they do not always wash themselves very clean in the winter, they are weak, they cannot do their duty nobly, they cannot do more than just to wash their hands and faces. Poor meek, weak souls who cannot do their duty."

Concurrent with NB9, #4, #5

*

Ms Note #13 re [MA 16]

Omitted text from First Draft, preceding line 43:

"Yes George Dehning was a good Anglo-saxon as now we know them. He was strong in sporting and in washing and he did the latter very often. No he was not german at all in his washing.

Concurrent with NB9, #4, #5

*

Ms Note #14 re [MA 17]

Original from First Draft of Final Draft text, lines 6 and 7:

"Yes George Dehning was not as german in his washing, and yet he was not all-over Anglo-saxon.

Concurrent with NB9, #4, #5

*

Ms Note #15 re [MA 17]

Original of corrected text, lines 26 and 27:

"They called her Hortense for that was both elegant and not german."

Changed to: … "elegant and not new then."

Corresponds to NB9, #5 and to NB1, #14

*

Ms Note #16 re [MA 19, 20, 22]

Inserted in final text: MA 19, lines 14–44; MA 20, line 22 to 21, line 3; MA 22, lines 21–26.

Corresponds to NB9, #6 and #8

*

Ms Note #17 re [MA 28]

Omitted text, following line 43:

"Oh young man, if you are not one of the strong men of this earth, beware how you take to wife the daughter and the sister loving and loyal of simple, sane, considerate men. Her family feeling and her pure devotion to the tradition of her early home will make a test that you must needs be bravely made to pass. Be doubly warned, attractive and weak brother, be sharply on your guard for it is a woman from such a family life who is so often taken by the glitter and the lightness of your thin and eager nature, your temper selfish and demanding, but when the close life of the marriage comes, she looks to find in you weak creature that you are the power and support, the honesty and steady courage she has always known and hence will spring your woe and loathesome sadness that begins and never has an end. Brother weak pleasant selfish brother, beware."

*

Ms Note #18 re [MA 33]

Omitted text from First Draft, following line 14:

"Face to face with nakedness in the soul of a man, poorly made by God, she shuddered and grew sick."

Replaced by inserted text in ***Final Draft: lines 11–44****.*

*

Ms Note #19 re [MA 36]

Omitted text, following line 27:

"Yes it is true and you must all listen to me while I say it. To whatever cause we must attribute the gentle attenuation, the thin imagination and the superficial sentiment of American expression in their writing and in almost all their painting, for so certainly do we mostly do it, to whatever one of the causes each one of us think we can say, yes there we have it, we never can give reason for abuse it, that our landscape, with it has not deep quality in it, it is there for us all to see it. Yes our prospects certainly do show it, the earth has been strongly handled every time to make it, whatever they are the concentratred strong meadows of northern New England, the delicate contours of the Connecticut hills in the rich flowing uplands of the middle South that give us an English understanding or the Spanish desert spaces of the West or the bare sun-burst foothills of California that make the Western sun-lover feel that to be in Tuscany is to be at home. No it is not for need of strongly featured out of doors that we must use the old world, it is for an accomplished harmony between a people and their land, for what understanding here of the thing we tread, we the children of one generation. However let us take comfort, beginnings are important, nay to a modern world almost more important than the fullfillment [sic], and so we go cheerily on with our story."

> *Corresponds to and expands treatment of the theme of "the burden on us moderns" in Note #70, which was written for the First Draft.*

*

Ms Note #20a re [MA 47]

Omitted text, following line 30:

"As I was saying people with queer ways in them, ways that come from the nature of them that they shall be free inside them, need an old world to content them. It takes time to make queer people and to make others that can know them, time and a certainty as to a place and means. Custom passion and a feel for mother earth are needed to breed vital singularity in any man and alas how poor we are in all these three."

*

Ms Note #20b re [MA 49]

Omitted text, following line 36:

"But what were the queer ways in him that so often made his children feel uncomfortable beside him.

"One thing that was queer about him was his way of walking. He was always walking when he was not eating or sleeping or talking. Always in the evening when he was at home he would be walking up and down the room to do his thinking and he would keep all his money jingling either in his pockets with his hands constantly moving or free in his hands changing and dropping and throwing it as if were so kind of game he was playing and always he was walking up and down and always thinking. Sometimes he would be talking to himself when he was impatient in his thinking."

> *Corresponding text in NB9, #9: General correspondence with the long note in NB11, #7 re: Hersland's "queer ways" and the general credulity of the "scientific" Herslands.*

*

Ms Note #21 re [MA 50]

Original of corrected text, ***lines 4–8****:*

"And then as I was saying he was a big man and he was very fond of eating and he liked to buy things that looked good to him."

"Sometimes it was a big dead wild goose that had appealed to him to take home for cooking and he would carry it with the head hanging and the feathers and the blood sticking to his clothing without his ever knowing there was anything queer about him. Sometimes it was a water-melon that he had found that promised to be a very good red sweet one and it would always be a very big one, he never liked to undertake anything that was not large in its beginning. The only time in his life he ever took..." [etc, as in final draft.]

*

Ms Note #22 re [MA 31ff.]

*The name "Hissen" in final draft is "Heisman" in this early draft. [See Ms Note #3 for MA 6] Notes NB-MA #25, 54; DB #41; NB-*C #5, #8 use "Heisman."*

Also, "Henry Dehning" in final draft is "Herman" in the early draft.

*

Ms Note #23 re [MA 54]

Following line 20, crossed out text:

"~~When the children were little children and she~~"

Planning Note opposite par.2:

"Now go on describe relation to household repeat the [richness?] of her in the general atmosphere, governess cooks etc. incident of doubling wages, for father of governess etc. etc. Relation to husband, relation to children once more dwelt upon."

*

Ms Note #24 re [MA 56]

Omitted text, following line 6:

"She had not yet learned as she did in her later living not to be with the people who were the natural people for her to have in her daily living."

Line 14: The name "Miller" is converted to "Schiller."

Line 29: The name "Schiller" is converted to "Shilling" in final draft.

Corresponds to NB14, #3, which uses the name "Schiller."

*

Ms Note #25 re [MA 67]

Deleted text [rewritten as final text in MA 67, par. 1–2]:

"So that these who are us can be better understood in us we must keep with us the the [sic] knowledge of the men and women who as our true parents made us and so we must have in us a lively sense of the mothers and the fathers who mixed together and so we came to be in us and we must realize inside us their ~~marriages~~ lives and marriages and feelings ~~and~~ all things in them that must be important to us. And we must know how they came to be married and make us and the kinds of important feelings inside them that make them individual beings for us."

*

Ms Note #26 re [MA 67]

Ms. corrections in following paragraph [correspond to final text, MA 67, par. 2]:

"In the slow history of three of those in the lives of Martha Alfred and young David Hersland and how they came each one to have their kind of important individual feeling inside them, in this slow history of them the thing that we have as a beginning is the history of Fanny Heisman and David Hersland, "

etc., continues as in MA 67, line 20ff.

LK GS's revision of this first-draft passage was possibly done in 1908 to conform to the novel's new focus on the three Hersland children. The original idea of p. 67, par 2 was that "the slow history" was of the young generation's forebears. The later insertions change the "slow history" to that of "the three of those who are to be always in this history … Martha Alfred and David Hersland."

*

Ms Note #27 re [MA 68]

*Two single yellow sheets inserted in front cover of mss. vol. 5a, out of order. Mss. volume 5a begins with **p. 68.***

Planning Note for MA 53, lines 3–37:

"Start in later and tell how it was never so with her children, her important feeling."

*

Ms Note #28 re [MA 68]

General planning Note for the two chapters on Mr and Mrs. Hersland, and Mrs. Hersland and the Servants, ending on MA 285:

"Just begin now to tell how they called on them with the children etc and then dropped out of their lives and begin experience with the servants. The Lies girls, Mary Gruenhagen fat cook turnovers, the Richardsons etc. and from that generally educational conditions and development to the children grown up mother getting sick, and then history of Martha."

*

Ms Note #29 re [MA 78]

Note on blank page facing page with text of MA 78, par. 1.

"Mrs. Schiller, Sophie Schiller & Pauline Schiller

Doodles: Cartoon-like pictures of the three Schillers, six drawing in all.

"She is a great fat one who is all straight down in front when she sits."

Draft of text about Mrs. Shilling, for MA 78, lines 31–32.

The "fatness" of Mrs. Shilling and her daughter Sophie is dwelled on in MA 78, line 31 to 80, line 6.

*

Ms Note #30 re [MA 98]

Following line 14:

Planning Note for MA 99, line 34f.

"wooden in tobacco shop and her daughter."

Following line 14:

Deleted text:

"they are like a dream to all the others of them who are in the same house with them."

*Concurrent with Note #94a; NB-*C #32 mentions "wooden faces" in other contexts; and Note #98, a planning note for MA 98–261.*

*

Ms Note #31a re [MA 196]

[On front cover of ms. "vol. 13, first draft", which begins with ***p. 196, line 2*** *and* ***ends p. 212, line 42.]*** *[The 6th volume of the MA ms.]*

"In this book dog's eared for Martha et al."

No dog's eared page detectable in this ms. volume.

*

Ms Note #31b re [MA 196]

Inside back cover of ms. vol. 13, first draft, (actual 6th volume) beginning ***p. 196****, ending* ***p. 212.***
Inside back cover, written upside down:

"The Life and death
of the good Anna
by
Jane Sands.

in pencil:

corrections from original.

Six last leaves of volume are sliced out, all written on in ink.

On back cover:

"Vol. III"

*

Ms Note #32 re [MA circa p. 214]

Inside front cover of ms. volume 7, beginning ***p. 214:***

"In final reading remember Madeleine only stayed two years."

*

Ms Note #33 re [MA 226]

Following line 5:

Planning Note for MA 227, line 44ff.

"Go on now with the types and pairs and history of love affairs."

"Pairing" in love and friendship—Weininger's point—begins on MA 221, line 15.

*

Ms Note #34 re [comment re: MA ms for pp.240–257]

LK First draft of text for **p. 240, line 22 to p. 257, line 3** are written on the versos of previous text from **pp. 222–237**. Appears to be scratch paper draft preceding penciled draft in the ms. volumes, which in turn were converted into ink copy in the volumes called, in the Yale Collection boxes, MA's "Final Draft."

*

Ms Note #35 re [MA 243]

Following line 17:

"Use this in beginning again about Mrs. Hersland use it again as a contrast for Madeleine Weiman."

Planning Note for repeating in substance MA 243, lines 18–44

At bottom of page, referring to same paragraph:

"Later in other book use it as a type study, servant girl type, etc."

"Other book" is A Long Gay Book, *being written concurrently.*

*

Ms Note #36 re [MA -unlocated note]

"do this different

David Hersland in his daily living had many things in him, ~~he had his business living, he had his country city living, he had his children's living, he had his wife's living he~~ He had his own way of living. The way a man has of thinking, his way of beginning and his way of ending."

*

Ms Note #37 re [MA 248]

Opposite line 1:

"(begin here to introduce Madeleine Weiman and Mrs. Hersland."

*

Ms Note #38 re [MA 253]

Preceding line 1:

"Start again with the reverse and so lead up to the respective characters of Mrs. H. & M. Weiman, and her family."

Corresponds to Note #82, with text on Madeleine Weiman's "possession" of Mrs. Hersland

*

Ms Note #39 re [MA 233–236]

Upside down on bottom of ms. page from section between MA 234, 236

"Go on now to discuss the way Mary was not content with Mabel's marrying, the trouble between them then beginning again with some money Mary had left to her and then back to the Hersland living and governesses."

*

Ms Note #40 re [MA 238]

Following line 32:

"Want to discuss quantity in character and success and failure tomorrow."

Planning Note for MA 238, line 35 to 239, line 7.

*

Ms Note #41 re [MA 273]

Following line 17:

"Describe a little more the feeling in Mrs. Hersland the kind of woman she was."

*

Ms Note #42 re [MA 275]

Following line 41:

"Description of resisting winning & yielding winning in Mrs. Hersland & Madeleine.

Concurrent with NB8, #5, in which text for this passage is set for MA 275, lines 30–33.

*

Ms Note #43 re [MA 285]

*Inside back cover of ms. volume 8, for **pp. 266–285**, which ends the chapter on Mr. and Mrs. Hersland*

"Use the copy when first is bad."

GS note to A. Toklas.

*

Ms Note #44 re [MA 296]

Following line 20:

"Use this general discussion before Martha Hersland and Hodder meet. Will throw the umbrella in the mud story."

"Discussion" refers to whole passage on "not knowing it in children" and "loving repeating in children", MA 295, line 44ff. But the "discussion"—of old and new themes—beginning here, extends for almost 100 pages before the "throw the umbrella in the mud story" appears on MA 388.

*

Ms Note #45 re [MA 378]

Corresponds to Note #109 and Ms Note #56b on verso of MA 378

Ms. copybook #19 includes MA text to ***p. 304, line 35****. The first sentence of MA 304, line 36, at the bottom of ms. page, is then crossed out, and the rest of the copybook pages (more than half) are sliced out, leaving two leaves at the end of the copybook in which the following note appears:*

"Use Mrs. Hodder the present like Mrs. Merle in the portrait of a lady, ow[n]s those she needs for loving to the point of renouncing herself for them."

*

Ms Note #46 re [Unlocated]

In ms. volume #19, on flyleaf under back cover, written upside down:

"The tragedy of the Linden sisters
(Etta spinster & Mary Berenson)
theme. married to B.B."

*Possibly corresponds to NB-*J #17*

"Probably use the tragedy of the Cone sisters as a big episode in other book,"

i.e., A Long Gay Book, *being written concurrently.*

*

Ms Note #47 re [MA 332]

Following line 20:

"(a little resume of the one and then to go on how knowing this one helped with others and then general question of resemblances.)"

*

Ms Note #48 re [MA 333]

On reverse of ms. page for MA 333, lines 5–28:

"Go on with description of Harriet and why she is damned.
"The spirit that denies is suffered to do evil this one did none therefor deceiving, denied in the same breath as affirmed and both being complete expressions and neither coming off not conscious of a struggle, not conscious of reality, do this to-morrow and then my conviction of her damnation and then the kind she was resistant and need at the same time. Told her so made her touch reality."

"sordid tenacity in holding on to God.
"Then resemblances then the other ways of learning by kinds of men and women. for resistance and on proud[?] attacking.
"Begin to describe my understanding of H."

> *MA 329, line 44 to 331, line 16, describes Harriet's "denying of the meaning of her being," and the resolution of GS's understanding of her.*
>
> *Corresponds to Note #1, the "Caliban" note, and its lengthy treatment of Harriet during the period of her suicide-crisis and "seeing God."*

*

Ms Note #49 re [MA 338]

Following line 27:
"(Confusion) (moments of seeing every kind of way) now consider only one meaning, later consider other meanings."

*

Ms Note #50 re [MA 352]

Following line 9:
"Muggy resisting being she needed engulfing, she was even then with the rest of her resisting. Always otherwise there was no yielding. Apparent giving."

*

Ms Note #51 re [MA 357]

Following line 34:
"(Claribel.)"

*

Ms Note #52 re [MA 364]

Written upside down at bottom of ms. page containing the beginning of MA 364, par. 4:
"Go on with description of how I learn[ed] to know Etta with fluctuation during and after and not sin[c]e too clear sometimes etc."

LK This entry not related to p. on which it appears. Might be for the "Linden Sisters" portrait, noted above in Ms Note #46

*

Ms Note #53 re [MA 366]

Following line 4:

"Then do Sam and then Chalfin run themselves by their minds."

Sam Wolfe is analyzed in NB-E, #12, and is the [---] th of the ten examples described in MA 362ff.

*Chalfin and "running himself by his mind" is analyzed and referred to in NB-A #3, NB-E #14, NB-C #20, NB-*B #20 and NB-*B #24.*

*

Ms Note #54 re [MA 368]

Following line 37:

"affection for objects[?] playing with women and protecting them"

*

Ms Note #55 re [MA 371]

Following line 34:

"various ways couldn't explain him. Leo's suggestion that perhaps he was not a unit, cleared it up. Not slow-minded like Claribel contrast in natures said he was slow-minded, made the trouble. [Word?]'s rationalizing power below the quality of his experiences when he has them, fine[?] quality of experiences and good quality of mind made him baffling. Came out believed in them both equally and results later in life as mind was more dominant became [five illegible words.]"

LK Notes #54, #55 summarize the difficulty of understanding Bernard Berenson "as a whole one" and correspond to notes NB-E #5, NB-E #6, and NB-E #7. These notes are the basis of the text in MA 368, line 4 to 372, line 34.

Leo's suggestion that perhaps he was not a unit: is used as the conclusion to the analysis, **lines 24–34**.

*

Ms Note #56a re [MA 378]

On bottom of ms. sheet, below text of MA 378, beginning of ***par. 7:***

A doodle: Three separately circled names:

Mabel **Annette Rosenshine** **A R**

*

Ms Note #56b re [MA 378]

Two pages verso in ms., with draft of text for MA 378, and Planning Notes, as follows:

First page:

"In some the nature in them is clear in that one when they are very young, in some when they are young, in some when they are not so young, in some when they are old ones. Always in each one it is there repeating, sometimes someone knows it in each one, sometimes someone will know it in every one that one is ever knowing."

Second page:

"One little boy does -
something to another little boy who does not like it, he shows no signs of reacting to it, the little boy who does not like it. He seems not to remember to be angr, or to have forgotten it, his eeaction is so slow to it. Then he hits out and after the first little boy is surprised at it. This often happens when one little boy does something to another little boy who does not like it."
"This is a nature in them when] repeat it with she, and then discuss its meanings and then
"This comes as introduction to the umbrella in the mud.
"Work it up that throw the umbrella in the mud might be an expression of dep. ind, or ind dep. like Martha Hersland."

Corresponds to Note #109

*

Ms Note #57 re [MA 378]

Third page verso in ms. for MA 378, and upside down: Planning Note for earlier section of MA:

"To-morrow why not the Weiman family again then go on to a full history of Madeleine from the beginning, her knowing Mrs. Hersland and her feeling about her gradually developing (lady etc) and then her family nagging and so on to Martha."

*

Ms Note #58 re [MA 384]

Following line 20:

"Bertha"

*

Ms Note #59 re [MA 415]

Following line 37:

"What she knew of the life around her."

*

Ms Note #60 re [MA 428] [Date: "Oct. 25, 1909"]

For dating:

The Ms draft text for MA 428, line 42 to 429, line 3. Text immediately preceding the inserted text from Fernhurst*—is written on verso of envelope addressed to "Monsieur Leo Stein / 27 Rue de Fleurus / Paris" and dated "25–10–09." A printed return address on envelope: "Envoi de G. Baranger Fils, Librairie / 5, Rue des Saints-Peres, Paris."*

*

Ms Note #61 re [MA 443]

Following line 20:

"Copy out of little book about virtue and religion and then go on about Hodder and Edstrom, and others."

Little book: NB3, #6, from which is copied MA 443, lines 30–43.

"then go on about Hodder and Edstom and others:"

Planning Note for MA 444, line 1 to 452, line 44, in which Hodder = Philip Redfern, and Edstrom = Lathrop, and then Johnson.

*

Ms Note #62 re [MA 444]

Following line 31:

"Copy again big book edstrom[?] etc. and then begin a long discussion of Edstrom, a long description of him."

The "copying" of the Note on Edstrom (about "forgetting his emotion… and so it must have been the other ones fault") begins on MA 446, line 9 and continues to line 42. The Note is recapped briefly on MA 447, lines 4–16. The "long discussion" in these lines merely paraphrases the original Note.

*

Ms Note #63 re [MA 445]

Following line 17:

"go on from here and copy to the end of 'he never ceased to fail."

*

Ms Note #64 re [MA 447]

Following line 38:

"To the ending of his living, he was true to the completest experience he had had in him."

"Commence to copy."

*

Ms Note #65 re [MA 461]

Following line 22:

"Go into morality of reaction and expediency[?] in personality to women honor[?]"

*

Ms Note #66 re [MA 464]

Following line 23:

"The type of sensitiveness in the three of them then what happened to each ending up with Martha."

*

Ms Note #67 re [MA 470]

Following line 28:

"(copy out of black book about hersland.)"

Copied and expanded text out of grey book [Note #73], in MA 470, line 34 to 471, line 18.

*

Ms Note #68 re [MA 477]

Beginning of Alfred Hersland chapter:

Epilogue.

~~Alfred Hersland~~

*

Ms Note #69 re [MA 477]

Following line 15:

"Repeat this putting virtue in place of distinction."

*

Ms Note #70 re [MA 477]

Following line 20:

"Perhaps begin again with this."

*

Ms Note #71 re [MA 480]

Preceding line 1:

Ms. text, quoted from MA 443, par. 4 and MA 444, par. 1; which in turn was copied from NB3, #6, with this note written above:

"repeat with different focus."

*

Ms Note #72 re [MA 480]

Following line 37:

"(Use before discussion of Mike's virtue:"

This is followed by draft of text for MA 480, line 38 to 481, line 14.

Then, an insertion in ink, following MA 481, line 39:

"Some do not know they have certainty in them. Some have it and do not know it until it is acting. Some even then are not certain that they have it in them. Some have it and lose it while they are speaking.

Use Bianco."

Draft of text, expanded in MA 481, line 18 to 482, line 14.

Michael Stein is the general paradigm for discussions of "concrete and general" virtue, beginning MA 486, line 38ff. Major discussion of Michael in relation to "concrete and general" virtue is in MA 489–493.

Corresponds to Note #112.

*

Ms Note #73 re [MA 482]

Following line 14:

"Leave out into book."

*

Ms Note #74 re [MA 482]

Following line 35:

"About the perfect joy of first recognition, if anybody else knows it, you cannot have it.

~~One can make a book they are writing a very queer~~

Paraphrased and enlarged on, in MA 485, lines 33–40.

*

Ms Note #75 re [MA 496]

Following line 12:

"For many it will be cheap. Saying g night [sic] religion, importance[?], virtues."

*

Ms Note #76 re [MA 506]

Following line 6:

"Sally"

*

Ms Note #77 re [MA 510]

Following line 18:

"St. Katherine, Mme Demarez, Mrs. Edstrom, Harriet."

*

Ms Note #78 re [MA 520]

Following line 21:

"Now just solidly describe Alfred Hersland as a boy and everything Bertha + A. Rosenshine + Sternberger + F. Jacobs, just begin."

*

Ms Note #79 re [MA 536]

On verso of sheet containing text for MA 536, par. 2, a note from Alice Toklas:

"We arrived here Thursday"

*

Ms Note #80 re [MA 536]

Following line 17:

"Whether they should have met Henrys at concert or theatre."

They already had, in MA 535, line 36.

*

Ms Note #81 re [MA 547]

Following line 4:

"Leo Friedman Purman et al."

*

Ms Note #82 re [MA 554]

Following line 18:

A long paragraph describing two men of the "resisting engulfing" kind is here omitted. The text, in ms. vol. 32, was set aside by Gallup, and so marked.

*

Ms Note #83 re [MA 559]

Following line 26:

~~"Some more about N."~~

*

Ms Note #84 re [MA 560]

Following line 31:

"Full story of Aunt F. & Leo."

> *Reference to Aunt Fanny in* ***lines 37–39****, who added things up by "one and one and one." See A. Toklas note on Aunt Fanny, in her comment on Note #32.*

*

Ms Note #85 re [MA 562]

Following line 7:

"Amiable intentions, gentle aspiration."

Following line 13:

"Amiable intentions, gentle aspiration."

> *Corresponds to NB-H, #6, #15*

*

Ms Note #86 re [MA 563]

Following line 18:

"Story of Weber Sally realizing herself, and both [later?] fight [word] with every one, Matisse picture, [two words] of Albert [Marquet]."

*

Ms Note #87 re [MA 564]

Following line 7:
"Use to begin Weber & Albert. Johnson thats just the way I do it and it comes simple why should you say it is complicated. Do you see."

*

Ms Note #88 re [MA 568]

Following line 39:
"Emotion of dominating by stern action."

*

Ms Note #89 re [MA 571]

Following line 11:
"Tell story of intuition. Intuition from timidity with men, hw she nearly received[?] a man who kind of hypnotised her. Intuition was so much more stupid than she, timidity and wanting to be attacking."

*

Ms Note #90 re [MA 571]

Verso of page of text for MA 571, par. 1, interspersed with draft of text for this paragraph:

"Gracie [Gassette]"

"Gracie's bragging, hitting in every direction the way a boy does when he has not learned swimming, or in fighting when fighting is not an attacking in him. her yogism, story of her intuition, liking to discipline. Mme. Matisse also, weary when alone with men, afraid in a way like I am."

*

Ms Note #91 re [MA 602]

Following line 39:
"Carrie., Etta Alice & me. Nina & Russell. Sterne and his ladies. Hersland and Julia Dehning."

*

Ms Note #92 re [MA 614]

Following line 14:
"Description of the Dehnings."

*

Ms Note #93 re [MA 617]

Following line 5:

"I hate my Aunt Pauline. Yes I do. I hate my Aunt Pauline."

Following line 29:

"I hate my Aunt Pauline."

Following line 41:

"I hate my Aunt Pauline."

*

Ms Note #94 re [MA 619]

Following line 6:

"Uncle Sol making money giving advice, ways of eating, not a very nervous but slightly sudden one.

make him like Fred."

*

Ms Note #95 re [MA 620]

Following line 16:

"Dehning family living, Julia Dehning. Playfulness and humor. Contrast between Bird & Fred, Sally and Mike. Sensitive and enthusiasm."

*

Ms Note #96 re [MA 621]

Following line 25:

"Describe family living. Julia Dehning. Tell about any social life to me—Alice."

*

Ms Note #97 re [MA 622]

Following line 33:

"Julia Dehning at home. All Dehnings. Loving and marrying and ambition."

*

Ms Note #98 re [MA 624]

Following line 6:

"Continue real description of Julia-Bird."

*

Ms Note #99 re [MA 626]

Following line 43:
"Tell the early and middle history this way once."

*

Ms Note #100 re [MA 632]

Following line 3:
"Go on now with the different kinds of sensitiveness. Edstrom, Hutch, Leo, Sally, Alice, Mary Berenson, Bird, Mrs. Perkins, Frank Jacott, Matisse, brother Mosey, Francis, typical cold American."

*

Ms Note #101 re [MA 637]

Following line 36:
"Dehning family living in a little more detail and then Julia & Alfreed together. General descriptions."

*

Ms Note #102 re [MA 638]

Following line 8:
"Dehning family living in a little more detail and then Julia & Alfred together, general descriptions."

*

Ms Note #103 re [MA 639]

Following line 7:
"Begin more description of Julia coming to know Alfred, what various ones thought of them and of this marriage."

*

Ms Note #104 re [MA 642]

Following line 30:
"The description of loving being in Julia Dehning & then in Alfred Hersland and the relation in Julia of her being loving to family living,—the loving being in Julia and the stupid being in her and the family living in her, and then more loving being in her."

*

Ms Note #105 re [MA 643]

Draft of text for MA. lines 35 and 36, with Roman numerals above and below text, as follows:

"This is to be now more description of

I IV III II

loving, and quarreling, and marrying, and family living."

II I III III II II I IV

*

Ms Note #106 re [MA 644]

Following line 7:

Draft of text for MA 644, lines 8–9:

"Julia and Alfred and Dehning family living and loving and learning and quarreling."

> *The passage immediately following this text is concurrent with NB-M, #17, in which the original entry specifying the names of the subjects being discussed is corrected to read "one" instead of the subjects' names. The passage is in MA 644, line 38 to 645, line 25.*

*

Ms Note #107 re [MA 644]

Opposite ***par. 2:***

"Julia and Alfred each one in daily living, aspiration, ambition, taste, feeling, moral being, quarreling, family living."

*

Ms Note #108 re [MA 648]

Following line 13:

"Describe whole question of honesty, Therese and B.B."

*

Ms Note #109 re [MA 648]

Note inserted into body of text, MA 648, lines 19–20:

Over the words "so terribly:"

"Me and Therese."

*

Ms Note #110 re [MA 657]

Following line 8:
~~"The marriage and coming hostilities and meeting young David."~~

Draft of text for lines 9 and 10:
"Loving being in each one of them, what mother and father and each one felt toward every other one just after the marrying. Some loving feeling then in each one of them."

*

Ms Note #111 re [MA 659]

Following line 25:
"Perhaps put it in"

refers to text below:
"Mrs. Dehning started in to get pride in son-in-law and daughtrer.
Mrs. Dehning having then " " " " " "
Hortense's pleasure, George's acquiescence. Julia knew she certainly was learning them anything."

*

Ms Note #112 re [MA 663]

Following line 11:
"Go one now about affairs and Bird and Pauline and young David and beginning smash and Alfred."

*

Ms Note #113 re [MA 663]

Following line 38:
"~~Trouble~~."

*

Ms Note #114 re [MA 664]

Following line 31:
"Election, others, Pat Moore Alfy Minnie Mason."

*

Ms Note #115 re [MA 665]

Following line 9:
"Roosevelt, Pat Moore, Minnie Mason, young David, Alfred in living, smash, and smash in Gossols. How the Dehnings felt and what they gradually did."

*

Ms Note #116 re [MA 667]

Following line 34:
"Julia & Alfred, Mrs. Dehning and all of them. Slow development of family feeling about it all."

*

Ms Note #117 re [MA 675]

Following line 4:
"Negroes, interest [or: intent?] in job, Sally et al, emotion real. Harriet experience not real, Nelly values not real, Mike experience and values real, emotion when carried on in direction of reality not lackng sense for living, even I[?] a married woman. Drops out of them they don't drop it, Sally."

*

Ms Note #118 re [MA 678]

Following line 30:
"I'd like to begin now. yes I would."

*

Ms Note #119 re [MS p.685]

Following line 25:
"Married living. Leo. Children needing handling for being living. Claribel, Hortense & Jakey, Sally Mikey, A. & me, Alfred & Julia."

*

Ms Note #120 re [MA 679]

Following line 36:
"Go on with sense for living. Give cases. everybody.

*

Ms Note #120a re [MA 684]

Following line 26:
"Married living. Leo, Georgiana wants everything to be in the world, not wanting anything but knowing that that is all in the world."

*

Ms Note #121 re [MA 686]

Following line 4:
"Go on now with this."

*

Ms Note #122 re [MA 687]

Following line 19:
"Pride

and then definition of egotism in relation to succeeding."

*

Ms Note #123 re [MA 689]

Following line 6:
"Detailed account of what happened to each one of them. Alfred & Julia."

*

Ms Note #124 re [MA 691]

Following line 35:
"More detail of Alfred's life. More detail of Julia's life. Go on with it."

*

Ms Note #125 re [MA 694]

Following line 22:
"Describe Pat Moore. Alfy."

*

Ms Note #126 re [MA 694]

Following line 27:
"Describe how Pat sounded and how he felt about the others and how he had his genius and how he was and wasn't a friend."

Corresponds to Note #124, an inclusive Planning Note which begins with this passage and anticipates the writing to the end of this chapter, MA 695–719.

*

Ms Note #127 re [MA 695]

Following line 19:

"Moore and hersland and Young and Flint & Minnie Mason and David Hersland."

*

Ms Note #128 re [MA 697]

Following line 27:

"Minnie Mason with each one and marrying."

*

Ms Note #129 re [MA 704]

Following line 24:

"Go on now, begin again with the list."

*

Ms Note #130 re [MA 708]

Following line 42:

"How Julia came to know each of them and so for now finish them and her up."

*

Ms Note #131 re [MA 709]

Following line 20:

"How Julia came to know each of them and so finish them and her up."

Used as draft of text for MA 708, lines 43–44.

*

Ms Note #132 re [MA 711]

Preceding line 1:

"Miriam., in relation to [Nina?] and go on with the others."

*

Ms Note #133 re [MA 714]

Following line 33:

"~~Go to bed sleepyhead~~"

*

Ms Note #134 re [MA 716]

Following line 3:

"Coming back again. Anything to say. Yes but I don't know what."

*

Ms Note #135 re [MA 717]

Following line 2:

"Finish up Alfred now."

*

Ms Note #136 re [MA 727]

On verso of sheet with text of MA 727, par. 1.

A doodle:

Drawing of a very tall figure in profile with an enormously protruding stomach embracing a very short figure with head turned forward and serene expression on features, and cheek resting on the profile of the protruding stomach. [AT and GS??]

*

Ms Note #137 re [MA 769]

Following line 31:

"Go on with the one explaining[?] regular but not [two words?] irregular teaching. Hersland was not like that, and then go on a little more about teaching and then go on to the end of teaching, and how some would have been ones learning if they had had teachers really knowing something. L. & food. Diet strictures."

*

Ms Note #138 re [MA 776]

Following line 23:

"Talk about living being in each one."

*

Ms Note #139 re [MA 782]

Following line 7:
"Francis Leo 22 [word?] Helene Pablo Nadel[man]."

*

Ms Note #140 re [MA 785]

Following line 6:
"Start with Leon and his thinking experiencing, meaning and telling, and tell about others."

*

Ms Note #141 re [MA 787]

Following line:25:
"Thinking, meaning, experiencing, boasting."

*

Ms Note #142 re [MA 788]

Used for text, MA 788, line 29–30.
"Thinking boasting, listening remembering forgetting, feeling, and meaning, and telling."

*

Ms Note #143 re [MA 790]

Opposite ***par. 1:***
"Feeling and thinking about ones [insert: about that one] being going on being living, thinking, boasting, listening, remembering, forgetting, feeling and meaning and telling.

Pach and Bruce"

*

Ms Note #144 re [MA 791]

Following line 25:
"David like Weininger in his experience in relation to his generalisation. Clarity of thought and feeling, L. clarity of thought but not of feeling. not of experiencing. David befogs clarity by desiring to have every woman [insert: in some ways] a beautiful one, some thinking of somethings to being completed

things, does not befog it but making anything a transparent thing."

*

Ms Note #145 re [MA 795]

Following line 7:

Eight doodles, and a rectangular hole cut into paper as though one of the doodles was removed. Followed by doodle-like text:

"Bless blessed blessing WENT TO TOWN RIDING ON A PONY Blessed BLESS BLESSING BLESS BLESSED BLESSING Blessing."

*

Ms Note #146 re [MA 797]

Following line 35:

"Youth."

*

Ms Note #147 re [MA 798]

Doodles accompanied by doodle-like printing and script:

"Youth YOUTH YOUTH
WHY DO SOME GET MORE TIRED RUNNING AROUND.
Some kind of ultimate
Magazine Story."

*

Ms Note #148 re [MA 801]

Following line 25:

"Camping, out of doors, shooting, feelings about such things.
HO FOR THE OPEN."

*

Ms Note #149 re [MA 806]

Following line 13:

"The way the boy jumped relation of Leon to that type of acting and fighting and self-consciousness, and entering into anything and impulsiveness & Leo, and Sayen."

*

Ms Note #150 re [MA 808]

Following line 12:

"Go on with youth and interests and activities. Sayen, etc. etc."

*

Ms Note #151 re [MA 814]

Following line 39:

Go on with how David Hersland was not one completely explaining or completely asking. Get him going."

*

Ms Note #152 re [MA 817]

Following line 43:

"Go on with young life and relation to others. Frank et al."

*

Ms Note #153 re [MA 818]

Following line 30:

Doodles, in doodle printing:

"ed yes I go to b I go to bed. Yes I go to bed. Do I go to b"

In an exaggeratedly soft, gentle hand:

"Beautiful is the day, yes, not the night, the night is not beautiful, it is nothing, yes it is nothing."
"Some are certain"

*

Ms Note #154 re [MA 821]

Preceding line 1:

"Leon & Arthur. Leon and girls."

*

Ms Note #155 re [MA 822]

Following line 11:

"Leon and Arthur and the crowd. Leon and girls."

*

Ms Note #156 re [MA 824]

Following line 3:

"Leon's relations with people when young etc. and how he took advice and how he never was intimate"

*

Ms Note #157 re [MA 826]

Following line 29:

"David Hersland as a boy
Arthur & sports and climbing and companionship."

Following line 31:

"David hersland as a boy:"

> *Planning Note for MA 836, line 3 to 837, line 2.*
>
> *Concurrent with Note #157, above the ms. text of the portrait of "Picasso." The Picasso portrait is consequently to be dated September-October 1911.*

*

Ms Note #158 re [MA 830]

Following line 43:

"Blessed! Bless Blessed Blessing."

*

Ms Note #159 re [MA 831]

Following line 412:

Doodle print:

"Yes I have been to Rome."

*

Ms Note #160 re [MA 831]

Following line 11:

"Leon & the crowd and Arthur.
" " his family."

Doodle print:

"My dear. A young man married is a young man marred. Yes.
oh yes."

This last, decorated with eight devices that look like inverted Christmas trees.

*

Ms Note #161 re [MA 836]

Following line 2:

"Leon philosophy, love & friends.
" & the crowd.
" & family.
" as small boy."

Doodle print:

"... No No I will will I"

*

Ms Note #162 re [MA 837]

Following line 2:

"Leon as small boy Camb. crowd, Arthur phil, love, friends, family, tramping, companionship"

Concurrent, and identical with, Long Gay Book Note #127.

*

Ms Note #163 re [MA 845]

Following line 8:

"Go on to his relations with people and in respect to changes in them."

*

Ms Note #164 re [MA 850]

Following line 4:

"Tell more about David's decisions."

*

Ms Note #165 re [MA 851]

Following line 28:

"Go on with youth, smells etc. eating etc. pairs, riding and marbles and games, and companions, his thinking"

Concurrent with and part of Note #125.

*

Ms Note #166 re [MA 853]

Verso of sheet with text for MA 853, par. 6:

"May. alight[?] ms.
Harriet. book
Mrs. Doge Villa Curonia Arciotri[?] Florence."

*

Ms Note #167 re [MA 855]

Following line 25:

"David & his companions."

*

Ms Note #168 re [MA 857]

Following line 22:

"Go on then. David & noises at different times
" " dullness
" " gentleness."

Doodle print:

"~~martyr to a literary effort."~~

Doodle script:

"~~Yes I have been to Rome yes I have yes I have, yes I have been to Rome.~~
Yes I have been to Rome."

*

Ms Note #169 re [MA 859]

Following line7:

written on inside of back cover of ms. volume

Doodle print:

"~~Men, women, Aeroplanes, Spades, Rock Horses~~."

Rest of entry crossed out and illegible.

*

Ms Note #170 re [MA 859]

Following line 2:

"dullness"

*

Ms Note #171 re [MA 859]

Written inside front cover of ms. volume:

Doodle print:
"Yes I have been to Rome"

*

Ms Note #172 re [MA 860]

Following line 26:
"Gentleness, school, judgment, L.C. Miss B. poetry material[or: unnatural?]."

*

Ms Note #173 re [MA 861]

Following line 31:

Doodle print on top of first page of ms volume:
"By a tuft of hair under each ear."

*

Ms Note #174 re [MA 862]

Following line 32:
"(go on to daily life and comrades and college mates and interests in him and by him and ladies and games.)"

*

Ms Note #175 re [MA 864]

Following line 36:
"Go on with daily life and companions. Loving and college. Women and decisions."

*

Ms Note #176 re [MA 865]

Following line 35:
"Go on with his life."

Doodle print:

"It is enough now take away my life for I am no better than my Fathers."

*

Ms Note #177 re [MA 867]

Following line 27:

"Describe love affairs, me, boys & men, Olga, Mabel Earle. Poetry, eating."

Corresponds to Note #52, which is a general planning note for MA 866 to end of chapter, MA 904.

*

Ms Note #178 re [MA 868]

Following line 36:

"Describe love affairs, me, boys and men, Olga, Mabel Earle, poetry, eating, thinking about N. how verifies details but does not question the implications, hair splitting—remembers the detail was wrong not the whole was right, different in art, not in phil. and eat."

*

Ms Note #179 re [MA 869]

Following line 2:

"Go on to his love affairs and comrades and Olga and me."

*

Ms Note #180 re [MA 869]

Following line 41:

"Go on with out of doors and friends and funny[?] feelings, olive trees and Cambridge and Leon's and Mabel in his efforts to enter into [word?] and how it was always a little artificial."

*

Ms Note #181 re [MA 872]

Following line 16:

"Go on with love affairs. Mabel & me, Olga."

*

Ms Note #182 re [MA 872]

Following line 29:

"Go on with rizzling[?] and relation to the crowd as to enjoyment and Mabel etc. Melodrama me. the end of that crowd life and then that Olga."

*

Ms Note #183 re [MA 872]

Following line 37:

"Go [on] with his love affairs Mabel me & Olga, and his friends and not friends, and Alfred's brother-in-law Fred Stein, and his intellectual development Julia Can't do anything with her. Can do something more with him. Cannot do anything more with her. Can do something more with him."

*

Ms Note #184 re [MA 873]

Following line 36:

"Go on with advice get it more definite"

*

Ms Note #185 re [MA 874]

Following line 38:

"Go on with love affairs and [work?] and friends and Fred Stein."

Doodle print:

"N o u g h said"

*

Ms Note #186 re [MA 877]

Following line 32:

"Go on with education and love affairs and [wondering?] and Olga & Arthur, & Fred, and Mabel & me & the rest. Francis et al and then the break of it all and active life and then solitary teaching with the young and then death."

*

Ms Note #187 re [MA 884]

Following line 18:

"Go on to his love affairs, relation to Alfred's family separation his attitude, attitude to his own family job in the East, love[?] and food and normal[?] life and death and defeat and possible chance and death and end and end."

*

Ms Note #188 re [MA 886]

Following line 5:

"Go on with relation to Julia etc and sadness of failing to understand and of conflict and of coming close together understanding and then it is as it was."

*

Ms Note #189 re [MA 887]

Following line 23:
"Indian walk[?] effect[?] in his relations."

*

Ms Note #190 re [MA 888]

Following line 19:
"Make new[?] friends[?] just his quality and his relation to Alfred George & Julia and old Mr. Dehning & Mrs. Dehning."

*

Ms Note #191 re [MA 889]

Corresponds in substance to Note #125, written for MA 851.

Following line 14:
"Get the relation of clear thinking and giving advice strongly enough and not completely clearly thinking in relation to Julia & George and Alfred, relation of going to be doing some other thing in relation to them not their doing some other thing, going to be a different way in being one being living to himself inside him Then being one eating some one thing, completely eating, completely not eating some one thing."

*

Ms Note #192 re [MA 891]

Following line 14:
"Leon Solomons. He could walk well."

*

Ms Note #193 re [MA 891]

Following line 42:
"Describe what he did influence, talk, work, and defeat & work, and family troubles and death."

*

Ms Note #194 re [MA 893]

Following line 27:

"Leon & Bird,
Needing something."

*

Ms Note #195 re [MA 894]

Following line 41:

"Go on with relation to Dehnings."

*

Ms Note #196 re [MA 895]

Following line 22:

"Clairvoyance eating. Mind."

*

Ms Note #197 re [MA 897]

Following line 8:

"How Bird knew him and told him. Go into the
George knew him " " " ganze megillah.
Hortense " " " " "

*

Ms Note #198 re [MA 897]

Following line 35:

"Go on with relation to Julia."

*

Ms Note #199 re [MA 898]

Following line 15:

"Go on with relation to Julia."

*

Ms Note #200 re [MA 899]

Following line 14:

"Go on with David's career & Julia."

*

Ms Note #201 re [MA 899]

Following line 35:
"He was not completely forgetting. Make definite his character, his relation to his family, to ideas, to religion, to passion, to beauty, [to work, to morality, to sadness,] to death, to success, to friends and loneliness to success to death and then make him dead. Finis."

*

Ms Note #202 re [MA 901]

Following line 22:
"His being different from any other one."

*

Ms Note #203 re [MA 903]

From "Epilogue." Only one draft of "Epilogue" is extant, consisting of 345 numbered pages. ***Epilogue ms, p. 15****, draft of text from MA 908, line 7ff.*

Top of ***p. 15*** *is sliced off, and remainder of a "doodle" note ends:*
"Yes Yes Yes Yes" etc and 23 "No"s printed on top of page.
Concurrent with Notes #55 and #120.

*

Ms Note #204 re [MA 910]

Epilogue ms, p. 60.

Following line 34:

An inserted note in ink, apparently testing a new pen:
"Yes I have been to Rome. Yes I have been to Rome. Yes. Yes Yes. No I don't like this pen. I like the other one. I certainly do like the other one."

*

Ms Note #205 re [MA 914]

Epilogue ms, p. 135

Following line 32:
"Singing to me singing to me. The cuckoo bird is singing in the cuckoo tree singing to me oh singing to me.
Come firefly and light up baby's nose.
All I know[?] of a certain she[?] Io sono qui Io sono qui Io sono solo Io sono

aqui."

Song appears in A Lyrical Opera Made By Two, *published in* Operas and Plays.

*

Ms Note #206 re [MA 916]

Epilogue ms, p. 160

Following line 6:

"This is no time to go to bed. No. Yes."

*

Ms Note #207 re [MA 917]

Corresponds to Note #126, which is repeated in part and in substance in Ms Notes #208, 209, 210, 213, 214, 215, 216, 217, 218.

Epilogue ms, p. 186

Following line 19:

"Edstroms, don't know what will happen, don't understand other ones, don't know what they will do, duty and how it is felt and done."

*

Ms Note #208 re [MA 918]

Epilogue ms, p. 201

Following line 12:

"Edstroms, don't understand others A.& N. don't know what the[y] will do M. & S. Duty and how it is felt and done. Fred and Amy & his pa & ma and sisters[?]."

"W h y s h o u l d t h e s p i r i t o f m"

"All story-books will do cause all of them are true."

*

Ms Note #209 re [MA 919]

Epilogue ms, p. 220

Following line 17:

"Edstroms, Don't understand others A. & N. Mabel Dodge & Constan[c]e etc etc. Duty and how it is felt and done. Fred & Amy & his pa & his ma."

*

Ms Note #210 re [MA 920]

Epilogue ms, p. 231

Following line 2:

"Don't understand others. A & N., Mabel & Constance, L & any one, Duty and how it is felt and done. Fred and Amy & his pa his ma."

*

Ms Note #211 re [MA 920]

Epilogue ms, p. 232

Within line 5, following: "it is done again:"

"Edstrom & Mrs.

He was interested in eating. He was a very fat one."

LK "David and Mrs." is the title of Edstrom portrait in GS original MS for portrait. Note #150 covers notes for this portrait, dated c. Pre-Sept 1911

*

Ms Note #212 re [MA 920]

Epilogue ms, p. 243

Following line 27:

A sort of decoration at the top of the page, written alternately in pencil and ink. The inked text is here underlined, but not in ms. A doodle print, probably GS's rather than AT's:

"Yes. Yes. Y Yes. Y Yes Y My Y dearest Y is Y all Y my Y love. Y Y Y"

"Duty and how it is felt and done."

*

Ms Note #213 re [MA 920]

Epilogue ms, p. 244

Following "done by some one" in line 3:

"Don't understand others A. & N. Mabel & Constance. Le[sic] and another one. Duty and how it is felt and done. Fred and Amy and his pa and ma."

*

Ms Note #214 re [MA 921]

Epilogue ms, p. 256

Following line 13:

"Don't understand others A & N. Mabel & Constance. B.B. & Ollie & B. Mosey & ~~Fred~~ family. Duty and how it is felt and done. Fred & Amy & his pa & his ma."

*

Ms Note #215 re [MA 922]

Epilogue ms, p. 270

Preceding line 1:

"Don't understand others. A & N. Mabel & Constance B.B. & Ollie & B. Mosey & family. Duty and how it is felt and done. Fred & Amy & his pa & his ma."

*

Ms Note #216 re [MA 922]

Epilogue ms, p. 278

Following line 18:

"Don't understand [insert: others] A. & N. Mabel & Constance B.B. & Ollie & B. Mosey & families. Duty and how it is felt and done. Fred and Amy & his pa and ma. All [sic] ones and how they come to be dead."

*

Ms Note #217 re [MA 923]

Epilogue ms, p. 289

Following line 4:

"Don't understand others. A, & N. Mabel & Constance B.B. & Ollie & B. Mosey and families. Duty and how it is felt and done. Fred & Amy & his pa & his ma. Old ones and how they come to be dead."

*

Ms Note #218 re [MA 923]

Epilogue ms, p. 305

Following line 38:

"Don't understand others. A & N. Mabel & Constance. B.B. & Ollie & B.

Mosey and families. Duty and how it is felt and done. Fred Amy & his pa & his ma. Old ones and how they come to be dead."

***

D. *The Making of Americans*. A Page-by-Page Summary

The following page-by-page summary of *The Making of Americans* provides, in addition to a precis of its narrative, a detailed record of the System's development. Concurrently, it underscores Gertrude's running confessional to the reader of her own responses to her text as it is being composed.

*

Chapter One (Part One)
The Dehnings and The Herslands

Introductory

MA 3–6 As Stein planned it, the novel was to recount the story of three generations—her grandfathers', her father's and "our own" in order that we may "know ourselves." But this did not become articulated as its intention until its third draft, which was begun in 1908. And before that draft was completed, in 1911, the novel's intention was to alter again, and in fact several times over. But none of these several intentions were altogether obliterated; all are in evidence to some degree and for some stretch of pages. But through all these overlays of focus, style and direction, what was most lost to the reader's glancing eye was the tale that was to be told.

The first 78 pages of the novel are a mix of her first (1902–3) and second (1906–1908) draft texts which anticipate little more than a tale of two sisters and their unhappy marriages: Julia Dehning's and her sister Hortense's. bounder, a man who has the gall to marry her with the secret desire of getting her father's solidly respectable name to cover for his shady dealings in the stock market. And that story is based on the lurid tale of Stein's New York cousin Bird Stein (the "Eastern" family of the novel) and her marriage and scandalous divorce to a Lucius Sternberger. The case dragged through the New York courts and the New York newspapers for several years and involved not only wrangles over money but over the custody of their two children. And Stein during all that time was close to Bird, was her cultural mentor, in fact, for which Bird, a not remarkably gifted intelligence, showered Gertrude with gratitude and love. Until the fateful day came, in 1906, when both Gertrude and her brother Leo turned with epistolary violence on Bird as well as her lawyer and friend, Howard Gans, (the Notebooks have scraps of the drafts of Gertrude's letters to Bird from Paris to New York, and reveal a level of vituperation that suggests residues of resentment on Gertrude's part that her "influence" over Bird was displaced and forgotten, now that the trials were over, and Bird was set to marry her lawyer, Howard Gans.) So the New York Steins became the novel's Dehning family, and Gertrude's Uncle Solomon (her father's very successful brother) became Herman (or Henry) Dehning, and Aunt Pauline (who disliked Gertrude because she was never clean and whom Gertrude detested for her bourgeois vulgarity) became Jenny Dehning ("whom one might like better the more one saw her less.")

THE DEHNING FAMILY

6 Henry Dehning's father—his speech
7 Henry Dehning [= GS's Uncle Sol]
8 Henry Dehning's speech— "Yes, I say to you children…"
9 Jenny Dehning [= GS's Aunt Pauline]
10 Adolph [= Meyer Stein] Sol and his trip to America [see Meyer Stein obit]
11–12 Parents of Jenny Dehning
14 Julia Dehning—description
15 George Dehning—description
15 Washing
16–17 George and Hortense Dehning—description
18 "Dependent loyal upgazing sweetness" in Hortense
18 "Heroical sweetness" in Julia

The ambition of these early pages is clearly moderate, and very much under the influence of the English novels Gertrude had been devouring for years. Many more pages of this story were written—the final version carries only the episode of Julia's loving contest with her father over her choice of husband, which she wins, and the very "culturine" (a California word for the horrors of bourgeois cultural aspirations) preparations for her marriage and her new home. What happened to those pages? They're gone—torn out of the copybook in which the second draft was written—but they represent the writing of two years, from 1906 to 1908, and how much of that thrown-away writing was folded into the final version we'll never know.

JULIA'S MARRIAGE

19 Julia & preparations for marriage
19 Julia & "passionate tempers" and their disillusion
20 Julia's youth and experience with Jameson
21 Alfred Hersland—& "singularity"
21 ***GS to Reader:*** "Brother Singulars… we fly to… an older world"
21 "The Herslands were a Western family"

22 Art & Julia & "The spare American imagination"
23 Julia's campaign with her father
26 "RESISTANCE FIGHTING" in Julia
28 The Dehning home—description: "Good solid riches"
29 Story-books and teaching the young
30 Julia's marriage and her new home
31 The new home: "the simple line and burlap"
31 "The spare American emotion" & dull furniture and interiors

Possibly the introductory pages on the "Western" family, the Herslands (MA 33–78) were culled from those lost pages. Only possibly, because the quality and focus of the writing of these pages is light years from the clumsy prose of those first pages on the Dehnings. The Herslands are of course her own family, and the three children, Alfred, Martha and David, are pulled out of Michael (her oldest brother), Martha (herself plus her older sister Bertha) and Leo. But much was added to these three fictional characters from other friends, other relations. Alfred, for example, was compounded of Bird's first husband Lucius Sternberger as the suitor and then husband of Julia as well as brother Michael, and several others enter into fictional Alfred, who becomes in the final version so complex and difficult a character to pin down that Gertrude's confessed failure to encompass him becomes one of the most significant developments in the novel, largely responsible for Gertrude's abandonment of her later, carefully constructed, monumental characterology. And David is of course her brother Leo, but more importantly, he is drawn from Stein's most admired friend at college, her collaborator and almost lover, Leon Solomons as well as, and significantly, herself.

THE HERSLAND FAMILY

33 Beginning of Mr and Mrs Hersland chapter
33–34 ***GS to Reader:*** "Bear it in your mind my reader… not an ordinary novel"; story of "a decent family progress"
34 ***GS to Reader:*** "Middle class middle class" paean
34 [recap] "Herslands were a western family"
34 David Hersland, the father—introduction
35 Gossols—introduced
35 Martha after her divorce (mentioned)
35 The ten-acre place in Gossols—description: "generous sweating" etc.
36 Leo—who died a glutton

(Pages 36–70) Some of the most magnificent prose in the novel is contained in these pages—the description of the journey of the family out of Germany to America, the incredibly beautiful description of old man Hissen's death ("it was a great death that met him… and so he, dying of old age, without struggling, met himself by himself in his dying… he was all one, living, dying, being, and religion.")

THE HERSLAND GRANDPARENTS

36 Grandmother Martha (father David's mother)— "back straight, flat and firmly supporting"
37–41 The movement from Germany to America
37 Grandfather David—introduced
42 [recap] Leo died a glutton—his children's fate
42 2nd generation: five Hersland children—three daughters, two sons.
42 Grandfather David—description
42 His "IMPORTANT FEELING IN RELIGION"
42 ***GS to Reader:*** The father "we must soon be realizing so that we can understand our own being"
43 Grandfather David's "not strong to keep going"
43 Fanny Hissen—introduced
43 the sister of David Hersland—mentioned
43 Fanny Hissen's mother—the "gentle little hopeless one… trickling" tears
44 GS QUOTE: "Solomon said of laughter" in re: Fanny's mother.

Mr. Hersland is plainly a portrait of Stein's father, his idiosyncrasies detailed almost anecdotally—but this description of her father turns out to be the novel's farewell to novelistic descriptive convention. A new strategy is suggested, not yet fully evident, in these pages—the strategy of defining "character" by its relation to itself—that is, "the feeling of oneself to oneself inside him." And this is the tentative beginning of Stein's "layering" in character analysis.

MR, DAVID HERSLAND, THE FATHER

45 Mother Fanny H— "not important to her children"
45 Father David H—and "pounding on the table"
45 The children "growing up to be strong… and free"
46 The children's battle against the Father
46 David H and education of his children
47 The ten-acre place—description
47 Young David and "what life meant to him to make it worth his living"
47 Alfred H: the "singularity to be free" left to him— "a poor thing but our own"
47 ***GS to Reader:*** [recap] "Brother Singulars"
48 David H "hardening" his children—his queer ways—the children "a little

	ashamed of him"
49	[recap and expands] David H description as above—and his "queer ways"
49–51	David H "in the street in his walking" and the cake shop incident
51	David H "AS BIG AS ALL THE WORLD AROUND HIM" introduced
52	[recap and expands] David H and his ways of educating his children

MRS. FANNY HERSLAND, THE MOTHER

53	Fanny H—full description
53	"a little temper in her… power with servants and governesses" etc.
54–55	"the pride in her"— "cut off from rich living"—visiting her rich family
56	THE SHILLINGS: Sophie, Pauline, & Fanny's "first important feeling" re: them.
56	Fanny H—[recap] of "hurt… angry… stubborn feeling"
57	THE HISSENS (Fanny's family)— "joyful—gentle pride—no important feeling of themselves"
58	The Hissen mother, and her "dreary trickling"
58	The Hissen father, and his "importance in religion"
58–59	The Hissen people—description
59–61	Old Hissen (father)—his children "shut up" with him—later, when they were gone, had his religion, and a tolerating spirit
61–62	Children asking him to leave when married—tells them the story of the "priest:", which ends, "I did not do any asking."
63	Hissen's "GREAT DEATH:"— "met himself by himself" in his dying.
64	The eldest Hissen daughter "gloomy and hard" in her religion.
64	[recap] Fanny Hersland and the Shillings
65–66	The Hissen stubborn feeling—other Hissens [end of Hissen analysis]
66	David Hersland and Fanny Hissen marriage—arranged by his sister.
67	[recap] The Hersland children's pre-history— "how they made us"
68	The later history of Alfred and David Hersland: when they were with the Hissens in Bridgepoint [summary]
68–69	In American teaching, "marrying is just loving" [extensive description]

(Pages 70–77) In the Spring of 1908, Gertrude initiated an almost completely new take on the novel, threw away the (1906–08) two years of writing, and holding on to only a few pages of it, started anew. "Begin this new thing," she writes in her Notebooks. The question is—why? and at what?

The "new thing" was a major break with the tradition of narrative writing and the description of "character." A concept is beginning to form in these pages that divorces narrative from the linear progression, of regular storytelling, and substitutes for it a different relation to the matter of the story being told. What's that relation? It's this: the story, from beginning to end, is present and so to speak simultaneously visible, and the narrator is free to dart from one part of it to another in the freedom of knowing that it's all there, already existing—not coming into being—its dimensions already circumscribed in the narrator's mind and imagination, all parts of it already fixed, all parts equally present and equally available for a moment's "viewing." But the "parts" of the tale, if not coming to light in a temporal sequence, are not understood to be free of temporal sequence. Much of the "narration" in the novel is, so to speak, "sign-posting," pointing, mentioning later moments in the tale and underscoring their place in the sequence, pointing to their position in the chronology, reminding the reader again and again of how the temporal "parts" of the story fit into that chronological sequence. But the narrator is relatively free of it—not chained to the progression of the story's narrative links.

That freedom has, and had for Stein, immeasurable consequence. It changed the shape, even the purpose and meaning, of narrative. The narrative becomes merely the ground for a deeply personal discursiveness, one that, though tied somewhat to the necessity of limning all the parts of the tale (a tale now more implicit than explicit, more template than primary matter,) is off on correlative intellectual adventures. They have to do with narrative, but they are not, as we commonly understand the purposes of narrative, narrative. What do they do instead? They explore the rationale, the ground, of narrative, its justification, its possibility as a thing that can be known.

Two things must be understood: one, that Stein's story was in fact already told—in those thrown away drafts—so it was for her in fact actually already an object—or as she was to call that kind of thing later on, a uniformly visible "landscape." And two, for Stein, the ground of narrative was the total realization of "characters." But this in a radical sense. The "knowing" of character entailed for her—what Otto Weininger, whom she was reading just then with powerful enthusiasm, called it—knowing "the last touch of human being." Of course, the absolute consonance of author with character's subjectivity is no novel ambition in the writing of novels. But the approach to seizing on, and learning to be at one with, a character's subjectivity, is in Stein distinctly novel. It entailed the absolute oneness with the inside, and at the same time the almost god-like positioning of the character within a universal schema of characterology on the outside. That was the ambition formulating at this time [during the writing of pp. 70–77], and just before, and forever after—at least until the late 1910's, during the writing of the Alfred Hersland chapter, when the endeavor finally overwhelmed her, and she acknowledged not only defeat, but because of defeat, a sort of personal dying. How she began the building of this schema from these first pages on, and what it was in its several transformations, I'll put into a separate document to be called, oddly, The Schema. From it, you'll be able to follow the rest of this summary-cum-index, and I believe the strategy and the coherence of the novel will become very clear. So—no more of these bold-faced interlinear paragraphs.

70–77	DAVID HERSLAND'S SISTER WHO ARRANGES MARRIAGE [In the notebooks, "Begin this new thing... Mrs. Matisse and Mrs. Rosenshine"]
77	[recap] Fanny Hersland—her marriage—her three children
77–85	THE SHILLINGS—EXTENDED DESCRIPTION
78	Flabby Mrs. Shilling, fat Sophie and slimmer Pauline
78	Their queerness—a "hole" in them
78	Mrs. Shilling: big dough, empty head, a baby head.
78	"LIKE MILLIONS OF THEM" [first used here]
79	Sophie: "many millions like her."
79	Fat and thin sisters—their unprotected surface
80	Mrs. Hersland meets the Shillings—her relation to each of them
81	"MANY MILLIONS" of each kind— [early formulation]
85	[recap] The Herslands in Gossols—no other rich people near them
85	Mr Hersland, "big as all the world in his beginning"
86	His loving his wife—she, "a flower to him"
86	His way of needing a woman to content him
86	"Herman Dehning" [renamed; earlier, was "Henry Dehning"]
86	Three strong men who needed "women to content them:" David Hersland, Herman Dehning and David's sister's husband.
86–87	David Hersland and the kind of woman he needed to content him
87	David Hersland and his need to fight with men
87–88	David Hersland and his relation to his wife: "a flower but mostly a woman"
88–89	Summary of David Hersland's later life, when Mrs. Hersland was dead [never detailed in the later pages of the novel]
89	David Hersland with rich business men, but Mrs. Hersland with no rich people living near her
90	The Herslands and their neighbors' "poor queer kind of living"
90	Mr. Hersland's impatient feeling when his troubles were beginning
90	Gossols—the ten-acre place and the children's joyous living [recapped]
90	The three Hersland children's opposition to their father
91	Mrs Hersland, and her visits to rich people

91	The children visiting the rich people with Mrs Hersland, and hating it
92–93	Gossols -The children's and Mrs. Hersland's "half-country, half-city living" 92–93 Mrs. Hersland as the mistress of governesses, servants, etc.
94–95	Mrs. Hersland and the children's half-country, half-city living [recapped]

THE FAMILIES NEAR THE HERSLANDS IN GOSSOLS

95–96	The families near the Herslands, and their mysterious ways of earning a living
96–97	Their daily living, eating, sleeping, etc.
97	They were "queer, but good enough"
98	First family description: the mother and three daughters—Anna, Cora and Bertha and their father, who worked all day.

FEELING OF "EXISTENCE"

98	Mr. Hersland's greeting of the father gave him the "feeling of real existence"
99	Men who have no "feeling of existence" except with other men
99	The mother of the family, and her "wooden" face
100	For the Hersland children, this mother had character, and existence

"IMPORTANT" FEELING

100	But she had no feeling of "past, present or future", and no "feeling of importance"
100–101	The mother and the children had no "history", and no changes—just repeating
102–103	Anna, the eldest, grew up beautiful. A change not expected, but carried for the family no surprise.
104	Anna had less "existence" but more "importance" than her mother
104–105	Cora had less existence, but more importance than her mother
104	The existence and importance in the mother and father
105	The slower changes in Cora, her uncertain feeling. Not "solid"
105–106	Bertha had less existence, but more than the father. Slow changes, felt little alive inside her, and got no feeling of importance from those around her.
106–107	This family, recapped.
108	The families near the Herslands [recapped]; each different in living, in earning a living, in religion, etc.
108	THE RICHARDSONS [Second family]; Father, and Eddy and Lily; the father ill from smoking; the family's uncertainties; their ways of having importance in religion
109	All three had importance in religion; it was a part of them, like eating.
109	The ways of having importance in religion
110–112	Religion kept Richardson continuous and existing

111	About washing. The meanings of eating and sleeping re: religion.
112–115	The families near the Herslands [recapped], and the three Hersland children
113	The three Hersland children becoming "more entirely of" the people near them
113	The later history of the children [recapped, summarized]; Their mother "lost among them" and scared.
113	Mrs. Hersland's later life, and her death [anticipated, summarized]
113	Mrs. Hersland and the children and the Shillers [recapped]
115–160	MR HERSLAND AND THE EXTENDED ANALYSIS OF MEN
115	Begins analysis of Mr. Hersland, and the repeated refrain:

THERE ARE MANY KINDS OF MEN

115–117	KINDS: "each repeating" themselves, and "many millions like them"—"knowing all the kinds"
115	INDIVIDUAL FEELING in some kinds, not in others
116	***GS to Reader:*** kinds are becoming clearer and clearer
116	The mixing of kinds
116	"Individual being" makes it seem that one is not like millions of others [an illusion]
117	One kind: feels "as big as all the world around him" in his beginnings, but then "shrinks" from his outside. But he keeps up till the end [and variations of the type]
117	Mr. Hersland is always so in his beginnings, until he is old
118	Mr. Hersland and his children's fear of him, which they lose as they grow up
119	But "beginning was all of living to him"; and his ways of educating, doctoring, eating
120	For many, the meaning of eating is: "EATING IS DYING"
120	Mr. Hersland and eating, and "filling up everything around him"
121	His "big ways," in some of his ways, "Arabian Nights." [i.e., his sexuality]
122–123	[Recapped:] His eating, doctoring, education
123	Martha was like him, Alfred was not. David "had another kind of bigness."
124–125	[recapped] His nature came out "every minute in his living" with his wife and children
125–127	The ten-acre place and the children: their schooling, and the differences in their feelings toward their father: variously lonely, scared, angry, troubled, etc.
128	"REPEATING" in the children

PRIDE

128	Different kinds of Pride;

Pride and the children:
Their education; the many kinds of teaching their father gave them [school, governesses, at home, etc.]

NATURES MIXED WITH FUNDAMENTAL NATURES

129 The children's natures mixed up with their fundamental natures
129 The children's doctoring, castor oil, the Chinese doctor, the queer blind man.
129 Playing cards with their father—begins with them, then says, "Finish up"

MRS HERSLAND RECAP:

130–133 Her "important feeling"; her half-country, half-city living; Mrs. Hersland and the poor people around her; her relation to her dependents [servants, governesses, etc.]
133–134 Madeleine Wyman [first mention], and relation to Mrs. Hersland
134 Mrs. Hersland's visit to her family in Bridgepoint
135 [recapped] the three children's fear of the father—the sons standing up to him
136 [recapped] Mr. Hersland later in life "needed a woman to fill him"

KINDS OF MEN

136 Mr. Hersland as example [recap]
136 The "mixtures" of kinds—differences in individuals—quality of kinds

BOTTOM LEVEL

136 Bottom is the strongest level
137 "Each one" = bottom + quantity of bottom + mixtures of other kinds (on top)
137–138 [recap of] the "big beginning" kind and the "mixture" in Mr. Hersland (extended analysis of him)—and, later in life, his developing "irritation"

REPEATING

139 In men, after middle living, it settles, and "repeating is clearer"
139 In women, not as much. In babies, not very much, and can't show it
140 Mr Hersland—his mixture—in middle living, he's still not clear. To the "poor people," he was a "queer man" in middle living
141 In both men and women, the variations and differences in their repeating
142–143 Mr. Hersland and the men working with him and their understanding of him—and his children—and the business men, who were afraid of him—and his blustering, his pushing people away, his fighting
144–148 [Lengthy recap] of Mr. Hersland
148 Summary of above recap
149 TEXT: "A man in his living has many things inside him"—re: his bottom nature, his mixtures, etc.

149 TEXT: "The feeling of himself to himself" (and variations of this)

CHAPTER ONE (PART TWO)
MRS. HERSLAND AND THE SERVANTS

[THE STRUCTURE OF PERSONALITY: FIRST FULL EXPOSITION]

150 TEXT: "A man in his living has many things inside him:" to wit: feeling himself to himself, way of beginning, ending, working, loving, having anger, eating, drinking, doctoring, sleeping, fighting, fearing, believing, being important inside, showing his importance to others. Some of these are stronger than others, but all are always there.

BOTTOM; TOP

151 "Bottom"— "Mixture"—"Top"—"Unmixed top or tops" (and Mr. Herland)

152 "Mixtures" (varieties)

FLAVOR

152 Bottom and "flavor"

153 Bottom and Mixing (varieties) [extended exposition]

153 "Feeling themselves to themselves"—and as conscious feeling (varieties)

LOVING [AS FUNDAMENTALLY ATTACKING AND RESISTING]

154 "Loving" as attacking, as wallowing, as melting, as resisting, etc.

SEXUAL BASIS CLEARER IN MEN

154 Kinds of ways of having loving—some from the bottom nature—some not from the bottom nature

155–157 Mr. Hersland's "loving"—the mixture in him—his wife "outside" of him—his middle living [recapped]—his "individual feeling" [recapped]

157 "Important feeling" in men and women—their ways of having it

157 Mr. Hersland's "individual feeling"—his "splitting himself to himself" because of his children

"SALE" [OR, "DIRTY" SEXUALITY]

158 For some, the "grimy little dirt" in loving— [recap of attacking, etc.]—and Mr. Hersland's loving—his wife—later in life, needed "filling" [recapped]

159 Mr. Hersland in family living—as husband, father, etc. [recapped]

159 [Transition to] Mrs. Hersland—as wife, mother, mistress of servants.

MRS. HERSLAND AND BEING LONESOME

160 Being lonesome—and escaping lonesomeness in men and women

161 Being lonesome and the feeling of reaching "the last end of a bad thing"—and ways of losing it

162 Mrs. Hersland's mother's "dreary trickling" [recapped]

162 Mrs. Hersland and her small "important feeling" and her lonesomeness

WOMEN AND "WAYS OF HAVING LOVING"

162 Women and ways of having loving—and Mrs. Hersland's loving [recapped]

DEPENDENT INDEPENDENT AND INDEPENDENT DEPENDENT

163 Two basic types of women's loving: (their "bottom nature")

Type I: Those who love those who need them (The other one's love gives them "strength in domination")

Type I: Those who love the one they need (they "subdue the one they need for loving" and "own" them)

165 Dependent independence = "those who own the ones they need to love them"

Independent dependence = "those who love only those who need them" from which they derive "strength in domination."

165 Mrs. Hersland = dependent independent

166 Mrs. Hersland—her important feeling, her resisting, etc. [recapped]

RESISTING

166 Women and kinds of resisting—patient resisting, concentrated, attacking, etc.

167 Women and religion. Mrs. Hersland and religion.

167 Women's "aggressive optimism", —do not feel they reach "the last end of a bad thing"

168 Madeleine Wyman, dependent independent

168 [Bridge to Servants:] Mrs. Hersland's 3 governesses, her seamstresses

SERVANT QUEERNESS AND LONESOMENESS

169 Servant queerness and lonesomeness

RESISTING AND ATTACKING

169 Mrs. Hersland and subduing those who need her

169–170 Independent Dependent and Dependent Independent [recap and expanded]

170 Servant queerness from lonesome living [recap]

171 German women servants—no queerness; Mrs. Hersland and German servants

SERVANT GIRL NATURE

172 First servant's history—had "servant girl nature"

173 Servant girl nature = no attacking, no ind dep. Mrs. Hersland and servant girl nature. But some servant girls were ind dep.

CHILDISH NATURE

174 Childish nature—mostly men

SCHOOL GIRL NATURE

174 "grimy little girl"— "just before adolescence"— "School girl nature" (See NB-A #7 on "Emily [Dawson]'s dancing steps")

[GS' EXPANDED SCOPE FOR BOOK—FIRST MENTIONED HERE]

175 ***GS to Reader:*** Book will be "a history of everyone who was or is or will be living"

175 First servant

176 Second servant: cook, foreign, dep ind, servant girl nature

176–177 "Servant girl nature" variants and elaboration

PAIRS IN LOVING [CF. WEININGER]

178 ***GS to Reader:*** Problem with words: Hard to "describe" with words, since some words "describe all of them," the dep ind, and the ind dep as well.

178 Dep ind and ind dep always "pair off"

IMPATIENT FEELING

178 ***GS to Reader:*** "Sometime there will be a history of every kind of impatient feeling"

179 Servants and impatient feeling. Mrs. Hersland and living with servants.

179 "Sometime, a history of everyone" [recap]

"LAST TOUCH OF BEING" [CF. WEININGER]

180 The "last touch of being" that a history can give everyone.

180 And all the ways kinds are connected—dep ind and ind dep [recap]

181 Mrs. Hersland and living with servants, and training them

181 Mrs. Hersland and injured and angry feeling[recap]

181 "sometime a history of everyone" [recap]

182 Living on the Ten-acre place—the three children—relation to everyone [recap]

SERVANT TYPES: SERVANT—SERVANT GIRL—SERVANT MISTRESS—MISTRESS SERVANT

182 The servant types

183 ***GS to Reader:*** A history of everyone—listening to the repeating of each one's bottom nature—feeling the *whole* of each one by looking hard and slowly—and so every history must be a long one.

184–185 ***GS to Reader:*** [Her anxiety] Anxious feeling about the whole of living, and about kinds. Historical curiosity.

186 [recap] Servant queerness—impatient and anxious feeling

186 [recap] In repeating, the whole of one comes out

187 One servant girl—her submission. Left employ to take care of a sick

	brother.
187	[recap] Servants and dep ind and ind dep
187	Mrs. Hersland and training servants and her important feeling
188	Mrs. Hersland and her trouble with servants' families—her injured and angry feeling

SENSE OF VIRTUE

189	The sense of virtue of the ind deps with their angry feeling—their outraged goodness. Not Mrs. Hersland, a dep ind.
189–191	Mrs. Hersland resisting, not attacking, because she does not have that sense of virtue.
191	Sometimes "repeating with a little changing"—sometimes copying with no changing, etc.
192	[recap] Bottom repeating—hard to describe—sometime, a history of everyone

LILLIAN ROSENHAGEN

193	The first seamstress, Lillian Rosenhagen. her stupid and anxious feeling.
194–196	Her mother, her queerness, her sister Cecilia—and repeating.

STUPID BEING

196–197	Lillian R and stupid being, and anxious being
198	Lillian and Cecilia

SPINSTER

199	Cecilia—spinster—mixture of impatient, angry, injured, stupid being
200–201	Lillian R summary—Cecilia R summary

MARY MAXWORTHING

201	Mary Maxworthing—not an "instrument" nature, but close

INSTRUMENT NATURE

202–203	Instrument nature = ind dep—described—ways of conquering bottom weaknesses
203	Mary Maxworthing not entirely an instrument nature [recap]
204	M. Maxworthing described—her difference from Martha Hersland and Julia Hersland to be described later
205	M Maxworthing and her relation to instrument nature [continued]
205	Instrument natures combined with bottom attacking, or weakness, or sensitive, etc. who "live other people's lives"

OLGA

205	Olga [mentioned as instrument], sister of first governess
205	M Maxworthing, and Mrs. Hersland's relation to her, to Mabel Linker, to Lillian R, as instruments

205 ***GS to Reader:*** "I like to tell it better in women… clearer… know it better… a little"

MABEL LINKER

205 M Maxworthing story begins. She and Mabel Linker
206–207 M Maxworthing and stupid being—and ind dep
207–223 [MAXWORTHING, LINKER, BABY STORY]
222 M Maxworthing and M Linker as a "pair"
222 ***GS to Reader:*** "Sometimes there will be a history of FIVE of them"
223–236 [MABEL LINKER STORY in re: MAXWORTHING]

PRACTICAL AND SORDID

224 M Linker and Instrument nature, and rel. to practical and sordid. But not earthy nature.
225 Instruments: will do Martha H, Julia H, Maxworthing, Linker and governess in relation to. DIAGRAM [first mention]
225 Instruments as ind dep—as attacking

EARTHY NATURE

226–227 Dep ind and earthy being—attacking etc. [variants] [recap]
227 Repeating: within each one gives to each on contentment
GS to Reader: When there will be a "description of all repeating", then "there will be contentment" [Introduction to Martha Chapter]
228–230 Story of Maxworthing and Linker continued—Linker idolizing Maxworthing— "Angel Mabel, Mabel is an angel"

NEGATIVE EGOTISM

231 Maxworthing and Linker and "negative egotism"
232 Ways of egotism—active, passive, negative, etc.
232–236 Maxworthing and Linker [recap plus end of story]

GOVERNESSES

236 First Governess is Martha—and her sister Olga
237–238 Governess Martha and stupid being and Olga—Story of Martha

SUCCESSFUL LIVING

238–239 Governess Martha and successful living—and dep ind—and concentration—and the Herslands
240–241 Sister Olga and spinster nature—vague bottom—attacking—silly
241 Later, Alfred [in Alfred chapter] makes fun of Olga

SECOND GOVERNESS

241–243 Second governess married a baker—the whole of her "stupid"—passive stupidity
244 Second governess and Mr. Hersland—and his new beginnings through

governesses

MEN'S LOVING

245 Men's loving as: dissipation, resting, cleaner attacking, as old men, etc.
245–246 Mr. Hersland and men's loving and governesses—and his middle living—habits
247 Mr Hersland and choosing the second governess—his new beginning
248 Mr. Hersland and his loving and his bottom nature [recap]
248–249 Mrs. Hersland [recap: summary description, in preparation for Madeleine Wyman episode]

MADELEINE WYMAN

250–285 [Madeleine Wyman and Mrs. Hersland relation and story]
252 Wyman and owning Mrs. Hersland—and children angry
253–256 Wyman and Mrs. Hersland and stupid being—and the "subduing power" in both

MARTHA HERSLAND

256 "Daughter Martha that year missed annual promotion"
257 Wyman family: the mother and father
257 Fearful being, cowardly being
258 Mr. Hersland and his liking women—in middle age giving advice to women
259 Mr Hersland and Wyman—and talking education to her—and she listening to him
259 Mrs. Hersland feeling "strongest in her whole living" with M Wyman
260–261 Wyman family: Louise, Frank and Helen Wyman.
261 John Summer and M Wyman—she marries him
262–263 Mr. Wyman: dep ind, earthy, instrument; Mrs. Wyman: ind dep, concentrated, attacking
263 Stupid being and the six Wymans.
264–266 M Wyman and John Summer—and education
265–266 [See NB8 #4:] "Madeleine Wyman had had a pretty good education" etc.
266 Helen Wyman: spread and vague
267 Louise Wyman: concentrated like mother
268 Frank Wyman: vague like father

EFFICIENT NATURE

269 M Wyman: not an "efficient" nature, but concentrated, and with a certain power
270 M Wyman marriage to John Summer [recap]—and her relation to the three Hersland children [recap]
271–274 The Hersland family and the Wyman family [recap]

"completed friendly feeling" of understanding.

311 Second Example:

ALICE TOKLAS

Began "in pieces"—a "succession" in repeating, not a whole one—then her way of loving repeats long enough "to make a whole one"—then "back in pieces." The problem: this type are in pieces—nothing dominates, not mind, not bottom, not emotion, not other natures.

MELODRAMA

312–313 This type "resorts to melodrama" to "make them whole to themselves" and to others. But Pride, not melodrama, is what is natural to them. With melodrama gone, there's nothing to guide one in understanding—so again in pieces, even though "illuminated"—Remained so, though "loving was louder than other pieces." Then—realized this *was* the complete understanding: whole in loving for short times, and in pieces most of the time.

313–332 Third Example:

HARRIET LEVY

313 Learned her quickly—heard of her before meeting her—then "looked intensely" and she was complete.

314 Possessed GS—gave meaning to DAMNATION—told her to "loosen" GS, and so was gentler, did not possess GS.

315–317 Harriet was never puzzling, no pieces, real bottom, "dominating"

317 [Detour—back to First Example: Annette Rosenshine:]
Gave all her loving to everyone, but there was no place for her in living—she was "explained" by everyone with "specific good reason"—but then, after years, louder repeating made understanding of her as a whole one complete to GS.

318–322 Harriet connects to first example in this way: everyone who knew her agreed, so no one helped. But her reality was: her "intense tenacity to negation"

322–328 [Lengthy recap and expansion of GS's way of learning and telling]

328–342 [Begins again with Learning, Knowing, Telling—and dovetails with exposition of "Resemblance"]

342 - on [The "Kinds"]

330 Harriet—a complete one, but GS was discouraged by Harriet holding on to "a wrong meaning" of herself—and GS urging her to give it up with "more knowing", and -

HARRIET SEES GOD

331 when GS told her that "denying" was her meaning, Harriet had a sudden

revelation which "came as religion"—and then Harriet stopped "gripping" and started accepting.

LEARNING RESEMBLING

332–343	[Learning Resembling]
333	Ways of making "kinds"
334	"Grouping" kinds begins
335	Learning "kinds"—bottom resembling—grouping—mixing it up—confusions from last learning—so, needs new grouping—then, suddenly, it all loses all meaning—again, a new beginning—and finally, grouping comes right.
336	"Grouping themselves:"—how a group of men, a group of women, did it for GS.
339	Ways of knowing kinds: the two main kinds: dep ind and ind dep, but—complications: because of mixing, disguising, complex using. Still, a certain number of kinds becoming clearer.
340	The confusions resulting from doing *one* person's resembling, and how they change—but still, "never throw anything out"
341	False starts—contradictions—new direction. Must have *one whole one* for comparison—if arbitrary must always begin again—and learn new variations
342	An early grouping of men: (by resemblance to someone else:)

[GENERAL DIVISION OF KINDS: RESISTING AND ATTACKING]

343	RESISTING kind: earthy, slow. Variations: solid, frozen, dried, etc. the character of the resisting kind: no quick or poignant reactions—quickest when "muddy bottom" is dry and almost wooden.
344–345	"Bottom Being": neither good nor bad, etc., but of the *kind* of good or bad, etc. "Bottom substance" is in lumps, or liquid, or metallic etc. [variations]
346–347	[recap of above]

EMOTION VS. SENSATION

347	In Resisting being, "Emotion is not as poignant as a sensation is"; In Attacking being, "Emotion is as quick and poignant as a sensation is"

RELATION TO THE OBJECT

348	In Attacking Kind: relation to the object in terms of its use, its beauty, its symbolism, etc.: which is "nastily disguised materialism"
348	In Resisting Kind: the nervousness— "slow-moving, and going too fast" [See note re: conversation with Sally]
348	***GS to Reader:*** "I am all unhappy in this writing" because nervous and driving, and so, unhappy in the telling

349 Resisting Kind: its substance: solid, liquid, holes, etc.
Attacking Kind: its substance: pulpy, slimy, gelatinous, etc.

349–350 First Attacking type GS knew—was so slow, almost resisting, gelatinous.

350 Attacking Kind: [variations and combinations with different "tops"]

351 THE SIX—A PRELIMINARY STUDY OF THE RESISTING KIND

352–353 The First: ANNETTE ROSENSHINE
A resisting kind, and not baffling—flattered by everyone because she had no "place" in living. But—it became clear that she "needed to own those she need for loving" But since she resisted yielding, she never owned anyone. And never yielded to "engulfing" except when "drowned."

353 The Second: Resisting, but this once *can* engulf.

353–354 The First: almost drowned, bottom so thin and watered, could not cling.

VANITY

The Second: bottom of thicker fluid, so could engulf—but didn't need anyone—sense of superiority, sense of completely engulfing what she needed—so, complete vanity, complete superiority to anyone.

354–355 The First: resisting being "her way of attacking," but couldn't win in loving or in fighting. So, only reckless attacking.

EFFICIENCY

355 Both high in efficiency, but the First was neither good nor bad in it, but it was *strong* in her
The Second: engulfing herself is her power; need not doing anything for anyone to give her a sense of owning. So—efficiency not interesting to her, though good enough.

356 [recap of above]

357 The Third: CLARIBEL CONE
Seemed resisting at bottom, but actually the opposite—an attacking bottom, but it came through a long-winded top, and so she seemed the resisting kind
[See Note NB-E #5 on Claribel: "not slow minded but long-winded"]

ROMANTICS

358 The problem for the Third kind: see everything in themselves except their bottom nature, and so, though the bottom determines their history, seeing everything else in themselves, they are "romantic in the contemplation of their personality."

359 The Fourth: NAPOLEON
A contradiction of top and bottom: See themselves as "guided by an unchanging destiny". But the bottom is opposite from their tops—if the bottom is attacking, the top is resisting, and vice versa. So they have the

romantic feeling that their destiny is unchanging.

360 The Fifth: all their nature, top and bottom, is one—yet there's a contradiction.

An attacking kind, but contradictory and puzzling. In this kind, loving is attacking, and so strong is it that it overflows into nervous boing, and is an excess of passion.

GS to Reader: This kind is still puzzling. But is all this a "fabrication" No, she insists, I'm certain of it.

NERVOUS BEING

363 So, "excess of passion" leads to "nervous being draining them" So they *seem* to be repressed, but are not. Really, they have attacking being, but not much attacking action.

MORAL CONVICTION

363 Also, they are opportunists, succeeding in living and in a feeling of moral conviction. Have no instinct for the quality in people, but want to understand only how to use them.

"HERBERT SPENCER KIND OF MAN"

363 Also, opportunistically embraces a moral conviction, then builds a complete system from it. So—mostly successful.

365 And so adds up to: "a curious spectacle of opportunism, moral conviction, rationalizing passion, nervousness, and much love and emotion."

365 Their minds: highly rationalizing from the beginning—and so becomes a conviction and a principle in living. But—the rationalized system "does not grow from experiencing."

RUN THEMSELVES BY THEIR MINDS

366 Run themselves by their minds.

BERNARD BERENSON

366 BB of this kind, with his "fixed scheme of living for grace and beauty"

366–372 Extremely detailed analysis of BB (as one of the TEN MEN who run themselves by their minds), and of other of the ten with different "rationalized convictions"—which could be about women, religion, socialism, intellectual, etc.

373–375 The Fifth [GS's count]:

"NEVER FINISHED ANYTHING" (BRUCE? CHALFIN?)

A resisting kind—all one kind—who "fail to succeed in living"

DETOUR: Resisting Being—its variants—can be quick on the surface if it is active. Variants in these [at length.]

Exalted nature, not petty, but never decently good to anyone. Explanation: their bottom mass not entirely dry [etc.]. Always said: this thing failed, so began again.

376 The Sixth: little bottom (turgid, resisting) and two top natures. Elegance and luxury "a need for such a one." Vanity—separation from contact with anyone—need for indolence and elegance—affection for beauty, and a conviction for steady, unexalted, slightly ambitious working -

377 and ends as "excessive spontaneous equilibration"

378 [Preparation for Martha Chapter, part two:]

REPEATING AND RESEMBLANCE IN BABIES, IN CHILDREN

378–379 Resemblance in babies and children, but lose their resemblance later. — Delayed reaction in young boys; their changes later.

380 Not clear in children, from a single incident, whether they are of attacking or resisting kind. (Various ways in which everyone sees everyone—of being confusing and uncertain—of seeing the whole one.)

CHAPTER TWO (PART TWO)
MARTHA HERSLAND

382 The *effect* of coming together as a whole one [variations]

383 Never coming together, and remaining as little *lumps*

BERTHA STEIN [GS'S SISTER]

384–388 Lengthy description: ind dep, but an "undifferentiated mass." Bertha "completely fluid", ind dep "in solution"; the prototype of the ind dep at its most fluid.

MARTHA HERSLAND

The same as Bertha, but more concentrated.

"I WILL THROW THE UMBRELLA IN THE MUD"

388 The incident from Martha's childhood narrated. Its meaning: hard to tell—whether dep ind or ind dep—from the one incident.

389 Martha and the umbrella—hard to know in children

MAPS

389–392 Knowing a place from a map—gratifying. And like a map known before, finding oneself like one's father or mother in middle age, is astonishing, gratifying and terrifying

393 [recap] "one little boy…" and "umbrella in the mud"

394 Begins Martha history—Gossols—she knew children in public school

395 How she was known to others—Summary of entire Martha history - [recap] the Hersland children and the children in the nearby small houses

396 David closest to those children, Alfred least, Martha like David.

397 [Detour:] Ways of disguising Being.

398	[recap] Martha is Bertha but more concentrated ***GS to Reader:*** Uncomfortable, and "wants to turn away" when describing Martha-Bertha
399	Martha's death wish (wished she died when still a bay)—the feeling of ind dep's about life and death—[recap] Can't know anyone from some thoughts or acts.
400–401	Some ind dep's wishing for death don't succeed by attacking—like Martha
402	Ind deps and ways of living and ways of being understood
403	Bertha's almost static attacking, and so resembles resisting—it becomes nervous and stupid being—and Martha was this, but less.
404–405	Martha in school and the governesses at home—the trouble for her—[recap] half-country, half-city living and schooling
405	[Anticipates:] Martha, after later marriage troubles, returns home
406–407	[recap] Martha a whole one—governess interference—Martha not pleasing—umbrella incident—other children's thoughts about Martha
407–408	Mr Hersland and Martha—both ind dep—his feeling—to: his final impatient feeling
409–411	Relation of Martha and Mr Hersland as ind deps—their relations in later life—Martha's governess troubles—Martha's relation to neighboring poor children
412	Martha and the little boy "who wanted to do loving"
413	Its failure and Martha's confusion Martha "not interesting" to anyone—and her future separated her from the other children

MAN HITTING WOMAN WITH UMBRELLA ON CALIFORNIA STREET

414	Introduction to story—[recap] Martha's nature
415	Martha and the Madeleine Wyman experience—which caused Martha further concentration
416	[recap] Martha and the poor people—future separated her from them
417	Martha and the family of Anna, Cora and Bertha—Martha and the Banks boys—and the Rodman boys—and Martha not interesting to them
418	Mr and Mrs Hersland's relation to Martha: annoyed, and not close—Martha and her brothers—Martha and her school teachers
419–420	[recap] Martha as ind dep—and Bertha & Martha—the poor people
421	Alfred and Mr Hersland story: take care of your sister sooner or later—Alfred: "I'll take mine later" Mr Hersland angry that Martha with poor people and not home studying
422	Harry Brenner, the boy who wanted to do loving
423	Mr Hersland and the poor people's cooking, a good lesson for Martha
424	[recap] Full summary of above

424 Martha sees man hitting woman on California street—marks the end of her living thus far
425 Martha and John Davidson—played music together and sang—[recap]: Martha as baby, then young etc.
426 "Man hitting woman" cause "shock and commotion" in Martha—and a forward movement (to get a university education)
427 College begins—the beginning of definite feeling in Martha
428 [full recap] family, Gossols, etc.
429–440 [Inserted from the earlier *Fernhurst* story]
429 Philip Redfern—early life with mother and father
430 Both see son differently
431 What he learned from them—goes to college, but a "democratic western college"
432–433 Philip and Martha— "you are a comrade and a woman"—incident with brother of John Davidson
433 Marriage failure—they live in "armed neutrality"
434 Miss Charles, the Dean—Miss Dounor—the first tea
435–436 Miss Dounor's "transfigured" innocence—Philip meets her—Martha's awkward interruption

TWENTY-NINE YEARS OLD CONDITION

437 Philip and twenty-nine years old condition, and American vocation—and Miss Dounor's readiness
438 Their love—the three now "two and an extra"—French and American attitudes
439 The gossip—Miss Charles warns Martha
440 Martha sees letter— "she had her evidence"
440 ***GS to Reader:*** "Categories" that once had meaning now have none—you have to "lose words"
441 Analysis of Redfern—in the end, a failure
442 "Johnson when he forgets his emotion" [See Note #73: Edstrom when he "forgets his emotion" etc.]

VIRTUOUS BEING

442 Forgetting emotion and self-deception later—analysis of how these do it: Edstrom, Frank Jacott, May Bookstaver, Sarah Stein, Alfred Hodder (who is the paradigm for Philip Redfern)
443–444 [See NB3, #6] "Out of their virtue, make a god"—ways of conceiving of themselves—make, out of love of themselves, a part of their virtuous and religious feeling
444 Philip makes a virtue out of his weakness
444 "Lathrop" [i.e., Edstrom] "tells a lie as if it were the truth and I tell the

truth as if it were a lie"

"SIMPLE SENSUOUS AND PASSIONATE"

445 Philip was that to himself, "and that was the whole of him" - The rest of his life—first literary career, then politician—always failed

ROMANTIC—LORD BYRON—OSCAR WILDE

445 Johnson [Edstrom] expanded—story of Hapgood's manuscript—Edstrom, romantic through weakness. All these: "Romantic, heroic, beautiful, saintly, by the weakness in them"—and so, boasting and sentimental

HACKART AND SARAH STEIN

446 Hackart, dramatic, also Sarah Sands [Stein]—[recap] Johnson forgets his emotion—self-righteous.

447 Philip on guard—giving them their revenge—his reputation

VIRTUE AND VIRTUOUS FEELING

448 Everyone's importance to himself—finding his "distinction", which is his virtue

448–450 The problem of having "the feeling of being distinguished"
GS to Reader: "One day will work out whole problem"—and the problem of "sentimental feeling" and how they reach these certainties

450 "Certainty" comes from their nature—the various ways of having it, and sustaining and living with it

451 Philip's way: "telling what it was right for him to tell" and feeling it was so natural and so right that it was not a part of "virtuous feeling"—his being on guard a "virtue"—and chivalry made necessary his weakness—and being on guard, running away [i.e. Edstrom—his wisdom]

452 [recap] Johnson attributes yielding to weakness—and Philip being on guard

[453–457] [Cora Dounor Description]

453–455 A puzzle: about someone else's way of loving, or of buying things, or of being angry, etc.
GS to Reader: Despairing, melancholy, discouraged. A sad thing, that no one will probably ever know the complete history of anyone, or have complete understanding Making and recopying mistakes, accounting for them—missing things in people for a complete history. "Repeating missed is like beauty not seen"

455 Being a "brute," and being "sensitive." Will discuss the three women in relation to these categories

457 Martha: of those with sensitive feeling, but then becomes "nervous anxious quivering vibratory, and then nothing can touch them"

REACTIVE VS. PERSONAL [I.E., SELF-DIRECTIVE] NATURE

457 Miss Charles less "reactive" than "self-directive"

458 Cora Dounor—all sensitive reactive, but could plan to hurt the other two To Redfern, she was gentle, sensitive, intelligent, but could plan attacking

458 ***GS to Reader:*** Despairing—knows all three women, "but not poignantly enough". Also, so confusing, and could be wrong, therefore, despair.

459 The three women to be discussed re: "reactive" and "personal" natures

460 [recap] ***GS to Reader:*** hard to know them

461 Cora Dounor—punishing others for making claims—delicate pride, no melodrama

[462–469] [Miss Charles Analysis]

GENERAL AND CONCRETE MORALITY

462 General and concrete morality—moral aspirations and immoral desires

463 Miss Charles—egotistic sensual nature emerges (from moral aspirations)—then her courage to live that—the courage this kind need "to make aspirations out of their being"—as example: buying clocks or handkerchiefs (violating general opinion and good taste.)

464 [recap and expands] personal and reactive living

465 Miss Dounor—complete in loving and complete understanding in desiring—made Redfern a saint—failed against Mrs. Redfern's attacking

466–467 Miss Charles—became a reformer, with aggressive attacking. Then, slow steady domination Then, achieved a generalized conviction in relation to her concrete living.

468–469 [recaps and expands above]

[469–476] [Martha Redfern Analysis]

469 Martha leaving Redfern at the time of Alfred marrying Julia.

470 Her traveling, till the death of Redfern women laughed at her—and she, never understanding
[See NB6, #9: "A little crazy like Selina is now"]

471 Mr. Hersland losing his fortune. Martha's annoying him: sugar in his coffee, holding his coat—his impatient feeling—he, now "shrunk away"

472–475 Mr. Hersland's failure—but can't know for certain till his death

476 [Bridge to Alfred Hersland Chapter]

CHAPTER THREE (PART ONE)
ALFRED HERSLAND AND JULIA DEHNING

THE LONG GAY BOOK

479 ***GS to Reader:*** When finished with this book, will start on "the long gay book"—but actually, already started it.

BEING VIRTUOUS

479 Virtue and the feeling of being distinguished by it

480–481 Virtue making kinds of morality—and kinds of religion—certainty and ways of arriving at it—and having it

482 Certainty and virtue and important feeling
GS to Reader: Unhappy "that everyone is a little queer to me"

DISILLUSIONMENT IN LIVING

483 ***GS to Reader:*** "Disillusionment in living" is finding that no one agrees with you completely in anything

484 ***GS to Reader:*** The next chapter—on David Hersland—will be a history of his disillusionment and death

485 The shock of being "no longer young"—young ones realizing this—their reaction: some kill themselves—an agony to them, but still, not really grasped

DAVID HERSLAND AND "THE NEED FOR LIVING"

485 David Hersland "trying to be certain from day to day what there was in living that could make it necessary for him"

485 Disillusionment—the shock of discovering that even those fighting *for* you don't completely agree with you. So— "Write for yourself and strangers"
GS to Reader: You write a book—a silly one and you're ashamed—and then after you're laughed at as crazy [LEO], the joy of one person liking the same thing [ALICE]—"and never again can you feel ashamed or afraid"

MASTERS AND SCHOOLS

486 Preparation for later discussion of "masters and schools"

486 GS puzzled about jealousy in love which is then denied.
[See NB-H #8: "From the way Alice goes on about Annette…"]

CONCRETE AND GENERAL

486 Concrete thinking, acting, and general thinking acting

486–487 Aspirations and convictions created by quick reaction to others, to books, to family traditions, etc. Causes one to "live the being of those others making them" rather than having the power to create one's living from the being inside oneself

MASTERS AND FOLLOWERS

488 Masters and followers [or, schools] to be developed later in David chapter.

488 "Measure" in living—measure in living for the followers (someone to be like), and measure in living for the masters, who have no model.

TEXT: "IT HAPPENS VERY OFTEN THAT A MAN HAS IT IN HIM…"

489 Story of the man who wrote letters of moral advice to his daughter—effect: rebounded on him, left him paralyzed

MIKE STEIN AND ALLEN AND BUTTERFLY STORY

489 Father and son and butterfly story

490 Concrete and general—for young men teaching others to be strong—for old men (sexual morality) just "trying to keep warm"

491 [recap and expand] Concrete and general

492 All this, to be used in relation of Alfred Hersland and Henry Dehning

492–493 [recap and variations] Concrete and general

LEO AND FRED STEIN, MASTER AND FOLLOWER

492 Example: George Dehning's [Fred] seeing David H [Leo] as a genius, the strongest scholar

494 Subject of this chapter will be Alfred H in relation to Henry D.

495 ***GS to Reader:*** "Disillusion, when one realizes cannot make anyone change"

495–496 Believing: one believing that others cannot believe what they believe—examples: Women of the Plymouth Brethren, and those who believe rivers can't flow north

497 Building up others' convictions, "their loving and virtue and religion"

497–498 Building up a conviction in "the one following", so that even when the master is not there or is himself not certain, the other one will go on doing the task religiously

"DEAD IS DEAD"

498–499 "To be dead is to be really dead" and the variations of this—in religion, can believe both that it is and it isn't—or that it is only partly "dead," is really active, instinctive living—or that ":dead" is really "living" (as in religion)—or can be "equilibrated" to the opinion opposite to living action

ROMANCE LEGEND IDEAL AND VIRTUOUS FEELING

500–505 Ways of having virtuous feeling—the Romantic self, as for example, "as chaste." Another way: being certain of having the ideal by leaving out a part of themselves. Another way: present ideal transcends the previous one (example: last love was not real, this one is really real.) Another: this "bad" is just a habit; can change habit. Another: It's myself, so it's different from same bad thing in another; in me, it's not bad, it's me. Another: building up sense of virtue piece by piece. Another: SOUNDING BOARD: the suggestion of another feels as though you anticipated it, and so it's your own opinion. [See Note #161 re: SARAH STEIN and the Portrait entitled: TWO]

505 TEXT: "Some out of their virtue make a god…"

SARAH STEIN

506 Her "feeling of original creation from an anticipated suggestion." Happens "resoundingly" and "quicker than chain lightning." The weakness, though—she must be supported by close company.

507 ***GS to Reader:*** "I have been relieving myself enough now of my wisdom" Promises in this chapter to alternate between the early life of Julia Dehning and of Alfred Hersland

[Note: from here on, GS begins her repeated efforts to encompass the "whole" of Alfred Hersland, and reports her increasing and repeated failure to do so. This is essentially the burden of the chapter]

507 ***GS to Reader:*** Alfred "is very clear inside me… I am full up with him"

508 ***GS to Reader:*** "Am full up with Alfred and the children young, then older, then with Julia" etc.

DEAD IS DEAD

508 [Lengthy recap of] Old man Hissen, the grandfather "who was religion". In him, concrete and general virtue were the same. For him, dead is dead was not a contradiction of religion.

508 ***GS to Reader:*** Alfred H is "always nearer to my understanding," but there are still difficulties.

508 To understand Alfred H, GS begins a series of descriptions of different groups: those who have "religious desiring" and those who have "fear and idealization."

509 ***GS to Reader:*** "Still waiting"

509 Alfred H is dep ind—resisting.

509 First example: Those who have fear, knowing that dead is dead, and are afraid.

510 Second example: Those who have the fear of this, and turn it into a "generalized conviction of religion and virtue." [Alfred's kind]

511 Third example: Know dead is dead and slip out of it by claiming "a world without ending" (eternity), and work this up as "loving" in them, and so "own the thing they need for loving"

SENSITIVE AND VIRTUOUS FEELING AND RELIGION

512 [Preparation for:] the contrast with Julia's kind, who have "sensitiveness and religion" and virtuous feeling [i.e., the *feeling* that they are virtuous.]—The attacking kind—And preparation for: Mr. Dehning and old men—their virtuous feeling, and George and Hortense Dehning and theirs (to be described in the next chapter)

512 Alfred H—a mixture of Old Man Hissen and Grandfather David

513 ***GS to Reader:*** Waiting

513 Alfred H—is the "engulfing resisting kind"

513–514 Julia— "the root of her being is intensity of emotion"—goes with her religion—her kind seem ruled by religion or virtue, but really only the intensity of their own emotion

514 ***GS to Reader:*** "Waiting is pleasant… a certain drowsiness… etc. etc."

514 Alfred H—the "temper" stirring in him as a boy, as a man

515 Begins Alfred Hersland story: as a baby—as helping Martha to her freedom—as example to David—problem of being the oldest son but not the oldest child

516 ***GS to Reader:*** "Saddening" to know repeating is going on, and that being young or middle aged or old seems not real, and existence seems not real—so it is "dreary to be writing it"— "Now have no one in my feeling. Am waiting"

517 No one has any age inside him—so will not put it into Alfred.

518 [recap] Alfred H's history summarized

518 ***GS to Reader:*** "Am almost through waiting"

518 Alfred and "family living"

518–519 ***GS to Reader:*** The difficulty of realizing another—and of realizing no one—shares this, "like a little boy suddenly realizing he is alone, and howling." Alfred now "completely in pieces" for her—and so, "must begin again"

519 [recap] | Alfred and family living—expanded

520 Alfred and Mother's holding his clothes in closet when he's gone [See notes NB-MA #3, NB9, #9.]

520–521 ***GS to Reader:*** Everything in pieces, no use going on, everything is a thing without end— "no reason to me why the world should go on" if "in repeating nothing gives me the sensation of a completed one." It is pointless putting together kinds unless each one becomes a whole one to me

522 Alfred not too passionate, or affectionate, or good or bad—sometimes virtuous, ambitious, aspiring, didactic

522 [recap] Alfred—engulfing ind dep kind—and religion

522 ***GS to Reader:*** Alfred H still in pieces

523 Alfred—the gamut from tyrannical to meek, success to failure—thought possibly he could save himself by "a little religion", or owning someone near

523–525 Six Variants of Alfred H's kind:

524 First Example: Not too successful—impersonal, just and kind— "dead is dead" but vaguely uncertain—not engulfing—needed to own only *one*

Second Example: Engulfing and passionate—but action only "niggling"—wanted to have passion and despair, but it came to nothing

Third Example: Completely concentrated—passionate murky engulfing -, therefore active, and loving without trouble to him—so active, that he never knew he was engulfing—interested only in what he was needing just then—pleasant

525 Fourth Example: "Dead is dead" so must stay alive, seize everything "to keep by him", and then dead is not dead, and if it were, what then? A *noble* man, not affected. Not trusted, but to some, attractive

Fifth Example: "Murky passionate resistance"—but intermittently so. Effect on him: sometimes quick, charming, a musician. Sometimes just quiet, and sometimes, uncontrollable temper. "Twice in his life, loving. but both times a trouble to him because not strong in persisting"— "not too successful in living"

Sixth Example: Efficient, active, practical, somewhat aggressive resistance—slightly sentimental, very successful. [Preparations: Four like him will possibly be in David H chapter]

526–531 Alfred history "begins again" [recap] his half-country, half-city living—his "rich surface of aesthetic feeling"— "mixed" feeling at this stage—knew mother's "never cut off" feeling—family feeling—playing with friends

BANKS BOYS—ALBERT AND GEORGE

531 Alfred's friends: the Banks boys—Albert drawing pistol—shoemaking

LOUIS CHAMPION, FRANK AND WILL RODDY, THE FISHERS, THE HENRYS

532–536 The Roddys: cigar stand—jail—Martha and the boys—Alfred threatens her: "Will tell father"—beginning feeling "good citizen, eldest son"—other friends: the Fishers, the Henrys'—Alfred and OLGA (sister of first governess) and the Wymans.

ARRAGON, IDA HEARD

536–537 Alfred's music teacher, Arragon—Ida Heard, the schoolteacher

537–538 ***GS to Reader:*** Knowing what people will do from minute to minute— "I am one such"—and "how wrong I can be"—because I HAVE NO DRAMATIC IMAGINATION for what people will do, only for what is already done. Have "constructive imagination" for the being already in them.

539 ***GS to Reader:*** "Sometime I will make more of this—later in my living" and will illustrate it.

539 [recap] Alfred in Gossols

539–540 ***GS to Reader:*** My difficulty "in using a new word since it must have more me very existent being." "I am just now feeling a learning in me for some words I have just been beginning using in my writing."

ALICE TOKLAS AND SARAH STEIN

540–541 ***GS to Reader:*** "Loving loving more than loving me" which makes "the whole one a piece," and then I must begin all over again to make her a whole one.
Realizing "whole ones" and "pieces" in relation to Sally ["not original but anticipatorily suggestible"] and in relation to Alice ["completely loving, and then not completely loving."]

541 [recap] Description of Alfred H's kind

542 ***GS to Reader:*** My astonishment at discovering that some talk differently to me than to others—so need to start again "realizing"

542 [recap] Alfred H a subdivision of engulfing resisting kind, active and aspiring, but a "piece" to everyone

543 Contradictions: examples of "in pieces": Milkman story and "I can only love a dark one" story.

543 ***GS to Reader:*** Re: "in pieces": "Not really caring anymore"

544–545 [recap and large expansion:] Alfred H kind:
(1) The "earthy" ones: things exist as "earth", not the use or emotion about them So—emotion is not "poignant s sensation" in them.
(2) The "lying" ones: Say not what they're thinking, so difficult to know whether they know the relation between their saying and what happened. So—must know *all* the being in them to know whether they are lying, or feeling, or afraid, etc., and so—very difficult to know the complete one.

543–573 THE TWENTY KINDS OF RESISTING [ALFRED H] BEING:

545–546 First example: Have *generalised* feeling of ideal aspiration—and *concrete* feeling for material "seizing and holding". *General* feeling that dead is really dead, so—happily should be married to one of faith. —Sensitive, slow-reacting, a little fearful, impersonal, somewhat loving

547 Second example: Appear strong, solid, decent, etc.—generally very successful. But—some too much pride, too much romantic imagination. Not "wooden" as in a live tree, which is sensitive, but "wooden" as in useful, solid, dead wood. —Pleasant, loyal, reliable—give impression of being very strong.—Their lack: not truly individual being but "the cream of the school men" [i.e., followers].

548 ***GS to Reader:*** "Just now, I am an altogether discouraged one"

548–549 Third example: Complete "instrument" type. [GS knows one in particular] "Vibrates like a violin"—Loves a resisting one (like himself) because needs complete "influencing". When older, with no beauty, will have fixed ideas, and maybe a little crazy.

549 ***GS to Reader:*** "Some day WILL WRITE A BOOK WITH PAIRS AND

THREES AND FOURS AND FIVES OF THEM" [i.e., Long Gay Book?]

549–550 Fourth example: [GS knows four men, all engulfing, otherwise different, as follows:]

[1] engulfing, gayly juicy in him, but—need someone to start him, except in dancing and loving. A little fussy, like father, and then reflects that. Seems not engulfing, but is really completely so.

550–551 [2] Fifth example: Despairing one, not supporting himself by working, but always hoping. When young, was vigorously aspiring; older, not vigorous in anything but always hopeful. Engulfing resisting in type, but never engulfed or resisted anything.

[3] Sixth example: So confused, that learning him was very important, led to learning a great deal. Dry inside, outside gently affectionate, ambitious, vain. A "piece", not a whole one. A lovely one.

551–552 [4] Seventh example: *Not* a lovely one. Engulfing in the following way: If woman thrusts herself at him, he swallows her in nibbles. To himself, he is noble, heroic, completely good. To his wife, completely good, lovely. She, not completely engulfed, but wanting to be.

552–553 Eighth example: Thick, murky engulfing. Always wrote poems before threatening suicide. In youth, not adroit but reckless, funny, almost foolish. Mother interferes in marriage—not very interesting to women—when older, stingy and suspicious—still older, popular with men. Both attacking and resisting alive in him, but no motion toward either.

553–554 Ninth example: Murky passionate resisting, but not really engulfing—completely disturbed in loving—relates to Grandfather Hissen in religion but—though not completely a lost one, is lost in loving and in religion, and afraid to be rescued. When young, a complete idealist—always elegant and graceful. In religion and in loving, "loses the feeling after the emotion" so has to begin again. Mastered by someone, so not completely a failure.

554–555 Tenth example: Complete vanity, no pride. These seize what they need, desire complete success, feel what they need for distinction, but no feeling for the thing itself. They "engulf" everything that can give them distinction. Have the need to judge whether anyone has distinction. So—need to be taught to recognize distinction in others.

VOLLARD

556–559 Eleventh example: Inquisitiveness, curiosity and suspicion. The Vollard anecdote with Matisse: "And this door—to the hall or the garden?" Attention wanders, so tries to catch it. Resisting, but not engulfing.

suspicion, a pleasant feeling for him. So—always asking questions, possibly for winning, manouvering, or even cheating.

558 [recap] Suspicion—and variants

559–560 Twelfth example: Resisting and sensitive about equal in this one—not engulfing. Quick developing, early flowering, so tries to be slower, but can't. Could only own the one he needed for loving by sending her away, then making another one love him.

AUNT FANNY—COUNTING [SEE: NOTE #32]

560–562 Thirteenth example: A gentle pleasant one, often injured and then fairly angry. Her children were "a piece of her cut off", equal to her, and "she was as they were." Once out of suspicion defended someone when it was not her business to interfere—so, nice and honest, but one time did a not pretty thing. Her way of recognizing real existing was by "counting by one and one and one." Had suspicion "only as injured feeling". (Story of telling tale about one cousin to another cousin.)

PRITCHARD—CANNONBALL ON COTTON

562–563 Fourteenth example: Amiable and ideal in aspiration, "large worded and hesitating in expression" "Cannon ball lying on a field of cotton" [See NB-H #15.]

563 ***GS to Reader:*** "Cannon ball" metaphor was borrowed. Not GS way of describing at all.

563–571 [*Note*: 15th, 16th, 17th and 18th examples have this in common: they would be resisting "if they could ever have true emotion". But because their sensitiveness connects stimuli to other things (suspicion, sentimentality, sexual passion, etc.) does not allow these stimuli to reach their bottom nature. So—they never have emotion, and in a sense have no bottom, and so are recognizable as resisting types only by resemblance to other groups.]

563–565 Fifteenth example: Sensitive and complete suspicion, completely important to themselves inside them. Their suspicion emerges in their providing the reason and motive in another one that reflects badly on themselves, because they are wicked or jealous or stupid, etc. Stories exemplifying this:

- One didn't get back the five cents he loaned because the other one knew he wouldn't ask for it, and so took advantage;
- "You'll be successful in teaching" translates to "You can't paint, so teach"
- "You'll be successful in the city" translates "city work is rotten, so you'll fit in"

565 ***GS to Reader:*** "I am a rare one"—one of the few who know that others "are really believing what they're believing", and therefore, I don't make the mistake of attributing wicked or jealous motives of others toward me. [Really?? What about Roche's and Leo's "motives" in criticizing the novel??]

565–567 Sixteenth example: Turn sensitiveness, before they have a real emotion about it, PROBABLY not into suspicion but into cleverness or self-protection or sexual CORA DOUNOR passion. Before marriage, this one was emotional, dark, expressive. After marriage, submissive, indifferent, timid, fat. Explanation: Before, nothing reached her bottom, but became sentimental sensibility. Now that's lost too, so illusion of "dark, emotional" etc., is gone too.

GS ON CONCEALING IDENTITIES

567 ***GS to Reader:*** "Last week I saw this one" Told her I would write it up, and this one objected. GS assured her "this one will not know that it is this one." Still she objected.

567–568 Seventeenth example: Everything in her was cleverness and "self-protection from any stimulation." So—never any emotion about a *thing*. Felt world owed it to her to force the emotion out of her, but never grateful when it did. Wanted faith and its conviction and emotion, and then, she felt sure, she would see everybody as a better person.

568 Eighteenth example: Would be resisting if she had any real emotion in her. Thinks of it as her sexual emotion. One can know this kind's "resisting being" only from resemblances to the really resisting.

568–569 Nineteenth Example: A resisting being who is continually attacking. And so not easy to describe.

GS to Reader: Will try "slowly thinking". "I am thinking now of this one."

MELODRAMA

Not engulfing, but thought she was, and so she had "much emotion of dominating with stern action." Because she had the emotion of engulfing, her talk was often "melodramatic." With animals or her children, she thought herself engulfing, but really was not. Just resisting and sensitive.

569–571 Twentieth Example: Resisting, not engulfing, but out of fear, thought of herself as attacking—the way a drowning boy splashes about. So scared that she hit out in all directions. Bragged about her quick, poignant emotion and vigorous thinking. But really a timid soul and scared. She knew she was always afraid with a man. This type attack, but it is not their real way—which is resisting—so they fail in love.

572 ***GS to Reader:*** Knows more about this kind, but is impatient with writing about them now.

573 ***GS to Reader:*** She herself is resisting, is slow in action and feeling. When she is not, she is not certain that she was really listening. Still, it is best for her to be even slower. "When I have not been right, there must be something wrong." This is GS's way of suffering: things being without meaning for her. Because "to be completely right and certain is... to be

like the earth, complete and fructifying."

574 ***GS to Reader:*** Sometime will deal with "secrecy" in the resisting kind.

SECRECY I

574–575 These—LENA, MARIA, HETTY—are the resisting kind who have parallels to the attacking kind.

"LENA, MARIA, HETTY ADAPT THEMSELVES TO ANYONE WHO IS INTERESTING" and do so to feel power in themselves, and to feel the knowing of the other one in themselves. [Variations of this.]

CORRELATIVE RESISTING AND ATTACKING GROUPS

ALFRED H BEGINS:

575 Alfred Hersland is resisting engulfing, entirely.

576 Alfred H and the basic kinds of dependent independent types—in religion, in family living, in marriage. Some try to engulf "in order to be lost and swallowed by the other one."

Alfred H is "a little" passionate, affectionate, a good and bad success;

Alfred H is "a lot" ambitious, and possibly has religion. And he has a lot of weakness.

577 GS THEME: PASSION AND AFFECTION—THEIR RELATION AND DIFFERENCE.

577–578 The foreign musician Alfred H knew when he was young. He inspired affection ARRAGON for beautiful things. He was a puzzle until one understood that he had "inspired affection, not passion." When young, his affection was "so poignant" that he had a "passionate understanding" of beautiful things. But when older, he couldn't make up the "beautiful luxury" he needed, and so he awoke in others the creation of the beauty he needed. And so Arragon had passion, but it was not poignant. It *was,* though, brilliant, emotional, and sentimental.

578 Another one—like Arragon, an independent dependent with passion, but a really passionate creating, seizing, attacking kind.

579 ***GS to Reader:*** Was mistaken earlier about Cora Dounor. She is really of the resisting kind. And GS will use the "sister of the first governess" later as an example of "Border Cases."

GS, CORA DOUNOR AND 'BORDER CASES'

579 [Recap:] In attacking kind, the emotion is poignant as a sensation—the use and purpose of things, and everything in relation to other things are to them the "primary [proof of their] existing."

579 Arragon [recapped and expanded.]

580 ***GS to Reader:*** "Sometime, will be able to make diagrams. Already made MAKING several." Sometime, will make a complete one, "and that

DIAGRAMS will be a very long book about each kind of men and women." and 'A LONG GAY BOOK'

580 ARRAGON— "ATTACKING PASSION" as a "highly suggestible emotion."

MARTHA REDFERN and JULIA and the "attacking passion:" both so stupidly using "attacking passion" so as to equal "obstinate resistance" to everything. [And variation on "attacking passion."]

581 ***GS to Reader:*** When she has the "simple certainty" of kinds, it is a "pleasant completed" feeling, and calming. The idea of Death is not discouraging. Instead, it becomes a "quiet, somber feeling", and not a fear.

582 Arragon [expanded]— "not succeeding"

GS to Reader: It all is getting diffuse and facile. So, GS tells herself, "begin again" about the "independent dependent passionate" ones.

582–583 Another man (following Arragon) who had passionate poignancy, but always felt that things were "holding him back." Was nervous about this, so he "seized" on creating more and more.

583 [Recap of] "Dead" and "sombre thing" and so it is important that each one is one, and each one is of a kind.

GS: "I AM IMPORTANT IN THIS THING."

584–585 Alfred H and Arragon [recapped and expanded.] Arragon's small musical influence on Alfred H.

586 ***GS to Reader:*** [THE DEFECATION ANALOGY] It should all be coming out "without pressing or straining," leaving her "pleasantly empty." And GS "not content" with description of Arragon.

586 "Border Cases" [recapped and expanded.]

587 ***GS to Reader:*** GS thinking her analyses and descriptions now are "all foolishness", but then recovers.

ALFRED H (CONTINUED)

587–588 Alfred H [recaps:] his poignant sensation is more than his emotion. [Now she adds:] Curiosity and imagination can be disconnected from basic "things as existing", and so can become mere cleverness, and is therefore "a piece," not a whole, of living.

588–589 "OLGA WHO WAS IDA" and Alfred H and their love letters, and Arragon knowing her.

589–590 "TWO SILLY ONES" of the flavor group—silly because they think that flavor is disconnected from any source. [expanded]

590–591 "OLGA" and her nervous, crazy way of asking everyone to be her lover. Two sides to her: her "nervous sexual asking" and her stupid, stagnant, bottom being.

ALFRED H IN BRIDGEPOINT

591–593	Alfred H in Bridgepoint with the Hissen relatives, and his "pleasant living" there.
593	***GS to Reader:*** "There is comfort for a great author inside one" who lives lonely, sighing and sombre, to say that "pleasant living is a pleasant thing."
593–594	ALFRED H AND HIS LOVE AFFAIR IN BRIDGEPOINT, his first. His Aunt is against it—winter comes—the girl goes away. His friends there, etc.
594–595	***GS to Reader:*** Wishes to have complete lists of everyone, and with diagrams of them. But no one else is interested, or "completely hearing."
596	[Recaps and expands:] Alfred H in Bridgepoint, summary of whole experience up to his marrying Julia Dehning.
596	Alfred H is resisting type, Julia D is attacking type.
597	[Recaps and expands:] resisting and attacking. Adds: The confusion in understanding "RESISTING MYSTICISM."

CHAPTER THREE (PART TWO)
ALFRED HERSLAND AND JULIA DEHNING

598	Pleasant living and Alfred H's uncertainty about it.
599–600	Alfred H's first realization of his importance to himself came with his first loving. Alfred H and "himself to himself" [expanded.]
601	All know the reasons for their own success or failure, but not that of others. Alfred H and Mr. Dehning.
602	ALFRED H AND JULIA DEHNING MARRY. He is "aspiring," she is "exciting." Their marriage not successful, and their loving.
	GS to Reader: She could make lists, and know one, two, many.
602–603	Everyone is a "nice" one, and their loving, and suspicion. "This one is seriously a nice one."
604	Loving [expanded.] Loving and the "nice one."
	GS to Reader: "I AM LOVING JUST NOW EVERY KIND OF LOVING."
605	Prejudices about different ways of loving.
	Loving [expanded to:] attacking and resisting kinds. Variations on "attacking" love and on "resisting" love.
606	***GS to Reader:*** THAT SHE SLOWLY LOST HER PREJUDICES ABOUT WAYS OF LOVING.
606	Love—its puzzles and variations.
607	About two "resisting" kinds who are always on fire—and so, not resisting anything.

608 ***GS to Reader:*** "I AM NOW A HAPPY PERSON."

608 There are many women loving someone who seems "burning" but is really solid wood.

609 GS begins again: Julia has "no bottom stimulation."

609 ***GS to Reader:*** GS's misery once, when she was jealous of successful ones [i.e., BIRD STEIN'S family] because she thought that she herself would end in failure.

610–611 [Recaps and expands:] Learning Alfred H and Julia D.

611 ***GS to Reader:*** "Desolate" and "sulking" because she is not "hearing all repeating." And is also "a little tired now with all this beginning again and again."

611–613 The differences between the Herslands and the Dehnings. Mr. Dehning so diffused in his resisting that he seems to be attacking. Mrs. Dehning is harsh in her attacking. Mrs. Dehning's worry that when she dies, Mr. D will marry again. She is worried for her children.

614 Introduces (anticipating end of story) the Dehning children struggling to prevent Mr. D's second marriage. Repeats their "pleasant family living," and Julia's "attacking."

615–620 Expanded description of Mr. Dehning's whole life, and when he was sick (later), and expanded descriptions of both Mr and Mrs Dehning together.

620–621 ***GS to Reader:*** She is feeling helpless, "learning but not grasping." Always, she was "halting" in realizing, but NOW SHE IS LEARNING FROM SOMEONE [i.e., ALICE TOKLAS], and is not sure, being a resisting type, that she enjoys "this new way."

622–623 Dehning family living—and Julia's "nervous being"—and Mrs. Dehning's feeling that she's not deserving her troubles.

624–625 ***GS to Reader:*** "All the ways of living" are "crowding" on GS, and she is "resisting" so she can "slowly realize."

625–627 [Continues:] Julia and "attacking" and honest and way of loving babies.

627 The difficulty of admitting to oneself that one doesn't feel what one is supposed to feel. One can't admit it out of fear, or out of sentiment, or etc. This, and its relation to Julia.

628–639 Julia and her lacking a sense for living, and not knowing her own feeling, and when she is crude and stupid, she is not really harsh, and her courage. In attacking and resisting, variations in behavior: can be harsh, crude, sweet, etc. etc.

630 [Recap re: BERTHA and MARTHA HERSLAND:] Both attacking, but in Bertha, so much wobble, and in Martha so much "indeterminate nervous excitement" that in both, it seemed like resisting.

631 ***GS to Reader:*** She wishes that she would be the only one who could

explain the being in everyone.

631–633 Variations on SENSITIVENESS IN ATTACKING.

633–634 ***GS to Reader:*** On learning all the ways of attacking, and GS not understanding all there is to know of sensitiveness in attacking.

634–635 Julia resisting changing in her attacking; and wanting to "learn"; and her relation to sensitiveness and teaching [and variations on these]; and the feeling sure that "THE LAST END OF A BAD THING" could not happen; and her "right" conviction.

636 Julia being given teaching, and so making life a moral operation.

637 And those who are given teaching, but learn nothing.
And those who learn religion, and feel that God is loving them.

638 [Recap of:] Dehning family living and pleasant living.

639 Mr. Dehning—his being ready for listening (to Alfred H), and his feeling of importance, and he and his other children, George and Hortense, and his sense for living.

640 Julia having "no emotion of ambition" but the intention of it. And Alfred who had the "emotion of ambition."

640–641 [Recap of:] Dehning family living.

641–642 Alfred H and Julia' marriage—their loving and quarreling, and what they remembered for, and from, quarreling.

642–643 [Recap of:] Loving in the attacking and resisting kinds.

643 The effects of "a new way of living."

644–645 JULIA AND FURNISHING AND DRESSING ETC., TO BE "A COMPLETED THING".

645 Julia and her PERSONAL IDEAL, i.e., going toward something, and then "sticking there in that thing." And different ways of others having a "personal ideal."

646 ***GS to Reader:*** [Recap of:] GS "a happy one" when "learning being."

646 Julia and Alfred and their quarreling, and [recap of:] Julia, and in their marriage,

"NOT REALLY FAILING AND NOT REALLY SUCCEEDING."

647 [Recap of:] Julia and her courage, and her learning, and her generous emotion in attacking, and her honest motive.

647 Julia and Alfred—[Recap:] "not really failing, not really succeeding," and their aspiration.

648 Alfred and Julia—and being certain about another's belief in their [i.e., Alfred and Julia's] loving and honesty and goodness and thinking.

649 ***GS to Reader:*** Not right now "terribly in a twitter" about being certain.

649–652 ALFRED AND HONESTY: Mr. Dehning and Julia discover that he is not honest. Their own honesty, and their judging of honesty. And [recap

	of:] honesty and loving.
653	***GS to Reader:*** Her feeling about young girls "feeling their being" which she has "delicately inside me"—but not about boys.
653–655	[Recap of:] Julia and Mr. Dehning, and loving feeling.
655–656	Remembering as a young one being tired or disturbed or sick—and Julia not remembering such things.
657	[Recap of:] Julia and loving being. "SWEET ONES" in the Dehning family—and Julia. [See notes re: Dehning girls "sweetness… loyal upgazing" etc.]
658	***GS to Reader:*** Would like to be in love with everyone so that she could "know all loving being."
658	Julia and her need for completely passional loving.
659	[Recap of:] Alfred H and the Dehnings.
659	MORAL CONVICTION: The strength needed to do without it. Julia, though, needed it completely, and in her marriage, not getting it through "learning."
660	The Dehning family, and its relation to Alfred's and Julia's marriage.
661	[Recap of:] Alfred H needing "something" for real living, and telling what he needed, and telling Mr. Dehning his need.
662	***GS to Reader:*** She is beginning to like conversation—which she never did before—as a successful diversion.
662	[Recap of] Mr. Dehning listening to Alfred.
663	Alfred beginning success. And [recap of] Julia and her dutiful side, and her stupid side.
663	***GS to Reader:*** "I AM A WISE ONE." She could be happy "if everyone was certain that she was a wise one," but likes it that she is not certain of this, which is "nicely disturbing."
663–664	[Recap of:] Ambition as an emotion or as an intention. Ambition and older people, who none at all is "sweet."
664	Alfred's ambition as a "complete aspiration." Mr. Dehning's loan to him.
664	***GS to Reader:*** GS recapping succeeding and failing, and now making groups of success and failure types.
665	***GS to Reader:*** Beginning to feel hope again in one day writing the complete history of men and women.
665	[Recap of:] Alfred and Julia and their quarreling.
666	DEFINITION OF QUARRELING: Not letting the attacking win by attacking, or the resisting win by resisting.
666–667	Mr. Dehning refuses to go into Alfred's house, convinced of his dishonesty—and Julia's feeling about his dishonesty.

667 [Recap of:] Alfred and the Dehnings about "ambition."

667–670 [Recaps and expands:] Honest reputation and Alfred and Julia and Mr. Dehning.

670–671 Alfred and Julia—their children, and their divorce.

671–672 ***GS to Reader:*** Feeling she is "getting old" in herself. And she asks: "How can anything be different from what it is?"

672 Being PRACTICAL, and having a SENSE FOR LIVING [and variations.]

673 [Recap of:] Succeeding and failing.

674 ***GS to Reader:*** She is putting everything else aside to focus on "sense for living."

675 Discussion of "Sense for living" begins: Examples: (1) has sense only for "each little piece of living", (2) one had a dull sense for living until married, and then more of it, (3) three who have a complete sense for living, and are always successful and winning, and trusting no one under them—of these, the really successful, there are three: one has a big business, one is always making something larger for him to be in, and one is known now internationally [Picasso.]

676 Changes in age—young, old, older—and sense for living; and changing one's size—fat, thin, etc.—and sense for living.

677 ***GS to Reader:*** It's never dull for her that they repeat themselves, but what can be dull is *what* they repeat.

677 SENSE FOR LIVING: EXAMPLES SPELLED OUT:

677 First example: One who was succeeding, but won't be remembered.

678 [Recap of:] Sense for living

679 [Recap of:] Sense for living in Julia and Alfred

679 "EIGHT HERE TONIGHT" none of whom had sense for living.

679–681 The eight exemplified.

682 [Recap of:] Julia and Alfred married living; and their success in re: sense for living.

683 Married ones: GS begins a series on them

A LONG GAY BOOK

684–685 ***GS to Reader:*** Possibly, a history of everyone will soon be finished.
[Recap of:] GS knowing everything and everyone, etc.

685 Julia and Alfred married and their "being in living."

686 Julia's "being in living."

GS'S MULTIPLE CATEGORIES TO BE USED FOR 'EACH ONE

687 GS analyzing these categories in each one: Pride, Egotism, Vanity, Ambition, Succeeding and Failing—and begins variations on these.

687 Example: One who was leading with no one following, and so "dying." [ADELE?]

	GS to Reader: "I won't be seeing this one again."
688	Two more examples
688	Continues Julia and Alfred story: Julia came to know David Hersland; she was not married again. The history of their marriage from Alfred's point of view.

MINNIE MASON AND PATRICK MOORE

689	Alfred's later life: married Minnie Mason; knew Patrick Moore. Later in his life—his little sense for living, his aspirations, and his ending as 'no success, no failure.'
691	Julia dead' Alfred has no children with Minnie Mason. Julia's and Alfred's children:
	GS to Reader: "And I am not finding it very interesting knowing what was happening later to their children."
691	Julia's later life—her courage—Alfred's loving, but not of Julia—their separation.
692	Alfred's friends, and "some" [variations]: Patrick Moore, Mackinly Young, James Flint.
693–694	Mackinly Young—a musician—artistic—his power of working—his sense for living— "so slow like molasses, almost stopped, so could learn nothing helpful for living."
694–695	James Flint mentioned; Patrick Moore described.
695	***GS to Reader:*** Wants to get completely the sense of Success-Failure, and is not interested in people re: their being good or bad, clean or dirty, rich or poor, etc.
696–697	Success-Failure in Moore, Young, Flint, Alfred and Minnie.
697	Intro to description of Minnie Mason
697–698	One who knew all of these was one "loving with intensity of emotion of feeling a thing being powerful."
698	***GS to Reader:*** [Recaps] knowing repeating, being full up with it and knowing it, but "I will not just now again be mentioning this thing."

MINNIE MASON

688–689	Description of Minnie Mason: she was "loving very much and very often," was married once, before Alfred; loving with Alfred, and they were "succeeding quite well in marrying."
700	[Recap of:] Julia and sense for living, and her goodness as a 'purpose.'

RELATION BETWEEN LOVING AND THE FEELING OF ETERNITY

701	Women who love "with the whole of them" can give to the man the feeling that "infinite and eternal" have real meaning, a sense of "no beginning and no ending", "the awe-inspiring feeling of realizing an eternal thing."

702 Julia's friends listed: David H, James and his wife Miriam Cranach, Theodore Summers, William Beckling, Helen Cooke, Rachel Sherman, Charles Kohler, Arthur Keller, Linder Herne, etc. etc.

703–707 Descriptions of Theodore Summers, Miriam Cranach, William Beckling, and Julia's life with these friends. Then, Miriam Cranach, William Beckling, Miss Ortenreid.

708 ***GS to Reader:*** Certain she is a wise one, but sad that everyone will not know this. Nevertheless, reconciled to the fact of her own wisdom, and that another may get it alone, and that all won't be known to everyone.

709 Preparation for David H Chapter and his "coming to be dead." GS will develop living—dead—and living-dead.

GS to Reader: "And so for now to finish them and her [Julia] up." Julia and death and unhappiness, and her success-failure, and her knowing friends.

710 ***GS to Reader:*** "Telling someone yesterday evening" about the difference between "concentration in expressing experiencing" and "experiencing." One sees Expression in its formulations [painting, books, etc.], but GS, through repeating, can see all this and its relation to "being."

711 "A QUEER THING" that (1) one wants to give what the other doesn't want, (2) that one remembers and sees what the other cannot, (3) that one realizes the other is seeing, and can't share it, (4) and that GS herself "sees nothing when another sees it, can realize his seeing it, but 'I' can't."

MORAL BEING

712 An earnest one, a moral one, not succeeding in living. Expecting much from himself, but knew that neither his father nor mother nor brother were "earnest in living."

712 Amusing to see others realize moral being in another.

712 ***GS to Reader:*** "I have sometimes been helping some, with… steady struggling and earnest attention… to be a good one in their living."

SICKNESS AND DEATH

713 Knowing sickness and death in a family.

Julia older, and never married William Beckling.

714 Knowing the being in oneself, frightened by it, glad of it, etc. [variations]

714–715 Realizing the being in people at different ages—and GS knowing this realization.

715 Alfred and Julia as old ones. Minnie married to Alfred, knew David, and was nice to him.

716 [Full recap of:] Alfred and Julia loving. (and to be more of Julia in the David chapter.)

GS LEARNING ABOUT MONEY [RADCLIFFE INCIDENT]

717–718 Incident of GS putting off paying for lessons at Radcliffe, and her difficulty in realizing another one's way of living, as well as difficulty in remembering one's own.

718–719 GS concludes chapter with summary of "being in living" of Alfred, Martha, Julia, and all the friends mentioned in the chapter.

CHAPTER FOUR (PART ONE)
DAVID HERSLAND

723 ***GS to Reader:*** "I DO ASK SOME" if they would like it if they learned they were illegitimate, or with "a low kind of blood."

723–724 ***GS to Reader:*** "What AM BELIEVING?" That I'm not sure what I mean by anything I am saying—or of the being in loving—or of the being in living—or of the meaning in her or in him—or what I would or would not do for someone—or of my knowledge of death—or of liking or not liking, being satisfied or not, to hear about death.

725 Some stubborn about letting themselves be convinced. Some judging someone foolish when they are actually governed by real standards for themselves.

725 [Mentions in passing:] David dead before middle aged.

725 ***GS to Reader:*** "I am coming to know" middle aged people "as young ones." A difficult thing to do. Also, difficult to realize someone as dead, and not growing older.

726 ***GS to Reader:*** GS coming to know more different age groups.
[Recap:] David dead before middle living.
GS's "knowing" gradually spreading to children
[Recap] David dead before middle living.

726–727 ***GS to Reader:*** "No one will listen while I am talking." Some do [variations, the fat, the thin, etc.] GS once thought some were believing her, but no.

BEGINNING OF PARALLEL SENTENCES: POSITIVE, THEN NEGATIVE

728 GS begins here the repetition of same sentence as first positive, then negative statement, e.g., "This one is believing. This one is not believing." etc.

729 The history of DAVID to begin now, re: his talking and listening.

729 ***GS to Reader:*** GS laments [in recap] that she can't experience all the being in everyone.

730 DAVID's history proper begins: his country living, arranging clothes, walking around things, thinking, etc. And his and others' "saying and

listening."

BEGINNING OF THE COLLAPSE OF THE SYSTEM:

730–732 ***GS to Reader:*** Discovers that "there are not so many kinds of men and women after all," but each one of the same kind is different. Each is always the same age to himself, and so is everyone else, and so is the world to him. Therefore, none can tell the whole history of anyone "going on being." "Listening:" doesn't help in this, but examples of every age living simultaneously does help. Knowing family living can help, but mostly nothing helps. So—GS won't try.

733 DAVID interested in listening and talking. So—GS will soon describe people listening and talking—in living, in dying, in loving, in ways of going on living, in eating.

734 The BEING IN DAVID [followed by one description after another of his "being" in relation to the above "ways."]

735–736 DAVID'S Gossols living when he was younger.
DAVID would have liked to like every kind of woman, and to think of all of them as beautiful.

736 Succeeding—GS realizing it in some—it is active in some, and succeeding and being interesting.

737 ***GS to Reader:*** Trying to realize being

737 [Recap] Introduction to "DAVID living."

737 ***GS to Reader:*** Troubled that each one is experiencing things in their own way. Doesn't want to change it, but is troubled by it.

738 [Recap] Succeeding and not succeeding—realizing experiencing.

738 DAVID knowing many people.

WOMEN IN LOVE AND DAVID

739–740 Women in love and their feeling in "directing" someone. Their feeling of importance in this. Each woman in this acts according to her kind.
DAVID's reaction to women in love: Submission.

740 [Recap] Some come to be dead, and David, before middle age.

741–742 No one is certain anyone else is "completely living their living," or realizing the full meaning of their living. Some certain that others are certain (and the changes and confusions in their "saying.")

743 DAVID's beginning -early life: a little one—not remembering—interested in some—the youngest Hersland because:

'TWO OTHER HAD NOT GONE ON LIVING'

743 He hears about the two dead children before, and so he was born—and so, thinking "living is a queer thing"—and so "needed to be certain he needed to be living," and the meaning of his need.

RELATION TO THE OBJECT: FULL DESCRIPTION OF VARIANTS

744–745 1. Relation to object as object existing solidly, (not its character or its expression)

2. Relation to object as its character (its particularity) and its expression (i.e., its way of telling its particularity)

3. Relation to object as solid, character and expression, and also the emotion about them.

4. Relation to object as emotion about his expression (i.e., to use "his beautiful means of expression on.")

5. Relation to object for needing a practical realization of things.

6. Relation to object only as a means of expression, because since this is all that really exists, there's no practical need for realizing "the thing as existing"

7. Relation to object for realizing objects as in relation to other things.

746 DAVID as interesting to some. Then [recap of] whole introduction and description of David.

746–748 "TWO KNOW EACH OTHER VERY WELL ALL THEIR LIVING"—and, their real knowledge of one another—and their certainty of the other one's knowledge—and their talk with others of the other one's being, etc.

748 [Recap] DAVID interesting. —People talking in different ways—and David's talking—and the reactions to his death.

748 DAVID and Gossols and talking and listening

"ONE SEEING AND ONE SITTING"

749 GS observes someone calling another stupid and uninteresting, while everyone is listening to the other. He is right, though, and knows it, because he is the same. And DAVID always enjoying observations of this kind.

749 DAVID young—playing—believing—reading—talking—listening—deciding—being listened to while deciding—liking "going on living."

750 DAVID's friend questioning whether he is should be marrying "that one" and then does. Puzzling, but David not too interested.

751 Being thankful at being shown how to live meaningfully.

752 GS questions: does everyone want the same thing? [and variations]

GS STRATEGY FOR CONTINUING— "BUT NOT THIS EVENING"

752 Her strategy: She will say often that "she knows there is being" in people, so often that she can just look at it and then leave it. And so, she will go on "fooling and mixing up" in David's history— "but not this evening."

752–753 Some not interested, some interested "in being living." David interested.

753–754 DAVID young—liked "being living." David wondering at how others earned money in Gossols. David knowing people and wondering about this.

"ANGRY FEELING" AND DAVID

755–766 Angry feeling, and the feeling about angry feeling—how it changes people—the Herslands knowing angry feeling—David knowing it—[variations in] David's angry feeling—and Alfred's—and Martha's.

LEO STEIN?? AND EARLY SCHOOLING

766–771 Angry feeling toward one teaching. David certain of the wrong teaching—changes later—David pleasant and unpleasant to his teachers—David believing teachers "know nothing of what they are teaching"—David asking questions and teacher couldn't answer—the close connection of angry feeling and being taught.

"One" knew no one was teaching him when he was young, because he was sure he knew, when he was older, how it should be done. But felt no desire to teach [his reasons].

GS criticism of him: He knew "thinking," yes, but not its individual relation to each one's individual experience.

770 DAVID like this one, and yet not at all like him because he "wanted to be needing to teach."

770–771 DAVID reaction to a governess at home—pleasant, and then not pleasant, but overall not serious. And none of them "regularly teaching anything to him."

771 DAVID and "one" re: the need for early teaching, and the uselessness of teaching.

RELATION OF THINKING AND FEELING

771 The relation of thinking and feeling [and variations]

ASKING AND ADVISING

772 An adviser says, "You asked me, so I told you, though you say it's a trouble to you."—Then the "asking" ones, and their angry feeling. When they are sure the adviser is no longer important, then they can ask again without angry feeling.

773 DAVID as adviser.

774 Example of getting angry: the "sharp knives and scissors" example—Martha listening to DAVID's advice—David listening to advice—listening to advice and angry feeling—not recognizing it in oneself when angry feeling is there.

775 DAVID and not recognizing his inner angry feeling because he didn't have full realization of his "feeling being."—And telling Martha—and variations of the relation between angry feeling and the certainty of being a dead one.

776 This relation, in relation to DAVID.

776 Angry feeling, and being certain of life.

777 DAVID and being certain of understanding everything. DAVID and angry feeling

777–778 DAVID and "Some" and their variations of feelings about others [silly, annoyed, disappointed, etc.]

778 DAVID and being angry and being impressed by those having certainty—the kinds of certainty about everything—this, and angry feeling.

"CLEAR THINKING AND EXPRESSING"

779 The certainty that clear thinking goes along with clear expression of it and clear emotion about it, and conviction.
DAVID, though, had not complete emotion, but clear thinking, adequate expression, and nearly absolute conviction

779 The primacy of experience over "thinking", which is partial. Primacy of experience vs. primacy of conception.
Cf. Leo Stein in notebooks, re: experience and thinking.
Leo's "not including all experience."

779–781 DAVID and full thinking and full experiencing. Being logical in thinking, and knowing the *amount* of one's experiencing.

SPIRITUALITY AND IDEALISM

779 To "some", spirituality and idealism mean only "completest intensification of experiencing," not transcending experiencing [variations]

"SAYING AND MEANING"

782–783 The relation between saying and meaning—meaning, saying, and being certain [variations] The way one means something. The relation between ways of experiencing and expressing and kinds (the groups of types.)

784 DAVID and knowing one's kind.
DAVID and variations of saying in relation to meaning.

785 DAVID interested in all relations of experience as experience and thinking as thinking.
DAVID and "strong feeling" and thinking and telling about it.

"COMPLETELY CLEARLY THINKING"

786–787 Those who remember what happened when they were feeling [variations]
DAVID and "completely clearly thinking" and boasting about it.

BOASTING

788 DAVID and "boasting" about "being living" and being listened to. And David interested in this.

789–790 DAVID and relation to change in feeling. And his relation to having delicate feeling and "beautifully talking about it."

"THINKING TO MAKE A COMPLETE, A BEAUTIFUL THING"

791 DAVID "with 'thinking,' to make a complete thing", and his "wanting to be needing… any woman to be a really beautiful one."

DAVID DEAD (I)

792 And variations in responses to his being dead.

DAVID AND BABIES

792–793 DAVID and not having babies—and babies not being completely interesting.

IMAGINING

794 Imagining [and variations]—telling and imagining

DAVID "BEING A YOUNG ONE" AND "JUMPING"

795–796 DAVID "being a young one". Jumping, and caring, and remembering it [etc.]

796 [Recaps] Responses to David's death, and David young and forgetting it.

797 Young ones certain that nothing exists—and David

797–798 [Recaps] Remembering being young and jumping and talking about it.

RESEMBLANCES

798 Finding resemblances in others and laughing about it—and having angry feeling about it—and being excited by it.

799 DAVID beginning living—and those to whom no one is every young.

800 DAVID and those who "need to listen", the reasons for this, and variants for different ages.

801 [Recap] DAVID's young living—being interested—later remembering it—and enjoying it.

802 Breathing.

802 DAVID liking being young, and his doing things then.

DREAMING

803 Young ones and dreaming

"DOING ONE THING AND DOING IT AGAIN"

803–804 Successions of unspecified acts, i.e., "each one doing one thing and doing it again, and doing another thing and another thing", etc.—and the need for it.

805 Completely living to oneself and doing something and others knowing it.

806 DAVID knowing he is a young one.

807 [Recap] DAVID jumping.

808 DAVID being young and knowing death.

808 DAVID being young and talking and knowing many

809 DAVID being young and feeling oneself existing

810 DAVID being uncertain made both these things true

(1) that existing is nothing, and

(2) that existing is something.

810–811 DAVID (and GS personally) wanting to know how old the other is, because this may be the explanation for why they do as they do.

WONDERING ABOUT EXISTING

811–812 DAVID knowing someone, and both knowing and not knowing his existing—and wondering about such a thing.

"BEING FRIGHTENED"

812 DAVID and ways of being frightened [and variations]

813 Asking why one does anything. The answer: to satisfy the wanting to do it—and responses to this.

814 DAVID and not completely asking about this.

815 Though many thought he *was* asking, and would one day explain. —and David listening to explanations of this—not completely.

"DAVID NOT NEEDING"

816 DAVID not needing to explain everything.

[Recap] David as young one and ways of doing then

817 DAVID and those *needing* to be of a certain age group.

DAVID deciding and directing as a young one.

818 DAVID being young, and experiencing it, and also experiencing that he was *not* a young one.

818–819 DAVID certain of being young, and certain about others being young, and of others' "clearly thinking" and not "clearly thinking"—and others certain about *his* clearly thinking—and David's telling of it.

820 DAVID's need and want to be "clearly thinking."

CHAPTER FOUR (PART TWO)
DAVID HERSLAND

"BEING PLEASED"

821 Being pleased to be with David [and variations]

822 DAVID's knowing others, and their liking knowing him

823 DAVID and his listening, clearly thinking, telling, feeling, and his need for these—but mostly needing "clearly thinking."

"UNDERSTANDING"

824 There is another being—and wanting to tell him—and usually deciding not to—and knowing the other will never do what he has to anyhow—and hoping no one else understanding will either.

824–825	[Recap of above]—but the understanding one is sure he will surprise the other.
825	DAVID's understanding of someone and someone's understanding of him—and their feeling—and their not telling.
826	One asking David to explain his not understanding David.

THE TWO DEAD CHILDREN

826	DAVID and the Hersland parents and the two dead children who came before.
827–828	Hersland living, and DAVID'S own living inside him—and his knowing and not remembering it—and his doing and saying things someone said he did and said.

SAYING AND BEING HEARD

829	DAVID and saying and being heard—his knowing and not knowing of his saying and doing—and he doing some things alone.

ASTONISHING

830	DAVID and what he said astonishing others [and variations]

UNDERSTANDING DAVID'S BEING

831	DAVID liking and understanding the meaning of an act—and David's acts—and liking and not liking his "being existing."

DAVID'S CLEARLY THINKING AND CLEARLY FEELING

832	[Recaps and expands] David clearly thinking and clearly feeling—and completely thinking and feeling—and his wanting and needing these things.

LIKING

833	Some liking and telling—and David's friends liking and not liking him—and expansion of this
834	Being certain and not certain about the meaning of liking [and variants] DAVID and those who know that they like or not like, and that they need the meaning of it or don't.

DAVID TROUBLING

835	DAVID needing both things to live: (1) the certainty that living has meaning, and (2) the certainty that it does not.
835	DAVID "troubling and not troubling"

DAVID AS A BOY DESCRIBED

836	DAVID as a boy described as gentle, daring, weak, strong, —a long long compendium of adjectives.

DAVID AND SOMEONE'S AFFECTION FOR HIM

837–838 "Someone ran after him"—a "silly" one—an incident of David's—and David's realization of affection in someone running after him.

"PEOPLE COME TOGETHER"

838–839 "People come together" to see, hear, do, forget, remember, feel someone do something [comprehensive variations on this] and "being together"—and David's feeling about this.

DAVID BEING SAD

840–841 DAVID wanting and not wanting to be a sad one—and David being sad enough—and David's interest in sadness.

842 DAVID not knowing he was living "in one way of living"—and his not complete interest in particular ways of living

"LITTLE BY LITTLE THEY ARE NOT SO YOUNG" AND BEING TOSSED

842 "Not so young" and being "tossed"—tossing and regular rhythm.

"LIKE A MAP"

844 Seeing one's own changes is "like a map"—how "the real thing" is like the description. [*Note*: The first sentence of the novel is echoed here.]

844 DAVID noticing changes—first, in the "middle of beginning middle living"—and his excitement of discovery—and his satisfaction in it.

845 DAVID feeling change as a boy—and the certainty of his feeling—his feeling something in the beginning—and then not—and then, sad—and then, troubled—and then deciding about the troubled ones he knew—and then, deciding about himself—but not completely interested.

"WRITING DOWN EVERY DAY… BEING A TROUBLED ONE"

846 DAVID being troubled [and variants]—David as a boy "feeling things"—and not interested—But when young, could have been "writing down every day" about being a troubled one

847 DAVID when older, and "clearly feeling and clearly thinking"—and not interested in having been very little—and not remembering—and David then interested in being bigger.

848–849 [Recap] David getting bigger, remembering, being interested, writing it all down

DECIDING

849 DAVID deciding—and puzzling—and wondering about deciding

SMELLING

850 DAVID smelling—and this causing people to remember—and DAVID interested in this

850–852 [Recap] Young ones, etc. [Cf. Note #125]

"SHE SAYS GO GO AND I GO"

853 DAVID "wanting to be needing to be such a one" (one coming and going on command)

SORROWING

853 DAVID and gloominess and sorrow

THE NUMBERS OF PEOPLE AROUND DAVID

854 DAVID "with one, two, four, six" etc.

855–856 [Recap] Clearly thinking, deciding, sorrowing, smelling.

856 Noise—heard and not heard, etc.

DULLNESS

857 Being certain someone is a dull one, certain someone is not a dull one, etc.

"A GENTLE THING… TO BE NO LONGER LIVING"

857 "A gentle thing to be not any longer living" [and variants]

857–860 DAVID a noisy one—hearing noises—not needing and needing, etc.—DAVID not a dull one [extended]

"A COMPLETE THING"

860–861 Some do a complete thing, with a beginning, middle and end, which is a gentle thing to have done. DAVID not gently seeing anything as a complete thing.

DAVID AND FAMILY LIVING

861–862 DAVID and doing things the way his family did them—and his not thinking of it—and those who understood he was not "family living".

"IT CAN BE KNOWN… ONE IS LIVING EVERY DAY"

862–863 DAVID and "living every day" [variants and extended]—and "it can be known all day and every day."

863 DAVID dead at beginning of middle living.

863–864 DAVID knowing he was living every day [recap and expanded]

EATING AND DECIDING

864–865 DAVID eating and *deciding* about eating

"NEEDING THAT THERE BE NO SUCCEEDING IN LIVING"

865 DAVID every day "being himself inside himself"

865 DAVID needing to express the feeling that "there was no succeeding in living"

866 DAVID longing to realize "a completely different thing"

BEING LISTENED TO IF LOVED

866 DAVID certain that no one "could completely listen to him unless they loved him"

867 One who almost completely loved him, and David's understanding of this love's incompleteness. And *her* incompleteness in listening to "all of him." DAVID and his thinking.

THINKING ABOUT THINKING

867 DAVID "completely thinking about thinking", and
DAVID and his need of "knowing he was one."
869–871 DAVID and his "needing another one," and
DAVID and his "liking to enjoy things the way he used to enjoy them"

LOVING ONE AND TELLING

871–872 DAVID loving one and telling her and showing it to her.

EACH ONE IS ONE

872 DAVID remembering that "each one is one", and completely remembering this, and certain of it.

DAVID AND ADVICE

872–873 DAVID giving advice to someone and interested in doing it.
874 [Recap] DAVID's knowing and understanding.
DAVID and his need to love "a completely beautiful one."

DAVID AND HIS FRIENDS

875 DAVID's certainty re: which of his friends felt he was one of them—and their knowing him [expanded]

SUCCEEDING AND EXISTING

876 Some of his friends "needed to express that succeeding was not existing."—and David's need and not need of this.
876–877 DAVID and doing "some other thing" sometime.
877 DAVID's certainty that "anyone is different from another one."
878 DAVID's "completely clear feeling" of what he was feeling, and his "extraordinarily completely clear" expression of it. —and his working at being certain he was "one being living"—and his incomplete need of this.

DAVID'S PREDICTIONS

878–879 Some who had faith in David's predictions
Cf. Notebooks re: David's failure.
879 DAVID's need for succeeding in living—if he had "gone on living" he would not have succeeded, but he would not have needed it them.
880 DAVID's certainty that no one's thinking could be more complete than his.
DAVID's not needing to be certain that he needed another one.

TRANSITION TO DAVID'S DEATH

880 DAVID and no use going on living when he no longer needed to be

living—and David's deciding and not completely deciding about living.

881 Those who are "not interested" in living, but do not mention it.

DAVID "A QUITE QUIET ONE, A QUITE GENTLE ONE"

882 DAVID and "quietly enough" living, and teaching.

882–883 DAVID and not being remembered as he is now: the "quite quiet one"—and they not needing to remember him so—and one who was certain he was not the "quite quiet one" now—and those who needed to remember him so.

DAVID WITH ALFRED H AND JULIA

883 Alfred H married, and David knew his friends -

884 and knew George Dehning, and
DAVID remembering his father and sister Martha, and
DAVID knowing Julia and all her friends.

885 DAVID stopping telling about enjoying things with former friends, and -
DAVID knowing people now—and explaining living—and his interest in this—and his telling it to one—and wondering whether this one would keep on needing him to tell it.
Cf. Notebooks re: David's third love, and the reason for its failure.

886 DAVID not sad— [recap of] knowing Alfred, Julia, George—and
DAVID "convincing Julia"—and
DAVID being "listened to enough" by George and

887 Alfred not being too close to David—and
DAVID being completely convincing about his understanding and his thinking
DAVID not determined in this, just naturally certain.

888 DAVID not repeating that thinking is existing, nor completely using it.

DECIDING ABOUT EATING

888–889 DAVID deciding about eating, and his need for this—and the need that others understand—and telling Mr. Dehning about it—and his *urging* his understanding—and [recap of] clearly thinking and needing meaning—and David "clearly telling" to some, but not repeating again and again.
Cf. Notebooks re: Leo's fasting.

"EATING ONE THING"

889 DAVID "needing to eat one thing."

DAVID DOING AND WORKING

890 DAVID wanting to need succeeding and doing and working.

DAVID UNDERSTANDING

890 DAVID "continuous and clear" in his understanding and advising some

"to go on with his understanding,"

891 DAVID "might have fought" for his understanding, but no one needed to fight him.

DAVID ALONE

891 DAVID alone and not suffering in it, but working, thinking, and almost clearly, and -

DAVID "not commencing again and again" in living.

DAVID UNDERSTANDING LIVING

892 DAVID's interest in other's thinking, but not completely, and

DAVID'S almost understanding daily living, and

DAVID'S need to understand that living is existing, and

DAVID'S expressing, not telling again and again, almost completely interested "in this thing"

DAVID'S going on living and his understanding of it.

893–894 DAVID, Julia, George and Alfred—difference in not needing something.

DAVID not needing succeeding, not needing another, not needing being certain that living is existing, not needing giving Julia anything.

Julia not needing to have David's understanding—and George not needing [expanded] n.d. Alfred not needing [expanded]

DAVID NOT NEEDING ANYTHING

894 DAVID not needing anything (going on living, etc.) and

DAVID "completely not eating some things."

895 DAVID "keeping his mind open" and Julia keeping her mind open.

DAVID AND THE DEHNINGS

896–897 The Dehnings knowing David—Mr Dehning's way—Mrs. Dehning's way—Julia's way.

897–898 The Dehnings knowing Alfred H—David telling Julia—Julia telling David—David knowing Julia—David giving her advice—David at the end knowing George more and Alfred less.

898 George knew David before David knew the other Dehnings—George not forgetting David after his death

899 Hortense Dehning knowing David—giving advice—while thinking of David when he was dead

DAVID'S LAST PHASE BEFORE DEATH

899 DAVID eating only one thing—and not—strong—completely clearly thinking—beginning success and not beginning success—his no need to remember anything -

900 DAVID "not needing" being dead one—eating only one thing—but not really needing anything—and "not completely filling anything in

completely clearly expressing"

901 DAVID—understanding—mentioning—expressing—thinking.
DAVID "not feeling being completely different" but being different—forgetting and not forgetting being different.

DAVID'S DEATH

902 DAVID "had come to be a dead one."—had not been one fighting—eaten only one thing—had done only his chosen thing.

RESPONSES TO DAVID'S DEATH

913–914 Some knew, some did not, some regretted, some wondered—some wanting to know him in after-life, some remembered "his having been a dead one, his having been a living one."

EPILOGUE

907 "Anyone comes to be a dead one" -
Some believing, some not, in another's doing things differently -
Anyone understanding—doing, believing, etc.

CF. NOTE #55

908 What someone does when something will happen

CF. NOTE #54

908–909 Old ones and feelings about death.
909–910 [Recap of] Kinds of men and women;
"There can be lists"

'FAMILY LIVING' VARIATIONS TO END OF EPILOGUE

911–914 Families [and variations]
914–915 "Anyone can have heard anything."
"Saying something" in family living [and variations]
"It is time" in family living that … [and variations]
916 "There is no time" to begin in family living [and variations]
917 "Being" and "doing" in family living [and variations]
918–919 "Standing" and "doing something"
918–925 Being a dead one in family living, "doing" in family living, being an old one in family living, "remembering some such thing." of family living.

***

Cited Works by Gertrude Stein

MA *The Making of Americans, Being A History of A Family's Progress* (Paris: Contact Editions, 1925; New York: A. & C. Boni, 1926) Page references match those in the 1995 Dalkey Archive edition.

EA *Everybody's Autobiography* (New York: Random House, 1937)

TWO *Two: Gertrude Stein and Her Brother*, in volume 1 of the Yale edition of the unpublished writings of Gertrude Stein. (Books for Libraries Press, Freeport, N.Y, 1969)

ABT *The Autobiography of Alice B. Toklas*, in Selected Writings of Gertrude Stein (New York: Vintage, 1990)

LGB *A Long Gay Book*, Published in *Matisse, Picasso and Gertrude Stein: with Two Shorter Stories*; (Paris: Plain Edition, 1933) Page references match those in the 2000 Dover edition.

Geography and Plays, (Boston: The Four Seas Company, 1922)

The Mother of Us All published in *Last Operas and Plays* (New York: Rinehart and Company, 1949)

Portraits and Prayers (New York. Random House, 1934)

Fernhurst, Q.E.D, and Other Early Writings (New York: Liveright, 1971)

The Geographical History of America or The Relation of Human Nature to the Human Mind (New York: Random House, 1936).

A Lyrical Opera Made by Two, published in *Operas and Plays* (Paris: Plain Edition, 1932)

Saints and Singing, a Play, published in *Operas and Plays.*

Gertrude Stein. Writings, 1903–32 (New York: Library of America, 1998)

Made in the USA
Las Vegas, NV
23 December 2021